Lecture Notes in Computer Science

Lecture Notes in Artificial Intelligence   **14282**

Founding Editor

Jörg Siekmann

Series Editors

Randy Goebel, *University of Alberta, Edmonton, Canada*
Wolfgang Wahlster, *DFKI, Berlin, Germany*
Zhi-Hua Zhou, *Nanjing University, Nanjing, China*

The series Lecture Notes in Artificial Intelligence (LNAI) was established in 1988 as a topical subseries of LNCS devoted to artificial intelligence.

The series publishes state-of-the-art research results at a high level. As with the LNCS mother series, the mission of the series is to serve the international R & D community by providing an invaluable service, mainly focused on the publication of conference and workshop proceedings and postproceedings.

Vadim Malvone · Aniello Murano
Editors

Multi-Agent Systems

20th European Conference, EUMAS 2023
Naples, Italy, September 14–15, 2023
Proceedings

 Springer

Editors
Vadim Malvone
Télécom Paris
Paris, France

Aniello Murano
Universitá degli Studi di Napoli Federico II
Naples, Italy

ISSN 0302-9743 ISSN 1611-3349 (electronic)
Lecture Notes in Artificial Intelligence
ISBN 978-3-031-43263-7 ISBN 978-3-031-43264-4 (eBook)
https://doi.org/10.1007/978-3-031-43264-4

LNCS Sublibrary: SL7 – Artificial Intelligence

This Springer imprint is published by the registered company Springer Nature Switzerland AG
The registered company address is: Gewerbestrasse 11, 6330 Cham, Switzerland

Paper in this product is recyclable.

Preface

This volume constitutes the proceedings of the 20th European Conference on Multi-Agent Systems (EUMAS 2023), held in September 2023 in Naples, Italy. In the past two decades, we have seen an enormous increase of interest in agent-based computing and multi-agent systems (MAS). This field is set to become one of the key intelligent systems technologies in the twenty-first century. The EUMAS conference series aims to provide the main forum for academics and practitioners in Europe to discuss current MAS research and applications.

EUMAS 2023 followed the tradition of previous editions: Oxford 2003, Barcelona 2004, Brussels 2005, Lisbon 2006, Hammamet 2007, Bath 2008, Agia Napa 2009, Paris 2010, Maastricht 2011, Dublin 2012, Toulouse 2013, Prague 2014, Athens 2015, Valencia 2016, Evry 2017, Bergen 2018, Thessaloniki 2020 (virtual), Israel 2021 (virtual), and Düsseldorf 2022. Like them, EUMAS 2023 aims to provide–in academic and industrial efforts–the prime European forum for presenting, encouraging, supporting, and discussing activity in the research and development of multi-agent systems as the annual designated event of the European Association for Multi-Agent Systems (EURAMAS).We are grateful for the guidance provided by the EURAMAS Board.

The peer-review process carried out by the 83 Program Committee (PC) members put great emphasis on ensuring the high quality of accepted contributions. These papers were presented at EUMAS 2023 and are contained in this volume. Each submission to EUMAS 2023 was peer reviewed by at least three PC members in a single-blind fashion. Out of 47 submissions, the PC decided to accept 24 full papers and 5 short papers for oral presentation. In addition, EUMAS 2023 was preceded by a Doctoral Consortium (PhD Day) at which 16 talks were given by PhD students, who presented their previous results, ongoing work, and future research plans. Sixteen short papers summarizing such contributions to the PhD Day are also contained in this volume. We thank Angelo Ferrando and Munyque Mittelmann for organizing the PhD Day, sifting through the submissions, and selecting them for presentation.

In addition to the papers contained in this volume, the EUMAS 2023 program was highlighted by two great keynote talks given by Orna Kupferman (Hebrew University, Israel) and Ana Paiva (University of Lisbon, Portugal).

Among the accepted papers, chose the best ones based on their review scores during the conference. The award recipients were invited to submit an extended version of their outstanding papers for fast-track publication in the Journal of Autonomous Agents and Multi-Agent Systems (JAAMAS). In addition, selected authors were invited to extend their contributions for a special issue of SN Computer Science.

We thank the authors for submitting their work to EUMAS 2023; the PC members of EUMAS 2023 as well as the additional reviewers for reviewing the submissions; the participants for traveling to Naples, listening to and giving great talks, and making this conference a wonderful event; the invited speakers for their excellent talks; the editors of JAAMAS for inviting the award recipients to extend their papers and enjoy a fast-track publication process; the editors of SN Computer Science for supporting a special issue of extended selected papers; the local organizing committee; our sponsors; and Springer for sponsoring the Best Paper Award.

July 2023

Vadim Malvone
Aniello Murano

Organization

Program Committee

Alessandro Abate	University of Oxford, UK
Natasha Alechina	Utrecht University, The Netherlands
Francesco Amigoni	Politecnico di Milano, Italy
Carlos Areces	Universidad Nacional de Córdoba, Argentina
Guy Avni	University of Haifa, Israel
Reyhan Aydogan	Delft University of Technology, The Netherlands
Matteo Baldoni	Università di Torino, Italy
Cristina Baroglio	Università di Torino, Italy
Nick Bassiliades	Aristotle University of Thessaloniki, Greece
Francesco Belardinelli	Imperial College London, UK
Raphaël Berthon	RWTH Aachen University, Germany
Dietmar Berwanger	CNRS, France
Antonis Bikakis	University College London, UK
Vittorio Bilo	University of Salento, Italy
Filippo Bistaffa	IIIA-CSIC, Spain
Thomas Bolander	Technical University of Denmark, Denmark
Vicent Botti	Universitat Politècnica de València, Spain
Patricia Bouyer	CNRS, France
Robert Bredereck	TU Clausthal, Germany
Valentin Cassano	Universidad Nacional de Córdoba, CONICET, Argentina
Cristiano Castelfranchi	Institute of Cognitive Sciences and Technologies, CNR, Italy
Francesco Chiariello	University of Naples Federico II, Italy
Paul Davidsson	Malmö University, Sweden
Louise Dennis	University of Manchester, UK
João Dias	Faculty of Science and Technology, University of Algarve, Portugal
Piotr Faliszewski	AGH University of Science and Technology, Poland
Angelo Ferrando	University of Genoa, Italy
Nicoletta Fornara	Università della Svizzera italiana, Switzerland
Tim French	University of Western Australia, Australia
Maira Gatti de Bayser	Microsoft, Brazil
Raffaella Gentilini	University of Perugia, Italy

Charlotte Gerritsen	Vrije Universiteit Amsterdam, The Netherlands
Nicola Gigante	Free University of Bozen-Bolzano, Italy
Rica Gonen	Open University of Israel, Israel
Valentin Goranko	Stockholm University, Sweden
Umberto Grandi	University of Toulouse, France
Davide Grossi	University of Groningen, The Netherlands
Dimitar Guelev	Bulgarian Academy of Sciences, Bulgaria
Zahia Guessoum	LIP6, Sorbonne Université and Université de Reims Champagne-Ardenne, France
Julian Gutierrez	Monash University, Australia
Magdalena Ivanovska	BI Norwegian Business School, Norway
Franziska Klügl	Örebro University, Sweden
Panagiotis Kouvaros	Imperial College London, UK
Martin Lackner	Vienna University of Technology, Austria
Stéphane Le Roux	ENS Paris-Saclay, France
Marin Lujak	University Rey Juan Carlos, Spain
Vadim Malvone	Télécom Paris, France
Jerusa Marchi	Federal University of Santa Catarina, Brazil
Enrico Marchioni	University of Southampton, UK
Nicolas Markey	IRISA, CNRS & Inria & Univ. Rennes 1, France
Francisco S. Melo	Instituto Superior Tecnico/INESC-ID, Portugal
Jakub Michaliszyn	University of Wrocław, Poland
Marco Montali	Free University of Bozen-Bolzano, Italy
Aniello Murano	University of Naples Federico II, Italy
Pavel Naumov	University of Southampton, UK
Gethin Norman	University of Glasgow, UK
Andrea Omicini	Alma Mater Studiorum–Università di Bologna, Italy
Nir Oren	University of Aberdeen, UK
Arno Pauly	Swansea University, UK
Wojciech Penczek	Institute of Computer Science of PAS, Poland
Laurent Perrussel	IRIT - Universite de Toulouse, France
Mickael Randour	F.R.S.-FNRS & UMONS - Université de Mons, Belgium
Anna Helena Reali Costa	Universidade de São Paulo, Brazil
Rasmus K. Rendsvig	University of Copenhagen, Denmark
Alessandro Ricci	University of Bologna, Italy
Juan Antonio Rodríguez Aguilar	IIIA-CSIC, Spain
Rosaldo Rossetti	University of Porto, Portugal
Jörg Rothe	Heinrich-Heine-Universität Düsseldorf, Germany
Emilio Serrano	Universidad Politécnica de Madrid, Spain
Sonja Smets	University of Amsterdam, The Netherlands

Nikolaos Spanoudakis	Technical University of Crete, Greece
Sharadhi Alape Suryanarayana	University of Oulu, Finland
Nimrod Talmon	Ben-Gurion University of the Negev, Israel
Paolo Turrini	University of Warwick, UK
Leon van der Torre	University of Luxembourg, Luxembourg
Wiebe van der Hoek	University of Liverpool, UK
Serena Villata	CNRS, Université Côte d'Azur, France
George Vouros	University of Piraeus, Greece
Bożena Woźna-Szcześniak	Jan Dlugosz University in Częstochowa, Poland
Neil Yorke-Smith	Delft University of Technology, The Netherlands
Martin Zimmermann	Aalborg University, Denmark

Additional Reviewers

Invited Speakers Abstracts

Game-Theoretic Perspectives in Reactive Synthesis

Orna Kupferman

Hebrew University, Israel

Overview

The classical definition of reactive synthesis assumes a single-component system interacting with a single-component environment. The setting corresponds to a zero-sum two-player game, where the objectives of the system and the environment are complementary. Realistic settings are much richer. In addition to systems composed of cooperative components, many systems nowadays lack a centralized authority and involve selfish users, giving rise to multi-agent systems in which the agents have their own objectives, and thus correspond to non-zero-sum games. Classical game theory concerns non-zero-sum games for economy-driven applications such as resource allocation, pricing, bidding, and others. The talk surveys concepts and ideas from game theory that have been or are waiting to be explored and used in the context of synthesis.

Engineering Social Capabilities in Human-Centered AI

Ana Paiva

INESC-ID, IST, University of Lisbon, Portugal

Overview

Social agents, chatbots or social robots have the potential to change the way we interact with technology. As they become more affordable, they will have increased involvement in our daily activities with the ability to perform a wide range of tasks, communicate naturally with us, and thus, partner with humans socially and collaboratively. But how do we engineer social capabilities in our AI systems? How do we guarantee that these agents are trustworthy? To investigate these ideas we must seek inspiration in what it means to be social and build the technology to support hybrid teams of humans and AI. In this talk, I will discuss how to engineer social capabilities in agents and illustrate it with some case studies, discussing the challenges, recent results, and the future directions for the field of social AI.

Contents

Multiple Attribute List Aggregation and an Application to Democratic Playlist Editing

Eyal Briman[✉] and Nimrod Talmon

Ben-Gurion University, Beersheba, Israel
briman@post.bgu.ac.il

Abstract. We present a social choice model that incorporates time-based constraints, where the goal is to produce an ordered list that satisfies both agent preferences (based on approval ballots) and global constraints. First, we analyze the general model, showing that it is generally NP-hard, but admits polynomial-time algorithms for a special case; we also develop heuristic solutions for the general case. Furthermore, we explore potential applications of the model and demonstrate its relevance by focusing on the use case of democratic playlist editing. In this scenario, our aim is to generate a playlist that reflects agent preferences for a given set of musical tracks while also considering soft constraints regarding the sequencing and transitions of tracks over time. We illustrate how the problem of democratic playlist editing can be translated into our model, and present simulation results where we apply our heuristics to solve specific instances of the problem. We contend that our results are promising, not only for the specific use case of democratic playlist editing, but also for a plethora of other use cases that we introduce here.

1 Introduction

Social choice theory examines collective decision-making processes by aggregating individual preferences to reach a collective choice or outcome [2]. In the standard setting of single-winner elections, a single alternative is chosen from a set of alternatives, based on group preferences. Moving beyond single-winner elections, in multi-winner elections—which formally generalize single-winner elections – a set of candidates or alternatives is selected, following agent preferences [12]. Going even further, in participatory budgeting – which formally generalizes multi-winner elections – a set of projects, each with its cost, is selected while respecting agent preferences and a given budget.

We argue that advancements in social choice many times correspond to the desire of having collective decision-making tools that aggregate agent preferences and output *increasingly complex outputs*. Our proposed social choice model can be viewed from this angle; and, correspondingly, the aggregation methods that we develop can be seen as computational tools that are able to aggregate agent preferences and output fairly structurally-involved outputs. In particular, we consider a social choice setting that consists of the following ingredients:

© The Author(s), under exclusive license to Springer Nature Switzerland AG 2023
V. Malvone and A. Murano (Eds.): EUMAS 2023, LNAI 14282, pp. 1–16, 2023.
https://doi.org/10.1007/978-3-031-43264-4_1

- A set of elements out of which a subset shall be selected (similar to a multi-winner election);
- where these elements have certain numerically-valued attributes that shall be taken into consideration (formally generalizing participatory budgeting);
- and where the selected subset of elements shall be ordered (similarly to ranking elements, such as in proportional ranking [28]).

We describe our setting formally in Sect. 3. Essentially, we formulate a multi-objective optimization problem that balances between two considerations:

- First, the ordered subset (i.e., list) that we output shall respect agent preferences (we model this aspect by aiming to maximize the score of the output list according to some multi-winner voting rule);
- second, the trend or pattern of the attribute values over time within the output list (we model this aspect by aiming to minimize the distance of the corresponding patterns to "ideal", predefined patterns).

Through the use of mathematical optimization techniques and the development of effective heuristics, our model provides a robust framework for tackling diverse use-cases that involve multi-attribute decision problems in which an output list is to be agreed upon. While in this paper we concentrate on a specific application – namely, of democratic playlist editing – below we first describe several potential applications of our model. Consider the following applications:

- **Democratic Planning:** Consider the task of some cooperative manufacturing plan for highly logistic complex products, sensitive products, or products with occasional or seasonal demand. We aim to optimize different attributes based on the social choice, ideal demand changing over time, the ideal stock and inventory changing over time, and different measures such as service quality type 1 or 2, which will ideally change over time to minimize costs.
- **Democratic Scheduling:** Democratic scheduling of jobs in a cooperative using a multi-attribute approach that includes, e.g., job type and its corresponding agent groups.
- **Democratic Media:** Creating content that serves different functions for various attributes over time, for example, a TV series or a movie. The amount of stress/relief or happiness/sadness that the show/movie creates in the viewer's experience as the season or movie evolves can be measured.

In Sect. 3 we provide our formal model, which we argue fits all these applications. Then, in Sect. 7 we describe a different application over which we demonstrate the applicability of our model as well as the suitability and quality of several heuristic solutions that we propose for the model. The concrete application that we concentrate on in this paper is of *democratic playlist editing*:

- **Democratic Playlist Editing:** Producing a musical playlist - perhaps to accompany a podcast, movie, TV show, theater or dance, where there should be changes in different attributes over time, such as tempo, loudness, and emotions that will be expressed through the music (using chords, scales, and other musical tools).

1.1   Paper Structure

After discussing some related work (in Sect. 2), we go on to describe our formal model (in Sect. 3).

Then, as the aspect of our model that corresponds to respecting agent preferences is both crucial to our model as well as general, in Sect. 4 we describe how to capture different multi-winner rules in our model. We go on to provide a computational analysis of our general model (in Sect. 5) and to describe various general heuristics that we propose for solving instances of the general model (in Sect. 6).

We continue to describe the problem of democratic playlist editing in detail and in a formal way (in Sect. 7) and to report on computer-based simulations that we have performed on real-world and artificial data to evaluate the relevance and the quality of our algorithms (in Sect. 8).

We conclude in Sect. 9 with a discussion on the implications of our research and on promising future research directions.

2   Related Work

In this section, we discuss relevant related work in three areas: multi-attribute social choice, proportional ranking, and multi-attribute scheduling. Indeed, these three areas of study are the basis for the model presented in this work.

First, however, we would like to mention some related work that does not directly fall within these three areas:

- First, as our model can be viewed as a time-based social choice model, we mention ongoing work regarding the aggregation of continuously-changing agent preferences [1].
- Second, in our work, we draw inspiration from work that combines social choice aspects with recommendation systems, such as the work of Burke et al. [7], that evolves around the exploration of dynamic fairness-aware recommendation systems using multi-agent social choice.
- Third, our multi-attribute setting also has some connections with work on the group activity selection problem [9].

2.1   Multi-attribute Social Choice

Multi-attribute social choice involves aggregating preferences of a group over alternatives with multiple attributes. Our work focuses on a multi-attribute setting where each element has a vector of numerical attribute values [5, 8, 16]. Various works explore social choice settings with different attributes, such as democratic parliamentary elections aiming for proportional representation of attributes like gender and race in society [4, 6, 22, 23, 27].

2.2 Proportional Ranking

Traditional approval voting ranks alternatives based on the percentage of approving voters, but it may not accurately reflect the preferences of the population. The proportional ranking model addresses this by interleaving alternatives supported by different groups of agents, reflecting relative popularity. It emphasizes sorting candidates to ensure proportional committees, considering candidate diversity and order. This model finds applications in recommendation systems, hiring, committee elections, and liquid democracy [28]. In our work, we aim to generate rankings with a broader scope than Skowron et al. [28]. Specifically, in Sect. 7, we consider proportionality in collaborative playlist editing, where tracks are ranked based on acoustic features, popularity, and proportional representation. We also mention other related works [14,18].

2.3 Multi-attribute Scheduling

The single-machine scheduling problem involves finding the optimal order of tasks on a single machine to minimize the total completion time or other objectives. Multi-attribute scheduling extends this by considering multiple objectives and constraints. It aims to find a schedule that satisfies constraints while optimizing objectives like completion time or resource utilization [15,20]. Our model generalizes the multi-attribute single-machine problem, emphasizing multi-objective optimization and incorporating the social choice aspect.

3 Multi-Attribute List Aggregation (MALA)

In this section, we present the formal model of Multi-Attribute List Aggregation (MALA). An instance of MALA consists of the following ingredients:

1. A set of y attributes, denoted with their index $q \in [y]$.
2. A set of m elements, $C = \{c_1, \ldots, c_m\}$. Each element c_i, $i \in [m]$, for each attribute $q \in [y]$, has some numerical value; we define c_i^q to be the numerical value of element i for attribute q (so, in particular, $c_i^q \in \mathbb{R}$).
3. A value $k \leq m$, $k \in \mathbb{N}$; this is the desired size of the list that is the output of the instance.
4. A set of z so-called Ω constraints, denoted by $\{\Omega_1, \ldots, \Omega_z\}$. Below we describe what is an Ω-constraint: in particular, an Ω-constraint is defined by a tuple (q, F, d, w); next we describe what are q, F, d, and w:
   - $q \in [y]$ is the index of some attribute.
   - $F := \{f_1, \cdots, f_t\}$ is a family of t vectors, each of length k; formally, $f_\ell \in \mathbb{R}^k$, $\ell \in [t]$. We use a square brackets notation for vectors; i.e., for $\ell \in [t]$, $s \in [k]$, we write $f_\ell[s]$, $f_\ell[s] \in \mathbb{R}$, to denote the value of the s'th element of f_ℓ. (Intuitively, each of these vectors corresponds to some ideal behavior of the output list with respect to attribute q).

- d is a metric that returns a distance between two real-valued vectors of length k. Formally, $d : \mathbb{R}^k \times \mathbb{R}^k \to \mathbb{R}$; i.e., d is a function that takes two vectors of length k and returns a numeric value that we interpret as their distance; and it shall be a metric. (Intuitively, the metric d quantifies how close-to-ideal is the output list to at least one of the ideal vectors, with respect to the attribute q; note that we will use d only to evaluate the distance between some possible solution and some vector of F.)
- $w \in \mathbb{R}$, is the weight that the Ω-constraint gets. (Intuitively, it corresponds to the importance of that Ω-constraint.)

An instance of MALA as described above defines a cost for each possible *solution* to it. To describe what it is, let *solution* be some possible solution to an instance of MALA; first, formally, *solution* shall satisfy the following:

- *solution* $\in C^k$; i.e., *solution* is a vector of k elements, each from C.
- For $s_1 \neq s_2$, it holds that $solution[s_1] \neq solution[s_2]$; i.e., there can be no repetitions.

Below we describe the *cost* of a possible solution *solution*:

- First, the cost of a solution *solution* with respect to a specific Ω-constraint $\Omega = (q, F, d, w)$ is, roughly speaking, the weight (w) multiplied by the distance (according to d) between the values of the elements of the solution for the attribute q to the vector of F that is the closest to it; formally, we define:

$$cost(solution, \Omega) = w \cdot min_{f \in F} d(f, solution^q),$$

where $solution^q \in \mathbb{R}^k$ is the vector containing the values of the elements of the solution with respect to the attribute q; formally, $solution^q[s] := solution[s]^q$, $s \in [k]$.
- Second, the cost of a solution *solution* with respect to an instance of MALA $MALA$ (that contains z Ω-constraints) is defined naturally as the summation of its cost with respect to each of the Ω-constraints; formally, we define:

$$cost(solution, MALA) = \sum_{i \in [z]} cost(solution, \Omega_i).$$

Given an instance of MALA $MALA$, we are looking for a solution *solution* of minimum cost; formally, we are looking for the following:

$$\arg \min_{\substack{solution \in C^k \\ solution[s_1] \neq solution[s_2] \\ \text{for } s_1 \neq s_2}} cost(solution, MALA)$$

Consider the following toy example.

Example 1. Jimmy would like to prepare food to take to work and needs to decide what to bring to each of his three meals, during the day. His decision is based on 3 attributes: (1) personal preferences, (2) calories, (3) and sugar.

His candidates are: (1) apple, (2) orange, (3) omelette sandwich, and (4) tuna sandwich. Each candidate is defined by its unique attributes' values. Jimmy also sets his ideal attribute values for each one of the three meals and the importance of each attribute. Thus, the formal instance – denoted by $MALA$ – is given by (with some specific data):

- $y = 3$;
- $k = 3$
- Ω-constraints:
  - q_1= apple, q_2= orange, q_3= omelette sandwich, q_4= tuna sandwich.
  - $F_1 = \{f_1\}$, where $f_1[1] = 10, f_1[2] = 10, f_1[3] = 10$;
  - $F_2 = \{f_2, f_3\}$, where $f_2[1] = 80, f_2[2] = 600, f_2[3] = 60$, and where $f_3[1] = 100, f_3[2] = 500, f_3[3] = 80$;
  - $F_3 = \{f_4, f_5\}$, where $f_4[1] = 0, f_4[2] = 20, f_4[3] = 0$, and where $f_5[1] = 0, f_5[2] = 0, f_5[3] = 0$;
  - d_i is the ℓ_1 norm, for each $i \in [3]$;
  - $w_1 = 1, w_2 = 0.5, w_3 = 0.8$.
- $C = \{c_1, c_2, c_3, c_4\}$ with jimmy's preferences given by: $c_1^1 = 7, c_1^2 = 95, c_1^3 = 19, c_2^1 = 4, c_2^2 = 60, c_2^3 = 12, c_3^1 = 5, c_3^2 = 530, c_3^3 = 15, c_4^1 = 10, c_4^2 = 570, c_4^3 = 50$;

Now let us observe a possible $solution_1$: [apple, omelette sandwich, orange] from the perspective of the cost of each of the Ω-constraints:

$$cost(solution_1, MALA)$$

$$= \sum_{i=1}^{3} w_i \cdot (min_{f_\ell \in F_i} d_i(f, solution^{q_i}))$$

$$= 1 \cdot (|10 - 7| + |10 - 5| + |10 - 4|)$$

$$+ 0.5 \cdot (|100 - 95| + |500 - 530| + |80 - 60|)$$

$$+ 0.8 \cdot (|0 - 19| + |20 - 15| + |0 - 12|) = 70.3.$$

4   Committee Scoring Rules Using MALA

Next, we will demonstrate the versatility of the MALA model for various voting rules. Our model is specifically designed for democratic settings, making it applicable to a wide range of use cases, including committee elections. One notable example is the Democratic Playlist Editing problem, which we will discuss in detail later.

Approval Voting and Borda Count: In the case of selecting a committee, the ideal approval score or Borda count would be achieved if all "n" agents voted or ranked the same "m" candidates, indicating a consensus. To model this, we represent the perfect approval score and Borda count as a vector of size "k," where each candidate's score is a constant value representing the number of votes or ranking positions they received from the "n" agents. Thus, this vector serves as an upper bound for calculating the cost of a given solution. Formally, we define:

- Each candidate's voting score is given by: voting score$(c_1) = \sum_{i=1}^{n} c_{i,1} \cdots$, voting score$(c_m) = \sum_{i=1}^{n} c_{i,m}$, and $c_{i,j} \in 0, 1$ or $c_{i,j} \in 0, 1, \cdots, k$ indicates the approval or ranking of candidate $j \in [m]$ by agent $i \in [n]$.
- $F_1 = f_1$, where in approval voting $f_1[s] = n$, and in Borda count $f_1[s] = n \cdot k$, for all $s \in [k]$.
- $d =$ any metric distance, such as ℓ_1 or ℓ_2.

PAV Score: The PAV (Proportional Approval Voting) score assigns scores to candidates based on the number of votes they receive, with the goal of allocating seats to candidates proportionally to their support, while also considering the number of available seats. In our model, each agent approves or disapproves of certain elements. We introduce a PAV cost constraint to represent the "loss" of the potential PAV score. This model can also be extended to OWA-based rules [13]. For each agent $v_j \in v_1, \cdots, v_n$ voting on elements $c_1, \cdots, c_m$, we create an Ω-constraint, and its distance will be the "PAV-cost," reflecting the "loss" of the potential PAV score. The following definitions apply:

- $q \in [m]$ corresponds to every agent.
- $solution[s]^j = 1$ if agent j approves of candidate i and 0 otherwise, for all $solution \in C^k$.
- $F = \{f_1\}$, $f_1 = \{[1]^k\}$.
-

$$d(x, y) = \begin{cases} \sum_{j=1}^{k-\ell_1(x,y)} \frac{1}{j}, & \ell_1(x, y) < k \\ 0, & else \end{cases}$$

Given such individual agent Ω-constraints, adding a weight vector of all "1" results in the realization of PAV as an instance of MALA.

5   Computational Analysis

To study the computational complexity of MALA we consider its decision variant, in which we are given an additional input that is the maximum total cost for which existence of a solution above is to be decided. First, we observe that, following the formulation described above of PAV as a MALA instance, NP-hardness is established [3]. Next we show that MALA is also NP-hard even with only 2 constraints.[1]

---

[1] There is a delicate point here with respect to the representation of the input. We discuss consequences of this to different applications in Sect. 9, but here, for the formal hardness statement and proof, it is crucial to describe the representation of the input that affects the length of the input. So, in particular, it is sufficient to assume that the F vectors in the input are given explicitly, while the d metrics are given as black-boxes of length $O(1)$.

Theorem 1. *The MALA Decision Problem is NP-hard.*

Proof. We provide a reduction from the subset-sum problem [21], where an instance X containing x_i, $i \in [n]$ is a "yes-instance" if a subgroup $X' \subset X$ exists that satisfies $|X'| = \frac{n}{2}$ and $\sum_{x_i \in X'} x_i = \frac{\sum_{x_i \in X} x_i}{2} = \frac{B}{2}$. To build an input for the MALA decision problem given the subset-sum input, we set the following Ω-constraints:

- **q** - We have a MALA problem with two identical attributes: q_1, q_2 having $c_i^1 = c_i^2 = x_i$ for all i.
- **F** - We set $F_1 = f_1$ where $f_1^j = 0$, and $F_2 = f_2$ where $f_2^j = M$, for all $j \in [k]$ (vector's length), where $M = \sum_{x_i \in X} x_i$.
- **d** - We create two distances based on the ℓ_1 distance between two given vectors:

$$d_1(vector_1, vector_2) = \begin{cases} 1, & \ell_1(vector_1, vector_2) > \frac{B}{2} \\ 0, & \ell_1(vector_1, vector_2) \leq \frac{B}{2} \end{cases}$$

$$d_2(vector_1, vector_2) = \begin{cases} 1, & \ell_1(vector_1, vector_2) > \frac{M \cdot n}{2} - \frac{B}{2} \\ 0, & \ell_1(vector_1, vector_2) \leq \frac{M \cdot n}{2} - \frac{B}{2} \end{cases}$$

- **Weights**- We set $w_1 = w_2 = \frac{1}{2}$.

We formulate the MALA model as a decision problem - Given all candidates C and: Ω-constraints, we want to determine if there exists a subset $X' \subseteq X$ such that $\sum_{i=1}^{2} cost(X', \Omega_i) = 1$. If such a subset X' exists, then $\sum_{x_i \in X'} x_i = \frac{\sum_{x_i \in X} x_i}{2} = \frac{B}{2}$. Conversely, if $c_{i,1} = c_{i,2}$, for all i, $F_1 = F_2$, $d_1 = d_2$, and $X = q_1 = q_2$, we can reduce the problem to the subset sum problem where $|X| = n$. In this case, if there exists a subset $X' \subseteq X$ such that $|X'| = \frac{n}{2}$ and $\sum_{x_i \in X'} x_i = \frac{\sum_{x_i \in X} x_i}{2} = \frac{B}{2}$, then $\sum_{i=1}^{2} cost(X', \Omega_i) = 1$. Thus, the MALA decision problem is NP-hard even with just two attributes, contradicting our polynomial assumption of the problem.

Observation 1. *It is worth noting that there are some polynomially-computable cases of MALA. For example, when the task is to choose an ordered sub-list of musical tracks that contains tracks with the most votes and is ordered by a non-ascending or non-descending tempo (speed of the track).*

6   Algorithms

Since our problem has been shown to be NP-hard, we have developed several heuristic algorithms to obtain a good solution within a reasonable time frame. In this study, we have chosen to test two main algorithms: Genetic and Simulated Annealing. Both of these heuristics are suitable for solving similar combinatorial optimization problems that have complex search spaces and multiple objectives.

To simplify the testing process, we make the assumption that each vector family, denoted as F, which describes optimal behavior over time or sequence of some feature q, has a finite set. (This assumption will be discussed further in the Outlook section.) In each of the heuristics explained here, we aim to find the ordered sub-group of k elements out of a total group of m elements that would minimize the weighted summation of costs defined by Ω-constraints.

Genetic Algorithm - The algorithm begins by generating an initial population of candidate solutions, each represented as a set of parameters. The cost of each solution is calculated based on the problem at hand. The population is then sorted based on the descending cost, and the best solution is identified. In each iteration, the algorithm updates the population size using adaptive population sizing techniques, which adjust the number of solutions in the population based on their performance. The crossover and mutation probabilities, which control the exploration and exploitation of the search space, are also updated adaptively [24]. New solutions are generated through crossover or mutation operations, ensuring that there are no repetitions among the solutions. The cost of each new solution is calculated, and the population is sorted again. If the best solution in the new population has a lower cost than the current best solution, it is updated accordingly. The algorithm continues iterating until the specified total run time is reached. Finally, the best solution found throughout the iterations is returned as the output of the algorithm.

Simulated Annealing - The algorithm starts by generating an initial random solution. It then sets the initial cooling rate and temperature, which are problem-dependent and determine the exploration-exploitation balance. Additionally, a number of iterations for a random start are specified to allow for more diverse exploration. During each iteration, the algorithm calculates the cost of the current solution and compares it to the minimal cost found so far. If the current cost is lower, the minimal cost is updated accordingly. The algorithm also computes the probability of accepting a worse solution based on an adaptive cooling rate [19]. If the probability allows accepting a worse solution, the minimal cost is updated. To explore the search space, a random element and index are generated. If the generated element is included in the solution, it is swapped with the element at the generated index. Otherwise, the element at the generated index is replaced with the generated element. The temperature is decreased using the cooling rate, gradually reducing the exploration ability of the algorithm. The process continues until the specified total run time is reached. Finally, the best solution found throughout the iterations is returned as the output of the algorithm.

7 The Democratic Playlist Editing Problem

The focus now shifts to the democratic playlist editing issue, specifically the problem of creating a playlist with a specific logic or theme. This problem, known as the Democratic Automated Generation Playlist Problem, involves a group of friends attempting to create a playlist. In this section, we will discuss this problem and its formulation using MALA. The Automated Generation Playlist Problem involves creating a playlist by selecting tracks from a given list based on their musical attributes, such as scale, key, tempo (beats per minute), time signature, loudness, valence (optimism), danceability, and more. The Democratic Automated Generation Playlist extends the original problem by allowing a community to vote on whether to include tracks in a playlist. Playlist editors and critics usually look for the following three measures in a playlist [17, 26]:

1. **Coherence of tracks** - Listeners tend to like playlists with tracks that correspond (musically and lyrically) to each other homogeneously. In order to model the coherence of a feature using MALA, we must find the vector of some constant value. It will serve as a reference to measure the extent of the coherence of the attribute's behavior over time or over a sequence of events. Thus, we need to search all the positive constant vectors in order to find the most suitable one for $Solution[q]$ over time. Formally:
   - q corresponds to c_i^q.
   - $F = \{f_1, f_2, \cdots, f_t\}$ having $f_i[s] = p, i \in [t], p \in \mathbb{R}$, for all $s \in [k]$.
   - $d = \ell_1$ or ℓ_2

2. **Smooth transitions between two consecutive tracks** - Smooth transitions are highly valued by users as they provide a seamless progression of attributes, whether in sequence or over time. The primary objective of these transitions is to maintain a consistent flow while minimizing abrupt changes in attributes value's direction over time.
   - $q_{j \in 0, \cdots, k-1}$ address a particular attribute, and e, the maximum explicit number of direction changes it values can undergo.
   - $F = \{f_1, f_2, \cdots, f_t\}$ having $f_i = \mathbb{R}^k, i \in [t]$,
     such that $0 \leq \sum_{s=2}^{k-1} \delta(sign(f_i[s] - f_i[s-1]), sign(f_i[s+1] - f_i[s])) \leq e \in [k-1]$,
     $\delta(x, y) = 0$ if $x = y$, else $\delta(x, y) = 1$.
   - $d = \ell_1$ or ℓ_2.
   This modeling of smooth transitions as well as coherence, is in contradiction to our initial assuming of a finite set of functions F. Because the modeling of these qualities depend on the attribute's behaviour and the actual suggested tracks; we do not have a way of predicting what would be the ideal set of functions, and so we can only approximate by giving a few reasonable functions (a finite set of vectors).

3. **Diversity** - Like many democratic parliaments that ensure seats for different groups in society (such as women and minorities) to maintain a proportional representation of society, a playlist should aim for representation of different attributes of the given tracks, including genres (e.g., jazz, pop, rock, reggae, Brazilian, Afro-beat, Indian), scales (e.g., major and minor), time signatures (e.g., even and odd beat division of a track), and ranges of tempo (e.g., Largo (very slow), Adagio (slow), Andante (medium-slow), Moderato (medium), Allegro (medium-fast), and Presto (fast)).While the two measures

before where based on numerical valued attributes, this measure is based on categorical valued attributes. Formally:

- q corresponds to $c_i^q \in [r]$ having $r = |P^q|$, and P^q to be the set of categories associated with attribute q.
- $F = \{f_0, f_1, \cdots, f_t\}$, $f_i = \{f_i[s] | s \in k, f_i[s] \in [r], freq(f_i[s], f_i) = \pi_{p \in P^q}\}$ having π_p to be the optimal proportion of each category of attribute q.
- $d = \ell_1$ or ℓ_2

In conclusion, the Democratic Automated Generation Playlist Problem involves selecting an ordered subset of k tracks from a set of total m musical tracks that satisfy both the user's own taste and some musical constraints.

Example 2. A community of 3 music lovers decided to collaboratively edit a three sized democratic playlist (i.e., k = 3) out of a 5 sized list of tracks (i.e., candidates). Each track has the following musical features and meta-data. After each member of the group has selected three tracks from the given list of tracks we assemble them into a binary-requirements-matrix where 1 represents if a track i was chosen by agent j:

Number	Name	Artist	Album	BPM	Scale	Loudness
1	"I Wish"	Stevie Wonder	"Songs In the Key of Life"	106	B flat minor	−10.4
2	"Thriller"	Michael Jackson	"Thriller"	139	E flat minor	−3.7
3	"So What"	Miles Davis	"Kind of Blue"	138	C major	−17.27
4	"Oye Como Va"	Carlos Santana	"Abraxas"	128	G major	−13.21
5	"Reelin' in the Years"	Steely Dan	"Can't Buy a Thrill"	135	D major minor	−17.34

	Track 1	Track 2	Track 3	Track 4	Track 5
agent 1	0	1	1	0	1
agent 2	0	1	1	1	0
agent 3	1	0	1	0	1

We aim to create a 3-track playlist that maximizes: (1) social welfare of the listeners while maintaining (2) coherence in beats per minute (BPM) among the tracks. This coherence ensures that all tempos of tracks are close to either 120 (medium tempo) or 180 BPM (fast tempo). We will explore both a potential "good" solution and a potential "bad" (or "expensive") solution for the given example, using distance ℓ_1 and measured by explicit F vectors:

- $F_{welfare} = F_1 = \{f_1\}$ where $f_1[1] = 3, f_1[2] = 3, f_1[3] = 3$
- $F_{BPM\ coherence} = F_2 = \{f_2, f_3\}$ where $f_2[1] = 120, f_2[2] = 120, f_2[3] = 120$, and where $f_3[1] = 180, f_3[2] = 180, f_3[3] = 180$.

Social welfare is given the weight $w_1=5$ and BPM coherence of tracks is given the weight of $w_2=0.5$.

- Good solution: $\sum_{i \in [2]} \text{cost}([track5, track3, track2], \Omega_i)$ =
  $5 \cdot \text{cost}([track5, track3, track2], \Omega_1) + 0.5 \cdot \text{cost}([track5, track3, track2], \Omega_2) =$
  $5 \cdot (|2-3| + |3-3| + |3-2|) + 0.5 \cdot (|135-120| + |138-120| + |139-120|) = 36.$
- Worst solution: $\sum_{i \in [2]} \text{cost}([track1, track2, track4], \Omega_i)$ =
  $5 \cdot \text{cost}([track1, track2, track4], \Omega_1) + 0.5 \cdot \text{cost}([track1, track2, track4], \Omega_2) =$
  $5 \cdot (|1-3| + |2-3| + |1-3|) + 0.5 \cdot (|106-120| + |139-120| + |128-120|) = 45.5.$

8   Experimental Analysis

To evaluate the quality of the heuristics discussed earlier, we conducted a simulation of the Democratic Playlist Editing problem modeled as a MALA-optimization problem.

8.1   Experimental Design

We generated ten 700-track playlists from Spotify's "Top 10,000 Songs Of All Times" playlist[2]. For each instance, we applied the discussed algorithms to find an ordered sub-list of 250 tracks that minimized the cost within a ten-minute run. The heuristic parameters were set as follows: simulated annealing and sequential simulated annealing with a temperature of 1000°, an initial cooling rate of 0.003, and a random start every 1000 iterations. Genetic Algorithm was initialized with an initial crossover probability of 0.85, an initial population size of 100, and a maximum population of 5000. The costs were normalized using a 100-random algorithm, which generated 100 random permutations and selected the one with the minimal cost. This allowed us to calculate the average cost per minute for all 10 instances.

We selected three audio features from Spotify's API out of 13 available features [10]: Energy (0.0 to 1.0 score representing intensity and activity), Tempo (measured in beats per minute), and Danceability (0.0 to 1.0 score representing suitability for dancing). These features were chosen for their significant impact on playlist formation.

Approval scores were added to each track using an artificial society of 20 agents. An algorithm was used to generate a list of 700 integers, ensuring a sum of 5000. The algorithm randomly and uniformly generated approval ballots, divided the remaining sum by the remaining iterations, and updated the list accordingly. If there was a remaining sum, it was distributed incrementally to randomly selected indices until reaching zero. Next, we generated 10 families of functions (represented as vectors), each one containing 50 different 250-sized vectors. These functions within each family can be divided into two types:

---

[2] https://open.spotify.com/playlist/1G8IpkZKobrIlXcVPoSIuf.

1. We aimed for an ideal behavior of certain attributes over time, specifically smooth transitions for BPM and energy, with 1–3 direction changes to ensure smoothness along the playlist. This resulted in a total of 6 families of functions.
2. We defined an ideal static value to measure the coherence of attributes, where changes in direction are 0 and the slope (i.e., the size of change between two consecutive tracks) is 0. This applies to BPM, danceability, energy, and approval score, with the latter only including one vector/function of "all 20s".

We developed an algorithm that takes in the minimum number of direction changes, a range for the first variable in the vector (distributed uniformly), a range for the slope between consecutive variables in the vector (distributed uniformly), and the minimum and maximum values to set the range of legal values in the vector. The algorithm generates the initial direction ($+$ or $-$) uniformly and k indexes in the range of 2–248, where k is the number of direction changes and $index_i - index_{i+1} \geq 2$. Whenever the algorithm reaches one of the indexes, or if the value of the current variable is greater than the maximum value or smaller than the minimal value, a change of direction will occur. Finally, we set the distance d as ℓ_1 and generated a weight for each Ω-constraint combination, including:

1. Energy weights for 0, 1, 2, and 3 changes of direction over time. These weights were generated uniformly between 1 to 3, taking into account the involvement of energy in creating a playlist.
2. Tempo weights for 0, 1, 2, and 3 changes of direction over time. These weights were generated uniformly between 0.0001 to 0.001, as tempo was deemed to be a feature of less importance in our simulation.
3. Danceability weight for 0 changes of direction over time. These weights were generated uniformly between 3 to 4, aiming to create a highly danceable playlist.
4. Approval score weight for 0 changes of direction over time. These weights were generated uniformly between 4 to 5, with the intention of creating a playlist of popular tracks.

We also tested a greedy algorithm as an additional reference, wherein we preformed a local search for the most suitable track to fit into every location in the list. Finally, we performed another simulation to measure the time required for the simulated annealing algorithm to reach half the value of zRandom on 10 different instances of different sizes (selected randomly), ranging from 30 tracks to 240, in jumps of 30.

8.2   Results and Analysis

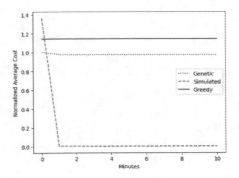

Fig. 1. Algorithms's Cost Over a 10 min Run.

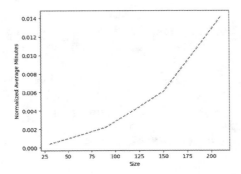

Fig. 2. SA Average Time VS Size of Playlist - until $SA\ cost = 0.5 \cdot (zRandom\ cost)$.

The results in Fig. 1 show that the simulated annealing algorithm achieved the lowest normalized cost quickly, with genetic algorithms performing worse. Figure 2 confirms that the simulated annealing algorithm takes longer to reach half the value of zRandom as the instance size increases. These results suggest that the simulated annealing algorithm explores a wider range of solutions compared to the more restrictive genetic algorithm, which converges slower due to maintaining parental order. Alternatively, the suboptimal tuning of initial parameters, such as adaptive crossover probability and population size, may explain the genetic algorithm's performance and could be improved with additional tuning techniques. These results suit the findings of Piotr Faliszewski et al [11] on effective heruistics for committee scoring rules.

9 Outlook

In future research, we suggest exploring the following directions:

- **Logical constraints:** Currently, we assume finite family functions F, limiting the model's applicability. Extending the model with logical predicates (P) as Ω-constraints could overcome this limitation and allow for the formulation of desired attribute behaviors over time.
- **Time-axis:** In playlist editing, considering variable song durations would require treating functions F as continuous functions, with the optimization problem involving a constraint on the summation of selected elements' time. This change from our current assumption of equal song durations can offer added flexibility to the process.
- **Several dimensions:** While our model is one-dimensional, considering a variant with multiple dimensions could be valuable for democratic editing of graphical illustrations or other multidimensional scenarios.
- **Heuristic solutions:** While we employed three standard heuristics, exploring alternative algorithmic solutions, such as constructing a linguistic model tailored to the MALA instance using Ngrams [25], may yield improved results.
- **Computational analysis:** Investigating both tractable and intractable special cases of MALA can enhance our understanding of the model's applicability and provide insights into its computational complexity, in particular by examining different types of distances in the Ω constraints.

References

1. Anonymous personal communication. Continuous preference aggregation in one dimension (2023)
2. Arrow, K.J., Sen, A., Suzumura, K.: Handbook of Social Choice and Welfare, vol. 2. Elsevier, Amsterdam (2010)
3. Aziz, H.: Proportional representation in approval-based committee voting and beyond (2018)
4. Aziz, H.: A rule for committee selection with soft diversity constraints. Group Decisi. Negot. **28**(6), 1193–1200 (2019). https://doi.org/10.1007/s10726-019-09634-5
5. Bossert, W., Peters, H.: Multi-attribute decision-making in individual and social choice. Math. Soc. Sci. **40**(3), 327–339 (2000)
6. Brederecek, R., Faliszewski, P., Igarashi, A., Lackner, M., Skowron, P.: Multiwinner elections with diversity constraints. In: Proceedings of the AAAI Conference on Artificial Intelligence, vol. 32 (2018)
7. Burke, R., Mattei, N., Grozin, V., Voida, A., Sonboli, N.: Multi-agent social choice for dynamic fairness-aware recommendation. In: Adjunct Proceedings of the 30th ACM Conference on User Modeling, Adaptation and Personalization, pp. 234–244 (2022)
8. Burke, R., Mattei, N., Grozin, V., Voida, A., Sonboli, N.: Multi-agent social choice for dynamic fairness-aware recommendation. In: Adjunct Proceedings of the 30th ACM Conference on User Modeling, Adaptation and Personalization, UMAP 2022 Adjunct, pp. 234–244. Association for Computing Machinery, New York, NY, USA (2022)

9. Darmann, A., Elkind, E., Kurz, S., Lang, J., Schauer, J., Woeginger, G.: Group activity selection problem. In: Goldberg, P.W. (ed.) WINE 2012. LNCS, vol. 7695, pp. 156–169. Springer, Heidelberg (2012). https://doi.org/10.1007/978-3-642-35311-6_12
10. Duman, D., Neto, P., Mavrolampados, A., Toiviainen, P., Luck, G.: Music we move to: Spotify audio features and reasons for listening. PLoS ONE **17**(9), 1–18 (2022)
11. Faliszewski, P., Lackner, M., Peters, D., Talmon, N.: Effective heuristics for committee scoring rules. In: Proceedings of the AAAI Conference on Artificial Intelligence, vol. 32 (2018)
12. Faliszewski, P., Skowron, P., Slinko, A., Talmon, N.: Multiwinner voting: a new challenge for social choice theory. Trends Comput. Soc. Choice **74**(2017), 27–47 (2017)
13. Faliszewski, P., Skowron, P., Slinko, A., Talmon, N.: Committee scoring rules: Axiomatic characterization and hierarchy. CoRR, abs/1802.06483 (2018)
14. Goldsmith, J., Lang, J., Mattei, N., Perny, P.: Voting with rank dependent scoring rules (2014)
15. Gupta, S.K., Kyparisis, J.: Single machine scheduling research. Omega **15**(3), 207–227 (1987)
16. Gupta, S., Jain, P., Saurabh, S.: Well-structured committees. In: Bessiere, C., (eds.) Proceedings of the Twenty-Ninth International Joint Conference on Artificial Intelligence, IJCAI-20, pp. 189–195. International Joint Conferences on Artificial Intelligence Organization, vol. 7 (2020). Main track
17. Ikeda, S., Oku, K., Kawagoe, K.: Analysis of music transition in acoustic feature space for music recommendation. In: Proceedings of the 9th International Conference on Machine Learning and Computing, ICMLC 2017, pp. 77–80. Association for Computing Machinery, New York, NY, USA (2017)
18. Israel, J., Brill, M.: Dynamic proportional rankings. arXiv preprint arXiv:2105.08043 (2021)
19. Karabin, M., Stuart, S.J.: Simulated annealing with adaptive cooling rates. J. Chem. Phys. **153**(11), 114103 (2020)
20. Karger, D., Stein, C., Wein, J.: Scheduling algorithms (2010)
21. Karp, R.M.: Reducibility among Combinatorial Problems, pp. 85–103,D US, Boston, MA (1972)
22. Lang, J., Skowron, P.: Multi-attribute proportional representation. Artif. Intell. **263**, 74–106 (2018)
23. Lian, J.W., Mattei, N., Noble, R., Walsh, T.: Using order weighted averages to assign indivisible goods. In: The conference Paper Assignment Problem (2018)
24. Lobo, F.G., Lima, C.F.: A review of adaptive population sizing schemes in genetic algorithms. In: Proceedings of the 7th Annual Workshop on Genetic and Evolutionary Computation, GECCO 2005, pp. 228–234. Association for Computing Machinery, New York, NY, USA (2005)
25. McFee, B., Lanckriet, G.R.: The natural language of playlists. In: ISMIR, vol. 11, pp. 537–541 (2011)
26. Pauws, S., Eggen, B.: Realization and user evaluation of an automatic playlist generator. J. New Music Res. **32**(2), 179–192 (2003)
27. Sikdar, S.K.: Optimal Multi-Attribute Decision Making in Social Choice Problems. Rensselaer Polytechnic Institute (2018)
28. Skowron, P., Lackner, M., Brill, M., Peters, D., Elkind, E.: Proportional rankings, Markus Brill (2016)

On the Graph Theory of Majority Illusions

Maaike Venema-Los[1](✉)(iD), Zoé Christoff[1](iD), and Davide Grossi[1,2](iD)

[1] University of Groningen, Groningen, The Netherlands
{m.d.los,z.l.christoff,d.grossi}@rug.nl
[2] University of Amsterdam, Amsterdam, The Netherlands

Abstract. The popularity of an opinion in one's direct circles is not necessarily a good indicator of its popularity in one's entire community. For instance, when confronted with a majority of opposing opinions in one's circles, one might get the impression that one belong s to a minority. From this perspective, network structure makes local information about global properties of the group potentially inaccurate. However, the way a social network is wired also determines what kind of information distortion can actually occur. In this paper, we discuss which classes of networks allow for a majority of agents to have the wrong impression about what the majority opinion is, that is, to be in a 'majority illusion'.

Keywords: majority illusion · social networks · graph colorings

1 Introduction

When making decisions, people often use information from the decisions of others in their circles and are influenced by those. For instance, if a lot of people around you buy a specific brand, vote for a specific political party, or have a specific opinion, you are more likely to buy, vote, or think the same (see e.g. [14,17]).

However, one's view of 'the world around' might be distorted by the social network one is in, and one might as a result misrepresent one's situation with respect to the overall population. A well-known example of this is the so-called 'friendship paradox' [9]: agents in a network are likely to get the impression that their popularity is lower than average because their friends have more friends than they do. Similarly, on the basis of what they can see of others around them, agents might get the wrong impression with respect to how popular their opinions are in the entire population. Indeed, the proportions of opinions an agent observes in its neighborhood are not necessarily a representative sample of their overall distribution in the population.

From this local sampling, one could for instance get the impression that they disagree with the majority of the population on a particular opinion and get influenced by this impression when taking their decisions. As a consequence, one could in principle influence what people will decide by changing the network structure to tweak the distribution of opinions/behavior agents see locally. Figure 1 (a), (b), and (c) illustrate this: rewiring a few edges is sufficient to make all nodes observe a different majority in their neighborhood.

V. Malvone and A. Murano (Eds.): EUMAS 2023, LNAI 14282, pp. 17–31, 2023.
https://doi.org/10.1007/978-3-031-43264-4_2

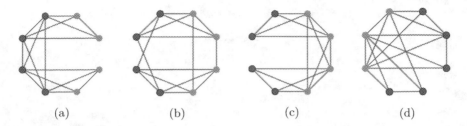

(a)　　　　　　　(b)　　　　　　　(c)　　　　　　　(d)

Fig. 1. (a), (b), and (c) have the same proportion of blue and red nodes but nodes see different distributions in their neighborhood: in (a), all nodes have a majority of red neighbors; changing two edges results in all nodes seeing a tie (b); changing two more edges makes nodes have a majority of blue neighbors (c). (d) is an example of a majority-majority-illusion: a majority (the red nodes) have more blue than red neighbors, while red is the actual global 'winner'. (Color figure online)

A paradigmatic example is polling bandwagon effects [19] in political decision making: if, for any reason, citizens prefer not to vote on a losing party, a party could increase the chances of *actually* winning by making a lot of voters *think* it is winning. The idea of manipulating the network towards this end, so-called 'information gerrymandering', is introduced in [4,20] and shown to potentially lead to undemocratic decisions. Similar phenomena have been observed in a variety of social networks [15].

In this paper, we examine which networks allow for which types of distortion between local and global opinion representations. We focus on a specific type of network distortion, 'majority illusion' as introduced by [15], where an agent observes that more than half its neighbors are in a certain state, while in the total network, less than half of the agents are in this state. An example is shown in Fig. 1d: if all nodes were to believe that their neighborhood was representative of the entire network, the red nodes would believe that the majority of nodes in the network is blue, while in reality it is red. Whether it is possible for such illusions to exist, and if so, for how many agents, depends on the network structure. On the one hand, not all networks allow for most agents to be under this type of majority illusions. On the other hand, there exist network structures in which even all agents can be under a majority illusion. In this paper we focus on the possibility of a *majority* of agents being in a majority illusion. The network in Fig. 1d is an example of such a 'majority-majority illusion'.

Related Work. The concept of majority illusion was first introduced in [15], to show how network structures can distort individual observations. Computational simulations are used to study to which extent the majority illusion can occur in scale-free, Erdős-Rényi networks, and several real-world networks, and show that networks in which high-degree nodes tend to connect to low-degree nodes are most susceptible to this illusion.

In [20] a voter game is modeled with two competing parties to show that majority illusions can be used for the purposes of 'information gerrymandering', that is, influencing people's votes by misrepresenting the opinion of the group to them. The authors predict this by a mathematical model and confirm their results with a social network experiment with human participants. They find that information gerrymandering can even take place when all agents have the same amount of influence (the same degree).

In [10], the computational complexity of majority illusions is studied. A q-majority illusion is defined, where at least a q fraction of agents are under majority illusion, and it is shown that the problem of deciding whether or not a given network can be colored into a q-majority illusion is NP-complete for $q > \frac{1}{2}$. Whether it also holds for $q \leq \frac{1}{2}$ is left as an open question. Since majority illusions can in some situations have detrimental effects and are generally regarded as undesirable, they also study the problem of eliminating an illusion from a network by adding or deleting edges. The problem to identify whether it is possible to change the network in such a way that the number of agents with a q-majority illusion is below a given bound is also shown to be NP-complete for $q > \frac{1}{2}$.

Contributions. We study the possibility of majority illusion in its weak and strict versions, in different classes of graphs. Section 2 introduces our framework, definitions and terminology. In Sect. 3, we prove that a weak version of the majority illusion can occur on *all* network structures. In Sect. 4, we provide some stronger results on specific classes of networks: graphs with odd degrees, properly 2-colorable graphs, and regular graphs. Table 2 gives a summary of which graphs allow for which type of majority illusions.

2 Preliminaries

Binary Opinion Networks and 2-Colored Graphs. A social network (a simple graph) $G = \langle V, E \rangle$ consists of a finite set V agents (nodes/vertices), and a set E of (undirected irreflexive) edges between agents. If two agents are connected by an edge, we call them neighbors. We assume that no agent is a neighbor of itself. We write N_i for the set of neighbors of i and d_i for its degree $|N_i|$. Each agent holds a binary opinion on a single issue. Since binary single-issue opinion distributions can be seen as graph 2-colorings, we will borrow the terminology of vertex colorings, and use the terms 'color' and 'opinion' interchangeably. We write c_i to refer to agent i's color and c for the 2-coloring of the graph ($c : V \rightarrow \{red, blue\}$). A 2-colored graph is a triple $C = \langle V, E, c \rangle$. Thoughout the paper, the term 'colored graph' refers to such 2-colored graph.

Majority Illusion and Opposition: Intuitions. In such opinion networks (or 2-colored graphs), we are concerned with three types of information: individual opinions, local majority opinions, and global majority opinions. Any two of these three types of opinions can be in agreement or not. We systematize and illustrate all possible relations between the above types of opinions in Table 1.

Different fields have been studying disagreement between the different types of information mentioned above. On the one hand, in social network science and social choice theory, an agent is under *majority illusion* when its neighborhood majority disagrees with the global majority [10,15]. On the other hand, graph theory has concerned itself with the disagreement between a node's color and the color of its neighbors: a proper coloring requires that no two adjacent nodes are of the same color, that is, that everybody disagrees with all of their neighbors. A generalisation of that concept is that of majority-coloring [1,5,13], where no agent agrees with most of its neighbors. We call the local disagreement faced by an agent in a majority coloring *majority opposition*. In such a situation, one might have the impression that they belong to a global minority. For instance, in Fig. 1d all nodes might have this impression, while it is only true for the blue ones. When all agents are under this impression, then some of them must be mistaken, it must be some sort of illusion. Clearly, the two concepts of majority illusion and opposition are related. In this paper, we explore this relation to get results about majority illusions.

Formal Definitions. We start by introducing some notions to be able to talk about which opinion is prevalent in a network, be it locally or globally. Given a set S of agents such that $|S| = n$ and a coloring c, a color x is a *majority winner* of S (we write $M_S = x$) if $|\{i \in S \mid c_i = x\}| > \frac{n}{2}$. When neither color is a majority winner among S (there is a tie), we will write $M_S = tie$. We say that an agent is under majority *illusion* if both the agent's neighbourhood and the entire network have a majority winner (no tie) but they are different. This definition is equivalent to that in [10].

Definition 1 (majority illusion). Given a colored graph $C = \langle V, E, c \rangle$, an agent $i \in V$ is *under majority illusion* if $M_{N_i} \neq$ tie and $M_V \neq$ tie and $M_{N_i} \neq M_V$. A graph is in a *majority-majority illusion* if more than half of agents are under majority illusion.

We can generalise this strict definition to weaker cases. First, there exists a weaker type of disagreement between local and global majorities: the cases where exactly one of the two is a tie. Second, the majority of agents under an illusion can also be weak, when exactly half of the agents are under illusion. The corresponding generalisations of majority illusion includes both types of weakening:

Definition 2 (weak versions of majority illusion). Given a colored graph $C = \langle V, E, c \rangle$, agent $i \in V$ is under *weak-majority illusion* if $M_{N_i} \neq M_V$. A graph is in a *majority-weak-majority illusion* if more than half of the agents are under weak-majority illusion. A graph is in a *weak-majority-(weak-)majority illusion* if at least half of the agents are under (weak-)majority illusion.

As indicated in Table 1, while it is the strict version of the majority illusion that is studied by [15][1], and by [10], it is the weak version of majority opposition

---

[1] They use the strict version throughout the paper, except for Fig. 1 where the illusion can be weak.

Table 1. Possible combinations of local and global majority winners, and presence or absence of majority opposition and majority illusion. We assume w.l.o.g. that the color of the relevant individual (highlighted in the exemplary illustrations) is red, otherwise just swap 'red' and 'blue' everywhere. ✗ indicates absence of the opposition/illusion, ✓ indicates presence of the opposition/illusion, 'weak' indicates the presence of a weak-majority opposition or a weak-majority illusion.

	local majority	majority opposition	global majority	majority illusion
	red	✗	red	✗
	red	✗	tie	weak
	red	✗	blue	✓ [15,10]
	tie	weak [1,5,13]	red	weak
	tie	weak [1,5,13]	tie	✗
	tie	weak [1,5,13]	blue	weak
	blue	✓	red	✓ [15,10]
	blue	✓	tie	weak
	blue	✓	blue	✗

that is studied by [1,5], and [13]. As far as we know, the strict majority opposition and the weak majority illusions have not been studied before. Furthermore, note that, in the same network, different agents can be under a weak-majority illusion with respect to different opinions, since it is possible that exactly half of the nodes in the network are of one color and half of the nodes of the other color.

Before proceeding, we introduce some extra terminology. When an agent is under majority illusion and all its neighbors all have the same color, we say that agent is in *unanimity illusion*. Similarly, when all agents are under a (weak)-majority illusion, we will call it a *unanimity-(weak-)majority illusion*. We say that *an illusion is possible* for a graph $G = \langle V, E \rangle$ if there exists a coloring c such that $C = \langle V, E, c \rangle$ is in the respective illusion.

3   Illusions in Arbitrary Networks

Our overall goal is to discover which social networks allow for majority illusions to occur. Since this is equivalent to asking which graphs can be colored in some specific way, we build on existing results from vertex colorings to obtain results about majority illusions. Recall that a coloring is called *proper* when no two neighbors are assigned the same color. The weaker notion of majority coloring [1, 13] is immediately relevant to us. In a majority coloring, each vertex is in what we described as majority opposition: at least half of its neighbors are of a different color than its own. For coherence with the rest of the paper, we call this a *weak majority coloring* here:

Definition 3 (weak majority 2-coloring). A weak majority 2-coloring of a graph $G = \langle V, E \rangle$ is a 2-coloring c such that, for each $i \in V : M_{N_i} \neq c(i)$.

A graph is called weak majority 2-colorable if there exists a weak majority 2-coloring of it. Given a colored graph, we call *monochromatic* the edges between nodes of the same color, and *dichromatic* the ones between nodes of different colors.

Remark 1. The main result involving majority colorings is credited to [16] in the literature [1,5]: every graph is weak majority 2-colorable. The proof strategy for this result is commonly described as easy and relying on a simple 'color swapping mechanism' that can only reduce the total number of monochromatic edges in the network. However, [16] itself focuses on multigraphs and is of a much wider scope. Therefore, to make the paper self-contained, we provide both a proof of the general result in Appendix 1 and below a proof of the related lemma, crucial to our main result, Theorem 1.

Lemma 1. *Let* $G = \langle V, E \rangle$ *be a graph, and let* c *be a 2-coloring of* G *that minimizes the number of monochromatic edges. Then,* c *is a weak majority 2-coloring of* G.

Proof. Let E_M be the set of monochromatic edges and $E_D = E \backslash E_M$ the set of dichromatic edges in graph G colored by c. Assume for contradiction that there is a node $i \in V$ that is an endpoint of strictly more monochromatic edges (we write E_{M_i} for the set of such edges) than dichromatic edges (E_{D_i}): $|E_{M_i}| > |E_{D_i}|$. Consider now a second 2-coloring c' of G that only differs from c with respect to i's color, i.e., c' assigns the same color as c did to all nodes except for i: $c_i \neq c'_i$. Let us write E'_M for the new set of monochromatic edges, and E'_{M_i} and E'_{D_i} for the new sets of monochromatic and dichromatic edges from i. Given that $|E'_{M_i}| = |E_{D_i}|$ and $|E'_{D_i}| = |E_{M_i}|$, we now have $|E'_{D_i}| > |E'_{M_i}|$ and $|E_{M_i}| > |E'_{M_i}|$. Given that no other edge of the graph is affected by this change, the total number of monochromatic edges is smaller with coloring c' than it was with c: $|E_M| > |E'_M|$. But since we started by assuming that c was such that $|E_M|$ was minimal, this is a contradiction.   □

We now use the existence of such a majority coloring to prove the following general result:

Theorem 1. *For any graph* $G = \langle V, E \rangle$, *a majority-weak-majority illusion is possible.*

Proof. Let $G = \langle V, E \rangle$ be a graph and let c be a 2-coloring of G that minimizes the total number of monochromatic edges. By Lemma 1, c is a weak majority 2-coloring of G. Two cases:

- $M_V \neq tie$. Assume w.l.o.g. that $M_V = red$. Since c is a weak majority coloring, for any red vertex i, $M_{N_i} \in \{blue, tie\}$, and therefore $M_{N_i} \neq M_V$. Hence, a majority of the nodes (the red ones) is under (possibly weak) majority illusion: we have a majority-weak-majority illusion.
- $M_V = tie$. Two cases:
  - If $|\{i \in V : M_{N_i} \in \{blue, red\}\}| > \frac{|V|}{2}$, we have a majority-weak-majority illusion.
  - Otherwise (if $|\{i \in V : M_{N_i} = tie\}| \geq \frac{|V|}{2}$) choose a node j with $M_{N_j} = tie$ and define a new coloring c' that is equal to c for all nodes except for j: $c'_j \neq c_j$. Since j has as many blue as red neighbors, this does not change the total number of monochromatic edges in the graph. Therefore, c' is also a coloring that minimizes this number. Hence, by Lemma 1, c' is also a weak majority 2-coloring of G. Now, we have $M_V = c'_j$, and we can apply the logic of the first case: Assume w.l.o.g. that $c'_j = red$. Since c' is a weak majority coloring, for any red vertex i, $M_{N_i} \in \{blue, tie\}$. It follows that a majority of the nodes has $M_{N_i} \neq M_V$: we have a majority-weak-majority illusion. $\square$

One of the results in [10] is that checking whether or not a network allows for a *majority-majority* illusion is NP-complete[2]. Here, in stark contrast, we see that there is no need for checking whether a network allows for a majority-*weak*-majority illusion, since Theorem 1 shows that it is always the case.

4   Illusions in Specific Network Classes

While the above solves the question of the existence of *weak* majority illusions, we now aim to understand when the *strict* version of the illusion can occur. In order to obtain results in that direction, we turn to some classes of graphs with well-known global properties. Note that the results from this section are not intended to describe realistic classes of social networks but can instead be seen as a starting point for the systematic analysis of the types of graphs that allow for majority illusions. We focus on graphs with only odd-degree nodes, properly 2-colorable graphs, and regular graphs.

---

[2] [10] does not actually speak about a majority-majority illusion, but about 'at least a fraction of q agents is under majority illusion', with $q > \frac{1}{2}$. The fact that it then also holds for majority-majority illusion follows from that 'more than half' is equivalent to 'at least some fraction q where q is more than half' since we only have to consider rational numbers.

4.1   Graphs with Odd Degrees

Theorem 2. *For any graph $G = \langle V, E \rangle$ such that for all $i \in V, d_i$ is odd, a majority-weak-majority illusion is either a unanimity-weak-majority illusion or a majority-majority illusion.*

Proof. Let $G = \langle V, E \rangle$ be such that for all $i \in V$, d_i is odd. By Theorem 1, there exists a coloring of G that induces a majority-weak-majority illusion. Consider any such coloring c. Two cases:

- $M_V = tie$. For all $i \in V$, since d_i is odd, $M_{N_i} \neq tie$ and therefore $M_{N_i} \neq M_V$: we have unanimity-weak-majority illusion.
- $M_V \neq tie$. Assume w.l.o.g. that $M_V = red$. Since G is in a majority-weak-majority illusion, $|\{i \in V : M_{N_i} \in \{blue, tie\}\}| > \frac{|V|}{2}$, but since for all i, d_i is odd, this implies that all those vertices cannot have a tie: we have $|\{i \in V : M_{N_i} = blue\}| > \frac{|V|}{2}$, a majority-majority illusion.

$\square$

The intuition is that an agent with odd degree cannot see a tie in its neighborhood, which causes either *all* agents a to be in weak-majority illusion if there is a global tie, or, if there is no global tie, a majority of agents to be in a majority illusion.

Given a graph coloring we can define a 'swappable node' as a node whose neighbors all have at least 2 (so 3 for odd degree) more nodes of one color than nodes of the other color. Then, a corollary of Theorem 2 is the following:

Corollary 1. *For a graph $G = \langle V, E \rangle$ such that for all $i \in V, d_i$ is odd, if the coloring c witnessing that majority-weak-majority illusion is possible induces that $M_v = tie$ and that there is at least one $j \in V$ that is 'swappable', a weak-majority-majority illusion is possible.*

Proof. W.l.o.g. assume $c_j = red$ and define c' which is equal to c for all nodes except that $c'_j = blue$. Since c was a majority 2-coloring, all red nodes had more than half blue neighbors. Since j's neighbors all had a margin of at least 2 and nothing except j's color changed, all red nodes except j still have more than half blue neighbors in c'. Hence, half of the nodes are under majority illusion. $\square$

4.2   2-Colorable Graphs

In the same way as we used the existence of a majority coloring to obtain results about the existence of majority illusions we can also use the existence of a special type of weak majority colorings, the proper colorings, to obtain results about majority illusions in 2-colorable graphs.

Lemma 2. *Any proper 2-coloring of a graph $G = \langle V, E \rangle$ is either a majority-majority illusion or a unanimity-weak-majority illusion.*

The idea of the proof is similar to that of Theorem 2: no node can see a tie among its neighbors.

Proof. Let c be a proper 2-coloring of G. Two cases:

- If $M_V \neq tie$, then w.l.o.g. assume that $M_V = red$. Since more than half the nodes are red and all red nodes have a majority of blue neighbors, we have a majority-majority illusion.
- If $M_V = tie$, then all the nodes are under weak-majority illusion, since for all nodes, all neighbors are the other color. We have a unanimity-weak-majority illusion.

□

Both cases used in the above proof are cases of majority-*weak*-majority illusions (which were already guaranteed to exist by 1), but we can also show the existence of the strict majority illusion in two different cases. First, when the number of nodes is odd, there cannot be a global tie, so by using the first case in Lemma 2 we get the following proposition :

Proposition 1. *For any properly 2-colorable graph $G = \langle V, E \rangle$ with $|V|$ odd, a majority-majority illusion is possible.*

Proof. Let c be a proper 2-coloring of G. Since $|V|$ is odd, $M_V \in \{red, blue\}$, we can use the first case of the proof of Lemma 2: W.l.o.g. assume $M_V = red$. Since more than half of the nodes are red and all red nodes have only blue neighbors (since c was a proper 2-coloring), we have a majority-majority-illusion.   □

Second, when the color of a node can be swapped if needed, we can solve a tie:

Proposition 2. *For any properly 2-colorable graph $G = \langle V, E \rangle$ with some $i \in V$ such that for all $j \in N_i$ $d_j > 2$, a weak-majority-majority illusion is possible.*

Proof. Let c be a proper coloring of G. Two cases:

- If $M_V \neq tie$, then conformingly to Lemma 2, we have a majority-majority illusion.
- If $M_V = tie$, then swap the color of node i: let c' assign the same colors as c to all other nodes but $c'_i \neq c_i$. Now $M'_V = c'i$. W.l.o.g. say $c_i = blue$ and $c'_i = red$. All of i's neighbors are also red and have now exactly one red neighbor (i), and more than one blue neighbor. Therefore, all red nodes except for i have more than half of their neighbors blue. Therefore, exactly $\frac{|V|}{2}$ of the nodes are in a situation of majority illusion.   □

In [10], the complexity of checking whether a network admits (what we call) a weak-majority-majority illusion was left as an open problem. Propositions 1 and 2 show that by checking whether a graph is properly 2-colorable (which can be done in polynomial time [6]) and whether there exists a node whose neighbors all have degree larger than 2 or whether the number of nodes is odd, we can know that a graph admits a (weak-)majority-majority illusion. Still this does not give us the complexity of checking whether a network admits a weak-majority-majority-illusion: while this is a sufficient condition for a graph to allow for a (weak-)majority-majority illusion, it is not a necessary condition.

4.3 Regular Graphs

In [2], theoretical analysis and experiments where human subjects were asked to perform estimation tasks are used to study the influence of network structure on the wisdom of crowds. The authors find a remarkable difference between centralized networks, where the degree distribution varies a lot between nodes, and decentralized (regular) networks, in which all nodes have the same degree, regarding what social influence does to the accuracy of the estimates of individuals (when individual's estimates are based on a weighted average of their own belief and the beliefs of their neighbors). They show that in decentralized networks, social influence significantly improves individual accuracy and the group mean estimate. Furthermore, an overview of research about collective intelligence by Centola [7] mentions several studies about decentralized networks in practical applications: in decentralized networks, political polarization and biases about climate change and immigration are reduced [3,11], and social influence reduced biases about the risk of smoking [12], as well as (implicit) race and gender biases in clinical settings [8]. Since decentralized/regular networks seem to be beneficial for group accuracy and bias reduction, we wonder whether they also are 'good networks' in terms of the distortion we study: to what extend they allow for majority illusions. According to [15], differences between the degrees of nodes and their neighbors are one of the main factors enabling majority illusion. Therefore, one would expect that regular networks, where all nodes have the same degree, make majority illusions less likely. Nevertheless, we show that majority illusions (beyond the ones given by Theorem 1) are also possible in regular networks.

A k-regular network is a network in which all nodes have degree k. We start by considering the simplest cases of regular network: simple cycles, where $k = 2$, and complete networks, where $k = |V| - 1$.

Proposition 3 (simple cycles). *For any 2-regular graph $G = \langle V, E \rangle$, a (weak-)majority-majority illusion is not possible.*

Proof. Let $G = \langle V, E \rangle$ be any 2-regular graph. A node can only be under majority illusion if both of its neighbours are of the minority color. Every minority-colored node can serve as a neighbour for at most two nodes. Thus, to give at least half of the nodes a majority illusion, there must be at least $\frac{|V|}{2}$ nodes in the minority color, which is a contradiction with being a strict minority.   □

However, a majority-weak-majority illusion is possible, according to Theorem 1, and it is easy to find one (which we leave as an exercise to the reader).

Proposition 4 (weak-majority-majority illusion in complete graphs). *For any complete graph $G = \langle V, E \rangle$ (i.e. a k-regular graph with $k = |V| - 1$), a (weak-)majority-majority illusion is not possible.*

Proof. This is a corollary of Proposition 8 in Appendix 2. If $|V| = n$, according to Proposition 8, a weak-p-q illusion can occur iff there is an integer x such that $q(n - 1) < x < qn$ and $n - x \geq pn$. This implies that a majority-weak-majority illusion can occur iff there is an integer x such that $\frac{n-1}{2} < x < \frac{n}{2}$ and $n - x \geq \frac{n}{2}$. Clearly, there is no x that satisfies the first requirement.   □

We know (by Theorem 1) that a majority-*weak*-majority illusion is always possible on complete graphs too. We can go further and specify the types of colorings under which these graphs are in such an illusion.

Proposition 5 (majority-weak-majority illusion in complete graphs). *A complete 2-colored graph $G = \langle V, E, c \rangle$ is under majority-weak-majority illusion if and only if:*

- *the difference in numbers of nodes of each color is one; or*
- *the number of nodes of each color is equal, then it is under unanimity-weak-majority illusion.*

Proof. If the difference in numbers of nodes of each color is one, assume w.l.o.g. that $M_V = red$. Then for all red nodes r, $M_r = tie$, so we have a majority-weak-majority illusion. If the number of nodes of each color is equal, we have $M_V = tie$ but every node will observe a majority of the other color: we have a unanimity-weak-majority illusion.   □

We return to the analysis of general regular graphs. The number of minority-colored neighbours needed for an illusion gives a restriction on the possible values of k depending on $|V|$:

Proposition 6 ((weak-)majority-majority illusion in k-regular graphs). *Let $G = \langle V, E \rangle$ be a k-regular graph with $|V| = n$. If a (weak-)majority-majority illusion is possible on G, then n and k must satisfy:*

- $k \leq n - 4$ *if n and k are even;*
- $k \leq n - 3$ *if one of n and k is even and one is odd.*

Proof. This is a direct corollary of Proposition 9 in Appendix 2.   □

Example 1. Consider a k-regular graph $G = \langle V, E \rangle$ with $|V| = 6$ and $k = 4$. For any node to be in a majority illusion, at least 3 of its neighbours have to have a different color than the global majority color. Assume that the global majority color is red. Then there are at least 4 red nodes and therefore only 2 nodes can be blue. Therefore, no node can have 3 or more blue neighbours.

The number of available edges of the minority color brings another requirement on the relative values of $|V|$ and k for the strictest version.

Proposition 7 (majority-majority illusion in k-regular graphs). *Let $G = \langle V, E \rangle$ be a k-regular graph with $|V| = n$. If a majority-majority illusion is possible on G, then n and k must satisfy:*

- $n \geq \frac{2(3k+2)}{k-2}$ *(assuming $k \geq 3$) if n and k are even;*
- $n \geq \frac{2(3k+1)}{k-1}$ *(assuming $k \geq 2$) if n is even and k is odd;*
- $n \geq \frac{3k+2}{k-2}$ *(assuming $k \geq 3$) if k is even and n is odd.*

Proof. If G is in a majority-majority illusion, there are more than half of the nodes of one color. W.l.o.g., assume that this majority color is red, and that the minority color is blue.

- When n and k both are even, in order for a majority-majority illusion to exist, at least $\frac{n}{2}+1$ nodes have to be red. Nodes with an illusion have to have at least $\frac{k+2}{2}$ blue neighbours. Then, there have to be at least $\frac{n}{2}+1$ such nodes with an illusion. Thus there have to be at least $\frac{k+2}{2}(\frac{n}{2}+1) = \frac{(k+2)(n+2)}{4}$ edges to a blue node. Hence, there must be at least $\frac{(k+2)(n+2)}{4k}$ blue nodes because every blue node can have at most k edges. Since at least $\frac{n}{2}+1$ nodes were red, there are at most $\frac{n}{2}-1$ left over to be blue, so this means that $\frac{(k+2)(n+2)}{4k}$ must be at most $\frac{n}{2}-1$. This is equivalent to $n \geq \frac{2(3k+2)}{k-2}$ assuming that $k>2$;
- When n is even and k odd, in order for a majority-majority illusion to exist, at least $\frac{n}{2}+1$ nodes have to be red. Nodes with an illusion have to have at least $\frac{k+1}{2}$ blue neighbours. Then, there have to be at least $\frac{n}{2}+1$ such nodes with an illusion. Thus there have to be at least $\frac{k+1}{2}(\frac{n}{2}+1) = \frac{(k+1)(n+2)}{4}$ edges to a blue node. Hence, there must be at least $\frac{(k+1)(n+2)}{4k}$ blue nodes because every blue node can have at most k edges. Since at least $\frac{n}{2}+1$ nodes were red, there are at most $\frac{n}{2}-1$ left over to be blue, so this means that $\frac{(k+1)(n+2)}{4k}$ must be at most $\frac{n}{2}-1$. This is equivalent to $n+2 \leq k(n-6)$, which means $n \geq \frac{2(3k+1)}{k-1}$ assuming that $k>1$;
- When k is even and n odd, in order for a majority-majority illusion to exist, at least $\frac{n+1}{2}$ nodes have to be red. Nodes with an illusion have to have at least $\frac{k+2}{2}$ blue neighbours. Then, there have to be at least $\frac{n+1}{2}$ such nodes with an illusion. Thus there have to be at least $\frac{k+2}{2} \cdot \frac{n+1}{2}$ edges to a blue node. Hence, there must be at least $\frac{(k+2)(n+1)}{4k}$ blue nodes. Since at least $\frac{n+1}{2}$ nodes were red, there are at most $\frac{n-1}{2}$ left over to be blue, so this means that $\frac{(k+2)(n+1)}{4k}$ must be at most $\frac{n-1}{2}$. This is equivalent to $n \geq \frac{3k+2}{k-2}$ assuming that $k>2$.

$\square$

Example 2. Consider a k-regular network with $|V|=6$ and $k=3$. Let us assume that red is the global majority color, so we have at least 4 red nodes and at most 2 blue nodes. Then any node with a majority illusion has at least 2 blue neighbours. Since for a majority-majority illusion there have to be at least 4 nodes with an illusion, there are at least $4 \cdot 2 = 8$ edges to blue nodes necessary. However, since we have at most 2 blue nodes that each have only 3 edges, this is not possible.

For any n and k (with $k>2$ and n or k even) satisfying the above constraints, we can find a k-regular graph of size n that has a majority-majority illusion. Note that this does not mean that for any k-regular graph of size n we can find a coloring that gives a majority-majority illusion, because there exist many different regular graphs with the same n and k. We only show that, for all

(a) Color 7 nodes red and 5 nodes blue. Draw lines from red to blue nodes,

(b) until each red node has $\lfloor \frac{k}{2} + 1 \rfloor = 4$ connections to a blue node.

(c) Add an edge (green) such that all blue nodes have 6 edges.

(d) Draw a regular graph (purple) of the remaining edges between the red nodes.

Fig. 2. Example of the algorithm for Theorem 3, with $n = 12$, $k = 6$.

Table 2. The (im)-possibility of majority illusions on different classes of graphs. ✓ indicates that the illusion is possible on all graphs of the class, ✗ indicates that the illusion is not possible on any graph in the class, ✓ / ✗ indicates that the illusion is possible on some but not all graphs of the class. For the majority-weak-majority illusion, some stronger results are shown. References to the relevant results are given.

Class of graphs	majority-weak-majority		weak-maj.-majority	majority-majority
All graphs				
Graph with only odd-degree nodes		(Thm. 2)	✓ / ✗	
2-colorable graphs	majority-majority or unanimity-weak-majority			
2-colorable graphs with $|V|$ odd		(Lem. 2)	✓ (Prop. 1)	
2-colorable graphs with $i \in V : \forall j \in N_i : d_j > 2$	✓ (Thm. 1)		✓ (Prop. 2)	✓ / ✗
2-regular graphs			✗ (Prop. 3)	
Complete graphs with $|V|$ even	unanimity-weak-majority (Prop. 5)			
Complete graphs with $|V|$ odd			✗ (Prop. 4)	

combinations of n and k not excluded by our previous results, there exists at least one such graph with the illusion, and that we know how to find it.

Theorem 3. *Let n and k be any two integers such that $k > 2$ and k or n is even. If the requirements of Propositions 6 and 7 are met, there exists a k-regular graph $G = \langle V, E \rangle$ with $|V| = n$ on which a majority-majority illusion is possible.*

Proof sketch. We prove this by construction: we give an algorithm that takes as input n and k and returns a regular graph with n nodes of degree k that has a majority-majority illusion. The algorithm and a proof that the algorithm outputs the desired graph are given in Appendix 3. See Fig. 2 for an example with 12 nodes of degree 6.

Propositions 6 and 7 and Theorem 3 together give necessary and sufficient conditions for n and k for the existence of a k-regular graph with $|V| = n$ nodes on which a majority-majority illusion is possible.

5   Conclusion and Outlook

We studied weak and strong versions of the majority illusion. Using results about majority-colorings, we proved that no network is immune to majority-weak-majority illusion, and that some classes of graphs are not immune to stronger types of illusions either. The results are summarized in Table 2. We also provided an algorithm to find a k-regular graph of size n with a majority-majority illusion, when it exists.

The most natural direction for further research is to broaden the scope of our study: first, as we have initiated with Appendix 2, by considering proportions other than majority; and second, by considering classes of graphs that are more realistic as social networks, including not necessarily irreflexive ones. Moreover, beyond verifying their sheer possibility, we keep measuring the likelihood of such illusions for future work.

A different direction is to investigate the relation between majority illusions and *majority logic* [18], which can 'talk about' local majorities, but not about global majority. We propose to enrich the logic with a global majority operator, to express the results from this paper. The idea is elaborated on in Appendix 4.

Last but not least, it would be interesting to measure the impact of proportional illusions on specific social phenomena. For instance, how do they affect opinion diffusion dynamics in a population? How do they interact with polling effects? And how do they relate to better known types of illusions, such as the above-mentioned 'friendship paradox' [9]?

Acknowledgments. We thank the anonymous reviewers of EUMAS 2023 for their helpful comments. Zoé Christoff acknowledges support from the project Social Networks and Democracy (VENI project number Vl.Veni.201F.032) financed by the Netherlands Organisation for Scientific Research (NWO). Davide Grossi acknowledges support by the Hybrid Intelligence Center, a 10-year program funded by the Dutch Ministry of Education, Culture and Science through the Netherlands Organisation for Scientific Research (NWO).

References

1. Anholcer, M., Bosek, B., Grytczuk, J.: Majority choosability of countable graphs (2020)
2. Becker, J., Brackbill, D., Centola, D.: Network dynamics of social influence in the wisdom of crowds. Proc. Natl. Acad. Sci. **114**(26), E5070–E5076 (2017). https://doi.org/10.1073/pnas.1615978114
3. Becker, J., Porter, E., Centola, D.: The wisdom of partisan crowds. Proc. Natl. Acad. Sci. **116**(22), 10717–10722 (2019). https://doi.org/10.1073/pnas.1817195116

4. Bergstrom, C.T., Bak-Coleman, J.B.: Information gerrymandering in social networks skews collective decision-making. Nature **573**, 40–41 (2019). https://doi-org.proxy-ub.rug.nl/10.1038/d41586-019-02562-z

5. Bosek, B., Grytczuk, J., Jakóbczak, G.: Majority coloring game. Discrete Appl. Math. **255**, 15–20 (2019). https://doi.org/10.1016/j.dam.2018.07.020

6. Brown, J.I.: The complexity of generalized graph colorings. Discrete Appl. Math. **69**(3), 257–270 (1996). https://doi.org/10.1016/0166-218X(96)00096-0

7. Centola, D.: The network science of collective intelligence. Trends Cognit. Sci. **26**(11), 923–941 (2022). https://doi.org/10.1016/j.tics.2022.08.009

8. Centola, D., Guilbeault, D., Sarkar, U., Khoong, E., Zhang, J.: The reduction of race and gender bias in clinical treatment recommendations using clinician peer networks in an experimental setting. Nat. Commun. **12**(1), 1–10 (2021). https://doi.org/10.1038/s41467-021-26905-

9. Feld, S.L.: Why your friends have more friends than you do. Am. J. Sociol. **96**(6), 1464–1477 (1991). http://www.jstor.org/stable/2781907

10. Grandi, U., Lisowski, G., Ramanujan, M.S., Turrini, P.: On the complexity of majority illusion in social networks (2022). https://doi.org/10.48550/ARXIV.2205.02056

11. Guilbeault, D., Becker, J., Centola, D.: Social learning and partisan bias in the interpretation of climate trends. Proc. Natl. Acad. Sci. **115**(39), 9714–9719 (2018). https://doi.org/10.1073/pnas.1722664115

12. Guilbeault, D., Centola, D.: Networked collective intelligence improves dissemination of scientific information regarding smoking risks. PLoS ONE **15**(2), 1–14 (2020). https://doi.org/10.1371/journal.pone.0227813

13. Kreutzer, S., Oum, S., Seymour, P., der Zypen, D.V., Wood, D.R.: Majority colourings of digraphs. Electr. J. Comb. **24**(2) (2017). https://doi.org/10.37236/6410

14. Lazarsfeld, P.F., Merton, R.K.: Friendship as a social process: a substantive and methodological analysis. Freedom Control Mod. Soc. **18**, 18–66 (1954)

15. Lerman, K., Yan, X., Wu, X.Z.: The "majority illusion" in social networks. PLoS ONE **11**(2), 1–13 (2016). https://doi.org/10.1371/journal.pone.0147617

16. Lovász, L.: On decomposition of graphs. Studia Sci. Math. Hungar. **1**, 237–238 (1966). https://www.scopus.com/inward/record.uri?eid=2-2.0-0013497816&partnerID=40v&md5=e9e8f87de7efa20945f4217ca9ee1124

17. McPherson, M., Smith-Lovin, L., Cook, J.M.: Birds of a feather: homophily in social networks. Ann. Rev. Sociol. **27**(1), 415–444 (2001). https://doi.org/10.1146/annurev.soc.27.1.415

18. Pacuit, E., Salame, S.: Majority logic. In: Proceedings of the Ninth International Conference on Principles of Knowledge Representation and Reasoning, KR 2004, pp. 598–605. AAAI Press (2004). https://dl.acm.org/doi/10.5555/3029848.3029925

19. Schmitt-Beck, R.: Bandwagon Effect, pp. 1–5. John Wiley and Sons, Ltd (2015). https://doi.org/10.1002/9781118541555.wbiepc015

20. Stewart, A.J., Mosleh, M., Diakonova, M., Arechar, A.A., Rand, D.G., Plotkin, J.B.: Information gerrymandering and undemocratic decisions. Nature **573**(7772), 117–121 (2019). https://doi.org/10.1038/s41586-019-1507-6

Qualitative Uncertainty Reasoning in AgentSpeak

Michael Vezina[1][(✉)] [iD], Babak Esfandiari[1], Sandra Morley[2], and François Schwarzentruber[3]

[1] Carleton University, Ottawa, ON, Canada
michaeljvezina@cmail.carleton.ca, babak@sce.carleton.ca
[2] Individual Researcher, Toronto, Canada
[3] Univ Rennes, IRISA, CNRS, Rennes, France
francois.schwarzentruber@ens-rennes.fr

Abstract. This paper presents an extension of AgentSpeak using dynamic epistemic logic (DEL) to reason about uncertainty. The extension relies on minimal AgentSpeak syntax to describe uncertainty, while augmenting the language with possibilistic reasoning via modalities. We apply the extension to a realistic navigation example with partial observability and vary the amount of uncertainty to evaluate scalability. Scalability is compared with an existing extension which relies on a less expressive form of DEL. We find that DEL's increased expressiveness comes with a linear cost in computational complexity.

Keywords: BDI · AgentSpeak · Uncertainty · Dynamic Epistemic Logic

1 Introduction

Belief-Desire-Intention (BDI) is a model for developing intelligent agents based on the principles of practical reasoning in humans [12]. BDI is rooted in modal logic, where one may reason about the *beliefs*, *desires*, and *intentions* of the agent.

AgentSpeak is an abstract programming language based on the principles of BDI, but removes itself from the modal logic roots of BDI in favour of a simple and practical implementation [15]. AgentSpeak is solely focused on capturing the agent's beliefs, desires, and intentions and fails to capture other important aspects of agent-oriented development such as reasoning about uncertainty [13].

To provide AgentSpeak with the ability to reason about uncertainty, we look to dynamic epistemic logic (DEL). DEL is a modal logic that captures belief uncertainty through the use of possible world semantics [2]. This paper introduces DEL-AgentSpeak (D-AS), an AgentSpeak extension that enables for reasoning about uncertainty through the modalities and expressive *event models* provided by DEL.

2   Background and Related Work

2.1   AgentSpeak

AgentSpeak is a BDI-based abstract agent-oriented programming language, which provides the operational semantics required for agent operation [15]. The programming language Jason [8] realizes AgentSpeak, providing an interpreter for its Prolog-based syntax and an implementation of the operational semantics. We use AgentSpeak/Jason interchangeably throughout the paper. An AgentSpeak program is composed of five main elements:

- **Beliefs** are explicit ground literals ℓ stored in a belief base, including perceptions from the environment.
- **Rules**, ℓ_r :- φ, are implicit beliefs ℓ_r formed under a belief condition φ.
- **Goals**, !ℓ, represent the agent's desires to be fulfilled.
- **Events**, reflect the addition (+) or deletion (−) of beliefs or goals, and are handled by *plans*.
- **Plans**: $te : c \leftarrow b$. The execution of a plan is based on the triggering event (te), a belief precondition (or context, c), and a sequence of instructions in the body (b). Instructions can include belief modifications (+ℓ, −ℓ), sub-goals (!ℓ), and actions (ℓ).

Listing 1.1 presents an illustrative AgentSpeak program with initial beliefs on Lines 1 and 2, a rule on Line 3, an initial goal on Line 4, and a plan on Line 5. In this example, `+!plan` will execute given the grounded context `rule(1)`, and will result in the action `act(1)`.

```
1  bel(1).
2  bel(2).
3  rule(X)  :- bel(X) & X <= 1.
4  !plan.
5  +!plan : rule(X) <- act(X); ....
```
Listing 1.1. Illustrative AgentSpeak Program.

The works presented in this paper extend the functionality of beliefs in AgentSpeak to allow for the specification of uncertainty. As such, we also provide a formal definition for the logical consequences (or entailment) of beliefs.

In AgentSpeak, beliefs and rules are housed in a belief base B. The agent is said to believe a conjunction of literals, φ, when φ is derived from B: $B \models \varphi$. A literal, ℓ, is a consequence of B if there exists a most-general unifier (MGU), θ, satisfying either of these conditions:

- It corresponds with a belief, b, such that $b = \ell\theta$, or
- It matches a rule, ℓ_r :- $\ell_1 \wedge \cdots \wedge \ell_n$, where $B \models (\ell_1 \wedge \cdots \wedge \ell_n)\theta'$ and $\ell_r\theta' = \ell\theta$.

A conjunction, $\varphi = \ell_1 \wedge \cdots \wedge \ell_n$, becomes a consequence of B if there exists an MGU, θ, such that $B \models (\ell_1 \wedge \cdots \wedge \ell_n)\theta$. We use $B \models_\phi \varphi\theta$ to obtain ϕ, an equivalent rewritten form of φ, containing the conjunction of ground beliefs in B that resulted in the consequence of $\varphi\theta$, i.e., ϕ is an equivalent rule-free rewritten form of $\varphi\theta$. The functions presented in this paper use this rewritten form to provide compact definitions that apply to both explicit and implicit beliefs.

2.2   Uncertainty Reasoning in AgentSpeak

In the existing literature, AgentSpeak has been extended using quantitative approaches to uncertainty in various works, such as those presented in [3,5]. These methodologies leverage probability theory, providing a precise approach to uncertainty reasoning. However, precision may not always be achievable or ideal, especially in scenarios where probabilistic distributions are not easily accessible. Moreover, these quantitative strategies typically rely on numerical representations of uncertainty within the agent's program. Given the symbolic nature of AgentSpeak syntax, incorporating these numerical elements often results in less streamlined solutions for uncertainty reasoning, thereby increasing difficulties during program development and maintenance [19].

On the other hand, symbolic uncertainty reasoning strategies, such as those proposed in [9,14], employ modalities and rankings to reason about uncertainty. Modal-based symbolic approaches are often favoured over other symbolic formalisms owing to AgentSpeak's roots in a modal logic (BDI). The alignment of AgentSpeak with modal logic (i.e., epistemic logic) for uncertainty provides an elegant description of uncertainty in the language. Although these strategies integrate well with AgentSpeak, they typically depend on logically complex dialects that are computationally infeasible, and hence, are largely theoretical and lack practical implementations [13,19].

In 2022, Vezina and Esfandiari introduced an approach to uncertainty reasoning in AgentSpeak, referred to as "PAL-AgentSpeak" (P-AS) [19]. P-AS extends AgentSpeak using public announcement logic (PAL). PAL is a restricted form of DEL, where public announcement events capture monotonic knowledge change about a static environment. Unfortunately, due to PAL's limited abilities, P-AS faces several non-trivial logical limitations that impact the general applicability of the extended language.

The reliance of P-AS on PAL restricts it to monotonic change, that is, our certainty of a static environment only increases as events occur. This severely limits the types of uncertainty that can be modelled with P-AS. For instance, PAL struggles to capture simple changes such as moving locations on a map due to its inability to model changes in state (also known as *ontic effects*).

Vezina and Esfandiari proposed an ad hoc workaround to capture movement using P-AS, which requires the anticipation of all resulting action-states at compile time and manual management of these states at run time. The author's have acknowledged that their presented workaround lacks soundness, generalizability, and elegance, and that it places unrealistic expectations on the agent at compile time.

Our paper aims to address these limitations in a sound, generalizable, and elegant manner by integrating DEL, a more expressive logic for change, with AgentSpeak. However, this integration is not a straightforward task, as it requires additional transformational semantics to fully represent DEL's expressive capacity within AgentSpeak. D-AS facilitates the comprehensive representation of DEL with AgentSpeak syntax, offering a declarative and idiomatic approach to express change within an AgentSpeak program.

In summary, while several approaches have attempted to introduce uncertainty reasoning into AgentSpeak, each has its limitations. This paper presents a new integration with DEL, aiming to overcome these challenges and provide a more comprehensive and practical solution for uncertainty management in AgentSpeak.

2.3   Dynamic Epistemic Logic

Dynamic epistemic logic (DEL) is a modal logic for reasoning about the statics and dynamics of knowledge [18]. Let P be a non-empty finite set of atomic propositions. A non-dynamic epistemic formula φ is given by the grammar:

$$\varphi ::= p \mid \neg\varphi \mid \varphi_1 \vee \varphi_2 \mid B\varphi.$$

where $p \in P$. The construction $B\varphi$ is read as 'the agent believes φ'. We introduce DEL with S5 semantics for knowledge, however, we use the term 'belief' to stay consistent with terminology used in AgentSpeak. The dual $\hat{B}\varphi = \neg B\neg\varphi$ represents a *possible* belief φ.

An S5 epistemic model $M = (W, V)$ provides semantics to the entailment of these formulae, where: W is a set of possible worlds and $V : W \to 2^P$ is a valuation that maps worlds to propositional states. Given a *pointed world* $w \in W$ used for entailment, entailment of truth conditions (boolean cases omitted) are: $M, w \models p$ iff $p \in V(w)$; and $M, w \models B\varphi$ iff for all $u \in W$, $M, u \models \varphi$. Entailment semantics for belief formulae $B\varphi$ are independent of any world $w \in W$ and can be simplified to $M \models B\varphi$.

A DEL event model $\varepsilon = (E, pre, post)$ captures the dynamics of uncertainty. E is a set of possible events, $pre(e)$ is an epistemic formula representing the precondition for event e, and $post(e)$ assigns an epistemic formula $post(e, p)$ to each proposition $p \in P$. We say that $post(e) = \backslash$ is *trivial* when $post(e, p) = p$ for all p. The application of an event model ε to an epistemic model M is a new epistemic model $M' = M \otimes \varepsilon$. The worlds in M' are pairs (w, e) in which the precondition of e holds in w, and in which we reassign the truth values of propositions according to *post*. Formally, the updated model M' is defined to be (W', V') where: $W' = \{(w, e) \in W \times E \mid M, w \models pre(e)\}$, and $V'((w, e)) = \{p \in P \mid M, w \models post(e, p)\}$.

Example 1 presents the navigation problem used throughout this paper while simultaneously demonstrating how we can naturally model the problem's uncertainty using DEL. In Sect. 8, we present an elegant agent-oriented solution to this problem using D-AS.

Example 1 (Navigation Problem). Consider the navigation problem introduced in [19], which is based off of the 2019 Multi-Agent Programming Contest (MAPC). The MAPC is a yearly contest that aims to simulate realistic environments by posing large-scale uncertainty problems and tight deliberation deadlines. The MAPC, specifically the navigation problem, represents a general class of uncertainty reasoning where modelling and reasoning about uncertainty is required in order to make a decision in the absence of probabilistic information [19]. An agent, Bob, knows the grid map (see Fig. 1) but is uncertain of his actual location, as he only perceives surrounding obstacles. Bob must navigate to the *goal cell.*

Fig. 1. The Known Map Definition.

We represent Bob's location with $\texttt{loc}(X,Y)$. Note that all directions are relative: $d \in \{\downarrow, \uparrow, \leftarrow, \rightarrow\}$. The corresponding initial epistemic model is $M_{\text{nav}} = (W, V)$ where:

$$W = \{w_{xy} \mid (x,y) \in \{0,\ldots,4\}^2 \setminus \{(1,2),(2,2)\}\}$$

$$V(w_{xy}) = \{\texttt{loc}(x,y)\} \cup$$

$\qquad px \qquad \{\texttt{loc}(x,y) \Rightarrow \texttt{obs}(d) \mid \text{obstacle in direction } d \text{ at } xy\} \cup$

$\qquad px \qquad \{\texttt{loc}(x,y) \Rightarrow \texttt{dir}(d) \mid \text{direction } d \text{ in shortest path to goal from } xy\}$

Bob is initially placed at $(1,1)$ and his partial observability allows him to perceive the obstacle at $(1,2)$, represented via $\texttt{obs}(\downarrow)$. The revealing of this fact is encoded by the event model $\varepsilon_{\texttt{obs}(\downarrow)} = (E, pre, post)$ with $E = \{e\}$, $pre(e) = \texttt{obs}(\downarrow)$, and $post = \setminus$. The resulting model $(M'_{\text{nav}} = M_{\text{nav}} \otimes \varepsilon_{\texttt{obs}(\downarrow)})$ eliminates all but two possible worlds (locations) that hold $\texttt{obs}(\downarrow)$: $\texttt{loc}(1,1)$ and $\texttt{loc}(2,1)$.

In order to get to the goal location, Bob now moves in the direction modelled by both possible locations: $\texttt{dir}(\rightarrow)$. The action $move(\rightarrow)$ is captured by $\varepsilon_{\rightarrow} = (E, pre, post)$ where:

- $E = \{e_{xy} \mid (x,y) \text{ is a non-obstacle cell}\}$,
- $pre(e_{xy}) = \texttt{loc}(x,y)$,
- $post(e_{xy}) = \begin{cases} \{\texttt{loc}(x,y)) = \bot, \texttt{loc}(x+1,y)) = \top\} & \textit{if } x \le 3 \\ \setminus & \textit{Otherwise} \end{cases}$

This event model captures the movement of the agent from each valid (i.e., non-edge) location to it's right-adjacent cell. The result $(M''_{\text{nav}} = M'_{\text{nav}} \otimes \varepsilon_{\rightarrow})$ contains the right-adjacent locations of all previous possible locations (inc. relevant obstacle and direction propositions): $(2,1)$ and $(3,1)$.

3   Methodology Overview

In general, the goal of D-AS is to provide a richer reasoning experience through the capturing of uncertainty and the explicit ability to query about the beliefs it considers certain and/or possible. This integration is achieved by assigning various transformational semantics to AgentSpeak, enabling the translation from AgentSpeak code into DEL models, formulae, and operations. In order to achieve this using DEL, we introduce three necessary operations: *model creation* (Sect. 4), *model updates* (Sect. 5), and *model queries* (Sect. 6).

D-AS utilizes a proposition-based form of DEL, as it provides linear computational complexity properties [16]. As such, the methodology we present in the following sections involve the transformation of literals into propositional formulae, referred to as *propositionalization* (see [11]).

4 Model Creation: Initializing an Epistemic Model

D-AS constructs the initial epistemic model based on the agent's initial beliefs. The model creation process of D-AS is based on the process introduced for P-AS by Vezina and Esfandiari [19], but introduces critical improvements. D-AS utilizes a SAT solver for model creation, a methodology that is inherently sound and can be generalized to other domains based on formulae described in the agent's program.

The standard AgentSpeak language lacks the ability to explicitly define uncertainty. Similar to P-AS, D-AS allows the agent to declare initial uncertainty through the use of **range** beliefs. The initial epistemic model is created based on the propositionalization of standard beliefs, **range** beliefs, and *constraints*, whose processes will be discussed in the following sub-sections. Once a propositional description of the initial belief state is obtained, a SAT solver is used to identify all satisfiable propositional solutions. These solutions are then used to populate the possible worlds in the initial epistemic model.

4.1 Propositionalizing Standard Beliefs

Explicit beliefs are simply ground literals. For a ground literal ℓ, propositionalization (denoted by pr) is trivial: we assign it a unique propositional symbol $pr(\ell) = \ell_{pr}$. Given a grounded expression ϕ, $pr(\phi)$ simply replaces ℓ with $pr(\ell)$ for all $\ell \in \phi$ and $\neg pr(\ell)$ for all $\neg \ell \in \phi$.

4.2 Propositionalizing Ranged Beliefs

Initial uncertainty of ℓ is declared through a ranged belief with the form: **range**(ℓ). Ranged beliefs simply indicate that the agent is uncertain about the truth value of ℓ. Ranged beliefs are propositionalized differently than standard beliefs to reflect uncertainty.

The ground ranged belief **range**(ℓ) is propositionalized as follows: $pr_{Ran}(\ell\theta) = pr(\ell\theta) \vee \neg pr(\ell\theta)$. Note that although the resulting propositional sentence is a tautology, it is necessary for the SAT solver to generate the correct propositional states.

We also obtain all positive and negated forms of ranged literals for grounding purposes. Given belief base B, the function $ran(B) = \{\ell\theta, \sim\ell\theta \mid B \models \texttt{range}(\ell)\theta\}$ provides the necessary grounding set. Additionally, given $R = ran(B)$ and a literal formula φ, the notation $(B \cup R) \models \varphi$ is used to obtain the consequences of φ using both ranged literals in R and any beliefs in B.

4.3 Propositionalizing Constraints

The agent may also know the condition(s) (e.g., φ) where the truth of a ranged belief $\texttt{range}(\ell)$ is known; these are indicated through the use of standard belief rules, e.g., $\ell \text{ :- } \varphi$. To incorporate these belief conditions into the initial epistemic model, we propositionalize their rule-free forms.

Given a set R of ranged literals and belief base B, the function $cons(R, B) = \{(\ell\theta, \phi) \mid (B \cup R) \models_\phi \ell\theta \ \ s.th. \ \ell \in R\}$ obtains pairs containing the ranged literal and MGU $\ell\theta$, and the rule-free condition ϕ resulting in the consequence of $\ell\theta$ given beliefs and ranged literals. Given a pair $(\ell\theta, \phi)$, we propositionalize the rule-free truth condition as follows: $pr_{Con}(\ell\theta, \phi) = (pr(\phi) \Rightarrow pr(\ell\theta))$.

4.4 Creating the Initial Epistemic Model

Given a belief base B and set of ranged literals R, we start the model creation process by obtaining all propositional sentences which describe the initial belief state of the agent, obtained via the following function:

$$all\_cons(B, R) = \{pr(\ell) \mid \ell \in B\} \cup \{pr_{Ran}(\ell) \mid \ell \in R\}$$
$$px \cup \{pr_{Con}(\ell\theta, \phi) \mid (\ell\theta, \phi) \in cons(R, B)\}$$

We then generate a set of possible worlds that conform to these sentences. This is done by finding all satisfiable solutions to the set of propositional sentences (S). Let $at(S)$ be the atomic propositions used by the formulae in S. The generation of the epistemic model is defined as: $gen\_model(S) = \langle W, V \rangle$, where: $W = \{w \in 2^{at(S)} \mid w \models S\}$, and $V(w) = w$, where $w \models S$ indicates that all formulas of S hold in w.

5 Model Updates: Updating the Epistemic Model

In AgentSpeak, belief events $+\ell$ and $-\ell$ represent the addition and deletion of a literal ℓ, respectively. The effects of these events on uncertainty will vary depending on the inherent meaning of belief ℓ; e.g., a movement event $(+\texttt{move}(\rightarrow))$ impacts the agent's beliefs differently than the perception of an obstacle $(+\texttt{obs}(\downarrow))$.

In P-AS, all belief events are treated the same, i.e., as monotonic epistemic change. As a result, P-AS fails to effectively capture change for many domains, including the navigation example.

By default, all belief events in D-AS are treated as ontic change. In cases where the default assumption (ontic change) is insufficient, D-AS allows the agent to capture the DEL event model associated with belief events through the use of "on" plans. Using ontic change as the default mode for belief events impacts the belief state in a way that is equivalent to standard AgentSpeak, and thus allows D-AS to be backwards-compatible with standard AgentSpeak programs. We introduce each belief update mode in more detail below.

5.1   Default Belief Event Models

In D-AS, belief additions and deletions are modelled as simple ontic changes when no corresponding "on" plans are available. Given a belief event trigger te, we create a corresponding default DEL event model: $def\_ev(te) = (E, pre, post)$ with: $E = \{te\}$, $pre(te) = \top$, $post(te, \ell) = \top$ (if $te = +\ell$) or $\bot$ (if $te = -\ell$). If the model given by $def\_ev(te)$ does not sufficiently capture the effects of the belief event te, the agent can override the default DEL event model through the use of *"on"* plans.

5.2   *"On"* Plans: Overriding Default Event Models

D-AS allows for a more intricate description of belief change through *"on"* plans. "On" plans contain a special trigger literal $on(\ell)$, which are seen as a meta-description of the epistemic/ontic effects of a belief event ℓ.

Given a belief event $+\ell$ (or $-\ell$) where ℓ is a ground literal, a standard AgentSpeak plan $te\colon c \leftarrow b$ is assigned *"on"* plan semantics when $te = +on(\ell)$ (resp. $te = -on(\ell)$). The plan is transformed into a corresponding DEL event model where the context and body are transformed into the pre- and post-condition(s), respectively.

Given a plan library P and triggering event te, we use $RelPlans(P, te)$ as defined by AgentSpeak's operational semantics in [8] to obtain a set of relevant plans (p, θ) with plan p and unifier θ. We use the function $rel\_on(P, te)$ to find all relevant *"on"* plans in P that correspond with te, where: $rel\_on(P, +\ell) = RelPlans(P, +on(\ell))$ or $rel\_on(P, -\ell) = RelPlans(P, -on(\ell))$.

Given a set R_{On} of relevant *"on"* plans and a belief base containing ranged literals B_R, we must ground all *"on"* plans using B_R before transforming into a corresponding DEL event. $AppPlans(B_R, R_{On})$ is another Jason-provided function which we use to find the applicable *"on"* plans from the relevant plans in R_{On} whose contexts are grounded consequences of B_R[1].

Transforming "On" Plans into DEL Event Models. D-AS transforms an applicable "on" plan (a, θ) with plan a and MGU θ, into its corresponding DEL event as follows: (a, θ) is the event's designated identifier and $pre((a, \theta)) = pr(Ctxt(a)\theta)$ is the plan context serving as the event pre-condition. Within the plan body $Body(a)\theta$, belief additions and deletions are interpreted as ontic effects, providing us with event post-conditions:

---

[1] Do not confuse *AppPlans* for *AppPlans'* defined in Sect. 6.

$$post((a, \theta)) = \begin{cases} (pr(\ell), \top) & if +\ell \in Body(a)\theta \\ (pr(\ell), \bot) & if -\ell \in Body(a)\theta \end{cases}$$

Grounding Literals from Ontic Changes. Since ontic changes in "on" plans introduce new literals that may be involved in the grounding of future queries and updates, we define the following function, which allow us to extract new literals from the additive ontic changes in a set of ground "on" plan pairs A.

$$ontic\_lits(A) = \{\ell, \neg\ell \mid (a, \theta) \in A \ where \ +\ell \in Body(a)\theta\}$$

5.3   Creating a DEL Event Model

Given a triggering event te and a set of applicable "on" plans A, we create a corresponding DEL event model for te (or use the default event model when $A = \emptyset$). The following function returns the appropriate DEL event model:

$$del\_em(A, te) = \begin{cases} \langle E = \{(a, \theta) \in A\}, pre((a, \theta)), post((a, \theta)) \rangle & if \ A \neq \emptyset \\ def\_ev(te) & else, \ A = \emptyset \end{cases}$$

6   Model Queries: Querying the Epistemic Model

Standard plan contexts allow the agent to express belief preconditions (i.e., a conjunction of literals), which are used to determine the applicability of a plan for execution. The standard AgentSpeak language is not expressive enough to explicitly query uncertainty in the plan contexts. To address this, we introduce the possibility operator $\mathbf{poss}(\ell)$ which allows the agent to query whether it considers ℓ to be possible. The methodology introduced in this section is identical to the model querying process presented for P-AS in [19], which enriches plan contexts with the ability to reason about both certain and possible beliefs by delegating the evaluation of belief (and possibility) queries to the epistemic model.

Using the epistemic model to evaluate a plan context requires a transformation into an equivalent epistemic formula. We assign a new semantic meaning to belief queries of the form $\mathbf{poss}(\ell)$, given any literal ℓ, where the possibility modality $\hat{B}$ is used to reason about ℓ. All non-$\mathbf{poss}$ queries in the plan context will be assigned the standard belief modality B – this is equivalent to standard belief queries in AgentSpeak.

Given a ground rule-free conjunction φ, $tr(\varphi)$ is an epistemic formula obtained by assigning the appropriate modalities to each propositionalized literal.

$$tr(\mathbf{poss}(\ell)) = \hat{B} \ pr(\ell)$$
$$tr(\ell) = B \ pr(\ell)$$
$$tr(\varphi_1 \wedge \varphi_2) = tr(\varphi_1) \wedge tr(\varphi_2)$$

Note that ℓ in the definition to represent a standard literal, i.e., $\ell \neq \mathbf{poss}(\_)$.

6.1   Evaluating Formulae

Given an epistemic model M, and ranged belief base $B_R = B \cup R$ with belief base B and set of ranged literals R, we use the following function to evaluate a plan context φ: $eval_{\langle M, B_R \rangle}(\varphi) = \{\theta \mid B_R \models_\phi \varphi\theta \text{ s. th. } M \models tr(\phi)\}$.

In AgentSpeak, plan contexts are used in determining applicability of a relevant plan (p, θ) with plan p and unifier θ – achieved in AgentSpeak by a function $AppPlans$. Given M and B_R from above, and a set of relevant plan pairs R_P, we provide an updated definition that evaluates plan contexts according to the semantics discussed previously: $AppPlans'(M, B_R, R_P) = \{(p, \theta \circ \theta') \mid (p, \theta) \in R_P \text{ and } \theta' \in eval_{\langle M, B_R \rangle}(Ctxt(p))\}$.

7   Operational Semantics

Operational semantics are presented as semantic rules defining transition relations between D-AS configurations: $\langle ag, C, T, S \rangle$. For brevity, we extend a minimal subset of Jason's configuration definition [8]. Extended components are bolded.

- ag (agent state). Belief base ag_B holds initial beliefs/rules, ag_{ps} holds all plan definitions, $\boldsymbol{ag_R} = ran(ag_B)$ holds all ranged literals, and $\boldsymbol{ag_M} = gen\_model(all\_cons(ag_B, ag_R))$ holds the initial epistemic model generated based on the constraints defined by the belief base.
- C (circumstances). C_E is a set of event tuples (te, ι) with an event te raised by intention ι.
- T (transition system). T_R and T_{Ap} contain relevant and applicable plans as tuples (p, θ), with plan p and MGU θ.
- S (current step) is one of the standard Jason steps: ProcMsg, SelEv, ApplPl, SelAppl, SelInt, etc.

Note that the model creation operation, which initializes the agent's epistemic model ag_M, occurs during the initialization of this configuration and does not occur within the reasoning cycle itself. This ensures a minimal impact on the time-sensitive reasoning cycle. The model update and query operations occur within the reasoning cycle and are described by the semantic rules presented in the following sub-sections.

7.1   Model Update Semantics

In D-AS, we apply DEL events described by the agent's *"on"* plans which match a given belief event. This process is captured by the semantic rules in Fig. 2, which override the default AgentSpeak semantic rules for belief addition and deletion events using the functions provided in Sect. 5. Boxed operations are those introduced by D-AS.

$$\frac{T_{\iota} = i[head \leftarrow +b; h]}{\langle ag, C, T, \mathsf{ExecInt} \rangle \rightarrow \langle ag', C', T', \mathsf{ClrInt} \rangle} \quad \textbf{(AddBel)}$$

$$\text{where} \begin{cases} ag'_B = ag_B + b \\ C'_E = C_E \cup \{\langle +b, \top \rangle\} \\ T'_{\iota} = i[head \leftarrow h] \\ C'_I = (C_I \setminus \{T_{\iota}\}) \cup \{T'_{\iota}\}) \\ \boxed{A = AppPlans(ag_B \cup ag_R, rel\_on(ag_{ps}, +b))} \\ \boxed{ag'_R = ag_R \cup ontic\_lits(A)} \\ \boxed{ag'_M = ag_M \otimes del\_em(A, +b)} \end{cases}$$

$$\frac{T_{\iota} = i[head \leftarrow -b; h]}{\langle ag, C, T, \mathsf{ExecInt} \rangle \rightarrow \langle ag', C', T', \mathsf{ClrInt} \rangle} \quad \textbf{(DelBel)}$$

$$\text{where} \begin{cases} ag'_B = ag_B - b \\ C'_E = C_E \cup \{\langle -b, \top \rangle\} \\ T'_{\iota} = i[head \leftarrow h] \\ C'_I = (C_I \setminus \{T_{\iota}\}) \cup \{T'_{\iota}\}) \\ \boxed{A = AppPlans(ag_B \cup ag_R, rel\_on(ag_{ps}, -b))} \\ \boxed{ag'_R = ag_R \cup ontic\_lits(A)} \\ \boxed{ag'_M = ag_M \otimes del\_em(A, -b)} \end{cases}$$

Fig. 2. Semantic Rules for Belief Addition/Deletion.

7.2   Model Query Semantics

In standard AgentSpeak, the agent selects an event (from C_E) and finds a set T_R of relevant plans (p, θ) where p is a plan whose trigger unifies (via MGU θ) with the selected event. Applicable plans are relevant plans whose context is a consequence of the agent's current beliefs. As shown in Fig. 3, D-AS provides new semantic rules for the step AppPl. We rely on function definitions from Sect. 6 to provide new semantic rules that compute the set of applicable plans T_{Ap} by evaluating relevant plan contexts using the epistemic model. Boxed operations are those introduced by D-AS.

$$\frac{\boxed{AppPlans'(ag_M, ag_B \cup ag_R, T_R) \neq \{\}}}{\langle ag, C, T, \mathsf{AppPl} \rangle \rightarrow \langle ag, C, T', \mathsf{SelAppl} \rangle} \quad \textbf{(Appl)}$$

$$\text{where} \left\{ \boxed{T'_{Ap} = AppPlans'(ag_M, ag_B \cup ag_R, T_R)} \right.$$

Fig. 3. Evaluate Applicability of Plans Based on the Epistemic Model.

8   Application and Evaluation

In this section, we apply D-AS to the MAPC's navigation problem and evaluate its performance and scalability. The MAPC serves as a general representation of the class of uncertainty faced by autonomous agents in practice and thus aims to model realistic uncertainty scenarios [1]. By applying D-AS to the MAPC domain via the navigation example, we are demonstrating that D-AS is not limited to a single domain, but rather, that it is applicable to an entire class of realistic uncertainty problems.

8.1 Application

Listing 1.2 provides the D-AS program for the navigation problem. The range rule on Line 1 succinctly defines the uncertainty of locations (0,0) to (4,4). The standard rule on line 2 is interpreted as a constraint on the truth values of locations by asserting mutual exclusivity. Lastly, the two beliefs on Line 3 state that we know obstacle locations (1,2) and (2,2) are not valid locations.

The plans on Lines 8 and 9 are assigned *"on"* semantics (Sect. 5). Respectively, these plans provide the relevant DEL event models for two events: +obs($\downarrow$) and +move($\rightarrow$), which correspond to $\epsilon_{obs(\downarrow)}$ and $\epsilon_{\rightarrow}$ from Example 1.

Lastly, the +!*nav* plan on line 10 allows us to reason about movement directions, which allow us to make a decision that is based on the locations we currently consider possible.

```
1   range(loc(X, Y)) :- .in([X,Y],[[0,0]..[4,4]]).
2   ~loc(X, Y) :- loc(X2, Y2)&(X, Y)\==(X2,Y2).
3   ~loc(1, 2). ~loc(2, 2).
4   obs(down) :- loc(1, 1) | loc(2, 1).
5   dir(right) :- loc(1, 1) | loc(2, 1).
6   ... // Etc. for all obs/dir
7   !nav.
8   +on(obs(D)) : obs(D).
9   +on(move(right)) : loc(X, Y) <- -loc(X, Y); +loc(X+1, Y).
10  +!nav : dir(D) & poss(dir(D)) <- move(D); ...
```

Listing 1.2. D-AS program for navigation.

The D-AS program presented above allows us to localize the agent by managing which locations we consider possible, and by eliminating impossibilities as the agent perceives its environment. Interestingly, this D-AS program also represents a solution to a much more general problem, i.e., the ability of the agent to make concrete and stable decisions while faced with varying facets of uncertainty. This is a problem that most autonomous agents face; this problem is aggravated due to the lack of uncertainty reasoning capabilities in the standard AgentSpeak language. D-AS solves this problem by providing a general, yet elegant, solution to capturing and reasoning about uncertainty.

8.2 Evaluation

This section evaluates the scalability of D-AS[2] to measure its impact on the agent's reasoning cycle. Due to the lack of symbolic approaches to uncertainty

---

[2] D-AS implementation: https://github.com/MikeVezina/epistemic-jason. We use the DEL reasoner and SAT solver included in *Hintikka's World* [17].

reasoning in the literature, P-AS is the only comparable extension which can be relied upon as a performance benchmark. The evaluation methodology used in this section scales the navigation application, measuring the time it takes to perform model creations, updates, and queries – this is identical to the methodology used to evaluate P-AS [19], allowing us to provide a direct comparison.

Although our evaluation relies on the MAPC navigation example, the main goal of our evaluation is to present the worst-case computational complexity trends. These results are general and can be interpreted regardless of the agent's chosen domain.

Additionally, our chosen evaluation parameters are scaled based on the scale constraints provided by the 2019 MAPC. Owing to the MAPC's aim of simulating realistic uncertainty scenarios, the chosen scale and constraints facilitate an understanding of D-AS's practical performance. This is made possible by providing us with results and trends indicative of how D-AS performs under more realistic conditions [1]. In the following sub-sections, we compare P-AS and D-AS with respect to their model creation, update, and query performance.

Model Creation. Figure 4 graphs the time it takes for P-AS and D-AS to create an initial epistemic model (with $|W|$ worlds) from a set of initial beliefs and rules.

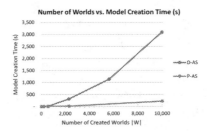

Fig. 4. Model Size vs. Model Creation time (s).

These results show that P-AS performs significantly better during model creation. P-AS relies on an ad hoc approach to model creation, which lacks the capability to generalize to other uncertainty domains. D-AS provides a generalizable model creation approach via SAT solving, but this comes at the cost of computation time. The worst-case time complexity for D-AS model creation is exponential, with respect to the agent's initial beliefs. In practice, there are efficient SAT solving algorithms which may out-perform ad hoc techniques [4]; this is left to be explored as future work. Additionally, this additional computation time may be justifiable since model generation can be invoked offline and cached, i.e., it does not have to impact the agent's time-sensitive reasoning cycle.

Model Update. Model update times measure the time it takes to apply an event model to the current epistemic model. Figure 5 compares the time it takes D-AS and P-AS to update the epistemic model, given $|E|$ events in the event model and $|W|$ worlds in the current epistemic model. Since P-AS uses PAL, it is limited to single-event (public announcement) event models where $|E| = 1$; with D-AS, we test two scenarios: $|E| = 1$ and $|E| = 2$, though D-AS is capable of expressing any number of events. Note that $|E|$ is dictated by the number of applicable *"on"* plans defined by the agent for a given belief event.

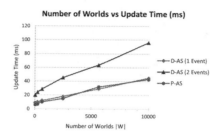

Fig. 5. Model size vs. model update time (ms).

P-AS and D-AS perform the same when there is a single-event event model $|E| = 1$. In the case where an agent expresses multi-event models in D-AS, the model update time increases linearly with a factor of $|E|$ due to DEL's update semantics.

Model Querying. Figure 6 compares the time it takes P-AS and D-AS to model-check 100 ground belief queries, with respect to the number of worlds in the current model $|W|$. Both P-AS and D-AS perform identically when querying, since the entailment semantics of formulae are the same for both PAL and DEL.

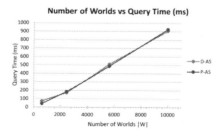

Fig. 6. Model Size vs. Model Querying Time (100 formulae, ms).

To conclude, P-AS is limited in its expressiveness. D-AS provides a higher level of expressiveness due to its more extensive semantics, but comes with a higher computational cost when these higher forms of expressiveness are used by the agent.

9   Conclusion

D-AS is a DEL-based extension for reasoning about uncertainty in AgentSpeak which addresses various non-trivial limitations encountered by Vezina and Esfandiari's P-AS [19]. D-AS enables the general creation of any initial epistemic model via propositionalization of the initial belief state and the use of a SAT solver. Unlike P-AS, the model creation methodology used in D-AS are general and can capture descriptions for domains other than the MAPC and the navigation problem. D-AS also assigns semantics to "on" plans which allow the agent to specify the impact that belief events have on the epistemic model. Lastly, P-AS lacked formal operational semantic definitions which are crucial to the description of any AgentSpeak-based language. This paper presented the necessary operational semantic definitions for D-AS, including its model creation, update, and querying operations.

D-AS and P-AS have similar performance and scalability, with a couple of exceptions. Although model creation is faster with P-AS, their approach is ad hoc and thus limited to the navigation example. At the cost of performance, D-AS is able to provide a sound and generalizable model creation process, which can be applied to domains other than the navigation problem. Additionally, the model creation process can occur offline and the model can be cached.

During model updates, we see that P-AS and D-AS perform the same when D-AS is limited to the expressability provided by P-AS (i.e., single-event event models). As soon as the agent requires the additional expressability provided by the "on" plans (i.e., DEL event models), computation time grows linearly with the magnitude of uncertainty.

Both AgentSpeak and DEL are widely-used in multi-agent settings – naturally, future work for D-AS involves multi-agent transformational semantics; however, multi-agent reasoning comes at an additional methodological and computational cost [16] and is thus left to be explored as future work. Additionally, since D-AS leverages the full power of single-agent DEL, it lends itself to knowledge-based programs [10] that rely on DEL (e.g., [20]), and DEL planning domains, such as robotics and security [6,7].

We hope to see D-AS integrated into Jason and other AgentSpeak-based languages, as D-AS provides powerful semantics for capturing belief change and reasoning about uncertainty in a manner that is elegant and would be useful for any agent domain involving uncertainty.

Acknowledgements. We acknowledge the support of the Natural Sciences and Engineering Research Council of Canada (NSERC).

References

1. Ahlbrecht, T., Dix, J., Fiekas, N., Krausburg, T.: The multi-agent programming contest. In: Ahlbrecht, T., Dix, J., Fiekas, N., Krausburg, T. (eds.) MAPC 2021. Lecture Notes in Computer Science, vol. 12381, pp. 3–20. Springer, Cham (2020). https://doi.org/10.1007/978-3-030-88549-6_1

2. Baltag, A., Renne, B.: Dynamic Epistemic Logic. In: Zalta, E.N. (ed.) The Stanford Encyclopedia of Philosophy. Metaphysics Research Lab, Stanford University, Winter 2016 edn. (2016)
3. Bauters, K., McAreavey, K., Liu, W., Hong, J., Godo, L., Sierra, C.: Managing different sources of uncertainty in a BDI framework in a principled way with tractable fragments. J. Artif. Intell. Res. **58**, 731–775 (2017). https://doi.org/10.1613/jair. 5287
4. Beskyd, F., Surynek, P.: Domain dependent parameter setting in SAT solver using machine learning techniques. In: Rocha, A.P., Steels, L., van den Herik, J. (eds.) ICAART 2022. Lecture Notes in Computer Science, pp. 169–200. Springer International Publishing, Cham (2022). https://doi.org/10.1007/978-3-031-22953-4_8
5. Biga, A.A., Casali, A.: G-jason: An extension of jason to engineer agents capable to reason under uncertainty. In: Proceedings of 14th Intelligent Agent and Systems Workshop (2014)
6. Bolander, T., Andersen, M.B.: Epistemic planning for single-and multi-agent systems. J. Appl. Non-Class. Logics **21**(1), 9–34 (2011)
7. Bolander, T., Charrier, T., Pinchinat, S., Schwarzentruber, F.: Del-based epistemic planning: decidability and complexity. Artif. Intell. **287**, 103304 (2020). https://doi.org/10.1016/j.artint.2020.103304
8. Bordini, R.H., Hübner, J.F., Wooldridge, M.: Programming Multi-agent Systems in AgentSpeak using Jason. John Wiley & Sons, Hoboken (2007)
9. Casali, A., Godo, L., Sierra, C.: g-BDI: a graded intensional agent model for practical reasoning. In: Torra, V., Narukawa, Y., Inuiguchi, M. (eds.) MDAI 2009. Lecture Notes in Computer Science, vol. 5861, pp. 5–20. Springer, Berlin (2009). https://doi.org/10.1007/978-3-642-04820-3_2
10. Fagin, R., Halpern, J.Y., Moses, Y., Vardi, M.Y.: Reasoning About Knowledge. MIT Press, Cambridge (1995). https://doi.org/10.7551/mitpress/5803.001.0001
11. Genesereth, M., Kao, E.: Introduction to Logic, 3rd edn. Morgan & Claypool Publishers, Synthesis Lectures on Computer Science (2016)
12. Georgeff, M.P., Rao, A.: An abstract architecture for rational agents. In: Proceedings of the Third International Conference on Principles of Knowledge Representation and Reasoning, pp. 439–449 (1992)
13. Herzig, A., Lorini, E., Perrussel, L., Xiao, Z.: Bdi logics for BDI architectures: Old problems, new perspectives. KI - Künstliche Intell. **31**(1), 73–83 (2017). https://doi.org/10.1007/s13218-016-0457-5
14. Jago, M.: Epistemic logic for rule-based agents. J. Logic Lang. Inf. **18**(1), 131–158 (2009). https://doi.org/10.1007/s10849-008-9071-8
15. Rao, A.S.: Agentspeak(L): BDI agents speak out in a logical computable language. In: Van de Velde, W., Perram, J.W. (eds.) MAAMAW 1996. Lecture Notes in Computer Science, vol. 1038, pp. 42–55. Springer, Berlin (1996). https://doi.org/10.1007/BFb0031845
16. Schwarzentruber, F.: Epistemic reasoning in Artificial Intelligence. Habilitation thesis, University of Rennes (2019)
17. Schwarzentruber, F.: Hintikka's world: agents with higher-order knowledge. In: Proceedings of the Twenty-Seventh International Joint Conference on Artificial Intelligence, IJCAI-18, pp. 5859–5861. International Joint Conferences on Artificial Intelligence Organization (2018). https://doi.org/10.24963/ijcai.2018/862
18. Van Ditmarsch, H., van Der Hoek, W., Kooi, B.: Dynamic Epistemic Logic, vol. 337. Springer, Cham (2007). https://doi.org/10.1007/978-1-4020-5839-4

19. Vezina, M., Esfandiari, B.: Epistemic reasoning in Jason. In: Proceedings of the 21st International Conference on Autonomous Agents and Multiagent Systems, AAMAS 2022, pp. 1328–1336. International Foundation for Autonomous Agents and Multiagent Systems, Richland, SC (2022)
20. Zanuttini, B., Lang, J., Saffidine, A., Schwarzentruber, F.: Knowledge-based programs as succinct policies for partially observable domains. Artif. Intell. **288**, 103365 (2020)

JaKtA: BDI Agent-Oriented Programming in Pure Kotlin

Martina Baiardi[✉][ID], Samuele Burattini[ID], Giovanni Ciatto[ID],
and Danilo Pianini[ID]

Department of Computer Science and Engineering (DISI),
Alma Mater Studiorum—Univerisità di Bologna,
Via dell'Università 50, 47522 Cesena (FC), Italy
{m.baiardi,samuele.burattini,giovanni.ciatto,danilo.pianini}@unibo.it
https://www.unibo.it/sitoweb/m.baiardi/en,
https://www.unibo.it/sitoweb/samuele.burattini/en,
https://www.unibo.it/sitoweb/giovanni.ciatto/en,
https://www.unibo.it/sitoweb/danilo.pianini/en

Abstract. Multi-paradigm languages are becoming more and more popular, as they allow developers to choose the most suitable paradigm for each task. Most commonly, we observe the combination of object-oriented (OOP) and functional programming (FP), however, in principle, other paradigms could be hybridised. In this paper, we present JaKtA, an internal DSL adding support for the definition of belief-desire-intention (BDI) agents in Kotlin. We believe is a first step to investigate the blending of Agent-Oriented Programming (AOP) with other popular paradigms and we discuss the opportunity and value of doing so with an internal DSLs. Finally, through JaKtA, we show how this can already lead to compactly and expressively create BDI agents that smoothly interoperate with the host language, its libraries and tooling.

Keywords: BDI · AgentSpeak(L) · DSL · Kotlin · JaKtA

1 Introduction

Many modern mainstream programming languages natively support multiple programming paradigms, thus allowing programmers to use the most appropriate abstractions for the job at hand without the need to adapt their mind to a syntax and tooling different to the one they are acquainted with. Most frequently, we observe the combination of object-oriented (OOP) and functional programming (FP) paradigms: some notable examples are OCaml [16], which adds object-orientation on top of the functional paradigm; Java, that since version 8 supports some functional abstractions on top of OOP [17] via the *lambda expressions* and

This work has been partially supported by the CHIST-ERA IV project "EXPECTATION", and by the Italian Ministry for Universities and Research (G.A. CHIST-ERA-19-XAI-005).

the *stream API*; and Scala, that since its conception has been designed with both OOP and FP in mind [24].

To the best of our knowledge, however, no mainstream programming language currently features *native* support for the agent-oriented programming paradigm (AOP), especially the beliefs–desires-intentions (BDI) model. The current state of the art includes several stand-alone programming languages that support BDI agents programming following the well-known AgentSpeak(L) [22] semantics—such as Jason [3], Astra [9], and GOAL [13]. However, using and maintaining stand-alone languages can be burdening, especially when the community of contributors is small, since languages usually require several tools to be usable in practice (e.g., content assistants, syntax highlighters, linters, checkers, debuggers, etc.) whose development and maintenance adds upon the cost of the language itself— potentially causing the ecosystem to evolve slowly, and thus hindering adoption.

In this paper, we propose a solution to both the availability in the mainstream and the tooling support of BDI languages, by leveraging a recent trend in modern programming languages: the construction of *internal* domain-specific languages (DSLs), namely, carefully designed APIs that capture problem-specific abstractions into a syntax providing ergonomics akin to that of a dedicated language, but still letting users rely on the tooling and ecosystem of the host language, as well as transparently use abstractions from other paradigms on a per-need basis. Thus, inspired by the successful Jason AOP language, we present Jason-like Kotlin Agents (JaKtA): a Kotlin internal DSL meant to seamlessly integrate BDI agents into a mainstream programming language, adding AOP to Kotlin as an additional paradigm, retaining its toolchain, libraries, and OOP/FP abstractions. We show that the internal DSL approach can blur the (usually neat) boundary between the two paradigms, promoting a more natural and seamless interaction. Moreover, since the code using the DSL abstractions is still valid code in the host language, we show that the tooling of the host language can be used immediately, with no need for additional support software to be developed and maintained.

The remainder of this paper is organised as follows: in Sect. 2, we present DSL engineering and we summarise the state of the art of BDI languages, then in Sect. 3 we discuss the design and the main features of JaKtA, and we show how it can be used to compactly and expressively create BDI agents that smoothly interoperate with the Kotlin ecosystem; in Sect. 4 we assess the effectiveness of our internal DSL approach by showing, through practical examples, how it can simplify the development of BDI agents in some conditions; and finally, in Sect. 5, we conclude the paper by discussing some limitations of our approach, as well as some future research directions stemming from it.

2   Background

This work lays on two pillars: DSL engineering (specifically, internal Kotlin DSLs) and BDI agents programming. In this section, we briefly introduce them by discussing the principles behind the creation of DSLs and we explain how and why modern languages support the creation of *internal* DSLs. We also provide a comparison among existing BDI programming frameworks from the literature, discussing how syntactical aspects may impact their interoperability and versatility.

2.1   DSL Engineering

As introduced in Sect. 1, DSLs are programming languages tailored to specific domains: they expose the domain model entities and their interactions as first-level abstractions. However, there is no rule on which amount of domain-specificity makes a language a DSL: at some level, every language is domain-specific, with the specific domain being the *paradigm* the language is rooted in. For instance, we argue that even the Agent Speak Language (ASL) can be seen as a DSL modelling the domain of BDI agents.

From a technical perspective, DSLs can be classified into two broad categories [24]: *external*, if they are stand-alone, with their own custom syntax and compiler/interpreter; and *internal*, if they are embedded in a host language and rely on the syntactic and semantic features of the host. From the point of view of the host language, internal DSLs are indistinguishable from ordinary libraries (indeed, as C++ inventor Bjarne Stroustrup used to say, "library design is language design" [25]), their distinction is usually driven by their *purpose*[1]. Consequently, internal DSLs might *in principle* be realised in any language; *in practice*, however, the host language syntactic flexibility directly reflects on the ergonomics of any internal DSL. For this reason, several recent languages (e.g., Scala, Kotlin, Ruby) provide syntactic features specifically tailored to the constructions of internal DSLs. Despite these features simplify the adoption of internal DSLs, they cannot provide the same expressiveness of an external DSL, as they are still bound to the host language syntax, for example, in the case of Kotlin each DSL statement must be enclosed in a curly braces block.

Selecting whether an internal or external DSL is best for the problem at hand is a matter of trade-offs: as discussed, internal DSLs have limited syntactic flexibility that could result in a less expressive language, but, in turn, they inherit from their host: *(i)* the tooling (IDE support, build systems, linters, debuggers, profilers, and so on), reducing the maintenance burden; *(ii)* the libraries, reducing the need for ad-hoc solutions; and *(iii)* the abstractions, allowing the DSL to be used in conjunction with other paradigms. Together, these aspects may also lower the learning curve for those already acquainted with the host language, possibly favouring wider adoption.

2.2   BDI Paradigm and Programming Languages

The philosopher Michael Bratman described humans' practical reasoning via the "beliefs, desires, intentions" (BDI) framework, as a way to explain future-directed

---

[1] https://www.martinfowler.com/bliki/DslBoundary.html.

decision-making [4]. Successively, the framework was formalised by means of modal logics [8], and then turned into an abstract semantics for computational agents: AgentSpeak(L) [22]. Computational agents are *autonomous* entities [19] situated into an *environment* they can perceive and affect; they interact either directly or stigmergically through the environment [23]. The classical implementation of BDI agents, based on the Procedural Reasoning System (PRS) [12], is characterized by four main abstractions, namely: **beliefs:** a set of facts and rules constituting the agent's *epistemic* memory; **desires:** a set of goals, (possibly partial) descriptions of the states of the world the agent wants to achieve, test, or maintain; **intentions:** a set of tasks the agent is currently committed to; **plans:** a set of *recipes* representing the agent's procedural memory.

Table 1. Comparison of the identified practical features across several common BDI agent programming languages. Columns denote languages, rows denote features. JaKtA is the language proposed in this paper: it is reported here for to ease comparison. In non-textual cells, symbol ✓ indicates the feature availability, × unavailability, and ~ that we were not able to find conclusive evidence.

	JaKtA	Jason [3]	SPADE-BDI [20]	PHIDIAS [10]	Astra [9]	JACK [26]	Jadex [21]	GOAL [13]
DSL Type	internal	external	both	internal	external	external	external	external
Hosting Syntax	Kotlin	AgentSpeak(L) extension	Python	Python	custom Java extension	custom Java extension	XML Java annotations	custom Prolog extension
Execution Platform	JVM	JVM	Python	Python	JVM	JVM	JVM	JVM
Direct interop.	Any JVM language	Any JVM language	Python	Python	Any JVM language	Any JVM language	Any JVM language	SWI-Prolog
Paradigm blending	✓	×	✓	✓	✓	✓	×	✓
Type safety	✓	×	×	×	✓	✓	✓	✓
Reuse mechanisms	Any Kotlin mechanism	file incl., ext. actions	Any Python mechanism	Any Python mechanism	agent extension	reusable plans	selective file incl	reusable plans, beliefs, goals, and agents
Logic Programming	✓	✓	×	✓	×	×	×	✓
License	Apache 2.0	LGPL v3	GPL v3	MIT	GPL v3	Proprietary	GPL v3	GPL v3

Since its introduction, the community produced many programming languages for BDI agents. Most of them are either based on or inspired by the AgentSpeak(L) semantics. In this section, we compare several major BDI agent programming languages from a software engineering perspective. Details about the comparison are reported in Table 1. There, columns represent BDI languages, while rows represent features that those languages may (or may not) have.

As far as BDI agent programming languages are concerned, our comparison is focussing on those languages which appear to have some running software implementation which is actively maintained and used by the community. Hence, we build upon the recent work by Calegari *et al.* [5], which surveys the state-of-the-art of logic-based agent-oriented technologies, and we select the ones aimed at supporting general-purpose BDI agents programming.

Conversely, as far as features are concerned, in the remainder of this section we discuss the most relevant ones, namely: *(i)* **DSL type** (internal or external); *(ii)* **hosting syntax**, i.e., which syntax the DSL is embedded in (for internal DSLs) or based upon (for external DSLs); *(iii)* **execution platform**, i.e. which runtime platform the language runs upon; *(iv)* **direct interop**erability, i.e., whether other languages can be called from within the BDI language (and, in that case, which ones); *(v)* **paradigm blending**, i.e., whether it is possible to mix, in the same source and scope, AOP and other abstractions; *(vi)* **type safety** i.e., the ability of the compiler/interpreter to intercept (most) type errors ahead-of-execution; *(vii)* **reuse mechanisms**, i.e., whether and how it is possible to parameterise and reuse partial or entire MAS specifications; *(viii)* **logic programming** support, i.e. the capability to rely upon the mechanisms of unification and backtracking to represent and manipulate BDI data structures; and, finally, *(ix)* **license**.

DSL Type and Hosting Syntax. The former feature categorizes BDI languages as either *external* or *internal* DSL, or possibly both of them. Conversely, the latter feature provides further details about the DSL syntax. The two features are strictly related, as they both refer to the syntax of the language. In fact, for internal DSLs, one may be interested in understanding which syntax the DSL is embedded in, whereas, for external DSLs, we further describe the derivation of the syntax. Accordingly, for internal DSLs, the hosting syntax is quite straightforward: both SPADE-BDI and PHIDIAS are hosted by Python. Conversely, external DSLs' syntaxes are built as extensions or refinements of well-known languages. For instance, while Jadex relies on XML, GOAL extends Prolog [15], and Jason extends AgentSpeak(L); whereas Astra and JACK extend Java.

Execution Platform. The execution platform is the runtime environment which is required for running a given BDI language—as well as the MAS described through it. It is worth highlighting that several programming languages may be executed on the same platform. This is the case, for instance, in Kotlin, Java, and Scala which are all executed on the JVM platform. The execution platform is a relevant feature, as it may affect the portability of the MAS, as well as its interoperability with other systems and languages. Accordingly, while SPADE-BDI and PHIDIAS target the Python platform, the other languages target the JVM platform.

Direct Interoperability. This feature concerns the ability of the agent programming language to interact with the hosting language constructs. Specifically, this feature is about which other languages the BDI language at hand can directly call, exploiting the hosting language interoperability mechanisms. For instance, every language targetting the JVM can directly call all the other JVM languages. However, this is not the case for Jadex, which is implemented on Java, but exploits XML files for MAS specification.

Paradigm Blending. This is a *syntactical* feature of languages whose syntax mixes AOP constructs with the hosting language ones—for instance, by letting developers exploit both AOP and OOP constructs, if the hosting language is OO. Notice that the opposite situation may also occur. In fact, some languages enforce a clear separation among high-level AOP constructs (e.g. belief, goals, plans) and the hosting language ones (e.g. classes, functions, etc.). This separation may for instance be enforced by requiring the AOP portions of a MAS to be written in separate files. For instance, in Python-based BDI languages such as SPADE-BDI and PHIDIAS, AOP specifications consist of Python classes and methods. Conversely, Astra, JACK, and GOAL allow exploiting Java or Prolog libraries, respectively. Finally, Jason, and Jadex strongly separate AOP from OOP. There, MAS are composed by scripts describing agent specifications, and by actions/environment specifications. The former only support AgentSpeak(L)-compliant constructs, whereas the latter are ordinary Java code.

Type Safety. This feature refers to the presence of a strong type checker for the BDI language at hand, which may proof check agents specifications at compile-time. Solutions having a tight interoperability with Java, such as Astra, JACK, and Jadex, come with this feature; whereas the others do not. Other languages – such as Jason, SPADE-BDI, PHIDIAS, and GOAL – come with a more flexible syntax—as they rely on weakly-typed hosting languages such as Prolog or Python.

Reuse Mechanisms. This feature refers the presence of abstraction mechanisms supporting the reuse of partial MAS specifications. As far as this feature is concerned, we observe great variety among the surveyed languages. Some rely on bare file include mechanisms. This is the case, for instance, of Jason – which supports the inclusion of ASL files into other ASL files, by path –, and Jadex—which supports referencing XML or Java files into other XML files. Furthermore, virtually all surveyed solutions support the abstraction and reuse mechanisms of the hosting language, if any. This implies, for instance, that solutions based on an OO hosting language may take advantage of OOP abstraction mechanisms such as sub-typing and inheritance for the OO portions of their MAS specifications. Some solutions may also expose high-level, agent-oriented notions – such as agents or plans – as first-class syntactical constructs. In other words, they may support ad-hoc syntaxes for writing agents or plans. This is the case, for instance, of Astra, JACK, and GOAL. When this is the case, first-class abstraction can be re-used along the MAS specification. For example, Astra supports writing agents specifications extending other agents specifications.

Logic Programming Support. This feature is about whether BDI languages rely on full-fledged logic programming as the preferred means to represent and manipulate BDI data structures—e.g. beliefs, goals, etc. This is the case, for instance, of Jason, PHIDIAS, and GOAL, which use logic terms and clauses to represent beliefs, goals, plans, and events. They also rely on logic unification and resolution as the basic mechanism to manipulate these data structures to implement the BDI reasoning cycle.

License. This feature is about which license BDI solutions are distributed with. Notably, most solutions come with an open-source license, and their source code is freely available and inspectable on the Web. The only exceptions are JACK, which is proprietary, closed-source software, and GOAL which allegedly has an open-source license, despite we were not able to find the source code on the Web.

3   A Kotlin DSL for BDI Agents

We now let the analysis from Sect. 2.2 drive our selection of core features, that will lead, in turn, to the actual implementation of a DSL for BDI agents.

We want our DSL to be familiar for BDI experts and, at the same time, to look idiomatic to the community of mainstream developers. One way to achieve the first goal is to reach AgentSpeak(L) compliance (i.e., to fulfill its operational semantic), as AgentSpeak(L)-inspired languages are very popular within the AOP community. Concerning the second goal, it can be achieved by letting the DSL (and the underlying agent interpreter) be compliant with the API, the syntax, and the stylistic conventions of some mainstream language of choice. Programmers from both communities must be able to blend paradigms, writing pieces of code that mix BDI abstractions with the ones of the chosen mainstream language. Together with the will to inherit the existing reuse mechanisms of a mainstream language, these aspects led us to choose an *internal* DSL.

As a BDI agent programming language, we also require our DSL to be compliant w.r.t. a set of features, discussed below. First, the language should support strong typing, and possibly type inference, in order to keep types as hidden as possible. It should also support modularity and reusability at various levels, there including *(i)* agent specifications, *(ii)* plan libraries and/or individual plans, *(iii)* belief bases or goal sets, as well as *(iv)* internal and external actions. This implies all such syntactical categories could be in principle written in separate files and composed in the finest way possible. Writing all such categories in a single file should be supported as well.

The DSL should support an explicit notion of *environment*, which in turns supports the pluggability of custom *external* actions – i.e., custom functionalities that agents may invoke to support perception and actuation – as well as the pluggability of custom message passing mechanisms—hence virtually supporting distributed communication among agents. As far as pluggability is concerned, MAS specification written in JaKtA should also support the addition of custom *internal actions* on individual agents – i.e., custom functionalities supporting the inspection/modification of agents' internals –, as well as the choice of the most adequate concurrency model for the MAS at hand—i.e., roughly, the strategy by which agents' concurrent execution is scheduled by the OS.

Finally, the DSL should support full-fledged logic programming syntax and semantics in dealing with BDI data structures representation and manipulation.

A more nuanced pick is the selection of the target host language. There are several elements to consider, including the target platform and its portability across multiple platforms (as we want to maximise the range of potential target runtimes), the existing ecosystem (as we want to leverage existing libraries and tools), the language's popularity (as we want to let the agent-orientation be available to the widest possible audience), the type safety, and, of course, the specific language features that could be leveraged for the construction of a DSL.

We considered several languages, including Java, Scala, Kotlin, Python, Ruby, C#, and Typescript. From the point of view of syntactic flexibility we favored Scala, Kotlin, and Ruby, as they provide machinery specifically meant to allow the construction of DSLs. We then discarded Ruby, as we wanted a statically typed language. We picked Kotlin over Scala despite the latter having a better type system (supporting, for instance, path-dependent and higher-kinded types [14]) for merely practical reasons: *(i)* Scala 3 recently broke retro-compatibility with Scala 2, and, at the time this work was realised, many libraries and tools were not yet available for the new version; *(ii)* we expect Kotlin popularity to grow faster than Scala's in the future, as Google picked Kotlin as reference language for the Android ecosystem[2], and *(iii)* there are emerging libraries in Kotlin that are meant for data science, e.g.: *KotlinGrad*[3], *KMath* [18], *KotlinDL*[4], and *Kotlin Dataframe*[5]. Combined with a Kotlin-based solution for MAS, these tools may hopefully pave the way towards the combination of MAS and data science.

3.1 Architecture and Implementation Details

It is worth mentioning that some required features are not merely syntactical as they require support from the underlying BDI agent interpreter. This is the case, for instance, of features supporting the pluggability of custom message passing mechanisms as well as the choice of the most adequate concurrency model for the MAS at hand. For this reason, JaKtA comes with its own BDI execution engine. Designing from scratch required significant effort, but it also allowed us to decouple agent specifications and their execution, and opened to the possibility to target multiple platforms by leveraging the Kotlin capability to do so.

The JaKtA framework then includes three main modules, namely: *(i)* the JaKtA DSL, *(ii)* the JaKtA BDI interpreter, and *(iii)* the concurrency management module. Notably, the DSL is built on top of the BDI interpreter, which in turn is built on top of the concurrency management module.

In principle, other languages could reuse the BDI interpreter by replacing the DSL module. For instance, a Jason's parser or a new Scala internal DSL for AOP could be plugged on top of the existing BDI interpreter, enjoying, respectively, the Kotlin debug tools and a reduced implementation effort.

The concurrency management module defines how agents are coupled with threads, allowing the same specification to be executed on one or more threads, depending on the application at hand. However, because of space limitations, in the remainder of this paper we focus upon the syntactical aspects of JaKtA, leaving the discussion of the underlying interpreter and concurrency module – as well as the challenges and the opportunities they bring – to future works.

The framework has been released, free and open-source. It is available on GitHub[6] and Maven Central[7] and archived on Zenodo [2].

---

[2] https://developer.android.com/kotlin/first.
[3] https://github.com/breandan/kotlingrad.
[4] https://github.com/Kotlin/kotlindl.
[5] https://github.com/Kotlin/dataframe.
[6] https://github.com/jakta-bdi/jakta.
[7] https://search.maven.org/artifact/it.unibo.jakta/jakta-dsl.

3.2   JaKtA's syntax

JaKtA DSL syntax is strongly inspired by Jason and it is AgentSpeak(L)-compliant. The entry point is the **mas** block, inside whose scope all the elements composing a BDI MAS can be defined:

```
mas { environment { ... }; agent("jedi") { ... }; agent("sith") { ... } }
```

In the **environment** block, users define the external actions that agents can use, as well as what agents can perceive. External actions include communication primitives that can be implemented to send messages of a predefined type to agent message boxes that are reified as part of the environment. Achieving compliance with different agent communication languages (e.g. KQML [11] as used in Jason) requires a further definition of the types of messages an agent can send and how such types are interpreted in the agent lifecycle.

```
mas { environment {
  actions { // definition of the external actions for this environment
    action(create, ...) { addAgent(...) }
    action(talk, ...) { sendMessage(recipient, ...) }
  }
}}
```

Agents are named entities created with the **agent** function. These few syntactic elements are enough to show a hint of how blending paradigms can be leveraged to build complex systems in a few lines of code. In the following example, we mix OOP, FP, and AOP: we fetch the rooster of three Italian football teams from a public website, we extract the names through a regular expression, and then we create one agent for each player:

```
mas { // BDI specification
  fun allPlayers(team: String) = // Object-oriented style
    Regex("""<span class="card-title">((\w+|\s)+)<\/span>""").findAll(
      URL("https://analytics.soccerment.com/en/team/$team").readText()
    ).map { it.groupValues[1] } // Monadic manipulation (functional)
  listOf("napoli", "milan", "juventus")
    .flatMap(::allPlayers) // Functional style (higher-order function)
    .forEach { agent("$player playing for $team") { ... }/* BDI style */}
}
```

In this example, we exploit JaKtA for the MAS definition, the OOP paradigm to deal with the regular expression match and data extraction from the group, and the functional paradigm to monadically map teams to players.

Agents' body is a collection of **beliefs**, **goals**, internal **actions** and **plans** defined in homonym blocks. Beliefs are represented as a logic theory, namely a collection of *facts* and *rules* expressed in a logic programming fashion. JaKtA directly leverages, and exposes as API, the logic programming toolkit for Kotlin 2P-KT [6] and its internal DSL for Prolog [7].

For instance, in the following, we define one fact (zero is a natural number) and a logic rule defining the 'successor' relation among natural numbers:

```
mas { agent("gauss") { beliefs {
  fact { natural_number(zero) }
  rule { natural_number(successor(X)) impliedBy natural_number(X) }
}}}
```

Goals can indicate either something that the agent wants to `achieve` or something that it wants to `test` (discover). Test goals prioritize the consultation of the knowledge base over the execution of plans.

```
mas { agent("player1") { goals { achieve(victory(X)); test(has_won(Y)) } } }
```

Internal actions can access and modify the agent's state. In the following snippet, an internal action is used to modify the knowledge base of an agent, changing the team it cheers for:

```
mas { agent("turncoat fan") { actions {
  action(changeTeam, 1 /*this parameter is the arity*/) {
    removeBelief(cheeringFor(X))
    addBelief(cheeringFor(argument(0) /*positional access to parameters*/))
  }
}}}
```

Finally, plans describe which operations the agent is capable to perform; inheriting the successful model of Jason, in JaKtA they are composed of a **triggering event** deciding whether the plan is *relevant*, an optional **context** restricting its *applicability*, and a **body** with the implementation. The triggering event can be a goal/belief invocation/addition (+) or failure/deletion (-), in the form: `[+|-]<triggering event> onlyIf {<context>} then {<body>}`. If a logical expression is present in the context block (prefixed by `onlyIf`), it is then used to vet the relevant plan; and if the plan is selected for execution the sequence of operations and actions contained in its body (prefixed by `then`) is performed. In the following example, we showcase the expressivity of blended paradigms by creating a Kotlin function using AOP in JaKtA to verify the Collatz conjecture [1] for a given number:

```
fun collatz(number: Int) = mas { agent(collatz) {
  goals { achieve(collatz(number)) }
  plans {
    +achieve(verify(X)) // We reached 4 for the second time: it's a cycle
      .onlyIf { found(4).fromSelf }
      .then { Print("Collatz Conjecture verified!"); execute(stop) }
    +achieve(collatz(X)) // We reached an even number: divide by 2
      .onlyIf { X.isEven() and (R `is` X.intDiv(2)) }
      .then { achieve(verify(R), true); +found(X); achieve(collatz(R)) }
    +achieve(collatz(X)) // We reached an odd number: multiply by 3 and add 1
      .onlyIf { X.isOdd() and (R `is` ((X * 3) + 1)) }
      .then { achieve(verify(R), true); +found(X); achieve(collatz(R)) }
  }
}}}
```

4   JaKtA in practice: running example

In this section, we show how JaKtA compares with a reference AOP technology (Jason) through a running example in terms of *(i)* multi-paradigm integration, and meta-programming, *(ii)* abstraction, re-use and type safety; and *(iii)* tooling and ecosystem. The case we select is meant to highlight the benefits of paradigm blending: we want to write a multi-agent modelling a TicTacToe match played on a $N \times N$ board, where N is only known at runtime. For the sake of conciseness, we keep the example deliberately minimal, and we only report the code of a single player. The full code of the example is available on a public repository[8].

The agent may perceive the environment (the board) via percepts of the form cell(X, Y, Z), where X and Y are the coordinates of the cell, and $Z \in \{e, x, o\}$ is the symbol contained in the cell. The agent may also perceive the beginning of a turn via the turn(x) (resp., turn(o)) percept, and may place a symbol in a cell of the environment using the put(X, Y, Z) *external* action—which also passes the turn. The agent's play strategy is the following: *(i)* if there are N of your (resp. the other player's) marks aligned in a row, declare victory (resp. defeat); *(ii)* if there are $N-1$ of your (resp. the other player's) marks aligned and the Nth cell in the same direction is empty, write your mark in that cell; *(iii)* put a cross in random empty cell.

There are four alignement directions, so the agent's belief base can host:

```
aligned(Cells) :- vertical(Cells) | horizontal(Cells) | diagonal(Cells) |
    antidiagonal(Cells).
```

The critical part of the scenario, however, is dealing with a grid of *unknown size*. For a simple 3×3 case, the problem can be dealt with via four couples of rules in the form:

```
⟨alignment⟩([cell(X, Y, S)]) :- cell(X, Y, S).
⟨alignment⟩([cell(X, Y, S1), cell(A, B, S2) | OtherCells]) :-
    cell(X, Y, S1) & cell(A, B, S2) & A-X=⟨dx⟩ & B-Y=⟨dy⟩ &
    ⟨alignment⟩([cell(A, B, S2) | OtherCells]).
```

where meta-variable ⟨*alignment*⟩ can be: vertical, horizontal, diagonal, and antidiagonal, while ⟨*dx*⟩, ⟨*dy*⟩ are in 1, 0, or -1. Under these premises, for a 3×3 simplified scenario, the plans dealing with victory, loss, and random choice may be written in Jason as:

```
+turn(x) : aligned([cell(_,_,x),cell(_,_,x),cell(_,_,x)]) <- .print('I won')
+turn(x) : aligned([cell(_,_,o),cell(_,_,o),cell(_,_,o)]) <- .print('I lost')
+turn(x) : cell(X,Y,e) <- put(X,Y,x)
```

whereas plans making the final move can be written as:

```
+turn(x) : aligned([cell(_,_,x),cell(_,_,x),cell(X,Y,e)]) <- put(X,Y,x)
+turn(x) : aligned([cell(_,_,x),cell(X,Y,e),cell(_,_,x)]) <- put(X,Y,x)
+turn(x) : aligned([cell(X,Y,e),cell(_,_,x),cell(_,_,x)]) <- put(X,Y,x)
```

Plans impeding the victory of the opponent would be very similar.

This way of writing plans, however, does not scale well with the size of the board: a $N \times N$ board would count $2N + 3$ plan statements with a guard mentioning N cells. There are no good strategies to handle these situations in pure Jason (i.e. without using external tools to generate code), while they can be managed by relying on alternative paradigms in JaKtA.

---

[8] https://github.com/jakta-bdi/jakta-examples.

Multi-paradigm Integration and Meta-Programmability. The same application in JaKtA could be created by defining a *parametric* MAS via an ordinary Kotlin function with a parameter:

```
fun ticTacToe(gridSize: Int = 3) = mas {
  require(gridSize > 0);
  environment { from(GridEnvironment(gridSize)) ; actions { action(Put) } }
  player(mySymbol="x", otherSymbol="o", gridSize=gridSize)
  player(mySymbol="o", otherSymbol="x", gridSize=gridSize)
}
```

The function declares a MAS whose environment of type `GridEnvironment` of size `gridSize` supporting an external action `Put` (defined elsewhere). The two players are agents returned by the `player` extension function:

```
fun MasScope.player(mySymbol: String, otherSymbol: String, gridSize: Int) =
  agent("$mySymbol-agent") {
    beliefs {
      alignment("vertical",dx=0,dy=1); alignment("horizontal",dx=1,dy=0)
      alignment("diagonal",dx=1,dy=1); alignment("antidiagonal",dx=1,dy=-1)
      setOf("vertical", "horizontal", "diagonal", "antidiagonal")
        .forEach { rule { aligned(L) impliedBy it(L) } }
    }
    plans {
      detectVictory(mySymbol, gridSize)
      detectDefeat(mySymbol, otherSymbol, gridSize)
      makeWinningMove(mySymbol, gridSize)
      preventOtherFromWinning(mySymbol, otherSymbol, gridSize)
      randomMove(mySymbol)
    }
  }
```

Notably, the function exploits multiple paradigms to construct agent specifications via AOP meta-programming. For instance, predicate `aligned/1` is defined in a `forEach` loop, while predicates `vertical/1`, `horizontal/1`, and `(anti)diagonal/1` are defined by calling the `alignment` function, which parametrically builds rules to compute alignments along the four major directions:

```
fun BeliefsScope.alignment(name: String, dx: Int, dy: Int) {
  val first = cell(A, B, C); val second = cell(X, Y, Z)
  rule { name(listOf(second)) impliedBy second }
  rule { name(listFrom(first, second, last = W)) .impliedBy(
      first, second, (X - A) arithEq dx, (Y - B) arithEq dy,
      name(listFrom(second, last = W))) }
}
```

With no paradigm blending, based on the bare AgentSpeak(L) syntax, the rules would have needed to be copied and modified to support multiple cases instead.

Plans are defined by means of Kotlin functions as well: JaKtA plans can have names, meta-parameters, and leverage decomposition. For instance, victory and defeat detection are implemented with functions parametric in the symbol of the player and size of the grid:

```
fun PlansScope.detectVictory(myMark: String, size: Int) =
  detect(myMark, myMark, size) { Print("I won!") }
fun PlansScope.detectDefeat(myMark: String, otherMark: String, size: Int) =
  detect(mySymbol, otherMark, size) { Print("I lost!") }
```

and both rely on a generic `detect` function implementing a *template plan*:

```
fun PlansScope.detect(me:String,oth:String,s:Int,action:BodyScope.()->Unit) =
    +turn(me) onlyIf { aligned((1..s).map { cell(oth) }) } then(action)
```

Finally, we show how *plan generation* can be realised in JaKtA by showing the implementation of `makeWinningMove`:

```
fun PlansScope.winningMove(myMark:String, gridSize:Int, mark:String=myMark) =
    allPermutationsOf(cell(X, Y, e), cell(mark), size - 1).forEach {
        +turn(myMark) onlyIf { aligned(it) } then { Put(X, Y, myMark) }
    }
```

There, `gridSize` plan statements are generated, one for each possible position of the empty cell in a line containing $N-1$ cells with the same mark. Once again, the definition is parametric in the size of the grid and the symbol of the current agent. In this way, the JaKtA code would work with all possible values $N > 0$, whereas the corresponding AgentSpeak(L) code would need to be tailored on a single value of N.

We believe that reusable units of agent behaviour such as template plans and plan generation, made possible by intertwining multiple paradigms, promote abstraction, reuse, and allow for improved code-organization.

Code Organisation, Reuse, and Type Safety. Proper organisation is important to the understandability and extensibility of any program. For instance, in our example, separating the belief base from the plan library may be useful to change the latter in order to implement different strategy. The main reuse technique in Jason (similar for many other external AOP DSLs) is plain file inclusion, performed with statements of the form `include("path/to/file.asl")`. The mechanism is simple, but arguably limited and relatively unsafe, as the actual result of the inclusion will be known at runtime.

Instead, JaKtA inherits the abstraction mechanisms of Kotlin: programs can be suitably split into different pieces, at different levels of granularity (package, file, class, function). Pieces may be either individual beliefs, plans, actions, or agents, or even groups of them. Furthermore, JaKtA's (Kotlin's) reusable abstractions are *type-safe*: one cannot, for instance, include a belief where a plan is expected, and consistency is verified at compile time by the Kotlin compiler.

Tooling and Ecosystem. An indirect benefit of internal DSLs is the availability of inheriting the rich ecosystem of tools of the host language. We quickly exemplify in Fig. 1 comparing how JaKtA and Jason are supported by two commonly used IDEs: Visual Studio Code (VSCode) and IntelliJ Idea. We install, in both cases, the latest version of the Jason and Kotlin plugins; notably, we developed nothing specific for JaKtA, so everything that is displayed came with no development and maintenance cost. As the figure shows, we get code highlighting and content assist for both languages in VSCode, although, thanks to Kotlin's type system, we obtain better completion suggestions. It is also worth noting that the suggestions for Jason are in the form of code snippets and have no real contextual relevance. On IntelliJ Idea, however, we have no highlighting or assist of any kind for Jason beyond the tools the IDE provides for plain text files: in fact, no Jason plugin for Idea exists, users coming from that IDE need to adapt to a new one, or developers need to invest time and resources into developing one. Opposedly, JaKtA is fully supported in any IDE featuring Kotlin support (at the time of writing, this includes VSCode, Idea, Android Studio, Eclipse, and Atom[9]).

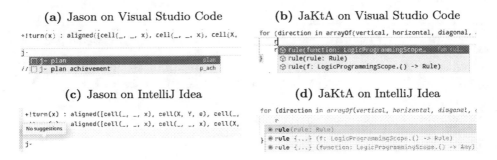

(a) Jason on Visual Studio Code   **(b)** JaKtA on Visual Studio Code

(c) Jason on IntelliJ Idea   **(d)** JaKtA on IntelliJ Idea

Fig. 1. IDE support for Jason and JaKtA compared Visual Studio Code (top) and IntelliJ Idea (bottom). By inheriting the tools made for Kotlin, JaKtA is fully supported in both IDEs with no need for additional development or maintenance.

Additionally, leveraging Kotlin as host language allows JaKtA code to be smoothly embedded in Android applications. The TicTacToe example described above has also been tested on Android[10], as demonstrated by Fig. 2. JaKtA is available on Maven Central, and can thus be imported as an ordinary dependency in any Android project, at the cost of a single line in the projects' Gradle build file.

Fig. 2. The TicTacToe MAS running on Android.

---

[9] https://kotlinlang.org/docs/kotlin-ide.html.
[10] code available at: https://github.com/jakta-bdi/jakta-android-example.

5   Conclusion, Limitations, and Future Work

In this paper, we introduce JaKtA: an internal DSL for BDI agent programming, written in Kotlin, that strives to achieve true paradigm blending of AOP, OOP, and FP in a mainstream language. We show how JaKtA can be used to implement a simple BDI agent, and how paradigm blending can be used to achieve improved modularity, and to build reusable BDI elements, thus providing value to the authors of AOP software. Moreover, we show that, with no need for dedicated components or tools, and thus with no additional development and maintenance cost for the language developers, JaKtA is already supported by most popular IDEs, as it can rely on the existing infrastructure of its host language. Additionally, we argue that JaKtA could enable more developers to get in touch with AOP, since it does not require newcomers to learn a new language, and/or adopt new tools.

Limitations. Approaching the problem through internal DSLs provides several benefits already discussed, but they come at the expense of syntactic flexibility induced by the host language (with different languages having imposing different constraints). Thus, due to the features of Kotlin, differences among JaKtA and AgentSpeak(L) are unavoidable. Indeed, only a fixed subset of symbols can be overloaded in Kotlin. For instance, while the unary logical operator ! can be overridden in Kotlin, the binary Elvis operator ?: cannot. Thus, JaKtA's syntax favors explicit keywords such as `achieve` and `test` to represent achievement and test goals, respectively. Many syntactical design choices in JaKtA were driven by the need to find appropriate Kotlin representations of Jason-inspired entities. As a result, JaKtA's syntax may be more verbose than Jason's: the choice between external and internal DSLs, in general, imposes a trade-off between conciseness and reuse.

Concerning runtime behaviour, JaKtA's architecture has been designed to separate the concurrency model from the agent specification. The implementation discussed in this work relies on a sequential implementation, but different concurrency models are under active development and will be explored in a future work.

Future Work. In the future, our research efforts will follow four main directions. Firstly, we plan to improve JaKtA to fully support Kotlin multiplatform facilities, thus enabling the exploitation of a single language and interpreter for running BDI systems on top embedded devices (Kotlin/Native) as well as in Web (Kotlin/JavaScript), mobile (Kotlin/Android), and general-purpose (Kotlin/JVM) applications. Second, with the help of the concurrency management module developed for JaKtA (which we plan to describe in detail in another work), we intend to investigate how different concurrency models may impact the design and performance of MASs, both in real-world and simulated scenarios. Along this line, we will also investigate how JaKtA can be integrated with mainstream simulation frameworks, to provide better support to the development of distributed MASs and we will attempt to compare how JaKtA relates to other

AOP technologies in terms of performance to understand whether the possibility to change the concurrency model can achieve performance gains. Finally, we will look for ways to improve the syntax of the DSL, in order to increase its readability and to thin the gap between the OOP and AOP.

References

1. Andrei, S., Masalagiu, C.: About the collatz conjecture. Acta Inform. **35**(2), 167–179 (1998). https://doi.org/10.1007/s002360050117
2. Martina, B., Ciatto, G., Pianini, D.: Semantic Release Bot: jakta-bdi/jakta: v0.3.0 (2023). https://doi.org/10.5281/zenodo.7900584
3. Bordini, R.H., Hübner, J.F., Wooldridge, M.J.: Programming Multi-agent Systems in AgentSpeak using Jason. Wiley, Hoboken (2007). http://eu.wiley.com/WileyCDA/WileyTitle/productCd-0470029005.html
4. Bratman, M., et al.: Intention, Plans, and Practical Reason, vol. 10. Harvard University Press Cambridge, MA (1987)
5. Calegari, R., Ciatto, G., Mascardi, V., Omicini, A.: Logic-based technologies for multi-agent systems: a systematic literature review. Auton. Agents Multi-Agent Syst. **35**(1), 1:1–1:67 (2021). https://doi.org/10.1007/s10458-020-09478-3
6. Ciatto, G., Calegari, R., Omicini, A.: 2P- Kt: a logic-based ecosystem for symbolic AI. SoftwareX **16**, 100817:1–100817:7 (2021). https://doi.org/10.1016/j.softx.2021.100817
7. Ciatto, G., Calegari, R., Siboni, E., Denti, E., Omicini, A.: 2P- Kt: logic programming with objects & functions in Kotlin. In: Calegari, R., Ciatto, G., Denti, E., Omicini, A., Sartor, G. (eds.) WOA 2020–21th Workshop "From Objects to Agents". CEUR Workshop Proceedings, vol. 2706, pp. 219–236. Sun SITE Central Europe, RWTH Aachen University, Aachen, Germany (2020). http://ceur-ws.org/Vol-2706/paper14.pdf, 21st Workshop "From Objects to Agents" (WOA 2020), Bologna, Italy, 14–16 September 2020. Proceedings
8. Cohen, P.R., Levesque, H.J.: Intention is choice with commitment. Artif. Intell. **42**(2–3), 213–261 (1990). https://doi.org/10.1016/0004-3702(90)90055-5
9. Collier, R.W., Russell, S., Lillis, D.: Reflecting on agent programming with AgentSpeak(L). In: Chen, Q., Torroni, P., Villata, S., Hsu, J., Omicini, A. (eds.) PRIMA 2015. LNCS (LNAI), vol. 9387, pp. 351–366. Springer, Cham (2015). https://doi.org/10.1007/978-3-319-25524-8_22
10. D'Urso, F., Longo, C.F., Santoro, C.: Programming intelligent IoT systems with a python-based declarative tool. CEUR Workshop Proceedings, vol. 2502, pp. 68–81. CEUR-WS.org (2019). https://ceur-ws.org/Vol-2502/paper5.pdf
11. Finin, T., Fritzson, R., McKay, D., McEntire, R.: KQML as an agent communication language. In: Proceedings of the Third International Conference on Information and Knowledge Management, pp. 456–463. CIKM 1994, Association for Computing Machinery, New York, NY, USA (1994). https://doi.org/10.1145/191246.191322
12. Georgeff, M.P., Lansky, A.L.: Reactive reasoning and planning. In: AAAI. vol. 87, pp. 677–682 (1987)
13. Hindriks, K.V.: Programming rational agents in GOAL. In: El Fallah Seghrouchni, A., Dix, J., Dastani, M., Bordini, R.H. (eds.) Multi-Agent Programming, pp. 119–157. Springer, Boston, MA (2009). https://doi.org/10.1007/978-0-387-89299-3_4

14. Johann, P., Polonsky, A.: Higher-kinded data types: syntax and semantics. In: 34th Annual ACM/IEEE Symposium on Logic in Computer Science, LICS 2019, Vancouver, BC, Canada, 24–27 June 2019, pp. 1–13. IEEE (2019). https://doi.org/10.1109/LICS.2019.8785657

15. Körner, P., et al.: Fifty years of prolog and beyond. Theory Pract. Log. Program. **22**(6), 776–858 (2022). https://doi.org/10.1017/S1471068422000102

16. Leroy, X., Doligez, D., Frisch, A., Garrigue, J., Rémy, D., Vouillon, J.: The OCaml system: Documentation and user's manual. INRIA **3**, 42

17. Mazinanian, D., Ketkar, A., Tsantalis, N., Dig, D.: Understanding the use of lambda expressions in Java. Proc. ACM Program. Lang. **1**(OOPSLA), 85:1–85:31 (2017). https://doi.org/10.1145/3133909

18. Nozik, A.: Kotlin language for science and Kmath library. In: AIP Conference Proceedings, vol. 2163(1), 040004 (2019). https://doi.org/10.1063/1.5130103

19. Omicini, A., Ricci, A., Viroli, M.: Artifacts in the a&a meta-model for multi-agent systems. Auton. Agents Multi Agent Syst. **17**(3), 432–456 (2008). https://doi.org/10.1007/s10458-008-9053-x

20. Palanca, J., Rincon, J.A., Carrascosa, C., Julián, V., Terrasa, A.: A flexible agent architecture in SPADE. In: Dignum, F., Mathieu, P., Corchado, J.M., De La Prieta, F. (eds.) Advances in Practical Applications of Agents, Multi-Agent Systems, and Complex Systems Simulation. The PAAMS Collection, PAAMS 2022. Lecture Notes in Computer Science, vol. 13616, pp. 320–331. Springer, Cham (2022). https://doi.org/10.1007/978-3-031-18192-4_26

21. Pokahr, A., Braubach, L., Lamersdorf, W.: Jadex: a BDI reasoning engine. In: Bordini, R.H., Dastani, M., Dix, J., El Fallah Seghrouchni, A. (eds.) Multi-Agent Programming. MSASSO, vol. 15, pp. 149–174. Springer, Boston, MA (2005). https://doi.org/10.1007/0-387-26350-0_6

22. Rao, A.S., Georgeff, M.P.: Modeling rational agents within a BDI-architecture. In: Allen, J.F., Fikes, R., Sandewall, E. (eds.) Proceedings of the 2nd International Conference on Principles of Knowledge Representation and Reasoning (KR 1991). Cambridge, MA, USA, 22–25 April 1991, pp. 473–484. Morgan Kaufmann (1991)

23. Ricci, A., Piunti, M., Viroli, M.: Environment programming in multi-agent systems - an artifact-based perspective. Auton. Agent. Multi-Agent Syst. **23**(2), 158–192 (2011). https://doi.org/10.1007/s10458-010-9140-7

24. Riti, P.: Practical Scala DSLs: Real-World Applications Using Domain Specific Languages. Apress, Berkeley, CA (2018). https://doi.org/10.1007/978-1-4842-3036-7

25. Stroustrup, B.: The C++ Programming Language, 3rd edn. Addison-Wesley, Boston (1997)

26. Winikoff, M.: JACK™ intelligent agents: an industrial strength platform. In: Bordini, R.H., Dastani, M., Dix, J., El Fallah Seghrouchni, A. (eds.) Multi-Agent Programming. MSASSO, vol. 15, pp. 175–193. Springer, Boston, MA (2005). https://doi.org/10.1007/0-387-26350-0_7

Integrating Ontologies and Cognitive Conversational Agents in On2Conv

Zeinab Namakizadeh Esfahani[1], Débora Cristina Engelmann[2],
Angelo Ferrando[1], Massimiliano Margarone[3], and Viviana Mascardi[1(✉)]

[1] Università degli Studi di Genova, Genova, Italy
n.e.zainab@gmail.com, {angelo.ferrando,viviana.mascardi}@unige.it
[2] Faculdades Integradas de Taquara, Taquara-RS, Brazil
deboraengelmann@faccat.br
[3] SPX LAB, Genova, Italy
m.margarone@spxlab.com

Abstract. Multiagent systems have been successfully used in many domains. Being social, they are expected to communicate with human users in natural language. Nevertheless, the natural interaction between agents and humans is still challenging. Chatbot technologies are a key enabler to boost the communication between humans and software agents, but few technical solutions exist that make the agents' reasoning capabilities easily accessible by a human user via a chatbot and, on the other hand, the chatbot's answers more controllable and explainable. Dial4JaCa is one of such tools. It creates a bridge between Dialogflow and the JaCaMo cognitive-oriented and symbolic AI-based framework: the user's interface is a Dialogflow chatbot allowing the user to interact in natural language, and the backend implementing the reasoning and performing required actions is a JaCaMo agent. However, in Dial4JaCa the consistency between data that feed the JaCaMo agent and those that feed the Dialogflow chatbot must be guaranteed by the developer via an error-prone and tedious manual process. By taking an ontology describing the domain of interest in input and generating both the skeleton for the JaCaMo agent's behaviour and the intents for the Dialogflow chatbot, On2Conv improves Dial4JaCa robustness and reliability, and moves one step towards an explainable integration of agents and chatbots.

Keywords: Conversational agents · Cognitive agents · BDI agents · Ontologies

1 Introduction

With the recent widespread interest in using chatbots in different areas, research on making them as intelligent as possible has gained attention. Powerful chatbot platforms now offer Machine Learning techniques, especially Large Language Models, LLM [30], and in particular Generative Pre-Trained Transformers [24] such as OpenAI's ChatGPT[1] and GPT-4[2], to detect – besides many other things – the user's intent from an utterance. The GPT hype seems unstoppable: at January 2023, according to a study of the UBS Swiss bank, ChatGPT was estimated to be the fastest growing app ever[3].

The hype also brings issues. On March 14th, 2023, the offices of the European Parliament shared a first draft on General Purpose Artificial Intelligence like ChatGPT, proposing some obligations for the providers of these AI models and responsibilities for the different economic actors involved[4]. The draft suggests that throughout their lifecycle, ChatGPT and similar models will have to undergo external audits testing their performance, predictability, interpretability, corrigibility, safety and cybersecurity in line with the European AI Act's strictest requirements. On March 31st, ChatGPT was banned by the Italian data protection authority over privacy concerns[5]. It was restored on April 28th, but France and Spain had shared similar worries in the meantime.

The concerns of authorities, scientists and citizens about the use of blackbox General Purpose Artificial Intelligence and the ongoing debate suggest that the benefits of integrating chatbots – even last-generation ones – with intelligent agents equipped with logic-based reasoning capabilities should be better explored. Indeed, the benefits of this integration might be twofold. On the one hand, users might talk to agents in natural language, removing the interaction barrier that is still preventing the large adoption of intelligent agents – and in particular of cognitive, logic-based ones – by the industry and by people on the street. On the other hand, thanks to the symbolic approach underneath the agent, the user-agent conversation might be controlled, monitored, explained, and steered towards directions implemented in the agent's reasoning rules.

For instance, let us consider a user that asks a health assistant agent *"I am really scared by these three symptoms together: blurred vision, increased thirst and need to urinate often"*; ChatGPT would try to reassure the user by answering *"I understand that these symptoms can be concerning, but it's important not to panic. [...] The most common cause of these symptoms is diabetes, which can be easily diagnosed with a blood test."*[6]. However, the health assistant agent must be aware of its user's gender, age, medications, and it should be able to reason about them and their relations.

Let us suppose that the user is Bob, a male following Fluoxetine therapy. The three symptoms might be side effects of the medication, although they are not frequent ones. The health assistant agent should be aware that Bob takes Fluoxetine because of his illness anxiety disorder and should not mention diabetes as a common cause of these symptoms, at least in its first answer,

---

[1] https://openai.com/blog/chatgpt, accessed on May 2023.

[2] https://openai.com/research/gpt-4, accessed on May 2023.

[3] https://www.reuters.com/technology/chatgpt-sets-record-fastest-growing-user-base-analyst-note-2023-02-01/, accessed on May 2023.

[4] https://www.euractiv.com/section/artificial-intelligence/news/leading-eu-lawmakers-propose-obligations-for-general-purpose-ai/, accessed on May 2023.

[5] https://www.bbc.com/news/technology-65139406, accessed on May 2023.

[6] Query-Answer experimented on May 5th, 2023.

not to alarm Bob. ChatGPT's *"it's important not to panic"* statement does not seem the best advice for a patient with an anxiety disorder, who might react with panic! Rather, the health assistant agent might report the conversation to the physician in charge of Bob, to keep her updated and let her intervene if it is the case, and keep on interacting with Bob in a reassuring way, without overdramatizing the situation.

If the user is Alice, a 35 years old female following a Clomiphene Citrate therapy, hopefully, the reason for the three symptoms together might be not diabetes but a desired pregnancy. Clomiphene Citrate is a fertility medication that can cause blurred vision, and pregnancy may increase thirst and the need to urinate. The assistant agent might then answer *"Alice, why not trying a pregnancy test today?"*.

These reactions targeted to the user's needs can be possible only if, besides being equipped with natural language understanding capabilities, the agent is also aware of concepts like medications, what they are taken for, their side effects, the user's diseases, their symptoms, and it is able to reason on them to provide a personalised answer.

To move a first step towards tackling the challenges above, we designed, implemented and tested **On2Conv** to translate the domain knowledge represented in an **On**tology into a **Conv**ersational cognitive agent based on Dial4JaCa [10,11]. In Dial4JaCa, the chatbot-like interface towards the user and the agent behind must be fed by manually generated input represented in two different formats. These two representations have to be generated and kept consistent by the human developer, who is hence exposed to an error-prone process.

By using On2Conv, the two representations of the input for the chatbot-like interface and the JaCaMo agent are instead generated in an automatic fashion starting from the same piece of knowledge, the ontology. This approach ensures that "Every piece of knowledge must have a single, unambiguous, authoritative representation within a system" [18] – the ontology in this case – and solves one of the main engineering issues that we experimented while using Dial4JaCa. As a further advantage, being an "an explicit specification of a conceptualization" [15], the ontology where the domain information is stored can be used in the early requirement analysis stages to allow the developers, the domain experts, the clients and the users to reach an agreement about the domain of interest and the relationships among concepts therein.

The structure of the paper is the following: Sect. 2 introduces the background and the works related to On2Conv. Section 3 presents its design and implementation. Section 4 discusses the features of the ontology that feeds On2Conv and shows some experiments carried out in the domestic violence domain. Finally, Sect. 5 concludes by highlighting some future directions.

2   Background and Related Work

Dialogflow [2] is a *lifelike conversational AI with state-of-the-art virtual agents* developed by Google. It allows users to create personal chatbots, namely conversational agents equipped with intents, entities, and fulfillment.

During a conversation between humans, a human speaker can utter different types of sentences, each one with a different intentional meaning. That meaning can be identified as the *intent* of that sentence. In order to explain the map between sentences and intents to the Dialogflow chatbot, the agent's developer should provide examples of sentences that convey that intent, for each intent that is relevant for the application.

The fulfillment is a sort of help from home: if the agent cannot answer messages for some specific intent, those messages are forwarded to an external, specialized source that is waiting. Fulfillment provides a field where the user can insert the URL address of the service to query. The service at that address will be consulted only for those intents that require it; in that case, Dialogflow will wait for the answer and will forward it to the user.

JaCaMo [4] is a framework for Multiagent Programming that combines:

(1) Jason [5], for programming autonomous agents characterised by mentalistic notions like beliefs, goals, desires, intentions, and ability to reason;
(2) CArtAgO [1,27], for programming environment artifacts;
(3) MOISE [16], for programming multiagent organisations.

Jason is a language inspired by the Beliefs-Desires-Intentions (BDI) paradigm [7, 26] that implements the logic-based AgentSpeak(L) language [25]. The Jason elements that are more relevant for programming one individual, cognitive agent are:

– Beliefs: the set of facts the agent knows,
– Goals: the set of goals the agent wants to achieve,
– Plans: the set of pre-compiled, operational plans the agent can use to achieve its goals.

Finally, Dial4JaCa [10,11] provides a bridge between Dialogflow or Rasa[7] [3] conversational agents and Jason agents.

As far as the related work is concerned, the strong connection between agents and semantic web technologies, and ontologies in particular, is as old as the semantic web itself [17]. Also, the connection between agents and chatbots is at the basis of the notion of "conversational agents", agents able to conversate with a human user, that started to flourish in the nineties [8,19,23].

When we move to connections between BDI agents and chatbots, however, the literature is scarce and, most often, the BDI paradigm is used as a theoretical framework, rather than as a technological tool.

As an example, the paper by Miliauskas and Dzemydiene [21] presents a non implemented architecture for a BDI chatbot assistant in a travel planning

---

[7] An open-source framework for building chat and voice-based AI assistants.

domain. Sirocki's Master Thesis [28] aims at aiding 113, the national suicide prevention center for The Netherlands. While the conversational agents design was based upon the BDI architecture, the technological solutions neither adopted any AgentSpeak-like, declarative agent programming language, nor implemented the standard BDI engine. The application domain is however similar to ours, suggesting that chatbots that need to be "psychologically aware and competent" might benefit from being designed and/or implemented as cognitive agents. The paper by Sugumar and Chandra [29] explore factors influencing the adoption of chatbots for financial sectors by emphasising on the role of user desires in addition to human beliefs. The BDI architecture is not used during the chatbot design stages, but only as a framework to represent the factors which the users expect to get from AI technologies for their adoption (*beliefs*), the user's future *desires*, and their *intentions* to adopt chatbots for financial services.

The normative agent system to prevent cyberbullying presented by Bosse and Stam [6] is old, but closer to our approach from a technological point of view. It consists of multiple agents implemented in Jason that control users' norm adherence within virtual societies: the agents continuously monitor the behaviour of the visitors – in particular, their communicative behaviour –, communicate with each other to maintain shared beliefs of the visitors' characteristics, and apply punishments and rewards to influence their behaviour. To the best of our knowledge, however, the most recent works in this research strand are all related to Dial4JaCa and include the implementation of a conversational agent to support hospital bed allocation [9], RV4JaCa (Runtime Verification for JaCaMo) that aims to control the dialogue flow in a MAS [12], and VEsNA (Virtual Environments via Natural language Agents) [14] that enhances the design of virtual environments by exploiting Dialogflow, JaCaMo, and Unity for building the dynamic virtual environment, and letting human users immerse in it.

3   On2Conv Design and Implementation

On2Conv is meant to fill the gap among cognitive agents (in particular, BDI agents implemented in the AgentSpeak(L) language), conversational agents (in particular, chatbots implemented in DialogFlow), and ontologies (in particular, OWL ontologies).

It is implemented in Java using Eclipse Version 2021-12, and Gradle[8] as the builder. It builds on top of JaCaMo, the OWL API[9] as the API to manage ontologies, and Dialogflow ES as the platform to build the chatbot-like interface. On2Conv is available to the research community on GitHub, https://github.com/znesss/Ontology-to-JaCaMo_and_Dialogflow.

Figure 1 shows how to use On2Conv in conjunction with Dial4JaCa, to automatically generate the Dialogflow chatbot and the JaCaMo cognitive agent. At the bottom of the figure, the core element, namely the domain ontology modeled using the OWL language [20], is shown. The ontology feeds both the Dialogflow

---

[8] https://gradle.org/, accessed on May 2023.
[9] http://owlcs.github.io/owlapi/, accessed on May 2023.

interface, shown at the top of the figure as a cube, via files in JSON format[10], and the JaCaMo back-end, via AgentSpeak (.asl) files. The purple box tagged with "File Generation by On2Conv" represents the On2Conv system that is in charge of creating these files based on the ontology knowledge, ready to be imported into JaCaMo and Dialogflow.

On the JaCaMo side there are two different agents implemented in Jason: the com_agent and the onto_agent. The first is the agent whose skeleton .asl code is generated by On2Conv, while the second is in charge of interacting with the ontology in order to find out the correct answers based on the recognized intent's parameter values. The com_agent plans must be completed by the developer, but their skeleton is coherent by design with the Dialogflow intents, since both are generated starting from the same source of knowledge, namely the ontology.

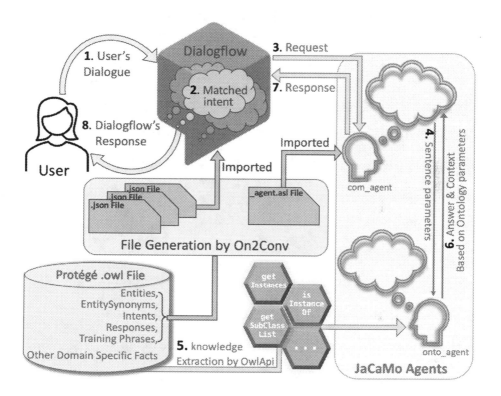

Fig. 1. Methodology to use On2Conv.

After receiving the user's sentence (**1**), Dialogflow automatically matches it with an intent (**2**). Intents are generated by On2Conv based on the ontology knowledge, namely the intent names, training phrases associated with them, and their entities. Hence, we are sure that the matched intent's entities are present

---

[10] https://www.json.org/json-en.html, accessed on May 2023.

in the ontology for further queries by the JaCaMo agents. The matched intent may have been set to send a request to JaCaMo agents to infer and answer. The existing Dial4JaCa system is represented by the cyan arrows labelled as **3** and **7**, it manages the execution of the response and request services, converting the request to a list of key values. The cyan arrow **5** represents the use of Onto4JaCa[11] [13], which is responsible for providing the methods for the plans that query the ontology, shown by the cyan hexagons. Upon receiving the request, the `com_agent` selects a suitable plan, among those generated by On2Conv and completed by the developer, for sending a message containing necessary parameters to the `onto_agent`, and receives the answer from it. This interaction is shown by numbers **4** and **6**. Dialogflow responds to the user with the received answer, and any possible context provided by the JaCaMo agents (**8**).

On2Conv reads an ontology and produces output to feed the Dialogflow interface, and the JaCaMo agents. Figure 2 shows the interaction between a chatbot developer and On2Conv, where the modules represent On2Conv major methods. On2Conv is equipped with an interface developed by `WindowBuilder` Editor[12], a bi-directional Java GUI designer.

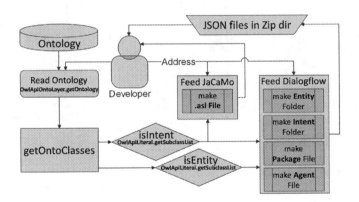

Fig. 2. On2Conv - Chatbot Developer view.

After loading the ontology and choosing a folder to store the JSON and .asl generated from the ontology, the developer will receive messages confirming that the files are created.

The process of generating these files starts with extracting the classes of the ontology as a list and passing them to methods that manage them in order to extract the information needed, and to create the suitable representation in JSON (then compacted into a zip file) and in .asl file.

---

[11] https://github.com/DeboraEngelmann/Onto4JaCa, accessed on May 2023.
[12] https://www.eclipse.org/windowbuilder/, accessed on May 2023.

As far as the files to feed JaCaMo are concerned, the JaCaMo plans are created with triggering events and contexts corresponding to the intents of ontology and written on the .asl files. The chatbot developer should add the desirable parameter values among those received in the plan's triggering event to the belief base, make the appropriate query, and send it to `onto_agent`. The generated .asl file already contains the plans which build the response message to be sent to Dialogflow, based on the answer received from `onto_agent`.

On the Dialogflow side, the input .zip file consists of JSON format files each carrying distinct information such as entity properties, their entries, training phrases properties, and other items. After importing the zip file, the chatbot developer has to 1. go through all the intents, 2. associate all the entity values of each training phrase with the appropriate entity name in the parameters box, 3. toggle on the required field of parameter[13], 4. set the input context, and 5. turn on the fulfilment option for the intents aimed to redirect to MAS in JaCaMo.

4   Ontology Development and Experiments

Figure 3 shows the interaction between the expert in charge for defining the domain-related concepts that will characterize the ontology ("*the expert*" in the sequel), and the developer of the multiagent system that will take advantage of On2Conv ("*the developer*" in the sequel). The ontology's structure is shown in Fig. 4.

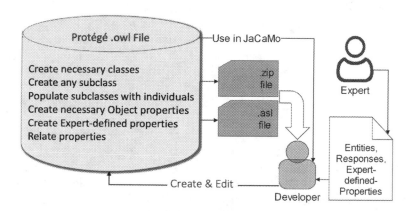

Fig. 3. Ontology Development.

The creation of the ontology is likely to be an iterative process, requiring interactions between the *expert* and the *developer*, and may follow some well known ontology engineering methodology like the Ontology Development 101

---

[13] This step should be done only in case there are plans in `onto_agent` on JaCaMo side attempting to unify the literal values with variables.

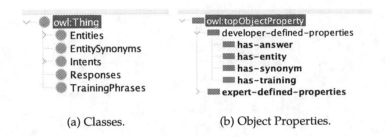

(a) Classes.   (b) Object Properties.

Fig. 4. Ontology Structure.

guide [22]. The second step proposed in that guide, is "consider reusing existing ontologies". Ontology sharing and reuse is one of the main motivations for On2Conv, besides improving the Dial4JaCa engineering. Given that an ontology to be used as input for On2Conv must respect some constraints related to its structure and hierarchy, we provide further and ad-hoc instructions on On2Conv ontology development (or adaptation for reuse) at https://github.com/znesss/ Ontology-to-JaCaMo_and_Dialogflow/wiki#onto-development.

There are two sources for the information to be integrated into the ontology. The first is a dialogue chart that must be designed by the *developer*, with the help of the *expert*, considering as many scenarios as possible. This chart may contain simple short conversations as "User: Hello, how do I look today?", "Bot: You look fantastic, Dalia." or rather complex ones as "User: Hello, what do you suggest me to read?", "Bot: Tell me more about your list of favourite genres and writers, Dalia.", "User: The last book I enjoyed reading was Quaderno proibito".

This dialogue chart helps the *developer* to identify topics (Intents) the user's sentence has to be matched with, in order for the agent to provide a suitable answer. Such sentences are categorised as the training phrases of that intent. During this process, entities detected to be used as a word to help the answer-generation are marked to be later added to their own proper class inside the Entity class.

The second source of information is the knowledge coming from the *expert*, that will feed the Entities class. For instance, if the *expert* provides the fact that "Setting clear goals, making plans, eliminating distractions, and taking breaks can help people focus and stay motivated.", the *developer* might create an Entity named MotivationBooster and include taking_breaks as instance.

After making the list of Intents, Entities, Training phrases, Responses, and Entity Synonyms, the developer has to create the classes with the same names and include their items as the subcategories or individuals. Following that, the properties linking these classes have to be defined. An object property must relate individuals to individuals only. Therefore, in order to relate each intent to multiple training phrases, the *developer* has to create individuals inside each intent class. These individuals may represent subcategories of their parent class, and in addition to allowing the *developer* to incorporate more *expert* knowledge by defining a more comprehensive ontology, their use is enabling the developer to relate them with training phrases through the property has-training. Table 1 shows the domain and range of the four properties that the *developer* must instantiate.

Table 1. Developer-defined-properties.

Name	Domain	Range
has-training	Intents	TrainingPhrases
has-entity	TrainingPhrases	Entities
has-synonym	Entities	EntitySynonyms
has-answer	Intents	Responses

As an example of ontology to be used to feed On2Conv we introduce donna-MAMi for creating a motivational agent for women experiencing domestic violence. The donnaMAMi structure is shown in form of tree in Fig. 5. Not all the classes are shown for lack of space.

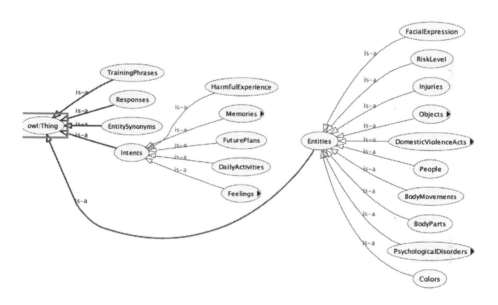

Fig. 5. Tree-like view of donnaMAMi.

In donnaMAMi, Intents include DailyActivities, Feelings, FuturePlans, Memories, hence topics that may be dealt with during a conversation between a woman and the motivational agent; some Intents are broken into sub-classes and may have instances (individuals). Also, some Intents are more related with the domestic violence domain, such as HarmfulExperience.

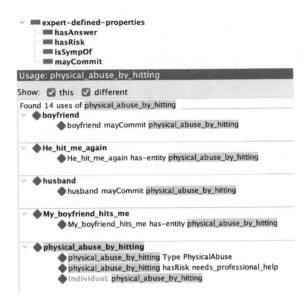

Fig. 6. expert-defined-properties.

Entities are designed to incorporate the domain dependent concepts. Take the entity Emotional Abuse for example. Its instances come from the expert that should be a psychologist with experience in the domestic violence domain, and are used to conclude the degree of the abuse, in order to generate acceptable response and/or take appropriate action. DomesticViolenceActs, Psychologi-calDisorders, and RiskLevel are the entities developed entirely based on the psychology domain texts that we consulted in order to design the donnaMaMi ontology, given the absence of a domain *expert* in the team.

Figure 6 shows an example of how the *expert* might define relations. For example, both a husband and a boyfriend may commit physical abuse by hitting, and some examples of sentences that are related to this kind of abuse are "He hit me again", represented in the ontology as an individual identified by the name He_hit_me_again, and "My boyfriend hits me".

Further examples of relations between the individuals for the daily conversations are provided in Fig. 7. The expert-defined-properties shown in Fig. 6 have hasAnswer, hasRisk, isSympOf, mayCommit as sub-properties, and the list might be further expanded. For example, hasRisk links an individual of DomesticViolenceActs (a subclass of Entities class) to an individual of RiskLevel which is an Entities' sub-class as well. This information is used by the reasoning system to find out the risk level of specific a domestic violence act.

It is also possible to include in the expert-defined-properties, the properties linking an Intents individual to an Entities individual, or vice-versa. For instance in donnaMAMi ontology, isSympOf's domain is NegativeFeelings, and its range is PsychologicalDisorder which is referring to the fact that any

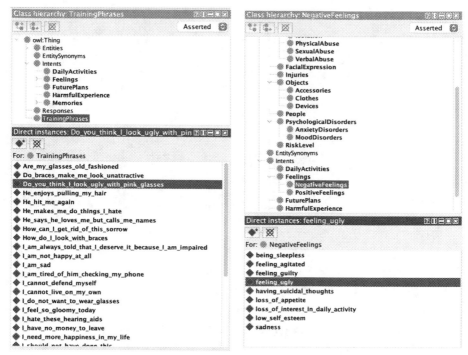

(a) Training Phrases Individuals.   (b) Intent Individuals.

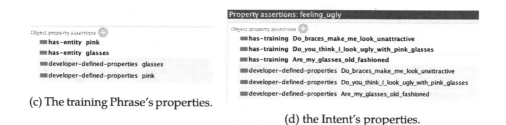

(c) The training Phrase's properties.

(d) the Intent's properties.

Fig. 7. donnaMAMi Ontology Example.

negative feeling the user is talking about may lead to a psychological disorder. Therefore, the part of knowledge provided by the *expert* can be related to the topics of the conversations going on between the chatbot and the user devised by the *developer*.

The sentences inserted in the donnaMAMi instances are used to automatically generate training sentences for Dialogflow as shown in Fig. 8.

⊛   HarmfulExperience

Fig. 8. Training phrases for the Dialogflow HarmfulExperience Intent generated starting from the `donnaMAMi` ontology.

On the other hand, Listing 1.1 shows the Jason plan of the `com_agent` agent, named `donnaMAMi_com_agent` in this instance of the MAS, also automatically generated by On2Conv and then edited by the developer to add domain dependent behaviour. As anticipated in Sect. 3, the `com_agent` acts as an interface between Dialogflow and the ontology. The plan shown in Listing 1.1 deals with the case of having recognized "HarmfulExperience" as the intent of the user's sentence (second line, representing the context of the Jason plan). The `com_agent` actions in the plan's body are aimed at sending a request for the correct answer to the `onto_agent`, named the `donnaMAMi_onto_agent` in this MAS (last line), after the parameters of the intent are properly managed. The `donnaMAMi_onto_agent` is in charge of looking for the correct answer in the ontology. At this stage of the On2Conv development, we were mainly focused on the On2Conv implementation and on its coherence. Although the plan shown in Listing 1.1 mainly implements a simple reactive behaviour, without any logical reasoning, Jason natively supports logic-based reasoning on the agents' beliefs that are represented in an explicit, symbolic way. The examples of sophisticated integration of knowledge and deduction of new facts presented in the Introduction can indeed be implemented in Jason thanks to its support to Prolog-like rules. While we do not claim that this implementation would be effortless, we believe that it would bring significant advantages in terms of code readability, shareability, and explainability, supporting a transparent approach to modern Artificial Intelligence.

```
1  +!responder(RequestedBy, RespId, IntentName, Params, Contexts)
2      : (IntentName == "HarmfulExperience")
3  <-  !delprevparams;
4      for ( .member(X,Params) ) { +X; };
5      ?param("PhysicalAbuse",ABUS); ?param("BodyParts",BD);
6      ?param("Injuries",INJ); ?param("People",PPL);
7      .send(donnaMAMi_onto_agent,askOne,
8          answerHarmfulExperience(ABUS, BD, INJ, PPL, RespId)).
```

Listing 1.1. Jason plan for the donnaMAMi_com_agent edited after being generated starting from the **donnaMAMi** ontology.

Finally, in Fig. 9, two different scenarios for a specific context are shown. The context is **needs_professional_help** when "any" person "has done/does/is doing" any "physical harm" to the user. In the first scenario (Fig. 9a), if the user does not provide the necessary information (in the tested case: person), she will be prompted by the chatbot to mention it, to take the best action based on the answer. The second scenario (Fig. 9b) copes with the situation where an injury is detected in the uttered sentence of the user. In this case, the priority is to tell the user to call the ambulance. Besides from taking care of the context generation, the type of injury is extracted, therefore the agent answers with "Have you called the ambulance?" to suggest the user to immediately do it, in a gentle, non assertive way.

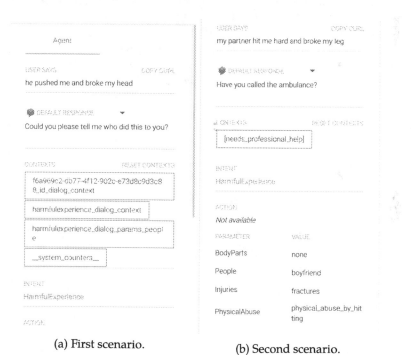

(a) First scenario.   (b) Second scenario.

Fig. 9. Experiments: generating the correct context for the conversation based on what the user says.

5   Conclusions and Future Work

In this paper, the On2Conv tool to generate the files for feeding the Dialogflow and JaCaMo agents starting from information stored in an ontology has been presented. On2Conv adds robustness to the agents communicating through Dial-4JaCa, and makes the development process faster and less error-prone eliminating duplication of information, as suggested by the "Don't repeat yourself" (DRY) software engineering principle.

The feasibility of the methodology using On2Conv is explored through the development of the donnaMAMi ontology and its exploitation to create a MAS. The donnaMAMi MAS has been tested by the authors with sample sentences that a user may utter in a simplified world. Although no tests were carried out in a real-world environment with any possible sentence about domestic violence, the test sentences were chosen wisely to cover as many aspects as possible in order for the MAS reasoning power to be evaluated.

To improve the donnaMAMi ontology and to move the experiment outside the boundaries of academia, we are currently interacting with the SAVE THE WOMAN Italian association of social promotion[14].

Born in 2020, SAVE THE WOMAN is responsible for promoting and disseminating digital solutions against gender-based violence. One of these solutions is the **NONPOSSO**PARLARE (**ICANNOT**TALK) chatbot, developed by SPX under the guidance of one of the authors of this paper. In the last two years **NONPOSSO**PARLARE has been integrated in more than twenty women assistance portals, collecting – in a fully anonymous, GDPR-compliant way – valuable information on how victims use digital tools to ask help. We are currently evaluating how we can integrate the **NONPOSSO**PARLARE chatbot with ontological knowledge and with reasoning capabilities, thanks to On2Conv.

During the development of On2Conv and of its experimentation we relied on our own sensitivity and common sense to address the psychological aspects related with domestic violence. With the help of the SAVE THE WOMAN on the field staff, however, the donnaMAMi ontology and the agents' reasoning mechanism might be made more realistic and once injected into **NONPOSSO**PARLARE, they might make it more competent and solid.

References

1. Cartago. https://cartago.sourceforge.net/
2. Dialogflow documentation. https://cloud.google.com/dialogflow/docs/
3. Introduction to rasa open source & rasa pro. https://rasa.com/docs/rasa/
4. Boissier, O., Bordini, R.H., Hübner, J.F., Ricci, A., Santi, A.: Multi-agent oriented programming with JaCaMo. Sci. Comput. Program. **78**(6), 747–761 (2013). https://doi.org/10.1016/j.scico.2011.10.004
5. Bordini, R.H., Hübner, J.F., Wooldridge, M.J.: Programming Multi-agent Systems in AgentSpeak using Jason. Wiley, Hoboken (2007)

---

[14] https://www.savethewoman.org/, accessed on May 2023.

6. Bosse, T., Stam, S.: A normative agent system to prevent cyberbullying. In: Boissier, O., Bradshaw, J., Cao, L., Fischer, K., Hacid, M. (eds.) Proceedings of the 2011 IEEE/WIC/ACM International Conference on Intelligent Agent Technology, IAT 2011, Campus Scientifique de la Doua, Lyon, France, 22–27 August 2011, pp. 425–430. IEEE Computer Society (2011). https://doi.org/10.1109/WI-IAT.2011.24

7. Bratman, M.: Intention, Plans, and Practical Reason. Harvard University Press, Cambridge, MA (1987)

8. Cassell, J., et al.: Embodiment in conversational interfaces: Rea. In: Williams, M.G., Altom, M.W. (eds.) Proceeding of the CHI 1999 Conference on Human Factors in Computing Systems: The CHI is the Limit, Pittsburgh, PA, USA, 15–20 May 1999, pp. 520–527. ACM (1999). https://doi.org/10.1145/302979.303150

9. Engelmann, D.C., Cezar, L.D., Panisson, A.R., Bordini, R.H.: A conversational agent to support hospital bed allocation. In: Britto, A., Delgado, K.V. (eds.) Intelligent Systems - 10th Brazilian Conference, BRACIS 2021, Virtual Event, 29 November – 3 December 2021, Proceedings, Part I. Lecture Notes in Computer Science, vol. 13073, pp. 3–17. Springer, Cham (2021). https://doi.org/10.1007/978-3-030-91702-9_1

10. Engelmann, D.C., et al.: Dial4jaca - a demonstration. In: Dignum, F., Corchado, J.M., de la Prieta, F. (eds.) Advances in Practical Applications of Agents, Multi-Agent Systems, and Social Good. The PAAMS Collection - 19th International Conference, PAAMS 2021, Salamanca, Spain, 6–8 October 2021, Proceedings. Lecture Notes in Computer Science, vol. 12946, pp. 346–350. Springer, Cham (2021). https://doi.org/10.1007/978-3-030-85739-4_29

11. Engelmann, D.C., et al.: Dial4jaca - a communication interface between multi-agent systems and chatbots. In: Dignum, F., Corchado, J.M., de la Prieta, F. (eds.) Advances in Practical Applications of Agents, Multi-Agent Systems, and Social Good. The PAAMS Collection - 19th International Conference, PAAMS 2021, Salamanca, Spain, 6–8 October 2021, Proceedings. Lecture Notes in Computer Science, vol. 12946, pp. 77–88. Springer, Cham (2021). https://doi.org/10.1007/978-3-030-85739-4_7

12. Engelmann, D.C., Ferrando, A., Panisson, A.R., Ancona, D., Bordini, R.H., Mascardi, V.: Rv4jaca - towards runtime verification of multi-agent systems and robotic applications. Robotics **12**(2), 49 (2023). https://doi.org/10.3390/robotics12020049

13. Engelmann, D.C.: Intentional dialogues in multi-agent systems based on ontologies and argumentation. Ph.D. thesis, Pontifícia Universidade Católica do Rio Grande do Sul and University of Genoa (Double-degree) (2023)

14. Gatti, A., Mascardi, V.: Vesna, a framework for virtual environments via natural language agents and its application to factory automation. Robotics **12**(2), 46 (2023). https://doi.org/10.3390/robotics12020046

15. Gruber, T.R.: A translation approach to portable ontology specifications. Knowl. Acquis. **5**(2), 199–220 (1993)

16. Hannoun, M., Boissier, O., Sichman, J.S., Sayettat, C.: MOISE: an organizational model for multi-agent systems. In: Monard, M.C., Sichman, J.S. (eds.) IBERAMIA/SBIA -2000. LNCS (LNAI), vol. 1952, pp. 156–165. Springer, Heidelberg (2000). https://doi.org/10.1007/3-540-44399-1_17

17. Hendler, J.A.: Agents and the semantic web. IEEE Intell. Syst. **16**(2), 30–37 (2001). https://doi.org/10.1109/5254.920597

18. Hunt, A., Thomas, D.: The Pragmatic Programmer: From Journeyman to Master. Addison-Wesley, Boston [etc.] (2000). http://www.amazon.com/The-Pragmatic-Programmer-Journeyman-Master/dp/020161622X

19. Massaro, D.W., Cohen, M.M., Daniel, S., Cole, R.A.: Chapter 7 - developing and evaluating conversational agents. In: Hancock, P. (ed.) Human Performance and Ergonomics, pp. 173–194. Handbook of Perception and Cognition (Second Edition), Academic Press, San Diego (1999). https://doi.org/10.1016/B978-012322735-5/50008-7, https://www.sciencedirect.com/science/article/pii/B9780123227355500087

20. McGuinness, D.L., Van Harmelen, F., et al.: OWL web ontology language overview. W3C Recommendation **10**(10), 2004 (2004)

21. Miliauskas, A., Dzemydiene, D.: An approach to designing belief-desire-intention based virtual agents for travel assistance. In: Lupeikiene, A., Matulevicius, R., Vasilecas, O. (eds.) Joint Proceedings of Baltic DB&IS 2018 Conference Forum and Doctoral Consortium co-located with the 13th International Baltic Conference on Databases and Information Systems (Baltic DB&IS 2018), Trakai, Lithuania, 1–4 July 2018. CEUR Workshop Proceedings, vol. 2158, pp. 94–103. CEUR-WS.org (2018). https://ceur-ws.org/Vol-2158/paper10.pdf

22. Noy, N.F., McGuinness, D.L.: Ontology development 101: A guide to creating your first ontology (2001). https://protege.stanford.edu/publications/ontology_development/ontology101.pdf

23. Nugues, P., Godéreaux, C., El Guedj, P.O., Revolta, F.: A conversational agent to navigate in virtual worlds. In: Proceedings Dialogue Management in Natural Language Systems. Twente Workshop on Language Technology, vol. 11, pp. 23–33 (1996)

24. Radford, A., Narasimhan, K., Salimans, T., Sutskever, I.: Improving language understanding by generative pre-training (2018). https://gwern.net/doc/www/s3-us-west-2.amazonaws.com/d73fdc5ffa8627bce44dcda2fc012da638ffb158.pdf

25. Rao, A.S.: Agentspeak(l): BDI agents speak out in a logical computable language. In: de Velde, W.V., Perram, J.W. (eds.) Agents Breaking Away, 7th European Workshop on Modelling Autonomous Agents in a Multi-Agent World, Eindhoven, The Netherlands, 22–25 January 1996, Proceedings. Lecture Notes in Computer Science, vol. 1038, pp. 42–55. Springer, Cham (1996). https://doi.org/10.1007/BFb0031845

26. Rao, A.S., Georgeff, M.P., et al.: BDI agents: from theory to practice. In: Icmas, vol. 95, pp. 312–319 (1995)

27. Ricci, A., Piunti, M., Viroli, M., Omicini, A.: Environment programming in CArtAgO. In: El Fallah Seghrouchni, A., Dix, J., Dastani, M., Bordini, R.H. (eds.) Multi-Agent Programming, pp. 259–288. Springer, Boston, MA (2009). https://doi.org/10.1007/978-0-387-89299-3_8

28. Sirocki, J.: Design and evaluation of a conversational agent model based on stance and BDI providing situated learning for triage-psychologists in the helpline of 113 suicide prevention (2019). master Thesis, Delft University of Technology

29. Sugumar, M., Chandra, S.: Do i desire chatbots to be like humans? Exploring factors for adoption of chatbots for financial services. J. Int. Technol. Inf. Manag. **30**(3), 38–77 (2021)

30. Vaswani, A., et al.: Attention is all you need. In: Guyon, I., et al. (eds.) Advances in Neural Information Processing Systems 30: Annual Conference on Neural Information Processing Systems 2017, 4–9 December 2017. Long Beach, CA, USA, pp. 5998–6008 (2017). https://proceedings.neurips.cc/paper/2017/hash/3f5ee243547dee91fbd053c1c4a845aa-Abstract.html

Exploiting Reward Machines with Deep Reinforcement Learning in Continuous Action Domains

Haolin Sun[(✉)][iD] and Yves Lespérance[iD]

York University, Toronto, Canada
{sun0907,lesperan}@yorku.ca

Abstract. In this paper, we address the challenges of non-Markovian rewards and learning efficiency in deep reinforcement learning (DRL) in continuous action domains by exploiting reward machines (RMs) and counterfactual experiences for reward machines (CRM). RM and CRM were proposed by Toro Icarte *et al.* A reward machine can decompose a task, convey its high-level structure to an agent, and support certain non-Markovian task specifications. In this paper, we integrate state-of-the-art DRL algorithms with RMs to enhance learning efficiency. Our experimental results demonstrate that Soft Actor-Critic with counterfactual experiences for RMs (SAC-CRM) facilitates faster learning of better policies, while Deep Deterministic Policy Gradient with counterfactual experiences for RMs (DDPG-CRM) is slower, achieves lower rewards, but is more stable. Option-based Hierarchical Reinforcement Learning for reward machines (HRM) and Twin Delayed Deep Deterministic (TD3) with CRM generally underperform compared to SAC-CRM and DDPG-CRM. This work contributes to the ongoing development of more efficient and robust DRL approaches by leveraging the potential of RMs in practical problem-solving scenarios.

Keywords: Deep Reinforcement Learning · Reward Machines

1 Introduction

In *reinforcement learning (RL),* an agent interacts with the environment by performing actions in each state, receiving a reward signal in return and the agent's goal is to learn a policy (mapping observations to actions) that maximizes the expected cumulative reward and improves its policy from past experiences.

In simple discrete action domains, like turn-based games with finite states and actions, basic RL algorithms such as Q-learning [23] suffice to quickly find the optimal policy. However, in more complex *continuous action domains* like autonomous driving, where variables like acceleration and steering angle have infinite domains, the agent cannot try all possible actions. Consequently, Q-learning fails to identify actions with the highest expected rewards and determine the optimal policy, and struggles to explore the state space effectively. *Deep*

© The Author(s), under exclusive license to Springer Nature Switzerland AG 2023
V. Malvone and A. Murano (Eds.): EUMAS 2023, LNAI 14282, pp. 83–99, 2023.
https://doi.org/10.1007/978-3-031-43264-4_6

reinforcement learning (DRL) was developed to address hard RL problems such as those in continuous action domains. DRL combines neural networks' understanding capabilities with RL's decision-making, allowing agents to tackle more complex problems in such domains [7].

Reward functions in RL algorithms are typically "black boxes". As a result, learning requires extensive interaction with the environment, consuming significant time and computational resources. However, if the agent can access the reward function's internal structure and understand the task's high-level idea, it can leverage this information to expedite optimal policy learning.

To provide agents access to the reward function, Toro Icarte *et al.* proposed using finite state machines called *reward machines (RMs)* [20–22], which define a novel form for reward functions that support certain non-Markovian task specifications. The reward is non-Markovian when it doesn't just depend on the current world state but on the whole history. A reward machine can define multiple forms of reward functions, including concatenation, loops, and conditional rules. It can also decompose a complex task into subtasks, revealing each subtask's reward function to the agent. The RM is assumed to be fully known to the agent; as the agent transitions between RM states, the specific subtask's reward is returned, enabling state-by-state learning and thus allowing the agent to conduct less exploration and speed up the learning. Reward machines offer flexible expression, allowing tasks to be represented using Linear Temporal Logic over infinite or finite traces (LTL/LTL$_f$) [4,15] or other formal languages before translation into a reward machine. A related approach is that of "restraining bolts" [3], where LTL$_f$ restraining specifications are compiled into automata and used in RL to ensure that the learned behavior conforms to them [1]. Another related approach is called "logically constrained RL" [9], where one specifies rules about the finite set of actions that are allowed in a given state, avoiding an exhaustive update over the whole state space, thus guiding the agent to learn more efficiently and conform to desired behaviors.

To utilize an RM's structure, Toro Icarte *et al.* proposed a novel approach called *counterfactual experiences for reward machines (CRM)* [20,22]. CRM leverages reward function information from RMs during agent-environment interactions to generate synthetic experiences, helping the agent make more explicit judgments about RM states thus accelerating learning speed.

Reward machines can be applied in both discrete and continuous action domains. In discrete action domains, Toro Icarte *et al.* enhanced the learning efficiency of existing RL and DRL algorithms by combining reward machines with Q-learning [23] and Double DQN [10], where RM-based Q-learning can converge to the optimal policy. However, in continuous action domains, only DDPG [12] and option-based Hierarchical Reinforcement Learning (HRL) [19] have been combined with reward machines. As new deep RL algorithms emerged, the performance of DDPG and option-based HRL has become less prominent, with some newly proposed algorithms surpassing their performance. To address this issue and further improve the learning efficiency of RM-based algorithms in continuous action domains, we focused on two aspects in our work.

First, we combined CRM with two widely used and well-performing deep RL algorithms, Soft Actor-Critic (SAC) [8] and Twin-Delayed Deep Deterministic Policy Gradient (TD3) [6]. We call the resulting algorithms Soft Actor-Critic with CRM (SAC-CRM) and Twin-Delayed Deep Deterministic Policy Gradient with CRM (TD3-CRM).

Next, we expanded the range of tasks tested compared to prior experiments, e.g., [22]. Based on the RM model, we defined six new tasks in two different continuous action domains. We ran experiments and compared the performance of existing and new RM-based deep RL algorithms and analyzed reasons for performance differences. Through these experiments, we found that SAC-CRM was generally the best-performing algorithm among those studied. The learning speed and reward values it achieved within the specified learning steps were generally the best amongst all the algorithms.

2 Preliminaries

2.1 Reward Machines in RL

Reward Machines. To support non-Markovian rewards, Toro Icarte *et al.* [20–22] introduced a novel reward function form called the *reward machine (RM)*. Formally, given a set of propositional symbols $\mathcal{P}$, a set of (environment) states S, and a set of actions A, a reward machine (RM) is a tuple $\mathcal{R}_{PSA} = \langle U, u_0, F, \delta_u, \delta_r \rangle$ where U is a finite set of states, $u_0 \in U$ is the initial state, F is a finite set of terminal states (where $U \cap F = \emptyset$), δ_u is the state-transition function, $\delta_u : U \times 2^{\mathcal{P}} \to U \cup F$, and δ_r is the state-reward function, $\delta_r : U \to S \times A \times S \to R$.

Consider a simple example where our agent (see Fig. 1) is a cheetah-like robot, as in the OpenAI Gym Half-Cheetah domain [2], and the task is to start from an arbitrary point between A and B, first go to point A, then to B and then C, then back to B, then back to C again, and then finally to point D to receive a reward of 1000 (which is Task 3 of the Half-Cheetah domain in Sect. 4). The agent can move in this 2D environment by choosing the moving angle and force to apply at each joint. Notice that this task involves non-Markovian rewards.

Fig. 1. An example RM environment (Half-Cheetah).

Also, since the agent starts far from point D, and the task contains multiple back-and-forth operations (e.g., to do pick ups and deliveries), if the task description only specifies the final goal of reaching point D, the agent must spend significant time exploring. However, using a reward machine (RM) allows the task to be decomposed into subtasks by introducing multiple RM states to

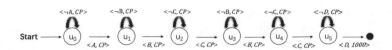

Fig. 2. The automaton for the task.

represent each intermediate reward function. With this, the agent can learn to reach each point sequentially, thus getting closer to the target with each sub-task. This approach reduces exploration time and improves learning efficiency. The automaton for this task is shown in Fig. 2. In this automaton, the reward value is a small control penalty CP for transitions among the non-terminal RM states u_0 to u_5, and when the agent reaches point D while in u_5, it arrives at the terminal RM state, and it will receive a reward value of 1000. In this environment, the set of propositional symbols $\mathcal{P}$ can be defined as $\mathcal{P} = \{A, B, C, D\}$, where event $e \in \mathcal{P}$ occurs when the agent is at location e. To assign truth values to symbols in $\mathcal{P}$, a labelling function $L : S \times A \times S \to 2^{\mathcal{P}}$ will be needed. L can assign truth values to symbols in $\mathcal{P}$ given an environment experience (s, a, s'), where s' is the resulting state after executing action a from the environmental state s. In the example, U is the set of all the non-terminal RM states, including $\{u_0, u_1, u_2, u_3, u_4, u_5\}$; F is the set of the terminal RM state, which is the state after u_5. When the agent reaches point A, the state-transition function δ_u will transfer the agent's current RM state from u_0 to u_1 (otherwise it remains in u_0), and it will transfer the RM state from u_1 to u_2 when the agent reaches point B, and so forth. When the agent reaches point D, a terminal state, the state-reward function δ_r will give the agent a reward of 1000.

MDPRM. In traditional reinforcement learning, the underlying environment model of the agent is assumed to be a *Markov Decision Process* (MDP) [5]. An MDP is a tuple $\mathcal{M} = \langle S, A, r, p, \gamma, \mu \rangle$, where S is a finite set of states, A is a finite set of actions, $r : S \times A \times S \to R$ is the reward function, $p(s_{t+1} \mid s_t, a_t)$ is the transition probability distribution, $\gamma \in (0, 1]$ is the discount factor, and μ is the initial state distribution where $\mu(s_0)$ is the probability that the agent starts in state $s_0 \in S$. By using reward machines, the agent learns in the environment considering not only the environmental state s_t at time t, but also the RM state u_t at time t. The extra consideration of the RM state u_t changes the learning environment from a traditional MDP to a *Markov Decision Process with a Reward Machine (MDPRM)* [20–22]. A *Markov Decision Process with a Reward Machine (MDPRM)* is a tuple $\mathcal{T} = \langle S, A, p, \gamma, \mu, \mathcal{P}, L, U, u_0, F, \delta_u, \delta_r \rangle$, where S, A, p, γ and μ are defined as in an MDP, $\mathcal{P}$ is a set of propositional symbols, L is a labelling function $L : S \times A \times S \to 2^{\mathcal{P}}$, and U, u_0, F, δ_u, and δ_r are defined as in a reward machine. In an MDPRM, the policy learned by the agent then changes from $\pi(a \mid s)$ to $\pi(a \mid s, u)$, and the experience changes from $\langle s, a, r, s' \rangle$ to $\langle s, u, a, r, s', u' \rangle$. It can be seen that MDPRMs are regular MDPs when considering the cross-product between the environmental states S and the

RM states U. As such, standard RL algorithms can learn in MDPRMs by using the *cross-product* of environment and RM states [1,11].

CRM. To exploit the information provided by the RM, Toro Icarte *et al.* proposed a method called *Counterfactual experience for Reward Machines (CRM)* [20,22]. CRM also learns policies over the cross-product $\pi(a \mid s, u)$, but uses counterfactual reasoning to generate *synthetic* experiences. In CRM, the RM will go through every RM state $\bar{u} \in U$ after each action, and use the state transition function $\delta_u (\bar{u}, L(s, a, s'))$ to determine the next RM state $\bar{u}'$; the agent will also receive a reward of $\bar{r}$ using the reward transition function $\delta_r(\bar{u})(s, a, s')$. That is, instead of just providing the actual experience in an MDPRM, the RM can now provide one experience per RM state. In this manner, after taking just one action, the agent will get to know whether the action could cause a transition in any of the RM states and what the reward would be if that happened. In other words, the agent will be able to determine precisely whether its current action, made in the current environmental state, would have an impact on any subtask. This greatly improves the efficiency of the agent's exploration.

2.2 Deep RL Algorithms

Deep Deterministic Policy Gradient (DDPG). Deep Deterministic Policy Gradient (DDPG) [12] is an off-policy deep reinforcement learning algorithm that incorporates an actor-critic architecture to address complex, continuous control problems. DDPG utilizes two distinct neural networks, namely the actor network and the critic network. The actor network is responsible for learning the optimal policy, while the critic network approximates the optimal Q-function, which estimates the expected reward of taking a given action in a given state.

In DDPG, the actor network takes the current environment state as input and outputs a continuous-valued action derived from the current policy. The critic network estimates the value of state-action pairs based on the actor network's output. By adopting a deterministic policy gradient approach, DDPG is able to effectively handle continuous action spaces, while the incorporation of experience replay and target networks stabilizes the learning process.

Option-Based Hierarchical Reinforcement Learning (HRL). Option-based Hierarchical Reinforcement Learning (HRL) [19] is a framework for efficiently learning and planning in complex environments with long-term goals and multiple abstraction levels. In HRL, agents learn a set of subgoals, or "options", which can be combined to create high-level plans. Options serve as reusable subroutines learned through experience. During training, agents learn intra-option policies to achieve each subgoal and inter-option policies for transitioning between subgoals. This allows agents to navigate complex environments by decomposing problems into smaller, more manageable subtasks. Thus a key advantage of HRL is its ability to reduce the amount of training needed, particularly in tasks involving long action sequences.

Soft Actor-Critic (SAC). Soft Actor-Critic (SAC) [8] is an off-policy deep
RL algorithm specifically designed for continuous control tasks. SAC aims to
concurrently maximize the policy's entropy and its cumulative return, i.e., obtain
an agent that succeeds at the task while acting as randomly as possible. To do
this, it incorporates an entropy term into the Q-function:

$$Q^{\pi}_{soft}(s,a) = \mathop{\mathbb{E}}_{s_t, a_t \sim \rho_\pi} \left[\sum_{t=0}^{\infty} \gamma^t r\left(s_t, a_t\right) + \alpha \sum_{t=1}^{\infty} \gamma^t H\left(\pi\left(\cdot \mid s_t\right)\right) \mid s_0 = s, a_0 = a \right]$$

where entropy is defined as: $H(P) = \mathop{\mathbb{E}}_{x \sim P}[-\log P(x)]$.
Adding this entropy component enables deeper exploration of the state space,
which is crucial in continuous control tasks characterized by high-dimensional
state and action spaces.

The maximum entropy model offers several advantages, including making
the fewest assumptions about the environment's unknown information while
matching observed data. This approach ensures that the model remains robust
and adaptable to various environments. Furthermore, by controlling the entropy
value, the agent can maintain a high level of exploration capability. This prevents
the agent from prematurely converging to a local optimum and allows for the
discovery of more optimal solutions in complex problem domains.

Twin Delayed Deep Deterministic Policy Gradient (TD3). Twin
Delayed Deep Deterministic Policy Gradient (TD3) [6] is an off-policy deep RL
algorithm for continuous control tasks, improving upon the original Deep Deterministic Policy Gradient (DDPG) algorithm by addressing several limitations.
A primary enhancement in TD3 is the use of two critic networks instead of one,
estimating the value of state-action pairs and reducing overestimation bias. TD3
also employs delayed policy updates, updating the policy less frequently than
the critic networks to decrease policy update variance and stabilize learning.
Another notable feature of TD3 is target policy smoothing, which adds noise
to actions selected by the actor network, regularizing the policy and increasing
its robustness to environmental perturbations. This is especially beneficial in
continuous control tasks where minor action changes significantly impact the
agent's behavior.

For more technical details about these algorithms, see [18].

3   Adapting Deep RL Algorithms with Reward Machines

Toro Icarte *et al.* [20, 22] proposed a variant of DDPG that incorporates the CRM
approach, calling it DDPG-CRM. Concurrently, they introduced an options-
based Hierarchical Reinforcement Learning (HRL) algorithm that learns options
to move between states of a RM, which they call HRM. The integration of CRM
into DDPG is achieved by initially modifying the learning environment to suit
the Markov Decision Process with a Reward Machine (MDPRM), followed by

the inclusion of counterfactual experiences into the replay buffer. Instead, HRM applies DDPG to learn the option policies while employing Deep Q-Network (DQN) [13] to learn the high-level policy. In this work, we incorporate the CRM approach into two additional deep RL algorithms that are currently widely recognized for their strong performance, namely Soft Actor-Critic (SAC) [8] and Twin Delayed Deep Deterministic Policy Gradient (TD3) [6]. Note that we also experimented with combining CRM with PPO [17] but the performance/learning efficiency was very poor, see [18] for details. PPO is an on-policy RL method and it is not clear how counterfactual experiences can be incorporated effectively in such approaches.

3.1   Soft Actor-Critic (SAC) with CRM

First, we use SAC as a base and propose a new algorithm, SAC-CRM, that takes advantage of the task structure that the RM has made visible. In SAC-CRM, the agent still uses the entropy value from the baseline SAC when updating the Q-function and continues the Energy-Based Policy model from the baseline SAC. In contrast to the baseline, SAC-CRM changes the type of the actual experience compared to the baseline SAC and also adds counterfactual experiences to the replay buffer. The pseudocode of SAC-CRM is shown in Algorithm 1.

In SAC-CRM, the learning environment becomes an MDPRM, so the RM experience will be added to the replay buffer. The actual experience learned by the agent will change from the original $\langle s, a, r, s' \rangle$ to $\langle s, \bar{u}, a, \bar{r}, s', \bar{u}' \rangle$, where $\bar{u}$ and $\bar{u}'$ are the RM states before and after the action a, and $\bar{r}$ is the reward given by the reward machine. Also, CRM will generate one counterfactual experience for each RM state after the agent takes an action (see line 7 in Algorithm 1). To generate the counterfactual experiences, the agent will traverse each RM state $\bar{u} \in U$ after making an action. If the agent's action in $\bar{u}$ causes the environmental state s change to the next environmental state s', then the next RM state will be calculated by the state-transition function, which is $\bar{u}' = \delta_u \left(\bar{u}, L \left(s, a, s' \right) \right)$, and the agent will receive a reward given by the state-reward function, which is $\bar{r} = \delta_r(\bar{u}) \left(s, a, s' \right)$. CRM generates one counterfactual experience for each RM state. The expression of the counterfactual experience set is:

$$\{(s, \bar{u}, a, \delta_r(\bar{u}) \left(s, a, s' \right), s', \delta_u \left(\bar{u}, L \left(s, a, s' \right) \right)) \mid \bar{u} \in U\}$$

Correspondingly, SAC-CRM will learn the information provided by CRM when updating the policy. Specifically, the agent will consider both the actual experience and counterfactual experiences. In terms of reward, the agent will now consider the RM reward provided by the state-reward function. At this point, since the agent learns in an MDPRM, SAC-CRM will not only consider the actual environmental state but the cross-product of the environmental state and the RM state, as well as the counterfactual experiences provided by CRM (line 9 to line 15 in Algorithm 1). Note that we follow [8] and maintain two independent Q functions and use the minimum of the two in the policy improvement step (line 15) to mitigate positive bias. The updated policy is selected by minimizing

Algorithm 1. Soft Actor-Critic with counterfactual experiences for RMs (CRM).

Input: initial policy parameters θ, Q-function parameters ϕ_1, ϕ_2, empty replay buffer $\mathcal{D}$, labelling function L, a finite set of states U, a finite set of terminal states F, state-transition function δ_u, state-reward function δ_r, initial RM state $u_0 \in U$

1: Set target parameters equal to main parameters $\phi_{\text{targ},1} \leftarrow \phi_1, \phi_{\text{targ},2} \leftarrow \phi_2$
2: Initialize $u \leftarrow u_0$ and $s \leftarrow \text{EnvInitialState}()$
3: **repeat**
4:     Observe state s and select action $a \sim \pi_\theta(\cdot \mid s, u)$
5:     Execute a in the environment and observe next state s'
6:     Compute the reward $r \leftarrow \delta_r(u)(s, a, s')$ and next RM state $u' \leftarrow \delta_u(u, L(s, a, s'))$, and done signal d to indicate whether s' is terminal
7:     Set experience $\leftarrow \{(s, \bar{u}, a, \delta_r(\bar{u})(s, a, s'), s', \delta_u(\bar{u}, L(s, a, s')), d) \mid \bar{u} \in U\}$
8:     Store experience in replay buffer $\mathcal{D}$
9:     If s' is terminal or $\bar{u} \in F$, reset environment state.
10:    **if** it's time to update **then**
11:        **for** j in range (however many updates) **do**
12:            Randomly sample a batch B of transitions from $\mathcal{D}$
13:            Compute targets for the Q functions:

$$y\left(\bar{r}, s', \bar{u}', d\right) = r + \gamma(1-d)\left(\min_{i=1,2} Q_{\phi_{\text{targ},i}}\left(s', \bar{u}', \tilde{a}'\right) - \alpha \log \pi_\theta\left(\tilde{a}' \mid s', \bar{u}'\right)\right),$$

$$\tilde{a}' \sim \pi_\theta\left(\cdot \mid s', \bar{u}'\right)$$

14:            Update Q-functions by one step of gradient descent using

$$\nabla_{\phi_i} \frac{1}{|B|} \sum_{(s, \bar{u}, a, \bar{r}, s', \bar{u}', d) \in B} \left(Q_{\phi_i}(s, \bar{u}, a) - y\left(\bar{r}, s', \bar{u}', d\right)\right)^2 \quad \text{for } i = 1, 2$$

15:            Update policy by one step of gradient ascent using

$$\nabla_\theta \frac{1}{|B|} \sum_{s, \bar{u} \in B} \left(\min_{i=1,2} Q_{\phi_i}\left(s, \bar{u}, \tilde{a}_\theta(s, \bar{u})\right) - \alpha \log \pi_\theta\left(\tilde{a}_\theta(s, \bar{u}) \mid s, \bar{u}\right)\right)$$

where $\tilde{a}_\theta(s, \bar{u})$ is a sample from $\pi_\theta(\cdot \mid s, \bar{u})$ which is differentiable wrt θ via the reparametrization trick.
16:            Update target network with

$$\phi_{\text{targ},i} \leftarrow \rho \phi_{\text{targ},i} + (1 - \rho)\phi_i \quad \text{for } i = 1, 2$$

17:        **end for**
18:    **end if**
19: **until** convergence or maximum training step reached

---

the distance between it and the energy-based policy (EBP) for the Q function, where the distance is measured via Kullback-Leibler divergence.

3.2   Twin Delayed Deep Deterministic Policy Gradient (TD3) with CRM

We chose Twin Delayed Deep Deterministic Policy Gradient (TD3) as another algorithm to integrate with CRM. The integration process is similar to SAC-CRM and involves two steps. First, we added reward machine information to the actual experience, which includes current and next RM states and the RM reward. Then, we added counterfactual experiences to the replay buffer.

Because the learning environment becomes an MDPRM, we need to include reward machine information in the actual experience. Specifically, we added the cross-product of the environmental states and the RM states to the actual experience, as well as the reward provided by the reward machine, changing the agent's experience from $\langle s, a, r, s' \rangle$ to $\langle s, u, a, r, s', u' \rangle$. Then, we added counterfactual experiences by generating a corresponding counterfactual experience for each RM state after the agent executes each action. This experience contains the next RM state $\bar{u}'$ calculated using the state-transition function $\delta_u(\bar{u})$ and the RM reward $\bar{r}$ calculated by the state-reward function $\delta_r(\bar{u})$, which is the same form as the counterfactual experience in SAC-CRM.

For more details about all these algorithms, see [18]; the code is available at https://github.com/haolinsun0907/Exploiting_RMs_with_DRL).

4   Experimental Evaluation

In this section, we test the proposed algorithms (SAC-CRM and TD3-CRM) in two continuous action domains, comparing their performance with existing algorithms (DDPG-CRM and HRM). The test environments are the Half-Cheetah (2D) and Ant (3D) domains in OpenAI Gym [2]. All CRM-based algorithms have a batch size of $100n$, where $n = |U|$ represents the number of non-terminal RM states. For HRM, option policies are learned using DDPG, and the high-level policy is learned using DQN. The batch size of HRM is $100n$, where n represents the available options. The neural networks for all algorithms use two hidden layers with 256 units and $RELU$ activation functions.

In both domains, the agent's task involves reaching multiple points in a specific order, making the rewards non-Markovian. This tests each algorithm's ability to control the agent's movement by coordinating its limbs, as well as CRM's impact on task completion. The efficiency of the baseline algorithms determines the agents' movement speed, affecting the steps required to reach target points. Additionally, since the environments are RM environments with complex tasks, it is difficult for the agent to learn to complete the task using only the baseline algorithm running over the cross-product of the environment and reward machine states. To substantiate this assertion, we conducted a performance comparison between the baseline SAC and DDPG running over the cross-product states versus their counterparts, SAC-CRM and DDPG-CRM, that generate counterfactual experiences. The test results (on the Half-Cheetah Tasks 1 and 2 below) revealed a significant performance boost when counterfactual experiences were utilized, thus underscoring their pivotal role in enhancing the efficacy of these algorithms; see [18] for details. CRM provides more specific task information, improving the agent's learning efficiency in completing multi-target point tasks.

4.1   Results in the Half-Cheetah Domain

In the Half-Cheetah domain, our first experimental environment, the agent is a cheetah-like robot with six joints, see Fig. 1. The robot must learn to control these joints to stand, move forward, or backward. It chooses how much force to apply to each joint per step, resulting in an infinite action space. The continuous state space includes each joint's location (coordinates' values on the plane) and velocity. We will test the new and existing algorithms on four tasks, including one original task defined by Toro Icarte *et al.* [20,22] (Task 1). The tasks are:

- **Task 1**: Starting between points A and B, first go to point B, then repeatedly go back and forth between A and B.
- **Task 2**: Starting between points A and B, first go to point A, then to B, then to C, then back to B, and then A, and repeat indefinitely.
- **Task 3**: Starting between points A and B, first go to point A, then to B, then C, then back to B, then to C again, then reach point D and stop.
- **Task 4**: Starting between points A and B, either go to point A or to B, then go to point C, and finally reach point D and stop.

We will use these tasks to test and compare the performance of our new algorithms, SAC-CRM and TD3-CRM, against [22]'s RM-based algorithms, DDPG-CRM and HRM. For all tasks, the agent starts from an arbitrary position between points A and B. Following the original approach in [22], to prevent the agent from ceasing exploration, the agent receives a small negative reward value, called *Control Penalty (CP)*, after each RM state transition.

Figure 3 displays the performance of the evaluated algorithms. The horizontal axis represents the total number of training steps (three million), while the vertical axis indicates the total reward received by the agent within an episode (of 1,000 training steps). Different coloured lines represent the mean episode reward among 10 trials for each algorithm, and the shaded area indicates the range between the highest and lowest episode rewards for each trial. Note that the results for the first task with DDPG-CRM and HRM, initially presented by Toro Icarte *et al.* [22], were reconfirmed in our study. After repeating the task ten times, we found our results consistent with theirs.

It can be seen that SAC-CRM outperforms all other algorithms in this domain, exhibiting faster learning speeds and higher reward values. In Task 1, SAC-CRM achieves the same performance level as the second-best performer, DDPG-CRM, in 150,000 training steps-up to 20 times faster. The mean reward value after two million training steps for SAC-CRM is about 30% higher than DDPG-CRM. With a highest episode reward of around 11,000, SAC-CRM can complete the task approximately 11 times in one episode, three more than DDPG-CRM. SAC-CRM also excels in the other tasks, demonstrating the fastest learning speed and highest episode reward.

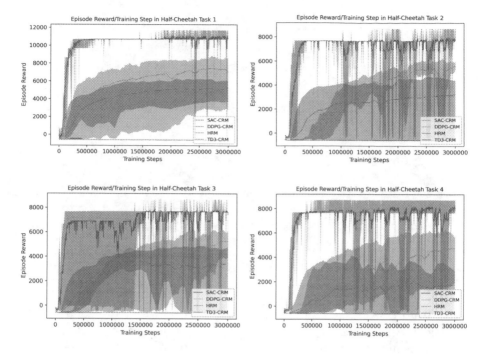

Fig. 3. Results in Half-Cheetah domain.

Other algorithms do not perform as well as SAC-CRM. DDPG-CRM ranks second, with more stable learning curves than SAC-CRM. HRM performs reasonably well but has lower rewards than SAC-CRM and DDPG-CRM. TD3-CRM fails to complete the task within the training period (without counterfactual experiences, it works effectively in the easier tasks).

4.2   Results in the Ant Domain

We further tested the algorithms' performance in the Ant domain to increase the environment and task complexity. The Ant robot is a 3D robot with a torso and four legs, each with two links. The main goal is to coordinate the four legs by applying torques to the eight hinges, allowing movement in any direction on the plane. The state space (coordinates of the joints in 3D space) and action space (torque on the joints) are also continuous, similar to the Half-Cheetah domain.

The Ant domain was chosen for several reasons. First, it is a 3D environment, providing a larger moving space and more diverse states. Second, the Ant robot's higher number of joints requires more complex movement coordination, making learning more difficult. Consequently, the Ant domain is ideal for testing the performance of RM-based algorithms in a more complex environment.

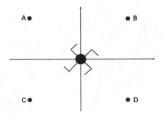

Fig. 4. The abstract representation of Ant.

We will test three tasks in the Ant environment, which has designated points similar to the Half-Cheetah domain. Figure 4 shows an abstract representation of the domain. In all three tasks, the ant robot starts at a random location near the origin:

- **Task 1**: Starting nearby the origin, go to point B, then repeatedly move between points A and B.
- **Task 2**: Starting nearby the origin, go to points A, B, and C sequentially, then back to B, A, and repeat indefinitely.
- **Task 3**: Starting nearby the origin, choose either point A or B, go to the chosen point, then to points C and D. From point D, return to the chosen point (A or B) and stop.

Figure 5 displays the learning curves of all algorithms across tasks. Only SAC-CRM and DDPG-CRM achieve significant rewards within the specified learning steps, while the other algorithms do not.

It can be seen that SAC-CRM outperforms all other algorithms, demonstrating faster learning and higher reward values compared to DDPG-CRM. This is primarily due to SAC's greater exploration capability. In the Ant domain, the agent's movement expands to backward, forward, left, and right, increasing the movement space. SAC's high exploration tendency enables it to try new directions and explore joint coordination more effectively, improving movement speed faster than other algorithms. Conversely, DDPG-CRM's exploration rate diminishes as it learns, resulting in slower performance improvement.

Notably, HRM performs poorly in the Ant domain, with a significant performance gap compared to the Half-Cheetah domain. Although it quickly finds local optimal solutions, HRM's policies often get stuck in local optima. In the Half-Cheetah domain, lower environmental complexity allows the agent to rely on local optimal policies for relatively high rewards. However, in more complex environments, the gap between local and global optimal policies widens, and local optimal policies become insufficient for obtaining high rewards, resulting in HRM's poor performance in the Ant domain.

Lastly, TD3-CRM's performance remains weak, similar to its results in the Half-Cheetah domain.

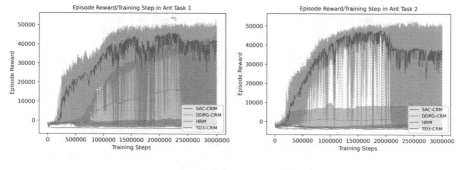

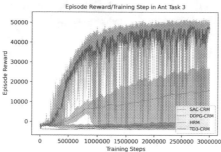

Fig. 5. Results in Ant domain.

5   Discussion

Performance of SAC-CRM. The experimental results reveal that SAC-CRM consistently outperforms the other tested RM-based algorithms across all tasks, demonstrating superior learning speed and policy quality. Its advantage is particularly pronounced in the more complex Ant domain. Therefore, SAC-CRM is deemed the optimal choice for all tasks in both Half-Cheetah and Ant domains explored in this paper.

The standout performance of SAC-CRM can be attributed mainly to its unique entropy-based policy update mechanism. In our continuous experimental environments, numerous action combinations influence the agent's movement, some leading to failure, some to slow progress, and others to rapid advancement. The entropy-based mechanism encourages extensive exploration, enabling the policy to avoid early local optima and maintain high exploration levels while maximizing reward value.

Furthermore, SAC-CRM's success is bolstered by its generation of stochastic policies. In the continuous action domain, multiple optimal actions often exist in a specific state. Unlike deterministic policies, which limit the discovery of better action combinations by outputting a unique action, SAC-CRM saves all available actions in a given state, allocating their probabilities based on their Q-values. This broader 'vision' in action selection allows more frequent testing of different action combinations, accelerating learning for complex tasks such as multi-limb robot control.

Performance of DDPG-CRM. Despite not achieving the highest rewards in most tasks, DDPG-CRM displays consistent performance, outshining other RM-based algorithms in stability, especially compared to SAC-CRM.

However, DDPG-CRM's drawbacks include its slow learning speed and lower rewards compared to SAC-CRM. The experimental results show that in all tasks, DDPG-CRM lags behind SAC-CRM in both learning speed and reward achieved. This gap widens in the more complex Ant domain. Due to its deterministic policy learning, DDPG-CRM is less exploratory, limiting the agent's capacity to seek better action combinations. Moreover, its traditional Q-function-based learning may overestimate Q-values, causing premature convergence to a local optimum.

In summary, DDPG-CRM is robust and stable, making it a viable choice for simpler environments like Half-Cheetah when stability is more important than optimal performance. However, its reward output falls short compared to SAC-CRM, making it less suitable for complex environments like the Ant domain.

Performance of HRM. The experimental results show that HRM performs reasonably well in the Half-cheetah domain. While not as efficient as SAC-CRM, it achieves comparable performance to DDPG-CRM in learning speed and reward, and it also often surpasses DDPG-CRM in early training stages.

However, HRM's performance declines sharply in the more complex Ant domain. This is due to HRM's predisposition to find local optima. HRM has no guarantee of convergence to a global optimum, which becomes problematic as the gap between local and global optima widens in complex environments. Thus, while HRM performs well in low-complexity settings, it becomes less effective in more complex environments. Note that HRM's performance depends on it using a good decomposition for the task; but we think that the RM-based task decompositions are reasonably good for our test tasks.

Performance of TD3-CRM. TD3-CRM's performance in all tasks is far from ideal, earning the lowest rewards among all the evaluated algorithms. The reason appears to be a conflict between CRM and TD3's policy updating mechanism.

First, TD3-CRM assigns the lower Q-value to an action using two learned Q-functions. This works well in MDPs, where Q-values are often overestimated, but not in MDPRMs. In an MDPRM, the RM information is critical for the agent to transfer from one RM state to another; specifically, the actions that can make the RM state change usually have high Q-values, which encourage the agent to keep using these actions to make transitions between the RM states. Nevertheless, TD3 always tries to "underestimate" the Q-values, which will avoid these beneficial actions.

Furthermore, TD3's target policy smoothing regularization, which adds noise to actions, restricts optimal action selection and steers the agent towards close alternatives instead. This contrasts with CRM's encouragement for the agent to execute optimal actions that trigger RM state changes. Consequently, this contradiction confuses the agent, causing infrequent correct actions and resulting in poor performance.

6   Conclusion

Training a practical deep RL agent for specific scenarios typically requires extensive training data and time. Furthermore, agents often face complex tasks with non-Markovian rewards, making learning high-quality policies from limited information a significant challenge. Therefore, observing more information and fully utilizing it is crucial for improving training efficiency.

Our research is inspired by previous work on reward machines and deep RL algorithms, particularly the work by Toro Icarte *et al.* [20,22]. Our contributions include extending two mainstream deep RL algorithms, SAC and TD3, to exploit reward machine models and counterfactual experiences, yielding two new reward machine-based algorithms, SAC-CRM and TD3-CRM. In order to simulate the tasks that an intelligent agent might encounter in the real world, we introduced seven different task types in two simulated continuous action domains. We evaluated experimentally the performance of all RM-based deep RL algorithms across these tasks. We found that the newly proposed SAC-CRM performed best in most tasks.

For future work, there are several key areas of focus. First, more extensive parameter tuning could potentially enhance algorithm performance, as the current uniform parameters may not allow for optimal performance. Second, expanding experimental evaluations to include a wider variety of tasks and domains would allow for more comprehensive robustness testing and a better understanding of the environments and tasks best suited for each algorithm. Third, finding ways to stabilize the policies of SAC-CRM, which currently fluctuate in learning curves across tasks, could make it a more robust algorithm. Fourth, incorporating Automated Reward Shaping [14] into CRM-based algorithms may further improve learning speed by providing intermediate rewards for subtask completion. Fifth, it's worth exploring ways to combine CRM and on-policy deep RL algorithms such as PPO [17] and TRPO [16]. This could further expand the use cases for RM and CRM. Lastly, applying these RL algorithms to real-world hybrid domains, which involve both discrete and continuous decision variables, could offer more practical solutions to real-world problems, expanding their usability beyond the purely continuous control problems they currently address.

Acknowledgements. Work supported by the National Science and Engineering Research Council of Canada and York University.

References

1. Brafman, R.I., Giacomo, G.D., Patrizi, F.: LTLf/LDLf non-markovian rewards. In: McIlraith, S.A., Weinberger, K.Q. (eds.) Proceedings of the Thirty-Second AAAI Conference on Artificial Intelligence, (AAAI-18), the 30th Innovative Applications of Artificial Intelligence (IAAI-18), and the 8th AAAI Symposium on Educational Advances in Artificial Intelligence (EAAI-18), New Orleans, Louisiana, USA, February 2–7, 2018, pp. 1771–1778. AAAI Press (2018). https://www.aaai.org/ocs/index.php/AAAI/AAAI18/paper/view/17342

2. Brockman, G., Cheung, V., Pettersson, L., Schneider, J., Schulman, J., Tang, J., Zaremba, W.: OpenAI Gym. CoRR abs/1606.01540 (2016), http://arxiv.org/abs/1606.01540

3. De Giacomo, G., Iocchi, L., Favorito, M., Patrizi, F.: Restraining bolts for reinforcement learning agents. In: The Thirty-Fourth AAAI Conference on Artificial Intelligence, AAAI 2020, The Thirty-Second Innovative Applications of Artificial Intelligence Conference, IAAI 2020, The Tenth AAAI Symposium on Educational Advances in Artificial Intelligence, EAAI 2020, New York, NY, USA, February 7–12, 2020, pp. 13659–13662. AAAI Press (2020). https://ojs.aaai.org/index.php/AAAI/article/view/7114

4. De Giacomo, G., Vardi, M.Y.: Linear temporal logic and linear dynamic logic on finite traces. In: Rossi, F. (ed.) IJCAI 2013, Proceedings of the 23rd International Joint Conference on Artificial Intelligence, Beijing, China, August 3–9, 2013. pp. 854–860. IJCAI/AAAI (2013). http://www.aaai.org/ocs/index.php/IJCAI/IJCAI13/paper/view/6997

5. Feinberg, A.: Markov decision processes: discrete stochastic dynamic programming (Martin L. Puterman). SIAM Rev. **38**(4), 689 (1996). https://doi.org/10.1137/1038137

6. Fujimoto, S., van Hoof, H., Meger, D.: Addressing function approximation error in actor-critic methods. In: Dy, J.G., Krause, A. (eds.) Proceedings of the 35th International Conference on Machine Learning, ICML 2018, Stockholmsmässan, Stockholm, Sweden, July 10–15, 2018. Proceedings of Machine Learning Research, vol. 80, pp. 1582–1591. PMLR (2018). http://proceedings.mlr.press/v80/fujimoto18a.html

7. Guillen-Perez, A., Cano, M.: Learning from oracle demonstrations - a new approach to develop autonomous intersection management control algorithms based on multiagent deep reinforcement learning. IEEE Access **10**, 53601–53613 (2022). https://doi.org/10.1109/ACCESS.2022.3175493

8. Haarnoja, T., Zhou, A., Abbeel, P., Levine, S.: Soft actor-critic: off-policy maximum entropy deep reinforcement learning with a stochastic actor. In: Dy, J.G., Krause, A. (eds.) Proceedings of the 35th International Conference on Machine Learning, ICML 2018, Stockholmsmässan, Stockholm, Sweden, July 10–15, 2018. Proceedings of Machine Learning Research, vol. 80, pp. 1856–1865. PMLR (2018). http://proceedings.mlr.press/v80/haarnoja18b.html

9. Hasanbeig, M., Kroening, D., Abate, A.: LCRL: certified policy synthesis via logically-constrained reinforcement learning. In: Ábrahám, E., Paolieri, M. (eds.) QEST 2022. LNCS, vol. 13479, pp. 217–231. Springer, Cham (2022). https://doi.org/10.1007/978-3-031-16336-4_11

10. van Hasselt, H., Guez, A., Silver, D.: Deep reinforcement learning with double q-learning. In: Schuurmans, D., Wellman, M.P. (eds.) Proceedings of the Thirtieth AAAI Conference on Artificial Intelligence, February 12–17, 2016, Phoenix, Arizona, USA, pp. 2094–2100. AAAI Press (2016). http://www.aaai.org/ocs/index.php/AAAI/AAAI16/paper/view/12389

11. Lacerda, B., Parker, D., Hawes, N.: Optimal policy generation for partially satisfiable co-safe LTL specifications. In: Yang, Q., Wooldridge, M.J. (eds.) Proceedings of the Twenty-Fourth International Joint Conference on Artificial Intelligence, IJCAI 2015, Buenos Aires, Argentina, July 25–31, 2015, pp. 1587–1593. AAAI Press (2015). http://ijcai.org/Abstract/15/227

12. Lillicrap, T.P., et al.: Continuous control with deep reinforcement learning. In: Bengio, Y., LeCun, Y. (eds.) 4th International Conference on Learning Repre-

sentations, ICLR 2016, San Juan, Puerto Rico, May 2–4, 2016, Conference Track Proceedings (2016). http://arxiv.org/abs/1509.02971

13. Mnih, V., et al.: Human-level control through deep reinforcement learning. Nature **518**(7540), 529–533 (2015). https://doi.org/10.1038/nature14236

14. Ng, A.Y., Harada, D., Russell, S.: Policy invariance under reward transformations: theory and application to reward shaping. In: Bratko, I., Dzeroski, S. (eds.) Proceedings of the Sixteenth International Conference on Machine Learning (ICML 1999), Bled, Slovenia, June 27–30, 1999, pp. 278–287. Morgan Kaufmann (1999)

15. Pnueli, A.: The temporal logic of programs. In: 18th Annual Symposium on Foundations of Computer Science, Providence, Rhode Island, USA, 31 October - 1 November 1977, pp. 46–57. IEEE Computer Society (1977). https://doi.org/10.1109/SFCS.1977.32

16. Schulman, J., Levine, S., Abbeel, P., Jordan, M.I., Moritz, P.: Trust region policy optimization. In: Bach, F.R., Blei, D.M. (eds.) Proceedings of the 32nd International Conference on Machine Learning, ICML 2015, Lille, France, 6–11 July 2015. JMLR Workshop and Conference Proceedings, vol. 37, pp. 1889–1897. JMLR.org (2015). http://proceedings.mlr.press/v37/schulman15.html

17. Schulman, J., Wolski, F., Dhariwal, P., Radford, A., Klimov, O.: Proximal policy optimization algorithms. CoRR abs/1707.06347 (2017). http://arxiv.org/abs/1707.06347

18. Sun, H.: Exploiting Reward Machines with Deep Reinforcement Learning in Continuous Action Domains. Master's thesis, EECS Dept., York University, Toronto, Canada (2022)

19. Sutton, R.S., Precup, D., Singh, S.: Between MDPs and semi-MDPs: a framework for temporal abstraction in reinforcement learning. Artif. Intell. **112**(1–2), 181–211 (1999). https://doi.org/10.1016/S0004-3702(99)00052-1

20. Toro Icarte, R.: Reward Machines. Ph.D. thesis, University of Toronto, Canada (2022). http://hdl.handle.net/1807/110754

21. Toro Icarte, R., Klassen, T.Q., Valenzano, R.A., McIlraith, S.A.: Using reward machines for high-level task specification and decomposition in reinforcement learning. In: Dy, J.G., Krause, A. (eds.) Proceedings of the 35th International Conference on Machine Learning, ICML 2018, Stockholmsmässan, Stockholm, Sweden, July 10–15, 2018. Proceedings of Machine Learning Research, vol. 80, pp. 2112–2121. PMLR (2018). http://proceedings.mlr.press/v80/icarte18a.html

22. Toro Icarte, R., Klassen, T.Q., Valenzano, R.A., McIlraith, S.A.: Reward machines: exploiting reward function structure in reinforcement learning. J. Artif. Intell. Res. **73**, 173–208 (2022). https://doi.org/10.1613/jair.1.12440

23. Watkins, C.J.C.H., Dayan, P.: Q-learning. Mach. Learn. **8**, 279–292 (1992). https://doi.org/10.1007/BF00992698

A Comprehensive Presentation of the Jadescript Agent-Oriented Programming Language

Federico Bergenti[1](✉), Stefania Monica[2], and Giuseppe Petrosino[2]

[1] Dipartimento di Scienze Matematiche, Fisiche e Informatiche, Università degli Studi di Parma, Parma, Italy
federico.bergenti@unipr.it
[2] Dipartimento di Scienze e Metodi dell'Ingegneria, Università degli Studi di Modena e Reggio Emilia, Reggio Emilia, Italy
{stefania.monica,giuseppe.petrosino}@unimore.it

Abstract. Jadescript is an agent-oriented programming language based on JADE that aims to become a dependable tool for the construction of industrial-strength multi-agent systems. This paper contributes to this objective by providing researchers and practitioners with a comprehensive description of Jadescript that discusses the most relevant features attained in several years of continuous development. In particular, this paper focuses on how Jadescript promotes the adoption of some ideas taken from agent-oriented programming by providing direct support for agent-oriented abstractions, like messages and ontologies, by encouraging the use of event-driven programming to govern interactions, and by allowing fine-grained task management using behaviours. Finally, to illustrate the practical applicability of Jadescript, this paper presents in detail the implementation of a well-known election algorithm traditionally used to coordinate distributed systems.

Keywords: Agent-oriented software engineering · Agent-oriented programming · JADE · Jadescript

1 Introduction

In recent years, the design and the implementation of software agents have received significant attention from the literature on agents and *MASs* (*Multi-Agent Systems*). In this context, *JADE* (*Java Agent DEvelopment framework*) [2,3,6] stands as a prominent open-source software framework aligned to the fundamental ideas inspired by *AOP* (*Agent-Oriented Programming*) [31] and *AOSE* (*Agent-Oriented Software Engineering*) [8]. JADE was envisaged with the goal of creating a flexible and robust framework for the construction of agent-based software systems using the technology standardized by *FIPA* (*Foundation of Intelligent Physical Agents*) [30]. Since its creation, JADE have been used by several researchers and practitioners all over the world [6], and it has been successfully employed in a wide range of real-world applications (e.g., [5,7,11,16]). JADE is still a point of reference for researchers and practitioners working on agent-based software systems and for teachers lecturing on AOP and AOSE.

The longevity and the popularity of JADE attest its relevance, and they also bear evidence that JADE helped identify and promote some of the characteristic abstractions of AOP and AOSE. For example, during the development of JADE, it was understood that agents could be effectively managed using virtual machines named (agent) containers, which could be organized in (agent) platforms [6]. Platforms and containers can be distributed across several physical machines connected through an underlying network, and they can be made responsible to provide general-purpose services to agents like naming, discovery, and messaging. Note that JADE helped understand that these services are better considered as platform-level services, and they cannot be faithfully considered as agents, which is the approach that the first public FIPA specifications followed.

Despite the success of JADE and the importance of the ideas that it helped identify and promote, the development of agents and MASs with JADE comes with some inherent issues. Most notably, the use of JADE to develop agents and MASs implies the use of Java, which tends to obfuscate the adoption of the agent-oriented abstractions that JADE provides. For example, the extraction of a message from a message queue, its validation, its conversion to a processable form, and its dispatch to a suitable handler requires much boilerplate code and several nested conditional statements, which inevitably increase the complexity of the produced code. Actually, the inherent complexity of the Java code needed to use the agent-oriented abstractions that JADE provides can cause the introduction of subtle bugs. Therefore, programmers are constantly tempted to avoid the adoption of these abstractions in favor of lower level, but harmless, solutions.

Most of the issues inherent to the use of JADE for the construction of agents and MASs can be traced back to the adoption of Java to interface JADE, and therefore they can be alleviated by means of a dedicated language. This language could be specifically designed to ease the adoption of the agent-oriented abstractions that JADE offers in the spirit of *DSLs (Domain-Specific Languages)* [19]. Moreover, it could be designed to refine and extend these abstractions to provide programmers with a complete and coherent system level for the design and the implementation of agent-based software systems [4,9,14]. Actually, this language could support programmers in their everyday work while promoting the view of agents and MASs that JADE and FIPA advocate.

Jadescript [6] was envisaged some years ago [13] with the intent to break the strong connection that links JADE with Java, thus advancing previous related investigations [10]. Jadescript has undergone significant improvements since its last published report [12], and this paper offers an up-to-date presentation of the language that serves as a comprehensive reference for its major features. Also, this paper precisely cites the papers that originally introduced each discussed improvement, thus providing accurate references for further reading.

The major features that Jadescript exhibits are described throughout this paper highlighting the advantages and the disadvantages that they bring to the construction of software agents and agent-based software systems. These features recast, improve, and extend, using dedicated language constructs, the abstractions that JADE provides. The description of these features and constructs is enriched with sections of Jadescript code that demonstrate the use of these features and constructs in a nontrivial example. The chosen example shows how the distinguishing features of Jadescript, and its characteristic event-driven approach, can be used to implement a well-known distributed algorithm, thus emphasizing the ability of Jadescript agents to schedule concurrent tasks using behaviours and to communicate using messages and shared ontologies. The chosen example is an implementation of the bully algorithm [20], which is a well-known election algorithm [20] used to coordinate distributed systems.

In detail, the bully algorithm is a distributed algorithm designed to elect a leader among a group of participants. Each participant is associated with a unique identifier, and each participant knows the identifiers of all other participants. Identifiers are totally ordered, and therefore they can be used to order participants. When participants start, the participant with the highest identifier assumes the leadership. Then, the algorithm proceeds as follows:

1. A participant p detects that the current leader is inoperative;
2. The participant p sends a message to all other participants with higher identifiers to elect a new leader;
3. When a participant q answers to p, p gives up and q takes over by sending a message to all other participants with higher identifiers; but
4. If no participants answer, participant p becomes the new leader.

In the Jadescript implementation of this algorithm described in the remaining of this paper, the detection that the leader is inoperative is accomplished by periodically sending heartbeat messages and waiting for acknowledgements [21]. In detail, when a participant becomes the leader, it starts sending heartbeat messages every $H = 3$s to all other participants. Therefore, a participant can consider the leader as inoperative if the participant did not receive heartbeat messages from the leader for the last $T = 10$s, and when this happens, the participant starts a new election.

This paper is organized as follows. Section 2 describes the support for ontologies that Jadescript currently provides. Section 3 discusses how agents and their behaviours can be programmed using Jadescript. Section 4 describes the current support that Jadescript offers to handle events and messages. Finally, Sect. 5 concludes the paper and briefly outlines some planned future developments.

2   Ontologies in Jadescript

JADE and FIPA adopt (communication) ontologies [32] as the principal means to share the interpretation of the content of messages among communicating agents. Ontologies serve as shared conceptual frameworks that allows the agents in a MAS to effectively communicate and coordinate. For JADE, an ontology is a set of definitions that describe the structure of the concepts, the (agent) actions, the predicates, and the (atomic) propositions pertinent to a given application domain. JADE uses these structured descriptions only to improve the efficiency and the robustness of message passing.

Jadescript adheres to the approach to the use of ontologies that JADE and FIPA promote, but it provides ontologies not only to enable fruitful communication among agents but also to define structured data that can be used in the construction of the agents and their behaviours. In order to support this extended approach to the use of ontologies, Jadescript treats ontologies as organized packages of concepts, actions, predicates, and propositions.

In particular, Jadescript provides concepts to facilitate the manipulation of domain-specific structured data. Similarly, Jadescript provides actions to represent the actions that agents can perform, request, cancel, or, more generally, refer to. Concepts and actions can be optionally structured in terms of typed properties, and they have the possibility to extend other concepts and actions, respectively. Predicates and propositions are elements of an ontology that Jadescript provides to represent logical facts. Predicates are structured in terms of typed properties, while propositions are not structured. Note that, with the use of the `uses ontology` construct, agents and their behaviours can explicitly refer to an ontology, which causes the elements of the referenced ontology to be readily usable in the Jadescript code of the agents and their behaviours.

Both JADE and Jadescript allow ontologies to be structured into hierarchies. In particular, an ontology, in JADE or in Jadescript, can extend other ontologies to reuse the concepts, the actions, the predicates, and the propositions from referenced ontologies, and possibly introduce new elements. This hierarchical approach is supported by JADE to promote the reusability of ontologies pertaining to a specific application domain. However, Jadescript adopts this hierarchical approach with the twofold aim to promote the reusability of ontologies and to improve the modularization of the Jadescript code when ontologies are used to manipulate data in the agents and their behaviours.

JADE allows agents to use various types of data as the content of messages, such as serialized Java objects, bit arrays, and strings of characters. In contrast, Jadescript imposes a more stringent restriction on the content of messages, and it enforces agents to use only concepts, actions, predicates, or propositions. The shift from allowing arbitrary data types in the content of messages, like JADE does, to enforcing the use of ontologies, like Jadescript does, is a decision explicitly taken in the design of Jadescript to foster a well-founded approach to knowledge sharing and communication within a MAS. Essentially, the Jadescript agents in a MAS are forced to adhere to a common taxonomy that describes the relevant characteristics of the application domain in order to improve the characteristic interoperability and reusability of software agents [9].

Figure 1 shows the Jadescript code of the ontology used by the participants in the bully example. The ontology defines one proposition (`Alive`), one action (`ElectNewLeader`), and one predicate (`NewLeader`). The `Alive` proposition is used as the content of the heartbeat messages that the leader sends to the other

```
1  ontology Bully
2      proposition Alive
3      action ElectNewLeader
4      predicate NewLeader(newLeader as aid)
```

Fig. 1. The Jadescript code of the ontology used in the bully example, which defines one proposition (`Alive`), one action (`ElectNewLeader`), and one predicate (`NewLeader`) to be used as the content of messages exchanged by participants.

participants. The `ElectNewLeader` action is used as the content of the messages that participants send when they detect that the leader is inoperative. Finally, the `NewLeader` predicate is used as the content of the messages used to inform all participants about the identity of the newly elected leader.

3   Jadescript Agents and Their Behaviours

Jadescript treats agents as the fundamental building blocks of software, and one of the basic assumptions behind Jadescript is that a Jadescript agent is a JADE agent. Therefore, Jadescript agents can be deployed in JADE containers, and, when deployed, they are assigned unique *AIDs* (*Agent IDentifiers*) [3]. AIDs are totally ordered in the scope of a platform because JADE, following FIPA, uses a textual representation for AIDs. In Jadescript, AIDs are represented by values of type `aid`, which is one of basic data types that Jadescript provides [25]. Since Jadescript AIDs are JADE AIDs, the values of type `aid` can be compared using relational operators, such as < and <=. The total ordering of the AIDs in the scope of a platform is used in the bully example to order participants during elections to ensure that a participant send messages only to the participants with higher identifiers. In detail, a participant p gives up in favor of a participant q if the AID of p is strictly less than the AID of q.

Similarly to JADE agents, a Jadescript agent have a private state that comprises a lifecycle state, a message queue, a queue of active behaviours, and an application-specific state described in terms of a set of properties. To ensure autonomy, the state of an agent can be accessed and modified only by the agent and its behaviours, and an agent can be destroyed only by the container that hosts it. The Jadescript code of an agent specifies, among other things, the properties that form the application-specific state of the agent and the handlers that the agent uses when it is created and destroyed.

Figure 2 shows the Jadescript code of the participants in the bully example. The code starts by associating participants with the `Bully` ontology, whose Jadescript code is shown in Fig. 1. This association enables participants to readily refer to the elements of the `Bully` ontology, allowing participants, and their behaviours, to create, manipulate and, in particular, send and receive, elements of the ontology. Moreover, the Jadescript code shown in Fig. 2 specifies that the application-specific state of a participant is structured in terms of six properties. The first two properties are the period of the heartbeat messages and the time

```
1   agent Participant uses ontology Bully
2       property heartbeatPeriod = "PT3S" as duration
3       property timeoutInterval = "PT10S" as duration
4       property leader as aid
5       property knownParticipants as list of aid
6       property monitor as MonitorHeartbeat
7       property election as Election
8
9       on create with participants as list of text do
10          # The first AID in the list is the leader.
11          if participants matches [initialLeader|others] do
12              leader = initialLeader as aid
13              # Add the AIDs of the other participants to
14              # the list of participants.
15              for op in others do
16                  opAid = op as aid
17                  if opAid != aid of agent do
18                      add opAid to knownParticipants
19          activate DoHeartbeat every heartbeatPeriod
20          activate RespondElection
21          activate HandleLeaderChanges
22          if leader != aid of agent do
23              # If the agent is not the leader, monitor
24              # heartbeat messages from the leader.
25              activate monitor
26          else do
27              # Otherwise, destroy the leader after 10s.
28              activate SimulateTermination
29                  after "PT10S" as duration
30
31      procedure setLeader with newLeader as aid do
32          if newLeader = aid of agent do
33              # If the agent is the new leader, stop
34              # monitoring and inform the other participants
35              deactivate monitor
36              send message inform NewLeader(newLeader)
37                  to knownParticipants
38              activate SimulateTermination
39                  after "PT10S" as duration
40          else do
41              # If the leader is another participant, start
42              # waiting for heartbeat messages.
43              activate monitor
44          leader = newLeader
```

Fig. 2. The Jadescript code of the participants in the bully example.

interval used when awaiting for a heartbeat message or a response. The two subsequent properties are the AID of the current leader and the list of the AIDs of all participants. Finally, the last two properties refer to the two behaviours used by the participant to enact the bully algorithm, as described later in this section.

Note that Jadescript agents can use private functions, procedures, and event handlers to perform some of their tasks. Functions and procedures are used by agents to execute sections of parameterized code that, in the case of functions, can also compute a value. Event handlers are used to specify how agents react when interesting events occurs. For example, the Jadescript code of the participants in the bully example, shown in Fig. 2, contains the `setLeader` procedure and one `on create` handler. A participant that has just won an election uses the `setLeader` procedure to inform all other participants of the result of the election, and it changes its private state accordingly. The `on create` handler specifies what a participant should do as soon as it is created and activated in the platform. A participant receives upon creation the list of the AIDs of the participants, which includes its AID, and the `on create` handler initializes the private state of the participant before activating its main behaviours, which are different for the leader and for the other participants.

Besides functions, procedures, and event handlers, Jadescript offers a structured approach to model the tasks of the agents using behaviours. Actually, Jadescript agents can concurrently execute several behaviours using a cooperative scheduling strategy [3]. This approach, which originated in the preliminary JADE prototypes [6], renounces to parallelism within the agent to favor parallelism and distribution among the agents.

Just like agents, a Jadescript behaviour has a private state structured in terms of a set of properties. Moreover, a behaviour can contain private functions, procedures, and event handlers. Note that a behaviour can be restricted to be used only by specific agents by means of the `for agent` construct. This construct identifies which agents can create and use a behaviour, and it allows the behaviour to readily access and modify the private state of its agent, which is the agent that created the behaviour. In addition, the use of this construct allows a behaviour to readily use the functions and the procedures of its agent.

Jadescript offers two types of behaviours: one-shot behaviours and cyclic behaviours. One-shot behaviours represent tasks that are designed to be executed only once. After a one-shot behaviour has completed its execution, it is automatically removed from the queue of the active behaviours of its agent. This kind of behaviour is ideal to create atomic sequences of actions that are meant to be deferred. For example, the Jadescript code of the behaviour that the participants in the bully example use to simulate a fatal failure in shown in Fig. 3. This behaviour is used to keep the bully example interesting by simulating fatal failures in the current leader, which force the remaining participants to initiate the election of a new leader.

Differently from one-shot behaviours, cyclic behaviours are used for repeatable tasks. After each execution, a cyclic behaviour remains in the queue of the active behaviours of its agent, and it is rescheduled for subsequent executions until explicitly deactivated. Cyclic behaviours are essential for tasks that require waiting for specific events or for tasks that need to be repeated periodically.

```
1   one shot behaviour SimulateTermination
2       on execute do
3           log "Simulating termination."
4           do delete
```

Fig. 3. The Jadescript code of the one-shot behaviour used to simulate the fatal failure of the leader in the bully example.

Typically, cyclic behaviours consist of event handlers, with support functions and procedures, that are designed to react to specific events.

Every time an agent schedules a behaviour, it attempts to execute one of the event handlers of the behaviour. The attempts are performed in the order in which handlers are written in the Jadescript code of the behaviour, from top to bottom. If, after scheduling a cyclic behaviour, no applicable event handlers are found, the behaviour transitions to the waiting state to save computational resources. While in the waiting state, the behaviour remains idle until a new interesting event occurs. Once an interesting event has occurred, the behaviour transitions to the ready state, so it can be selected by the behaviour scheduler embedded in its agent. This approach allows Jadescript agents to efficiently manage cyclic behaviours, ensuring that they can promptly react to relevant events while saving resources during inactivity.

One-shot and cyclic behaviours form a versatile framework for agents to handle diverse tasks. This framework has been recently extended to support periodic and delayed executions [28]. In the current version of Jadescript, the activation of behaviours, expressed using the **activate** statement, can have arguments to detail when and how often the activated behaviour should be executed. These arguments are specified using the **at** keyword, the **after** keyword, or the **every** keyword. The **at** keyword can be used to precisely state when the activation should take place. The **after** keyword can be used to force a delay before the activation takes place. Finally, the **every** keyword can be used only with cyclic behaviours, and possibly with the **at** keyword or **after** keyword, to state that the activation is periodic and to specify its period. Similarly, the deactivation of behaviours can be delayed by using the **at** keyword or the **after** keyword in the scope of the **deactivate** statement. These recent improvements empower programmers to code tasks that are typical of distributed systems, such as managing timeouts or sending heartbeat messages.

Each participant in the bully example has two behaviours whose Jadescript code is shown in Fig. 4. The first is called monitor behaviour while the second is called heartbeat behaviour. The monitor behaviour is used by a participant to receive and process the heartbeat messages from the leader. When activated, this behaviour activates the election behaviour of the participant, which is available through the **election** property of the participant. The **timeoutInterval** property of the participant is used to determine for how long this activation should be delayed. Upon receiving an heartbeat message, the monitor behaviour of a participant postpones the activation of the corresponding election behaviour.

```
1  cyclic behaviour MonitorHeartbeat for agent Participant
2      on activate do
3          activate election after timeoutInterval
4
5      on message when performative = inform
6          and content = Alive
7          and sender = leader do
8          # Postpone the activation of the election.
9          activate election after timeoutInterval
10
11 cyclic behaviour DoHeartbeat for agent Participant
12     on execute do
13         # Only the leader sends heartbeat messages.
14         if leader = aid of agent do
15             send message inform Alive to knownParticipants
```

Fig. 4. The Jadescript code of the behaviours used to monitor (`MonitorHeartbeat`) and periodically signal (`DoHeartbeat`) the correct functioning of the leader.

Therefore, an election starts only when the leader fails to communicate with the other participants for a sufficiently long period of time. Note that the reception of heartbeat messages is handled by the monitor behaviour of a participant using a message handler. A comprehensive description of message handlers is available in Sect. 4. The heartbeat behaviour of a participant is executed by the participant with a period specified by its `heartbeatPeriod` property. At each execution, only the leader acts, and it broadcasts a message, whose content is `Alive`, to all other participants. Finally, note that both the monitor behaviour and the heartbeat behaviour use the `for agent` construct to access the private state of their participant.

4   Events and Messages in Jadescript

The messaging service that JADE provides is location-transparent, and therefore it allows agents in the same platform to communicate using asynchronous messages independently of their current hosting containers. This feature allows treating the network addresses of agents as low-level details that are subsumed by their AIDs. Actually, this feature abstracts away the complexities of low-level communication mechanisms. Therefore, a MAS based on JADE can be designed focusing only on agents and their tasks. Jadescript complements this feature with specific constructs that embrace event-driven programming, as follows.

Jadescript categorizes events in either internal or external. Internal events pertain to changes in the private state of an agent or in the private state of a behaviour, and they can be captured using specific event handlers. For example, the initial creation of an agent can be captured using an `on create` handler. Similarly, the ordered destruction of an agent can be captured using an `on destroy` handler. These two event handlers are also available to behaviours, which can also react to execution, activation, and deactivation events. An **on execute** handler is executed every time a behaviour is selected by the internal scheduler of its agent. An **on activate** handler is executed the first time a behaviour is selected after its activation. Finally, an **on deactivate** handler is executed when a behaviour is removed from the queue of the active behaviours of an agent, either explicitly via the **deactivate** statement or implicitly when the behaviour is done. The set of internal events has been recently extended to support exception handling [26]. Agents and behaviours can react to exceptions arising from procedure, functions, and event handlers by means of **on exception** handlers. A behaviour can explicitly fail by means of the **fail** statement, or it can implicitly fail because of uncaught exceptions. Agents can handle behaviour failures using **on behaviour failure** handlers, which provide the means to possibly reactivate failed behaviours.

Currently, Jadescript supports two types of external events: native events and message events. Native events are submitted to an agent using the Java API designed to support bidirectional interoperability between Jadescript agents and legacy Java code [27]. A native event has a content that is a predicate or proposition defined in one of the ontologies used by the agent. Therefore, predicates and propositions can be used to model conditions that occur in the local view of the environment that the agent has. Native events are essential to allow agents interfacing with their environment to support, for example, pervasive and ubiquitous agents (e.g., [1, 15, 22]). Similarly, message events occur when new messages are delivered to an agent. Upon arrival, a new message is always placed in the message queue of the agent by the messaging service of the platform. Every time an **on message** handler of an active behaviour is executed, it attempts to retrieve a message from this queue for further processing.

In Jadescript, a message always includes several properties. In particular, a message includes the AID of the sender and the list of the AIDs of the receivers. It includes a performative, which is a label that indicates the purpose of the communicative act performed by sending the message. It also includes the name of the ontology that the sender and the receivers are expected to share. Finally, it includes a content, which is defined in terms of the concepts, the actions, the predicates, and the propositions of the shared ontology. The **send message** statement can be used in Jadescript to construct and send messages to other agents, explicitly specifying the receivers, the performative, and the content. Note that Jadescript does not require programmers to specify the sender of a message or the ontology used in a message because the execution context of the **send message** statement can provide this information. Finally, note that Jadescript assumes that the content of a message is compatible with the performative of the message. For example, a **request** message can only contain an action, whereas an **inform** message can only contain a predicate or an atomic proposition. This restriction is not imposed by JADE because JADE does not even restrict the content of messages to rely on a shared ontology.

Agents can be programmed in Jadescript to selectively handle specific incoming messages by refining message handlers. This is primarily obtained with the use of a dedicated construct that associates an handler with the messages for which a specified Boolean expression evaluates to `true`. This expression refers to the properties of the incoming message and to the state of the agent to obtain a sophisticated condition that holds only for the messages that the handler can actually process on the basis of the state of the agent. Figure 4 shows the Jadescript code of behaviours that use message handlers to selectively decide which message to process. Note that if a message handler cannot process an incoming message because the message is not structured as expected or because the state of the agent is not appropriate, the message queue is left unchanged to give subsequent message handlers the opportunity to process the message.

It is worth noting that message handlers feature pattern matching to ease the construction of the condition that must hold for a message to be processed [23]. Pattern matching allows programmers to effectively deconstruct the content of the received messages by matching them against message patterns. A message pattern consists of a constant performative followed by a content pattern. A content pattern is an expression that can contain values, free variables, and placeholders. The values in a content pattern are compared for equality with the values of the corresponding properties of the received messages. When a match is successful, the content of the matching message is deconstructed, and the free variables of the content pattern are bound and made accessible in the scope of the handler. Pattern matching enhances the expressive power of Jadescript, enabling effective message selection while allowing programmers to focus on the parts of the received messages that are truly relevant for the message handlers.

Each participant in the bully example has two behaviours whose Jadescript code is shown in Fig. 5. The first is called leadership change behaviour while the second is called take over behaviour. The leadership change behaviour uses an `on message` handler that matches against messages whose performative is `inform` and whose content matches the pattern `NewLeader(l)`, where `l` is a free variable. If a message is actually processed by the handler, the `l` variable is bound to the AID of the leader. The value of `l` is then used to set the new leader by means of the `setLeader` procedure. This behaviour is always active for all agents to ensure that all agents in the MAS, including those who did not participate in the election, are aware of the leadership change caused by the successful conclusion of an election. The take over behaviour is used by a participant to take over in an election initiated by a participant with a lower AID. The message handler in this behaviour matches against messages whose performative is `propose` and whose content matches the content pattern `ElectNewLeader`. When a message that matches against this message pattern is received, the participant can decide whether to accept the proposal and takes over or not.

Finally, each participant in the bully example has two behaviours whose Jadescript code is shown in Fig. 6. The first is called election behaviour while the second is called terminate election behaviour. The election behaviour of a participant, which is accessed using the `election` property of the participant, has a property named `iAmCandidate` that acts as a Boolean flag. While true, the participant considers itself as a valid candidate for leadership. On the con-

```
1   cyclic behaviour HandleLeaderChanges for agent Participant
2        on message inform NewLeader(l) do
3            do setLeader with newLeader=l
4
5   cyclic behaviour RespondElection for agent Participant
6        on message propose ElectNewLeader when
7        sender < aid of agent do
8            send message accept_proposal ElectNewLeader
9                to sender
10           activate election
```

Fig. 5. The Jadescript code of two behaviours used to handle changes in leadership (HandleLeaderChanges) and to respond to election messages from other participants (RespondElection).

trary, while false, the participant does not consider itself as a valid candidate for leadership. When activated, the election behaviour sets its flag to true, stops the monitoring behaviour of the participant, and subsequently sends a propose message with content ElectNewLeader to all participants with higher AIDs. Finally, the election behaviour activates a terminate election behaviour with a delay equal to the value of the timeoutInterval property to perform an ordered termination of the election. The election behaviour provides a message handler designed to process messages whose performative is accept_proposal and whose content

```
1   cyclic behaviour Election for agent Participant
2        property iAmCandidate as boolean
3
4        on activate do
5            iAmCandidate = true
6            deactivate monitor
7            for p in knownParticipants do
8                if p > aid of agent do
9                    send message propose ElectNewLeader to p
10
11           activate TerminateElection after timeoutInterval
12
13       on message accept_proposal ElectNewLeader do
14           iAmCandidate = false
15
16  one shot behaviour TerminateElection for agent Participant
17       on activate do
18           deactivate election
19           if iAmCandidate of election do
20               do setLeader with newLeader=aid of agent
```

Fig. 6. The Jadescript code of two behaviours used to handle take over in elections (Election) and to perform the ordered termination of an election (TerminateElection).

matches the content pattern `ElectNewLeader`. When a message that matches this pattern arrives, the handler flips the flag to false, and the participant no longer considers itself as a valid candidate for leadership. The terminate election behaviour implements a timeout for the responses from the other participants. When activated, it deactivates the corresponding election behaviour to make the participant stop waiting for the responses from the other participants. Then, if the participant still considers itself as a valid candidate, the participant wins the election and terminates the election using the `setLeader` procedure. Otherwise, the participant remains idle, waiting for a message of leadership change.

5   Conclusion

Jadescript is an agent-oriented programming language based on JADE that aims to become a dependable tool for the construction of industrial-strength MASs. This paper contributes to this objective by providing a comprehensive and self-contained description of Jadescript that discusses the most relevant features of the language in detail and through an example.

Jadescript is a practical language, and the current implementation of its compiler is available at https://github.com/aiagents/jadescript. The compiler is bundled in a distribution with a dedicated plugin for the Eclipse IDE to support programmers in managing their Jadescript projects with the help of several wizards and a feature-rich text editor [24]. Moreover, the distribution includes a set of additional support tools and some documentation. Note that the distribution also provides a Java API that can be used to support bidirectional interoperability between Jadescript agents and legacy Java code [27].

Jadescript and its tools are under active and continuous development to explore new features and fix problems. Among the plethora of possible new features, the focus is now on the features that are expected to effectively promote the adoption of the agent-oriented abstractions that characterize AOP and AOSE without introducing excessive complexity for programmers. Actually, each explored new feature must be characterized by significant advantages for programmers so that the inevitable additional complexity is justified. This is the reason why the short term plans for the development of Jadescript include a dedicated and feature-rich support for interaction protocols [29].

Internal preliminary experiments highlighted the relevance of a dedicated support for interaction protocols in Jadescript. In particular, these experiments suggested that the early use of interaction protocols could promote a new design approach for agents and MASs in which the design could start with the specification of ontologies and interaction protocols. Jadescript, with its envisaged support for interaction protocols, will be a practical tool to specify ontologies and interaction protocols, and therefore it will be readily usable to bring design artifacts to executable code. Essentially, designers will be able to use Jadescript to design ontologies and interaction protocols for their MASs to establish executable specifications that will encompass the overall conduct of their MASs from a global perspective. Afterwards, the detailed implementation of agents and behaviours will take place in Jadescript with a local focus on all the aspects related to the effective implementation of the specific tasks of the agents. Essentially, the envisaged support for interaction protocols will enable compliance-by-construction matched with a sophisticated support for recovery strategies. Finally, it is worth noting that the envisaged support for interaction protocols is expected to be open to the integration of external tools like, for example, tools for runtime verification and monitoring [17,18], that programmers will be free to use to improve the quality of their software.

The programmers that use JADE already know and appreciate interaction protocols because JADE provides a comprehensive support for interaction protocols that includes the interaction protocols that FIPA standardized. Therefore, Jadescript is obviously expected to provide programmers with the possibility of using general-purpose interaction protocols and with the possibility of defining application-specific interaction protocols. In detail, the envisaged support for interaction protocols will allow associating interaction protocols with ontologies to provide programmers with an effective means to specify the content of acceptable messages. Moreover, by adopting the same constructs already available for messages, such as message handlers and pattern matching, the support for interaction protocols will allow specifying additional constraints on the content of acceptable messages. Finally, note that the current proposal for the new constructs designed to extend Jadescript with a dedicated support for interaction protocols matches the syntactic style of the rest of the language, seamlessly integrating these new constructs in the current language.

Acknowledgements. This work was partially supported by the Italian Ministry of University and Research under the PRIN 2020 grant 2020TL3X8X for the project *Typeful Language Adaptation for Dynamic, Interacting and Evolving Systems* (T-LADIES).

References

1. Adorni, G., Bergenti, F., Poggi, A., Rimassa, G.: Enabling FIPA agents on small devices. In: Klusch, M., Zambonelli, F. (eds.) CIA 2001. LNCS (LNAI), vol. 2182, pp. 248–257. Springer, Heidelberg (2001). https://doi.org/10.1007/3-540-44799-7_28
2. Bellifemine, F., Bergenti, F., Caire, G., Poggi, A.: Jade — a java agent development framework. In: Bordini, R.H., Dastani, M., Dix, J., El Fallah Seghrouchni, A. (eds.) Multi-Agent Programming. MSASSO, vol. 15, pp. 125–147. Springer, Boston, MA (2005). https://doi.org/10.1007/0-387-26350-0_5
3. Bellifemine, F., Caire, G., Greenwood, D.: Developing Multi-Agent Systems with JADE. Wiley Series in Agent Technology, Wiley, Hoboken (2007)
4. Bergenti, F.: A discussion of two major benefits of using agents in software development. In: Petta, P., Tolksdorf, R., Zambonelli, F. (eds.) ESAW 2002. LNCS (LNAI), vol. 2577, pp. 1–12. Springer, Heidelberg (2003). https://doi.org/10.1007/3-540-39173-8_1
5. Bergenti, F., Caire, G., Gotta, D.: Large-scale network and service management with WANTS. In: Industrial Agents: Emerging Applications of Software Agents in Industry, pp. 231–246. Elsevier (2015)

6. Bergenti, F., Caire, G., Monica, S., Poggi, A.: The first twenty years of agent-based software development with JADE. Auton. Agents Multi-Agent Syst. **34**(36), 1–19 (2020)
7. Bergenti, F., Franchi, E., Poggi, A.: Agent-based social networks for enterprise collaboration. In: Proceedings of the 20th IEEE International Workshops on Enabling Technologies: Infrastructure for Collaborative Enterprises (WETICE 2011), pp. 25–28. IEEE (2011)
8. Bergenti, F., Gleizes, M.P., Zambonelli, F. (eds.): Methodologies and Software Engineering for Agent Systems: The Agent-Oriented Software Engineering Handbook, Multiagent Systems, Artificial Societies, and Simulated Organizations, vol. 11. Springer, New York (2004)
9. Bergenti, F., Huhns, M.N.: On the use of agents as components of software systems. In: Bergenti, F., Gleizes, M.P., Zambonelli, F. (eds.) Methodologies and Software Engineering for Agent Systems: The Agent-Oriented Software Engineering Handbook. Multiagent Systems, Artificial Societies, and Simulated Organizations, vol. 11, pp. 19–31. Springer, Boston (2004). https://doi.org/10.1007/1-4020-8058-1_3
10. Bergenti, F., Iotti, E., Monica, S., Poggi, A.: Agent-oriented model-driven development for JADE with the JADEL programming language. Comput. Lang. Syst. Struct. **50**, 142–158 (2017)
11. Bergenti, F., Monica, S.: Location-aware social gaming with AMUSE. In: Demazeau, Y., Ito, T., Bajo, J., Escalona, M.J. (eds.) PAAMS 2016. LNCS (LNAI), vol. 9662, pp. 36–47. Springer, Cham (2016). https://doi.org/10.1007/978-3-319-39324-7_4
12. Bergenti, F., Monica, S., Petrosino, G.: A scripting language for practical agent-oriented programming. In: Proceedings of the 8th ACM SIGPLAN International Workshop on Programming Based on Actors, Agents, and Decentralized Control (AGERE 2018) at ACM SIGPLAN Conference Systems, Programming, Languages and Applications: Software for Humanity (SPLASH 2018). ACM (2018)
13. Bergenti, F., Petrosino, G.: Overview of a scripting language for JADE-based multi-agent systems. In: Proceedings of the 19th Workshop "From Objects to Agents" (WOA 2018). CEUR Workshop Proceedings, vol. 2215, pp. 57–62. RWTH Aachen (2018)
14. Bergenti, F., Poggi, A.: Exploiting UML in the design of multi-agent systems. In: Omicini, A., Tolksdorf, R., Zambonelli, F. (eds.) ESAW 2000. LNCS (LNAI), vol. 1972, pp. 106–113. Springer, Heidelberg (2000). https://doi.org/10.1007/3-540-44539-0_8
15. Bergenti, F., Poggi, A.: Ubiquitous information agents. Int. J. Coop. Inf. Syst. **11**(3–4), 231–244 (2002)
16. Bergenti, F., Poggi, A.: Developing smart emergency applications with multi-agent systems. Int. J. E-Health Med. Commun. **1**(4), 1–13 (2010)
17. Briola, D., Mascardi, V., Ancona, D.: Distributed runtime verification of JADE multiagent systems. In: Camacho, D., Braubach, L., Venticinque, S., Badica, C. (eds.) Intelligent Distributed Computing VIII. SCI, vol. 570, pp. 81–91. Springer, Cham (2015). https://doi.org/10.1007/978-3-319-10422-5_10
18. Ferrando, A., Ancona, D., Mascardi, V.: Decentralizing MAS monitoring with DecAMon. In: Proceedings of the 16th International Joint Conference on Autonomous Agents and MultiAgent Systems (AAMAS 2017). IFAAMAS (2017)
19. Fowler, M., Parsons, R.: Domain Specific Languages. Addison-Wesley, Boston (2010)
20. Garcia-Molina, H.: Elections in a distributed computing system. IEEE Trans. Comput. **C-31**(1), 48–59 (1982)

21. Gouda, M.G., McGuire, T.M.: Accelerated heartbeat protocols. In: Proceedings of 18th International Conference on Distributed Computing Systems (ICDS 1998), pp. 202–209. IEEE (1998)
22. Monica, S., Bergenti, F.: Hybrid indoor localization using WiFi and UWB technologies. Electronics **8**(3), 334 (2019)
23. Petrosino, G., Bergenti, F.: Extending message handlers with pattern matching in the Jadescript programming language. In: Proceedings of the 20th Workshop "From Objects to Agents" (WOA 2019). CEUR Workshop Proceedings, vol. 2404, pp. 113–118. RWTH Aachen (2019)
24. Petrosino, G., Iotti, E., Monica, S., Bergenti, F.: Prototypes of productivity tools for the Jadescript programming language. In: Proceedings of the 22nd Workshop "From Objects to Agents" (WOA 2021). CEUR Workshop Proceedings, vol. 2963, pp. 14–28. RWTH Aachen (2021)
25. Petrosino, G., Iotti, E., Monica, S., Bergenti, F.: A Description of the Jadescript Type System. In: Chen, J., Lang, J., Amato, C., Zhao, D. (eds.) DAI 2021. LNCS (LNAI), vol. 13170, pp. 206–220. Springer, Cham (2022). https://doi.org/10.1007/978-3-030-94662-3_13
26. Petrosino, G., Monica, S., Bergenti, F.: Robust software agents with the Jadescript programming language. In: Proceedings of the 23rd Workshop "From Objects to Agents" (WOA 2022). CEUR Workshop Proceedings, vol. 3261, pp. 194–208. RWTH Aachen (2022)
27. Petrosino, G., Monica, S., Bergenti, F.: Cross-paradigm interoperability between Jadescript and Java. In: Proceedings of the 15th International Conference on Agents and Artificial Intelligence (ICAART 2023), vol. 1, pp. 165–172. Science and Technology Publications (2023)
28. Petrosino, G., Monica, S., Bergenti, F.: Delayed and periodic execution of tasks in the Jadescript programming language. In: Omatu, S., Mehmood, R., Sitek, P., Cicerone, S., Rodríguez, S. (eds.) DCAI 2022. LNCS, vol. 583, pp. 50–59. Springer, Cham (2023). https://doi.org/10.1007/978-3-031-20859-1_6
29. Poslad, S.: Specifying protocols for multi-agent systems interaction. ACM Trans. Auton. Adapt. Syst. **2**(4), 15:-15:24 (2007)
30. Poslad, S., Charlton, P.: Standardizing agent interoperability: the FIPA approach. In: Luck, M., Mařík, V., Štěpánková, O., Trappl, R. (eds.) ACAI 2001. LNCS (LNAI), vol. 2086, pp. 98–117. Springer, Heidelberg (2001). https://doi.org/10.1007/3-540-47745-4_5
31. Shoham, Y.: Agent-oriented programming. Artif. Intell. **60**(1), 51–92 (1993)
32. Tomaiuolo, M., Turci, P., Bergenti, F., Poggi, A.: An ontology support for semantic aware agents. In: Kolp, M., Bresciani, P., Henderson-Sellers, B., Winikoff, M. (eds.) AOIS -2005. LNCS (LNAI), vol. 3529, pp. 140–153. Springer, Heidelberg (2006). https://doi.org/10.1007/11916291_10

Verifying Programs by Bounded Tree-Width Behavior Graphs

Omar Inverso[1], Salvatore La Torre[2], Gennaro Parlato[3(✉)],
and Ermenegildo Tomasco[1,2,3]

[1] Gran Sasso Science Institute, L'Aquila, Italy
[2] Università degli Studi di Salerno, Fisciano, Italy
[3] Università degli Studi del Molise, Pesche, Italy
gennaro.parlato@unimol.it

Abstract. We present a novel framework to reason about programs based on encodings of computations as graphs. The main insight here is to rearrange the programs such that given a bound k, each computation can be explored according to any tree decomposition of width k of the corresponding behaviour graph. This produces under-approximations parameterized on k, which result in a complete method when we restrict to classes of behaviour graphs of bounded tree-width. As an additional feature, the transformation of the input program can be targeted to existing tools for the analysis. Thus, off-the-shelf tools based on fixed-point, or capable of analyzing sequential programs with scalar variables and nondeterminism, can be used. To illustrate our approach, we develop this framework for sequential programs and discuss how to extend it to handle concurrency. For the case of sequential programs, we develop a compositional approach to generate on-the-fly tree decompositions of nested words, which is based on graph-summaries.

1 Introduction

Program computations are typically described as runs of flat transition systems with possibly infinitely many states. The basic information stored in a state is the current control location and the valuation of the statically allocated variables. Depending on the class of programs, a state can also store heap structures, the call stack and in general, additional *data structures* to handle concurrency (multiple call stacks, FIFO channels, etc.).

Computations can also be represented as graphs (*behaviour graphs*) where the nodes capture the basic (finite) information, and different types of edges are used to capture the transitions and the relations deriving from the use of the additional data structures (see [17]). For example, a stack can be captured by

This work was partially supported by INDAM-GNCS 2022 and 2023, AWS 2021 Amazon Research Awards, the MUR project 'Innovation, digitalisation and sustainability for the diffused economy in Central Italy', Spoke 1 MEGHALITIC, VITALITY Ecosystem, and FARB 2021–2023 grants Università degli Studi di Salerno.

V. Malvone and A. Murano (Eds.): EUMAS 2023, LNAI 14282, pp. 116–132, 2023.
https://doi.org/10.1007/978-3-031-43264-4_8

linking the pair of states corresponding to a push and a matching pop, a queue by linking an enqueue to a matching dequeue, and so on.

Several classes of behavior graphs can be defined depending on the aspects and the granularity of the information we wish to capture. Nested words naturally capture the control-flow structure of sequential programs [1], multiply nested words that of shared-memory multi-threaded programs and stack-queue graphs that of both distributed programs with recursive calls and sequential programs with queues and stacks [17], and more definitions are possible.

A very general result on the decidability of problems on classes of behaviour graphs is the decidability of MSO for all MSO-definable classes of graphs of bounded tree-width [5,6,17], which generalizes Courcelle/Seese's theorem [3,19]. For interesting classes of programs, many decidability results of relevant decision problems in verification, such as reachability, model-checking and decidability of linear temporal logics, are indeed subsumed by this general result.

A class of graphs has tree-width k if for each graph there is a tree decomposition of *width* at most $k + 1$, that is, the graph can be rearranged on a tree by assigning to each node a set of at most $k + 1$ graph vertices (*bag*) such that all vertices and edges are covered and vertices replicated in two nodes also belong to all the bags on the path connecting them. Essentially, for a behaviour graph G, a tree decomposition T of width k ensures that we can execute the computation described by G by checking the consistency of the information at each vertex (i.e., its program counter and variable valuation) locally to a node and its neighbors: in fact, to check the consistency across the edges of G, it is sufficient to consider one bag at a time, and to ensure that each vertex has the same information in any bag, it is sufficient to compare for each node the bags at the node and at its children.

This way of looking at the tree decompositions is the crucial intuition of the approach we present in this paper. We design a general framework for analyzing programs where given a parameter k, we transform an input program P such that the resulting encoding P' interprets the behaviours of P as described above, according to all the tree decompositions of width k of P behaviour graphs, and then P' is analyzed in a separate tool.

Our approach gives a novel and natural way of representing and analyzing systems and has several other features. First, each tree decomposition rearranges the transitions of a computation and gets a way to explore them in a totally independent order, and thus our approach is likely to be less sensitive to "pathological patterns". Second, the width of a tree decomposition gives a natural parameter for bounding the additional storage needed to explore the program computations, and thus we get under-approximation methods of adjustable precision for arbitrary classes of systems. Third, and probably more importantly, we get a general way to encode unbounded heap structures captured in configurations into a *thick* tree where we need to associate a fixed amount of data stored at each node. The tree encodings of computation graphs will allow us to encode complex features of programs (recursion, concurrency, heap, etc.) in a uniform way where we can exploit off-the-shelf solutions that compute the fixed point of finite relations or can check sequential programs with only scalar variables and non-determinism, to analyze these otherwise complex systems.

We develop our framework for sequential programs with recursive procedure calls and use as behaviour graphs the nested words augmented with the program counters and the variable valuations (*program nested words*). A crucial aspect is to find an efficient way to generate tree decompositions for this class of graphs. We introduce the concept of *shape of a program nested word* (pnw-shape) to summarize portions of program nested words. Namely, a pnw-shape is either a fragment of a nested word (*ground pnw-shape*), or a *merge* of two "compatible" pnw-shapes, or a *contraction* of a pnw-shape on a set of vertices. By compatible we essentially mean that the pnw-shapes can share nodes but edges do not overlap, and the contraction has the effect of keeping only the vertices in the contraction set and projecting on them the edges of the starting pnw-shape. Essentially, in the construction of a tree decomposition, we use these pnw-shapes to summarize the information of the portion of the nested word covered by the nodes of a subtree. In particular, we start from the leaves labeled each with a ground pnw-shape. At each internal node v, we add a ground pnw-shape which is compatible with the pnw-shape of the children of v, and compute the pnw-shape of v by first merging these three pnw-shapes and then contracting the resulting pnw-shape on the vertices of the ground one (which form the bag of v). We also provide a test for the root to ensure that the constructed tree is indeed a tree decomposition.

We outline a simple implementation of our approach as a code-to-code translation of C-like sequential programs that do not make use of dynamic memory allocation. The output of the transformation is a program that nondeterministically builds a tree decomposition using recursive procedure calls as in a DFS traversal of the tree. The ground program pnw-shapes are nondeterministically guessed, and the consistency of program counters and variable valuations associated to each vertex is checked for each edge (according to the semantics of the input program). Moreover, there are procedures to implement the tests, and the merging and contraction operations.

As a further contribution, we give an informal though detailed description on how this approach can be extended to handle concurrent shared-memory programs and how this relates to the sequentialization algorithms (see [2,4,9, 16,18] for a sample research). We believe that our approach can be extended to many other classes of programs and systems, such as concurrent programs with a weak memory model assumption, distributed programs, and programs with dynamic data-structures, to mention some.

2   Programs with Recursive Procedure Calls

We consider sequential programs with possibly recursive procedure calls. For the sake of simplicity and without loss of generality, we omit local variables and procedure parameters (in a procedure call, when needed, the values are passed through the global variables). Since we only admit global variables, henceforth we refer to them simply as variables.

Verifying Programs by Bounded Tree-Width Behavior Graphs 119

Var x, y;	procedure *boo* begin 3: $y := x$; 4: call *foo*; 5: assert(x=1); 6: call *foo*; 7: return; end	procedure *foo* begin 8: if $(y > 0)$ then 9: $y := y - 1$; A: call *foo*; B: else skip; fi C: return; end
procedure main begin 0: assume(x=1 || x=2); 1: call *boo*; 2: return; end		

Fig. 1. A sample program.

In the rest of the paper, we use program P of Fig. 1 as a running example. P is a simple program with three possible behaviours depending on the initial values of the variable x being 1, 2 or an other value. In the last case, the condition of the assume statement does not hold and thus the computation immediately halts. In the remaining cases, the procedures *boo* and *foo* get recursively called until the assert statement at program counter 5 is reached. Now, a computation with $x = 2$ violates the assertion, and thus reaches an *error* state, while a computation with $x = 1$ continues through the end of the procedure main.

Syntax. The BNF grammar on the right gives the formal syntax of programs (Fig. 2). A program starts with the declaration of a finite set of variables *Var* that are visible to all procedures. We assume variables range over some (potentially

$$\begin{aligned}
&\langle prgm \rangle ::= \ Var; \ \langle proc \rangle^+ \\
&\langle proc \rangle ::= \ \text{procedure } p \text{ begin } \langle pc\_stmt \rangle^+ \text{ end} \\
&\langle pc\_stmt \rangle ::= \ pc : \langle stmt \rangle; \\
&\langle stmt \rangle ::= \ g := \langle expr \rangle \mid \text{skip} \\
&\quad \mid \ \text{assume}(\langle pred \rangle) \mid \text{assert}(\langle pred \rangle) \\
&\quad \mid \ \text{if } \langle pred \rangle \text{ then } \langle pc\_stmt \rangle^+ \text{ else } \langle pc\_stmt \rangle^+ \text{ fi} \\
&\quad \mid \ \text{while } \langle expr \rangle \text{ do } \langle pc\_stmt \rangle \text{ do} \\
&\quad \mid \ \text{call } p \mid \text{return}
\end{aligned}$$

Fig. 2. BNF grammar of programs.

infinite) data domain $\mathbb{D}$, a language of expressions $\langle expr \rangle$ interpreted over $\mathbb{D}$, and a language of predicates $\langle pred \rangle$ over the variables. Thereafter, there is a declaration of a non empty list of *procedures*, among which one called main that is initially executed to start the program. Each procedure is formed by a nonempty sequence of labeled statements of the form $pc : \langle stmt \rangle$ where pc is the *program counter* (or *program location*) and $\langle stmt \rangle$ defines a simple language of C-like statements. We assume that each procedure has return as last statement.

For a program P, we denote with PC (resp., $Call$, Ret) the set of all program counters pc such that $pc : stmt$ (resp., $pc : \text{call } p$, $pc : \text{return}$) is a labeled statement of P. Furthermore, for every $pc \in Call$ we denote with $afterCall(pc)$ the (unique) program counter pc' such that $pc' : stmt$ is the statement that is executed after returning the procedure call with program counter pc.

Semantics. The semantics is given as a transition system. Each program can make procedure calls and manipulate variables. Thus, a state is a *configuration* of the form $\langle \nu, pc, St \rangle$ where ν is a valuation of the variables (i.e., $\nu : Var \mapsto \mathbb{D}$), $pc \in PC$ is a program counter, and St is the content of the call stack (i.e., the control locations of the pending procedure calls). A configuration $C = \langle \nu, pc, St \rangle$ is *initial* if pc is the program counter of the first statement of the procedure main and St is the empty stack.

The *transition relation*, denoted $\hookrightarrow$, is defined as usual. The control-flow statements update the program counter, possibly depending on a predicate (condition). The assignment statements update the variable valuation other than moving to the next program counter. At a procedure call, the current location of the caller (pc) is pushed onto the stack, and the control moves to the first location of the called procedure. At a return statement the control location at the top of the stack is popped, say pc, and the control moves to location $afterCall(pc)$.

A *computation* of a program is a sequence of configurations $C_0 C_1 \ldots C_n$ such that C_0 is initial, and $C_{i-1} \hookrightarrow C_i$ for every $i \in [1, n]$.

3   Graphs Representing Program Executions

In this section, we recall some definitions on graphs and define the notion of program nested word that we use in the rest of the paper to represent the executions of a program.

Multigraphs. A multigraph is a structure $G = (V, E_1, \ldots, E_n)$, where V is a finite set of vertices, and for each i, $E_i \subseteq V \times V$ is a set of directed edges. An edge $(u, v) \in E_i$ is also denoted as $u E_i v$. A multigraph $G = (V, E_i)$ is a *line graph* if there is an ordering of all vertices of G, say $v_0, v_1, \ldots, v_m$, such that $E_i = \{v_{j-1} E_i v_j \mid j \in [m]\}$.

Nested Words. A *nested word*[1] is a multigraph $(V, \rightarrow, \curvearrowright)$ where $(V, \rightarrow)$ is a line graph and $\curvearrowright$ is a matching edge relation such that for every $u, v, u', v' \in V$:

- if $u \curvearrowright v$ then $u \rightarrow^+ v$;
- if $u \curvearrowright v$, $u' \curvearrowright v'$ are distinct edges then (1) u, v, u', v' are all distinct nodes, and (2) if $u \rightarrow^+ u'$ then either $v \rightarrow^+ u'$ or $v' \rightarrow^+ v$.

Program Nested Words. We wish to look at the computations of a program via their behaviour graphs, i.e., finite graphs that carefully model with their edges the control-flow structure. In particular, we use as behaviour graphs the nested words annotated with the program counter (pc, for short) and the valuation of the variables of each *state*. We refer to such annotated nested words as *program nested words*. In Fig. 3, we give the behaviour graph of a computation of the program from Fig. 1 when $x = 1$ holds. The vertices of the nested word $v_0, \ldots, v_{17}$ are labeled with the corresponding pc in the program. Also, in the figure, we report the variable valuation at the beginning and update it at each node after an assignment. Moreover, the $\curvearrowright$-edges are represented as curved arrows and the $\rightarrow$-edges are represented as straight arrows. The $\rightarrow$-edges capture the linear ordering of the program states in the computation (and thus the *transitions* of the computation). The $\curvearrowright$-edges match the vertices corresponding to the pc of a call to a procedure to the pc of the next statement of the procedure that will be executed after returning the call (*return location*). Consider for example

---

[1] We assume that there are no unmatched calls and returns, differently from [1].

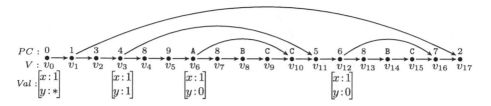

Fig. 3. Program nested word of a run of the program in Fig. 1.

$v_1 \curvearrowright v_{17}$, v_1 corresponds to the state that precedes the call to *boo* from **main** (with pc 1) and v_{17} corresponds to the state after returning from this call (with pc 2); also we have $v_1 \to v_2$, and v_2 corresponds to the begin of the first activation of *boo* (with pc 3).

Below, we give a logical characterization of program nested words. For the ease of presentation we assume that all the procedure calls in the computations are returned. Note that this is without loss of generality, since we can always append a possibly empty sequence of additional transitions (which are not actual program transitions and thus can be recognized as such) to match all pending calls in the call stack.

Definition 1 (PROGRAM NESTED WORD). *A program nested word of a program P with set of variables Var and set of program counters PC, is a tuple $(nw, Val, \overline{pc})$ where*

- $nw = (V, \to, \curvearrowright)$ *is a nested word; let $V = \{v_0, v_1, \ldots, v_n\}$ such that $v_{i-1} \to v_i$ for $i \in [1, n]$;*
- *Val and $\overline{pc}$ are labeling functions that map each vertex of V respectively with a valuation of Var and a program counter in PC such that $\overline{pc}(v_0)$ is the program counter of the first statement of procedure **main** and for $u, v, z \in V$:*
  - *if $u \to v$ then $\langle Val(u), \overline{pc}(u), st \rangle \hookrightarrow \langle Val(v), \overline{pc}(v), st' \rangle$, for some st, st';*
  - *if $u \curvearrowright v$ then $\overline{pc}(u) \in Call$, $\overline{pc}(v) = afterCall(\overline{pc}(u))$, and $\overline{pc}(z) \in Ret$ where $z \to v$;*
  - *if $\overline{pc}(u) \in Call$, then $u \curvearrowright v$ exists;*
  - *if $u \to v$ and $\overline{pc}(u) \in Ret$, then $z \curvearrowright v$ exists.*   □

From Executions to Program Nested Words and Back: Let $\pi = C_0 C_1 \ldots C_n$ be a computation of P, where $C_i = \langle \nu_i, pc_i, St_i \rangle$ for $i \in [0, n]$. For each $i \in [0, n]$ with $pc_i \in Call$, we say that i *matches* j if j is the smallest index such that $j > i$ and $St_j = St_i$. We denote with $NW(\pi)$ the tuple $(nw, Val, \overline{pc})$ where $nw = (\{v_0, \ldots, v_n\}, \to, \curvearrowright)$ is a nested word such that (1) $v_{i-1} \to v_i$ for $i \in [1, n]$, (2) $v_i \curvearrowright v_j$ iff i matches j in π, and (3) $Val(v_i) = \nu_i$ and $\overline{pc}(v_i) = pc_i$, for $i \in [0, n]$. We can show that $NW(\pi)$ is indeed a program nested word of P.

Vice-versa, consider a program nested word $pnw = (nw, Val, \overline{pc})$ of P and let $\{v_0, \ldots, v_n\}$ be the set of vertices of nw such that $v_{i-1} \to v_i$ for $i \in [1, n]$. We denote with $RUN(pnw)$ the sequence of configurations $C_0 C_1 \ldots C_n$ where denoting $C_i = \langle Val(v_i), \overline{pc}(v_i), St_i \rangle$, St_0 is the empty stack and for $i \in [1, n]$:

(1) if $\overline{pc}(v_{i-1}) \in Call$ then $St_i = \overline{pc}(v_{i-1}).St_{i-1}$ (procedure call), (2) if $v_j \curvearrowright v_i$ then $St_{i-1} = \overline{pc}(v_j).St_i$ (return from a call), (3) otherwise $St_i = St_{i-1}$ (internal move). We can show that $RUN(\pi)$ is indeed a computation of P.

Thus the following holds:

Theorem 1. *Given a program P there is a one-to-one mapping (modulo a vertex renaming) between the computations and the program nested words of P.*

4   Bounded Tree-Width Analysis of Programs

The main intuition behind our methodology is to use the tree decompositions of the behaviour graphs of a program, to guide the exploration of its computations.

Informally, a *tree decomposition* of a graph G is a binary tree whose nodes are labeled with sets of G vertices, which are called *bags*, such that every edge or vertex of G is covered by at least one bag, and if a vertex v belongs to two bags labeling two different nodes then all the bags on the unique path connecting such nodes also contain v. Figure 4(a) gives a tree decomposition of the program nested word of Fig. 3 where each bag is implicitly defined by the vertices of the graph that labels the node. A formal definition of tree decomposition is given at the end of this section.

We illustrate the role played by tree decompositions in our methodology on the sample program nested word of Fig. 3 and with respect to the above mentioned tree decomposition.

We augment the tree decompositions by adding to each node some edges of the graph such that each edge is mapped exactly to a node whose bag contains both of its endpoints (note that such a labeling is always possible since by definition each edge is covered by at least one bag). The tree decomposition of Fig. 4(a) is augmented in such a way.

Now, by assuming that we have an augmented tree decomposition for a program nested word of a program P (we will discuss in the next section how to generate efficiently such tree decompositions), we check that a labeling of each vertex in each bag with a program counter and a variable valuation of P forms a computation of P: that is, we can reconstruct a program nested word of P from the additional labeling and the tree decomposition.

Starting from the leaves, we locally check the consistency of the transitions captured by the edges in the bag. For example, in node n_5, we can check for the consistency of the program counters and variable evaluations of the vertices $v_6, v_7, v_8, v_9, v_{10}, v_{11}$ according to (1) the transitions of P corresponding to the $\rightarrow$-edges (v_6, v_7), (v_7, v_8), (v_9, v_{10}) and (v_{10}, v_{11}) and (2) the $\curvearrowright$-edge (v_6, v_{10}). Then, moving up to the parent of n_5, i.e., n_2, we do not need to keep the information for v_7, v_8, v_9, v_{10}, since all the edges involving them have already been examined (this is carefully captured by the tree decomposition that does not contain these vertices in the bag of n_2). However, we need to check that the program counter and the variable valuation associated with the vertices that are kept, i.e., v_6 and v_{11}, are the same as in n_2 and n_5.

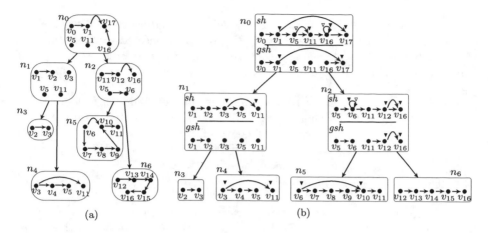

Fig. 4. Example of a tree decomposition (a) and an nw-shape tree (b) for the program nested word of Fig. 3.

In this use of tree decompositions, a bag associated with a node n is the *interface*, or the sticking vertices, of the portion of nested word corresponding to the subtree rooted at n with the rest of the computation. Thus, if we restrict to tree decompositions with bags of size bounded by a parameter k (the width), at each node we only need to track $O(k)$ information. By choosing $k \geq 3$, for the class of programs that we have defined, we can explore the whole set of computations of a program, as stated by Theorem 2 at the end of this section.

Tree Decompositions and Tree-Width. A *tree-decomposition* of a multigraph $G = (V, E_1, \ldots, E_n)$ is a pair $D = (T, \{bag_t\}_{t \in N})$, where T is a binary tree with set of nodes N, and $bag_t \subseteq V$ satisfying the following:

- for every $v \in V$, there is a node $t \in N$ such that $v \in bag_t$;
- for every i and $(u, v) \in E_i$, there is a node $t \in N$ such that $u, v \in bag_t$;
- if $u \in (bag_t \cap bag_{t'})$ then $u \in bag_{t''}$ for every T node t'' that lies on the unique path connecting t to t' in T.

The *width* of a tree decomposition $(T, \{bag_t\}_{t \in N})$ is the size of the largest bag in it, minus one; i.e. $max_{t \in N}\{|bag_n|\} - 1$. The *tree-width* of a graph is the *smallest* of the widths overall its tree decompositions.

Theorem 2 ([17]). *Any nested word has tree-width at most 2.*

5   Getting Tree Decompositions for Program Nested Words

In the description of our approach from the previous section, we assume that a tree-decomposition of a program nested word is given. Indeed, we compute such decompositions on the fly. For this, we need to carry in our *summaries* (at each node) some structural information about the portion of the nested word so far explored, such that we can correctly check portions of nested words separately, then combine them in the same structure, and in the end claim that we have constructed a valid tree decomposition for a computation of the program.

The Informal Scenario. Our notion of *summary* for nested words is a shape of a nested word, *nw-shape* for short. Informally, an nw-shape is either a fragment of a nested word (*ground nw-shape*), or a *merge* of two "compatible" nw-shapes, or a *contraction* of an nw-shape on a set of vertices. By compatible, we essentially mean that the nw-shapes can share nodes but the edges do not overlap. For example, each of the graphs labeling the nodes of the tree in Fig. 4(b) is an nw-shape.

In addition to the notation used for nested words, we also use the symbols ▼ and ▽ to annotate respectively that an end-point of a ⌒-edge is the actual one or it replaces one that has been abstracted away. In particular, for a ground nw-shape all the endpoints of a ⌒-edge are marked with ▼.

To generate a tree decomposition, we construct an nw-shape tree. In Fig. 4, we give an nw-shape tree for the nested word from Fig. 3. We start from the leaves that are assigned each with a ground nw-shape. For each internal node n, we add a ground nw-shape (marked with *gsh* below the line in each node) and compute a summary of the ground nw-shapes in the subtree rooted at n (marked with *sh* above the line). The summary is computed by merging the summaries at the children and the ground nw-shape of the current node, and then contracting the resulting nw-shape on the vertices of the ground nw-shape (note that at each node the nw-shape and the ground nw-shape have the same set of vertices).

For example, consider node n_1. The nw-shapes from nodes n_3 and n_4 just share the vertex v_3 and therefore can be merged (in fact they are compatible because when glued to v_3 there are no overlaps between the edges). Similarly, the resulting nw-shape can be merged with the ground nw-shape of n_1, and the resulting nw-shape has vertices v_1, v_2, v_3, v_4, v_5 and v_{11}. In the contraction, only v_4 gets abstracted away. The effect of the contraction is thus to remove v_4 and connect v_3 to v_5 to store the information that has already been explored in the space between v_3 and v_5.

The contraction is slightly more intricate when an endpoint of a ⌒-edge is abstracted away. In fact, in this case, the new endpoint (if any) is selected, among those that have not been removed, as the closest one which is included in the portion of the graph below the edge. In particular, the ⌒-edge from v_3 to v_{11} in n_1 is replaced (in the contraction) by the ⌒-edge from v_5 to v_{11} in n_0, and since v_5 is not the actual left endpoint of this edge, we annotate the left end of $v_5 ⌒ v_{11}$ with ▽. Also observe that in case there is no such vertex (both the endpoints are abstracted away and no vertices in the between are kept in the new set of vertices), the edge is canceled. This is in fact the case for the self-loop on v_6 in node n_2, which does not appear in the nw-shape of n_0.

There are two more conditions to ensure to obtain an nw-shapetree. First, the vertices of a ground shapein an internal node must contain all the vertices at the "borders" of the maximal lines defined by →-edges in the nw-shapes of its children and the endpoints of the $\curvearrowright$-edges that have not yet been added to the shapes of the subtree (see, for example, vertex v_{11} in n_2). Second, the nw-shape of the root must be entirely connected through the $\rightarrow$-edges (*linearly connected*) and should have all the endpoints of $\curvearrowright$ matched (*fully matched*).

An augmented tree decomposition is easily obtained from an nw-shape tree by retaining for each node just its ground shape. Since vice versa also holds, i.e., for each augmented tree decomposition there is a corresponding nw-shape tree, our method captures all the augmented tree decompositions of a program. Moreover, it can be implemented on the fly, with all operations being local.

Nested Word Shapes. Let $T = \{\triangledown, \blacktriangledown\}$ be an alphabet, where the symbol $\triangledown$ stands for *abstract*, and $\blacktriangledown$ stands for *concrete*.

Definition 2 (NESTED WORD SHAPES). *A nested word shape (nw-shape) is a tuple $S = (V, \Rightarrow, \rightarrow, \{\overset{t,z}{\curvearrowright}\}_{t,z \in T})$ where*

- V *is a finite set of vertices;*
- $(V, \Rightarrow)$ *is a line graph;*
- *the set of* linear edges $\rightarrow$ *is a subset of* $\Rightarrow$*;*
- *the set of the* matching edges $\curvearrowright = (\bigcup_{t,z \in T} \overset{t,z}{\curvearrowright})$ *where* $\overset{t,z}{\curvearrowright} \subseteq V \times V$ *and is such that (where $a, b, c, d, \in T$ and $u, v, x, y \in V$):*
  - *if $u \curvearrowright v$ then also $u \Rightarrow^* v$;*
  - *if $u \curvearrowright v$ and $x \curvearrowright y$, then the following does not hold:*
    * $u \Rightarrow^+ x \Rightarrow^+ v \Rightarrow^+ y$ *(matching edges do not cross);*
    * $(u, v) \neq (x, y)$ *and $v = x$ (call and return of distinct matching edges must not coincide);*
  - $u \overset{\blacktriangledown,\blacktriangledown}{\curvearrowright} u$ *does not hold;*
  - *at most one among $u \overset{\blacktriangledown,\triangledown}{\curvearrowright} v$, $u \overset{\triangledown,\blacktriangledown}{\curvearrowright} v$ and $u \overset{\blacktriangledown,\blacktriangledown}{\curvearrowright} v$ holds;*
  - *if $u \overset{a,b}{\curvearrowright} v$, $u \overset{c,d}{\curvearrowright} y$ and $y \Rightarrow^+ v$ then $a = \triangledown$;*
  - *if $u \overset{a,b}{\curvearrowright} v$, $x \overset{c,d}{\curvearrowright} v$ and $u \Rightarrow^+ x$ then $b = \triangledown$.*

S *is* ground *if all of its matching edges are concrete, that is, $\curvearrowright$ is exactly $\overset{\blacktriangledown,\blacktriangledown}{\curvearrowright}$. S is* linearly connected *if $\rightarrow$ is exactly $\Rightarrow$.* □

A *linear border* of a shape S is a vertex $u \in V$ without a linear successor or a linear predecessor, i.e., either $u \not\rightarrow v$ for each $v \in V$ or $v \not\rightarrow u$ for each $v \in V$.

Operations on Shapes. In the following, we fix $S = (V, \Rightarrow, \rightarrow, \{\overset{t,z}{\curvearrowright}\}_{t,z \in T})$, $S' = (V', \Rightarrow', \rightarrow', \{\overset{t,z}{\curvearrowright}'\}_{t,z \in T})$, and $S_i = (V_i, \Rightarrow_i, \rightarrow_i, \{\overset{t,z}{\curvearrowright}_i\}_{t,z \in T})$ for $i = 1, 2$.

An nw-shape S' is the *contraction* of an nw-shape S on a set of vertices $V' \subseteq V$, denoted $S' = contraction(S, V')$, if the following holds:

- $\Rightarrow'^*$ is the total order on V' induced by $\Rightarrow^*$;
- $\rightarrow'$ is the set of all pairs $(x, y) \in V' \times V'$ such that either (1) $x \rightarrow y$, or (2) there is a sequence of vertices $u_1, u_2, \ldots, u_m \in (V \setminus V')$ such that $x \rightarrow u_1 \rightarrow u_2 \rightarrow \ldots \rightarrow u_m \rightarrow y$.

– for each matching edge (u, v) of S, denote with $contraction_\frown(u, v)$ the pair (x, y) if the following holds:
  - $u \Rightarrow^* x \Rightarrow^* y \Rightarrow^* v$;
  - x is the smallest vertex $x' \in V'$ with $u \Rightarrow^* x'$; and
  - y is the greatest vertex $y' \in V'$ with $y' \Rightarrow^* v$.

For every $t, z \in T$, $\overset{t,z}{\frown}'$ is the minimal set containing all pairs (x, y) such that there exist $u, v \in V$ where (1) $u \overset{p,s}{\frown} v$ for some p, s, (2) $contraction_\frown(u, v) = (x, y)$, (3) $t = \blacktriangledown$ iff $u = x$ and $p = \blacktriangledown$, and (4) $z = \blacktriangledown$ iff $v = y$ and $s = \blacktriangledown$.

S is the *merge* of two nw-shapes S_1 and S_2, denoted $S = merge(S_1, S_2)$, if S is an nw-shape and the following holds:

– $V = V_1 \cup V_2$;
– $\Rightarrow_1, \Rightarrow_2 \subseteq \Rightarrow$;
– $(\rightarrow_1 \cap \rightarrow_2) = \emptyset$, and $\rightarrow = (\rightarrow_1 \cup \rightarrow_2)$;
– For every $t, z \in T$, $\overset{t,z}{\frown} = (\overset{t,z}{\frown}_1 \cup \overset{t,z}{\frown}_2)$.

Tree Decompositions via nw-Shapes. In an nw-shape tree $\mathcal{T}$, the vertices of the nw-shape are typed as either left ($\mathcal{L}$) or right ($\mathcal{R}$) endpoint of a matching edge, or none of them, with the meaning that $u \in \mathcal{L}$, resp. $v \in \mathcal{R}$, iff there is a ground nw-shape of $\mathcal{T}$ that contains an edge $u \overset{\blacktriangledown,\blacktriangledown}{\frown} v$.

Definition 3 (NW-SHAPE TREE). *An nw-shape tree $\mathcal{T}$ is a triple (T, sh, gsh) where T is a binary tree with set of nodes N, and sh and gsh label each node of T with respectively an nw-shape and a ground nw-shape such that for each $n \in N$ the following holds:*

– *if n is a leaf, then $sh(n) = gsh(n)$;*
– *if n is an internal node, denoting with n_1 and n_2 its left and right children and with V_n the set of the vertices of $gsh(n)$:*
  - *$sh(n) = contraction(S(n), V_n)$ where $S(n)$ is the merge of $sh(n_1)$, $sh(n_2)$ and $gsh(n)$;*
  - *denoting with $\mathcal{LR}$ the set of all vertices from $\mathcal{L} \cup \mathcal{R}$ that are not concrete endpoints of $\frown$-edges of $sh(n_1)$ and $sh(n_2)$, V_n contains $\mathcal{LR}$ and all the linear borders of $sh(n_1)$ and $sh(n_2)$;*
  - *if n is the root, then additionally $sh(n)$ is also linearly connected and fully matched, that is, all its vertices from $\mathcal{L} \cup \mathcal{R}$ are concrete endpoints of some $\frown$-edge.*

We denote with $G(\mathcal{T})$ the graph $\bigcup_{n \in N} gsh(n)$.   □

Note that in the above definition for each $n \in N$, $gsh(n)$ and $sh(n)$ have the same vertices and each edge of $gsh(n)$ is also an edge of $sh(n)$. By structural induction, it is possible to show that the graph obtained by the union of the ground nw-shapes of the leaves of a subtree is a ground nw-shape corresponding to a fragment of a nested word. When the nw-shape associated with the root of the subtree is also linearly connected and fully matched, then the resulting ground nw-shape corresponds to a nested word.

Lemma 1. *For any nw-shape tree $\mathcal{T}$, $G(\mathcal{T})$ is a nested word.*

For a nested word w denote with $\bullet\text{-}w\text{-}\bullet$ the nested word obtained from w by adding two new vertices v_L and v_R along with the edges $v_L \to v$ and $v' \to v_R$ where v denotes the first vertex and v' the last vertex of w according to $\to^*$.

From an nw-shape tree $\mathcal{T} = (T, sh, gsh)$ such that $G(\mathcal{T}) = \bullet\text{-}w\text{-}\bullet$, define $D(\mathcal{T}) = (T, \{V_n\}_{n \in N})$ where N is the set of nodes of T and V_n is the set of all the vertices of $sh(n)$ but v_L and v_R. By the definitions of nw-shape tree and tree decomposition, we get that $D(\mathcal{T})$ is a tree decomposition of w.

Vice versa, consider a tree decomposition $D = (T, \{B_n\}_{n \in N})$ of a nested word $w = (V, \to, \curvearrowright)$. Add to each bag B_n the vertices v_L and v_R and define:

- $\{\to_n\}_{n \in N}$ such that each edge $u \to v$ of w, belongs to exactly one $\to_n$ such that $u, v \in B_n$, and each of $v_L \to v$ and $v' \to v_R$ belongs to exactly one $\to_n$;
- $\{\curvearrowright_n\}_{n \in N}$ such that for each edge $u \curvearrowright v$ of w, $u \overset{\blacktriangledown,\blacktriangledown}{\curvearrowright} v$ belongs to exactly one $\curvearrowright_n$ such that $u, v \in B_n$;
- each $\Rightarrow_n$ is the total order on B_n induced by $\to^*$;
- $gsh(n) = (B_n, \Rightarrow_n, \to_n, \curvearrowright_n)$, $\mathcal{L} = \{u \mid u \curvearrowright v\}$ and $\mathcal{R} = \{v \mid u \curvearrowright v\}$.

Starting from the parents of the leaves of T we compute for each node n, $sh(n)$ as the contraction on V_n of the merge of $gsh(n)$, $sh(n_1)$ and $sh(n_2)$ where n_1 and n_2 are the children of n. By definition, we can show that $\mathcal{T} = (T, sh, gsh)$ is nw-shapeand $G(\mathcal{T}) = \bullet\text{-}w\text{-}\bullet$. Therefore, the following theorem holds.

Theorem 3. *For any nested word w, there exists a tree decomposition D of width k iff there exists an nw-shape tree $\mathcal{T} = (T, sh, gsh)$ such that $\bullet\text{-}w\text{-}\bullet = G(\mathcal{T})$ and each $gsh(n)$ has at most k vertices of w.*

Note that the additional vertices v_L and v_R do not correspond to any state of the program and are not really needed to have the above theorem. In fact, it would be sufficient to modify the definition of nw-shape tree such that a left (respectively right) linear border can be abstracted away as soon as a prefix (resp. a suffix) of the nested word has been explored.

Shapes and Shape Trees for Programs. We augment nw-shape and nw-shape trees with program counters and variable valuations. In particular, we define a *pnw-shape* inductively from portions of program nested words and with merging and contraction operations. The merging requires that a same vertex is labeled with the same program counter and the same variable valuation. Analogously to nw-shape trees, we define the *pnw-shape tree* with respect to the notion of pnw-shape.

For a mapping $f : A \to B$ and $C \subseteq A$, we denote with $f_{|C}$ the restriction of f to C. For mappings $f_i : A_i \to B_i$ $i = 1, 2$, we denote with $f_1 \cup f_2$ the mapping defined as $f_1(x)$ for each $x \in A_1$ and $f_2(x)$ for each $x \in A_2 \setminus A_1$.

Fix a program P. A *ground pnw-shape* $\mathcal{S}$ of P is a triple $(S, Val, \overline{pc})$ such that S is a ground nw-shape and there exists a program nested word $(nw, Val', \overline{pc}')$ of P such that S is a subgraph of nw, $Val = Val'_{|V}$ and $\overline{pc} = \overline{pc}'_{|V}$.

A *pnw-shape* $\mathcal{S}$ of P is either a ground pnw-shape or $\mathcal{S} = (S, Val, \overline{pc})$ is:

- the *contraction* of a pnw-shape, that is, there is pnw-shape $\mathcal{S}' = (S', Val', \overline{pc}')$ and denoting with V the set of vertices of S, $S = contraction(S', V)$, $Val = Val'_{|V}$ to V and $\overline{pc} = \overline{pc}'_{|V}$, or
- the *merging* of two pnw-shapes, that is, there are two pnw-shapes $\mathcal{S}_1 = (S_1, Val_1, \overline{pc}_1)$ and $\mathcal{S}_2 = (S_2, Val_2, \overline{pc}_2)$ for which, denoting with V the intersection of the sets of vertices of S_1 and S_2, $Val_1(v) = Val_2(v)$ and $\overline{pc}_1(v) = \overline{pc}_2(v)$ for every $v \in V$, then $S = merge(S_1, S_2)$, $Val = Val_1 \cup Val_2$ and $\overline{pc} = \overline{pc}_1 \cup \overline{pc}_2$.

Analogously to nw-shape tree, we define the *pnw-shape tree* with respect to the notion of pnw-shape. The definition is the same except that the merging and contraction operations apply to pnw-shape, and thus we omit further details.

6   Implementation

In this section, we briefly illustrate an implementation of the outlined approach, that is targeted to use a verifier of sequential programs (with recursive procedure calls), though also fixed-point translations in the style of [7,8,11] are possible.

The input program P is transformed into a program P' that is essentially composed of the main and five more procedures: contraction(S1,S2), check(S), ShapeTree(), merge(S1, S2) and CreateGroundShape(k). All the procedures except for ShapeTree() do not contain recursive calls.

Procedure main nondeterministically computes a pnw-shape S by calling ShapeTree and then calls check on it.

Procedure check verifies that S is indeed a pnw-shape that can label the root of a pnw-shape tree, i.e., it is linearly connected and fully matched. (Observe that fully matched within a program nw-shape-tree refers to all the vertices that are marked with a program counter from *Call* or correspond to the return states after a call.) If this is the case and the last vertex (according to the linear order) corresponds to an error state, then a statement assert(0) is reachable (which defines the error state in P').

Procedure ShapeTree (Fig. 5) computes the pnw-shape at the nodes of a possible pnw-shape tree. When invoked from main, it starts from the root. At each node, it guesses a ground nw-shape S by invoking CreateGroundShape. Then, nondeterministically, it decides whether the current node is a leaf or is internal. In the first case, S is returned,

```
shape ShapeTree() {
  shape S;
  S = CreateGroundShape(k);
  if (nondet()) {
    S1 = contraction(ShapeTree(),S);
    S2 = contraction(ShapeTree(),S);
    S  = merge(S, merge(S1,S2));
  }
  return S;
}
```

Fig. 5. Procedure ShapeTree.

otherwise two recursive calls to ShapeTree are done (one for the left child and the other for the right one). The pnw-shapes returned by these calls are meant to label the two children, then according to the definition of pnw-shape tree these are contracted and merged by respectively invoking procedures contraction and merge, thus obtaining the pnw-shape for the current node, that is returned.

Observe that `ShapeTree` exactly implements the properties of Definition 3. To minimize memory usage, we employ contraction of the children's nw-shapebefore merging them, eliminating the need for constructing an intermediate nw-shape containing 2k nodes.

The procedure `contraction` also ensures that S2 has as vertices all the linear borders of S1 along with the vertices corresponding to calls and return states that have not yet been matched with the ⌢-edges (which is required by Definition 3). Procedure `CreateGroundShape` nondeterministically generates a ground pnw-shapewith k vertices and for each edge of the nw-shape it ensures that the program counters of its endpoints conform to the meaning of the edge in the program (that is, a transition or the matching of a call and a return state). Furthermore, if an edge represents a transition, it guarantees the consistency of variable values at its endpoints with the transition's semantics.

7 Discussion

In this paper, we have presented a new methodology to perform software analysis. The main idea is to transform the input programs so that the exploration of the computations is guided by the tree decompositions of their behavior graphs. We have developed in detail our methodology for sequential programs with recursive procedure calls and without dynamic data structures.

In this section, we discuss how to extend our approach to concurrent programs and how it relates to sequentialization of concurrent programs. We then conclude with some remarks and future work.

Concurrent Programs. Concurrent programs consist of a finite number of threads where each of them is defined by a sequential program. All threads run in parallel and communicate through a finite number of shared variables according to the sequential consistency memory model (SC). A natural graph encoding for the computations of concurrent programs is the following. The behavior of each thread is modeled with a nested word. Further, the behaviour of the shared memory is represented by a line graph capturing the sequence of memory operations, where each vertex represents a unique read or write operation. Vertices of the nested words are labeled, as usual, with a program counter and a valuation of the global variables, while memory vertices are labeled with a valuation of the shared variables. A vertex u of a nested word that "reads" a shared variable for executing the local transition, it is linked through a *memory edge* to the memory vertex representing that operation. The direction of this edge is reversed if the vertex "writes" to a shared variable. Since each memory vertex u represents exactly one memory operation, u has exactly one memory edge incident on it. Of course, memory edges will never cross w.r.t. temporal events (as we assume SC). Let us call these behavior graphs *concurrent nested words* (*cnw*).

Concurrent nested words admit natural summaries that reflect their composition. A *concurrent nw-shape* (*cnw-shape* for short) is formed by a distinct nw-shape for each component nested word, and an additional *memory-shape* that is a nw-shape without matching edges. Additional care should be taken for the memory edges to avoid crossing. We have worked out the details of this representation. For example, a *contraction* operation on a cnw-shape can be accomplished by executing a contraction on each component nw-shape and the memory-shape. Furthermore, memory edges are contracted similarly to matching edges of nw-shapes. The *merge* operation is defined exactly as for nw-shapes. By defining *cnw-shape trees* using the same combination of operations seen for nw-shape trees, we can show an equivalent of Theorem 3 for the concurrent setting. In addition, a code-to-code translation for concurrent programs is again possible (it is similar to that described in Sect. 6). An essential point to note is that verification tools designed for sequential programs can be effectively reused for analyzing concurrent programs.

Here we convey the idea that our approach actually leads to a sort of *sequentialization* when applied to concurrent programs and implemented as a code-to-code translation to sequential programs. A sequentialization translates a concurrent program P into a nondeterministic sequential program P' that (under certain assumptions) behaves equivalently [9,16,18]. To make the approach effective, P' should not track the whole state space of the concurrent program, as in the cross product of the thread states. All sequentializations that have been proposed in literature only track one local state at a time and use k copies of the shared variables, for a given parameter k. Under these restrictions, such approaches can only cover a strict subset of computations in which each thread can at most interact k times with the other threads. These features are indeed desirable as we get a parameterized analysis technique that aims at exploiting as much as possible by tuning k for the underlying sequential verification tool. By increasing the parameter k, we can capture more computations, but this of course comes with a cost in terms of computational resources.

Our analysis schema inherits the favorable features of sequentializations while extending its coverage to a broader range of computations for the parameter k. By considering cnw-shapes with at most k nodes, we also track k copies of the variables (either global or shared), but cover all cnw of tree width k vs. existing sequentializations being only able to intercept a very small subset of them. Moreover, a different sequentialization must be designed to capture new classes of behavior (parameterized programs [10], thread creation [2,4], scope bounded [12,14,15], path bounded [13], etc.), while our schema is uniform for all of them.

Future Work. We believe that obtaining scalable solutions for sequential programs based on our approach will pave the way to lift such results to the concurrent settings. On the theoretical side, it would be interesting to study how computations of concurrent programs running under weak memory models can be modeled with behaviour graphs. Similarly, for distributed programs where the communication among threads happens through FIFO channels (see [17] for behaviour graphs of these programs). Further, we believe that our approach could be useful to reason about programs manipulating heaps. The intuition is that concurrent and distributed programs can be seen as sequential programs that use stacks for recursion and queues to simulate FIFO channels. We thus wonder whether our approach can be lifted to more general data structures.

References

1. Alur, R., Madhusudan, P.: Adding nesting structure to words. In: Ibarra, O.H., Dang, Z. (eds.) DLT 2006. LNCS, vol. 4036, pp. 1–13. Springer, Heidelberg (2006). https://doi.org/10.1007/11779148_1
2. Bouajjani, A., Emmi, M., Parlato, G.: On sequentializing concurrent programs. In: Yahav, E. (ed.) SAS 2011. LNCS, vol. 6887, pp. 129–145. Springer, Heidelberg (2011). https://doi.org/10.1007/978-3-642-23702-7_13
3. Courcelle, B.: The monadic second-order logic of graphs. I. Recognizable sets of finite graphs. Inf. Comput. **85**(1), 12–75 (1990). https://doi.org/10.1016/0890-5401(90)90043-H
4. Emmi, M., Qadeer, S., Rakamaric, Z.: Delay-bounded scheduling. In: Ball, T., Sagiv, M. (eds.) Proceedings of the 38th ACM SIGPLAN-SIGACT Symposium on Principles of Programming Languages, POPL 2011, Austin, TX, USA, 26–28 January 2011, pp. 411–422. ACM (2011). https://doi.org/10.1145/1926385.1926432
5. Enea, C., Habermehl, P., Inverso, O., Parlato, G.: On the path-width of integer linear programming. In: Peron, A., Piazza, C. (eds.) Proceedings Fifth International Symposium on Games, Automata, Logics and Formal Verification, GandALF 2014. EPTCS, Verona, Italy, 10–12 September 2014, vol. 161, pp. 74–87 (2014). https://doi.org/10.4204/EPTCS.161.9
6. Enea, C., Habermehl, P., Inverso, O., Parlato, G.: On the path-width of integer linear programming. Inf. Comput. **253**, 257–271 (2017). https://doi.org/10.1016/j.ic.2016.07.010
7. Grebenshchikov, S., Lopes, N.P., Popeea, C., Rybalchenko, A.: Synthesizing software verifiers from proof rules. In: Vitek, J., Lin, H., Tip, F. (eds.) ACM SIGPLAN Conference on Programming Language Design and Implementation, PLDI 2012, Beijing, China, 11–16 June 2012, pp. 405–416. ACM (2012). https://doi.org/10.1145/2254064.2254112
8. Hoder, K., Bjørner, N., de Moura, L.: μZ – an efficient engine for fixed points with constraints. In: Gopalakrishnan, G., Qadeer, S. (eds.) CAV 2011. LNCS, vol. 6806, pp. 457–462. Springer, Heidelberg (2011). https://doi.org/10.1007/978-3-642-22110-1_36
9. La Torre, S., Madhusudan, P., Parlato, G.: Reducing context-bounded concurrent reachability to sequential reachability. In: Bouajjani, A., Maler, O. (eds.) CAV 2009. LNCS, vol. 5643, pp. 477–492. Springer, Heidelberg (2009). https://doi.org/10.1007/978-3-642-02658-4_36
10. La Torre, S., Madhusudan, P., Parlato, G.: Sequentializing parameterized programs. In: Bauer, S.S., Raclet, J. (eds.) Proceedings Fourth Workshop on Foundations of Interface Technologies, FIT 2012. EPTCS, Tallinn, Estonia, 25th March 2012, vol. 87, pp. 34–47 (2012). https://doi.org/10.4204/EPTCS.87.4
11. La Torre, S., Madhusudan, P., Parlato, G.: Analyzing recursive programs using a fixed-point calculus. In: Hind, M., Diwan, A. (eds.) Proceedings of the 2009 ACM SIGPLAN Conference on Programming Language Design and Implementation, PLDI 2009, Dublin, Ireland, 15–21 June 2009, pp. 211–222. ACM (2009). https://doi.org/10.1145/1542476.1542500

12. La Torre, S., Napoli, M.: Reachability of multistack pushdown systems with scope-bounded matching relations. In: Katoen, J.-P., König, B. (eds.) CONCUR 2011. LNCS, vol. 6901, pp. 203–218. Springer, Heidelberg (2011). https://doi.org/10.1007/978-3-642-23217-6_14

13. La Torre, S., Napoli, M., Parlato, G.: A unifying approach for multistack pushdown automata. In: Csuhaj-Varjú, E., Dietzfelbinger, M., Ésik, Z. (eds.) MFCS 2014. LNCS, vol. 8634, pp. 377–389. Springer, Heidelberg (2014). https://doi.org/10.1007/978-3-662-44522-8_32

14. La Torre, S., Napoli, M., Parlato, G.: Reachability of scope-bounded multistack pushdown systems. Inf. Comput. **275**, 104588 (2020). https://doi.org/10.1016/j.ic.2020.104588

15. La Torre, S., Parlato, G.: Scope-bounded multistack pushdown systems: fixed-point, sequentialization, and tree-width. In: D'Souza, D., Kavitha, T., Radhakrishnan, J. (eds.) IARCS Annual Conference on Foundations of Software Technology and Theoretical Computer Science, FSTTCS 2012. LIPIcs, Hyderabad, India, 15–17 December 2012, vol. 18, pp. 173–184. Schloss Dagstuhl - Leibniz-Zentrum für Informatik (2012). https://doi.org/10.4230/LIPIcs.FSTTCS.2012.173

16. Lal, A., Reps, T.W.: Reducing concurrent analysis under a context bound to sequential analysis. Formal Methods Syst. Des. **35**(1), 73–97 (2009). https://doi.org/10.1007/s10703-009-0078-9

17. Madhusudan, P., Parlato, G.: The tree width of auxiliary storage. In: Ball, T., Sagiv, M. (eds.) Proceedings of the 38th ACM SIGPLAN-SIGACT Symposium on Principles of Programming Languages, POPL 2011, Austin, TX, USA, 26–28 January 2011, pp. 283–294. ACM (2011). https://doi.org/10.1145/1926385.1926419

18. Qadeer, S., Wu, D.: KISS: keep it simple and sequential. In: Pugh, W.W., Chambers, C. (eds.) Proceedings of the ACM SIGPLAN 2004 Conference on Programming Language Design and Implementation 2004, Washington, DC, USA, 9–11 June 2004, pp. 14–24. ACM (2004). https://doi.org/10.1145/996841.996845

19. Seese, D.: The structure of models of decidable monadic theories of graphs. Ann. Pure Appl. Log. **53**(2), 169–195 (1991). https://doi.org/10.1016/0168-0072(91)90054-P

Behavioral QLTL

Giuseppe De Giacomo[1,2] and Giuseppe Perelli[2(✉)]

[1] University of Oxford, Oxford, UK
[2] Sapienza University of Rome, Rome, Italy
perelli@di.uniroma1.it

Abstract. This paper introduces Behavioral QLTL, a "behavioral" variant of Linear Temporal Logic (LTL) with second-order quantifiers. Behavioral QLTL is characterized by the fact that the functions that assign the truth value of the quantified propositions along the trace can only depend on the past. In other words, such functions must be "processes" [1]. This gives the logic a strategic flavor that we usually associate with planning. Indeed we show that temporally extended planning in nondeterministic domains and LTL synthesis are expressed in Behavioral QLTL through formulas with a simple quantification alternation. While as this alternation increases, we get to forms of planning/synthesis in which contingent and conformant planning aspects get mixed. We study this logic from the computational point of view and compare it to the original QLTL (with non-behavioral semantics) and simpler forms of behavioral semantics.

1 Introduction

Since the very early time of AI, researchers have tried to reduce planning to logical reasoning, i.e., satisfiability, validity, logical implication [29]. However as we consider more and more sophisticated forms of planning this becomes more and more challenging, because the logical reasoning required quickly becomes second-order. One prominent case is if we want to express the model of the world (aka the environment) and the goal of the agent directly in Linear Temporal Logic (LTL). LTL has been often adopted also in Artificial Intelligence. Examples are the pioneering work on using temporal logic as a sort of programming language through the MetateM framework [7], the work on temporally extended goals and declarative control constraints [5,6], the work on planning via model-checking [9,17,18,20], the work on adopting LTL logical reasoning (plus some meta-theoretic manipulation) for certain forms of planning [10,12]. More recently the connection between planning in nondeterministic domains and (reactive) synthesis [35] has been investigated, and in fact it has been shown that planning in nondeterministic domains can be seen in general terms as a form of synthesis in presence of a model of the environment [3,11], also related to synthesis under assumptions [13,14].

However the connection between planning and synthesis also clarifies formally that we cannot use directly the standard forms of reasoning in LTL, such as satisfiability, validity, or logical implication, to do planning. Indeed the logical

V. Malvone and A. Murano (Eds.): EUMAS 2023, LNAI 14282, pp. 133–149, 2023.
https://doi.org/10.1007/978-3-031-43264-4_9

reasoning task we have to adopt is a nonstandard one, called *"realizability"* [16, 35], which is inherently a second-order form of reasoning on LTL specifications. So one question comes natural: can we use the second-order version of LTL, called QLTL (or QPTL) [40] and then use its classic reasoning tasks, such as satisfiability, validity and logical implication, to capture planning and synthesis?

In [10] a positive answer was given limited to conformant planning [37], in which we have partial observability on the environment and, in particular, we cannot fully observe the initial state and the environment response to agent actions, which however are deterministic. Hence, in conformant planning we need to synthesize plans/strategies that work (in the deterministic domain) in spite of the lack of knowledge. [10] shows that exploiting existential and universal quantifications, to account for the lack of knowledge, QLTL could actually capture conformant planning through standard satisfiability.

However, the results there do not apply when the environment is nondeterministic, as in contingent planning (with or without full observability) [37]. The reason for this is very profound. Any plan/strategy must be a *"process"*, i.e., a function that observes what has happened so far (the history), observes the current state, and takes a decision (conditional on what observed) on the next action to do [1]. QLTL instead interprets quantified propositions (i.e., in the case of planning, the actions to be chosen) through functions that have access to the whole traces, i.e., also the future instants, hence they cannot be considered processes. This is a clear mismatch that makes standard QLTL unsuitable to capture planning through standard reasoning tasks.

This mismatch is not only a characteristic of QLTL, but, interestingly, even of logics that have been introduced specifically for strategic reasoning such as Strategy Logic (SL) [15,32]. This has led to investigating the *"behavioral"* semantics in these logics, i.e., a semantics based on processes. In their seminal work [32], Mogavero et al. introduce and analyze the behavioral aspects of quantification in SL: a logic for reasoning about the strategic behavior of agents in a context where the properties of executions are expressed in LTL. They show that restricting to behavioral quantification of strategies is a way of both making the semantics more realistic and computationally easier. In addition, they proved that behavioral and non-behavioral semantics coincide for certain fragments, including the one corresponding to the well known ATL* [2], but diverge for more interesting classes of formulas, e.g., the ones that can express game-theoretic properties such as Nash Equilibria and the like. This has started a new line of research that aims at identifying new notions of behavioral and non-behavioral quantification, as well as characterize the syntactic fragments that are invariant to these semantic variations [24,25,33].

In this paper, inspired by the study of behavioral semantics in Strategy Logic, we introduce a simple and elegant variant of QLTL with a behavioral semantics. The resulting logic, called *Behavioral*-QLTL (QLTL$_B$), maintains the same syntax of QLTL, but is characterized by the fact that the functions that assign the truth value of the quantified propositions along the trace can only depend on the past. In other words such functions must indeed be *"processes"*. This makes QLTL$_B$

perfectly suitable to capture extended forms of planning and synthesis through standard reasoning tasks (satisfiability in particular).

In QLTL$_B$, planning for temporally extended goals in nondeterministic domains, as well as LTL synthesis, are expressed through formulas with a simple quantification alternation. While, as this alternation increases, we get to forms of planning/synthesis in which contingent and conformant planning aspects get mixed by controlling via quantification what is visible of the current history to take a decision on. For example, the QLTL$_B$ formula of the form $\exists Y \forall X \psi$ represents the conformant planning over the LTL specification (of both environment model and goal) ψ, as it is intended in [37]. Here we use $\forall X$ to hide in the history the propositions (a.k.a. *fluents*) that are not visible to the agent. Note that this could be done also with standard QLTL, since $\exists Y$ is put upfront as it cannot depend on the nondeterministic evolution of X. The QLTL$_B$ formula $\forall X \exists Y \psi$ represents contingent planning in fully observable domains [37], also known as *Strong Planning in Fully Observable Nondeterministic Domains* (FOND) [19,26], as well as LTL synthesis [35]. The QLTL$_B$ formula $\forall X_1 \exists Y \forall X_2 \varphi$ represents the problem of contingent planning under partial observability [37], also known as *Strong Planning in Partially Observable Nondeterministic Domains* (POND) [26]. Here, X_1 and X_2 are, respectively, the visible and hidden propositions controlled by the environment and the strategy corresponding to the Skolem function assigning the values to Y depends on the values of X_1 in the history so far but not on the values of X_2, which indeed remain non-observable to the agent. By going even further in alternation, we get a generalization of POND where a number the controllable variables of the agent depend individually on more and more environment variables. In other words, we have a hierarchy of partial observability over the whole history on which the various variable under the control of the agent can depend upon. Interestingly, if we consider the agent controlled variables as independent actuators, then this instantiates the problem of distributed synthesis with strictly decreasing levels of information studied in formal methods [22,31,36].

We study QLTL$_B$ by introducing a formal semantics that is *Skolem-based*, meaning that we assign existential values through Skolem-like functions that depend on the universal (adversarial) choice of the variables of interest. Specifically we restrict such Skolem function to depend only on the past and hence behave as processes/strategies/plans. As a matter of fact, such Skolem functions can be represented as suitable labeled trees, describing all the possible executions of a given process that receive inputs from the environment. We then study satisfiability in QLTL$_B$ and characterize its complexity as $(n+1)$-EXPTIME-complete, with n being the number of quantification blocks of the form $\forall X_i \exists Y_i$ in the formula. Note that this is substantially lower than the complexity of satisfiability for classic QLTL, which depends on the overall quantifier alternation in the formula, and in particular is $2(n-1)$-EXSPACE-complete. Interestingly, instantiating our satisfiability procedure we get an optimal technique for solving synthesis, and planning in nondeterministic domains, for LTL goals in the case of full observability and partial observability. Indeed, both the formula $\forall X \exists Y \psi$ for the case of full observability and the formula $\forall X_1 \exists Y \forall X_2 \varphi$ for the case of partial observability, include a single block of the form $\forall X_i \exists Y_i$, and hence satisfiability can be checked in 2-EXPTIME, thus matching the 2-EXPTIME-completeness of the two problems [30,35].

2   Quantified Linear Temporal Logic

Linear Temporal Logic (LTL) was originally proposed in Computer Science as a specification language for concurrent programs [34]. Formulas of LTL are built from a set Var of *propositional variables* (or simply variables), together with Boolean and temporal operators. Its syntax can be described as follows:

$$\psi ::= x \mid \neg\psi \mid \psi \vee \psi \mid \psi \wedge \psi \mid \mathbf{X}\psi \mid \psi\mathbf{U}\psi$$

where $x \in$ Var is a propositional variable.

Intuitively, the formula $\mathbf{X}\psi$ says that ψ holds at the *next* instant. Moreover, the formula $\psi_1\mathbf{U}\psi_2$ says that at some future instant ψ_2 holds and *until* that point, ψ_1 holds. We also use the standard Boolean abbreviations $\mathbf{true} := x \vee \neg x$ (*true*), $\mathbf{false} := \neg\mathbf{true}$ (*false*), and $\psi_1 \rightarrow \psi_2 := \neg\psi_1 \vee \psi_2$ (*implication*). In addition, we also use the binary operator $\psi_1\mathbf{R}\psi_2 \doteq \neg(\neg\psi_1\mathbf{U}\neg\psi_2)$ (*release*) and the unary operators $\mathbf{F}\psi := \mathbf{true}\mathbf{U}\psi$ (*eventually*) and $\mathbf{G}\psi := \neg\mathbf{F}\neg\psi$ (*globally*).

The classic semantics of LTL is given in terms of infinite traces, i.e., truth-value assignments over the natural numbers. More precisely, a *trace* $\pi \in (2^{\mathtt{Var}})^\omega$ is an infinite sequence of truth assignments over the set of variables Var, where $(\cdot)^\omega$ is the classic omega operator used to denote such infinite sequences. By $\pi(i) \in 2^{\mathtt{Var}}$, we denote the i-th truth assignment of the infinite sequence π. Along the paper, we might refer to finite *segments* of a computation π. More precisely, for two indexes $i, j \in \mathbb{N}$, by $\pi(i,j) \doteq \pi(i), \ldots, \pi(j) \in (2^{\mathtt{Var}})^*$ we denote the finite segment of π from it's i-th to its j-th position, where $(\cdot)^*$ is the classic Kleene's star used to denote finite sequences of any length. A segment $\pi(0,j)$ starting from 0 is also called a *prefix* and is sometimes denoted $\pi_{\leq j}$. Moreover, we sometimes use π_X to denote a trace over a subset $X \subseteq$ Var of variables, that is, we make explicit the range of variables on which the trace is defined.

We say that an LTL formula ψ is true on an assignment π at instant i, written $\pi, i \models_{\mathrm{LTL}} \psi$, if:

– $\pi, i \models_{\mathrm{LTL}} x$, for $x \in$ Var iff $x \in \pi(i)$;
– $\pi, i \models_{\mathrm{LTL}} \neg\psi$ iff $\pi, i \not\models_{\mathrm{LTL}} \psi$;
– $\pi, i \models_{\mathrm{LTL}} \psi_1 \vee \psi_2$ iff either $\pi, i \models_{\mathrm{LTL}} \psi_1$ or $\pi, i \models_{\mathrm{LTL}} \psi_2$;
– $\pi, i \models_{\mathrm{LTL}} \psi_1 \wedge \psi_2$ iff both $\pi, i \models_{\mathrm{LTL}} \psi_1$ and $\pi, i \models_{\mathrm{LTL}} \psi_2$;
– $\pi, i \models_{\mathrm{LTL}} \mathbf{X}\psi$ iff $\pi, i + 1 \models_{\mathrm{LTL}} \psi$;
– $\pi, i \models_{\mathrm{LTL}} \psi_1\mathbf{U}\psi_2$ iff for some $j \geq i$, we have that $\pi, j \models_{\mathrm{LTL}} \psi_2$ and for all $k \in \{i, \ldots j - 1\}$, we have that $\pi, k \models_{\mathrm{LTL}} \psi_1$.

A formula ψ is *true* over π, written $\pi \models_{\mathrm{LTL}} \psi$, iff $\pi, 0 \models_{\mathrm{LTL}} \psi$. A formula ψ is *satisfiable* if it is true on some trace and *valid* if it is true in every trace.

Quantified Linear-Temporal Logic (QLTL) is an extension of LTL with two *Second-order* quantifiers [39]. Its formulas are built using the classic LTL Boolean and temporal operators, on top of which existential and universal quantification over variables is applied. Formally, the syntax is given as follows:

$$\varphi ::= \exists x \varphi \mid \forall x \varphi \mid x \mid \neg\varphi \mid \varphi \vee \varphi \mid \varphi \wedge \varphi \mid \mathsf{X}\varphi \mid \varphi \mathsf{U}\varphi,$$

where $x \in \mathsf{Var}$ is a propositional variable.

Note that this is a proper extension of LTL, as QLTL has the same expressive power of MSO [39], whereas LTL is equivalent to FOL [23].

In order to define the semantics of QLTL, we introduce some notation. For a trace π and a set of variables $X \subseteq \mathsf{Var}$, by $\mathrm{Prj}(\pi, X)$ we denote the *projection* trace over X defined as $\mathrm{Prj}(\pi, X)(i) \doteq \pi(i) \cap X$ at any time point $i \in \mathbb{N}$. Moreover, by $\mathrm{Prj}(\pi, -X) \doteq \mathrm{Prj}(\pi, \mathsf{Var} \setminus X)$ we denote the projection trace over the complement of X. For a single variable x, we simplify the notation as $\mathrm{Prj}(\pi, x) \doteq \mathrm{Prj}(\pi, \{x\})$ and $\mathrm{Prj}(\pi, -x) \doteq \mathrm{Prj}(\pi, \mathsf{Var} \setminus \{x\})$. Finally, we say that π and π' *agree* over X if $\mathrm{Prj}(\pi, X) = \mathrm{Prj}(\pi', X)$.

Observe that we can reverse the projection operation by combining traces over disjoint sets of variables. More formally, for two disjoint sets $X, X' \subseteq \mathsf{Var}$ and two traces π_X and $\pi_{X'}$ over X and X', respectively, we define the combined trace $\pi_X \uplus \pi_{X'}$ as the (unique) trace over $X \cup X'$ such that its projections on X and X' correspond to π_X and $\pi_{X'}$, respectively.

The *classic* semantics of the quantifiers in a QLTL formula φ over a trace π, at instant i, denoted $\pi, i \models_c \varphi$, is defined as follows:

- $\pi, i \models_c \psi$ iff $\pi, i \models_{\mathrm{LTL}} \psi$ for every quantifier-free (LTL) formula ψ;
- $\pi, i \models_c \exists x \varphi$ iff there exists π' agreeing with π over $-x$ s.t. $\pi', i \models_c \varphi$;
- $\pi, i \models_c \forall x \varphi$ iff for each π' agreeing with π over $-x$, it holds that $\pi', i \models_c \varphi$;

A variable x is *free* in φ if it occurs at least once out of the scope of either $\exists x$ or $\forall x$ in φ. By $\mathtt{free}(\varphi)$ we denote the set of free variables in φ.

As for LTL, we say that φ is true on π, and write $\pi \models_c \varphi$ iff $\pi, 0 \models_c \varphi$. Analogously, a formula φ is *satisfiable* if it is true on some trace π, whereas it is *valid* if it is true on every possible trace π. Note that, as quantifications in the formula replace the trace over the variables in their scope, we can assume that π are traces over the set $\mathtt{free}(\varphi)$ of free variables in φ.

For convenience, and without loss of generality, QLTL is typically used in *prenex normal form*, i.e., according to the following syntax:

$$\varphi ::= \exists x \varphi \mid \forall x \varphi \mid \psi$$

where ψ is an LTL formula over the the propositional variables Var. Hence a QLTL formula in *prenex normal form* has the form $\wp\psi$, where $\wp = \mathtt{Qn}_1 x_1 \ldots \mathtt{Qn}_n x_n$ is a *prefix quantification* with $\mathtt{Qn}_i \in \{\exists, \forall\}$ and x_i being a variable occurring on a *quantifier-free* subformula ψ. Every QLTL formula can be rewritten in prenex normal form, meaning that such rewriting is true on the same set of traces. Consider for instance the formula $\mathsf{G}(\exists y (y \wedge \mathsf{X}\neg y))$. This is equivalent to $\forall x \exists y (\mathtt{singleton}(x) \to (\mathsf{G}(x \to (y \wedge \mathsf{X}\neg y))))$, with $\mathtt{singleton}(x) \doteq \mathsf{F}x \wedge \mathsf{G}(x \to$

$\mathtt{XG}\neg x$) expressing the fact that x is true exactly once on the trace[1]. A full proof of the reduction to prenex normal form can be found in [41, Section 2.3].

Recall that for a formula $\varphi = \wp\psi$ is easy to obtain the prefix normal form of its negation $\neg\varphi$ as $\overline{\wp}\neg\psi$, where $\overline{\wp}$ is obtained from $\wp$ by swapping every quantification from existential to universal and vice-versa. From now on, by $\neg\varphi$ we denote its prenex normal form transformation.

An *alternation* in a quantification prefix $\wp$ is either a sequence $\exists x \forall y$ or a sequence $\forall x \exists y$ occurring in $\wp$. A formula of the form $\wp\psi$ is of *alternation-depth* k if $\wp$ contains exactly k alternations. Following the notation introduced in [39], by k-QLTL we denote the QLTL fragment of formulas with alternation k. Moreover, Σ_k^{QLTL} and Π_k^{QLTL} denote the fragments of k-QLTL of formulas starting with an existential and a universal quantification, respectively.

Let $\wp$ be a quantification prefix. By $\exists(\wp)$ and $\forall(\wp)$ we denote the set of variables that are quantified existentially and universally, respectively. We say that two variables x and x' belong to the same *block* X if no alternation occurs between them, i.e., they are both of the same quantification type, together with any other variable occurring in between them in $\wp$.

Note that a QLTL formula $\wp\psi$ is equivalent to any formula $\wp'\psi$ where $\wp'$ is obtained from $\wp$ by shuffling variables belonging to the same block. For this reason, it is convenient to make use of the syntactic shortcuts $\exists X\varphi \doteq \exists x_1 \dots \exists x_k \varphi$ and $\forall X\varphi \doteq \forall x_1 \dots \forall x_k \varphi$ with $X = \{x_1, \dots, x_k\}$, being a block of variables in $\wp$. Formulas can then be written in the form $\mathtt{Qn}_1 X_1 \dots \mathtt{Qn}_n X_n \psi$ with $X_1, \dots X_n$ being *maximal blocks*, meaning that every two consecutive occurrences of them are of different quantification type. More formally, it holds that $\mathtt{Qn}_i = \exists$ iff $\mathtt{Qn}_{i+1} = \forall$, for every $i < n$.

Note that also the semantics of prenex QLTL formulas can easily be lifted in terms of quantification blocks.

For a QLTL formula φ, a trace π, and an instant i, we obtain that

- $\pi, i \models_\mathrm{c} \psi$ iff $\pi, i \models_\mathrm{LTL} \psi$, for every quantifier-free formula ψ;
- $\pi, i \models_\mathrm{c} \exists X\varphi$ iff there exists π' agreeing with π over $-X$ s.t. $\pi', i \models_\mathrm{c} \varphi$;
- $\pi, i \models_\mathrm{c} \forall X\varphi$ iff for each π' agreeing with π over $-X$, it holds that $\pi', i \models_\mathrm{c} \varphi$[2].

From now on, we might refer to variable blocks, simply as blocks. Moreover, with a slight overlap of notation, we write $X \subseteq \exists(\wp)$ to denote that the variables of the block X are existentially quantified in $\wp$.

The satisfiability problem consists in, given a QLTL formula φ, determining whether it is satisfiable or not. Note that every formula φ is satisfiable if, and only if, $\exists\mathtt{free}(\varphi)\varphi$ is satisfiable. This means that we can study satisfiability in QLTL for *closed* formulas, i.e., formulas where every variable is quantified.

Consider the formula $\varphi = \exists y(y \leftrightarrow \mathtt{G}x)$ with $\mathtt{free}(\varphi) = \{x\}$. This is satisfiable as, for example, the trace π obtained by combining π_x over $\{x\}$ taking always

---

[1] The reader might observe that pushing the quantification over y outside the temporal operator does not work. Indeed, the formula $\exists y \mathtt{G}(y \wedge \mathtt{X}\neg y)$ is unsatisfiable.

[2] Notice that now we are dealing with variable blocks and not single variables at the time.

the value true with the trace π_y over $\{y\}$ assigning true at the first instant satisfies $(y \leftrightarrow \mathsf{G}x)$. Notice that $\varphi = \exists y(y \leftrightarrow \mathsf{G}x)$ is satisfiable if and only if the close formula $\exists x \exists y(y \leftrightarrow \mathsf{G}x)$ is so. Analogously, φ is valid if and only if the close formula $\forall x \exists y(y \leftrightarrow \mathsf{G}x)$ is so.

Such problem is decidable, though computationally highly intractable in general [39]. For a given natural number k, by k-EXPSPACE we denote the language of problems solved by a Turing machine with space bounded by $2^{2^{\cdot^{\cdot^{\cdot^{2^n}}}}}$, where the height of the tower is k and n is the size of the input. By convention 0-EXPSPACE denotes PSPACE.

Theorem 1 [40]. *Satisfiability for k-QLTL is k-EXPSPACE-complete.*

3 Skolem Functions for QLTL Semantics

We now give an alternative way to capture the semantics of QLTL, which is in terms of (second order) Skolem functions. This will allow us later to suitably restrict such Skolem functions to capture behavioral semantics, by forcing them to depend only on the past history and the current situation.

Consider two variable blocks X and Y. By $X <_\wp Y$ we denote the fact that X occurs *before* Y in $\wp$. For a given existentially quantified block $Y \in \exists(\wp)$, by $\mathsf{Dep}_\wp(Y) = \{X \in \forall(\wp) | X <_\wp Y\}$ we denote the blocks to which Y depends on in $\wp$. Moreover, for a given set $F \subseteq \mathsf{Var}$ of variables, sometimes referred as the *free variables block*, by $\mathsf{Dep}_\wp^F(Y) = F \cup \mathsf{Dep}_\wp(Y)$ we denote the *augmented dependency*, taking into account the additional free block. Whenever clear from the context, we omit the subscript and simply write $\mathsf{Dep}(Y)$ and $\mathsf{Dep}^F(Y)$.

The relation defined above captures the concept of *variable dependence* generated by quantifiers and free variables in a QLTL formula. Intuitively, whenever a dependence occurs between two blocks X and Y, this means that the existential choices of Y are determined by a function whose domain is given by all possible choices available for X, be it universally quantified or free in the corresponding formula. This dependence is know in first-order logic as *Skolem function* and can be described in QLTL as follows.

Definition 1 (Skolem function). *For a given quantification prefix $\wp$ defined over a set $\mathsf{Var}(\wp) \subseteq \mathsf{Var}$ of variables, and a free block $F = \mathsf{Var} \setminus \mathsf{Var}(\wp)$, a function*

$$\theta : (2^{F \cup \forall(\wp)})^\omega \to (2^{\exists(\wp)})^\omega$$

is called a Skolem function over $(\wp, F)$ if, for all traces $\pi_1, \pi_2 \in (2^{F \cup \forall(\wp)})^\omega$ over $F \cup \forall(\wp)$ and for all blocks $Y \in \exists(\wp)$, it holds that

$$\mathit{Prj}(\pi_1, \mathsf{Dep}^F(Y)) = \mathit{Prj}(\pi_2, \mathsf{Dep}^F(Y)) \text{ implies } \mathit{Prj}(\theta(\pi_1), Y) = \mathit{Prj}(\theta(\pi_2), Y).$$

In other words, whenever π_1 and π_2 are equal over the variables to which block Y depends on, $\theta(\pi_1)$ and $\theta(\pi_2)$ are equal over the block Y.

Intuitively, a Skolem function takes traces of the free variables and (the blocks of) universally quantified variables and returns traces of (the blocks of) existentially quantified variables so that they depend only on the free variables and the universal variables that appear before them in the quantification prefix $\wp$.

Skolem functions can be used to give an alternative characterization of the semantics of QLTL formulas in prenex normal form. Given a trace π over $F \cup \forall(\wp)$, sometimes we denote the combined trace $\hat{\theta}(\pi) \doteq \pi \cup \theta(\pi)$, as if $\hat{\theta}$ *combines* the inputs and outputs outcomes of θ together.

Definition 2 (Skolem semantics). *A* QLTL *formula* $\varphi = \wp\psi$ *is Skolem true over a trace* π *at an instant* i, *written* $\pi, i \models_S \varphi$, *if there exists a Skolem function* θ *over* $(\wp, free(\varphi))$ *such that* $\hat{\theta}(\pi \cup \pi_{\forall(\wp)}), i \models_{LTL} \psi$, *for every possible trace* $\pi_{\forall\wp}$.

Intuitively, the Skolem characterizes the truth of a QLTL formula with the existence of a Skolem function that returns the traces of the existential quantifications as function of the variables to which they depend in the formula φ. The following theorem shows, the Skolem semantics is equivalent to the classic one. Therefore, for every formula φ and every trace π, it holds that $\pi \models_S \varphi$ if, and only if, $\pi \not\models_S \neg\varphi$.

Theorem 2. *For every* QLTL *formula* $\varphi = \wp\psi$ *and every trace* $\pi_F \in (2^F)^\omega$ *over the free variables block* $F = free(\varphi)$ *of* φ, *it holds that*

$$\pi \models_c \varphi \text{ if, and only if, } \pi \models_S \varphi.$$

Proof. The proof proceeds by induction on the length of $\wp$. For the case of $|\wp| = 0$ it holds that $\wp = \epsilon$ is the empty sequence. This means that $\varphi = \psi$ is variable free and the classic and Skolem semantics coincide with the LTL semantics. Therefore we obtain $\pi_F \models_c \psi$ iff $\pi_F \models_S \psi$.

For the case of $|\wp| > 0$ we prove the two implications separately. From the left to right direction, assume that $\pi_F \models_c \varphi$ and distinguish two cases:

- $\wp = \exists X\wp'$. Thus, there exists a trace $\pi_X \in (2^X)^\omega$ such that $\pi_F \cup \pi_X \models_c \wp'\psi$. By induction hypothesis, we have that $\pi_F \cup \pi_X \models_S \wp'\psi$ and so that there exists a Skolem function θ' over $(\wp', F \cup \{X\})$ such that $\hat{\theta}'(\pi_F \cup \pi_X \cup \pi') \models_{LTL} \psi$, for every $\pi' \in (2^{\forall(\wp')})^\omega$. Now, consider the Skolem function θ over $(\wp, F)$ defined as $\theta(\pi_F \cup \pi') = \theta'(\pi_F \cup \pi_X \cup \pi'_{-X}) \cup \pi_X$ for every $\pi' \in (2^{\forall(\wp)})^\omega$. This implies that $\hat{\theta}(\pi_F \cup \pi') \models_{LTL} \psi$ for every $\pi' \in (2^{\forall(\wp)})^\omega$, and so that $\pi_F \models_S \varphi$.
- $\wp = \forall X\wp'$. Then, it holds that $\pi_F \cup \pi_X \models_c \wp'\psi$ for every $\pi_X \in (2^X)^\omega$. By induction hypothesis, for every $\pi_X \in (2^X)^\omega$ there exists a Skolem function $\theta\pi_X$ over $(\wp', F \cup \{X\})$ such that $\hat{\theta}\pi_X(\pi_F \cup \pi_X \cup \pi') \models_{LTL} \psi$ for every $\pi' \in (2^{\forall(\wp')})^\omega$. Now, consider the Skolem function θ over $(\wp, F)$ defined as $\theta(\pi_F \cup \pi') = \theta_{\pi'_X}(\pi_F \cup \pi'_X \cup \pi'_{-X})$. It holds that $\hat{\theta}(\pi_F \cup \pi') \models_{LTL} \psi$ for every $\pi' \in (2^\wp)^\omega$, which means that $\pi_F \models_S \varphi$.

For the right to left direction, assume that $\pi_F \models_S \wp\psi$. Then, there exists a Skolem function θ over $(\wp, F)$ such that $\hat{\theta}(\pi_F \cup \pi) \models_{LTL} \psi$ for every $\pi \in (2^{\forall(\wp)})^\omega$. Here, we also distinguish the two cases.

- $\wp = \exists X \wp'$. Observe that $\text{Dep}^F(X) = F$. Then it holds that $\theta(\pi_F \uplus \pi)(X) = \theta(\pi_F \cup \pi')(X) = \pi_X$ for every $\pi, \pi' \in (2^{\forall(\wp')})^\omega$. Now, define the Skolem function θ' over $(\wp', F \cup \{X\})$ as $\theta'(\pi_F \uplus \pi_X \uplus \pi') = \text{Prj}(\theta(\pi_F \uplus \pi_X \uplus \pi'), -X)$ outputting the same as θ except for the trace of the block variable X. It holds that $\hat{\theta}'(\pi_F \uplus \pi_X \uplus \pi') \models_{\text{LTL}} \psi$ for each $\pi' \in (2^{\forall(\wp')})^\omega$ and so, by induction hypothesis, that $\pi_F \uplus \pi_X \models_c \wp' \psi$, which in turns implies that $\pi_F \models_c \exists X \wp' \psi$ and so that $\pi_F \models_c \varphi$.

- $\wp = \forall X \wp'$. Observe that $\forall(\wp) = \forall(\wp') \cup \{X\}$, and so that θ is also a Skolem function over $(\wp', F \cup \{X\})$. This implies that, for each $\pi_X \in (2^X)^\omega$, it holds that $\hat{\theta}(\pi_F \uplus \pi_X \uplus \pi') \models_{\text{LTL}} \psi$ for every $\pi' \in (2^{\forall(\wp')})^\omega$. By induction hypothesis, we obtain that, for every $\pi_X \in (2^X)^\omega$, it holds that $\pi_F \uplus \pi_X \models_c \wp' \psi$, which in turns implies that $\pi_F \models_c \exists X \wp' \psi$ and so that $\pi_F \models_c \varphi$.

4   Behavioral QLTL (QLTL_B)

The classic semantics of QLTL requires to consider at once the evaluation of the variables on the whole trace. This gives rise to counter-intuitive phenomena. Consider the formula $\forall x \exists y (\text{G} x \leftrightarrow y)$. Such a formula is satisfiable. Indeed, on the one hand, for the trace assigning for being always true to x, the trace that makes y true at the beginning satisfies the temporal part. On the other hand, for every other trace making x false sometimes, the trace that makes y false at the beginning satisfies the temporal part. However, in order to correctly interpret y on the first instant, one needs to know in advance the entire trace of x. Such requirement is practically impossible to fulfill and does not reflect the notion of *reactive systems*, where the agent variables at the k-th instant of the computation depend only on the past assignments of the environment variables. Such principle is often referred to as *behavioral* in the context of strategic reasoning, see e.g., [25,32].

Here, we introduce an alternative semantics for QLTL, which is based on the idea that the *existential variables are controlled by the agent* and the *universally quantified variables are controlled by the environment*. We require such control functions to be processes in the sense of [1], i.e., the next move depends only on the past history and the present, but not the future. Moreover the choices of the existential variables can depend only on the universal variables coming earlier in the quantification prefix. In other words this semantics allows for *partial observability* of the uncontrollable variables (i.e., the universally quantified variables). To formally define the semantics, we suitably constrain Skolem functions to make them behavioral, i.e., processes.

Specifically we introduce *behavioral* QLTL, denoted QLTL_B, a logic with the same syntax as of prenex normal form QLTL, namely:

$$\varphi ::= \exists x \varphi \mid \forall x \varphi \mid \psi$$

where ψ is an LTL formula over the the propositional variables Var. However, while the syntax is the same of QLTL, the semantics of QLTL_B is defined in terms of behavioral Skolem functions.

Definition 3 (Behavioral Skolem function). *For a given quantification prefix* $\wp$ *defined over a blocks of propositional variables* **Var** *and a block F of free variables, a Skolem function* θ *over* $(\wp, F)$ *is* behavioral *if, for all* $\pi_1, \pi_2 \in (2^{F \cup \forall(\wp)})^\omega$, $k \in \mathbb{N}$, *and* $Y \in \exists(\wp)$, *it holds that*

$$Prj(\pi_1(0, k), Dep^F(Y)) = Prj(\pi_2(0, k), Dep^F(Y))$$
$$implies$$
$$Prj(\theta(\pi_1)(0, k), Y) = Prj(\theta(\pi_2)(0, k), Y).$$

The behavioral Skolem functions capture the fact that the trace of existentially quantified variables depends only on the past and present values of free and universally quantified variables. This offers a way to formalize the semantics of QLTL$_B$ as follows.

Definition 4. *A* QLTL$_B$ *formula* $\varphi = \wp\psi$ *is true over a trace* π *in an instant* i, *written* $\pi, i \models_B \wp\psi$, *if there exists a behavioral Skolem function* θ *over* $(\wp, free(\varphi))$ *such that* $\hat{\theta}(\pi \cup \pi'), i \models_C \psi$ *for every* $\pi' \in (2^{free(\varphi) \cup \forall(\wp)})^\omega$.

A QLTL$_B$ formula φ is true on a trace π, written $\pi \models_B \varphi$, if $\pi, 0 \models_B \varphi$. A formula φ is *satisfiable* if it is true on some trace and *valid* if it is true in every trace. Consider again the formula $\varphi = \exists y(y \leftrightarrow Gx)$ with $free(\varphi) = \{x\}$, now in QLTL$_B$. This is satisfiable again. Indeed, consider the behavioral Skolem function θ such that $\theta(\pi_x)(0, 0) = \text{true}$ and $\theta(\pi_x)(0, k) = \text{false}$ for each $k > 0$. Now, for the trace π obtained by combining π_x over $\{x\}$ taking always the value true with the trace $\pi_y = \theta(\pi_x)$ over $\{y\}$ generated by the Skolem function θ, we have that π satisfies $(y \leftrightarrow Gx)$.

Again, notice that $\varphi = \exists y(y \leftrightarrow Gx)$ is satisfiable if and only if the close formula $\exists x \exists y(y \leftrightarrow Gx)$ is so. Indeed, now notice that the Skolem function chose both the values of x and y as needed in $(y \leftrightarrow Gx)$. However, the formula φ is not valid. Indeed, the closed formula $\forall x \exists y(y \leftrightarrow Gx)$ is neither satisfiable nor valid in QLTL$_B$ since, in order to set the value of y appropriately, one should be able to observe the whole trace π_x and, since behavioral Skolem functions depend only on history, this cannot be done. Observe that also the negation of $\forall x \exists y(y \leftrightarrow Gx)$ is not satisfiable. Indeed, the formula $\exists y \forall x(x \not\leftrightarrow Gy)$ cannot have a Skolem function that sets the values of y appropriately without seeing x at the first instant. This is a common phenomenon, as it also happens when considering the behavioral semantics of logic for the strategic reasoning [25,32].

Consider instead the formula $\varphi = \exists y G(y \leftrightarrow x)$. This is both satisfiable and valid. Indeed, in the case of satisfiability, the closed formula $\exists x \exists y G(y \leftrightarrow x)$ is satisfiable as the behavioral Skolem function can chose the values of x and y appropriately. For the case of validity, the closed formula $\forall x \exists y G(y \leftrightarrow x)$ is satisfiable, as the Skolem function can set the value of y in dependence of the history of values for x (in particular, the last one) in a suitable way. Instead the formula $\exists y \forall x G(y \leftrightarrow x)$ is not satisfiable (neither valid) since the Skolem function needs to chose the values for y independently (i.e., without observing) the values of x.

5   Capturing Advanced Forms of Planning in QLTL$_B$

In order to gain some intuition on QLTL$_B$, it is interesting to see how QLTL$_B$ can capture advanced forms of Planning. We assume some familiarity with Planning in AI, see [26,27]. In planning, we typically have a: *domain D* (here including the initial state) describing the dynamics of the environment, i.e., what happens when the agent performs its actions; a *goal G* that the agent has to accomplish in the domain. The various forms of planning can be seen as a game between the agent controlling the *actions* and environment controlling the *fluents*. Given an agent's action, the environment responds by setting the fluents according to the specification in D. The agent has to come up with actions that eventually enforce the goal G. Typically the goal is reaching a state with certain properties (values of fluents) but here we consider temporally extended goals, so the goal is a specification of desirable traces rather than states [5]. Here we consider several forms of planning where the fluents to the agent are: (i) totally invisible (*conformant planning*); (ii) totally visible –but not controllable (*contingent planning with full observability*); (iii) or partially visible (*contingent planning with partial observability*).

In the following, we assume to have a LTL formula φ_D that captures the domain D (including the initial state), and another LTL formula φ_g that captures the agent goal G. Such formulas are on fluents, controlled by the environment, for which we use the variables X possibly with subscripts, and actions, controlled by the agent, for which we used the variable Y possibly with subscripts. Notice that by using LTL to express the domain we can actually capture not only standard Markovian domains, but also non-Markovian ones in which the reaction of the environment depends on the whole history, as well as, liveness constrains on the environment dynamics. So φ_D can be seen as denoting the set of traces that satisfy the (temporally extended) domain specifications D.

The general formula for a planning problem is of the form: $\varphi = \varphi_D \rightarrow \varphi_g$, which says that on the infinite runs where the environment acts as prescribed by φ_D the goal φ_g holds [3,10]. Note that φ does not mention strategies but only traces, so it is not very useful in isolation to solve planning, i.e., to show the existence of a plan/strategy that guarantees φ independently of the environment's behavior. To capture this, we are going to use second order quantification of QLTL$_B$. In all the formulas below, the blocks X are the fluents and blocks Y are the actions (coded in binary for simplicity).

Consider the QLTL$_B$ formula $\exists Y \forall X \varphi$. This is looking for an assignment of the actions Y such that for every assignment of the fluents X the resulting LTL formula φ holds. This formula captures *conformant planning* [18]. Note that the values of Y, i.e., the choice of actions at each point in time, do not depend on X. That is the plan (the Skolem function deciding Y) does not see the evolution of the fluents X. This is the reason why the plan is conformant. Note also that in this case the fact that X are assigned through a behavioral Skolem function or any Skolem function is irrelevant, since we do not see the values of X anyway when choosing the Skolem function for Y (i.e., the plan). So this form of planning could be captured through standard QLTL as well.

Consider the QLTL$_\text{B}$ formula $\forall X \exists Y \varphi$. This states that at every point in time for every value of the fluents X there exists an action Y such that the resulting trace satisfies φ. This captures *contingent planning with full observability*, i.e., (strong) planning in *Fully Observable Nondeterministic Domains (FOND)* [19, 26]. Here the fact that Y at the current instant may depend only on the past and current values of X of the behavioral semantics is critical. Otherwise the choices of action Y would depend on the future values of fluents X, that is, the plan would **not** be a process but would forecast the future, which is usually impossible in practice. Note that with QLTL$_\text{B}$ formulas of the form $\forall X \exists Y \psi$, where ψ is an arbitrary LTL formula, we capture LTL synthesis (for realizing the LTL specification ψ) [35].

Now consider the QLTL$_\text{B}$ formula $\forall X_1 \exists Y \forall X_2 \varphi$. It is similar to the previous one but now we have split the fluents X into X_1 and X_2 and the actions Y are allowed to depend on X_1 but not on X_2. In other words, the Skolem function for Y may depend on the previous and current values of X_1 but does **not** depend on the values of X_2. This captures *contingent planning with partial observability*, i.e., (strong) planning in *Partially Observable Nondeterministic Domains (POND)*, where some fluents are observable (X_1) and some are not (X_2), and indeed the plan can only depend on the observable ones [26,28]. Note that with QLTL$_\text{B}$ formulas of the from $\forall X_1 \exists Y \forall X_2 \psi$, where ψ is an arbitrary LTL formula, we capture synthesis under incomplete information (for realizing the LTL specification ψ) [30]. Notice also that we can indeed include fairness assumptions in φ_D and hence in φ, so with some care, see [4], the above two QLTL$_\text{B}$ formulas can capture also strong cyclic plans [20,26].

As we allow more quantifier nesting we get more and more sophisticated forms of planning. For example the QLTL$_\text{B}$ formula $\forall X_1 \exists Y_1 (\ldots) \forall X_n \exists Y_n \varphi$ captures a centralized planning for multiple plan actuators with hierarchically reduced partial observability, with the innermost plan actuator, controlling Y_n, solving a FOND planning instance. Similarly, $\forall X_1 \exists Y_1 (\ldots) \forall X_n \exists Y_n \forall X_{n+1} \varphi$ captures a centralized planning for multiple plan actuators with hierarchically reduced partial observability, with the innermost plan actuator, controlling Y_n, solving a POND planning instance. Instead, $\exists Y_1 \forall X_1 (\ldots) \exists Y_{n-1} \forall X_{n-1} \exists Y_n \varphi$ captures a centralized planning for multiple plan actuators with hierarchically reduced partial observability, with the outermost actuator, controlling Y_1, solving a conformant planning instance and the innermost, controlling Y_n, solving a FOND planning instance. Similarly, $\exists Y_1 \forall X_1 (\ldots) \exists Y_{n-1} \forall X_{n-1} \exists Y_n \forall X_n \varphi$ captures a centralized planning for multiple plan actuators with hierarchically reduced partial observability, with the outermost actuator, controlling Y_1, solving a conformant planning instance and the innermost, controlling Y_n, solving POND planning.

Note that, these last forms of planning have never been studied in detail in the AI literature. However the corresponding form of synthesis has indeed been investigated under the name of *distributed synthesis* [22,36]. Distributed synthesis concerns the coordination of a number of agents, each with partial observability on the environment and on the other agents, so as to enforce together an LTL formula. Several visibility architectures among agents have been considered, including those that allow for *information forks*, that is, situations in which two agents receive information from the environment in a way that they cannot completely deduce the information received by the other agent. In general distributed synthesis is undecidable [36]. However, it has been proven that the absence of information forks is sufficient to guarantee the decidability of synthesis [22]. Specifically, without information forks it is possible to arrange the agents in a sort of information hierarchy, which leads to decidability [22]. Incidentally, this is the form of uniform distributed synthesis that is captured by the above QLTL$_B$ formulas. Indeed we will show later that solving a distributed synthesis with hierarchical information architectures can be done optimally by reduction to QLTL$_B$ satisfiability of the formulas presented above.

6   QLTL$_B$ Properties

Clearly, since QLTL$_B$ shares the syntax with QLTL, all the definitions that involve syntactic elements, such as free variables and alternation, apply to this variant the same way. As for QLTL, the satisfiability of a QLTL$_B$ formula φ is equivalent to the one of $\exists \mathtt{free}(\varphi)\varphi$, as well as the validity is equivalent to the one of $\forall \mathtt{free}(\varphi)\varphi$. However, the proof is not as straightforward as for the classic semantics case.

Theorem 3. *For every* QLTL$_B$ *formula* $\varphi = \wp\psi$, φ *is satisfiable if, and only if,* $\exists \mathit{free}(\varphi)\varphi$ *is satisfiable. Moreover,* φ *is valid if, and only if,* $\forall \mathit{free}(\varphi)\varphi$ *is valid.*

Proof. We show the proof only for satisfiability, as the one for validity is similar. The proof proceeds by double implication.

From left to right, assume that φ is satisfiable, therefore there exists a trace π over $F = \mathtt{free}(\varphi)$ such that $\pi \models_B \varphi$, which in turns implies that there exists a behavioral Skolem function θ over $(\wp, F)$ such that $\hat{\theta}(\pi \uplus \pi') \models_C \psi$ for every trace $\pi' \in (2^{\forall(\wp)})^\omega$. Consider the function $\theta' : (2^{\forall(\wp)})^\omega \to (2^{\exists(\wp)\cup F})^\omega$ defined as $\theta'(\pi') = \theta(\pi \uplus \pi') \uplus \pi$, for every $\pi' \in (2^{\forall(\wp)})^\omega$. Clearly, it is a behavioral Skolem function over $(\exists F\wp, \emptyset)$ such that $\hat{\theta}'(\pi') \models_{LTL} \psi$ for every $\pi' \in (2^{\forall(\wp)})^\omega$, which implies that $\exists F\varphi$ is satisfiable.

From right to left, we have that $\exists F\varphi$ is satisfiable, which means that there exists a behavioral Skolem function θ over $(\exists F\varphi, \emptyset)$ such that $\hat{\theta}(\pi) \models_{LTL} \psi$ for every $\pi \in (2^{\forall(\wp)\cup\{F\}})^\omega$. Observe that $\mathtt{Dep}^F(F) = \emptyset$, and so that $\theta(\pi)(F) = \theta(\pi')(F) = \pi_F$ for every $\pi, \pi' \in (2^{\forall(\wp)})^\omega$. Thus, consider the behavioral Skolem function θ' over $(\wp, F)$ defined as $\theta'(\pi'_F \uplus \pi) = \theta(\pi_F \uplus \pi)$, for every $\pi'_F \in (2^F)^\omega$ and $\pi \in (2^{\forall(\wp)})^\omega$, from which it follows that $\theta'(\pi_F \cup \pi) \models_{LTL} \psi$ for every $\pi \in (2^{\forall(\wp)})^\omega$, from which we derive that $\pi_F \models_B \wp\psi$, and so that φ is satisfiable.

Note that every behavioral Skolem function is also a Skolem function. This means that a formula φ interpreted as QLTL$_B$ is true on π implies that the same formula is true on π also when it is interpreted as QLTL. The reverse, however, is not true, as we have seen this when discussing the satisfiability of the formula $\varphi = \forall x \exists y (y \leftrightarrow Gx)$. Indeed, we have.

Lemma 1. *For every* QLTL$_B$ *formula* φ *and every trace* π *over the set* $\mathbf{free}(\varphi)$ *of free variables, if* $\pi \models_B \varphi$ *then* $\pi \models_C \varphi$. *On the other hand, there exists a formula* φ *and a trace* π *such that* $\pi \models_C \varphi$ *but not* $\pi \models_B \varphi$.

7   QLTL$_B$ Satisfiability

There are three syntactic fragments for which QLTL and QLTL$_B$ are equivalent. Precisely, the fragments $\Pi_0^{\mathrm{QLTL_B}}$, $\Sigma_0^{\mathrm{QLTL_B}}$, and $\Sigma_1^{\mathrm{QLTL_B}}$. Recall that $\Pi_0^{\mathrm{QLTL_B}}$ formulas are of the form $\forall X \varphi_{\mathrm{LTL}}$, whereas $\Sigma_0^{\mathrm{QLTL_B}}$ formulas are of the form $\exists Y \varphi_{\mathrm{LTL}}$. Finally, $\Sigma_1^{\mathrm{QLTL_B}}$ formulas are of the form $\exists Y \forall X \varphi_{\mathrm{LTL}}$. The reason is that the sets of Skolem and behavioral Skolem functions for these formulas coincide, and so the existence of one implies the existence of the other.

Theorem 4. *For every* QLTL$_B$ *formula* $\varphi = \wp\psi$ *in the fragments* $\Pi_0^{\mathrm{QLTL_B}}$, $\Sigma_0^{\mathrm{QLTL_B}}$, *and* $\Sigma_1^{\mathrm{QLTL_B}}$ *and every trace* π, *it holds that* $\pi \models_B \varphi$ *if, and only if,* $\pi \models_C \varphi$.

Proof. The proof proceeds by double implication. From left to right, it follows from Lemma 1. From right to left, consider first the case that $\varphi \in \Pi_0^{\mathrm{QLTL}}$. Observe that $\exists(\wp) = \emptyset$ and so the only possible Skolem function θ returns the empty interpretation on every possible interpretation $\pi \uplus \pi' \in (2^{\mathbf{free}(\varphi) \cup \forall(\wp)})^\omega$. Such Skolem function is trivially behavioral and so we have that $\pi \models_S \varphi$ implies $\pi \models_B \varphi$.

For the case of $\varphi \in \Sigma_0^{\mathrm{QLTL}} \cup \Sigma_1^{\mathrm{QLTL}}$, assume that $\pi, \models_S \varphi$ and let θ be a Skolem function such that $\theta(\pi \uplus \pi') \models_C \varphi$ for every $\pi' \in (2^{\forall(\wp)})^\omega$. Observe that, for every $Y \in \exists(\wp)$, it holds that $\mathtt{Dep}_\wp = \emptyset$ and so the values of Y depend only on the free variables in φ. Now, consider the Skolem function θ' over $(\wp, \mathbf{free}(\varphi))$ defined such that as $\theta'(\pi') \doteq \theta(\pi'_{\restriction \forall(\wp)} \uplus \pi)$. As θ is a Skolem function and $\mathtt{Dep}_\wp = \emptyset$, it holds that $\theta'(\pi')(Y) = \theta'(\pi'')(Y)$ for every $\pi', \pi'' \in (2^{\forall(\wp)})^\omega$ and so θ' is trivially behavioral. Moreover, from its definition, it holds that $\theta'(\pi \uplus \pi') \models_C \psi$ for every $\pi' \in (2^{\forall(\wp)})^\omega$, which implies $\pi \models_B \varphi$.

Theorem 4 shows that for these three fragments of QLTL$_B$, satisfiability can be solved by employing QLTL satisfiability. This also comes with the same complexity, as we just interpret the QLTL$_B$ formula directly as QLTL one.

Corollary 1. *Satisfiability for the fragments* $\Pi_0^{\mathrm{QLTL_B}}$ *and* $\Sigma_0^{\mathrm{QLTL_B}}$ *is PSPACE-complete. Moreover, satisfiability for the fragment* $\Sigma_1^{\mathrm{QLTL_B}}$ *is EXPSPACE-complete.*

We now turn into solving satisfiability for QLTL$_B$ formulas that are not in fragments $\Pi_0^{\mathrm{QLTL_B}}$, $\Sigma_0^{\mathrm{QLTL_B}}$, and $\Sigma_1^{\mathrm{QLTL_B}}$. Analogously to the case of QLTL, note that Theorem 3 allows to restrict our attention to closed formulas. We use an automata-theoretic approach inspired by the one employed in the synthesis of distributed systems [22,31,38]. Details about this construction are available in the appendix. We have the following.

Theorem 5. *Satisfiability of* n-QLTL$_B$ *is* $(n+1)$-*EXPTIME-complete.*

We close this section by observing that the above techniques for solving QLTL$_B$ satisfiability give us optimal techniques to solve conformant planning, contingent planing in FOND and contingent planing in PONDs in the case of LTL goals. Indeed for conformant planning we have to solve a formula of the form $\exists Y \forall X \varphi$ which belongs to $\Sigma_1^{\mathrm{QLTL_B}}$ and can be solved in EXPSPACE. On the other hand conformant planning for LTL goals is EXPACE-complete [21]. contingent planning in FOND is captured by a formula of the form $\forall X \exists Y \varphi$ which can be solved in 2-EXPTIME. On the other hand planning in FOND for LTL goals is 2-EXPTIME-complete –by reduction to synthesis [35]. Similarly, contingent planning in POND is captured by a formula of the form $\forall X_1 \exists Y \forall X_2 \varphi$, which although more complex than in the previous case still contains only a single block of the form $\forall X_i \exists Y_i$, and hence can still be solved in 2-EXPTIME. On the other hand planning in POND for LTL goals is 2-EXPTIME-complete –by reduction to synthesis under incomplete information [30].

Note also that this result gives us an optimal technique for solving synthesis and planing in nondeterministic domains for LTL goals. Indeed the QLTL$_B$ formulas that capture them requires a single block of the form $\forall X_i \exists Y_i$, and hence satisfiability can be checked in 2-EXPTIME, thus matching the 2-EXPTIME-completeness of the two problems.

8 Conclusion

We introduced a behavioral variant of QLTL. Our variant, QLTL$_B$, is based on the following ingredients. First, it uses the syntax of QLTL. Secondly, it interprets the existential quantifications $\exists Y$ as functions from histories to the next value of Y, where the variables observed over the histories are controlled by the nesting of quantification. Third, satisfiability over this logic corresponds to advanced forms of reactive synthesis with partial observability.

Recently, independently of our work, QLTL has been at the base of a proposal that shares with us a strategic nature [8]. As witnessed by the complexity characterization of satisfiability in the two cases, respectively $(n + 1)$-EXPTIME-complete, with n being the number of quantification blocks in our case, and 2-EXPTIME-complete in [8], our proposal looks at more sophisticated forms of strategies, with respect to partial observability over the histories. Deeper understanding on the relationship between the two approaches deserves further investigation.

Acknowledgements. This work was supported by MUR under the PRIN programme, grant B87G22000450001 (PINPOINT), the ERC Advanced Grant White-Mech (No. 834228), by the EU ICT-48 2020 project TAILOR (No. 952215), by the PRIN project RIPER (No. 20203FFYLK), the JPMorgan AI Faculty Research Award "Resilience-based Generalized Planning and Strategic Reasoning", and PNRR MUR project PE0000013-FAIR.

References

1. Abadi, M., Lamport, L., Wolper, P.: Realizable and unrealizable specifications of reactive systems. In: Ausiello, G., Dezani-Ciancaglini, M., Della Rocca, S.R. (eds.) ICALP 1989. LNCS, vol. 372, pp. 1–17. Springer, Heidelberg (1989). https://doi.org/10.1007/BFb0035748
2. Alur, R., Henzinger, T., Kupferman, O.: Alternating-time temporal logic. JACM **49**(5), 672–713 (2002)
3. Aminof, B., De Giacomo, G., Murano, A., Rubin, S.: Planning under LTL environment specifications. In: ICAPS, pp. 31–39. AAAI Press (2019)
4. Aminof, B., De Giacomo, G., Rubin, S.: Stochastic fairness and language-theoretic fairness in planning in nondeterministic domains. In: ICAPS, pp. 20–28. AAAI Press (2020)
5. Bacchus, F., Kabanza, F.: Planning for temporally extended goals. Ann. Math. Artif. Intell. **22**(1–2), 5–27 (1998)
6. Bacchus, F., Kabanza, F.: Using temporal logics to express search control knowledge for planning. Artif. Intell. **116**(1–2), 123–191 (2000)
7. Barringer, H., Fisher, M., Gabbay, D.M., Gough, G., Owens, R.: METATEM: an introduction. Formal Aspects Comput. **7**(5), 533–549 (1995)
8. Bellier, D., Benerecetti, M., Monica, D.D., Mogavero, F.: Good-for-game QPTL: an alternating hodges semantics. ACM Trans. Comput. Log. **24**(1), 4:1–4:57 (2023)
9. Bertoli, P., Cimatti, A., Roveri, M.: Heuristic search + symbolic model checking = efficient conformant planning. In: IJCAI 2001, pp. 467–472 (2001)
10. Calvanese, D., De Giacomo, G., Vardi, M.Y.: Reasoning about actions and planning in LTL action theories. In: KR 2002, pp. 593–602 (2002)
11. Camacho, A., Bienvenu, M., McIlraith, S.A.: Towards a unified view of AI planning and reactive synthesis. In: ICAPS 2019, pp. 58–67 (2019)
12. Cerrito, S., Mayer, M.C.: Bounded model search in linear temporal logic and its application to planning. In: de Swart, H. (ed.) TABLEAUX 1998. LNCS (LNAI), vol. 1397, pp. 124–140. Springer, Heidelberg (1998). https://doi.org/10.1007/3-540-69778-0_18
13. Chatterjee, K., Henzinger, T.A.: Assume-guarantee synthesis. In: Grumberg, O., Huth, M. (eds.) TACAS 2007. LNCS, vol. 4424, pp. 261–275. Springer, Heidelberg (2007). https://doi.org/10.1007/978-3-540-71209-1_21
14. Chatterjee, K., Henzinger, T.A., Jobstmann, B.: Environment assumptions for synthesis. In: van Breugel, F., Chechik, M. (eds.) CONCUR 2008. LNCS, vol. 5201, pp. 147–161. Springer, Heidelberg (2008). https://doi.org/10.1007/978-3-540-85361-9_14
15. Chatterjee, K., Henzinger, T.A., Piterman, N.: Strategy logic. Inf. Comput. **208**(6), 677–693 (2010). https://doi.org/10.1016/j.ic.2009.07.004
16. Church, A.: Logic, arithmetics, and automata. In: 1962 Proceedings of the International Congress of Mathematicians, pp. 23–35 (1963)
17. Cimatti, A., Giunchiglia, E., Giunchiglia, F., Traverso, P.: Planning via model checking: a decision procedure for AR. In: Steel, S., Alami, R. (eds.) ECP 1997. LNCS, vol. 1348, pp. 130–142. Springer, Heidelberg (1997). https://doi.org/10.1007/3-540-63912-8_81
18. Cimatti, A., Roveri, M.: Conformant planning via symbolic model checking. J. Artif. Intell. Res. **13**, 305–338 (2000)
19. Cimatti, A., Roveri, M., Traverso, P.: Strong planning in non-deterministic domains via model checking. In: AIPS, pp. 36–43. AAAI (1998)

20. Daniele, M., Traverso, P., Vardi, M.Y.: Strong cyclic planning revisited. In: Biundo, S., Fox, M. (eds.) ECP 1999. LNCS (LNAI), vol. 1809, pp. 35–48. Springer, Heidelberg (2000). https://doi.org/10.1007/10720246_3
21. De Giacomo, G., Vardi, M.Y.: Automata-theoretic approach to planning for temporally extended goals. In: Biundo, S., Fox, M. (eds.) ECP 1999. LNCS (LNAI), vol. 1809, pp. 226–238. Springer, Heidelberg (2000). https://doi.org/10.1007/10720246_18
22. Finkbeiner, B., Schewe, S.: Uniform distributed synthesis. In: LICS 2005, pp. 321–330 (2005)
23. Gabbay, D.M., Pnueli, A., Shelah, S., Stavi, J.: On the temporal basis of fairness. In: Abrahams, P.W., Lipton, R.J., Bourne, S.R. (eds.) POPL 1980, pp. 163–173 (1980)
24. Gardy, P., Bouyer, P., Markey, N.: Dependences in strategy logic. In: STACS 2018, LIPIcs, vol. 96, pp. 34:1–34:15 (2018)
25. Gardy, P., Bouyer, P., Markey, N.: Dependences in strategy logic. Theory Comput. Syst. **64**(3), 467–507 (2020)
26. Geffner, H., Bonet, B.: A Concise Introduction to Models and Methods for Automated Planning. Morgan & Claypool, San Rafael (2013)
27. Ghallab, M., Nau, D.S., Traverso, P.: Automated Planning - Theory and Practice, 1st edn., p. 635. Elsevier, Amsterdam (2004)
28. Goldman, R.P., Boddy, M.S.: Expressive planning and explicit knowledge. In: Proceedings of AIPS (1996)
29. Green, C.C.: Application of theorem proving to problem solving. In: IJCAI 1969, pp. 219–240 (1969)
30. Kupferman, O., Vardi, M.Y.: Synthesis with incomplete informatio. In: Barringer, H., Fisher, M., Gabbay, D., Gough, G. (eds.) Advances in Temporal Logic. Applied Logic Series, vol. 16, pp. 109–127. Springer, Dordrecht (2000). https://doi.org/10.1007/978-94-015-9586-5_6
31. Kupferman, O., Vardi, M.Y.: Synthesizing distributed systems. In: LICS 2001. pp. 389–398 (2001)
32. Mogavero, F., Murano, A., Perelli, G., Vardi, M.: Reasoning about strategies: on the model-checking problem. ACM TOCL **15**(4), 34:1–34:47 (2014)
33. Fijalkow, N., Maubert, B., Murano, A., Rubin, S., Vardi, M.Y.: Public and private affairs in strategic reasoning. In: Kern-Isberner, G., Lakemeyer, G., Meyer, T. (eds.) KR 2022 (2022). https://proceedings.kr.org/2022/14/
34. Pnueli, A.: The temporal logic of programs. In: FOCS-77, pp. 46–57 (1977)
35. Pnueli, A., Rosner, R.: On the synthesis of a reactive module. In: POPL, pp. 179–190. ACM (1989)
36. Pnueli, A., Rosner, R.: Distributed reactive systems are hard to synthesize. In: FOCS 1990, pp. 746–757 (1990)
37. Rintanen, J.: Complexity of planning with partial observability. In: ICAPS 2004, pp. 345–354 (2004)
38. Schewe, S.: Synthesis of distributed systems. Ph.D. thesis, Saarland University, Saarbrücken, Germany (2008)
39. Sistla, A., Vardi, M., Wolper, P.: The complementation problem for Büchi automata with applications to temporal logic. TCS **49**, 217–237 (1987)
40. Sistla, A.P.: Theoretical issues in the design and verification of distributed systems. Ph.D. thesis (1985)
41. Thomas, W.: Languages, automata, and logic. In: Rozenberg, G., Salomaa, A. (eds.) Handbook of Formal Languages, pp. 389–455. Springer, Heidelberg (1997). https://doi.org/10.1007/978-3-642-59126-6_7

Lorenzen-Style Strategies as Proof-Search Strategies

Matteo Acclavio[1(✉)] and Davide Catta[2]

[1] University of Southern Denmark, Odense, Denmark
acclavio@imada.sdu.dk
[2] Università degli studi di Napoli, Federico II, Naples, Italy

Abstract. Dialogical logic, originated in the work of Lorenzen and his student Lorenz, is an approach to logic in which the validity of a certain formula is defined as the existence of a winning strategy for a particular kind of turn-based two-players games. This paper studies the relationship between winning strategies for Lorenzen-style dialogical games and sequent calculus derivations. We define three different classes of dialogical logic games for the implicational fragment of intuitionistic logic, showing that winning strategies for such games naturally correspond to classes of derivations defined by uniformly restraining the rules of the sequent calculus.

Keywords: Dialogical Logic · Sequent Calculus · Game Semantics

1 Introduction

Dialogical logic is an approach to the study of logical reasoning, introduced by Lorenzen and his student Lorenz [21,22], in which the validity of a formula is defined as the existence of a winning strategy for a turn-based two-player game. These games are articulated as argumentative dialogues in which the *Proponent* player **P** (she/her) aims at showing that a given formula is valid, while the *Opponent* player **O** (he/him) aims at finding possible fallacies disproving it. More precisely, each play starts with **P** asserting a certain formula. **O** takes his turn and attacks the claim made by **P** according to its logical form. The player **P** can, either, defend his previous claim or counter-attack. The debate evolves following this pattern. The player **P** wins whenever she has the last word, i.e., when **O** cannot attack anymore without violating the game's rules.

Dialogical logic was initially conceived as a foundation for the meaning of the connectives and quantifiers of *intuitionistic logic*, and it has gradually become detached from its connection with intuitionism over the years, becoming a subject of research in philosophical logic [5,10,23,28], in the formal semantics of natural language [8,9], in proof theory [3,13,14,17,25,29,30] and inspiring a series of work in formal argumentation theory and multi-agent systems [6,20,24,26,27]. In proof theory, the soundness and completeness of a dialogical system is proved by establishing the equivalence between the existence of a winning strategy in specific games and the notion of validity in a given logic. This result is typically attained by defining a procedure that reconstructs a formal derivation from a winning strategy (and vice versa) in a sound and complete system for a given logic [3,12,13]. In this paper, we study the correspondence between

V. Malvone and A. Murano (Eds.): EUMAS 2023, LNAI 14282, pp. 150–166, 2023.
https://doi.org/10.1007/978-3-031-43264-4_10

certain classes of winning strategies for a given dialogic system and the structure of the corresponding formal derivations in the sequent calculus. We study winning strategies in which **P** moves are restricted according to **O** precedent moves (e.g., if **O** plays a move $A \rightarrow B$ as a response to a move of **P** of a special kind, then the **P** has to immediately reply to this move). We prove that for each of the classes of winning strategies we consider, we have a correspondence with a proof-search strategy in the sequent calculus GKi for the $\rightarrow$-fragment of intuitionistic logic [33]. This latter result is obtained by showing that it is possible to narrow the proof-search space in sequent calculus without losing the soundness and completeness of the sequent system (as, e.g., in focusing [4]) and that there is a straightforward correspondence between such focused proofs and winning strategies.

This work shows how interesting results on the combinatorics of proofs can be obtained using dialogic logic, whose methods are not as well known as the ones from more widely used proof systems such as analytic tableaux, sequent calculus and natural deduction. In fact, certain intuitive restrictions on the behavior of the players in dialogical games allows us to express proof search strategies allowing us to reduce the proof search space, without requiring convoluted definitions in sequent calculus. The techniques developed in this work pave the way for further investigations on the use of dialogical logic methods in designing proof systems with restricted research space.

Related Work. Various definitions of Lorenzen-style dialogue games have been proposed over the years; the definitions that have a more direct relevance to our work are those of *Felscher's E-dialogues* [12] and *Fermüller's E-dialogues* [3,13]. In an E-dialogue, each **O** move is either a challenge to the immediately preceding **P** move or a defense from it. In Felscher's E-dialogues there are no challenges directed toward atomic formulas, and **P** cannot assert an atomic formula unless **O** has already asserted it. On the contrary, in Fermüller's E-dialogue atomic formulas can be attacked, but only by **O** and both players can freely assert them without restrictions. In our definition, we choose a hybrid approach in which **P** can assert an atomic proposition freely as long as that assertion is a challenge against a previous **O** assertion, and in which **P** cannot assert an atomic proposition as a defense to a previous attack unless that proposition has already been asserted by **O**. The assertion of an atomic proposition can be attacked, but only by **O** and only if that assertion is a challenge.

Herbelin noted the formal correspondence between winning strategies for dialogical games and sequent calculus focusing proofs in his doctoral dissertation [17]. In the fifth chapter of the dissertation, Herbelin shows that winning strategies for E-dialogues (defined by Felscher in [12]), are in bijective correspondence with proofs of the LGQ sequent calculus. Herbelin's technique to transform winning strategies into sequent calculus proofs is very elegant and will be used by us (with slight modifications) to achieve the same result.

Another work that, in spirit, is closer to ours is the one presented by Stitch in [30]. In this work, the author studies a multi-agents variant of dialogical logic games. Such games are turn-based games in which a *coalition* of Proponents plays against an Opponent: when it is their turn, each of the Proponent can make a different move. The play is won by the Proponents if the Opponent cannot react to any of the Proponents's moves of the previous round. Stitch shows that Proponents winning strategies for such games correspond to derivations in a multi-conclusion variant of the already cited LGQ sequent calculus. Plays are formalized by Stitch as paths in a peculiar sequent calculus, and strategies as derivations of this sequent calculus. While there may be some similarities between Stitch's works and ours, it is essential to note the significant differences in the details. We here consider "traditional" dialogical games played by two players, and we obtain the correspondence with restricted sequent calculus proof by restricting the way in which the Proponent can play in a game. Moreover, we show how to transform winning strategies into derivations (and vice versa) directly without the need of defining an ad-hoc sequent calculus formalism.

Outline of the Paper. The paper is organized as follows: in Sect. 2 we state definitions on dialogical logic, defining different classes of plays and strategies. In Sect. 3 we introduce different sequent calculi for intuitionistic logic, obtained by restricting the rules of the sequent calculus GKi [33]. In Sect. 4 we show how to sequentialize winning strategy, that is, how to define a sequent calculus derivation associated to a given winning strategy, and we prove the correspondence between classes of winning strategies and classes of GKi derivations. In Sect. 5 we show the converse. In Sect. 6 we discuss the obtained results and future works.

2 Dialogical Logic

In this section we fix the notation and terminology, as well as the formal definitions on dialogical logic we use in this paper.

2.1 Notation and Terminology

We denote by $|\sigma|$ the **length** of a countable[1] **sequence** $\sigma = \sigma_1, \sigma_2, \dots$, by $\sigma_{\leq i}$ the **prefix** $\sigma_1, \dots, \sigma_i$. The **parity** of an element σ_i in σ is the parity of i. It is **even** or **odd** iff i is. Given two sequences σ and τ, we write $\sigma \sqsubseteq \tau$ if $\sigma = \tau_{\leq i}$ for a given $i \leq |\tau|$ and we denote by $\sigma \cdot \tau$ their concatenation.

A *tree* $\mathcal{T} = \langle \mathcal{N}, \mathcal{E} \rangle$ is a connected directed graph with a countable set of **nodes** $\mathcal{N}$ containing a special node $r \in \mathcal{N}$ called **root**, and such that the set of **edges** $\mathcal{E} \subset \mathcal{N} \times \mathcal{N}$ contains a unique edge $\langle x, y \rangle$ for every non-root node $y \in \mathcal{N}$. If $\langle x, y \rangle \in \mathcal{E}$, we say that x is the **parent** of y and that y is a **child** of x. A **path** (in $\mathcal{T}$) is a sequence of nodes $\mathcal{P} = x_1, x_2 \dots$ such that x_1 is the root of $\mathcal{T}$ and x_{i+1} is a child of x_i for all $i > 0$.

A **branch** is a maximal path. Given two nodes x and y, x is an **ancestor** of y and y is a **descendant** of x if there is a path containing x whose last element is y (note that every node is an ancestor and a descendant of itself). The **height** $|x|$ of a node x is the length of the (unique) path from the root to x. Thus, the root has height 1, a child of the root has height 2 and so on. The **height** of a tree is the maximal height of its nodes.

In this paper we consider **formulas** generated from a countable non-empty set of atomic propositions $\mathcal{A} = \{a, b, c, \dots\}$ and the implication connective $\rightarrow$ (and the parenthesis symbols). In the following, we may write $(A_1 \cdots A_n) \rightarrow c$ as a shortcut for

---

[1] We use the adjective *countable* in the standard mathematical sense: a set is countable iff it is in a one-to-one correspondence with a (finite or infinite) subset of the set of natural numbers.

$A_1 \to (\cdots \to (A_n \to c)\cdots)$. We consider the **implication fragments of intuition-istic logic** $\mathsf{IL}^\to$, defined as the smallest set of formulas containing each instance of the two axioms $A \to (B \to A)$ and $A \to (B \to C) \to ((A \to B) \to (A \to C))$ and closed for **modus ponens**, that is: if $A \in \mathsf{IL}^\to$ and $A \to B \in \mathsf{IL}^\to$ then $B \in \mathsf{IL}^\to$. We say that a formula F is **valild** if and only if $F \in \mathsf{IL}^{\to 2}$.

2.2 Dialogical Games

A **challenge** is a pair $\langle ?, s \rangle$ where s is either an occurrence of the symbol $\bullet$, in which case such a challenge is said **atomic**, or where s is formula F. A **defense** is a pair $\langle !, F \rangle$ where F is a formula. An **assertion (of F)** is a non-atomic challenge $\langle ?, F \rangle$ or a defense $\langle !, F \rangle$. A **move** is an assertion or an atomic-challenge. An **augmented sequence** is a pair $\langle \sigma, \phi \rangle$ where σ is a non-empty sequence of moves, and ϕ is a function mapping any σ_i with $i > 1$ to a $\sigma_j = \phi(\sigma_i)$ with opposite parity and such that $j < i$. A move σ_i in σ is called **P-move** (denoted σ_i^P) if i is odd, and **O-move** (denoted σ_i^O) if i is even. It is a **repetition** if there is $j < i$ such that i and j have opposite parity and σ_i and σ_j are assertions of the same formula.

Definition 1. *Let $\langle \sigma, \phi \rangle$ be an augmented sequence and $i \le |\sigma|$.*

*1. A challenge σ_i is **justified** whenever:*
   (a) either σ_i is an atomic-challenge and $\phi(\sigma_i)$ is an assertion of an atomic formula;
   (b) or $\sigma_i = \langle ?, A \rangle$ and $\phi(\sigma_i)$ is an assertion of a formula $A \to B$.
*2. A defense is σ_i is **justified** whenever:*
   (a) either σ_i and $\phi(\phi(\sigma_i))$ are assertions of a same atomic formula $a \in \mathcal{A}$ and $\phi(\sigma_i)$ is an atomic challenge;
   (b) or σ_i is an assertion of a formula B, $\phi(\sigma_i)$ is a justified challenge of the form $\langle ?, A \rangle$, and $\phi(\phi(\sigma_i))$ is an assertion of $A \to B$.

*If σ_i is a justified move, we say $\phi(\sigma_i)$ **justifies** σ_i and that σ_i **is justified** by $\phi(\sigma_i)$. A challenge σ_i is **unanswered** if there is no defense σ_k such that σ_k is justified by σ_i. A justified challenge σ_i is a **counterattack** if $\phi(\sigma_i)$ is a challenge. A **justified sequence** is an augmented sequence in which any move except the first one is justified.*

Definition 2 (Play). *A play for F is a justified sequence $\mathsf{p} = \langle \sigma, \phi \rangle$ starting with $\mathbf{P}$ defending F, that is, $\sigma_1 = \langle !, F \rangle$ and such that the following holds for any $1 < i \le |\sigma|$:*

*1. each **O**-move is justified by the immediately preceding **P**-move, that is, $\phi(\sigma_{2k}) = \sigma_{2k-1}$ for any $2k \le |\sigma|$;*
*2. each **P**-move (but the first) is justified by some preceding **O**-move. In particular, if $\mathbf{P}$ states a defense, such defense is justified by the last unanswered challenge stated by $\mathbf{O}$, that is, if $\sigma_{2k+1} = \langle !, F \rangle$, then $\phi(\sigma_{2k+1}) = \sigma_{2h}$ is the unanswered challenge with maximal $2h \le 2k$;*
3. if $\mathbf{P}$ state a defense and such a defense is an assertion of an atomic formula, then there must be another preceding $\mathbf{O}$ assertion of the same atomic formula. That is, if $\sigma_{2k+1} = \langle !, a \rangle$ with $a \in \mathcal{A}$, then σ_{2k+1} is a repetition;

---

[2] This definition of validity corresponds to the standard one i.e., valid in every Kripke model whose accessibility relation is a preorder and whose labeling is monotone. See e.g. [15,32].

4. *Only* **O** *can challenge assertions of atomic formulas and these assertions must be challenges. That is, if* $\sigma_i = \langle ?, \bullet \rangle$, *then i must be even and* $\phi(\sigma_i)$ *is a challenge.*

A play $\mathsf{p} = \langle \sigma, \phi \rangle$ *is finite if* σ *is. and its* **length** $|\mathsf{p}|$ *is the length* σ. *A move m is* **legal** *for* p *if* $\langle \sigma \cdot m, \phi \cup \{\langle m, \sigma_i \rangle\}\rangle$ *is a play for a* $i \leq |\sigma|$.

Definition 3 (Winning Condition). *The player* **P** *wins* *a play* $\mathsf{p} = \langle \sigma, \phi \rangle$ *if* σ *is finite and ends with a* **P**-*move* $\langle !, a \rangle$ *with* $a \in \mathcal{A}$. *Otherwise,* **O** *wins.*

We now define two particular types of plays: *Lorenzen-Felscher* plays, and *Stubborn* plays. In Lorenzen-Felscher plays **P** can assert an atomic formula only if **O** has already asserted it. In Stubborn plays once **P** starts challenging an assertion of a complex formula B, she will stubbornly continue to challenge the subformulas of that formula until **O** asserts an atomic formula.

Definition 4. *Let* $\mathsf{p} = \langle \sigma, \phi \rangle$ *be a play.*

1. p *is a* **Lorenzen-Felscher play** *(or* LF-*play) if any* **P**-*assertion of an atomic formula is a repetition. That is, if* $\sigma_{2k+1} \in \{\langle !, a \rangle, \langle ?, a \rangle \mid a \in \mathcal{A}\}$, *then there is* $h \leq k$ *such that* $\sigma_{2h} = \pm \langle \star, a \rangle$ *for* $\star \in \{?, !\}$
2. p *is a* **Stubborn play** *(or* ST-*play) if the following hold:*
   (a) *whenever* **O** *assert a complex formula* $A \to B$ *as a defense from a preceding challenge, then* **P**'s *next move is a challenge of such a formula. That is, if* $\sigma' \cdot m^{\mathbf{O}} \sqsubseteq \sigma$ *and* $m = \langle !, A \to B \rangle$, *then* $\sigma' \cdot m^{\mathbf{O}} \cdot n^{\mathbf{P}} \sqsubseteq \sigma$ *for a* $n = \langle ?, A \rangle$ *justified by* m.
   (b) *whenever* **O** *assert an atomic formula* c *as a defense from a preceding challenge, then* **P**'s *next move is a defense asserting* c. *That is, if* $\sigma' \cdot m^{\mathbf{O}} \sqsubseteq \sigma$ *and* $m = \langle !, c \rangle$, *then* $\sigma = \sigma' \cdot m^{\mathbf{O}} \cdot n^{\mathbf{P}}$ *where* $n = \langle !, c \rangle$.

Example 1. Consider the two following plays (both won by **P**). We represent a play $\langle \sigma, \phi \rangle$ as a sequence of moves. We represent the function ϕ by drawing directed edges from each move σ_i to the move $\phi(\sigma_i)$.

$p_1^{\mathbf{P}} = \langle !, a \to b \to ((b \to c) \to (a \to c)) \rangle$

$p_2^{\mathbf{O}} = \langle ?, a \to b \rangle$

$p_3^{\mathbf{P}} = \langle !, (b \to c) \to (a \to c) \rangle$

$p_4^{\mathbf{O}} = \langle ?, b \to c \rangle$

$p_5^{\mathbf{P}} = \langle !, a \to c \rangle$

$p_6^{\mathbf{O}} = \langle ?, a \rangle$

$p_7^{\mathbf{P}} = \langle ?, a \rangle$

$p_8^{\mathbf{O}} = \langle !, b \rangle$

$p_9^{\mathbf{P}} = \langle ?, b \rangle$

$p_{10}^{\mathbf{O}} = \langle !, c \rangle$

$p_{11}^{\mathbf{P}} = \langle !, c \rangle$

$p_1^{\mathbf{P}} = \langle !, a \to b \to ((b \to c) \to (a \to c)) \rangle$

$p_2^{\mathbf{O}} = \langle ?, a \to b \rangle$

$p_3^{\mathbf{P}} = \langle !, b \to c \to a \to c \rangle$

$p_4^{\mathbf{O}} = \langle ?, b \to c \rangle$

$p_5^{\mathbf{P}} = \langle !, a \to c \rangle$

$p_6^{\mathbf{O}} = \langle ?, a \rangle$

$p_7^{\mathbf{P}} = \langle ?, b \rangle$

$p_8^{\mathbf{O}} = \langle ?, \bullet \rangle$

$p_9^{\mathbf{P}} = \langle ?, a \rangle$

$p_{10}^{\mathbf{O}} = \langle !, b \rangle$

$p_{11}^{\mathbf{P}} = \langle !, b \rangle$

The play on the left is LF-play that is not a ST-play, while the one on the right is ST-play that is not an LF-play. Remark that each atomic challenge $\langle ?, \bullet \rangle$ is an **O**-move, and it is justified by a **P**-challenge asserting an atomic formula.

Definition 5. *Let A be a formula. The **game** for A is a pair $\mathcal{G}_A = \langle \mathcal{R}_A, \phi_A \rangle$ where $\mathcal{R}_A = \langle N_A, \mathcal{E}_A \rangle$ is a tree of moves and $\phi : N_A \to N_A$ is a map such that:*

1. *for each path $\mathcal{P}$ of $\mathcal{R}_A$, the pair $\langle \mathcal{P}, \phi_A|_{\mathcal{P}} \rangle$ is a play for A;*
2. *for each node v of $\mathcal{R}_A$, all and only the children of v are legal move of the play in $\mathcal{G}_A$ ending with v.*

*A node v of $\mathcal{G}$ is a **P-node** (resp. **O-node**) if is its height is odd (resp. even).*

   *A **strategy** for A is a pair $\mathcal{S} = \langle \mathcal{T}, \psi \rangle$ such that $\mathcal{T}$ is a subtree of $\mathcal{R}_A$ (and ψ is defined as the restriction of ϕ_A on the nodes in $\mathcal{T}$) in which every **O**-node has at most one child. It is **winning** when $\mathcal{T}$ is finite and any of its branch is a play won by **P**. A **Lorenzen-Felscher strategy** (resp. **Stubborn strategy**) is a strategy such that each branch of $\mathcal{S}$ is a LF-play (resp. a ST-play).*

Example 2. Below we provide a representation of Lorenzen-Felscher winning strategy (left) and of a winning Stubborn strategy (right) for the formula $a \to b \to ((b \to c) \to (a \to c))$ as tree of moves. As in Example 1 we represent the function ϕ by drawing directed edges from each move σ_i to the move $\phi(\sigma_i)$. However, we here we omit the edges with source an **O**-move because $\phi(\sigma_{2k+2}) = \sigma_{2k+1}$ for all $k \in \mathbb{N}$.

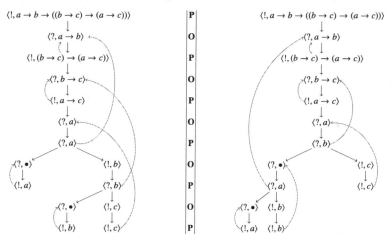

3   Sequent Calculus

In this section, we recall the definition of the sequent calculus GKi from [33] which is sound and complete for the logic $\mathsf{IL}^{\to}$. We then provide three classes of derivations obtained by imposing restrictions on rules applications, and we show that they are still sound and complete with respect to the same logic.

   A **sequent** is an expression $\Gamma \vdash C$ where C is a formula and Γ is a finite (possibly empty) multiset of formulas. A derivation $\mathscr{D}$ is a finite tree of sequents constructed using the rules in Fig. 1 in which each leaf is obtained by an Ax-rule and each non-leaf sequent is obtained by $\to^{\mathsf{R}}$-rule or a $\to^{\mathsf{L}}$-rule. A sequent $\Gamma \vdash C$ is GKi-provable if it admits a derivation in the sequent calculus GKi, whose root (or conclusion) is $\Gamma \vdash C$.

$$\frac{}{\Gamma,\underline{a} \vdash a} \; Ax \qquad \frac{\Gamma, A \to B \vdash \underline{A} \quad \Gamma, A \to B, \underline{B} \vdash C}{\Gamma, \underline{A \to B} \vdash C} \to^L \qquad \frac{\Gamma, \underline{A} \vdash B}{\Gamma \vdash \underline{A \to B}} \to^R$$

Fig. 1. Rules for the sequent calculus GKi. In each rule we have underlined its **principal** formula in the conclusion, and the **active** formulas in each premise.

Theorem 1 [33]. *The sequent calculus* GKi *is sound and complete for* IL$^\to$, *that is a formula F is valid if and only if $\vdash$ F is provable in* GKi.

We characterize derivations according to their shape.

Definition 6. *Let $\mathscr{D}$ be a derivation of some sequent $\Delta \vdash F$ in* GKi. *We say that:*

1. *$\mathscr{D}$ is a **strategic derivation** (or **S-derivation**) when each left-hand side premise of $\to^L$-rule of the form $\Gamma \vdash A \to B$ is the conclusion of a $\to^R$-rule;*
2. *$\mathscr{D}$ is a **LF-derivation** if the left-hand side premise of each $\to^L$-rule is always the conclusion of a $\to^R$-rule or an Ax-rule;*
3. *$\mathscr{D}$ is a **ST-derivation** if is a S-derivation and the active formula of the right-hand premise of each $\to^L$-rule in $\mathscr{D}$ is the principal formula of this premise. That is, if $\Gamma, A \to B, B \vdash C$ is the right-hand premise of a $\to^L$-rule, then either it is the conclusion of a Ax if $B = C$ is atomic, or it is the conclusion of a $\to^L$-rule. In both cases B is the principal formula of $\Gamma, A \to B, B \vdash C$*

Remark 1. Every **LF**-derivation is a **S**-derivation by definition. If a sequent $\Gamma \vdash C$ occurs in a **S**-derivation $\mathscr{D}$ as conclusion of a $\to^L$-rule and as left-hand premise of (another) $\to^L$-rule with principal formula $A \to B$, then $A = C$ and A is an atomic formula. Similarly, if a sequent $\Gamma, A \to B, B \vdash C$ is the right-hand premise of $\to^L$-rule in a **ST**-derivation, then C is atomic.

LF-derivations were introduced by Herbelin in the fifth chapter of his PhD thesis (where they are called **LGQ**-derivations [17]). Similarly, **ST**-derivations are a variant of derivations in the sequent calculus LJT, also introduced by Herbelin in [16]. The only difference is that the sequent calculus LJT contains an explicit contraction rule and operates over sequents of the form $\Gamma; A \vdash C$ or $\Gamma; \emptyset \vdash C$ with Γ set of formula occurences, and A and C formulas. The following lemma will prove useful later on.

Lemma 1 (Weakening admissibility). *If a sequent $\Gamma \vdash C$ admits an **ST**-derivation, then there is a **ST**-derivation $\mathscr{D}^\star$ of the sequent $\Gamma, \Delta \vdash C$ for any finite multiset Δ. Moreover, $\mathscr{D}^\star$ contains the same rules of $\mathscr{D}$ (with the same principal and active formulas).*

Proof. It suffices to consider the derivation $\mathscr{D}^\star$ obtained by adding Δ to any leaf of $\mathscr{D}$.

Since the sequent calculus GKi is a sound and complete with respect to IL$^\to$, we can prove that the set of **S**-derivations and the set of **LF**-derivations are also sound and complete with respect to IL$^\to$.

Theorem 2. *Let $\Gamma \vdash C$ be a sequent. It is* GKi-*provable iff it admits a **S**-derivation iff it admits a **LF**-derivation.*

Proof. The fact that any GKi-provable sequents admits a **LF**-derivation has been proved in [7]. We conclude since any **LF**-derivation is a **S**-derivation and any **S**-derivation is a derivation in GKi.

3.1   Games on Hyland-Ong Arenas

In order to prove that also the set of **ST**-derivations are sound and complete for $IL^\rightarrow$, we establish a correspondence between *winning innocent strategies* for games on Hyland-Ong Arenas [19] and **ST**-derivations. We then conclude by levering on the result of soundness and (full-)completeness of these winning strategies with respect to $IL^\rightarrow$.

Note 1. Both games in dialogical logic and game on Hyland-Ong arenas formalize proofs as winning strategies over games defined by a formula F. However, some terminology in these two paradigms identify objects of different nature. For this reason, we here list the main differences.

Dialogical Logic	Games on Hyland-Ong arenas
a play $\sigma_1, \sigma_2, \ldots$ starts $i = 1$ odd	a play $\tau_0, \tau_1, \ldots$ starts $i = 0$ even
a play starts with a **P**-move	a play starts with a **O**-move
a move is a subformula of F plus a polarity	a move corresponds to an atom in F

To facilitate distinguishing as much as possible the two formalisms, in games over Hyland-Ong arenas we denote the proponent **P** by • the opponent **O** by ∘.

Definition 7. *A **sink** of a directed acyclic graph $G = \langle V, \rightarrow \rangle$ is a vertex v such that $\langle v, w \rangle \notin \rightarrow$ for no $w \in V$. The **arena** of a formula F is the $\mathcal{A}$-labeled directed acyclic graph $[\![F]\!] = \langle V_{[\![F]\!]}, \overset{[\![F]\!]}{\rightarrow}, \ell \rangle$ (where $\langle V_{[\![F]\!]}, \overset{[\![F]\!]}{\rightarrow} \rangle$ is a directed acyclic graph, and ℓ a labeling function associating to each $v \in V_{[}[\![F]\!]]$ an atom $\ell(v) \in \mathcal{A}$) defined as follows:*

$$[\![a]\!] = \langle \{v\}, \emptyset, \ell(v) = a \rangle \quad \text{and} \quad [\![A \rightarrow B]\!] = \langle V_{[\![A]\!]} \cup V_{[\![B]\!]}, \overset{[\![A]\!]}{\rightarrow} \cup \overset{[\![B]\!]}{\rightarrow} \cup I, \ell_{[\![A]\!]} \cup \ell_{[\![B]\!]} \rangle$$

*with $I = \{(s_{[\![A]\!]}, s_{[\![B]\!]})\}$ where $s_{[\![A]\!]}$ and $s_{[\![B]\!]}$ are the unique (by construction) sink of $[\![A]\!]$ and $[\![B]\!]$ respectively. The **arena** of a sequent $A_1, \ldots, A_n \vdash B$ is defined as the arena $[\![(A_1 \cdots A_n) \rightarrow B]\!]$.*

Definition 8. *Let F be a formula. A **justified sequence** for F is a pair $\langle \tau, f \rangle$ where $\tau = \tau_0, \ldots, \tau_n$ is a non-empty sequence of **moves** (i.e., occurrences of vertices of $[\![F]\!]$), and f is a function mapping each τ_i with $i > 0$ in its **justifier** $f(\tau_i) = \tau_j$ for a $j < i$ such that $i + j$ is odd (i.e. if i is even, then j is odd and vice versa).*

*The **pointer** of a move τ_i with $i > 0$ is the pair $\langle \tau_i, f(\tau_i) \rangle$; we identify f with the set of pointers it defines. A move τ_i is a ∘-move (resp. •-move) if i is even (resp. i is odd).*

*A **view** is a justified sequence $\langle \tau, f \rangle$ such that:*

– *it is a **play**, that is, the initial move τ_0 is the sink of $[\![F]\!]$;*
– *it is ∘-**shortsighted**, that is, $f(\tau_i) = \tau_{i-1}$ for each non-initial ∘-move τ_i;*
– *it is •-**uniform**, that is, $\ell(\tau_i) = \ell(\tau_{i-1})$ for each •-move τ_i.*

Remark 2. By definition, it follows that each ∘-move (resp. •-move) is an occurrence of a vertex v of $[\![F]\!]$ having even (resp. odd) *distance* $d(v)$ from the sink $s_{[\![F]\!]}$ of $[\![F]\!]$, where the distance $d(v)$ is defined as the number of vertices in a path from v to $s_{[\![F]\!]}$ minus one. The proof that each of such a path in an arena has the same length is provided in [31].

The **predecessor** of a view is the result of deleting the final move (and its pointer); the converse is the **successor** relation.

Definition 9. *Let F be a formula. A **winning innocent strategy** (or **WIS**) Σ for F is a finite, non-empty prefix-closed set of views for F such that:*

1. *The view containing a single occurrence of the sink of $\llbracket F \rrbracket$ belongs to Σ;*
2. *Σ is ∘-**complete**: if $\langle \rho \cdot v, f \rangle \in \Sigma$ with v a •-move, then every successor of $\langle \rho \cdot v, f \rangle$ is in Σ;*
3. *Σ is •-**deterministic** and •-**total**: if $\langle \rho \cdot v, f \rangle \in \Sigma$ and v is an ∘-move, then exactly one successor of $\langle \rho \cdot v, f \rangle$ belongs to Σ.*

Theorem 3 [11, 19]. *A formula F is valid iff there is a **WIS** for F.*

Lemma 2. *Let $\Gamma \vdash F$ be a sequent. For any **WIS** Σ for $\Gamma \vdash F$ there is a canonically defined **ST**-derivation $\mathcal{D}_\Sigma$ of $\Gamma \vdash F$.*

Proof. The proof is by induction on the pair $\langle |\Sigma|, |F| \rangle$ where $|\Sigma|$ is the cardinality of Σ and $|F|$ is the height of F[3].

1. if $F = c$ is atomic, then Σ must contain the set of views $\{c^\circ, c^\circ \cdot c^\bullet\}$ where the justifier of $c^\bullet$ is c°. We have two cases
   (a) either $c^\circ \cdot c^\bullet$ is maximal in Σ, and by ∘-completeness we deduce that $\Gamma = \Delta, c$. In this case $\mathcal{D}_\Sigma$ is a proof of $\Delta, \underline{c} \vdash c$ obtained by an Ax-rule.
   (b) or $c^\circ \cdot c^\bullet$ is not maximal in Σ. By ∘-completeness, we conclude that $\Gamma = \Delta, (A_1 \cdots A_n) \to c$ for some Δ and $n \geq 1$. For each $i \leq n$ let a_i be the root of $\llbracket A_i \rrbracket$ and let Σ_i be the prefix-closed set of views containing each view of Σ that starts with a_i. We obtain that Σ_i is a **WIS** for $\Gamma \vdash A_i$ for any i and that $|\Sigma_i| < |\Sigma|$. By induction hypothesis, for each $i \leq n$ there is a canonically defined **ST**-derivation $\mathcal{D}_{\Sigma_i}$ of $\Gamma \vdash A_i$. By weakening admissibility (Lemma 1), we have a derivation $\mathcal{D}_{\Sigma_i}^\star$ of $\Gamma_i^\star \vdash A_i$ with $\Gamma_i^\star = \Gamma, (A_i \cdots A_n) \to c, \ldots, A_n \to c$ for any $i \in \{2, \ldots, n\}$. We define $\mathcal{D}_\Sigma$ as the following **ST**-derivation:

$$
\cfrac{
  \cfrac{\mathcal{D}_{\Sigma_1}}{\Gamma \vdash A_1}
  \quad
  \cfrac{
    \cfrac{\mathcal{D}_{\Sigma_2^\star}}{\Gamma_2^\star \vdash A_2}
    \quad
    \cfrac{
      \cfrac{\mathcal{D}_{\Sigma_n^\star}}{\Gamma_n^\star \vdash A_n} \quad \cfrac{}{\Gamma, (A_2 \cdots A_n) \to c, \ldots, A_n \to c, \underline{c} \vdash c}\text{Ax}
    }{
      \cfrac{\Gamma, (A_2 \cdots A_n) \to c, \ldots, \underline{A_n \to c} \vdash c}{\vdots}
    }
    \quad \Gamma, (A_3 \cdots A_n) \to c, (A_2 \cdots A_n) \to c \vdash c
  }{\Gamma, (A_2 \cdots A_n) \to c \vdash c}{\to}^L
}{\Gamma \vdash c}
$$

Notice that, in virtue on the restriction on the application of the $\to^L$-rule in **ST**-derivation, this is the unique way to define $\mathcal{D}_\Sigma$ from the derivations $\mathcal{D}_{\Sigma_1^\star}, \ldots, \mathcal{D}_{\Sigma_n}$.

---

[3] The height of a formula is the height of its construction tree.

2. If $F = A \rightarrow B$ then Σ is also a strategy for $\Gamma, A \vdash B$. Since $|B| < |A \rightarrow B|$, by induction hypothesis there is a **ST**-derivation $\mathscr{D}_\Sigma$ of $\Gamma, A \vdash B$ and we can conclude by the application of a $\rightarrow^R$-rule.

Theorem 4. *Let F be a formula. It is valid if and only if it admits a **ST**-derivation.*

Proof. If F is valid, then by Theorem 1 there is **GKi** derivation of $\vdash F$. By Theorem 3 there is a **WIS** Σ for $\vdash F$, therefore a **ST**-derivation $\mathscr{D}_\Sigma$ by Lemma 2. We conclude since the converse trivially holds because every **ST**-derivation is a **GKi**-derivation.

4   From Dialogical Logic Strategies to Derivations

In this section, we show how to associate to any winning dialogical strategy for a formula F a **S**-derivation of the sequent $\vdash F$. We first show how we associate a sequent to any **O**-move of a strategy.

Definition 10. *Let F be any formula and $S = \langle \mathcal{T}, \phi \rangle$ be a strategy for F. Recall that each path $\mathcal{P}$ of $\mathcal{T}$ is a sequence of moves. The **O-tree** of S is the tree $\mathcal{T}_O$ defined as follows:*

1. *the set of nodes of $\mathcal{T}_O$ contains each **O** node of $\mathcal{T}$, an additional node r and nothing else;*
2. *a node v of $\mathcal{T}_O$ is the parent of a node v' iff either $v = r$ and $v' = \mathcal{P}_2$ is the second move of a branch $\mathcal{P}$ in $\mathcal{T}$, or there is a branch $\mathcal{P}$ in $\mathcal{T}$ such that $v = \mathcal{P}_{2k}$ and $v' = \mathcal{P}_{2k+2}$.*

We recursively define the function Seq. *associating to any node v of $\mathcal{T}_O$ a sequent* Seq$(v) := \Gamma^v \vdash F^v$ *and it is defined as follows:*

1. *if $|v| = 1$, then v is the root r. Thus $\Gamma^v = \emptyset$ and $F^v = F$;*
2. *If $|v| = k + 1$, then there is a **P**-node t which is the parent of v in S and a node v' which is the parent of v in $\mathcal{T}_O$, with associated sequent* Seq$(v') = \Gamma^{v'} \vdash F^{v'}$.
   (a) *if $v = \langle ?, \bullet \rangle$, then t asserts an atomic formula b. We let $\Gamma^v = \Gamma^{v'}$ and $F^v = b$;*
   (b) *if $v = \langle ?, A \rangle$, then t asserts a formula $A \rightarrow B$. We let $\Gamma^v = \Gamma^{v'}, A$ and $F^v = B$;*
   (c) *otherwise $v = \langle !, B \rangle$ and we let $\Gamma^v = \Gamma^{v'}, B$ and $F^v = F^{v'}$.*

The following proposition states that the formulas asserted by **O** in the play ending with v are precisely those that are contained in Γ^v.

Proposition 1. *Let $S = \langle \mathcal{T}, \phi \rangle$ be a strategy and let $\mathcal{T}_O$ be its **O**-tree. For every node v of $\mathcal{T}_O$ and for every formula B we have that $B \in \Gamma^v$ if and only if there is an ancestor v' of v that asserts B.*

Proof. If $B \in \Gamma^v$, we can prove that there is an ancestor v' of v that asserts B by induction on $|v|$. If v is the root of $\mathcal{T}_O$, then the proposition is vacuously true. Otherwise we conclude by inductive hypothesis since either v is an assertion of B, and then $\Gamma^v = \Gamma^{v'}, B$ where v' is the parent of v, or $v = \langle ?, \bullet \rangle$, and then $\Gamma^v = \Gamma^{v'}$ where v' is the parent of v.

The converse implication immediately follows by the definition of Seq.

Given a winning strategy $\mathcal{S} = \langle \mathcal{T}, \phi \rangle$ for F, we can show that each leaf of $\mathcal{T}_O$ is labeled by a sequent that is conclusion of an Ax-rule of the sequent calculus.

Proposition 2. *Let $\mathcal{S} = \langle \mathcal{T}, \phi \rangle$ be a winning strategy and m a leaf of $\mathcal{T}$. If n is the parent of m in $\mathcal{T}$ and $m = \langle !, a \rangle$, then Γ^n is of the form $\Delta, a \vdash a$.*

Proof. Since $\mathcal{S}$ is winning, then m is the last move of a play p that is won by **P**. Consequently, by Condition 2 in the definition of play, m is a repetition. Thus the atom a has already been asserted by **O** in the play. By the definition of Seq, we deduce that $a \in \Gamma^n$.

Moreover, m is justified by a **O**-challenge t. As a consequence, t is either justified by an assertion of $B \to a$ for some formula B, or by an assertion $\langle ?, a \rangle$. By the definition of Seq, we conclude the formula F^t of the sequent associated by Seq to t is a. By the Condition 2 in the definition of play, any **O**-move $t_1, \ldots, t_k$ that is after t is a defense move. This implies, by definition of Seq, that $F^{t_i} = F^t$ for all i; therefore $F^t = F^n = a$.

The two following technical propositions will be used in the proof of Lemma 3.

Proposition 3. *Let $\mathcal{S} = \langle \mathcal{T}, \phi \rangle$ be a winning strategy, $\mathcal{T}_O$ be its **O**-tree and m a node of $\mathcal{T}_O$. If m is the parent of a defense move m' asserting B, then $A \to B \in \Gamma^m$ for some formula A.*

Proof. Let $\mathcal{B}$ be the unique branch of $\mathcal{S}$ containing both m and m', and let t be **P**-move that is the parent of m. By the definition of strategy, $\langle B, \phi|_B \rangle$ is a play. Consequently, m is justified by t and t must be a challenge asserting some formula A. This means that the **O**-move $\phi(t)$ is an assertion of $A \to B$. Since $\phi(t)$ is an ancestor of m, we conclude that $A \to B \in \Gamma^m$.

Proposition 4. *Let $\mathcal{S} = \langle \mathcal{T}, \phi \rangle$ be a winning strategy, $\mathcal{T}_O$ be its **O**-tree and m a node of $\mathcal{T}_O$. If m is the parent of m' and m' is counterattack asserting A, then $A \to B \in \Gamma^m$ for some formula B.*

Proof. The proof is entirely similar to the one of the previous proposition.

Definition 11. *Let $\mathcal{S} = \langle \mathcal{T}, \phi \rangle$ be a winning strategy, and $\mathcal{T}_O$ be its **O**-tree. We define a function Φ associating a tree of sequent $\mathcal{D}^v$ rooted in $\Gamma^v \vdash F^v$ to each node v of $\mathcal{T}_O$. Such a function is defined by recursion on the number of descendants of v.*

1. *If the number of descendant of v is one, then v is a leaf of $\mathcal{T}_O$. We associate to v a tree whose only node is $\Gamma^v \vdash F^v$.*
2. *Suppose that $\mathcal{D}^x$ is defined for all vertex of having at most $n \geq 1$ descendants and let v be a node with $k + 1$ descendants. Let t be the unique **P**-node of $\mathcal{T}$ such that v is the parent of t in $\mathcal{T}$:*
   (a) *If t is a challenge asserting some formula A, then there are two cases:*
       – *A is an atomic formula a, and v has (in $\mathcal{T}_O$) two children $v_1 = \langle ?, \bullet \rangle$ and $v_2 = \langle !, B \rangle$. Then the tree of sequents $\mathcal{D}^v$ is defined as follows:*

$$\frac{\mathcal{D}^{v_1} \qquad \mathcal{D}^{v_2}}{\Gamma, a \to B \vdash a \qquad \Gamma, a \to B, B \vdash C}{\Gamma, a \to B \vdash C} \to^L$$

where $\Gamma, a \to B \vdash a$ and $\Gamma, a \to B, B \vdash C$ are the sequents associated to v_1 and v_2 respectively.

- $A = A_1 \to A_2$ *and v has two children $v_1 = \langle ?, A_1 \rangle$ and $v_2 = \langle !, B \rangle$ (in $\mathcal{T_O}$) for some formula B. The tree of sequents $\mathcal{D}^v$ is*

$$\cfrac{\cfrac{\overset{\mathscr{D}^{v_1}}{\nabla}}{\Gamma, (A_1 \to A_2) \to B, A_1 \vdash A_2}}{\cfrac{\Gamma, (A_1 \to A_2) \to B, \vdash A_1 \to A_2}{\Gamma} \to R \qquad \cfrac{\overset{\mathscr{D}^{v_2}}{\nabla}}{\Gamma, (A_1 \to A_2) \to B, B \vdash C}}{\Gamma, (A_1 \to A_2) \to B \vdash C} \to L$$

where $\Gamma, (A_1 \to A_2) \to B, A_1 \vdash A_2$ and $\Gamma, (A_1 \to A_2), B \vdash C$ are the sequents associated to v_1 and v_2 respectively.

(b) *If t is a defense asserting $A \to B$, then v has a unique child $v_1 = \langle ?, A \rangle$ in $\mathcal{T_O}$ and $\mathcal{D}^v$ is defined as:*

$$\cfrac{\cfrac{\overset{\mathscr{D}^{v_1}}{\nabla}}{\Gamma, A \vdash B}}{\Gamma \vdash A \to B} \to R$$

Lemma 3. *For every winning strategy $S = \langle \mathcal{T}, \phi \rangle$, for every node v of $\mathcal{T_O}$, the tree of sequent $\mathcal{D}^v$ is a S-derivation of $\Gamma^v \vdash F^v$.*

Proof. The proof is by induction on the height of $\mathcal{D}^v$. If the height is 1, then the lemma is immediately established in virtue of Proposition 2. The inductive cases follow by induction hypothesis, by construction of $\mathcal{D}^v$ and by Propositions 3 and 4.

Theorem 5. *For any winning strategy $S = \langle \mathcal{T}, \phi \rangle$, the tree of sequent $\mathcal{D}^S$ associated to the root-node of $\mathcal{T_O}$ is a S-derivation of $\vdash F$, moreover:*

1. *if S is a Lorenzen-Felscher winning strategy, then $\mathcal{D}^S$ is a LF-derivation;*
2. *if S is a Stubborn winning strategy, then $\mathcal{D}^S$ is a ST-derivation.*

Proof. The fact that $\mathcal{D}^S$ is a S-derivation of $\vdash F$ follows immediately by Lemma 3. We only give a proof of (2) because the proof of (1) is easier.

Consider a sequent in $\mathcal{D}^S$ that is obtained by an application of a $\to L$-rule and let $\Gamma, A \to B, B \vdash C$ be its right-hand premise. We must show that B is the principal formula of this latter sequent. Remark that the sequent $\Gamma, A \to B, B \vdash C$ is associated to a O move $\langle !, B \rangle$ in $\mathcal{T_O}$. There are two cases: if $B = B \to B_1$, then since S is Stubborn, we must have that child t of $\langle !, B \rangle$ is a challenge $\langle ?, B_1 \rangle$. By the definition of the function Φ, the sequents associated to the child v_1 and v_2 are of the form $\Gamma, A \to B, B \vdash B_1$ and $\Gamma, A \to B, B, B_2 \vdash C$, this means that $B = B_1 \to B_2$ is the principal formula of $\Gamma, A \to B, B \vdash C$. The case in which B is an atomic formula is similar.

5   From Derivations to Dialogical Logic Strategies

In this section, we show how to transform any S-derivation of $\vdash F$ in a winning strategy for F. To do so, we define a function that associates to any path $\mathcal{P}$ of $\mathcal{D}$ a play for F.

Definition 12. *Let* $\mathcal{P} = S_1, \ldots, S_n$ *be a path in a S-derivation* $\mathcal{D}$ *of F. We associate with* $\mathcal{P}$ *a sequence of moves* $\sigma^{\mathcal{P}}$ *by induction on* $|\mathcal{P}|$

- *If* $|\mathcal{P}| = 1$ *then* $\sigma^{\mathcal{P}} = \langle !, F \rangle$;
- *if* $|\mathcal{P}| = n$ *and* $\mathcal{P} = \mathcal{P}', S$ *then we consider the following cases:*
    1. *If S is the conclusion of an* Ax-*rule whose principal formula is a, then:*
        (a) *if S is the premise of a* $\to^{\mathsf{R}}$-*rule then the principal formula of this last rule must be* $B \to a$ *for some formula B. We define* $\sigma^{\mathcal{P}} = \sigma^{\mathcal{P}'} \cdot \langle ?, B \rangle \cdot \langle !, a \rangle$;
        (b) *if S is the left-hand premise of* $\to^{\mathsf{L}}$-*rule, then the principal formula of this last rule must be* $a \to B$ *for some formula B; we define* $\sigma^{\mathcal{P}} = \sigma^{\mathcal{P}'} \cdot \langle ?, \bullet \rangle \cdot \langle !, a \rangle$;
        (c) *if S is the right-hand premise of a* $\to^{\mathsf{L}}$-*rule whose principal formula is* $C \to D$, *then we define* $\sigma_{\mathcal{P}} = \sigma_{\mathcal{P}'} \cdot \langle !, D \rangle \cdot \langle !, a \rangle$;
    2. *If S is the conclusion of an* $\to^{\mathsf{R}}$-*rule whose principal formula is* $A \to B$ *then:*
        (a) *if S is the left-hand premise of an* $\to^{\mathsf{L}}$-*rule, then* $\sigma^{\mathcal{P}} = \sigma^{\mathcal{P}'}$
        (b) *if S is the right-hand premise of an* $\to^{\mathsf{L}}$-*rule whose principal formula is* $C \to D$, *then* $\sigma^{\mathcal{P}} = \sigma^{\mathcal{P}'} \cdot \langle !, D \rangle \cdot \langle !, A \to B \rangle$;
        (c) *if S is the premise of an* $\to^{\mathsf{R}}$-*rule then, the principal formula of such a rule must be* $G \to (A \to B)$ *for some formula G. We define* $\sigma^{\mathcal{P}} = \sigma^{\mathcal{P}'} \cdot \langle ?, G \rangle \cdot \langle !, A \to B \rangle$.
    3. *If S is the conclusion of an* $\to^{\mathsf{L}}$-*rule whose principal formula is* $A \to B$ *then:*
        (a) *if S is the premise of a* $\to^{\mathsf{R}}$-*rule whose principal formula is* $C \to D$, *then* $\sigma^{\mathcal{P}} = \sigma^{\mathcal{P}'} \cdot \langle ?, C \rangle \cdot \langle ?, A \rangle$
        (b) *If S is the left-hand premise of a* $\to^{\mathsf{L}}$-*rule whose principal formula is* $C \to D$, *then C must be an atomic formula. We define* $\sigma^{\mathcal{P}} = \sigma^{\mathcal{P}'} \cdot \langle ?, \bullet \rangle \cdot \langle ?, A \rangle$.
        (c) *If S is the right-hand premise of* $\to^{\mathsf{L}}$ *whose principal formula is* $C \to D$, *then we define* $\sigma^{\mathcal{P}} = \sigma^{\mathcal{P}'} \cdot \langle !, D \rangle \cdot \langle ?, A \rangle$.

Proposition 5. *Let* $\mathcal{D}$ *be* **ST**-*derivation of* $\vdash F$, $\mathcal{P}$ *a path in* $\mathcal{D}$ *and* $\Gamma \vdash C$ *the last sequent of this path. If* $B \in \Gamma$, *then there is an* **O**-*move in* $\sigma^{\mathcal{P}}$ *that asserts B.*

Proof. By induction on the length of $\mathcal{P}$.

By the above proposition, if $\mathcal{P} = S_1, \ldots, S_n$ is a path of $\mathcal{D}$ and if a formula occurrence A is the principal formula of a $\to^{\mathsf{L}}$-rule in one of the S_i, then there is a **O**-move $\sigma_i^{\mathcal{P}}$ that asserts A. For any formula occurrence A, we denote by m_A the first move in $\sigma^{\mathcal{P}}$ that asserts such formula occurrence A.

Definition 13. *Let* $\mathcal{D}$ *be a S-derivation and let* $\mathcal{P}$ *be a path in* $\mathcal{D}$. *We define a function* $\phi^{\mathcal{P}}$ *from* $\sigma^{\mathcal{P}}$ *to* $\sigma^{\mathcal{P}}$ *by the following cases:*

1. $\phi^{\mathcal{P}}(\sigma_i^{\mathcal{P}}) = \sigma_{i-1}^{\mathcal{P}}$ *if* $\sigma_i^{\mathcal{P}}$ *is an* **O** *move;*
2. $\phi^{\mathcal{P}}(\sigma_i^{\mathcal{P}}) = m_A$ *if* $\sigma_i^{\mathcal{P}}$ *is a* **P** *move and* S_n *is the conclusion of a* $\to^{\mathsf{L}}$ *whose principal formula occurrence is A;*
3. $\phi^{\mathcal{P}}(\sigma_i^{\mathcal{P}}) = \sigma_k^{\mathcal{P}}$ *if* $\sigma_i^{\mathcal{P}}$ *is a* **P** *move and a defense, and* $\sigma_k^{\mathcal{P}}$ *is the last unanswered* **O** *challenge in* $\sigma_{\leq i-1}^{\mathcal{P}}$.

Lemma 4. *Let $\mathscr{D}$ be a S-derivation derivation of $\vdash F$. If $\mathcal{P}$ is a path in $\mathscr{D}$, then $\mathsf{p}^{\mathcal{P}} = \langle \sigma^{\mathcal{P}}, \phi^{\mathcal{P}} \rangle$ is a play for F. Moreover, if $\mathcal{P}$ is a branch of $\mathscr{D}$, then $\langle \sigma^{\mathcal{P}}, \phi^{\mathcal{P}} \rangle$ is won by* **P**.

Proof. Suppose that the proposition holds for any path whose length is at most $k \geq 1$ and let $\mathcal{P} = \mathcal{P}', S$ by a path of length $k + 1$. We should check that $\sigma^{\mathcal{P}'} \cdot m^{\mathbf{O}} \cdot n^{\mathbf{P}}$ and $\phi^{\mathcal{P}}$ forms a play where m and n are the two moves associated to S. There are as many cases as those detailed in the Definition 12 of $\sigma^{\mathcal{P}}$. We only consider some of them. Let t be the last move of $\sigma^{\mathcal{P}'}$.

- If S is obtained by an $\to^{\mathsf{L}}$-rule whose principal formula is $A \to B$ and S is the left-hand premise of another $\to^{\mathsf{L}}$-rule whose principal formula is $C \to D$, then $m = \langle ?, \bullet \rangle$, $n = \langle ?, A \rangle$, $\phi^{\mathcal{P}}(m) = t$ and $\phi^{\mathcal{P}}(n) = m_{A \to B}$. The move t is the **P** move associated to the last element $\Sigma \vdash G$ of $\mathcal{P}'$. This latter sequent is obtained by a $\to^{\mathsf{L}}$. Thus, by construction t is $\langle ?, C \rangle$, and since C is atomic, and t is a justified move by induction hypothesis, then m is justified. The move $m_{A \to B}$ is an **O**-move that asserts $A \to B$, since $n = \langle ?, A \rangle$ and $m_{A \to B}$ is justified by hypothesis, then m is justified as well.
- If S is obtained by an $\to^{\mathsf{R}}$-rule whose principal formula is $A \to B$ and S is the premise of another $\to^{\mathsf{R}}$-rule whose principal formula is $G \to (A \to B)$, then $m = \langle ?, G \rangle$, $n = \langle !, A \to B \rangle$, $\phi^{\mathcal{P}}(m) = t$ and $\phi^{\mathcal{P}}(n) = m$. The move t is associated to the last sequent $\Gamma \vdash G \to (A \to B)$ of $\mathcal{P}'$. This latter sequent is obtained by a $\to^{\mathsf{R}}$ with principal formula $G \to (A \to C)$ thus $t = \langle !, G \to (A \to C) \rangle$ and since t is justified by induction hypothesis, then also m is. The fact that n is justified is immediate.
- If S is obtained by an Ax-rule whose principal formula is a and S is the premise of $\to^{\mathsf{R}}$, then the principal formula of this rule must be $B \to a$ for some B. In this case $m = \langle ?, B \rangle$ and $n = \langle !, a \rangle$. Remark that $t = \langle B \to a \rangle$, and since t is justified by induction hypothesis, then also m is. By definition of $\phi^{\mathcal{P}}$, we have that $\phi^{\mathcal{P}}(n) = m$ and thus also m is justified. We should check that $n = \langle !, a \rangle$ is a repetition. This easily follows by observing that S must be of the form $\Delta, a, B \vdash a$ for some Δ and by applying Proposition 5.

The fact that $\mathsf{p}^{\mathcal{P}}$ is won by **P** whenever $\mathcal{P}$ is a branch, follows from the fact that the last move of $\mathsf{p}^{\mathcal{P}}$ must be $\langle !, a \rangle$ for some atom a.

Lemma 5. *Let $\mathscr{D}$ be a proof of $\vdash F$ and $\mathcal{P}$ a path in $\mathscr{D}$. The following holds:*

1. *if $\mathscr{D}$ is a **ST**-derivation then $\langle \sigma^{\mathcal{P}}, \phi^{\mathcal{P}} \rangle$ is a S-play;*
2. *if $\mathscr{D}$ is a **LF**-derivation then $\langle \sigma^{\mathcal{P}}, \phi^{\mathcal{P}} \rangle$ is a LF-play.*

Proof. Both statement are proven by induction on $|\mathcal{P}|$. We only detail the interesting case of (2), i.e., when $\mathcal{P} = \mathcal{P}', S$ and the last **O**-move of $\sigma^{\mathcal{P}}$ is a defense asserting either a complex formula $A \to B$ or an atomic formula a. By the construction of $\sigma^{\mathcal{P}}$, S can only be a sequent $\Gamma \vdash G$ that is the right-hand premise of a $\to^{\mathsf{L}}$ with principal formula $C \to (A \to B)$ (resp $C \to a$). As a consequence, G must be an atomic formula b, and thus either $\Gamma \vdash b$ is obtained by another $\to^{\mathsf{L}}$-rule or by an Ax-rule. In the former case, since $\mathscr{D}$ is a **ST**-derivation, then $A \to B$ is the principal formula of $\Gamma \vdash b$, and by construction of $\sigma^{\mathcal{P}}$ its last move must be $\langle ?, A \rangle$ and must be justified by $\langle !, A \to B \rangle$ and we can conclude. In the latter case, since $\mathscr{D}$ is an **ST**-derivation, then $b = a$ and $\Gamma \vdash G$ is $\Delta, a \vdash a$ for some multiset Δ. Thus, the last move of $\sigma^{\mathcal{P}}$ must be $\langle !, a \rangle$.

Let $\mathscr{D}$ be a S-derivation of $\vdash F$. Let $\mathscr{T}^{\mathscr{D}}$ be the tree in which any branch is equal to a $\sigma^{\mathcal{B}}$ for a branch $\mathcal{B}$ of $\mathscr{D}$. Let $\phi^{\mathscr{D}}$ be the union of all $\phi^{\mathcal{B}}$ for a branch $\mathcal{B}$ of $\mathscr{D}$.

Theorem 6. *If $\mathscr{D}$ is a S-derivation of $\vdash F$, then $S^{\mathscr{D}} = \langle \mathscr{T}^{\mathscr{D}}, \phi^{\mathscr{D}} \rangle$ is a winning strategy for F. Moreover, if $\mathscr{D}$ is a **LF**-derivation then $S^{\mathscr{D}}$ is a Lorenzen-Felscher strategy and if $\mathscr{D}$ is a **ST**-derivation, then $S^{\mathscr{D}}$ is a Stubborn strategy.*

Proof. Each branch of $S^{\mathscr{D}}$ is a play won by **P** in virtue of Lemma 4. The other conditions in the definition of strategy follows easily by the construction of the sequences composing $S^{\mathscr{D}}$. The fact that $S^{\mathscr{D}}$ is a Lorenzen-Felscher (resp. Stubborn) strategy when $\mathscr{D}$ is a **LF**-derivation (resp. **ST**-derivation) follows from Lemma 5.

Corollary 1. *Strategies, Lorenzen-Felscher Strategies and Stubborn Strategies are sound and complete for $\mathsf{IL}^{\rightarrow}$.*

We conclude by establishing that there is a bijective correspondence between the classes of winning strategies and derivations that we have considered.

Theorem 7. *The following statements hold:*

1. *The set of **S**-derivations is in one-to-one correspondence with the set of winning strategies;*
2. *The set of **LF**-derivations is in one-to-one correspondence with the set of Lorenzen-Felscher winning strategies*
3. *The set of **ST**-derivations is in one-to-one correspondence with the set of Stubborn winning strategies.*

Proof. The procedure we have used to transform winning strategies into derivations (see Definition 11) and the one we have used to obtain the converse result (see Definitions 12 and 13) are one the inverse of the other. Thus, the result follows.

6   Conclusion and Future Work

We have defined different classes of Lorenzen-style dialogical plays for intuitionistic logic by restricting the way in which **P** can play during a game. We have shown that winning strategies for such games naturally corresponds to particular GKi derivations obtained by limiting the application of GKis-rules in proof search procedures.

The correspondence between Stubborn strategies and **ST**-derivation, as well as the result we used to prove that the latter are sound and complete with respect to $\mathsf{IL}^{\rightarrow}$ (Lemma 2), suggest the existence of a one-to-one correspondence between these strategies and Hyland-Ong Winning Innocent Strategies. In future work, we want to study this correspondence in order to use dialogical logic to define denotational semantics of the simply typed lambda calculus [18], for which Hyland-Ong game semantics is a fully abstract denotational semantics [11, 19]. Moreover, the results in [1,2] would suggest a way to define a dialogical system for the constructive modal logic CK.

The semantics of formal argumentation systems are often specified through the help of concepts originated in dialogic logic (e.g. E-strategies see [24]). We think it would be interesting to study a more abstract version of our stubborn strategies in the context of formal argumentation.

Acknowledgments. The first author is supported by Villum Fonden, grant no. 50079. The second author is supported by the PRIN project RIPER (No. 20203FFYLK).

References

1. Acclavio, M., Catta, D., Straßburger, L.: Game semantics for constructive modal logic. In: Das, A., Negri, S. (eds.) TABLEAUX 2021. LNCS (LNAI), vol. 12842, pp. 428–445. Springer, Cham (2021). https://doi.org/10.1007/978-3-030-86059-2_25
2. Acclavio, M., Catta, D., Straßburger, L.: Towards a denotational semantics for proofs in constructive modal logic (2021). https://hal.archives-ouvertes.fr/hal-03201439. Preprint
3. Alama, J., Knoks, A., Uckelman, S.: Dialogues games for classical logic (short paper), pp. 82–86. Universiteit Bern (2011)
4. Andreoli, J.M.: Logic programming with focusing proofs in linear logic. J. Log. Comput. **2**, 297–347 (1992)
5. Barrio, E., Clerbout, N., Rahman, S.: Introducing consistency in a dialogical framework for paraconsistent logic (online 2018). Log. J. IGPL/Log. J. IGPL **28**(5), 953–972 (2020). https://halshs.archives-ouvertes.fr/halshs-01689148
6. Booth, R., Gabbay, D.M., Kaci, S., Rienstra, T., van der Torre, L.W.N.: Abduction and dialogical proof in argumentation and logic programming. In: Schaub, T., Friedrich, G., O'Sullivan, B. (eds.) ECAI 2014–21st European Conference on Artificial Intelligence, 18–22 August 2014, Prague, Czech Republic - Including Prestigious Applications of Intelligent Systems (PAIS 2014). Frontiers in Artificial Intelligence and Applications, vol. 263, pp. 117–122. IOS Press (2014). https://doi.org/10.3233/978-1-61499-419-0-117
7. Catta, D.: From strategies to derivations and back an easy completeness proof for first order intuitionistic dialogical logic (2022). https://hal.archives-ouvertes.fr/hal-03188862. Working paper or preprint
8. Catta, D., Moot, R., Retoré, C.: Dialogical argumentation and textual entailment. In: Loukanova, R. (ed.) Natural Language Processing in Artificial Intelligence—NLPinAI 2020. SCI, vol. 939, pp. 191–226. Springer, Cham (2021). https://doi.org/10.1007/978-3-030-63787-3_7
9. Catta, D., Stevens-Guille, S.J.: Lorenzen won the game, Lorenz did too: dialogical logic for ellipsis and anaphora resolution. In: Silva, A., Wassermann, R., de Queiroz, R. (eds.) WoLLIC 2021. LNCS, vol. 13038, pp. 269–286. Springer, Cham (2021). https://doi.org/10.1007/978-3-030-88853-4_17
10. Crubellier, M., Marion, M., McConaughey, Z., Rahman, S.: Dialectic, the dictum de omni and ecthesis. Hist. Philos. Logic **40**(3), 207–233 (2019)
11. Danos, V., Herbelin, H., Regnier, L.: Game semantics & abstract machines. In: Proceedings, 11th Annual IEEE Symposium on Logic in Computer Science, New Brunswick, New Jersey, USA, 27–30 July 1996, pp. 394–405. IEEE Computer Society (1996). https://doi.org/10.1109/LICS.1996.561456
12. Felscher, W.: Dialogues, strategies, and intuitionistic provability. Ann. Pure Appl. Logic **28**(3), 217–254 (1985). https://doi.org/10.1016/0168-0072(85)90016-8
13. Fermüller, C.G.: Parallel dialogue games and hypersequents for intermediate logics. In: Cialdea Mayer, M., Pirri, F. (eds.) TABLEAUX 2003. LNCS (LNAI), vol. 2796, pp. 48–64. Springer, Heidelberg (2003). https://doi.org/10.1007/978-3-540-45206-5_7
14. Fermüller, C.G.: Connecting sequent calculi with Lorenzen-style dialogue games. In: Paul Lorenzen-Mathematician and Logician, pp. 115–141 (2021)
15. Fitting, M.: Intuitionistic Logic, Model Theory and Forcing. North-Holland Pub. Co., Amsterdam (1969)

16. Herbelin, H.: A λ-calculus structure isomorphic to Gentzen-style sequent calculus structure. In: Pacholski, L., Tiuryn, J. (eds.) CSL 1994. LNCS, vol. 933, pp. 61–75. Springer, Heidelberg (1995). https://doi.org/10.1007/BFb0022247

17. Herbelin, H.: Séquents qu'on calcule: de l'interprétation du calcul des séquents comme calcul de λ-termes et comme calcul de stratégies gagnantes. Phd thesis, Université Paris 7 (1995). https://tel.archives-ouvertes.fr/tel-00382528/file/These-Her95.pdf

18. Hindley, J.R.: Basic Simple Type Theory. Cambridge Tracts in Theoretical Computer Science, vol. 42. Cambridge University Press (1997). Corrected edition, 2008

19. Hyland, M., Ong, L.: On full abstraction for PCF: I, II, and III. Inf. Comput. **163**(2), 285–408 (2000). https://doi.org/10.1006/inco.2000.2917, http://www.sciencedirect.com/science/article/pii/S0890540100929171

20. Kacprzak, M., Budzynska, K.: Reasoning about dialogical strategies. In: Graña, M., Toro, C., Howlett, R.J., Jain, L.C. (eds.) KES 2012. LNCS (LNAI), vol. 7828, pp. 171–184. Springer, Heidelberg (2013). https://doi.org/10.1007/978-3-642-37343-5_18

21. Lorenzen, P.: Logik und agon. Atti Del XII Congresso Internazionale Filosofia **4**, 187–194 (1958)

22. Lorenzen, P., Lorenz, K.: Dialogische Logik. Wissenschaftliche Buchgesellschaft [Abt. Verlag] (1978)

23. Mcconaughey, Z.: Existence, meaning and the law of excluded middle. A dialogical approach to Hermann Weyl's philosophical considerations. Klesis - Revue Philos. **46** (2020). https://hal.archives-ouvertes.fr/hal-03036825

24. Modgil, S., Caminada, M.: Proof theories and algorithms for abstract argumentation frameworks. In: Simari, G.R., Rahwan, I. (eds.) Argumentation in Artificial Intelligence, pp. 105–129. Springer, Boston (2009). https://doi.org/10.1007/978-0-387-98197-0_6

25. Pavlova, A.: Dialogue games for minimal logic. Log. Log. Philos. **30**(2), 281–309 (2020). https://doi.org/10.12775/LLP.2020.022, https://apcz.umk.pl/LLP/article/view/LLP.2020.022

26. Prakken, H.: Coherence and flexibility in dialogue games for argumentation. J. Log. and Comput. **15**(6), 1009–1040 (2005). https://doi.org/10.1093/logcom/exi046

27. Prakken, H., Sartor, G.: A dialectical model of assessing conflicting arguments in legal reasoning. Artif. Intell. Law **4**(3–4), 331–368 (1996). https://doi.org/10.1007/BF00118496

28. Rahman, S., Clerbout, N.: Constructive type theory and the dialogical approach to meaning. Baltic Int. Yearb. Cogn. Log. Commun. **8**, 1–72 (2013). https://doi.org/10.4148/1944-3676.1077, https://halshs.archives-ouvertes.fr/halshs-01225723

29. Rahman, S., Clerbout, N., Keiff, L.: On dialogues and natural deduction. In: Primiero, G. (ed.) Acts of Knowledge: History and Philosophy of Logic, pp. 301–336. College Publications, Tributes (2009). https://halshs.archives-ouvertes.fr/halshs-00713187

30. Sticht, M.: Multi-agent dialogue games and dialogue sequents for proof search and scheduling. In: Fiorentini, C., Momigliano, A. (eds.) Proceedings of the 31st Italian Conference on Computational Logic, Milano, Italy, 20–22 June 2016. CEUR Workshop Proceedings, vol. 1645, pp. 21–36. CEUR-WS.org (2016). https://ceur-ws.org/Vol-1645/paper_20.pdf

31. Straßburger, L., Heijltjes, W., Hughes, D.J.D.: Intuitionistic proofs without syntax. In: LICS 2019–34th Annual ACM/IEEE Symposium on Logic in Computer Science. pp. 1–13. IEEE, Vancouver (2019). https://doi.org/10.1109/LICS.2019.8785827, https://hal.inria.fr/hal-02386878

32. Troelstra, A., van Dalen, D.: Constructivism in Mathematics (vol. 2). Studies in Logic and the Foundations of Mathematics, vol. 123. North-Holland (1988)

33. Troelstra, A., Schwichtenberg, H.: Basic Proof Theory. Cambridge University Press, USA (1996)

SHAPE: A Framework for Evaluating the Ethicality of Influence

Elfia Bezou-Vrakatseli[1] ⬤, Benedikt Brückner[2] ⬤, and Luke Thorburn[1(✉)] ⬤

[1] King's College London, London, UK
{elfia.bezou_vrakatseli,luke.thorburn}@kcl.ac.uk
[2] Imperial College London, London, UK
b.brueckner21@imperial.ac.uk

Abstract. Agents often exert influence when interacting with humans and non-human agents. However, the ethical status of such influence is often unclear. In this paper, we present the SHAPE framework, which lists reasons why influence may be unethical. We draw on literature from descriptive and moral philosophy and connect it to machine learning to help guide ethical considerations when developing algorithms with potential influence. Lastly, we explore mechanisms for governing influential algorithmic systems, inspired by regulation in journalism, human subject research, and advertising.

Keywords: influence · manipulation · mental interference · nudging · choice architecture · suasion · persuasion · cognitive liberty · mental integrity · mental self-determination · freedom of thought · preference change

1 Introduction

Influence—which we define broadly as one agent taking an action that causes a change in another agent—is ubiquitous in multi-agent systems. If the agent being influenced is a person or is otherwise deserving of moral consideration, then it is widely accepted that some types of influence (e.g., blackmail, extortion) are unethical. In many settings where human communication is mediated by algorithms, however, the ethical status of influence is less clear. For example, interacting with a recommender system may change our preferences [25,43,64] and emotions [63], exposure to online political advertising can change our voting intentions [31], and interacting with large language models can change our opinions [10,58]. In such cases, it can be easier to sense that there may be an ethical principle being violated than to articulate the principle of concern.

There is a substantial body of work from descriptive and moral philosophy on concepts such as "influence" [102], "manipulation" [76], "mental interference" [37], "nudging" [91], "choice architecture" [94], "suasion" and "persuasion" [15], "cognitive liberty" [95], "mental integrity" [37], "mental self-determination" [21], freedom of thought [65], and preference change [25]. The definition of each of

© The Author(s), under exclusive license to Springer Nature Switzerland AG 2023
V. Malvone and A. Murano (Eds.): EUMAS 2023, LNAI 14282, pp. 167–185, 2023.
https://doi.org/10.1007/978-3-031-43264-4_11

these terms, and the situations in which the phenomena they describe can be considered ethical, are all contested. We do not attempt to stipulate definitions or resolve normative disagreements in this paper. Rather, we draw on this literature to highlight specific reasons why some types of influence might be unethical, and link these concerns to relevant work from computer science and artificial intelligence (AI). Our hope is that the framework created through this synthesis will help designers of algorithmic systems that influence people to think more concretely about the ethical considerations relevant to their work.

Before introducing the framework we would like to stress that not all influence is bad or morally questionable. Our definition of influence (given in the opening sentence of this article) is so broad as to encompass all causal relationships between agents. In this view, all human communication—much of which is beneficial—constitutes a form of influence. In particular, rational persuasion ("the unforced force of the better argument" [52]) is often delineated as being a morally acceptable form of communication, and hence influence [98]. Without aiming to provide a perfect characterisation of wrongful influence, our view is that influence is ethically acceptable unless it possesses a property which makes it wrongful, and this paper is an attempt to compile a list of such properties.

Method. To arrive at the SHAPE framework we conducted an extensive (but unstructured) literature search in order to compile a list of reasons why influence may be unethical. This longlist of reasons was iteratively grouped into sets of similar concerns, discussed, supplemented with additional literature searches, and re-grouped until we arrived at the current version of the framework. This process was not straightforward due to the fact that a number of categories have a non-negligible overlap, and our decisions about how to hierarchically arrange the relevant ideas are inevitably somewhat contingent and subjective. Additionally, we emphasise that this article is not a true systematic review, and the amount of literature relevant to the ethics of influence is vast. Nonetheless, we are confident that the chosen categories are informative, if not perfectly disjoint, and to the best of our knowledge we are the first to provide a framework to assess the ethicality of influential AI systems.

2   Concerns

In this section we develop our SHAPE (Secrecy, Harm, Agency, Privacy, Exogeneity) framework by listing reasons why influence may be unethical, drawing on work from moral philosophy and linking it to relevant concepts in computer science and AI. We do not claim that this list is comprehensive, but we do think it covers the most commonly-cited objections to influence. Similarly, we do not claim that this is a perfect taxonomy or that each of the reasons given is perfectly distinct from the others, but we do argue that the five groups of reasons—secrecy, harm, agency, privacy, and exogeneity—capture meaningful families of objections. The aim of the framework is to provide guidance about whether a particular instance of influence might be unethical to those in charge of designing the agent or process which exerts the influence. While the terms in

The SHAPE framework

Influence might be unethical if...

Secrecy (2.1)

  ... the influencee is not fully aware of the intent to influence
  ... the influencee is not fully aware of the means of influence

Harm (2.2)

  ... it causes harm

Agency (2.3)

  ... it removes options
  ... it imposes conditional costs or offers
  ... it occurs without consent
  ... it bypasses reason
  ... it is not able to be resisted

Privacy (2.4)

  ... it breaches an assumed contract regarding the use of personal information
  ... it is implicated in mass surveillance

Exogeneity (2.5)

  ... it serves exogenous rather than endogenous interests
  ... it gives one group power over another

Box 1. The SHAPE framework for considering the ethicality of influence.

the acronym give an overview of concerns, the corresponding sections provide a more detailed analysis for each. An overview of the framework summarising these reasons is given in Box 1, and a discussion of the concept of intent (which is relevant to all five reasons) is given in Box 2.

2.1 Secrecy

First, influence may be unethical if it involves *secrecy*. In the literature, variations of this idea have also been referred to as "covertness" [39], "deception" [72], "lying" [71], or "trickery" [76]. Articulating precise definitions for these terms is an open philosophical problem [67], but many have been proposed. The core idea is perhaps most neutrally defined as an "information asymmetry", where the influencer has more information than the influencee [35]. More narrowly, deception has been defined as any situation where an agent A intentionally causes another agent B to have a false belief, with necessary requirement that agent A does not believe it to be true [26].

Secrecy of all sorts may be wrong—when it is wrong—because it violates a moral norm or duty, specifically "a duty to take care not to cause another to form false beliefs based on one's behaviour, communication, or omission" [97], because it constitutes a breach of an implicit promise to be open and truthful [84], or because it constitutes a betrayal of trust [71]. The wrongness of secrecy may also in some cases be due to downstream consequences of the secrecy, rather than due to the secrecy itself. For example, some argue that when an intent to influence is hidden from the influencee, it is "less likely to trigger rational scrutiny" [76] and thus bypasses reason, reducing agency (Sect. 2.3).

That said, secrecy may not always be unethical, as in cases of "benevolent deception" [3]. For example, it may be beneficial for the rehabilitation of patients who have suffered stokes or other brain injuries if their physical therapist robot obfuscates their true progress towards recovery [19].

Here, we distinguish between two types of secrecy as it relates influence: secrecy of *intent* and secrecy of *means*.

Secrecy of Intent. Influence may be unethical if the influence is intended by the influencer, and the influencee is not fully aware of this intent. For example, a video deepfake [73] intended to influence public opinion in a certain direction (perhaps by misrepresenting the actions of a political figure) may be unethical because the people who are influenced are not made fully aware of this intention. Had they been aware, they would have assigned less credence to the information contained in the video [68].

Secrecy of Means. Influence may also be unethical if the influencee is not fully aware of the means by which they are being influenced. For example, a user interacting with a sophisticated social media recommender system may be fully aware that the algorithm is designed to maximise the total amount of time they spend on the platform—so there is no secrecy of intent—but be unaware of the strategies the recommender is employing to achieve this, such as through the occasional recommendation of content that is increasingly sympathetic to a conspiracy theory [105].

Technical Work. Of the many ethical objections to influence, secrecy has perhaps received the most attention in the context of AI. For example, the sizable literature on algorithmic transparency, explainability, and interpretability (see, e.g., [27,69]) represents an attempt to mitigate information asymmetries between AI systems and their human users. There is also an emerging literature that seeks to provide formal definitions of deception from a causal perspective, along with mechanisms for detecting it in AI systems [88,113,114,116]. Algorithmic agents can also fall prey to influence involving secrecy, as in cases of adversarial attacks [70], data-poisoning [70], reward function tampering [44], and manipulating human feedback [115].

2.2   Harm

Second, influence may be unethical if it causes *harm*. There are many different forms of harm, with some of the most prominent categories including reduced physical or mental well-being [78], bias [118], unfairness [118], or injustice [101]. In general, harm and related concepts such as "suffering" [56] are expansively but inconsistently defined. Definitions range from those that equate harm with any "physical or other injury or damage" [23], to those state harm is a condition of "interference with individual liberty", originating from the "harm principle" of John Stuart Mill [81], a definition which would liken harm to a reduction in agency (Sect. 2.3).

Ethical (if not legal) views on what does and doesn't count as harm are normative and contested, and this is notably true of harms that may arise from speech acts in algorithmically-mediated online fora. For example, "safe spaces" are viewed by some as a means of avoiding psychological harm and others as an institution which, if realised, inflicts epistemic harms [6]. Regardless of the position one takes in such debates, it seems defensible that there are many forms of harm which are widespread but not frequently well-articulated, and some of these harms can plausibly be promulgated by influential AI systems. One example of such harms has been labelled epistemic injustice [61]. Varieties of epistemic injustice include *testimonial injustice*, where an individual is discredited as a credible source of knowledge, and *hermeneutic injustice*, where an individual experiences reduced capacity to make sense of their own experiences due to a lack of a relevant framework, shared vocabulary, or common knowledge of a shared experience. Both forms of epistemic injustice may be exacerbated by language models or recommender systems, if such systems are heavily used and systematically privilege certain perspectives.

It should be emphasised that harm, while perhaps intrinsically injurious, need not always be unethical. A surgeon making a cut to a patient's skin to fix their broken leg may cause temporary harm and pain, but is arguably acting in the best interests of the patient. In such cases, influence would then not be unethical despite causing harm. The assessment of harmful influence is further complicated by the fact that it can be very hard to define when influence is actually harmful, particularly influence over mental properties such as preferences [25].

Technical Work. The concept of harm is a central topic among AI policymakers, with the prevention of harm being underscored as a critical principle for AI systems in the European Commission's report on trustworthy AI. The report asserts that AI systems should never cause adverse effects on any human being [54]. Harm, particularly in the physical sense induced by AI systems, has been scrutinized extensively within the domain of self-driving cars through thought experiments like the trolley problem [41].

Another significant area of research is AI in healthcare, where there is a strong emphasis on the minimization of harm potential. AI systems in healthcare are expected not only to elevate the well-being of individuals but also to consider the

---

Intent

When debating ethical considerations concerning AI systems, the concept of intent is highly relevant. The definition we have adopted for deception already encompasses the notion of intention, but it is easy to see that, for example, whether harm that was caused or a reduction of agency that took place was intended by a given agent also requires a more thorough definition of this notion. While the concept of intention may be somewhat easy to understand for humans, it becomes more obscure as soon as algorithmic agents are involved. Such agents may deploy deceptive, harmful or otherwise undesired strategies without human intention [65]. A key distinction is, thus, to be made between reprehensible actions that follow human intention and such actions that happen unintentionally (regarding the human responsible). In the case of deception in human-machine relations three distinct cases are: (1) the agent deceives as a result of human intention to deceive; (2) the agent deceives autonomously or incidentally without human intention; and (3) the agent deceives its designer [31].

Technical Work Intent in AI systems that deceive or manipulate is analysed in a number of works. It can be seen as a key dimension of manipulation, but may be hard to define and operationalise [27,62]. Helpful definitions of intent for algorithms may be derived based on notions from legal theory since parallels between judging whether a human intended to commit a crime and judging whether an artificial agent intended to perform an action such as deceiving its creator or causing harm to a user can be drawn [8]. However, even if suitable definitions are found, intent and causation tests may fail for black-box AI algorithms, implying that different approaches to the issue may be necessary [14].

Box 2. The concept of *intent*, as it relates to the ethics of influence.

potential psychological or mental harm they may cause, such as those resulting from discrimination or neglect [78].

A prominent challenge in this field is assigning responsibility when harm does occur, given the numerous actors typically involved in the development process. This issue is particularly salient in the context of recommender systems, which often serve to influence human behaviour. Even when these systems are designed with benevolent intentions—such as supporting healthy decision-making—they can unintentionally cause adverse effects [40].

2.3   Agency

Third, influence may be unethical if it reduces human *agency*, or related concepts such as "self-determination" [21] and "autonomy" [85]. There are many proposed definitions of agency [46]. One account defines agency as the act of an agent making use of its ability to act [90]. In this view, agency requires that executed actions are intended, and result in part from the agent's reasoning processes. To reduce human agency, then, is to disrupt the link between an agent's intentions or reasoning processes and their subsequent actions.

Several works link influence with a reduction in agency. Being influenced into performing an action reduces the agency of an individual, at least in terms of the decision about whether to perform that action [103]. Human agency is often characterised as having intrinsic moral value, and reductions in agency may be wrong regardless of whether that reduction in agency is paternalistic and results in improved welfare for the person affected. Not respecting the competency of an individual to make their own decisions is seen as a lack of appreciation of them being a rational agent [96] or even a degradation [75]. Perhaps more unambiguously, reduced agency can be wrong if it involves impairments to the psychological capabilities of the subject thought to be the basis for free will [100]. The wrongness of reductions in human agency may also stem from the fact that the interests of the affected agent are being devalued or deprioritised relative to those of the another party (see Sect. 2.5) [86,96].

However, it has also been argued that reductions in agency are not always wrong, and that rational agents often do not oppose influence that has this effect [22]. Instead, agency may be valuable instrumentally because is often a useful means to an end. We sometimes place ourselves in situations where we have reduced agency—such as following a recipe or studying a prescribed curriculum—if it helps to achieve a goal.

Here, we give five accounts of what it means for influence to reduce agency: removing options, imposing conditional costs or offers, influencing without consent, bypassing reason, or being irresistible. These are likely not mutually exclusive.

Removal of Options. Influence may be unethical if it removes options previously available to the influencee [49]. For example, an autonomous vehicle may in some implementations prevent its human driver from deciding to take a certain route to a destination that they otherwise would have taken. Options may be removed explicitly (by refusal) or implicitly (by a failure to provide an affordance that would enable the option). Options can also be removed effectively, without being absolutely removed, by imposing conditional costs (see below) that are so severe as to make the option untenable. Such removal of options, where the influenced party can be said to have no choice or no acceptable choice, has been labelled "coercion" [62,77,119].

Conditional Costs or Offers. Influence may be unethical if it imposes conditional costs or offers on the influenced depending on the action they choose to take, thus altering the relative appeal of different options. In philosophical literature, this type of influence is sometimes called "pressure" [76]. Conditional costs can be seen as a form of threat, though the severity of the threatened cost can vary significantly. Examples of costs that might be threatened include a loss of time or energy (e.g., nudging [101] or browbeating [12]), a loss of social status (e.g., peer pressure), or physical violence (e.g., kidnappers demanding a ransom).

It is possible to use carrots as well as sticks: the costs imposed may be opportunity costs. For example, the influencer may attach positive incentives or "offers" (e.g., money or status) to certain alternatives, which reduces the relative value of others [87]. Such incentives are not always unethical. For example, it is generally considered acceptable to offer salaries to influence people to work for you. Baron [12] suggests that such incentives are only unethical if they mean the influenced adopts a particular alternative for "the wrong sort of reason" [12]. Which sorts of reasons are considered wrong will be context specific.

Consent. Influence may be unethical if it occurs without (informed) consent, thus potentially ignoring a decision a person has made while exercising their agency [45]. For example, consent is plausibly the morally distinguishing factor between strenuous exercise and forced labour.

Bypassing Reason. Influence may be unethical if it bypasses human reason [51]. Mechanisms of influence which involve the bypassing of reason include: customised presentation of information, the flooding of agents with irrelevant information to crowd out relevant information, and the withholding of certain information [17]; exploitation of known imperfections in human decision-making such as group pressure [7]; exploitation of the "truth effect", which is the fact that frequent repetition of a statement increases the probability of individuals to find that statement to be true [53,92]; anchoring [5]; and appeals to emotion such as fear [57].

Irresistibility. Influence may be unethical to the extent that it is difficult to resist [17,28]. Attempts at influence can be made difficult to resist through the use of techniques such as flattery or seduction. Use of such techniques arguably reduces agency of those influenced. This has direct implications on the moral responsibility of an agent for their actions. Such responsibility has been claimed to not require "regulative control", i.e. access to alternative possibilities, but merely "guidance control" as control over the mechanism which steers their behaviour. An agent who is influenced into acting in a certain way through mechanisms they cannot resist is therefore not morally responsible for the consequences of their actions [47].

Technical Work. There is an emerging body of technical work that seeks to quantify degrees of agency, often from a causal perspective [29,60]. There has also been work that seeks to use AI to support human agency in certain contexts, such as in learning environments [34] or on social media platforms [59].

2.4   Privacy

Influence may also be unethical if it is made possible by a violation of *privacy*. Privacy is a fundamental aspect of our lives that refers to our ability to control access to our personal information. It encompasses the right to keep certain information about ourselves hidden from others and is vital for protecting our individuality, fostering trust, and preserving our personal freedom. The more information is known about a person, the greater the extent to which it is possible to identify mechanisms by which they can be influenced. Nissenbaum [74] identifies three privacy principles frequently cited when justifying privacy-enhancing laws: (1) limiting surveillance of citizens and use of information about them by agents of government, (2) restricting access to sensitive, personal, or private information, (3) curtailing intrusions into places deemed private or personal.

In the first years after the internet was established a number of very serious invasions of individual privacy were committed [110]. There is currently a consensus on condemning such actions, but the concern of privacy is still relevant and a very complex one. When training an agent, privacy can be inadvertently breached through data collection, data aggregation, predictions or third-party access [120]. One example of a practice that often raises privacy concerns is personalised ads. The extensive collection of user data raises concerns about the transparency of data collection practices and the potential for unauthorised access or misuse of personal information [109]. More generally, the personalised, virtual experience that such practices result in "fractures the public sphere into individual parallel realities" [110], while also being more likely to promote extreme content, and less likely to be noticed by experts who have historically been responsible for fact-checking (e.g., journalists).

As the concern of privacy is very complex, it is important to be able to identify the type of information that is private and which should therefore be protected (and not used without our consent). Ben and Lazar [13] distinguish between the following types of data: *training* (i.e., data collected to train predictive models) vs *targeting* (i.e., data used for targeting); *sensitive*[1] (i.e., data about a person that they might reasonably not want others to know) vs *nonsensitive*; and subdivide *sensitive* into *intrinsically sensitive*(i.e., if it is sensitive when considered on its own) vs *extrinsically sensitive* (if it is sensitive only when considered in combination with other data points). Privacy concerns arise when the training data consists of sensitive and nonsensitive information [11]; a model trained on that data can uncover a link between intrinsically nonsensitive properties P, Q, and R, and intrinsically sensitive property S. This means that if we have access to values for these non-sensitive properties for a user, the chances of successfully predicting S increase [13].

We address the privacy concern on two levels: as an individual breach of contract or trust, and as a wrong associated with collective surveillance.

Breach of Contract. Thinking back to the three privacy principles, principles (2) and (3) address the individual level. A privacy breach constitutes a violation of these principles. Principle (3) encompasses the traditional idea of *sanctity*, in support of the notion of people "shielding themselves from the gaze of others", whereas principle (2) encapsulates the nature of the information collected, and

---

[1] An extensive analysis of the notion of "sensitive information" and why it is critical can be found in [111].

potentially disseminated, which should be protected when it meets societal standards of intimacy, sensitivity, or confidentiality [74]. The ethical ramifications of influence encompass the broader societal implications of privacy violations; a breach of contract in these cases constitutes a degradation of human dignity. This extends beyond the individual level since individual privacy infringements can violate the right to privacy of other people, and the consequences of privacy losses are experienced collectively [110].

Surveillance. The issue of surveillance adds an extra layer to the aforementioned collective experience of privacy loss. The first of the three principles is dedicated to this concern, and it constitutes a special case of the more general principle of protecting individuals against unacceptable government domination. The right to privacy can thus also be understood by referring to general, well-defined, and generally accepted political principles addressing the balance of power [74] (See also Sect. 2.5). An invasion of the privacy of an agent gives others power over that agent [110]. On a societal level, citizens' autonomy is threatened when they lose their privacy. The more data are collected, the easier it becomes to anticipate the following actions of an individual, the more prone people become to influence, and the easier it becomes to justify this influence. Government surveillance becomes, thus, more powerful once they gain access to said data. This is a critical concern since "a largely unregulated tech industry is detrimental to free and democratic societies" [110].

Technical Work. While the most obvious approaches to mitigating privacy concerns relating to influence involve simply deciding whether or not to proceed with a given product deployment or research project, there is also research on technical approaches to respecting privacy in certain applications of influential AI. These include work on differential privacy [1,38] and contextual integrity [14,33].

2.5   Exogeneity

Lastly, influence may be unethical if it advances interests not held by the agent being influenced, a property we call *exogeneity*.

We present two articulations of unethical exogeneity in influence: the disparate advancing of exogenous and endogenous interests, and the exercise of power.

Exogenous Interests. Influence may be unethical if it advances exogenous goals or interests (those not held by the influencee) over endogenous goals or interests (those held by the influencee). In this account, the wrongness of influence stems not from the fact that the influencer benefits (they may not benefit), or from harm to the influencee in absolute terms (they may not be harmed), but from the relative advantaging of the interests of another agent over the interests of the influencee [13,76,86].

Power. Influence may also be unethical if it empowers one party over another, or constitutes an exercise of power of one party over another. There is considerable philosophical literature on how power is instantiated in technology [16], as well as related concepts including "control" and "domination" [9]. For example, manipulating the opinion of a single individual can be difficult [31], but widely-used recommender systems present a vector by which a minority might steer the opinions and behaviour of a larger population, through an accumulation of small or stochastic effects. Another example of power being abused is the use of AI-enabled ad targeting to influence election results [18].

Technical Work. Monitoring whose interests are being served through the use of an AI system lends itself naturally to questions of fairness, and there is substantial literature on both formal measures of fairness [82] and algorithms for promoting it [112]. Another relevant line of work relates the development of mechanisms for diffusing or decentralising the power that is exercised through the use of influential AI systems. This includes both technical social choice mechanisms for choosing objective functions [66], and the use of participatory institutions such as citizen assemblies [79] and collective response systems [32,80] to provide democratic oversight.

3 Governance of Influence

For the most part, the concerns listed in Sect. 2 point to general or abstract principles that can inform an understanding of the ethical status of different kinds of influence. In order for such an understanding to be widely adopted into the practices of those designing and building influential algorithmic systems, we need mechanisms for deciding, disseminating and enforcing what best practice looks like in specific, concrete terms. Here we point to three such mechanisms (professional cultures, ethics review processes, government regulation) via examples from other domains (scientific research with human subjects, journalism, advertising).

3.1 Professional Culture

In journalism there is minimal formal oversight of ethical practice, but nonetheless there is broad understanding of a core set of ethical principles which are reinforced by educational institutions, professional organisations, and workplace culture [48,89]. These principles commonly include mention of accuracy or truthfulness [83], objectivity or impartiality [117], and avoidance of harm through the use of anonymity or avoiding coverage of certain topics (e.g. suicide) [24,36]. Such principles informally govern influence in the context of journalism. Similar ethical principles exist in computer science, but these are not as widely adopted [20,30].

3.2   Institutional Ethics Reviews

Formal ethics review processes, such as those conducted by most academic institutions in advance of research that involves human subjects, are one way of formalising a consideration for the ethics of influence. Reviewers involved in such processes already grapple with the use of techniques such as deception or trickery to create experimental conditions [8], and with what it means to have meaningfully consented to be subject to such influence [55]. Examples of such review processes in practice are numerous, in AI research a number of prestigious conferences and journals have implemented such mechanisms through checklists and the provision of guidelines [99]. The same holds true for industry where the widespread deployment of AI-based algorithms has lead to the establishment of ethics review processes by large companies such as Adobe or Google [4,50].

3.3   Regulation

In many jurisdictions, the advertising industry is subject to laws that place limits on the content of advertising and the contexts in which certain types of advertising can appear. These often require that advertising avoid outright deception (e.g., truth-in-advertising laws) [106], and ban ads in contexts where they are thought to cause harm (e.g., the ban of gambling, alcohol, or fast food ads during childrens' programs or televised sports) [2,104]. Such laws formally specify classes of influence which are collectively deemed unacceptable in the context of advertising.

Since AI is a fast-moving field, implementing regulatory guidelines for it presents a challenge. Though not specifically targeted at AI systems, the European Union's General Data Protection Regulation (GDPR) sets out a number of rules which implicitly impose constraints on Artificial Intelligence as well [93]. These rules will be concretised by the Union's Artificial Intelligence Act which it aims to pass by the end of 2023 and which is specifically targeted at the regulation of AI Systems [42]. Further examples of planned AI regulation include the attempts in the United Kingdom where a white paper was recently published which will be used as the basis for the country's AI regulations [107] as well as the US which published a Blueprint for an AI Bill of Rights [108].

4   Conclusion

In this paper we have synthesised some of the most commonly cited reasons—captured by the acronym SHAPE—why influence can be unethical. Specifically, these are that influence can (1) involve *secrecy* regarding the intent or means of influence, (2) cause *harm*, (3) reduce human *agency* by removing options, imposing conditional costs or offers, occurring without consent, bypassing reason, or being irresistible, (4) violate *privacy* by relying on the use of private information in a way that breaches an assumed contract or being implicated in mass surveillance, and (5) advance *exogenous* interests at the expense of endogenous interests, or give one group power over another. We linked each of these general principles to relevant concepts from computer science and artificial intelligence, and described three models of ethical governance from other domains—professional culture which emphasises ethics, institutional ethics reviews, and regulation—which could be employed to translate such general principles into practice.

We envisage the SHAPE framework being used by designers of influential AI systems as a way to structure their thinking when considering the ethical impacts of their systems. For example, those building a product based on a large language model (LLM) might systematically work through Box 1, enumerating the examples of each of the SHAPE concerns that arise in the context of their product. These might include user-to-LLM feedback loops that are not understood by the user (*secrecy*), defamatory hallucinations (*harm*), affordances that require extra effort by users to surface certain perspectives in model outputs (*agency*), use of personal data to improve user retention (*privacy*), and adversely paternalistic choices in the design of the product (*exogeneity*), among others. Such a list could then be translated into a list of actions to be taken to remove or mitigate each of these ethical concerns.

For the most part, we have in this paper refrained from stipulating particular definitions or drawing definitive lines between ethical and unethical influence. Such decisions will likely be context-specific and contested, and our focus has instead been on drawing connections between work in philosophy and computer science. That said, it would be valuable for future work to consider the extent to which these concerns over influence could be made more precise by focusing on narrower domains, such as LLM-enabled chat interfaces or social media recommender systems.

Acknowledgements. The authors were supported by UK Research and Innovation [grant number EP/S023356/1], in the UKRI Centre for Doctoral Training in Safe and Trusted Artificial Intelligence (safeandtrustedai.org), co-located at King's College London and Imperial College London.

References

1. Abadi, M., et al.: Deep learning with differential privacy. In: Proceedings of the 2016 ACM SIGSAC Conference on Computer and Communications Security, pp. 308–318. CCS 2016, Association for Computing Machinery, New York, NY, USA (2016). https://doi.org/10.1145/2976749.2978318
2. Adams, J., Tyrrell, R., Adamson, A.J., White, M.: Effect of restrictions on television food advertising to children on exposure to advertisements for 'less healthy' foods: Repeat cross-sectional study. PLOS ONE **7**(2), 1–6 (2012). https://doi.org/10.1371/journal.pone.0031578
3. Adar, E., Tan, D.S., Teevan, J.: Benevolent deception in human computer interaction. In: Proceedings of the SIGCHI Conference on Human Factors in Computing Systems, pp. 1863–1872 (2013)
4. Adobe Inc.: AI Ethics. https://www.adobe.com/uk/about-adobe/aiethics.html
5. Adomavicius, G., Bockstedt, J.C., Curley, S.P., Zhang, J.: Do recommender systems manipulate consumer preferences? A study of anchoring effects. Inf. Syst. Res. **24**(4), 956–975 (2013). https://doi.org/10.1287/isre.2013.0497

6. Anderson, D.: An epistemological conception of safe spaces. Soc. Epistemology **35**(3), 285–311 (2021). https://doi.org/10.1080/02691728.2020.1855485
7. Asch, S.E.: Opinions and social pressure. Sci. Am. **193**(5), 31–35 (1955). https://doi.org/10.1038/scientificamerican1155-31
8. Athanassoulis, N., Wilson, J.: When is deception in research ethical? Clin. Ethics **4**(1), 44–49 (2009). https://doi.org/10.1258/ce.2008.008047
9. Aytac, U.: Digital domination: Social media and contestatory democracy. Polit. Stud. 00323217221096564 (2022). https://doi.org/10.1177/00323217221096564
10. Bai, H., Voelkel, J.G., Eichstaedt, J.C., Willer, R.: Artificial intelligence can persuade humans on political issues (2023). https://doi.org/10.31219/osf.io/stakv. https://osf.io/stakv/
11. Barocas, S., Nissenbaum, H.: Big data's end run around anonymity and consent. Priv. Big Data Public Good: Frameworks Engagem. **1**, 44–75 (2014)
12. Baron, M.: Manipulativeness. In: Proceedings and Addresses of the American Philosophical Association, vol. 77, no. 2, pp. 37–54 (2003). http://www.jstor.org/stable/3219740
13. Benn, C., Lazar, S.: What's wrong with automated influence. Can. J. Philos. **52**(1), 125–148 (2022). https://doi.org/10.1017/can.2021.23
14. Benthall, S., Gürses, S., Nissenbaum, H., et al.: Contextual integrity through the lens of computer science. Now Publishers (2017)
15. Berdichevsky, D., Neuenschwander, E.: Toward an ethics of persuasive technology. Commun. ACM **42**(5), 51–58 (1999). https://doi.org/10.1145/301353.301410
16. Bloomfield, B.P., Coombs, R.: Information technology, control and power: the centralization and decentralization debate revisited. J. Manage. Stud. **29**(4), 459–459 (1992)
17. Blumenthal-Barby, J.S.: A framework for assessing the moral status of manipulation, In: Weber, C.C.M. (ed.) Manipulation, pp. 121–134. Oxford University Press (2014)
18. Boine, C.: AI-enabled manipulation and EU law (2021). https://doi.org/10.2139/ssrn.4042321
19. Brewer, B.R., Fagan, M., Klatzky, R.L., Matsuoka, Y.: Perceptual limits for a robotic rehabilitation environment using visual feedback distortion. IEEE Trans. Neural Syst. Rehab. Eng. **13**(1), 1–11 (2005)
20. BCS, The Chartered Institute for IT: Code of conduct for BCS members (2022). https://www.bcs.org/media/2211/bcs-code-of-conduct.pdf
21. Bublitz, J.C., Merkel, R.: Crimes against minds: on mental manipulations, harms and a human right to mental self-determination. Crim. Law Philos. **8**(1), 51–77 (2014). https://doi.org/10.1007/s11572-012-9172-y
22. Buss, S.: Valuing autonomy and respecting persons: manipulation, seduction, and the basis of moral constraints. Ethics **115**(2), 195–235 (2005). https://doi.org/10.1086/426304
23. Cambridge dictionary (2023). https://dictionary.cambridge.org. Accessed 23 July 2023
24. Carlson, M.: Whither anonymity? journalism and unnamed sources in a changing media environment. In: Journalists, Sources, and Credibility, pp. 49–60. Routledge (2010)
25. Carroll, M., Hadfield-Menell, D., Russell, S., Dragan, A.: Estimating and penalizing preference shift in recommender systems. In: Proceedings of the 15th ACM Conference on Recommender Systems, pp. 661–667. RecSys 2021, Association for Computing Machinery, New York, NY, USA (2021). https://doi.org/10.1145/3460231.3478849

26. Carson, T.L.: Lying and Deception: Theory and practice. OUP Oxford, Oxford (2010)
27. Carvalho, D.V., Pereira, E.M., Cardoso, J.S.: Machine learning interpretability: a survey on methods and metrics. Electronics **8**(8), 832 (2019). https://doi.org/10.3390/electronics8080832. https://www.mdpi.com/2079-9292/8/8/832
28. Cave, E.M.: What's wrong with motive manipulation? Ethical Theor. Moral Pract. **10**(2), 129–144 (2007). https://doi.org/10.1007/s10677-006-9052-4
29. Chan, A., et al.: Harms from increasingly agentic algorithmic systems. In: Proceedings of the 2023 ACM Conference on Fairness, Accountability, and Transparency, pp. 651–666. FAccT 2023, Association for Computing Machinery, New York, NY, USA (2023). https://doi.org/10.1145/3593013.3594033
30. Association for Computer Machinery: ACM code of ethics and professional conduct (2018). https://www.acm.org/code-of-ethics
31. Coppock, A., Hill, S.J., Vavreck, L.: The small effects of political advertising are small regardless of context, message, sender, or receiver: evidence from 59 real-time randomized experiments. Sci. Adv. **6**(36), eabc4046 (2020). https://doi.org/10.1126/sciadv.abc4046
32. Coy, P.: Can A.I. and democracy fix each other? New York Times (2023). https://www.nytimes.com/2023/04/05/opinion/artificial-intelligence-democracy-chatgpt.html
33. Criado, N., Such, J.M.: Implicit contextual integrity in online social networks. Infor. Sci. **325**, 48–69 (2015). https://doi.org/10.1016/j.ins.2015.07.013
34. Deschênes, M.: Recommender systems to support learners' agency in a learning context: a systematic review. Int. J. Educ. Technol. High. Educ. **17**(1), 50 (2020). https://doi.org/10.1186/s41239-020-00219-w
35. Dierkens, N.: Information asymmetry and equity issues. J. Financ. Quant. Anal. **26**(2), 181–199 (1991)
36. Domaradzki, J.: The Werther effect, the Papageno effect or no effect? A literature review. Int. J. Environ. Res. Public Health **18**(5), 2396 (2021). https://doi.org/10.3390/ijerph18052396
37. Douglas, T., Forsberg, L.: Three rationales for a legal right to mental integrity. In: Ligthart, S., van Toor, D., Kooijmans, T., Douglas, T., Meynen, G. (eds.) Neurolaw. Palgrave Studies in Law. Neuroscience, and Human Behavior, pp. 179–201. Springer, Cham (2021). https://doi.org/10.1007/978-3-030-69277-3_8
38. Dwork, C.: Differential Privacy. In: Bugliesi, M., Preneel, B., Sassone, V., Wegener, I. (eds.) ICALP 2006. LNCS, vol. 4052, pp. 1–12. Springer, Heidelberg (2006). https://doi.org/10.1007/11787006_1
39. Dynel, M.: Comparing and combining covert and overt untruthfulness: on lying, deception, irony and metaphor. Pragmatics Cogn. **23**(1), 174–208 (2016)
40. Ekstrand, J.D., Ekstrand, M.D.: First do no harm: considering and minimizing harm in recommender systems designed for engendering health. In: Engendering Health Workshop at the RecSys 2016 Conference, pp. 1–2. ACM (2016)
41. Etzioni, A., Etzioni, O.: Incorporating ethics into artificial intelligence. J. Ethics **21**(4), 403–418 (2017). https://doi.org/10.1007/s10892-017-9252-2
42. European Parliament: EU AI Act: First regulation on Artificial Intelligence (2023). https://www.europarl.europa.eu/news/en/headlines/society/20230601STO93804/eu-ai-act-first-regulation-on-artificial-intelligence
43. Evans, C., Kasirzadeh, A.: User tampering in reinforcement learning recommender systems (2022)

44. Everitt, T., Hutter, M., Kumar, R., Krakovna, V.: Reward tampering problems and solutions in reinforcement learning: a causal influence diagram perspective. Synthese **198**(Suppl 27), 6435–6467 (2021)

45. Faden, R.R., Beauchamp, T.L.: A History and Theory of Informed Consent. Oxford University Press, Oxford (1986)

46. Ferrero, L.: An introduction to the philosophy of agency. In: The Routledge Handbook of Philosophy of Agency. Routledge (2022)

47. Fischer, J.M.: Responsibility and manipulation. J. Ethics **8**(2), 145–177 (2004). https://doi.org/10.1023/B:JOET.0000018773.97209.84

48. Frost, C.: Journalism Ethics and Regulation. Taylor & Francis, Milton Park (2015). https://books.google.co.uk/books?id=K5b4CgAAQBAJ

49. Garnett, M.: Agency and inner freedom. Noûs **51**(1), 3–23 (2017). http://www.jstor.org/stable/26631435

50. Google LLC: Google AI Review Process. https://ai.google/responsibility/ai-governance-operations/

51. Gorin, M.: Do manipulators always threaten rationality? Am. Philos. Q. **51**(1), 51–61 (2014)

52. Habermas, J.: Between Facts and Norms: Contributions to a Discourse Theory of Law and Democracy. The MIT Press, Cambridge (1996)

53. Hasher, L., Goldstein, D., Toppino, T.: Frequency and the conference of referential validity. J. Verbal Learn. Verbal Behav. **16**(1), 107–112 (1977). https://doi.org/10.1016/S0022-5371(77)80012-1

54. High Level Expert Group on Artificial Intelligence: Ethics Guidelines for Trustworthy AI (2019)

55. Hoeyer, K., Hogle, L.F.: Informed consent: the politics of intent and practice in medical research ethics. Ann. Rev. Anthropol. **43**(1), 347–362 (2014). https://doi.org/10.1146/annurev-anthro-102313-030413

56. Hofmann, B.: Suffering: harm to bodies, minds, and persons. In: Handbook of the Philosophy of Medicine, pp. 129–145 (2017)

57. Howard, P., Ganesh, B., Liotsiou, D., Kelly, J., François, C.: The IRA, social media and political polarization in the United States, 2012–2018. U.S, Senate Documents ((2019)

58. Jakesch, M., Bhat, A., Buschek, D., Zalmanson, L., Naaman, M.: Co-writing with opinionated language models affects users' views. In: Proceedings of the 2023 CHI Conference on Human Factors in Computing Systems. CHI 2023, Association for Computing Machinery, New York, NY, USA (2023). https://doi.org/10.1145/3544548.3581196

59. Kang, H., Lou, C.: AI agency vs. human agency: understanding human–AI interactions on TikTok and their implications for user engagement. J. Comput.-Mediated Commun. **27**(5), zmac014 (2022). https://doi.org/10.1093/jcmc/zmac014

60. Kenton, Z., Kumar, R., Farquhar, S., Richens, J., MacDermott, M., Everitt, T.: Discovering agents (2022)

61. Kidd, I.J.K., Medina, J., Pohlhaus Jr., G. (eds.): The Routledge Handbook of Epistemic Injustice. Routledge, London (2017). https://doi.org/10.4324/9781315212043

62. Kligman, M., Culver, C.M.: An analysis of interpersonal manipulation. J. Med. Philos. A Forum Bioeth. Philos. Med. **17**(2), 173–197 (1992). https://doi.org/10.1093/jmp/17.2.173

63. Kramer, A.D.I., Guillory, J.E., Hancock, J.T.: Experimental evidence of massive-scale emotional contagion through social networks. Proc. Natl Acad. Sci. **111**(24), 8788–8790 (2014). https://doi.org/10.1073/pnas.1320040111
64. Krueger, D., Maharaj, T., Leike, J.: Hidden incentives for auto-induced distributional shift (2020)
65. Lavazza, A.: Freedom of thought and mental integrity: The moral requirements for any neural prosthesis. Front. Neurosci. **12**, 82 (2018). https://doi.org/10.3389/fnins.2018.00082.https://www.frontiersin.org/articles/10.3389/fnins.2018.00082
66. Lee, M.K., et al.: WeBuildAI: participatory framework for algorithmic governance. Proc. ACM Hum.-Comput. Interact. **3**(CSCW), 1–35 (2019)
67. Levine, T.R.: Encyclopedia of Deception, vol. 2. Sage Publications, Thousand Oaks (2014)
68. Lewandowsky, S., Van Der Linden, S.: Countering misinformation and fake news through inoculation and Prebunking. Eur. Rev. Soc. Psychol. **32**(2), 348–384 (2021)
69. Linardatos, P., Papastefanopoulos, V., Kotsiantis, S.: Explainable AI: a review of machine learning interpretability methods. Entropy **23**(1), 18 (2021). https://doi.org/10.3390/e23010018. https://www.mdpi.com/1099-4300/23/1/18
70. Madry, A., Makelov, A., Schmidt, L., Tsipras, D., Vladu, A.: Towards deep learning models resistant to adversarial attacks. arXiv preprint arXiv:1706.06083 (2017)
71. Mahon, J.E.: Contemporary Approaches to the Philosophy of Lying. In: The Oxford Handbook of Lying. Oxford University Press, Oxford (2018). https://doi.org/10.1093/oxfordhb/9780198736578.013.3
72. Martin, C.W.: The Philosophy of Deception. Oxford University Press, Oxford (2009)
73. Mirsky, Y., Lee, W.: The creation and detection of deepfakes: a survey. ACM Comput. Surv. (CSUR) **54**(1), 1–41 (2021)
74. Nissenbaum, H.: Privacy as contextual integrity. Wash. L. Rev. **79**, 119 (2004)
75. Noggle, R.: Manipulative actions: a conceptual and moral analysis. Am. Philoso. Q. **33**(1), 43–55 (1996)
76. Noggle, R.: The ethics of manipulation. In: Zalta, E.N. (ed.) The Stanford Encyclopedia of Philosophy. Metaphysics Research Lab, Stanford University. Summer 2022 edn. (2022)
77. Nozick, R.: Coercion. In: Morgenbesser, M.P.S.S.W. (ed.) Philosophy, Science, and Method: Essays in Honor of Ernest Nagel, pp. 440–72. St Martin's Press, New York (1969)
78. World Health Organization, et al.: Ethics and governance of artificial intelligence for health: WHO guidance (2021)
79. Ovadya, A.: Towards platform democracy: Policymaking beyond corporate CEOs and partisan pressure. https://www.belfercenter.org/publication/towards-platform-democracy-policymaking-beyond-corporate-ceos-and-partisan-pressure
80. Ovadya, A.: 'Generative CI' through collective response systems (2023)
81. Peczenik, A., Karlsson, M.M.: Law, justice and the state: essays on justice and rights. In: Proceedings of the 16th World Congress of the International Association for Philosophy of Law and Social Philosophy (IVR) Reykjavík, 26 May-2 June, 1993, vol. 1. Franz Steiner Verlag (1995)
82. Pessach, D., Shmueli, E.: A review on fairness in machine learning. ACM Comput. Surv. **55**(3), 51:1–51:44 (2023). https://doi.org/10.1145/3494672
83. Porlezza, C.: Accuracy in journalism (2019). https://doi.org/10.1093/acrefore/9780190228613.013.773

84. Ross, W.D.: Foundations of Ethics. Read Books Ltd., Redditch (2011)
85. Rubel, A., Castro, C., Pham, A.: Autonomy, agency, and responsibility, pp. 21–42. Cambridge University Press (2021). https://doi.org/10.1017/9781108895057.002
86. Rudinow, J.: Manipulation. Ethics **88**(4), 338–347 (1978). https://doi.org/10.1086/292086
87. Sachs, B.: Why coercion is wrong when it's wrong. Australas. J. Philos. **91**(1), 63–82 (2013). https://doi.org/10.1080/00048402.2011.646280
88. Sahbane, I., Ward, F.R., Åslund, C.H.: Experiments with detecting and mitigating AI deception (2023)
89. Sanders, K.: Ethics and Journalism. SAGE Publications, Thousand Oaks (2003). https://books.google.co.uk/books?id=5khuTNSQ6rYC
90. Schlosser, M.: Agency. In: Zalta, E.N. (ed.) The Stanford Encyclopedia of Philosophy. Metaphysics Research Lab. Winter 2019 edn. Stanford University, Stanford (2019)
91. Schmidt, A.T., Engelen, B.: The ethics of nudging: an overview. Philos. Compass **15**(4), e12658 (2020). https://doi.org/10.1111/phc3.12658
92. Schwartz, M.: Repetition and rated truth value of statements. Am. J. Psychol. **95**(3), 393–407 (1982). https://doi.org/10.2307/1422132
93. E.P. for the Future of Science: Technology: the impact of the general data protection regulation (GDPR) on artificial intelligence (2020)
94. Selinger, E., Whyte, K.: Is there a right way to nudge? The practice and ethics of choice architecture. Soc. Compass **5**(10), 923–935 (2011). https://doi.org/10.1111/j.1751-9020.2011.00413.x
95. Sententia, W.: Neuroethical considerations: cognitive liberty and converging technologies for improving human cognition. Ann. New York Acad. Sci. **1013**(1), 221–228 (2004). https://doi.org/10.1196/annals.1305.014
96. Seymour Fahmy, M.: Love, respect, and interfering with others. Pacific Philos. Q. **92**(2), 174–192 (2011). https://doi.org/10.1111/j.1468-0114.2011.01390.x
97. Shiffrin, S.V.: Speech Matters: On Lying, Morality, and the Law. Princeton University Press, Princeton (2014). https://doi.org/10.1515/9781400852529
98. Spahn, A.: And lead us (not) into persuasion...? Persuasive technology and the ethics of communication. Sci. Eng. Ethics **18**(4), 633–650 (2012). https://doi.org/10.1007/s11948-011-9278-y
99. Srikumar, M., et al.: Advancing ethics review practices in AI research. Nat. Mach. Intell. **4**(12), 1061–1064 (2022). https://doi.org/10.1038/s42256-022-00585-2
100. Sripada, C.S.: What makes a manipulated agent unfree? Philos. Phenomenological Res. **85**(3), 563–593 (2012). https://doi.org/10.1111/j.1933-1592.2011.00527.x
101. Sunstein, C.R.: The ethics of nudging. Yale J. Regul. **32**(2), 413–450 (2015)
102. Sunstein, C.R.: The Ethics of Influence: Government in the Age of Behavioral Science. Cambridge University Press, Cambridge (2016)
103. Taylor, J.S.: Practical Autonomy and Bioethics. Routledge, New York (2009). https://doi.org/10.4324/9780203873991
104. Thomas, S.L., et al.: Young people's awareness of the timing and placement of gambling advertising on traditional and social media platforms: a study of 11–16-year-old's in Australia. Harm Reduction J. **15**(1), 51 (2018). https://doi.org/10.1186/s12954-018-0254-6
105. Thorburn, L., Stray, J., Bengani, P.: Is optimizing for engagement changing us? Understanding recommenders (2022). https://medium.com/understanding-recommenders/is-optimizing-for-engagement-changing-us-9d0ddfb0c65e

106. Tushnet, R.: Chapter 11: Truth and Advertising: The Lanham Act and Commercial Speech Doctrine. Edward Elgar Publishing, Cheltenham, UK (2008). https://doi.org/10.4337/9781848441316.00020
107. UK Department for Science, Innovation and Technology: A Pro-innovation Approach to AI Regulation (2023)
108. US Office of Science and Technology Policy: Blueprint for an AI Bill of Rights (2022)
109. Vold, K., Whittlestone, J.: Privacy, Autonomy, and Personalised Targeting: rethinking how personal data is used. Apollo-University of Cambridge Repository (2019). https://doi.org/10.17863/CAM.43129
110. Véliz, C.: Privacy is Power: Why and How You Should Take Back Control of Your Data. Transworld Digital, London (2020)
111. Wacks, R.: Personal Information: Privacy and the Law. Clarendon Press, Oxford (1989)
112. Waller, M., Rodrigues, O., Cocarascu, O.: Bias mitigation methods for binary classification decision-making systems: survey and recommendations (2023)
113. Ward, F.R., Everitt, T., Belardinelli, F., Toni, F.: Honesty is the best policy: defining and mitigating AI deception. https://causalincentives.com/pdfs/deception-ward-2023.pdf
114. Ward, F.R., Toni, F., Belardinelli, F.: A causal perspective on AI deception in games. In: Proceedings of the 2022 International Conference on Logic Programming Workshops (2022)
115. Ward, F.R., Toni, F., Belardinelli, F.: On agent incentives to manipulate human feedback in multi-agent reward learning scenarios. In: AAMAS, pp. 1759–1761 (2022)
116. Ward, F.R., Toni, F., Belardinelli, F.: Defining deception in structural causal games. In: Proceedings of the 2023 International Conference on Autonomous Agents and Multiagent Systems, pp. 2902–2904 (2023)
117. Ward, S.J.A.: Objectivity and bias in journalism (2019). https://doi.org/10.1093/acrefore/9780190228613.013.853
118. Weidinger, L., et al.: Ethical and social risks of harm from language models (2021). https://arxiv.org/abs/2112.04359
119. Wood, A.W.: Coercion, manipulation, exploitation. In: Manipulation: Theory and Practice. Oxford University Press, Oxford (2014). https://doi.org/10.1093/acprof:oso/9780199338207.003.0002
120. Zuboff, S.: The Age of Surveillance Capitalism. Public Affairs, New York (2019)

Modelling Group Performance in Multiagent Systems: Introducing the CollabQuest Simulation Game

Alejandra López de Aberasturi-Gómez[✉][ID], Jordi Sabater-Mir[ID], and Carles Sierra[ID]

Artificial Intelligence Research Institute, IIIA-CSIC, Barcelona, Spain
{alejandra,jsabater,sierra}@iiia.csic.es

Abstract. We present a novel model for studying group performance in collaborative multiagent teams. The model incorporates task interdependence and evaluation types as key factors influencing group dynamics. We propose a simulation game called CollabQuest, which will serve as a platform to explore the effects of these factors on collective performance within the context of collaborative project teams. The game involves agents collaborating to fill a common pool with a minimum amount of work within a limited number of turns, simulating a group work environment. By manipulating the composition of the group and the interdependence among agents, we plan to study how different types of tasks and evaluation approaches impact the behaviour and decision-making of agents. The model integrates intrinsic and extrinsic rewards, creating a tension between individual and collective interests, and reflecting real-world challenges. Through CollabQuest, we aim to gain insights into the challenges and strategies associated with multiagent systems in collaborative settings. This preliminary work lays the foundation for further research in the field of multiagent reinforcement learning and collective decision-making.

Keywords: Multiagent Reinforcement Learning · Group Productivity · Collaboration

1 Introduction

Collaborative skills are increasingly crucial in modern society, leading many countries to shift their educational systems towards promoting teamwork over the last few decades.

The traditional individualistic teaching approach, which encouraged competition among students until the 1970s, has given way to a more collaborative classroom setting since the 1980s. Innovative teaching strategies now focus on projects and teamwork, where students collectively engage their intellectual efforts within a group. In these group work scenarios, students are organized into teams of three to five members to collaboratively solve problems, explore concepts, answer questions, or create products. Each member can take on inter-dependent tasks that contribute to a common goal or participate in the same shared task.

Similarly, in the corporate world, individual-oriented industrial psychology and group-oriented psychology have been applied for more than half a century. However, according to Edgar H. Schein, "*organizational research and consulting practices still seem obsessed with reducing interactive phenomena into individual traits such as emotional intelligence*" [9]. In educational settings, the advantages of adopting this collaborative teaching approach have been observed [4]. However, implementing effective group teaching and leadership can be challenging, especially due to limited access to external resources like theoretical models or consultants. Consequently, the responsibility for fostering effective group dynamics often falls solely on teachers, who may lack the necessary theoretical background or tools to navigate this task successfully [1].

To address these gaps, we propose a computational model that studies the factors influencing the productivity of groups. Viewing group productivity as an objective measure of a workgroup's outcomes [2], we believe a well-designed and trained multiagent model can predict group performance in specific tasks. By leveraging this capability, we aim to optimize and facilitate group work. Collaborative skills are becoming increasingly important in our modern society, to the point that many countries have witnessed a paradigm shift in their educational systems towards increased teamwork through the last few decades.

This research makes several significant contributions to the field of collaborative performance in multiagent systems within group work contexts. Firstly, we propose a formal model that integrates theories from social psychology and game theory, providing a structured framework for investigating teamwork and decision-making processes. This model offers a novel approach to studying collaboration in groups and lays the foundation for our future work.

Additionally, we introduce the concept of the CollabQuest simulation game, which, although still in its early stages, holds great potential as an experimental platform for exploring the dynamics of collaborative performance. By manipulating factors such as group composition and interdependence, we expect that CollabQuest will allow researchers and educators to gain valuable insights into the challenges and strategies associated with group work. Through the exploration of these factors, we anticipate uncovering key dynamics that influence collaborative performance, thereby informing the design and implementation of effective interventions. As CollabQuest is still in its early stages, we envision its potential as an experimental platform for advancing our understanding of group performance and decision-making processes in multiagent systems

The paper is organized as follows: The next section outlines the key theories from social psychology and game theory that underpin our proposed model. Building upon the insights from the literature, Sect. 3 presents a formal model for investigating teamwork, offering a structured framework for studying collaborative decision-making processes. In Sect. 4, we propose the idea of the CollabQuest simulation game-a tool designed to examine how group performance might vary when modifying two critical internal factors: composition and interdependence. While CollabQuest is currently a work in progress, we envision it as an innovative experimental platform for exploring the dynamics of group performance and decision-making. Finally, Sect. 5 concludes the paper by discussing the potential applications and implications of the CollabQuest game in collaborative multi-agent systems, emphasizing its potential contribution to understanding group performance.

2   Group Work as a Mixed-Motive Game

Group productivity or group performance refers to the relationship between the resources available for a task and the outcome achieved. Each individual brings their own knowledge, motivations, and personality traits (among other elements) to the group, influencing and being influenced by the context and the other members of the team. The processes of group interaction (the relationships that build up and evolve among the individuals within the group) determine whether individuals will combine their resources appropriately to achieve the group's goals based on the task type the group needs to accomplish.

In psychology, theoretical models of group productivity agree that the internal factors shaping group performance are: **1)** the group members, **2)** the interdependences among group members caused by the task, and **3)** the processes of group interaction that occur among group members [7].

A very well-known taxonomy of group tasks in social psychology is owed to Ivan D. Steiner [10] and anchors on the relationship between what the individual and the group contribute to the assignment. This taxonomy distinguishes between:

1. Additive tasks: group productivity is the sum of individual productivity. For example, a group project where each member is assigned a specific section to research and write, and their individual contributions are combined to create a comprehensive report.
2. Compensatory tasks: group productivity is the average of individuals' productivity. For instance, in a group presentation, each member presents a different aspect of the topic, and the overall performance is evaluated based on the collective quality of their presentations.
3. Disjunctive tasks: the group selects the response or contribution of one of its members. For example, in a problem-solving task, the group's success depends on identifying the best solution provided by any member of the group.
4. Conjunctive tasks: all group members must contribute for the task to be finished. For instance, in a group fitness challenge, the group's success is determined by the ability of the least fit member to complete the tasks or exercises, and
5. Discretionary tasks: where there is no direct relationship between individual and group contributions. An example of a discretionary task is a brainstorming session where each member generates ideas individually, and the group's success depends on the overall quantity and quality of the ideas contributed.

When one or several group members exert less effort than their potential to achieve optimal performance in a collective task, it is referred to as motivation loss. One factor that can undermine motivation is *social loafing*. Social loafing is characterised by a decrease in individual contributions (working "less hard") when people work in a group and believe that others are also working, compared to when they work alone. Conversely, we can observe the opposite effect known as *social compensation*. Social compensation occurs when individuals put in extra effort when they anticipate lower performance from other group members [12]. This phenomenon arises from the desire to compensate for a perceived lack of skills or motivation among colleagues to successfully complete a task. The study suggests that people are more likely to work harder in a group setting compared to when they are working alone if **1)** at least one group member expects insufficient effort from others to achieve success, and **2)** the task holds significant importance to those individuals.

On the other hand, Steiner made a clear distinction between potential productivity, which represents what a group is capable of achieving, and actual productivity, which reflects what the group actually accomplishes. According to his theory, actual productivity can be calculated by subtracting the "lost" processes within the group from the potential productivity. These "lost" processes refer to factors that hinder the group from reaching its full potential. Steiner identified two such processes: the loss of motivation and the loss of coordination. It's important to note that Steiner also acknowledged the possibility of gains in addition to losses in group interaction processes. In addition, substantial efforts have been devoted in social psychology to studying audience effects like social facilitation and inhibition on productivity. This preliminary version will not cover these aspects, though. Instead, we will focus on elements that have the highest impact on group productivity without considering the effect of other group members' gaze.

In the context of group work, it is useful to view it as a *mixed-motive game*. A mixed-motive game, as defined in game theory, involves players whose preferences among outcomes partially align and partially conflict. This scenario motivates players to both cooperate and compete, similar to the dynamics of the Prisoner's Dilemma game. In a mixed-motive game, individuals face not only interpersonal conflict with others but also intrapersonal psychological conflict resulting from the clash of motives. In the context of group members working together, they share the common goal of collaborating to complete a group task. However, factors such as the evaluation system (*e.g.*, being assessed as a group *vs.* being assessed individually), the task structure (*e.g.*, whether the group product reflects the behaviour of a single member or the contributions of all members are combined), and the perceived cost of individual contributions create a psychological conflict. This conflict presents each member with the choice between cooperating with the rest of the group or pursuing personal interests (defecting) within the group context.

The notion of a social dilemma and the associated research paradigms are particularly suitable for studying settings where the task assessment is the same for all team members [5]. Specifically, in such a situation, the payoff structure that group members face seems similar to the dilemma of contributing to public goods: agents contribute their expertise over time to the service of the group and benefit from the evaluation of the task regardless of whether they have contributed or not, and without diminishing the evaluation received by others.

To represent situations involving mixed motivations that concern multiple decision makers (hereafter referred to as DMs) and extend over time, [6] define a Sequential Social Dilemma (SSD) as a general-sum Markov game, which may not necessarily be a cooperative one, where agents must learn an appropriate policy while coexisting with one another. Unlike social dilemmas in traditional game theory, in an SSD, cooperation or defection are labels that apply to policies (rather than actions), such that the cooperativeness of a policy becomes a gradable quality defined concerning a certain metric.

We understand that a group work scenario meets the necessary conditions to be modelled as an SSD, as it involves multiple DMs with general and possibly different, motivations who must interact over time. During their interactions, each individual must decide what contributions to make to the group while coexisting with and being affected by others. Therefore, we propose utilising the model of [6] to represent the internal elements of a group that, according to theory, primarily impact its performance, i.e., the group members, the interdependences caused by the task among group members, and the processes of group interaction that unfold. Further, we propose a game, CollabQuest, as a future simulation platform to explore the effects of these factors on collective performance.

Until recently, most previous work on policy search in multiagent systems took a prescriptive view: "What should each agent do?" The challenge of modelling games that were not purely cooperative (i.e., situations where there was no complete alignment of the goals of all the agents) led [6] to adopt an orthogonal approach, the descriptive one: "What social effects emerge when each agent uses a particular learning rule?" To answer this question, they use reinforcement learning.

Reinforcement learning implements goal-directed behaviour. Goals in reinforcement learning are formalised in terms of a signal, the reward, passing from the environment to the agent. The mission of a reinforcement learning agent is to maximise the expected value of the cumulative sum of a received reward signal [11] without being explicitly told how to do it (i.e., without the use of heuristics that facilitate the search for a solution to the problem). Shedding heuristics, in this case, is particularly advantageous, as in line with what has been mentioned before, structural factors, payoff systems and group phenomena conspire in a complex web of relationships that cannot be fully captured using hand-designed rules. A behavioural model based on the pursuit of a positive (extrinsic or intrinsic) reward signal naturally fits into this approach: based on theoretical assumptions about the motivations (external and internal) underlying behaviour, we design a reward function that takes these factors into account and observes the resulting social effects. This same approach has been advocated in seminal works such as [3].

3   Formal Model

As [2] proposed, we interpret group productivity as an objective measure of the outcomes of a workgroup, often involving the counting of items or tracking the achievement of milestones in a project. We assume that given a group task, there exists an objective and quantitative measure of group productivity in work units, denoted as $[W]$.

Definition 1 (Group Task). *We characterize a group task ∇ by a scalar $\mathcal{W}_\nabla$ representing the measure of group productivity (in work units) required to consider the task completed, a scalar T_∇ indicating the maximum time available for the group to complete the task and a label l_∇ indicating the typology of the task:*

$$\nabla := (\mathcal{W}_\nabla, T_\nabla, l_\nabla) \tag{1}$$

A group task will be considered accomplished after a time T with group productivity W if the following two conditions are simultaneously met:

$$\begin{cases} W \geq \mathcal{W}_\nabla \\ T \leq T_\nabla \end{cases} \tag{2}$$

In order to represent resources that the members of a group bring to the team, we introduce the concept of *expertise*:

Definition 2 (Expertise). *We define the expertise p^i of the i-th member of the group to solve a group task involving a single competency as a constant representing the amount of work that i can accomplish per unit of time applying that competency.*

$$p^i = \left(\frac{\mathrm{d}W}{\mathrm{d}t} \right)_i \tag{3}$$

In practice, we approximate the expertise of i as the ratio of the amount of work W^i that i can perform in a time interval to the duration of the interval:

$$p^i \approx \frac{W^i}{\Delta t} \tag{4}$$

So, the work units that i performs while working on the task during a time interval Δt are approximated by the product:

$$W^i \approx p^i \cdot \Delta t$$

3.1   Multiagent Reinforcement Learning

We consider a group task that involves a single competency, denoted as $\mathcal{W}_\nabla$, within a work scenario. Following Leibo et al.'s approach, we model this scenario as a Markov game. The participants in this game are identified as group members and are considered agents belonging to the set $\mathcal{J}$. By adopting a Markov game framework, we can capture the dynamics of the group task and analyze the interactions and decision-making processes of the individual agents within the collaborative setting. The task state $S_t \in \mathcal{S}$ represents the system's current state. The duration of an episode (*i.e.* the duration of a task) is limited by T_∇, but it can potentially end earlier if the end conditions in Eq. 2 are met. We discretize the time axis along which the agents interact, treating it as a game with turns. For instance, a time step might tick a new hour. At each time step or turn t, every agent has the option to allocate a certain percentage $A_t^i = a$, if any, of their turn time to contribute to the task. Although this is, of course, a simplification, it captures the temporally extended nature of the interaction and the fact that not every member of the group needs to engage in teamwork simultaneously with the rest of peers. In this context, the agents' agency is reflected through the time they choose to spend on the task, which we refer to as abstract *actions*. The available range of time percentages that an agent can choose to contribute from defines its set of possible actions, denoted as $\mathcal{A}$. Consequently, the joint action space becomes $\mathcal{A}^n$, where n represents the number of agents within the system $\mathcal{J}$. To denote a joint action of the entire agent system, we utilize the notation $\overrightarrow{a}$.

As outlined later, our model's transition function is represented by the label l_∇, which corresponds to the task type and determines how agents' contributions are combined to make progress in the task. We denote this transition function $\mathcal{P} : \mathcal{S} \times \mathcal{S} \times \mathcal{A}^n \longrightarrow [0, 1]$, as the function $\mathcal{P}(s'|s, \overrightarrow{a})$ that maps each tuple $(s', s, \overrightarrow{a})$ to a probability density value for each choice of s and $\overrightarrow{a}$. Each agent i has full observation of the task state s and learns a behaviour $\pi^i(a|s)$ guided by a reward signal R^i. Given a temporal discount factor $\gamma \in [0, 1]$, the state-value function at state $S_t = s$ for agent i when the joint policy is $\overrightarrow{\pi} = (\pi^1, ..., \pi^n)$ is defined as:

$$V_i^{\overrightarrow{\pi}}(s) = \mathbb{E}_{\overrightarrow{\pi}}\left[\sum_{k=0}^{\infty} \gamma^k R_{t+k+1}^i | S_t = s\right] \tag{5}$$

3.2   Task Type and Transition Function

As mentioned in the introduction, the most widely used taxonomy of tasks in group psychology distinguishes between additive, compensatory, disjunctive, conjunctive, and discretionary tasks. The task typology determines how the efforts of group members are combined to achieve a collective outcome, thus establishing task interdependences among them [7], as the performance of each group member in a group task depends to some extent on the performance of others.

In our model, the task type imposes constraints on how the work performed by group members is aggregated to transition to the next task state. While the agents' allocation of their turn time might introduce stochasticity, resulting in some noise when mapping effort to measured contributions, we will, for simplicity, treat these transitions deterministically as a starting point. Therefore, here we will focus on the subfamily of Markov Decision Processes (MDPs) within the broader class of Markov Games as our general framework.

The task state at time t, S_t, will be the accumulated group work units from the start of the episode until t, where $S_0 \doteq 0$. We focus on the first four types of tasks[1] and denote by $A_t^i = a$ the fraction of time that agent i decides to dedicate to working on the task in turn t. The total time dedicated by the set $\mathcal{J}$ of agents in turn t is represented by $\overrightarrow{A}_t = \overrightarrow{a}$. We group the expertise of all agents in $\mathcal{J}$ into a constant vector $\overrightarrow{p} = (p^1, ..., p^n)$. Let S_t be the current task state, $\overrightarrow{A}_t$ be the joint action of the group, and $\mathcal{W}_\triangledown$ be the productivity measure representing the completion threshold for the task. The transition functions $\mathcal{P}$ for the different task typologies are defined as:

Transition Function of an **Additive Task (A)**: In an Additive task, the group's performance is the sum of the individual contributions.

$$\mathcal{P}_A(S_{t+1} = s' | S_t = s, \overrightarrow{A}_t = \overrightarrow{a}) = \begin{cases} 1 & \text{if } s' = s + (\overrightarrow{p} \cdot \overrightarrow{a}^\top) \\ 0 & \text{otherwise} \end{cases}$$

Transition Function of a **Compensatory Task (X)**: In this case, the next state S_{t+1} is determined by the current state S_t, the collective actions $\overrightarrow{A}_t$, and the specific and normalised weights $\omega^i, i \in \mathcal{J}$ assigned to each agent in the system.

$$\mathcal{P}_X(S_{t+1} = s' | S_t = s, \overrightarrow{A}_t = \overrightarrow{a}) = \begin{cases} 1 & \text{if } s' = s + \sum_{i \in \mathcal{J}} \omega^i (p^i \cdot a^i) \text{ with } \sum_{i \in \mathcal{J}} \omega^i = 1 \\ 0 & \text{otherwise} \end{cases}$$

Transition Function of a **Disjunctive Task** (D): In a disjunctive task, the group's performance is determined by the achievement of at least one group member. Hence, the transition function for a disjunctive task must ensure that the group's progression depends on the maximum contribution among all members

$$\mathcal{P}_D(S_{t+1} = s' | S_t = s, \overrightarrow{A}_t = \overrightarrow{a}) = \begin{cases} 1 & \text{if } s' = s + \max_{i \in \mathcal{J}} \{ p^i \cdot a^i \} \\ 0 & \text{otherwise} \end{cases}$$

Transition Function of a **Conjunctive Task** (C): In a conjunctive task, the group's performance is contingent upon achieving the least performing member. Hence, the transition function for a disjunctive task must ensure that the group's progression relies on the least-performing member's contribution to task completion.

$$\mathcal{P}_C(S_{t+1} = s' | S_t = s, \overrightarrow{A}_t = \overrightarrow{a}) = \begin{cases} 1 & \text{if } s' = s + \min_{i \in \mathcal{J}} \{ p^i \cdot a^i \} \\ 0 & \text{otherwise} \end{cases}$$

3.3   Payoff System and Expected Reward

In addition to task interdependences, Nijstad's model [7] considers the interdependences caused among group members by the distribution of feedback and rewards. Consistent with major models in social psychology, the evaluation of a collective task (*i.e.*, the payoff system) can be of three types:

---

[1] We exclude discretionary tasks from our model since the way contributions of team members are aggregated is not determined in their definition.

1. **Promotive** of interdependence
2. **Contrient** or competitive, and
3. **Independent** (where each group member's evaluation depends solely on their own performance)

In our model, the payoff system partially determines the reward R_t^i received by the i-th agent in each turn. Specifically, we allow the reward R_t^i to have an intrinsic component representing the cost (effort) of collaborating for the public good, C_t^i, and an extrinsic component dependent on the payoff system, E_t^i, that serves as feedback for agents to discern between high and low-performing turns:

$$R_t^i = E_t^i - C_t^i$$

The expected reward function for an agent i in a turn t is:

$$r^i(s, \overrightarrow{a}) \doteq \mathbb{E}\left[R_t^i | S_{t-1} = s, \overrightarrow{A}_{t-1} = \overrightarrow{a}\right]$$

which can be decoupled as a sum of the form:

$$r^i(s, \overrightarrow{a}) = e^i(s, \overrightarrow{a}) - c^i(s, \overrightarrow{a}) \tag{6}$$

where $e^i(s, \overrightarrow{a})$ represents the external reward function received by agent i, and $c^i(s, \overrightarrow{a})$ represents the cost or effort incurred by agent i for dedicating a^i units of time.

As a starting point, we take $c^i(s, \overrightarrow{a}) \equiv f(a^i)$ (the expected cost of a turn for agent i is a function of the time dedicated to the task by i in that turn). Specifically, we propose that the expected cost is of the form $c^i(s, \overrightarrow{a}) = \beta^i \cdot a^i$, where β^i is a proportionality constant that may vary (or not) for each agent.

Regarding the expected extrinsic reward, we define the following functional forms for each type of evaluation:

Promotive Evaluation: In a promotive evaluation, the extrinsic reward received by each agent is solely based on the overall performance of the group. It does not take into account individual contributions or rankings within the team. The functional form for the expected extrinsic reward in a promotive evaluation can be defined as:

$$e^i(s, \overrightarrow{a}) = f(s, \overrightarrow{a}) \quad \text{for all } i$$

Here, $f(s, \overrightarrow{a})$ represents a function that determines the expected extrinsic reward based on the collective performance of the group, as indicated by the state s and the vector of actions $\overrightarrow{a}$. In this type of evaluation, all agents receive the same reward, promoting a sense of cooperation and shared success within the group. In such a situation, the payoff structure that agents face is similar to the dilemma of contributing to public goods. According to [8], there are two main characteristics that distinguish a public good: non-exclusion and non-rivalry. The first characteristic refers to the impossibility of denying the consumption or enjoyment of the good to any individual. The second characteristic is that the enjoyment of one person does not diminish the amount that others can consume. For instance, taxpayers face such a dilemma when their contributions are enjoyed by everybody, without the possibility of denying access to social security and public health to tax evaders. All the population would be better off if everybody payed their taxes, yet from a selfish perspective one maximises their payoff by exploiting the contributions and not reciprocating.

Promotive evaluation in teamwork is thus an instance of the public goods dilemma: cooperative agents contribute their expertise over time to the service of the group, and all agents benefit from the evaluation of the task regardless of whether they contributed or not. Plus, enjoyment of the evaluation by an agent does not diminish the evaluation received by others.

Competitive or Contrient *Evaluation:* In competitive evaluation, the extrinsic reward is based on the relative productivity or ranking of each individual within the group. The evaluation takes into account the proportion of an individual's productivity (represented by $p_i \cdot a_i$) compared to the productivity of others in the team $\mathcal{J}$:

$$e^i(s, \overrightarrow{a}) = f(\text{rank}^i(\overrightarrow{a}, \overrightarrow{p}))$$

In this expression, $\text{rank}^i(\overrightarrow{a}, \overrightarrow{p})$ represents the ranking of individual i based on their productivity within the group, considering both their contribution vector $\overrightarrow{a}$ and the expertise vector $\overrightarrow{p}$. The function $f(\cdot)$ maps the rank to a corresponding reward or outcome. The specific form of the function $f(\cdot)$ can vary depending on the specific context and criteria used for ranking individuals.

Hence, when this kind of evaluation is implemented, each member's grade reflects their rank within the group. For instance, educational systems in which the highest honours are awarded in a class based on the percentile that the student occupies are contrient.

Independent *Evaluation:* For independent evaluation, we can define it using a function that directly considers the individual's own performance without referencing the performance of others:

$$e^i(s, \overrightarrow{a}) = f(p^i, a^i)$$

Each individual is evaluated based on their expertise and effort, providing a sense of autonomy and independence in the evaluation process. An example of such an evaluation would be an educational system in which the highest honours are awarded if a student's performance satisfies a pre-established set of criteria.

In terms of the payoff system, it is important to clarify that the extrinsic reward E_t in non-terminal states should be contingent exclusively on the actions undertaken by the agents in $t - 1$. This approach enables the agents to discern between high-performing and low-performing turns, allowing them to assess and differentiate the effectiveness of their actions in contributing to the collective task.

To provide an example, let's consider a simplified **promotive** evaluation system where tasks are either pass or fail. In this system, the extrinsic reward E_t in non-terminal states is determined solely by the agents' actions. After each time step or turn, the agents receive a shared extrinsic reward of $E_t \propto (\overrightarrow{p} \cdot \overrightarrow{a}^{\top})$ based on their contributions.

In the case of terminal states, which represent evaluations performed by the instructor, an extrinsic reward can be designed. For instance, a reward of $E_t = 10$ can be assigned to a task that has been successfully completed, meeting the criterion $S_t \geq \mathcal{W}_{\nabla}$, while a reward of $E_t = -10$ can be allocated otherwise

4   CollabQuest: Unleashing Collective Potential

Finally, we present a baseline simulation game, CollabQuest, designed to replicate a teamwork environment and provide a structured platform for systematically studying group collaboration based on the model discussed earlier. The game aims to investigate how the performance of groups in tasks involving a single competency is predicted to vary when modifying two internal factors believed to be most predictive of group performance: **composition** and **interdependence**.

In CollabQuest, the collective goal of the agents is to fill a common pool with a minimum of tokens equivalent to $\mathcal{W}_{\nabla}$ units of work within a maximum of T_{∇} turns. If T_{∇} turns go by without successfully filling the common pool, the agents receive a negative reward representing failure. Each agent i is endowed with a skill level p^i that remains constant throughout the interaction. This skill level determines the value of the tokens for each player. For example, each token of a player with skill level $p^i = 2$ will have a value of 2. In each turn, each agent can contribute $A_t^i \in [a_{min}, a_{max}]$, so that we compute an agent's contribution in a turn as the product $p^i \cdot a^i$.

To create tension between individual and collective interests, CollabQuest incorporates both extrinsic and intrinsic rewards in the agent's decision-making process. The reward function for each agent at each time step consists of an extrinsic component and an intrinsic component that represents the cost of contributing to the public good. This tension reflects real-world scenarios, where individual incentives often conflict with the collective goal. While agents may be tempted to free-ride and benefit from the work of their peers in the short term, the success of the group and the avoidance of negative rewards depend on making sufficient contributions throughout the game

In future studies, we plan to apply a parsimonious methodology that draws inspiration from practices followed in the social sciences. This methodology will involve carefully manipulating the variables of group composition, interdependence, task type, and payoff system to gain valuable insights into their impact on group performance. Our aim is to conduct these studies in a rigorous and efficient manner.

To examine the influence of group composition, we will manipulate the number of agents, denoted as n, and the skill vector represented by $\overrightarrow{p}$. This will allow us to explore how different team sizes and skill distributions among group members affect overall performance outcomes.

Furthermore, we will intentionally manipulate interdependence by imposing specific task types and payoff systems (evaluation methods). For instance, to study the performance of a group of agents with different skill levels in an additive task under promotive evaluation, the transition function could be designed such that all contributions from all agents determine the successor state.

$$\mathcal{P}_{\mathrm{A}}(S_{t+1} = s' | S_t = s, \overrightarrow{A}_t = \overrightarrow{a}) = \begin{cases} 1 & \text{if } s' = s + (\overrightarrow{p} \cdot \overrightarrow{a}^{\top}) \\ 0 & \text{otherwise} \end{cases}$$

Similarly, to align with the promotive nature of the task, an equal extrinsic reward function would be uniformly employed for all agents:

$$E_t = \begin{cases} \overrightarrow{p} \cdot \overrightarrow{a}^{\top} & \text{for non-terminal states} \\ 10 \cdot \mathbb{I}(S_t \geq \mathcal{W}_{\nabla}) - 10 \cdot \mathbb{I}(S_t < \mathcal{W}_{\nabla}) & \text{for terminal states} \end{cases}$$

Notice that in non-terminal states, the extrinsic reward is contingent on the actions performed by the agents $\mathcal{J}$ in the previous turn, reflecting the immediate impact of their actions on the collaborative task. Conversely, in terminal states, the extrinsic reward assumes the role of a global evaluation by an instructor or leader, providing an overall assessment of the group's performance.

We believe that CollabQuest may serve as an effective model for studying team dynamics due to its ability to capture key elements of collaborative decision-making. By simulating the interactions among agents and considering factors such as composition and interdependence, CollabQuest has the potential to provide valuable insights into how teams perform in complex tasks according to social and group psychology models. The game's integration of intrinsic and extrinsic rewards creates a realistic tension between individual and collective interests, reflecting the dynamics often observed in group work scenarios.

Eventually, the insights gained from CollabQuest can inform team formation practices in group work settings. Educators and administrators can leverage the findings to design teams with complementary skills and diverse perspectives, fostering a teamwork environment where team members can benefit from each other's expertise.

5   Conclusions and Future Work

To conclude, this paper makes significant contributions to the study of collaborative performance in multiagent systems, particularly within educational and corporate contexts. Firstly, we present a formal model that offers a novel approach to investigating teamwork based on evidence from social psychology and game theory. As far as our knowledge extends, this is the first multi-agent reinforcement model specifically designed for group performance prediction.

Moreover, we introduce the CollabQuest simulation game as a foundational tool for exploring the dynamics of collaborative decision-making. This game will allow for the manipulation of important factors such as task interdependence and evaluation types, enabling researchers to gain insights into the underlying mechanisms that drive group dynamics. By varying the composition of the group and the interdependence among agents, we aim to uncover the challenges and strategies associated with collaboration in groups.

Through the integration of intrinsic and extrinsic rewards, CollabQuest creates a tension between individual and collective interests, mirroring real-world scenarios. Our preliminary work establishes a strong foundation for further research in the field of multiagent reinforcement learning. It opens up possibilities for enhancing educational and corporate outcomes by deepening our understanding of group work and decision-making processes.

We believe that this model and the CollabQuest simulation game hold great potential for informing the design and implementation of interventions that foster effective collaboration and maximise collective outcomes.

For the sake of simplicity, this preliminary work has focused solely on tasks that involve the application by the group members of a single competency. Moving forward, we plan to extend our research by investigating more complex scenarios involving tasks that require sets of d competencies, $\mathcal{C}$, such that $\mathcal{W}_\nabla$ is replaced by a d-dimensional vector $\overrightarrow{\mathcal{W}_\nabla}$.

We believe that this extension of the model will provide a foundation for studying collaborative performance in divisible tasks [10].

Additionally, we will explore the incorporation of other traits into the agents beyond their expertise. These efforts will pave the way for innovative approaches in collaborative multiagent systems and contribute to the advancement of effective teamwork.

References

1. Bolton, M.K.: The role of coaching in student teams: a "just-in-time" approach to learning. J. Manag. Educ. **23**(3), 233 (1999)
2. Campion, M.A., Medsker, G.J., Higgs, A.C.: Relations between work group characteristics and effectiveness: implications for designing effective work groups. Pers. Psychol. **46**(4), 823–847 (1993)
3. Jara-Ettinger, J., Gweon, H., Schulz, L.E., Tenenbaum, J.B.: The naïve utility calculus: computational principles underlying commonsense psychology. Trends Cogn. Sci. **20**(8), 589–604 (2016)
4. Johnson, D.W., Johnson, R.T.: An educational psychology success story: social interdependence theory and cooperative learning. Educ. Res. **38**(5), 365–379 (2009)
5. Kameda, T., Stasson, M.F., Davis, J.H., Parks, C.D., Zimmerman, S.K.: Social dilemmas, subgroups, and motivation loss in task-oriented groups: in search of an "optimal" team size in division of work. Soc. Psychol. Q. **55**, 47–56 (1992)
6. Leibo, J.Z., Zambaldi, V., Lanctot, M., Marecki, J., Graepel, T.: Multi-agent reinforcement learning in sequential social dilemmas. arXiv preprint arXiv:1702.03037 (2017)
7. Nijstad, B.A.: Group Performance. Psychology Press, London (2009)
8. Ostrom, V., Ostrom, E.: Public goods and public choices. In: Alternatives for Delivering Public Services, pp. 7–49. Routledge (2019)
9. Schein, E.H.: Organizational psychology then and now: some observations. Annu. Rev. Organ. Psychol. Organ. Behav. **2**(1), 1–19 (2015)
10. Steiner, I.D.: Group Process and Productivity. Academic Press, New York (1972)

11. Sutton, R.S., Barto, A.G.: Reinforcement Learning: An Introduction. MIT Press, Cambridge (2018)
12. Williams, K.D., Karau, S.J.: Social loafing and social compensation: the effects of expectations of co-worker performance. J. Pers. Soc. Psychol. **61**(4), 570–581 (1991)

Towards Developing an Agent-Based Model of Price Competition in the European Pharmaceutical Parallel Trade Market

Ruhollah Jamali[1]([⊠])(iD) and Sanja Lazarova-Molnar[2,1]

[1] The Maersk Mc-Kinney Moller Institute, University of Southern Denmark, 5230 Odense, Denmark
{ruja,slmo}@mmmi.sdu.dk
[2] Institute of Applied Informatics and Formal Description Methods, Karlsruhe Institute of Technology, 76133 Karlsruhe, Germany
sanja.lazarova-molnar@kit.edu

Abstract. The European pharmaceutical parallel trade refers to the practice of purchasing pharmaceutical products in one European Union (EU) member state at a lower price and reselling the products in another EU member state at a higher price. In the pharmaceutical market, pricing strategies are of utmost importance as the market structure and regulations allow only the lowest-priced product to gain market share, making it imperative for players to optimize their pricing decisions in order to remain competitive. Therefore, developing a dynamic and data-driven pricing strategy that takes into account market conditions, competitors' behaviors, and regulatory compliance is of interest to players involved in this market. In this paper, we demonstrate the potential of agent-based modeling as a tool for integrating mathematical modeling and economic concepts and investigating targeted pricing strategies in the pharmaceutical parallel trade market. We achieve this by utilizing agent-based modeling to evaluate and compare multiple pricing strategies through simulation. We aim to identify the challenges associated with developing a dynamic pricing approach in this complex market by showcasing the effectiveness of agent-based modeling. We contribute to the understanding of pricing strategies and their implications in the pharmaceutical parallel trade market.

Keywords: Agent-based modeling and simulation · Pricing strategy · Price competition · Pharmaceutical parallel trade

1 Introduction

The European pharmaceutical trade market incorporates the practice of parallel trade, also known as parallel importing, in which patented pharmaceutical

This work is partly funded by the Innovation Fund Denmark (IFD) under File No. 9065-00207B.

products are purchased in one EU member state at a lower price, repackaged to comply with another EU member state market's local legislation, and then resold in the destination state at a higher price. This is made possible by the EU's single market that allows for free movement of goods between member states [6]. There are several players involved in the pharmaceutical parallel trade market, including original manufacturers (also known as originators), parallel importers, wholesalers, retailers (pharmacies, supermarkets, and online retailers), and regulators. In this market, each player plays a unique role and interacts with others to bring pharmaceutical products to the end-users. The parallel trade market can benefit consumers as it increases the availability of cheaper medicines. However, it can also have a negative impact on pharmaceutical companies' profitability and competitiveness [7].

Decision-making processes in the pharmaceutical trade market are challenging as they involve multiple factors, such as market demand, dynamic supply chain, balancing profitability and affordability, regulations, and price competition. Investigating and quantifying even one of these factors could be a challenging assignment. For example, the price competition between parallel traders and the originator in a country's market can be intense, as all parties are vying for a share of the market and profits, whereas the parallel import framework allows parallel traders to offer the same products to consumers at a lower price than the original manufacturers [5]. The pricing strategy for players involved in the pharmaceutical parallel trade market is a complex process that takes into account various factors such as the price of the product in the origin country, transportation and logistics costs, tariffs, taxes, and the market demand in the target country.

Agent-based modeling and simulation (ABMS) enable the possibility to evaluate, analyze, and predict behaviors and interactions, especially under uncertainty as is common in complex processes such as economics interactions [19]. ABMS has advantages over other forms of modeling, like mathematical modeling, by facilitating the design of agents with relatively more autonomy, and has been applied in the field of economics for a number of purposes, such as analyzing market dynamics, the impact of regulations, and the study of financial markets [18]. Furthermore, running simulations that account for multiple initial assumptions can offer insights to guide decision-making, ultimately contributing to the maximization of economic efficiency and stability. In our previous work, we developed a simple agent-based model of the pharmaceutical parallel trade market involving two countries and demonstrated how this model could be beneficial for players involved in this market and how economists can use the model to investigate the pharmaceutical parallel trade market [9,10].

In the first agent-based model of the pharmaceutical parallel trade market, the competition between players is modeled as a Cournot competition where players compete to get a larger market share only by adjusting their sell quantities [10]. In subsequent work, we developed an initial pricing function for agents to investigate and demonstrate the ability of an agent-based model to simulate multiple scenarios of parallel trade of pharmaceuticals [8]. The primary objective of this study is to investigate the effect of various pricing strategies on the profitability of agents participating in the price competition of the pharmaceutical parallel trade market, through an agent-based modeling approach. The study aims to identify the challenges and opportunities associated with modeling pricing strategy and their implications on the market.

The rest of the paper is structured as follows: In Sect. 2, we present the agent-based model of the pharmaceutical trade market. Section 3 describes the agent-based model specification of the case study. Results and discussion of the case study are presented in Sect. 4. Lastly, a summary and outlook of the paper are provided in Sect. 5.

2   Description of the Parallel Trade Market Model

In this study, we model the price competition among multiple parallel traders and a manufacturer (or direct sellers) in the Danish pharmaceutical market using agent-based modeling. Our research utilizes the agent-based model to study pricing strategies and key factors that influence pricing strategies for the participants of the pharmaceutical market.

Parallel traders import medicine from foreign countries, repackage it to comply with Danish regulations, and sell it for profit, whereas manufacturers sell medicine directly in the market. In Denmark, the prices of medicinal products are determined by pharmaceutical companies (parallel traders and manufacturers) and sold at the same rate by all pharmacies. The Danish Medicines Agency does not regulate the prices set by the companies but rather ensures that prices are updated every 14 days (fortnight) and reported to relevant parties. Every fortnight, pharmaceutical companies that wish to sell a particular medicine must establish its price. The company that offers the lowest price for a medicine will be the offered brand for that medicine at all pharmacies in Denmark. If the company with the lowest price cannot deliver the market demand, pharmacies will proceed to offer the product from the company with the second lowest price, and so on. The system of fixed prices and free market competition helps maintain low prices for medicinal products. This framework creates a level of stability in the market by setting limits on the number of packages a company can deliver [2, 11].

This study extends our previous research [10] by expanding the agent-based model to account for the behavior of the players' pricing strategies during the price competition in the destination market. First, we describe the basis agent-based model of a pharmaceutical trade market that comprises two countries. Then, we define pricing strategies for the players involved in the market, resulting in an extended agent-based model of price competition in the market. The nature of price competition in the Danish pharmaceutical market is unique in that only the player with the lowest price can secure market share in a given fortnight, while others are unable to do so. Moreover, considering the narrow profit margin associated with parallel trading of pharmaceutical product and their expiry date, the decisions regarding timing and pricing can have a significant impact on participants' profitability. Consequently, it is crucial for participants in this market to explore and develop effective pricing strategies to gain an edge in the competition.

2.1 Agent-Based Model of Pharmaceutical Parallel Trade Market

Our agent-based model of the pharmaceutical parallel trade market is motivated by a game theory model of the parallel trade market between the United States and Canada and examines the impact of parallel trade on the profits of manufacturers and social welfare [17]. Two countries are involved in the game theory model, denoted as country I and country E as importer and exporter, correspondingly. The model commences with a pharmaceutical manufacturer (located in country E) negotiating the price of a patented medicine with the government of country I, which is modeled as Nash bargaining negotiation [16]. Subsequently, parallel traders purchase the medicine in country I and incur a transfer cost to repackage and move the medicine to country E. Then parallel traders compete with the manufacturer in the market of country E (where the manufacturer can sell the medicine at its desired price) to sell the medicine and maximize their profits, modeled using Cournot competition [4]. Cournot competition is an economic model that illustrates a business scenario wherein rival companies present a homogenous product and compete by determining their sales quantity in the market. The equilibrium price (P) for the medicine in the game theory model is calculated according to:

$$P = \begin{cases} \frac{1}{2}[1 - \frac{n(1 - 2(P_I+t))}{n + 2}], & \text{if } P_I \leq \frac{1}{2} - t \\ \frac{1}{2}, & otherwise \end{cases}, \qquad (1)$$

where P_I is the price of medicine in country I, n is the number of parallel traders engaged in the market, and t is the transfer cost for parallel traders.

In the agent-based model of the pharmaceutical parallel trade market, we consider the environment to be the same countries as in the game theory model. The model has three types of agents, i.e., government, manufacturer, and parallel trader. The simulation of our agent-based model consists of multiple steps that model the behavior of the manufacturer and traders in the pharmaceutical market of the two countries, I and E. In each step, the manufacturer and the government set the medicine price in country I using the Nash bargaining result same as the game theory model. The manufacturer then sells the product in country I, while traders evaluate the profitability of participating in country E's market considering the transfer cost. If traders participate in the market, they compete with the manufacturer and each other to sell a quantity of the medicine of interest. The price of the medicine in country E is calculated using a linear demand function that depends on the total quantity sold and the market size. The revenues for the manufacturer and traders are calculated at each step by reducing costs associated with sales. The manufacturer and traders adjust their market shares to maximize their revenue in each step. Fig 1 provides a high-level overview of the agent-based model. The agent-based model demonstrates the capability to replicate equilibrium prices observed in the game theory model.

Moreover, it offers the advantage of convenient adjustment of model parameters for agents, such as transfer cost, enabling further investigation of the market dynamics.

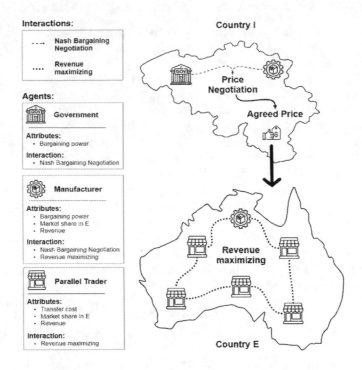

Fig. 1. Agent-based model of a pharmaceutical parallel trade market.

To modify our original agent-based model and investigate pricing strategies, we consider that the government and the manufacturer have already completed the negotiation, and the price of the medicine is fixed in country I (P_I). Parallel traders subsequently purchase the medicine at P_I. After incurring the transfer cost (t), parallel traders participate in price competition in country E by implementing individual pricing strategies that we elaborate on further in Subsect. 2.2. Through running multiple scenarios, we evaluate the effectiveness of each pricing strategy and investigate the impact of different criteria on price adjustment.

2.2   Pricing Strategy

Pricing is an important aspect of marketing and a crucial decision for businesses [3], as it is the only element that generates revenue. Developing a pricing strategy is an intricate task influenced by multiple factors, such as product type, company goals, and market trends. Different pricing approaches, such as price skimming, penetration pricing, bundling, promotion, and complementary pricing, work towards determining the optimal price level [12].

In our model, two distinct pricing strategies are employed by agents. The first strategy is cost-plus pricing, which is utilized by the manufacturer. This approach entails adding a margin to the cost of production of the medicine to determine its final price. Given the typical nature of the pharmaceutical market, where the demand for patented medicines is generally assumed to surpass the supply, it is reasonable to assume that the manufacturer would adopt a cost-plus pricing approach. In our model, the margin is calculated by considering a revenue margin parameter greater than zero. To determine the price, the revenue margin is multiplied by the cost of production and then added to the cost.

The second pricing strategy is employed by parallel traders, where they average a predicted price of the medicine and the price derived from the cost-plus pricing to arrive at their price for the next fortnight. Parallel traders utilize historical data to predict the market price for the next step. They can employ two methods to predict the market price: averaging the price of the market for the last K fortnights, or employing a linear regression model that considers demand, the prices of all players in the market, and the number of fortnight, to predict the price of the medicine for the next fortnight.

Every step or in the agent-based model represents a fortnight where all players involved in the market assess their revenue margin and adjust it based on their previous sales. They examine their revenue histories from the previous N fortnight and if their revenue in more than D fortnights were zero, which suggests that their price is not competitive, they reduce their revenue margin. Conversely, if they earned some revenue in more than T fortnights in the previous N fortnights, indicating the potential for higher profits with a higher price, they increase their revenue margin. The pseudocode presented in Algorithm 1 outlines a comprehensive pricing strategy for market participants.

Algorithm 1. Pricing algorithm for agents in the agent-based model of the danish pharmaceutical market.

---

   if Zero revenue for over D fortnights out of the last N: **then**
      Reduce revenue margin
   else if Positive revenue for over T fortnights out of last N: **then**
      Increase revenue margin
   else
      Keep current revenue margin
   end if
   $\hat{P} \leftarrow$ Predicted price of the market
   for Player in the market **do**
      $\overline{P} \leftarrow$ cost-plus pricing using revenue margin
      if Player is manufacturer: **then**
         $P \leftarrow \overline{P}$
      else
         $P \leftarrow (\overline{P} + \hat{P})/2$
      end if
   end for

2.3 The Agent-Based Model of Price Competition

In this model, there are two types of agents, termed manufacturer and trader, and the environment is the market, where all agents compete to sell a patented medicine produced by the manufacturer. In the following, we present the model in a structured manner, according to the guidelines in the Macal and North tutorial [13].

The first step towards presenting the model is defining the agents set, including agents' attributes and the rules governing their behavior. Both manufacturer and trader agents have eight attributes: 1) Warehouse capacity, which indicates their capacity to store the medicine in a market. 2) Stock, which indicates the number of available medicines in the warehouse. 3) Cost, which for the manufacturer indicates the production cost of the medicine, and for the trader indicates the total cost of buying, repackaging, and moving the medicine. 4) Revenue margin, which is used for cost-plus pricing. 5) Warehouse input, which indicates the number of medicine they are adding to their storage at every step. 6) N, which indicates the number of past fortnights they want to consider for revenue margin adjustment. 7) D, which is the a threshold for decreasing the revenue margin. 8) T, which is a threshold to increase the revenue margin. N, D, and T as presented in the pricing algorithm 1 are parameters representing the competitiveness of an agent in the market.

The second step is to define interaction rules. In each simulation step, both types of agents add a fixed amount of medicine to their warehouse, considering their warehouse capacity. Next, the agents will determine their selling prices for the upcoming fortnight, employing the pricing strategies outlined in Subsect. 2.2. The agent with the lowest price will then become the first seller in the market. If an agent can not provide the medicine for the market (the market demand is bigger than the agent's stock), the agent with the second lowest price start selling their medicine, and so on. Finally, all agents calculate their step revenue.

The Danish pharmaceutical market is the environment of our model. The environment has only one attribute, which is the market demand for medicine.

3 Case Study

In this section, we present the implementation details of the model presented in Sect. 2, aimed at evaluating the impact of pricing strategies and investigating agent-based model applications as a representative of the pharmaceutical market in Denmark. Here we are running our initial step towards developing an agent-based model of price competition. The model was developed using the Python programming language, and the Mesa library [14]. Our case study focuses on the competition surrounding the medication Apixaban, sold under the brand name Eliquis, which is used to treat and prevent blood clots and to reduce the risk of stroke in individuals with nonvalvular atrial fibrillation [1].

To generate the demand data for Apixaban, we utilized the Danish Health Data Authority website (https://medstat.dk/), which provides historical data on the volume of the drug sold in the Danish market. Given the limited size of the data set, we generated synthetic time series data from it using the SDV library [15]. We used the Gaussian Copula form SDV library, which is a tool to model the dependence structure of a set of variables by combining their marginal distributions with a copula function. This tool can generate synthetic time series data that captures the statistical characteristics of the original data. Additionally, the historical pricing data for the Danish market is publicly available from the Danish Medicine Agency (https://medicinpriser.dk/), which has a comprehensive record of the price development of all medicines on the market, updated on a bi-weekly basis since 1998. This data was employed to train the linear regression model used in the pricing strategy.

The parameter values utilized in the model implementation are based on available data for Apixaban. In our simulations, the warehouse capacity of the manufacturer was considered to be 10000 units of medicine, while that of the traders was set to 8000 units. The cost for the manufacturer was considered to be 400 DKK and 550 DKK for the traders. The initial revenue margin for the manufacturer was set at 0.7 and 0.3 for the traders. The warehouse input of the manufacturer in each step was set at 700 medicine units, while that of the traders was 450 medicine units. We use the variables N, D, and T in the model to define a player's competitiveness in the market in terms of their pricing behavior. Since the manufacturer operates in multiple countries, it was considered that they adopt a less competitive approach in the market and look over a longer window when adjusting their revenue margin. Therefore, the value of N was set at 20 for the manufacturer and less than 10 for the traders. D and T are thresholds that indicate the impact of market share on the pricing, with D and T being 2 and 18, respectively, for the manufacturer. This means that if the manufacturer does not have any sales in the market for 18 fortnights of the last 20, they will reduce their revenue margin by 0.01. If they have more than two sales in the last 20, they will increase it by the same amount.

The agent-based model of price competition in the pharmaceutical market of Denmark, developed in this study, provides a data-driven approach to investigating the market dynamics. This model offers the capability to examine the long-term impacts of various pricing strategies and provides insights into the behavior of market participants. Furthermore, the model can assist market players in exploring and determining the optimal approach to the market. In the following section, we will demonstrate the model's capabilities through multiple scenarios, highlighting its practical applications for players in the pharmaceutical market of Denmark.

4   Experiments and Results

The objective of the first scenario is to examine the impact of different pricing strategies on the total revenue of traders in the Danish pharmaceutical market. To accomplish this, four traders were considered, where two of them utilizing a simple price prediction technique by computing the average of the last five fortnights' prices and the other two employing linear regression to forecast the

next fortnight's price based on historical data. To differentiate their characteristics, different values of N, D, and T were assigned to each trader. Here, one of
the traders who employed averaging as their prediction technique was assigned
$N = 8$ while the other was assigned $N = 5$. The same was done for the traders
who utilized linear regression for price prediction. Additionally, $T = 4$ and $D = 2$
were assigned to all traders, while for the manufacturer, we set $N = 20$, $T = 18$,
and $D = 2$. We simulated the model for 1000 replications, each lasting 1000
steps, with a synthetic time-series market demand generated in each replication,
which varied and was independent of one run to another. We used the results of
this simulation experiment to determine the impact of competitiveness on the
total revenue of traders in the pharmaceutical market.

The simulation results showed that the trader who used averaging as the price
prediction method and had $N = 5$ had the highest average revenue of more than
65 million for the whole 1000 steps. The second place was occupied by the trader
who also employed averaging but had $N = 8$, with an average revenue of more
than 64.2 million. The third place was held by the trader who had $N = 8$ and
used linear regression as the price prediction method, with an average revenue
of more than 64 million. The trader who had $N = 5$ and used linear regression
as the prediction method had an average revenue of 63.8 million, which was the
lowest among all traders.

The simulation result indicates that using averaging as the price prediction
method was more beneficial for traders than linear regression under the current
assumptions. Moreover, the results suggest that being more aggressive in changing the revenue margin is more profitable for traders when using averaging as
the prediction method, whereas a different outcome might be expected when
using another prediction method. This highlights the importance of investigating different approach combinations in a market, as the combination could have
a completely different outcome than the expected one.

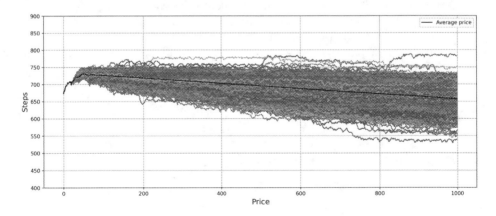

Fig. 2. Market price of the medicine over 1000 simulations.

Additionally, previous simulations can provide an overview of the future market price for the medicine while considering a projected demand for the medicine. Figure 2 illustrates the market price over simulations. Each colored line indicates an independent simulation, while the black one indicates the average of all simulations. In all simulations, the first 50 steps are historical data of prices. Since, in every simulation, a synthetic time-series market demand is generated, the medicine market price varies, which is aligned to the law of supply and demand in economics. However, the interesting observation from Fig. 2 is that price competition caused a diminishing trend in the market price over time.

The second scenario focuses on the manufacturer's behavior optimization in the Danish pharmaceutical market using our agent-based model. The simulation addresses a situation where the manufacturer aims to achieve the maximum profit per product sold in the Danish market over a period of two years, consisting of 104 fortnights. In this simulation, the manufacturer can adjust the parameters N, T, and S to reflect their anticipated market behavior and use historical data to predict the behavior of other market participants. Given the knowledge of the market's parameters, the manufacturer can then use the agent-based model to determine the optimal approach to attain their goal. In this scenario, we investigated the impact of varying values of parameter N on profit per product for the manufacturer in the Danish pharmaceutical market. Specifically, we considered values of 10 to 60 by step of 10 for N, where T was set as $N \times 0.9$ and D as $N \times 0.1$. To obtain robust results, we ran 500 simulations and calculated the 95% confidence intervals for profit per product for each value of N. The detailed results are presented in Fig. 3.

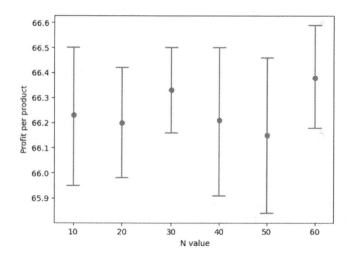

Fig. 3. Profit per product confidence interval for different values of N.

In the final scenario, we aimed to investigate the impact of new revenue margin adjustment criteria on traders' revenue in the Danish pharmaceutical market. Two additional criteria were introduced, one based on total revenue and another one based on volume sold, which were used to set the revenue margin values for each player. We ran the simulation for 1000 fortnights, repeated 1000 times, with one trader employing the previous criterion (count of zero revenue) explained in Subsect. 2.2, two using the new criteria, and the last trader considering all three criteria in an or clause (combined criterion). The results showed that the previous criterion, where traders only adjusted their revenue margin based on the number of zero revenue fortnights in the previous N fortnights, was the most profitable. The combined criterion was the second most profitable, while the total revenue and volume sold criteria ranked next. We also analyzed the profit per product for each trader and observed a similar order, with the gap between the first and second place being less than one. Our findings suggest that considering total revenue and volume sold does not necessarily lead to better pricing strategies for traders in the Danish pharmaceutical market, while employing the zero revenue count is the most profitable approach. Figure 4 provides a visualization of the 95% confidence intervals of total revenue and profit per product for all criteria.

5   Summary and Outlook

In this paper, we present an agent-based model of price competition in the Danish pharmaceutical market between a manufacturer and parallel traders. We demonstrated how this model can be used to analyze the long-term impact of pricing strategies on the market. Furthermore, the model facilitates participants in comprehending the behaviors of other market players in a structured and data-driven fashion by employing data-driven parameters. This model is an important step towards developing a data-driven model of price competition in the Danish pharmaceutical market, allowing players to explore optimal approaches to engage with the market. The presented model enables players to fine-tune their behaviors, particularly their pricing strategies, in order to achieve specific goals.

We ran multiple what-if scenarios with our agent-based model of the market to investigate the impact of different parameters on the players' revenue and profit per product. In our first simulation experiment, we investigated the impact of different pricing strategies on the traders' total revenue. In our second simulation experiment, we showed that the manufacturer could optimize their behavior in the market using our agent-based model to maximize their profit per product on sales. In our last simulation, we illustrated the impact of revenue margin adjustment criteria on total revenue and price per product of traders.

Our agent-based model of price competition in the Danish pharmaceutical market has the potential to become an effective tool for players to optimize their pricing strategies and understand their competitors' behavior. Our simulations indicate that the choice of price prediction method can have a significant impact on traders' total revenue. In this work, we explored and experimented with multiple pricing strategies and investigated various factors affecting the strategy. It is essential to acknowledge that the model presented in this study has yet

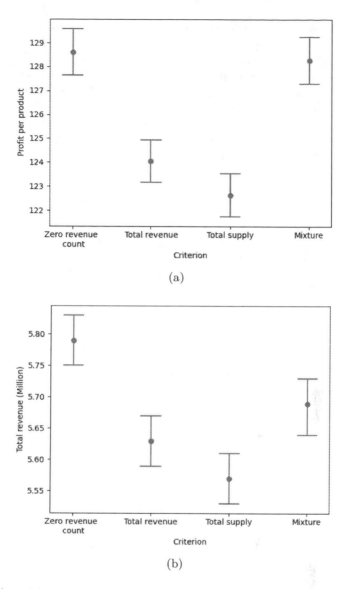

Fig. 4. 95% confidence intervals of (a) total revenue and (b) profit per product for all criteria included in pricing strategy.

to undergo a validation process, and further research is necessary to assess its reliability and effectiveness for real-world applications. While our initial findings appear promising, it is imperative to conduct additional testing and refinement to establish its potential for practical implementation. Future work will involve rigorous experimentation and simulation under diverse conditions and scenarios to assess the robustness of the approach, and to explore its benefits and limitations using historical data of the pharmaceutical parallel trade market.

Our agent-based model provides a framework to explore pricing strategies and optimize behaviors considering specific goals. In our future research, we aim to extend this model further to investigate the impact of other factors, such as the expiry date of available products, expected competitor's actions, type of behavior considering the product, development in purchase prices, and supply chain dynamics. Overall, our study highlights the importance of using data-driven approaches to understand and optimize behavior in complex markets such as the pharmaceutical industry.

References

1. Apixaban monograph for professionals. https://www.drugs.com/monograph/apixaban.html. Accessed 10 Feb 2023
2. Prices of medicine. https://laegemiddelstyrelsen.dk/en/reimbursement/prices/. Accessed 03 Feb 2023
3. Borden, N.H.: The concept of the marketing mix. J. Advert. Res. **4**(2), 2–7 (1964)
4. Cournot, A.A.: Researches into the mathematical principles of the theory of wealth. New York: Macmillan Company, 1927 [c1897] (1927)
5. Danzon, P.M.: The economics of parallel trade. Pharmacoeconomics **13**(3), 293–304 (1998)
6. Darba, J., Rovira, J.: Parallel imports of pharmaceuticals in the European union. Pharmacoeconomics **14**(Suppl 1), 129–136 (1998)
7. Enemark, U., Pedersen, K.M., Sørensen, J.: The economic impact of parallel import of pharmaceuticals (2006)
8. Jamali, R., Lazarova-Molnar, S.: Agent-based simulation of the pharmaceutical parallel trade market: a case study. In: The 14th International Conference on Ambient Systems, Networks and Technologies (2022)
9. Jamali, R., Lazarova-Molnar, S.: The relationship between agent-based simulation and game theory in the case of parallel trade. In: 2022 IEEE International Conference on Agents (ICA), pp. 36–41. IEEE (2022)
10. Jamali, R., Lazarova-Molnar, S.: Towards agent-based simulation of the parallel trading market of pharmaceuticals. In: 2022 IEEE International Conference on Parallel & Distributed Processing with Applications, Big Data & Cloud Computing, Sustainable Computing & Communications, Social Computing & Networking (ISPA/BDCloud/SocialCom/SustainCom). IEEE (2022)
11. Kaiser, U., Mendez, S.J., Rønde, T., Ullrich, H.: Regulation of pharmaceutical prices: evidence from a reference price reform in Denmark. J. Health Econ. **36**, 174–187 (2014)
12. Kienzler, M., Kowalkowski, C.: Pricing strategy: a review of 22 years of marketing research. J. Bus. Res. **78**, 101–110 (2017)
13. Macal, C.M., North, M.J.: Tutorial on agent-based modeling and simulation. In: Proceedings of the Winter Simulation Conference, 2005, p. 14. IEEE (2005)
14. Masad, D., Kazil, J.: MESA: an agent-based modeling framework. In: 14th PYTHON in Science Conference, vol. 2015, pp. 53–60 (2015)
15. Montanez, A., et al.: SDV: an open source library for synthetic data generation. Ph.D. thesis, Massachusetts Institute of Technology (2018)

16. Nash, J.: Two-person cooperative games. Econometrica: J. Econometric Soc. **21**, 128–140 (1953)
17. Pecorino, P.: Should the us allow prescription drug reimports from Canada? J. Health Econ. **21**(4), 699–708 (2002)
18. Tesfatsion, L.: Agent-based computational economics: a constructive approach to economic theory. In: Handbook of Computational Economics, vol. 2, pp. 831–880 (2006)
19. Vermeulen, B., Pyka, A.: Agent-based modeling for decision making in economics under uncertainty. Economics **10**(1), 20160006 (2016)

Using a BDI Agent to Represent a Human on the Factory Floor of the ARIAC 2023 Industrial Automation Competition

Leandro Buss Becker[1,5]([⊠]), Anthony Downs[2], Craig Schlenoff[2], Justin Albrecht[2], Zeid Kootbally[2], Angelo Ferrando[3], Rafael Cardoso[4], and Michael Fisher[1]

[1] University of Manchester, Manchester, UK
{leandro.bussbecker,michael.fisher}@manchester.ac.uk
[2] National Institute of Standards and Technology, Gaithersburg, MD, USA
{anthony.downs,craig.schlenoff,justin.albrecht,zeid.kootbally}@nist.gov
[3] University of Genova, Genova, Italy
angelo.ferrando@unige.it
[4] University of Aberdeen, Aberdeen, UK
rafael.cardoso@abdn.ac.uk
[5] Federal University of Santa Catarina, Florianópolis, Brazil

Abstract. The "Agile Robotics for Industrial Automation Competition" (ARIAC) is an international robotic competition carried out in a simulated factory floor using ROS 2 (Robot Operating System)/Gazebo. Competitors control one gantry robot, four AGVs, and many other elements/devices, overcoming a range of agility challenges in this simulated environment, and are provided with a scoring system to evaluate their performance during the tasks. This paper describes one of the agility challenges in ARIAC 2023, which pertains to a simulated human operator on the factory floor. In undertaking manufacturing tasks, competitors must avoid close proximity between the gantry robot and the human not to get penalized. The human operator is implemented as a Belief-Desire-Intention (BDI) agent in Jason. It is provided with a range of different potential types of behaviour in what concerns with how such human reacts when in proximity to the gantry robot. Three different personalities are presented, ranging from a minimally intrusive up to a very intrusive one. A preliminary analysis was conducted to evaluate the impact of using the developed Jason agent in the ARIAC 2023 competition.

Keywords: Robots in human environments · BDI agents · Jason/ROS

This work was supported by NIST in the USA and the UK's Royal Academy of Engineering through its Chair in Emerging Technologies scheme.

1   Introduction

Organised by the National Institute of Standards and Technology (NIST) since 2017, the Agile Robotics for Industrial Automation Competition[1] [5] (ARIAC) is an annual simulation-based competition which brings together researchers and practitioners to tackle challenges related to agile robotics that industry is facing.

ARIAC 2023 uses version 2 of the Robot Operating System (ROS 2)[2], an open-source framework that offers a comprehensive set of libraries and tools to develop robot software, in conjunction with Gazebo, a physics-based simulator. Together, ROS 2/Gazebo provide a flexible and efficient platform for designing, testing, and deploying robotics applications.

One of the main goals of ARIAC is to provide real-life manufacturing scenarios where humans and robots share a low-volume high-mix workload in a collaborative environment. As such, a new challenge has been introduced in ARIAC 2023, which consists of avoiding close contact between a human operator that moves around the factory floor making inspections and the robots present in the workcell. The workcell contains the following robots: (i) four AGVs that move forward or backward within a given straight lane, and (ii) one gantry[3] robot that consists of a manipulator mounted onto an overhead system that allows it to move along the entire factory floor.

It is our aim that the human operator can have different types of behaviours (from now on we refer to these types as personalities), varying the level of interference caused by the human operator to the gantry robot. The human operator must also attempt not to collide against the AGVs while they move within the factory floor. Figure 1 depicts the ARIAC 2023 simulation scenario.

It is required for the gantry robot not to get closer to the human operator than established in the ISO/TS 15066:2016 standard "Robots and robotic devices – Collaborative robots", which addresses the safety issue of robot speed and separation monitoring [6]. A similar restriction also applies for the AGVs. Competitors get penalized if such restrictions are not properly followed.

This paper concerns the implementation of the movement control strategy for the human operator. Given that Belief-Desire-Intention (BDI) agents [9] can emulate the cognitive reasoning of humans in a very natural way, this paradigm was selected to be used for controlling our human operator. More specifically, the implementation of our BDI agent is done in Jason [1], a well-known BDI programming language [2]. The challenge that we face is this work relates not simply with implementing the Jason agent, but also with how to properly integrate it within the complex ARIAC 2023 simulation environment. Moreover, it

---

[1] https://www.nist.gov/ariac.

[2] Certain commercial products or company names are identified here to describe our competition. Such identification is not intended to imply recommendation or endorsement by the National Institute of Standards and Technology, nor is it intended to imply that the products or names identified are necessarily the best available for the purpose.

[3] Gantry robots are also called Cartesian or Linear robots. In the ARIAC 2023 documentation it will be also referred to as ceiling robot.

is also a challenge how to guide competitors so that they can properly deploy all the tools needed to run our agent within the simulation environment.

The main contributions of this paper can be summarized are as follows: (i) we describe how to integrate the Jason BDI agent for controlling the human operator within the complex ARIAC 2023 simulation scenario; (ii) we detail how such agent is in fact programmed in Jason and how it interfaces with ROS 2/Gazebo. (iii) we analyze the impact of using such Jason agent in ARIAC 2023 from the final user (competitors) perspective, in what concerns the deployment and usage difficulties and also the impact in respect to the CPU utilization.

The remaining parts of this paper are organised as follows. Section 2 describes the ARIAC competition. Section 3 presents the software architecture of our solution. The developed Jason agent is detailed in Sect. 4. Our conclusions are presented in Sect. 5.

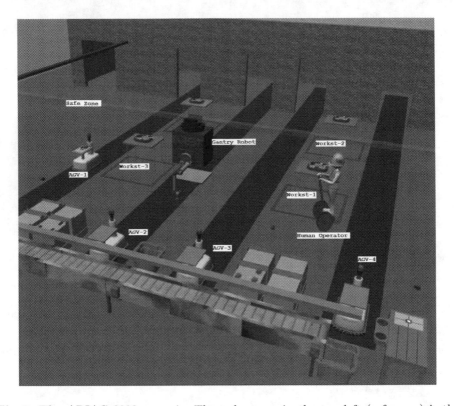

Fig. 1. The ARIAC 2023 scenario. The red square in the top left (safe zone) is the starting position of the human operator. The four blue squares below the tables are the workstations. AGV-1 is moving and the other three are stationary. The human operator is facing the gantry robot, but from the image it is not possible to guess its current personality: if *antagonistic* or *indifferent* it will move towards the gantry; if *helper* it will turn around and move back to the workstation-2. (Color figure online)

2   Agile Robotics for Industrial Automation Competition

ARIAC is an annual competition which aims to tackle challenges that industry is facing in agile robotics. The main goal of ARIAC is to test the agility of industrial robot systems and to enable industrial robots on shop floors to be more productive, more autonomous, and to require less time from shop floor workers. In ARIAC, agility is defined broadly to address: (1) task failure identification and recovery by robots, (2) automated planning to minimise (or eliminate) the up-front robot programming time when a new task is introduced, and (3) operation in fixtureless environments, where robots can sense the environment and perform tasks on parts that are not in predefined locations. The competition participants are required to develop a robot control system for a gantry robot in order to perform kitting operations in a simulated environment.

Prior to designing ARIAC in 2017, NIST explored existing robotics competitions to ensure none of them already addressed industrial robotics agility. The Amazon Picking Challenge [4] was one of the competitions related to challenges addressed in ARIAC. The competition assessed the capability of robots to perform some of the common pick and place operations that are currently performed by humans. The Robot Perception Challenge [7] was another competition which was relevant to agility challenges. The goal of this competition was to drive improvements in sensing and perception technologies for next-generation robots. ARIAC was designed to test and measure Industrial Robot Agility in a holistic sense, because no other competitions were covering that niche.

Figure 1 depicts the simulated environment where the ARIAC 2023 competition takes place. The gantry can move in the simulated environment to interact with objects in order to perform kitting for assembly tasks (announced dynamically during the simulation). A kit is an order for specific items, which can be found on shelves, on the conveyor belt, and in bins. The robot builds kits by picking up all the required items and placing them into one of the trays located on the automated guided vehicles (AGVs). When an order is completed, the AGV delivers the kit and a final score is given to the participants' systems. The final score takes into account many aspects, such as if the type/colour of the selected item matches the type/colour required by the order; the accuracy of products' pose in the tray; and the time taken by the control system to complete a kit (measured in simulation seconds).

The ARIAC 2023 competition has eight "agility challenges"[4]. They represent extra difficulties that competitors may face while performing kitting tasks. For example, competitors could face faulty and/or flipped parts to assemble. Challenges are sampled together in different "trials" that the competitors must overcome during the qualification and final rounds of the competition. Within the scope of this paper we focus on the "human operator" agility challenge.

---

[4] https://ariac.readthedocs.io/en/latest/competition/challenges.html.

2.1   Human Operator Agility Challenge

This challenge consists of inserting a human operator that navigates through the factory floor (workcell). In Fig. 1, it is possible to observe the presence of the human operator (on the right) facing the gantry robot (on the left). The goal of this challenge is to test the ability of the competitors' control system for the gantry robot to avoid collisions with the human operator, otherwise it will incur a penalization.

The simulated human operator will take one of the three personalities in a given trial. Note that, once a personality has been selected for a trial, it will not change during that trial. Even though the development and integration of changing a personality at runtime in ARIAC would be feasible, to simplify the evaluation of the competitor's controller, we opted for a static agent's personality. Regardless of the personality that the agent adopts, it was decided to avoid random moves and to make simplistic, predefined, movement patterns along the four workstations that simulate working/inspection tasks, something common for humans to do within a factory floor. The human operator agent will keep travelling to these workstations and working until the trial ends.

If the human operator and one of the robots get closer than a minimum safety distance (details for the calculation are provided in the next section), then the human is teleported to a safe zone (the top left position shown in Fig. 1). Exceptionally, the human operator is not teleported if it gets close to a non-moving (static) AGV. Moreover, if the teleport operation is caused for being too close to the gantry robot, then the competitor team gets penalised, which also implies disabling the gantry robot for 8 s; afterwards, the normal operation is resumed. In such case the human operator is teleported away purely to give time to the competitors to recover and to avoid situations where the human can behave too aggressively and keep the gantry in a deadlock.

The agent's personalities are as following:

1. *Indifferent*: The human operator follows a predetermined path, regardless of the location of the robots in the environment.
2. *Antagonistic*: The human operator purposefully moves towards the gantry robot to interfere with the robot's current task.
3. *Helpful*: The human operator will move to another workstation (changing direction to avoid the gantry) once the gantry robot is detected to be at a certain distance (`safety distance` × 2).

The *helpful* agent was designed to be minimally intrusive, and should rarely interfere the competition. On the other hand, the *antagonistic* agent is intended to be very intrusive, and is likely to frequently cause penalization to the competitors. We foresee that the *indifferent* agent is the one that will better judge the competitors' skills to avoid contact with the human operator.

2.2   Safety Distance Calculation

The safety distance between the human operator and the robots (gantry robot and AGVs) is derived from the ISO/TS 15066:2016 standard - "Robots and robotic devices - Collaborative robots", which addresses the safety issue of robot speed and separation monitoring [6]. ISO/TS 15066:2016 specifies that the minimum allowable distance between a robot and a human is

$$d_{min} = k_H(t_1 + t_2) + k_R t_1 + B + \delta$$

where t_1 is the maximum time between the actuation of the sensing function and the output signal switching devices to the off state, t_2 is the maximum response time of the machine (i.e., the time required to stop the machine), δ is an additional distance, based on the expected intrusion toward the critical zone prior to actuation of the protective equipment, k_H is the speed of the intruding human, k_R is the speed of the robot, and B is the Euclidean distance required to bring the robot to a safe, controlled stop.

3 Simulation Software Overview

Figure 2 illustrates the elements within the simulation scenario that are of interest for the developed BDI agent: the human operator, the four AGVs, and the gantry robot. The relevant related information about such elements – mainly location and speed – must be constantly updated within the agent, which can only actuate towards the human operator. The additional elements in the scene (shown in Fig. 1) are treated simply as obstacles that should be avoided by the navigation control algorithm running in ROS 2.

A relatively complex software architecture was built to support this simulation environment. Such software architecture is composed of several elements that include, mostly, artifacts from ROS 2 (nodes, topics, services, actions, plugins) and the Jason agent. Figure 3 depicts the elements of the proposed solution[5].

Analysing Fig. 3 from left to right, first there is the *task_manager* Gazebo plugin. It is in charge of initialising all the components that constitute the competition scenario. It is also in charge of publishing the */ariac/start_human* topic to start our Jason's *human–agent*, which was already launched but remains idle until a message on this topic is received. Continuing to the right of the figure, the agent can publish to the three topics at the bottom and subscribe to the two topics at the top, which are all related to the *human_control* ROS 2 node. This node also interacts with the *teleport* Gazebo plugin and with the *navigation stack* (part of the ROS 2 distribution).

4 The Human Agent

The Jason agent is in charge of the high-level control of the human operator. In the simulation, the human is represented as a robot with a human mesh on top of it. Representing the human as a robot allows the human to easily interact with other ROS elements in the simulation. The agent is responsible for controlling the

---

[5] Source code available at https://github.com/usnistgov/ARIAC.

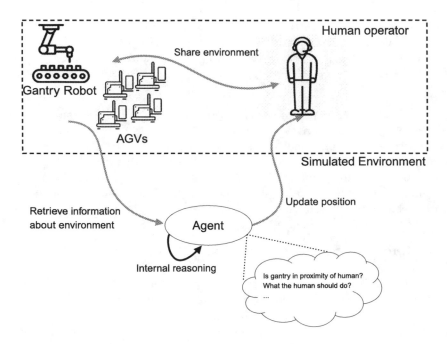

Fig. 2. Overview of the simulation environment from the BDI agent perspective.

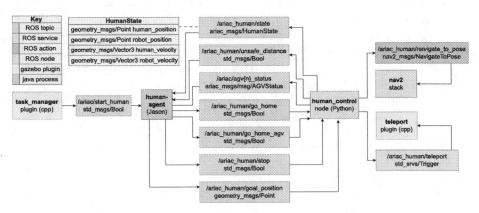

Fig. 3. Software architecture artifacts that support the adopted simulation scenario.

movements of the human, calling ROS 2 functions such as $move(x, y)$ and $stop()$. It must also be constantly updated about the position of the gantry robot and the AGVs, so that it can properly reason about the actions to be taken. It was decided that the human behaviour should be simple and predictable to a certain extent, i.e., there should be no random moves. Therefore, in general terms, the human operator must move around four predefined points of interest within the virtual factory's shop floor (the workstations). The default movement occurs in a clockwise basis starting at workstation 4 ($4 > 2 > 1 > 3 > 4 > \ldots$).

Jason programs are implemented separately into agent and environment programs. Agent programs consist of (in this order): initial beliefs and rules; initial goals; and plans. Plans are written with traditional AgentSpeak syntax [8] `triggering_event : context <- body.` wherein the `triggering_event` can be the addition/deletion of a `belief` or a `goal`, the `context` are the preconditions of the plan, and the `body` is a sequence of operations (`actions` or addition/deletion of `beliefs/goals`). Environment programs are written in Java and define the semantics of the actions that agents can execute, as well as providing the agent with environment perceptions.

4.1 Initial Beliefs and Initial Goal

The initial lines of code from the agent define a set of static beliefs that are used for orientation purposes. For instance, it defines the (x, y) coordinates of the four target positions (workstations 1 to 4), the first position for the robot to visit, and the order in which such positions should be visited (for either counterclockwise and clockwise movement directions).

Two beliefs can change at runtime: `working(Loc)` and `counterClockWise`. The first keeps track of the current station, so that the agent can derive the next target position; while the latter, if present in the agent's belief, indicates a counterclockwise movement direction (otherwise the agent adopts clockwise movement). The agent has one initial goal to wait for the *human_start* message.

4.2 Plans for Movement Control

The agent's main task is to keep the human operator moving through the predefined points. We implement this with two plans, with triggering events `+!work` and `+work_completed`, as shown in Listing 1.1. The first has a context used only to find the coordinates of the desired destination (ln.1)[6]. It then removes the belief that indicates the previous target location (ln.2), and sets the belief with the current target location (ln.3). Finally, it calls an external action in charge of activating the movement at the ROS node (ln.4). The `+work_completed` is triggered when the ROS node indicates that the human operator reached the target position. Its context is used to find the next location to be visited. There is an analogous version of this plan for the counterclockwise movement.

---

[6] 'ln.' will be used as abbreviation for *line* throughout the paper.

```
1   +!work(Loc) : location(Loc, X, Y, Z) <-
2       -working(_);
3       +working(Loc);
4       move(X, Y, Z).

6   +work_completed(_) : working(Loc) & next_loc(Loc,Next) &
        counterClockWise   <- !work(Next).
```

Listing 1.1. Main plans to move the human operator.

In the plan on Listing 1.2, the `+gantry_disabled(_)` belief is added when the gantry is disabled due the fact that the distance between the gantry and the human operator is violating the safety distance. This belief is added with a parameter for debugging purposes. Note the use of _ as in Prolog, which indicates that the term can be unified with anything (i.e., we do not care about its contents in this plan). A similar plan was created for when the human operator is too close to an AGV. The difference in the AGV case is that it calls a teleport service that does not penalise the competitor.

```
1   +gantry_disabled(_) : firstStation(ST) <-
2       .drop_all_desires;
3       teleport_safe; // stop + teleport to safe zone
4       .wait(8000);
5       !!work(ST).
```

Listing 1.2. Plan for when the Gantry is disabled.

In such a plan, the agent drops its own desires (ln.2) using an internal action (Jason predefined actions that do not interact with the environment). This is done to stop all goals currently executed by the agent (e.g., moving to a work-station). Then, we call an external action (implemented in the environment) to teleport the human operator to the safe location (ln.3). This is obtained on the Gazebo side by means of a custom plugin (developed as part of the human challenge integration in ARIAC). After that, the agent waits a fixed amount of time (ln.4); the latter is domain specific and has been decided to give time to the gantry's controller to restore its own tasks. At the end, the plan concludes by calling the `!work` once more, and restoring the standard movement of the human operator in the simulation by going to the first workstation.

4.3   Implementing Personalities

The human personality defines how it behaves in respect to the gantry position. This role is defined upon the agent's initialisation based on the parameter specified in a particular trial (we expect that in ARIAC 2023 there will be at least one trial with each personality). As mentioned in Sect. 2, the three possible personalities are *Indifferent*, *Antagonistic*, and *Helpful*.

In order to implement these three different personalities within the Jason agent, we provide three distinct implementations for the `+gantry_detected` perception. Each implementation lies in a different agent program file (*asl* extension), which is loaded according to the agent initialisation parameter. This perception is triggered when the human operator and the gantry get "too close". This distance, which is computed in Jason's *Environment* class, is defined as being twice the safety distance (calculated as shown in Sect. 2.2).

The implementation for the *indifferent* personality is proforma, as in fact it has no condition and does not take any action (it is just an empty plan). Therefore we only discuss here the implementations for the *antagonistic* and the *helpful* personalities, as follows.

The core part of *antagonistic* agent behavior is shown in Listing 1.3.

```
1  +gantry_detected(_) :
2         working(Loc) & next_loc(Loc,Next) <-
3      stop_movement;
4      .drop_all_desires;
5      move_to_gantry;
6      .wait("+work_completed(_)");
7      !!work(Next).
```

Listing 1.3. Jason code for the agent with the *antagonistic* personality.

It has a context that will always be **true** since it uses beliefs that are always supposed to be present in the belief base, but it is needed in order to allow identifying the destination that the human is currently moving to (ln.2). It first stops and cancels any navigation goal (ln.3), then it drops all desires (ln.4) and triggers an external action requiring the human to move towards the gantry (ln.5). Afterwards the plan remains blocked until it reaches the target position (ln.6). When this holds, it resumes moving to the next station (ln.7).

The core part of the *helpful* agent implementation is shown in Listing 1.4. It requires two distinct plans because it can be moving in either clockwise or counterclockwise directions. The agent keeps the internal belief `counterClockWise`, which is used in the plan contexts to reason about the current direction. If this belief is present (condition in ln.2), then the movement is counterclockwise, and the plan in ln.1–6 is triggered. Otherwise, if it is absent (condition in ln.9), the movement is clockwise, triggering the plan in ln.8–13. Besides having different contexts, each of them adjusts the direction in a different way (ln.5 versus ln.12) and resumes the movement towards a different destination (ln.6 versus ln.13).

The plans for the *helpful* agent are implemented as `atomic`, a predefined plan annotation available in Jason (@id[atomic] where id is a unique plan identifier) to stop considering concurrent intention stacks (i.e., only the intentions related to this plan can be selected). This is required because we do not want these plans to be interrupted while executing, otherwise the agent could lose track of its current movement direction.

```
1   @detected[atomic]
2   +gantry_detected(_) : working(Loc) & previous_loc(Loc,
       Prev) & counterClockWise <-
3      stop_movement;
4      .drop_all_desires;
5      -counterClockWise;
6      !!work(Prev).

8   @detectedCounter[atomic]
9   +gantry_detected(_) : working(Loc) & next_loc(Loc,Next) &
       not counterClockWise <-
10     stop_movement;
11     .drop_all_desires;
12     +counterClockWise;
13     !!work(Next).
```

Listing 1.4. Jason code for the agent with the *helpful* personality.

```
1   public class RosEnv extends Environment{
2    RosBridge bridge = new RosBridge();
3    ...
4    @Override
5    public void init(String[] args) {
6       super.init(args);
7       bridge.connect("ws://localhost:9090", true);
8       bridge.subscribe(SubscriptionRequestMsg.generate("
9       /ariac_human/state")
10       .setType("ariac_msgs/msg/HumanState")
11       .setThrottleRate(1)
12       .setQueueLength(1),
13      new RosListenDelegate() {
14       public void receive(JsonNode dt, String st) {
15        MessageUnpacker<HumanState> unpkr = new
              MesageUnpacker<HumanState>(HumanState.class);
16        HumanState m = unpkr.unpackRosMessage(dt);
17        gpX = m.robot_position.x; //store Gantry position
18        ... //same to y,z
19        double dis_robotHuman = calcDistanceRH(m);
20        double safe_dis     = calcSafeDistance(m);
21        if(dis_robotHuman>2*safe_dis){
22         Literal gDet=new LiteralImpl("gantry_detected");
23         gDet.addTerm(new NumberTermImpl(ctrDt++));
24         addPercept("human",gDet);
25      }  }  }
26      ); // END subscribe "/ariac_human/state"
27    ... //continue subscription to other ROS topics
28   } // END init()
```

Listing 1.5. *RosEnv* Jason's Environment with ROS–topics subscription.

4.4   The Environment Class

Jason's `Environment` class is responsible for performing the agents' interaction with the external world. In this case, the `Environment` class is responsible for subscribing to the ROS topics of interest and transforming the messages within them into perceptions for the agent. It is also responsible for implementing the agent's external actions, which in this case means publishing on ROS topics. The previous Fig. 3 presented the topics-of-interest for our human agent.

Our implementation is based in the ROS-A interface[7] [3] which makes use of the ROSBridge[8] library. Listing 1.5 shows our `RosEnv` class definition and its `init()` method, where subscriptions to ROS topics are defined (e.g., ln.8–26) and, when received, are transformed into perceptions for the agent (ln.21–23). In total, the agent subscribes to four ROS topics, as depicted in the Fig. 3.

The method `executeAction()` is responsible for decoding the required external action, as presented in ln.1–11 of Listing 1.6. An example of ROS–topic publication is given in ln.12–15. In total, the agent publishes four different ROS topics, as also depicted in the Fig. 3.

```
1   public boolean executeAction(String ag, Structure ac){
2     if (ac.getFunctor().equals("move")) { //
3         ... //get x,y,z "terms" from ac
4         move(x,y,z);
5     } else if (ac.getFunctor().equals("stop_movement"))
6         stop_moving();
7     ... //continue with other ext. actions
8     else return false;
9     informAgsEnvironmentChanged();
10    return true; // action successfully executed
11  }  ... //here starts the method's implementation
12  public void stop_moving() {
13    Publisher pub = new Publisher("/ariac_human/stop",
                "std_msgs/Bool", bridge);
14    pub.publish(new Bool(true));
15  }
```

Listing 1.6. External actions and ROS topic publishers.

4.5   Results and Additional Remarks

This section presents the preliminary analysis conducted to evaluate the impact of using the developed Jason agent in the ARIAC 2023 competition – a complete analysis should be done once the competition is finished. Such analysis is performed in terms of deployment and usage difficulties – from the final users (competitors) perspective – and also in respect to the impact on the computing resources utilization.

---

[7] https://github.com/rafaelcaue/jason-rosbridge.
[8] http://wiki.ros.org/rosbridge_suite.

The metric used to evaluate the users difficulties regards the number of related issues opened in the competition's Github[9]. From a total of 256 issues opened until the present moment, only 3 (1.2%) were related with the "human operator" agility challenge: #221, #229, and #245. The first issue was related with installation problems of two required artifacts, Java and ROS 2: (i) wrong JDK version, and (ii) missing ROS 2 *nav2-simple-commander* package. The issue #229 addressed the effects the human in proximity with the AGVs, and triggered some internal parameters tuning in our software. The last issue addressed difficulties for running the system within a Docker package.

Performance tests were conducted to evaluate the impact of the developed BDI-agents in respect to the computing resources utilization. Such tests were executed using a Linux Ubuntu 20.04 workstation with an Intel Core i9-10920X CPU with 24 cores at 3.50 GHz, 64 GiB of memory, and the NVIDIA GeForce RTX 3080 graphics card. ROS 2 Galactic was used. The *ps* command at 2 s intervals was used to log CPU utilization. The performance data was collected by running a 275 s long experiment. As the experiment script is launched it spawns 27 processes related with ROS 2/Gazebo and one process related with the Jason agent. For the ROS 2/Gazebo processes, the average CPU utilization was 510% (five cores entirely plus 10% of a sixth core). For the Jason process, the average CPU utilization was 6.5%. The Jason CPU usage decreased slightly over time. Overall, Jason required only 1.27% of the CPU portion used by ROS 2/Gazebo, which shows that it does not provide a significant overhead when observing the complete simulation system.

We recorded videos demonstrating the three different human personalities in action in the competition environment.[10] As the gantry is stopped close to the station 1, only the indifferent human will in fact reach this station – and then will continue moving up to the point that it gets teleported. The antagonistic human will change its direction towards the gantry before reaching station 1, and shortly after it will also get teleported. The helpful human will turn around as it gets close to the station 1 and will continue moving in the opposite direction.

5   Conclusions and Future Work

This paper presented what is considered to be the first use of BDI agents in the ARIAC competition. Amongst the challenges that we faced when implementing this agent, we highlight the high-level of complexity involving the software architecture of the ARIAC 2023 competition. Our Jason agent was required to interact with different components of the simulation environment, so that it could properly control the human operator in the simulation. Besides the Jason agent, including its environment, it was necessary to implement a couple of additional ROS 2/Gazebo components, such as the Python ROS node for movement control and the CPP Gazebo plugin to support the teleport operation.

---

[9] https://github.com/usnistgov/ARIAC/issues?q=is%3A+issue.

[10] Indifferent: https://youtu.be/5pqm5WSQNTw. Helpful: https://youtu.be/7CH4sko Os8c. Antagonistic: https://youtu.be/TQh9GQ1BbFw.

The conducted analysis presented evidences that using BDI technologies did cause significant overhead to the final users in terms of complexity for properly putting the system to run. More importantly, it did not lead to a significant overhead in terms of CPU utilization.

Even though the currently developed movement control for the human operator is simplistic if considering the full capacities of a BDI application, it serves as basis for more sophisticated/complex versions that will come in the future. This can, therefore, be seen as a successful initiative, which can also be observed as a pedagogical action towards evangelising the use of cognitive/BDI agents within non-agents developer communities, such as the robotics one, which is the community mostly involved with the ARIAC competition. We also understand this to be an initial seed towards spreading the use of cognitive agents within industrial automation environments.

As future work, we aim to analyse the practical effects (consequences) on competitors in the human challenge after ARIAC 2023 takes place, in especial in what concerns the impact of the three different personalities of the human operator.

References

1. Bordini, R.H., Hübner, J.F., Wooldrige, M.: Programming Multi-Agent Systems in AgentSpeak Using Jason. John Wiley & Sons, Hoboken (2007)
2. Cardoso, R.C., Ferrando, A.: A review of agent-based programming for multi-agent systems. Computers **10**(2), 16 (2021)
3. Cardoso, R.C., Ferrando, A., Dennis, L.A., Fisher, M.: An interface for programming verifiable autonomous agents in ROS. In: Bassiliades, N., Chalkiadakis, G., de Jonge, D. (eds.) EUMAS/AT -2020. LNCS (LNAI), vol. 12520, pp. 191–205. Springer, Cham (2020). https://doi.org/10.1007/978-3-030-66412-1_13
4. Correll, N., et al.: Analysis and Observations from the First Amazon Picking Challenge (2016)
5. Harrison, W., Downs, A., Schlenoff, C.: The agile robotics for industrial automation competition. AI Mag. **39**(4), 73–76 (2018)
6. Marvel, J.A.: Performance metrics of speed and separation monitoring in shared workspaces. IEEE Trans. Autom. Sci. Eng. **10**(2), 405–414 (2013)
7. Marvel, J.A., Hong, T.H., Messina, E.: 2011 solutions in perception challenge performance metrics and results. In: Proceedings of the Workshop on Performance Metrics for Intelligent Systems, pp. 59–63. ACM, New York, NY, USA (2012)
8. Rao, A.S.: AgentSpeak(L): BDI agents speak out in a logical computable language. In: Van de Velde, W., Perram, J.W. (eds.) MAAMAW 1996. LNCS, vol. 1038, pp. 42–55. Springer, Heidelberg (1996). https://doi.org/10.1007/BFb0031845
9. Rao, A.S., Georgeff, M.P.: BDI agents: from theory to practice. In: Lesser, V.R., Gasser, L. (eds.) Proceedings of the First International Conference on Multiagent Systems, pp. 312–319. The MIT Press, United States (1995)

Symbolic LTL$_f$ Best-Effort Synthesis

Giuseppe De Giacomo[1,2], Gianmarco Parretti[1(✉)], and Shufang Zhu[2(✉)]

[1] University of Rome "La Sapienza", Rome, Italy
{degiacomo,parretti}@diag.uniroma1.com
[2] University of Oxford, Oxford, UK
{giuseppe.degiacomo,shufang.zhu}@cs.ox.ac.uk

Abstract. We consider an agent acting to fulfil tasks in a nondeterministic environment. When a strategy that fulfills the task regardless of how the environment acts does not exist, the agent should at least avoid adopting strategies that prevent from fulfilling its task. Best-effort synthesis captures this intuition. In this paper, we devise and compare various symbolic approaches for best-effort synthesis in Linear Temporal Logic on finite traces (LTL$_f$). These approaches are based on the same basic components, however they change in how these components are combined, and this has a significant impact on the performance of the approaches as confirmed by our empirical evaluations.

1 Introduction

We consider an agent acting to fulfill tasks in a nondeterministic environment, as considered in Planning in nondeterministic (adversarial) domains [8,15], except that we specify both the environment and the task in Linear Temporal Logic (LTL) [3], the formalism typically used for specifying complex dynamic properties in Formal Methods [5].

In fact, we consider Linear Temporal Logic on finite traces (LTL$_f$) [11,12], which maintains the syntax of LTL [18] but is interpreted on finite traces. In this setting, we study synthesis [3,12,13,17]. In particular, we look at how to synthesize a strategy that is guaranteed to satisfy the task against all environment behaviors that conform to the environment specification.

When a winning strategy that fulfills the agent's task, regardless of how the environment acts, does not exist, the agent should at least avoid adopting strategies that prevent it from fulfilling its task. Best-effort synthesis captures this intuition. More precisely, best-effort synthesis captures the game-theoretic rationality principle that a player would not use a strategy that is "dominated" by another of its strategies (i.e. if the other strategy would fulfill the task against more environment behaviors than the one chosen by the player). Best-effort strategies have been studied in [4] and proven to have some notable properties: (*i*) they always exist, (*ii*) if a winning strategy exists, then best-effort strategies are exactly the winning strategies, (*iii*) best-effort strategies can be computed in 2EXPTIME as computing winning strategies (best-effort synthesis is indeed 2EXPTIME-complete).

© The Author(s), under exclusive license to Springer Nature Switzerland AG 2023
V. Malvone and A. Murano (Eds.): EUMAS 2023, LNAI 14282, pp. 228–243, 2023.
https://doi.org/10.1007/978-3-031-43264-4_15

The algorithms for best-effort synthesis in LTL and LTL$_f$ have been presented in [4]. These algorithms are based on creating, solving, and combining the solutions of three distinct games but of the same game arena. The arena is obtained from the automata corresponding to the formulas $\mathcal{E}$ and φ constituting the environment and the task specifications, respectively.

In particular, the algorithm for LTL$_f$ best-effort synthesis appears to be quite promising in practice since well-performing techniques for each component of the algorithm are available in the literature. These components are: (*i*) transformation of the LTL$_f$ formulas $\mathcal{E}$ and φ into deterministic finite automata (DFA), which can be double-exponential in the worst case, but for which various good techniques have been developed [6,10,16,22]; (*ii*) Cartesian product of DFAs, which is polynomial; (*iii*) minimization of DFAs, which is also polynomial; (*iv*) fixpoint computation over DFA to compute adversarial and cooperative winning strategies for reaching the final states, which is again polynomial.

In this paper, we refine the LTL$_f$ best-effort synthesis techniques presented in [4] by using symbolic techniques [5,7,22]. In particular, we show three different symbolic approaches that combine the above operations in different ways (and in fact allow for different levels of minimization). We then compare the three approaches through empirical evaluations. From this comparison, a clear winner emerges. Interestingly, the winner does not fully exploit DFA minimization to minimize the DFA whenever it is possible. Instead, this approach uses uniformly the same arena for all three games (hence giving up on minimization at some level). Finally, it turns out that the winner performs better in computing best-effort solutions even than state-of-the-art tools that compute only adversarial solutions. These findings confirm that LTL$_f$ best-effort synthesis is indeed well suited for efficient and scalable implementations.

The rest of the paper is organized as follows. In Sect. 2, we recall the main notions of LTL$_f$ synthesis. In Sect. 3, we discuss LTL$_f$ best-effort synthesis, and the algorithm presented in [4]. In Sect. 4, we introduce three distinct symbolic approaches for LTL$_f$ best-effort synthesis: the first (c.f., Subsect. 4.2) is a direct symbolic implementation of the algorithm presented in [4]; the second one (c.f., Subsect. 4.3) favors maximally conducting DFA minimization, thus getting the smallest possible arenas for the three games; and the third one (c.f., Subsect. 4.4) gives up DFA minimization at some level, and creates a single arena for the three games. In Sect. 5, we perform an empirical evaluation of the three algorithms. We conclude the paper in Sect. 6.

2 Preliminaries

LTL$_f$ *Basics. Linear Temporal Logic on finite traces* (LTL$_f$) is a specification language to express temporal properties on finite traces [11]. In particular, LTL$_f$ has the same syntax as LTL, which is instead interpreted over infinite traces [18]. Given a set of propositions Σ, LTL$_f$ formulas are generated as follows:

$$\varphi ::= a \mid (\varphi_1 \wedge \varphi_2) \mid (\neg\varphi) \mid (\bigcirc\varphi) \mid (\varphi_1 \,\mathcal{U}\, \varphi_2)$$

where $a \in \Sigma$ is an *atom*, $\bigcirc$ (*Next*), and $\mathcal{U}$ (*Until*) are temporal operators. We make use of standard Boolean abbreviations such as $\vee$ (or) and $\rightarrow$ (implies), *true* and *false*. In addition, we define the following abbreviations *Weak Next* $\bullet\varphi \equiv \neg\bigcirc\neg\varphi$, *Eventually* $\Diamond\varphi \equiv true\,\mathcal{U}\,\varphi$ and *Always* $\Box\varphi \equiv \neg\Diamond\neg\varphi$. The length/size of φ, written $|\varphi|$, is the number of operators in φ.

A *finite* (resp. *infinite*) *trace* is a sequence of propositional interpretations $\pi \in (2^{\Sigma})^*$ (resp. $\pi \in (2^{\Sigma})^{\omega}$). For every $i \geq 0$, $\pi_i \in 2^{\Sigma}$ is the i-th interpretation of π. Given a finite trace π, we denote its last instant (i.e., index) by $\mathsf{lst}(\pi)$. LTL$_f$ formulas are interpreted over finite, nonempty traces. Given a finite, non-empty trace $\pi \in (2^{\Sigma})^+$, we define when an LTL$_f$ formula φ *holds* at instant i, $0 \leq i \leq \mathsf{lst}(\pi)$, written $\pi, i \models \varphi$, inductively on the structure of φ, as:

- $\pi, i \models a$ iff $a \in \pi_i$ (for $a \in \Sigma$);
- $\pi, i \models \neg\varphi$ iff $\pi, i \not\models \varphi$;
- $\pi, i \models \varphi_1 \wedge \varphi_2$ iff $\pi, i \models \varphi_1$ and $\pi, i \models \varphi_2$;
- $\pi, i \models \bigcirc\varphi$ iff $i < \mathsf{lst}(\pi)$ and $\pi, i+1 \models \varphi$;
- $\pi, i \models \varphi_1 \mathcal{U} \varphi_2$ iff $\exists j$ such that $i \leq j \leq \mathsf{lst}(\pi)$ and $\pi, j \models \varphi_2$, and $\forall k, i \leq k < j$ we have that $\pi, k \models \varphi_1$.

We say π *satisfies* φ, written as $\pi \models \varphi$, if $\pi, 0 \models \varphi$.

Reactive Synthesis Under Environment Specifications. Reactive synthesis concerns computing a strategy that allows the agent to achieve its goal in an adversarial environment. In many AI applications, the agent has a model describing possible environment behaviors, which we call here an *environment specification* [2,3]. In this work, we specify both environment specifications and agent goals as LTL$_f$ formulas defined over $\Sigma = \mathcal{X} \cup \mathcal{Y}$, where $\mathcal{X}$ and $\mathcal{Y}$ are disjoint sets of variables under the control of the environment and the agent, respectively.

An *agent strategy* is a function $\sigma_{ag} : (2^{\mathcal{X}})^* \rightarrow 2^{\mathcal{Y}}$ that maps a sequence of environment choices to an agent choice. Similarly, an *environment strategy* is a function $\sigma_{env} : (2^{\mathcal{Y}})^+ \rightarrow 2^{\mathcal{X}}$ mapping non-empty sequences of agent choices to an environment choice. A trace $\pi = (X_0 \cup Y_0)(X_1 \cup Y_1)\ldots \in (2^{\mathcal{X}\cup\mathcal{Y}})^{\omega}$ is σ_{ag}-consistent if $Y_0 = \sigma_{ag}(\epsilon)$, where ϵ denotes empty sequence, and $Y_i = \sigma_{ag}(X_0, \ldots, X_{i-1})$ for every $i > 0$. Analogously, π is σ_{env}-consistent if $X_i = \sigma_{env}(Y_0, \ldots, Y_i)$ for every $i \geq 0$. We define $\pi(\sigma_{ag}, \sigma_{env})$ to be the unique infinite trace that is consistent with both σ_{ag} and σ_{env}.

Let ψ be an LTL$_f$ formula over $\mathcal{X}\cup\mathcal{Y}$. We say that agent strategy σ_{ag} *enforces* ψ, written $\sigma_{ag} \triangleright \psi$, if for every environment strategy σ_{env}, there exists a *finite* prefix of $\pi(\sigma_{ag}, \sigma_{env})$ that satisfies ψ. Conversely, we say that an environment strategy σ_{env} *enforces* ψ, written $\sigma_{env} \triangleright \psi$, if for every agent strategy σ_{ag}, every finite prefix of $\pi(\sigma_{ag}, \sigma_{env})$ satisfies ψ. ψ is *agent enforceable* (resp. *environment enforceable*) if there exists an agent (resp. environment) strategy that enforces it. An *environment specification* is an LTL$_f$ formula $\mathcal{E}$ that is environment enforceable.

The problem of LTL$_f$ reactive synthesis under environment specifications is defined as follows.

Definition 1. *The* LTL$_f$ *reactive synthesis under environment specifications problem is defined as a pair* $\mathcal{P} = (\mathcal{E}, \varphi)$, *where* LTL$_f$ *formulas* $\mathcal{E}$ *and* φ *correspond to an environment specification and an agent goal, respectively. Realizability of* $\mathcal{P}$ *checks whether there exists an agent strategy* σ_{ag} *that enforces* φ *under* $\mathcal{E}$, *i.e.,*

$$\forall \sigma_{env} \triangleright \mathcal{E}, \pi(\sigma_{ag}, \sigma_{env}) \models \varphi$$

Synthesis of $\mathcal{P}$ *computes such a strategy if it exists.*

A naive approach to this problem is a reduction to standard reactive synthesis of LTL$_f$ formula $\mathcal{E} \rightarrow \varphi$ [3]. Moreover, it has been shown that the problem of LTL$_f$ reactive synthesis under environment specifications is 2EXPTIME-complete [3].

3 Best-Effort Synthesis Under Environment Specifications

In reactive synthesis, the agent aims at computing a strategy that enforces the goal regardless of environment behaviors. If such a strategy does not exist, the agent just gives up when the synthesis procedure declares the problem *unrealizable*, although the environment can be possibly "over-approximated". In this work, we synthesize a strategy ensuring that the agent will do nothing that would needlessly prevent it from achieving its goal – which we call a *best-effort strategy*. *Best-effort synthesis* is the problem of finding such a strategy [4]. We start by reviewing what it means for an agent strategy to make more effort with respect to another.

Definition 2. *Let* $\mathcal{E}$ *and* φ *be* LTL$_f$ *formulas denoting an environment specification and an agent goal, respectively, and* σ_1 *and* σ_2 *be two agent strategies.* σ_1 *dominates* σ_2 *for* φ *under* $\mathcal{E}$, *written* $\sigma_1 \geq_{\varphi|\mathcal{E}} \sigma_2$, *if for every* $\sigma_{env} \triangleright \mathcal{E}, \pi(\sigma_2, \sigma_{env}) \models \varphi$ *implies* $\pi(\sigma_1, \sigma_{env}) \models \varphi$.

Furthermore, we say that σ_1 *strictly dominates* σ_2, written $\sigma_1 >_{\varphi|\mathcal{E}} \sigma_2$, if $\sigma_1 \geq_{\varphi|\mathcal{E}} \sigma_2$ and $\sigma_2 \not\geq_{\varphi|\mathcal{E}} \sigma_1$. Intuitively, $\sigma_1 >_{\varphi|\mathcal{E}} \sigma_2$ means that σ_1 does at least as well as σ_2 against every environment strategy enforcing $\mathcal{E}$ and strictly better against one such strategy. If σ_1 strictly dominates σ_2, then σ_1 makes more effort than σ_2 to satisfy the goal. In other words, if σ_2 is strictly dominated by σ_1, then an agent that uses σ_2 does not do its best to achieve the goal: if it used σ_1 instead, it could achieve the goal against a strictly larger set of environment behaviors. Within this framework, a best-effort strategy is one that is not strictly dominated by any other strategy.

Definition 3. *An agent strategy* σ *is best-effort for* φ *under* $\mathcal{E}$, *if there is no agent strategy* σ' *such that* $\sigma' >_{\varphi|\mathcal{E}} \sigma$.

It follows immediately from Definition 3 that if a goal φ is agent enforceable under $\mathcal{E}$, then best-effort strategies enforce φ under $\mathcal{E}$. Best-effort synthesis concerns computing a best-effort strategy.

Definition 4 ([4]). *The* LTL$_f$ *best-effort synthesis problem is defined as a pair* $\mathcal{P} = (\mathcal{E}, \varphi)$*, where* LTL$_f$ *formulas* $\mathcal{E}$ *and* φ *are the environment specification and the agent goal, respectively. Best-effort synthesis of* $\mathcal{P}$ *computes an agent strategy that is best-effort for* φ *under* $\mathcal{E}$*.*

While classical synthesis settings first require checking the realizability of the problem, i.e., the existence of a strategy that enforces the agent goal under environment specification [12,17], deciding whether a best-effort strategy exists is trivial, as they always exist.

Theorem 1 ([4]). *Let* $\mathcal{P} = (\mathcal{E}, \varphi)$ *be an* LTL$_f$ *best-effort synthesis problem. There exists a best-effort strategy for* φ *under* $\mathcal{E}$*.*

LTL$_f$ best-effort synthesis can be solved by a reduction to suitable DFA games and is 2EXPTIME-complete [4].

DFA *Game.* A DFA *game* is a two-player game played on a deterministic finite automaton (DFA). Formally, a DFA is defined as a pair $\mathcal{A} = (\mathcal{D}, F)$, where $\mathcal{D}$ is a deterministic transition system such that $\mathcal{D} = (2^{\mathcal{X} \cup \mathcal{Y}}, S, s_0, \delta)$, where $2^{\mathcal{X} \cup \mathcal{Y}}$ is the alphabet, S is the state set, $s_0 \in S$ is the initial state and $\delta \colon S \times 2^{\mathcal{X} \cup \mathcal{Y}} \to S$ is the deterministic *transition function*, and $F \subseteq S$ is a set of final states. We call $|S|$ the *size* of $\mathcal{D}$. Given a finite word $\pi = (X_0 \cup Y_0) \ldots (X_n \cup Y_n) \in (2^{\mathcal{X} \cup \mathcal{Y}})^+$, running π in $\mathcal{D}$ yields the sequence $\rho = s_0 \ldots s_{n+1}$ such that s_0 is the initial state of $\mathcal{D}$ and $s_{i+1} = \delta(s_i, X_i \cup Y_i)$ for all i. Since the transitions in $\mathcal{D}$ are all deterministic, we denote by $\rho = \mathsf{Run}(\pi, \mathcal{D})$ the unique sequence induced by running π on $\mathcal{D}$. We define the *product* of transition systems as follows.

Definition 5. *The product of transition systems* $\mathcal{D}_i = (\Sigma, S_i, s_{(0,i)}, \delta_i)$ *(with* $i = 1, 2$*) over the same alphabet is the transition system* $\mathcal{D}_1 \times \mathcal{D}_2 = (\Sigma, S, s_0, \delta)$ *with:* $S = S_1 \times S_2$*;* $s_0 = (s_{(0,1)}, s_{(0,2)})$*; and* $\delta((s_1, s_2), x) = (\delta(s_1, x), \delta(s_2, x))$*. The product* $\mathcal{D}_1 \times \ldots \times \mathcal{D}_n$ *is defined analogously for any finite sequence* $\mathcal{D}_1, \ldots, \mathcal{D}_n$ *of transition systems over the same alphabet.*

A finite word π is *accepted* by $\mathcal{A} = (\mathcal{D}, F)$ if the last state of the run it induces is a final state, i.e., $\mathsf{lst}(\rho) \in F$, where $\rho = \mathsf{Run}(\pi, \mathcal{D})$. The language of $\mathcal{A}$, denoted as $\mathcal{L}(\mathcal{A})$, consists of all words accepted by the automaton. Every LTL$_f$ formula φ can be transformed into a DFA $\mathcal{A}_\varphi$ that accepts exactly the traces that satisfy the formula, in other words, $\mathcal{A}_\varphi$ *recognizes* φ.

Theorem 2 ([11]). *Given an* LTL$_f$ *formula over* Σ*, we can build a DFA* $\mathcal{A}_\varphi = (\mathcal{D}_\varphi, F_\varphi)$ *whose size is at most double-exponential in* $|\varphi|$ *such that* $\pi \models \varphi$ *iff* $\pi \in \mathcal{L}(\mathcal{A}_\varphi)$*.*

In a DFA game $(\mathcal{D}, F)$, the transition system $\mathcal{D}$ is also called the *game arena*. Given σ_{ag} and σ_{env} denoting an agent strategy and an environment strategy, respectively, the trace $\pi(\sigma_{ag}, \sigma_{env})$ is called a *play*. Specifically, a play is *winning* if it contains a finite prefix that is accepted by the DFA. Intuitively, DFA games require F to be visited at least once. An agent strategy σ_{ag} is *winning* in

$(\mathcal{D}, F)$ if, for every environment strategy σ_{env}, it results that $\pi(\sigma_{ag}, \sigma_{env})$ is winning. Conversely, an environment strategy σ_{env} is *winning* in the game $(\mathcal{D}, F)$ if, for every agent strategy σ_{ag}, it results that $\pi(\sigma_{ag}, \sigma_{env})$ is not winning. In DFA *games*, $s \in S$ is a *winning* state for the agent (resp. environment) if the agent (resp. the environment) has a winning strategy in the game $(\mathcal{D}', F)$, where $\mathcal{D}' = (2^{\mathcal{X} \cup \mathcal{Y}}, S, s, \delta)$, i.e., the same arena $\mathcal{D}$ but with the new initial state s. By $\mathsf{W}_{ag}(\mathcal{D}, F)$ (resp. $\mathsf{W}_{env}(\mathcal{D}, F)$) we denote the set of all agent (resp. environment) winning states. Intuitively, W_{ag} represents the "agent winning region", from which the agent is able to win the game, no matter how the environment behaves.

We also define cooperatively winning strategies for DFA games. An agent strategy σ_{ag} is *cooperatively winning* in game $(\mathcal{D}, F)$ if there exists an environment strategy σ_{env} such that $\pi(\sigma_{ag}, \sigma_{env})$ is winning. Hence, $s \in S$ is a *cooperatively winning state* if the agent has a cooperatively winning strategy in the game $(\mathcal{D}', F)$, where $\mathcal{D}' = (2^{\mathcal{X} \cup \mathcal{Y}}, S, s_0, \delta)$. By $\mathsf{W}'_{ag}(\mathcal{D}, F)$ we denote the set of all agent cooperative winning states.

When the agent makes its choices based only on the current state of the game, we say that it uses a *positional strategy*. Formally, we define an *agent positional strategy* (a.k.a. *memory-less strategy*) as a function $\tau_{ag} : S \to 2^{\mathcal{X}}$. An agent positional strategy τ_{ag} *induces* an agent strategy $\sigma_{ag} : (2^{\mathcal{X}})^* \to 2^{\mathcal{Y}}$ as follows: $\sigma_{ag}(\epsilon) = \tau(s_0)$ and, for $i \geq 0$, $\sigma_{ag}(X_0 \ldots X_i) = \tau_{ag}(s_{i+1})$, where s_{i+1} is the last state in the sequence $\rho = \mathsf{Run}(\pi, \mathcal{D})$, with π being the finite sequence played until now, i.e., $\pi = (\sigma_{ag}(\epsilon) \cup X_0)(\sigma_{ag}(X_0) \cup X_1) \ldots (\sigma(X_0 \ldots X_{k-1}) \cup X_k)$. Similarly, we can define an *environment positional* strategy as a function $\tau_{env} : S \times 2^{\mathcal{Y}} \to 2^{\mathcal{X}}$. A positional strategy for a player that is winning (resp. cooperatively winning) from every state in its winning region is called *uniform winning* (resp. *uniform cooperatively winning*).

The solution to LTL$_f$ best-effort synthesis presented in [4] can be summarized as follows.

Algorithm 0 [4]. Given an LTL$_f$ best-effort synthesis problem $\mathcal{P} = (\mathcal{E}, \varphi)$, proceed as follows:

1. For every $\xi \in \{\neg \mathcal{E}, \mathcal{E} \to \varphi, \mathcal{E} \wedge \varphi\}$ compute the DFAs $\mathcal{A}_\xi = (\mathcal{D}_\xi, F_\xi)$.
2. Form the product $\mathcal{D} = \mathcal{D}_{\neg \mathcal{E}} \times \mathcal{D}_{\mathcal{E} \to \varphi} \times \mathcal{D}_{\mathcal{E} \wedge \varphi}$. Lift the final states of each component to the product, i.e. if $\mathcal{A}_\xi = (D_\xi, F_\xi)$ is the DFA for ξ, then the lifted condition G_ξ consists of all states $(s_{\neg \mathcal{E}}, s_{\mathcal{E} \to \varphi}, s_{\mathcal{E} \wedge \varphi})$ s.t. $s_\xi \in F_\xi$.
3. In DFA game $(\mathcal{D}, G_{\mathcal{E} \to \varphi})$ compute a uniform positional winning strategy f_{ag}. Let $W_{ag} \subseteq S$ be the agent's winning region.
4. In DFA game $(\mathcal{D}, G_{\neg \mathcal{E}})$ compute the environment's winning region $V \subseteq Q$.
5. Compute the environment restriction $\mathcal{D}'$ of $\mathcal{D}$ to V.
6. In DFA game $(\mathcal{D}', G_{\mathcal{E} \wedge \varphi})$ find a uniform positional cooperatively winning strategy g_{ag}.
7. **Return** the agent strategy σ_{ag} induced by the positional strategy k_{ag}, which is defined as follows: $k_{ag}(s) = \begin{cases} f_{ag}(s) & \text{if } s \in W_{ag}, \\ g_{ag}(s) & \text{otherwise.} \end{cases}$

4   Symbolic LTL$_f$ Best-Effort Synthesis

We present in this section three different symbolic approaches to LTL$_f$
best-effort synthesis, namely monolithic, explicit-compositional, and symbolic-
compositional, as depicted in Fig. 1. In particular, we base on the symbolic techniques of DFA games presented in [22], which we briefly review below.

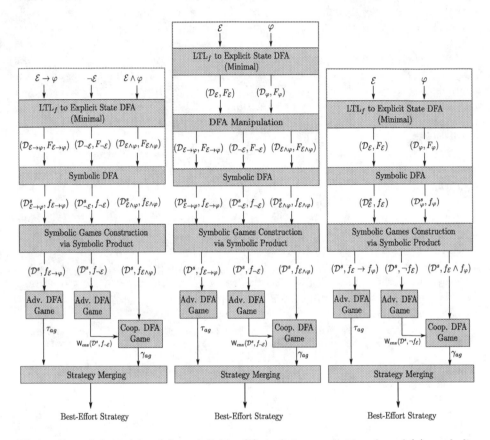

Fig. 1. From left to right, (a) monolithic, (b) explicit-compositional, and (c) symbolic-
compositional techniques to LTL$_f$ best-effort synthesis. In particular, $\mathcal{D}^s = \mathcal{D}^s_{\mathcal{E} \to \varphi} \times \mathcal{D}^s_{\neg \mathcal{E}} \times \mathcal{D}^s_{\mathcal{E} \wedge \varphi}$ in (a) and (b). $\mathcal{D}^s = \mathcal{D}^s_{\mathcal{E}} \times \mathcal{D}^s_{\varphi}$ in (c). The specific operations of the three
techniques are enclosed in red boxes.

4.1   Symbolic DFA Games

We consider the DFA representation described in Sect. 3 as an explicit-state representation. Instead, we are able to represent a DFA more compactly in a symbolic way by using a logarithmic number of propositions to encode the state

space. More specifically, the *symbolic* representation of $\mathcal{D}$ is a tuple $\mathcal{D}^s = (\mathcal{X}, \mathcal{Y}, \mathcal{Z}, Z_0, \eta)$, where $\mathcal{Z}$ is a set of state variables such that $|\mathcal{Z}| = \lceil \log |S| \rceil$, and every state $s \in S$ corresponds to an interpretation $Z \in 2^{\mathcal{Z}}$ over $\mathcal{Z}$; $Z_0 \in 2^{\mathcal{Z}}$ is the interpretation corresponding to the initial state s_0; $\eta \colon 2^{\mathcal{X}} \times 2^{\mathcal{Y}} \times 2^{\mathcal{Z}} \to 2^{\mathcal{Z}}$ is a Boolean function such that $\eta(Z, X, Y) = Z'$ if and only if Z is the interpretation of a state s and Z' is the interpretation of the state $\delta(s, X \cup Y)$. The set of goal states is represented by a Boolean function f over $\mathcal{Z}$ that is satisfied exactly by the interpretations of states in F. In the following, we denote symbolic DFAs as pairs $(\mathcal{D}^s, f)$.

Given a symbolic DFA game $(\mathcal{D}^s, f)$, we can compute a positional uniform winning agent strategy through a least fixpoint computation over two Boolean formulas w over $\mathcal{Z}$ and t over $\mathcal{Z} \cup \mathcal{Y}$, which represent the agent winning region and winning states with agent actions such that, regardless of how the environment behaves, the agent reaches the final states, respectively. Specifically, w and t are initialized as $w_0(\mathcal{Z}) = f(\mathcal{Z})$ and $t_0(\mathcal{Z}, \mathcal{Y}) = f(\mathcal{Z})$, since every goal state is an agent winning state. Note that t_0 is independent of the propositions from $\mathcal{Y}$, since once the play reaches goal states, the agent can do whatever it wants. t_{i+1} and w_{i+1} are constructed as follows:

$$t_{i+1}(Z, Y) = t_i(Z, Y) \vee (\neg w_i(Z) \wedge \forall X. w_i(\eta(X, Y, Z)))$$
$$w_{i+1}(Z) = \exists Y. t_{i+1}(Z, Y)$$

The computation reaches a fixpoint when $w_{i+1} \equiv w_i$. To see why a fixpoint is eventually reached, note that function w_{i+1} is *monotonic*. That is, at each step, a state Z is added to the winning region w_{i+1} only if it has not been already detected as a winning state, written $\neg w_i(Z)$ in function $t_{i+1}(Z, Y)$ above, *and* there exists an agent choice Y such that, for every environment choice X, the agent moves in w_i, written $\forall X. w_i(\eta(X, Y, Z))$.

When the fixpoint is reached, no more states will be added, and so all agent winning states have been collected. By evaluating Z_0 on w_{i+1} we can determine if there exists a winning strategy. If that is the case, t_{i+1} can be used to compute a uniform positional winning strategy through the mechanism of Boolean synthesis [14]. More specifically, by passing t_i to a Boolean synthesis procedure, setting $\mathcal{Z}$ as input variables and $\mathcal{Y}$ as output variables, we obtain a uniform positional winning strategy $\tau \colon 2^{\mathcal{Z}} \to 2^{\mathcal{Y}}$ that can be used to induce an agent winning strategy.

Computing a uniform positional cooperatively winning strategy can be performed through an analogous least-fixpoint computation. To do this, we define again Boolean functions $\hat{w}$ over $\mathcal{Z}$ and $\hat{t}$ over $\mathcal{Z} \cup \mathcal{Y}$, now representing the agent cooperatively winning region and cooperatively winning states with agent actions such that, if the environment behaves cooperatively, the agent reaches the final states. Analogously, we initialize $\hat{w}_0(\mathcal{Z}) = f(\mathcal{Z})$ and $\hat{t}_0(\mathcal{Z}, \mathcal{Y}) = f(\mathcal{Z})$. Then, we construct $\hat{t}_{i+1}$ and $\hat{w}_{i+1}$ as follows:

$$\hat{t}_{i+1}(Z, Y) = \hat{t}_i(Z, Y) \vee (\neg \hat{w}_i(Z) \wedge \exists X. \hat{w}_i(\eta(X, Y, Z)))$$
$$\hat{w}_{i+1}(Z) = \exists Y. \hat{t}_{i+1}(Z, Y);$$

Once the computation reaches the fixpoint, checking the existence and computing a uniform cooperatively winning positional strategy can be done similarly.

Sometimes, the state space of a symbolic transition system must be restricted to not reach a given set of invalid states represented as a Boolean function. To do so, we redirect all transitions from states in the set to a *sink* state. Formally:

Definition 6. *Let* $\mathcal{D}^s = (\mathcal{Z}, \mathcal{X}, \mathcal{Y}, Z_0, \eta)$ *be a symbolic transition system and* g *a Boolean formula over* $\mathcal{Z}$ *representing a set of states. The restriction of* $\mathcal{D}^s$ *to* g *is a new symbolic transition system* $\mathcal{D}'^s = (\mathcal{Z}, \mathcal{X}, \mathcal{Y}, Z_0, \eta')$, *where* η' *only agrees with* η *if* $Z \models g$, *i.e.,* $\eta' = \eta \wedge g$.

4.2 Monolithic Approach

The monolithic approach is a direct implementation of the best-effort synthesis approach presented in [4] (i.e., of Algorithm 0), utilizing the symbolic synthesis framework introduced in [22]. Given a best-effort synthesis problem $\mathcal{P} = (\mathcal{E}, \varphi)$, we first construct the DFAs following the synthesis algorithm described in Sect. 3, and convert them into a symbolic representation. Then, we solve suitable games on the symbolic DFAs and obtain a best-effort strategy. The workflow of the monolithic approach, i.e., **Algorithm 1**, is shown in Fig. 1(a). We elaborate on the algorithm as follows.

Algorithm 1. Given an LTL$_f$ best-effort synthesis problem $\mathcal{P} = (\mathcal{E}, \varphi)$, proceed as follows:

1. For LTL$_f$ formulas $\mathcal{E} \to \varphi$, $\neg\mathcal{E}$ and $\mathcal{E} \wedge \varphi$ compute the corresponding minimal explicit-state DFAs $\mathcal{A}_{\mathcal{E}\to\varphi} = (\mathcal{D}_{\mathcal{E}\to\varphi}, F_{\mathcal{E}\to\varphi})$, $\mathcal{A}_{\neg\mathcal{E}} = (\mathcal{D}_{\neg\mathcal{E}}, F_{\neg\mathcal{E}})$ and $\mathcal{A}_{\mathcal{E}\wedge\varphi} = (\mathcal{D}_{\mathcal{E}\wedge\varphi}, F_{\mathcal{E}\wedge\varphi})$.
2. Convert the DFAs to a symbolic representation to obtain $\mathcal{A}^s_{\mathcal{E}\to\varphi} = (\mathcal{D}^s_{\mathcal{E}\to\varphi}, f_{\mathcal{E}\to\varphi})$, $\mathcal{A}^s_{\neg\mathcal{E}} = (\mathcal{D}^s_{\neg\mathcal{E}}, f_{\neg\mathcal{E}})$ and $\mathcal{A}^s_{\mathcal{E}\wedge\varphi} = (\mathcal{D}^s_{\mathcal{E}\wedge\varphi}, f_{\mathcal{E}\wedge\varphi})$.
3. Construct the product $\mathcal{D}^s = \mathcal{D}^s_{\mathcal{E}\to\varphi} \times \mathcal{D}^s_{\neg\mathcal{E}} \times \mathcal{D}^s_{\mathcal{E}\wedge\varphi}$.
4. In DFA game $(\mathcal{D}^s, f_{\mathcal{E}\to\varphi})$, compute a uniform positional winning strategy τ_{ag} and the agent's winning region $W_{ag}(\mathcal{D}^s, f_{\mathcal{E}\to\varphi})$.
5. In DFA game $(\mathcal{D}^s, f_{\neg\mathcal{E}})$, compute the environment's winning region $W_{env}(\mathcal{D}^s, f_{\neg\mathcal{E}})$.
6. Compute the symbolic restriction $\mathcal{D}'^s$ of $\mathcal{D}^s$ to $W_{env}(\mathcal{D}^s, f_{\neg\mathcal{E}})$ to restrict the state space of $\mathcal{D}^s$ to considering $W_{env}(\mathcal{D}^s, f_{\neg\mathcal{E}})$ only.
7. In DFA game $(\mathcal{D}'^s, f_{\mathcal{E}\wedge\varphi})$, compute a uniform positional cooperatively winning strategy γ_{ag}.
8. **Return** the best-effort strategy σ_{ag} *induced* by the positional strategy κ_{ag} constructed as follows: $\kappa_{ag}(Z) = \begin{cases} \tau_{ag}(Z) & \text{if } Z \models W_{ag}(\mathcal{D}^s, f_{\mathcal{E}\to\varphi}) \\ \gamma_{ag}(Z) & \text{otherwise.} \end{cases}$

The main challenge in the monolithic approach comes from the LTL$_f$-to-DFA conversion, which can take, in the worst case, double-exponential time [11], and thus is also considered the bottleneck of LTL$_f$ synthesis [22]. To that end, we propose an explicit-compositional approach to diminish this difficulty by decreasing the number of LTL$_f$-to-DFA conversions.

4.3   Explicit-Compositional Approach

As described in Sect. 4.2, the monolithic approach to a best-effort synthesis problem $\mathcal{P} = (\mathcal{E}, \varphi)$ involves three rounds of LTL$_f$-to-DFA conversions corresponding to LTL$_f$ formulas $\mathcal{E} \rightarrow \varphi$, $\neg\mathcal{E}$ and $\mathcal{E} \wedge \varphi$. However, observe that DFAs $\mathcal{A}_{\mathcal{E} \rightarrow \varphi}$, $\mathcal{A}_{\neg\mathcal{E}}$ and $\mathcal{A}_{\mathcal{E} \wedge \varphi}$ can, in fact, be constructed by manipulating the two DFAs $\mathcal{A}_{\mathcal{E}}$ and $\mathcal{A}_{\varphi}$ of LTL$_f$ formulas $\mathcal{E}$ and φ, respectively. Specifically, given the explicit-state DFAs $\mathcal{A}_{\varphi}$ and $\mathcal{A}_{\mathcal{E}}$, we obtain $\mathcal{A}_{\mathcal{E} \rightarrow \varphi}$, $\mathcal{A}_{\neg\mathcal{E}}$ and $\mathcal{A}_{\mathcal{E} \wedge \varphi}$ as follows:

- $\mathcal{A}_{\mathcal{E} \rightarrow \varphi} = \mathsf{Comp}(\mathsf{Inter}(\mathcal{A}_{\mathcal{E}}, \mathsf{Comp}(\mathcal{A}_{\varphi})))$;
- $\mathcal{A}_{\neg\mathcal{E}} = \mathsf{Comp}(\mathcal{A}_{\mathcal{E}})$;
- $\mathcal{A}_{\mathcal{E} \wedge \varphi} = \mathsf{Inter}(\mathcal{A}_{\mathcal{E}}, \mathcal{A}_{\varphi})$;

where Comp and Inter denote complement and intersection on explicit-state DFAs, respectively. Note that transforming LTL$_f$ formulas into DFAs takes double-exponential time in the size of the formula, while the complement and intersection of DFAs take polynomial time in the size of the DFA.

The workflow of the explicit-compositional approach, i.e., **Algorithm 2**, is shown in Fig. 1(b). As the monolithic approach, we first translate the formulas $\mathcal{E}$ and φ into minimal explicit-state DFAs $\mathcal{A}_{\mathcal{E}}$ and $\mathcal{A}_{\varphi}$, respectively. Then, DFAs $\mathcal{A}_{\mathcal{E} \rightarrow \varphi}$, $\mathcal{A}_{\neg\mathcal{E}}$ and $\mathcal{A}_{\mathcal{E} \wedge \varphi}$ are constructed by manipulating $\mathcal{A}_{\mathcal{E}}$ and $\mathcal{A}_{\varphi}$ through complement and intersection. Indeed, the constructed explicit-state DFAs are also minimized. The remaining steps of computing suitable DFA games are the same as in the monolithic approach.

4.4   Symbolic-Compositional Approach

The monolithic and explicit-compositional approaches are based on playing three games over the symbolic product of transition systems $\mathcal{D}_{\mathcal{E} \rightarrow \varphi}$, $\mathcal{D}_{\neg\mathcal{E}}$, and $\mathcal{D}_{\mathcal{E} \wedge \varphi}$. We observe that given DFAs $\mathcal{A}_{\mathcal{E}} = (\mathcal{D}_{\mathcal{E}}, F_{\mathcal{E}})$ and $\mathcal{A}_{\varphi} = (\mathcal{D}_{\varphi}, F_{\varphi})$ recognizing $\mathcal{E}$ and φ, respectively, the DFA recognizing any Boolean combination of $\mathcal{E}$ and φ can be constructed by taking the product of $\mathcal{D}_{\mathcal{E}}$ and $\mathcal{D}_{\varphi}$ and properly defining the set of final states over the resulting transition system.

Lemma 1. *Let $\mathcal{A}_{\psi_1} = (\mathcal{D}_{\psi_1}, F_{\psi_1})$ and $\mathcal{A}_{\psi_2} = (\mathcal{D}_{\psi_2}, F_{\psi_2})$ be the automata recognizing LTL$_f$ formulas ψ_1 and ψ_2, respectively, and $\psi = \psi_1 \; op \; \psi_2$ denoting an arbitrary Boolean combination of ψ_1 and ψ_2, i.e., $op \in \{\wedge, \vee, \rightarrow, \leftrightarrow\}$. The DFA $\hat{\mathcal{A}}_{\psi} = (\hat{\mathcal{D}}_{\psi}, \hat{F}_{\psi})$ with $\hat{\mathcal{D}}_{\psi} = \mathcal{D}_{\psi_1} \times \mathcal{D}_{\psi_2}$ and $\hat{F}_{\psi} = \{(s_{\psi_1}, s_{\psi_2}) \mid s_{\psi_1} \in F_{\psi_1} \; op \; s_{\psi_2} \in F_{\psi_2}\}$ recognizes ψ.*

Proof. ($\rightarrow$) Assume $\pi \models \psi$. We will prove that $\pi \in \mathcal{L}(\hat{\mathcal{A}}_{\varphi})$. To see this, observe that $\pi \models \psi$ implies $\pi \models \psi_1 \; op \; \pi \models \psi_2$. It follows by [11] that $\pi \in \mathcal{L}(\mathcal{A}_{\psi_1}) \; op \; \pi \in \mathcal{L}(\mathcal{A}_{\psi_2})$, meaning that running π in $\mathcal{D}_{\psi_1}$ and $\mathcal{D}_{\psi_2}$ yields the sequences of states $(s_0^{\psi_1}, \ldots, s_n^{\psi_1})$ and $(s_0^{\psi_2}, \ldots, s_n^{\psi_2})$ such that $s_n^{\psi_1} \in F_{\psi_1} \; op \; s_n^{\psi_2} \in F_{\psi_2}$. Since $\hat{\mathcal{D}}_{\psi}$ is obtained through synchronous product of $\mathcal{D}_{\psi_1}$ and $\mathcal{D}_{\psi_2}$, running π in $\hat{\mathcal{A}}_{\psi}$ yields the sequence of states $((s_0^{\psi_1}, s_0^{\psi_2}), \ldots, (s_n^{\psi_1}, s_n^{\psi_2}))$, such that $(s_n^{\psi_1}, s_n^{\psi_2}) \in \hat{F}_{\psi}$. Hence, we have that $\pi \in \mathcal{L}(\hat{\mathcal{A}}_{\psi})$.

($\leftarrow$) Assume $\pi \in \mathcal{L}(\hat{\mathcal{A}}_\varphi)$. We prove that $\pi \models \psi$. To see this, observe that $\pi \in \mathcal{L}(\hat{\mathcal{A}}_\varphi)$ means that the run $\rho = (s_0^{\psi_1}, s_0^{\psi_2}) \ldots (s_n^{\psi_1}, s_n^{\psi_2})$ induced by π on $\hat{\mathcal{D}}_\psi$ is such that $(s_n^{\psi_1}, s_n^{\psi_2}) \in \hat{F}_\psi$. This means, by construction of $\hat{F}_\psi$, that $(s_n^{\psi_1}, s_n^{\psi_2})$ s.t. $s_n^{\psi_1} \in F_{\psi_1}$ op $s_n^{\psi_2} \in F_{\psi_2}$. Since $\hat{\mathcal{D}}_\psi$ is obtained through synchronous product of $\mathcal{D}_{\psi_1}$ and $\mathcal{D}_{\psi_2}$, it follows that $\pi \in \mathcal{L}(\mathcal{A}_{\psi_1})$ op $\pi \in \mathcal{L}(\mathcal{A}_{\psi_2})$. By [11] we have that $\pi \models \psi_1$ op $\pi \models \psi_2$, and hence $\pi \models \psi$. $\qquad\square$

Notably, Lemma 1 tells that the DFAs $\mathcal{A}_{\mathcal{E}\to\varphi}$, $\mathcal{A}_{\neg\mathcal{E}}$, and $\mathcal{A}_{\mathcal{E}\wedge\varphi}$ can be constructed from the same transition system by defining proper sets of final states. Specifically, given the DFAs $\mathcal{A}_\mathcal{E} = (\mathcal{D}_\mathcal{E}, F_\mathcal{E})$ and $\mathcal{A}_\varphi = (\mathcal{D}_\varphi, F_\varphi)$ recognizing $\mathcal{E}$ and φ, respectively, the DFAs recognizing $\mathcal{E} \to \varphi$, $\neg\mathcal{E}$, and $\mathcal{E} \wedge \varphi$ can be constructed as $\mathcal{A}_{\mathcal{E}\to\varphi} = (\mathcal{D}, F_{\mathcal{E}\to\varphi})$, $\mathcal{A}_{\neg\mathcal{E}} = (\mathcal{D}, F_{\neg\mathcal{E}})$, and $\mathcal{A}_{\mathcal{E}\wedge\varphi} = (\mathcal{D}, F_{\mathcal{E}\wedge\varphi})$, respectively, where $\mathcal{D} = \mathcal{D}_\mathcal{E} \times \mathcal{D}_\varphi$ and:

- $F_{\mathcal{E}\to\varphi} = \{(s_\mathcal{E}, s_\varphi) \mid s_\mathcal{E} \in F_\mathcal{E} \to s_\varphi \in F_\varphi\}$.
- $F_{\neg\mathcal{E}} = \{(s_\mathcal{E}, s_\varphi) \mid s_\mathcal{E} \notin F_\mathcal{E}\}$.
- $F_{\mathcal{E}\wedge\varphi} = \{(s_\mathcal{E}, s_\varphi) \mid s_\mathcal{E} \in F_\mathcal{E} \wedge s_\varphi \in F_\varphi\}$.

The symbolic-compositional approach precisely bases on this observation. As shown in Fig. 1(c), we first transform the LTL$_f$ formulas $\mathcal{E}$ and φ into minimal explicit-state DFAs $\mathcal{A}_\mathcal{E}$ and $\mathcal{A}_\varphi$, respectively, and then construct the symbolic representations $\mathcal{A}_\mathcal{E}^s$ and $\mathcal{A}_\varphi^s$ of them. Subsequently, we construct the symbolic product $\mathcal{D}^s = \mathcal{D}_\mathcal{E}^s \times \mathcal{D}_\varphi^s$, once and for all, and get the three DFA games by defining the final states (which are Boolean functions) from $f_\mathcal{E}$ and f_φ as follows:

- $f_{\mathcal{E}\to\varphi} = f_\mathcal{E} \to f_\varphi$.
- $f_{\neg\mathcal{E}} = \neg f_\mathcal{E}$.
- $f_{\mathcal{E}\wedge\varphi} = f_\mathcal{E} \wedge f_\varphi$.

From now on, the remaining steps are the same as in the monolithic and explicit-compositional approaches.

Algorithm 3. Given a best-effort synthesis problem $\mathcal{P} = (\mathcal{E}, \varphi)$, proceed as follows:

1. Compute the minimal explicit-state DFAs $\mathcal{A}_\mathcal{E} = (\mathcal{D}_\mathcal{E}, F_\mathcal{E})$ and $\mathcal{A}_\varphi = (\mathcal{D}_\varphi, F_\varphi)$.
2. Convert the DFAs to a symbolic representation to obtain $\mathcal{A}_\mathcal{E}^s = (\mathcal{D}_\mathcal{E}^s, f_\mathcal{E})$ and $\mathcal{A}_\varphi^s = (\mathcal{D}_\varphi^s, f_\varphi)$.
3. Construct the symbolic product $\mathcal{D}^s = \mathcal{D}_\mathcal{E}^s \times \mathcal{D}_\varphi^s$.
4. In DFA game $\mathcal{G}_{\mathcal{E}\to\varphi}^s = (\mathcal{D}^s, f_\mathcal{E} \to f_\varphi)$ compute a positional uniform winning strategy τ_{ag} and the agent winning region $\mathsf{W}_{ag}(\mathcal{D}^s, f_\mathcal{E} \to f_\varphi)$.
5. In the DFA game $(\mathcal{D}^s, \neg f_\mathcal{E})$ compute the environment's winning region $\mathsf{W}_{env}(\mathcal{D}^s, \neg f_\mathcal{E})$.
6. Compute the symbolic restriction $\mathcal{D}'^s$ of $\mathcal{D}^s$ to $\mathsf{W}_{env}(\mathcal{D}^s, f_{\neg\mathcal{E}})$ so as to restrict the state space of $\mathcal{D}^s$ to considering $\mathsf{W}_{env}(\mathcal{D}^s, f_{\neg\mathcal{E}})$ only.
7. In the DFA game $(\mathcal{D}'^s, f_\mathcal{E} \wedge f_\varphi)$ find a positional cooperatively winning strategy γ_{ag}.
8. **Return** the best-effort strategy σ_{ag} *induced* by the positional strategy κ_{ag} constructed as follows: $\kappa_{ag}(Z) = \begin{cases} \tau_{ag}(Z) & \text{if } Z \models \mathsf{W}_{ag}(\mathcal{D}^s, f_{\mathcal{E}\to\varphi}) \\ \gamma_{ag}(Z) & \text{otherwise.} \end{cases}$

5   Empirical Evaluations

In this section, we first describe how we implemented our symbolic LTL$_f$ best-effort synthesis approaches described in Sect. 4. Then, by empirical evaluation, we show that Algorithm 3, i.e., the symbolic-compositional approach, shows an overall best-performance. In particular, we show that performing best-effort synthesis only brings a minimal overhead with respect to standard synthesis and may even show better performance on certain instances.

5.1   Implementation

We implemented the three symbolic approaches to LTL$_f$ best-effort synthesis described in Sect. 4 in a tool called *BeSyft*, by extending the symbolic synthesis framework [20,22] integrated in state-of-the-art synthesis tools [6,9]. In particular, we based on LYDIA[1], the overall best performing LTL$_f$-to-DFA conversion tool, to construct the minimal explicit-state DFAs of LTL$_f$ formulas. Moreover, *BeSyft* borrows the rich APIs from LYDIA to perform relevant explicit-state DFA manipulations required by both Algorithm 1, i.e., the monolithic approach (c.f., Subsect. 4.2), and Algorithm 2, i.e., the explicit-compositional approach (c.f., Subsect. 4.3), such as complement, intersection, minimization. As in [20,22], the symbolic DFA games are represented in Binary Decision Diagrams (BDDs) [7], utilizing CUDD-3.0.0 [19] as the BDD library. Thereby, *BeSyft* constructs and solves symbolic DFA games using Boolean operations provided by CUDD-3.0.0, such as negation, conjunction, and quantification. The uniform positional winning strategy τ_{ag} and the uniform positional cooperatively winning strategy γ_{ag} are computed utilizing Boolean synthesis [14]. The positional best-effort strategy is obtained by applying suitable Boolean operations on τ_{ag} and γ_{ag}. As a result, we have three derivations of *BeSyft*, namely *BeSyft*-Alg-1, *BeSyft*-Alg-2, and *BeSyft*-Alg-3, corresponding to the monolithic, explicit-compositional, and symbolic-compositional approach, respectively.

5.2   Experiment Methodology

Experiment Setup. All experiments were run on a laptop with an operating system 64-bit Ubuntu 20.04, 3.6 GHz CPU, and 12 GB of memory. Time out was set to 1000 s.

Benchmarks. We devised a *counter-game* benchmark, based on the one proposed in [21]. More specifically, there is an n-bit binary counter and, at each round, the environment chooses whether to issue an increment request for the counter or not. The agent can choose to grant the request or ignore it and its goal is to get the counter to have all bits set to 1. The increment requests only come from the environment, and occur in accordance with the environment specification.

---

[1] https://github.com/whitemech/lydia.

The size of the minimal DFA of a counter-game specification grows exponentially as n increases.

In the experiments, environment specifications ensure that the environment eventually issues a minimum number K of increment requests in sequence, which can be represented as LTL$_f$ formulas $\mathcal{E}_K = \Diamond(add \wedge \bullet(add)\dots \wedge \bullet(\dots(\bullet(add))\dots))$, where K is the number of conjuncts. Counter-game instances may be realizable depending on the parameter K and the number of bits n. In the case of a realizable instance, a strategy for the agent to enforce the goal is to grant all increment requests coming from the environment. Else, the agent can achieve the goal only if the environment behaves cooperatively, such as issuing more increment requests than that specified in the environment specification. That is, the agent needs a best-effort strategy. In our experiments, we considered counter-game instances with at most $n = 10$ bits and $K = 10$ sequential increment requests. As a result, our benchmarks consist of a total of 100 instances.

5.3   Experimental Results and Analysis

In our experiments, all *BeSyft* implementations are only able to solve counter-game instances with up to $n = 8$ bits. Figure 2 shows the comparison (in log scale) of the three symbolic implementations of best-effort synthesis on counter-game instances with $n = 8$ and $1 \leq K \leq 10$. First, we observe that *BeSyft*-Alg-1 (monolithic) and *BeSyft*-Alg-2 (explicit-compositional) reach timeout when $K \geq 8$, whereas *BeSyft*-Alg-3 (symbolic-compositional) is able to solve all 8-bit counter-game instances. We can also see that *BeSyft*-Alg-1 performs worse than the other two derivations since it requires three rounds of LTL$_f$-to-DFA conversions, which in the worst case, can lead to a double-exponential blowup. Finally, we note that *BeSyft*-Alg-3, which implements the symbolic-compositional approach, achieves orders of magnitude better performance than the other two implementations, although it does not fully exploit the power of DFA minimization. Nevertheless, it is not the case that automata minimization always leads to improvement. Instead, there is a tread-off of performing automata minimization. As shown in Fig. 2, *BeSyft*-Alg-3, performs better than *BeSyft*-Alg-2, though the former does not minimize the game arena after the symbolic product, and the latter minimizes the game arena as much as possible.

On a closer inspection, we evaluated the time cost of each major operation of *BeSyft*-Alg-3, and present the results on counter-game instances with $n = 8$ and $1 \leq K \leq 10$ in Fig. 3. First, the results show that LTL$_f$-to-DFA conversion is the bottleneck of LTL$_f$ best-effort synthesis, the cost of which dominates the total running time. Furthermore, we can see that the total time cost of solving the cooperative DFA game counts for less than 10% of the total time cost. As a result, we conclude that performing best-effort synthesis only brings a minimal overhead with respect to standard reactive synthesis, which consists of constructing the DFA of the input LTL$_f$ formula and solving its corresponding adversarial game. Also, we observe that solving the cooperative game takes longer than solving the adversarial game. Indeed, this is because the fixpoint computation in the

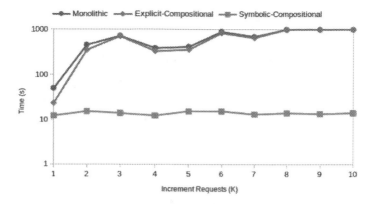

Fig. 2. Comparison (in log scale) of *BeSyft* implementations on counter game instances with $n = 8$ and $1 \leq K \leq 10$.

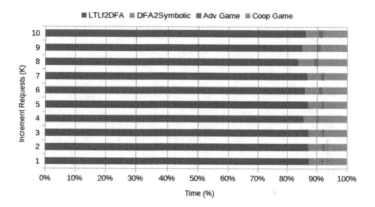

Fig. 3. Relative time cost of *BeSyft*-Alg-3 major operations on counter game instances with $n = 8$ and $1 \leq K \leq 10$.

cooperative game often requires more iterations than that in the adversarial game.

Finally, we also compared the time cost of symbolic-compositional best-effort synthesis with that of standard reactive synthesis on counter-game instances. More specifically, we considered a symbolic implementation of reactive synthesis that computes an agent strategy that enforces the LTL$_f$ formula $\mathcal{E} \rightarrow \varphi$ [10, 22], which can be used to find an agent strategy enforcing φ under $\mathcal{E}$, if it exists [3]. Interestingly, Fig. 4 shows that for certain counter-game instances, symbolic-compositional best-effort synthesis takes even less time than standard reactive synthesis. It should be noted that symbolic-compositional best-effort synthesis performs LTL$_f$-to-DFA conversions of LTL$_f$ formulas φ and $\mathcal{E}$ separately and combines them to obtain the final game arena without having automata minimization, whereas reactive synthesis performs the LTL$_f$-to-DFA conversion of formula $\mathcal{E} \rightarrow \varphi$ and minimizes its corresponding DFA. These results confirm

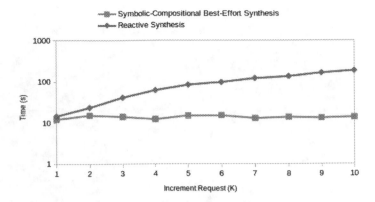

Fig. 4. Comparison (in log scale) of *BeSyft*-Alg-3 and implementations of symbolic LTL$_f$ reactive synthesis on counter-game instances with $n = 8$ and $1 \le K \le 10$.

the practical feasibility of best-effort synthesis and that automata minimization does not always guarantee performance improvement.

6   Conclusion

We presented three different symbolic LTL$_f$ best-effort synthesis approaches: monolithic, explicit-compositional, and symbolic-compositional. Empirical evaluations proved the outperformance of the symbolic-compositional approach. An interesting observation is that, although previous studies suggest taking the maximal advantage of automata minimization [20,21], in the case of LTL$_f$ best-effort synthesis, there can be a trade-off in doing so. Another significant finding is that the best-performing LTL$_f$ best-effort synthesis approach only brings a minimal overhead compared to standard synthesis. Given this nice computational result, a natural future direction would be looking into LTL$_f$ best-effort synthesis with multiple environment assumptions [1].

Acknowledgments. This work has been partially supported by the ERC-ADG White- Mech (No. 834228), the EU ICT-48 2020 project TAILOR (No. 952215), the PRIN project RIPER (No. 20203FFYLK), and the PNRR MUR project FAIR (No. PE0000013).

References

1. Aminof, B., De Giacomo, G., Lomuscio, A., Murano, A., Rubin, S.: Synthesizing best-effort strategies under multiple environment specifications. In: KR, pp. 42–51 (2021)
2. Aminof, B., De Giacomo, G., Murano, A., Rubin, S.: Planning and synthesis under assumptions. arXiv (2018)
3. Aminof, B., De Giacomo, G., Murano, A., Rubin, S.: Planning under LTL environment specifications. In: ICAPS, pp. 31–39 (2019)

4. Aminof, B., De Giacomo, G., Rubin, S.: Best-effort synthesis: doing your best is not harder than giving up. In: IJCAI, pp. 1766–1772 (2021)
5. Baier, C., Katoen, J.P.: Principles of Model Checking. MIT Press, Cambridge (2008)
6. Bansal, S., Li, Y., Tabajara, L.M., Vardi, M.Y.: Hybrid compositional reasoning for reactive synthesis from finite-horizon specifications. In: AAAI, pp. 9766–9774 (2020)
7. Bryant, R.E.: Symbolic Boolean manipulation with ordered binary-decision diagrams. ACM Comput. Surv. **24**(3), 293–318 (1992)
8. Cimatti, A., Pistore, M., Roveri, M., Traverso, P.: Weak, strong, and strong cyclic planning via symbolic model checking. AIJ **1–2**(147), 35–84 (2003)
9. De Giacomo, G., Favorito, M.: Compositional approach to translate LTL$_f$/LDL$_f$ into deterministic finite automata. In: ICAPS, pp. 122–130 (2021)
10. De Giacomo, G., Favorito, M.: Lydia: a tool for compositional LTL$_f$ /LDL$_f$ synthesis. In: ICAPS, pp. 122–130 (2021)
11. De Giacomo, G., Vardi, M.Y.: Linear temporal logic and linear dynamic logic on finite traces. In: IJCAI, pp. 854–860 (2013)
12. De Giacomo, G., Vardi, M.Y.: Synthesis for LTL and LDL on Finite Traces. In: IJCAI, pp. 1558–1564 (2015)
13. Finkbeiner, B.: Synthesis of reactive systems. Dependable Softw. Syst. Eng. **45**, 72–98 (2016)
14. Fried, D., Tabajara, L.M., Vardi, M.Y.: BDD-based Boolean functional synthesis. In: Chaudhuri, S., Farzan, A. (eds.) CAV 2016. LNCS, vol. 9780, pp. 402–421. Springer, Cham (2016). https://doi.org/10.1007/978-3-319-41540-6_22
15. Ghallab, M., Nau, D.S., Traverso, P.: Automated Planning - Theory and Practice. Elsevier, Amsterdam (2004)
16. Henriksen, J.G., et al.: Mona: monadic second-order logic in practice. In: Brinksma, E., Cleaveland, W.R., Larsen, K.G., Margaria, T., Steffen, B. (eds.) TACAS 1995. LNCS, vol. 1019, pp. 89–110. Springer, Heidelberg (1995). https://doi.org/10.1007/3-540-60630-0_5
17. Pnueli, A., Rosner, R.: On the synthesis of a reactive module. In: POPL, pp. 179–190 (1989)
18. Pnueli, A.: The temporal logic of programs. In: FOCS, pp. 46–57 (1977)
19. Somenzi, F.: CUDD: CU Decision Diagram Package 3.0.0. Universiy of Colorado at Boulder (2016)
20. Tabajara, L.M., Vardi, M.Y.: Partitioning techniques in LTL$_f$ synthesis. In: IJCAI, pp. 5599–5606 (2019)
21. Zhu, S., De Giacomo, G., Pu, G., Vardi, M.Y.: LTL$_f$ synthesis with fairness and stability assumptions. In: AAAI, pp. 3088–3095 (2020)
22. Zhu, S., Tabajara, L.M., Li, J., Pu, G., Vardi, M.Y.: Symbolic LTL$_f$ synthesis. In: IJCAI, pp. 1362–1369 (2017)

Robust Explanations for Human-Neural Multi-agent Systems with Formal Verification

Francesco Leofante$^{(\boxtimes)}$ (iD) and Alessio Lomuscio (iD)

Department of Computing, Imperial College London, London, UK
{f.leofante,a.lomuscio}@imperial.ac.uk

Abstract. The quality of explanations in human-agent interactions is fundamental to the development of trustworthy AI systems. In this paper we study the problem of generating robust contrastive explanations for human-neural multi-agent systems and introduce two novel verification-based algorithms to *(i)* identify non-robust explanations generated by other methods and *(ii)* generate contrastive explanations equipped with formal robustness certificates. We present an implementation and evaluate the effectiveness of the approach on two case studies involving neural agents trained on credit scoring and traffic sign recognition tasks.

Keywords: Robust Explainable AI · Formal Verification

1 Introduction

The forthcoming adoption of AI in modern societies has lead to the emergence of sophisticated multi-agent systems in which humans and artificial agents interact and collaborate [2,17,41]. Advances of deep learning [24] have facilitated the development of neural agents governed by neural networks (NNs) synthesised from data [1]. We call Human-Neural Multi-agent System (HNMAS) a system composed by humans and neural MAS interacting and communicating in view of achieving common and private goals. While HNMAS may offer rapid gains in terms of performance and generalisation, neural agents are known to produce outputs that are not normally intelligible to humans, thus hindering the deployment of HNMAS that can be trusted by human participants.

Some of the methods in the area of Explainable AI (XAI) are concerned with making NNs, and other learned models, more understandable to humans. A widely recognised factor contributing towards this goal is the availability of *explanations*, i.e., arguments supporting or contrasting the decisions taken by an NN. In particular, Contrastive Explanations (CEs) have attracted interest as they appear to ease human comprehension [22,32]. To understand what makes

---

Work partially supported by the DARPA Assured Autonomy programme (FA8750-18-C-0095), the UK Royal Academy of Engineering (CiET17/18-26) and an Imperial College Research Fellowship awarded to Leofante. This paper is an extended version of [26] presented at AAMAS 2023.

CEs advantageous, consider the classic scenario of a loan application, containing the features *employment status* unemployed, *loan term* 40 months and *loan amount* $1500, being classified by a bank's NN as rejected. A CE explaining this decision may consist of a slightly modified application where the loan amount is reduced to $1310 resulting in the application being accepted. This would give the applicant an explanation as to a possible change that would lead to the desired output. Explanations of this form have been found to elicit causal thinking in humans [7,31] and may thus play a crucial role in fostering trustworthy human-AI partnerships. Crucially, CEs are typically proposed as a tool to provide recourse to individuals that have been impacted by the decisions of an AI. It is therefore important that explanations are trustworthy and of high quality, and appropriate methods are developed to ensure that this is the case.

Several approaches have been proposed to compute CEs for NNs according to different quality criteria, such as *validity* and *proximity* [22,33,48], *plausibility* [20,22] and *actionability* [47]. We discuss these in Sect. 2. Our focus here is the criterion of *robustness*. Robustness has often been defined in terms of *robustness to input perturbations* [43,44], *robustness to changes in the NN parameters* [4,9,18,46] or *robustness to model multiplicity* [25,37]. While these notions are useful when considering NNs in isolation, other forms of robustness are equally important when humans are in the loop. In particular, *robustness to noisy execution*, i.e., the validity of CEs when implemented by humans in a noisy and inconsistent manner [38], has so far received little attention, but is an essential stepping stone towards building trustworthy interactions in HNMAS. Indeed, current algorithms generate explanations under the assumption that the human receiving a CE will follow the recourse recommendations it provides exactly. However, several studies have reported that this rarely happens in practical applications [3,38]. This may jeopardise the validity of CEs, thus reducing the trust humans put into their neural agent counterpart. Consider the loan example: if decreasing the loan amount to $1309 (as opposed to the recommended $1310) does not result in the application being accepted (thus invalidating the CE), the human may start questioning whether the explanations are actually capturing the decision making of the neural agent, defeating the original purpose for which the explanation was generated.

To remedy this, we propose an entirely novel approach to generate CEs that uses automated reasoning techniques to provide strong robustness guarantees. In particular, we put forward novel techniques to *(i)* formally assess the robustness of CEs and *(ii)* generate CEs with provable robustness certificates. To achieve this, we leverage recent advances in verification of neural networks (VNN) [6]. We establish a formal correspondence between the validation of robustness for a CE and the verification of absence of adversarial attacks in an NN. As we show, this enables us to *(i)* determine whether or not an explanation is robust and, *(ii)* synthesise explanations with rigorous mathematical guarantees on their robustness. The guarantees offered by our methodology provide users of CEs with a quantitative metric which can be used to evaluate the reliability of an explanation. For illustration, consider the loan example once more: using our approach, a bank would then be able to provide CEs together with robustness ranges within which explanations are *guaranteed to remain valid*, e.g., \$1310 $\pm$ 0.5. The user can then decide whether to accept this explanation, or ask for a new, more robust one. It can be seen, even from this simple example, that this kind of robustness guarantees can prove extremely useful in sensitive situations.

The rest of this paper is organised as follows. We discuss related work below and cover the necessary background in Sect. 2. We then introduce our main results in Sect. 3 and demonstrate their usefulness in Sect. 4 on two case studies involving credit scoring and traffic sign recognition. We then conclude in Sect. 5, where we discuss our results together with some avenues for future work. In summary, this paper proposes the first formal approach for the generation of CEs for HNMAS with strong robustness guarantees.

Related Work. Several approaches have been proposed to compute CEs for NNs based on continuous optimisation [8,22,30,35,48], Mixed-integer Linear Programming (MILP) [33,42] and Satisfiability Modulo Theories solving [20].

As CEs are increasingly used to guide decisions in areas with clear societal implications [10,39], their reliability has come under scrutiny. In particular, recent work has shown that algorithms based on gradient search can be highly sensitive to input perturbations and thus may result in radically different CEs being generated to explain very similar events [44].

Another line of work has shown that CEs often lack robustness with respect to changes in the model being explained [4,9,18,25,37,46]. As noted in [13], such fragility may denote that explanations are not capturing the actual decision-making process of the underlying neural model, thus casting doubts on their reliability.

Closely related to this work is [36], where the authors focused on a class of CEs known as counterfactual explanations (CFEs), and showed that many popular approaches to generate CFEs often return explanations that are indistinguishable from adversarial examples. This may have troublesome consequences within HNMAS, as the interaction between humans and neural agents on explanations may be misguided by explanations that are in fact just an artefact of the underlying model and do not explain anything about the agent's behaviour.

Finally, [38] considers the notion of *robustness to noisy execution* which is central to this work. The authors describe situations in which the validity of a CFE may be compromised by small perturbations directly applied to the explanation itself. The authors point out that such perturbations may naturally occur when humans try to implement the changes prescribed by a CFE. As we already argued in the introduction, this notion of robustness is particularly relevant to HNMAS, where fragile explanations may hinder a transparent interaction between humans and neural agents. While we target the same notion of robustness here, we note that the approach proposed in [38] is heuristic and incomplete, thus only providing probabilistic guarantees on whether an explanation may be invalidated on average. As such, this approach may fail to detect cases in which explanations may be invalidated. In contrast, we seek much stronger, formal guarantees that allow whether an explanation can be trusted to be identified.

2   Background

Notation. We consider neural agents implemented by feed-forward, ReLU-based NNs trained to solve classification problems. For ease of exposition, we consider binary classification tasks where a neural classifier computes a function $f : \mathcal{X} \to [0,1]$ mapping an input $x \in \mathcal{X}$ to a classification label $c \in \{0,1\}$. The input x is classified as 1 if $f(x) \geq 0.5$ and 0 otherwise. With an abuse of notation, we denote these outcomes as $f(x) = 1$ and $f(x) = 0$ respectively. However, our approach can be seamlessly applied to the multi-class setting as we demonstrate in Sect. 4. Finally, we use $\|\cdot\|_p$ to denote p-norms with the usual meaning.

Contrastive Explanations. CEs for neural classifiers have been formalised in the literature in different ways; following [22], we distinguish between *counterfactual explanations* and *semi-factual explanations*.

Counterfactual Explanations. Consider the loan example in the introduction and assume a loan application x_F was rejected by the bank's AI agent, i.e., $f(x_F) = 0$. The individual submitting x_F may want to interrogate the agent to understand what changes would be needed in their application for the loan to be accepted. An answer to this question may be given in terms of a counterfactual explanation, i.e., a set of changes that, if applied to x_F, results in another hypothetical application for which the loan is granted. A formalisation of counterfactual explanations (CFEs) can defined as follows.

Definition 1. *Given an input $x_F \in \mathcal{X}$ and a neural classifier f such that $f(x_F) = 0$, find $x \in \mathcal{X}$ such that: (i) $d(x, x_F) \leq \epsilon$ and (ii) $f(x) = 1$ where $d(\cdot, \cdot) : \mathcal{X} \times \mathcal{X} \to \mathbb{R}_+$ is a distance function, $\epsilon \in \mathbb{R}_{>0}$.*

A CFE thus corresponds to a new input x that is at most ϵ-far from the original input x_F that makes the classification flip. Common choices for the distance function are the normalised L_1 [48] or L_∞ [36] distances; w.l.o.g. we focus on the latter and thus consider $d(\cdot, \cdot) : \mathcal{X} \times \mathcal{X} \to [0,1]$.

While Definition 1 ensures the *validity* of a CFE, i.e., x is guaranteed to flip the classification of f, we highlight that previous work extended it to accommodate a host of different metrics. For instance, [33,48] enforce *proximity* by requiring that x be the nearest input that causes the classification to change, under the assumption that good CFEs lie in the vicinity of the input to be explained; this can be obtained by embedding Definition 1 into a simple binary search scheme minimising ϵ. Others require that CFEs be *plausible*; a common approach, also used here, is to enforce plausibility via domain-consistency [20], where counterfactual instances are restricted to the range of admissible values for the domain of features. Finally, [47] argued that CFEs should be *actionable*, i.e., they should only involve input features that can be modified by end-users (e.g., income vs age). This can be obtained by extending Definition 1 to enforce that changes only occur on selected (actionable) dimensions of the input space. While our focus in this work is mostly on *robustness to noisy execution*, we will later show how actionability can be seamlessly integrated in our proposal.

Semifactual Explanations. Consider the loan scenario once more. Assume an application x_F has been rejected again and this time the customer would like to know the margin by which their application was rejected. The agent may answer this question in terms of a semifactual explanation, describing changes that, if applied to x_F, would still result in a denied loan. A formalisation of semifactual explanations (SFEs) can be defined as follows.

Definition 2. *Given an input $x_F \in \mathcal{X}$ and a neural classifier f such that $f(x_F) = 0$, find $x \in \mathcal{X}$ such that: (i) $d(x, x_F) \geq \epsilon$ and (ii) $f(x) = 0$ where $d(\cdot, \cdot) : \mathcal{X} \times \mathcal{X} \to \mathbb{R}_+$ is a distance function, $\epsilon \in \mathbb{R}_{>0}$.*

SFEs thus describe hypothetical situations where the output of the classifier would not change, even if the input x_F were to be modified. Similarly to CFEs, additional requirements are often imposed on SFEs to improve their quality. A common choice is to require that explanations are obtained via large feature modification, i.e., x should be sufficiently distant from x_F to maximise its plausibility [22]; this can again be obtained by embedding Definition 2 into an optimisation scheme where the distance between the original input and the SFE is maximised. However, our main focus in this work will be on providing robustness guarantees for an SFE and we leave other properties for future work. As for the distance function $d(\cdot, \cdot)$, the same choices made for CFEs apply here.

Verification of Neural Networks. VNN is concerned with determining whether an NN satisfies an input-output specification defining allowed inputs and desired outputs. Several approaches have been developed for a wide range of neural architectures and specifications [1,5,11,12,14,15,19,21,23,29,40]. In this work we focus on local robustness [21,27,28], which is the most commonly studied property within the VNN literature, and is defined as follows.

Definition 3. *Consider an input x_F and a neural classifier f such that $f(x_F) = 0$ (resp. $f(x_F) = 1$). The neural classifier is said to be locally robust with radius $\epsilon \in \mathbb{R}_{\geq 0}$ if for all x such that $\|x - x_F\|_\infty \leq \epsilon$, we have that $f(x) = 0$ (resp. $f(x) = 1$).*

Informally, local robustness requires that the prediction of a neural network for a specific input x_F does not change drastically within a reasonably small neighbour, defined as an ϵ-ball under L_∞ norm. Common techniques to check whether a network satisfies local robustness, also used in this paper, include symbolic interval propagation [16,49] and reductions to MILP [5,29]. We refer to [6] for a recent summary of approaches and results in the VNN area.

3   Robust Explanations via Verification

In this section we propose to analyse robustness of explanations through the lens of formal verification of neural networks. By doing so, we will derive a new method to generate CEs equipped with formal robustness guarantees by construction. In addition, the method also enables human agents to analyse CEs via quantitative robustness metrics which they can use to filter out potentially problematic explanations, as we will show later in our experiments.

The notion of robustness that we study is tied to variations of a CE's classification with respect to changes in the CE that led to that classification. Intuitively, if a CE is modified slightly then the classification provided by the classifier for that new input should not change radically. If that is the case, as discussed in [13], it is likely to signify that the CE is an artefact of the classifier and does not represent, nor explain, its underlying classification logic.

Motivating Example. Consider a real loan application based on the Home Equity Line of Credity (HELOC) dataset (more details on this are provided in Sect. 4). HELOC contains instances corresponding to line of credit applications, such as the following one:

$$x_F = [62, 323, 1, 104, 14, 7, 7, 100, 0, 0, 8, 24, 2, 18, 0, 1, 1, 4, 100, 3, 1, 0, 36]$$

which corresponds to an application that was rejected by the bank's AI agent. Using an off-the-shelf CFE generation algorithm, we may obtain the following:

$$x = [62, 323, 1, 104, \mathbf{19.84}, 7, 7, 100, 0, 0, 8, 24, 2, 18, 0, 1, 1, 4, 100, 3, 1, 0, 36]$$

where increasing the 5-th element of x_F (highlighted in bold) results in the application being accepted. However, upon testing, we may actually discover that a very slight perturbation to a subset of features in x (highlighted in red) invalidates the CFE, i.e.,

$$x' = [61.8, 323, 1, 104, 19.84, 7, 7, 100, 0, 0, 8, 24, 2, 17.8, 0, 1, 1.2, 4.2, 100, 3, 1, 0, 36]$$

is again rejected. This lack of robustness is not in line with human intuition and expectations, which ultimately weakens the explanation power of the CFE. To remedy this, we propose an approach based on formal verification to mechanise the analysis and discovery of robust explanations.

3.1   Robust Counterfactual Explanations

We are interested in identifying *robust* CFEs for a neural classifier f and input x, $f(x) = 0$. Towards this end, the first question we address is whether a (possibly non-robust) explanation exists for a given input x. Answering this question requires solving the satisfaction problem introduced in Definition 1.

Proposition 1. *Deciding the existence of a CFE is NP-complete.*

Proof. Checking if an input x is indeed a CFE can be done in polynomial time by simply propagating x through f. This places the problem in NP. To show that the problem is NP-hard, observe that determining the existence of a CFE entails checking the satisfaction of a set of linear constraints encoding (i) that $d(x, x_F) < \epsilon$ (ii) the computation performed by f and (iii) that $f(x) = 1$. This problem has been shown to be NP-hard for ReLU-based classified here considered [21], which gives the result.

We now show that determining the existence of a CFE can be recast in terms of verification techniques.

Theorem 1. *The existence of a CFE for an input x_F and neural classifier f can be established by checking whether f violates local robustness on x_F for radius ϵ.*

Proof. If f satisfies local robustness on x_F with radius ϵ, then all other inputs x within distance ϵ will yield $f(x) = 0$, thus showing that no CFE exists for x_F (as per Definition 1). On the other hand, if f violates local robustness, at least one input x exists such that both conditions in Definition 1 are met.

Observation 1. *A complete procedure for determining the existence of a CFE can be derived from any complete procedure for verifying local robustness.*

Theorem 1 establishes a connection between CFEs and formal verification methods for neural networks, showing that the latter can be used to compute explanations. Furthermore, if the verification procedure is complete, then if an explanation exists, it will be obtained (computational limitations withstanding). However, this is not enough to conclude something about the robustness of an explanation. We therefore propose the following, novel formalisation.

Definition 4. *Consider an input x_F and a neural classifier f such that $f(x_F) = 0$. Let x be a CFE computed for x_F, i.e., $f(x) = 1$. The CFE x is said to be robust to noisy execution up to magnitude δ if for all inputs x' such that $\|x' - x\|_\infty \le \delta$, we have that $f(x') = 1$.*

For readability, we will use δ-robustness as a shorthand to indicate robustness to noisy execution up to magnitude δ. In a nutshell, δ-robustness requires that explanations remain valid across a (reasonably-sized) neighbourhood to ensure that small noise introduced by humans when implementing recourse recommendations cannot invalidate them.

Proposition 2. *Deciding whether a CFE x is δ-robust is CONP-complete.*

Proof. To see that the problem is in CONP, observe that a counterexample certificate is simply an input x' such that $\|x' - x\|_\infty \le \delta$ and $f(x') = 0$. To see that the problem is CONP-complete, consider its complement, defined as the problem of determining whether there exists an input x' such that $\|x' - x\|_\infty \le \delta$ and $f(x') = 1$. This is known to be NP-complete [21], giving the result.

Theorem 2. *The δ-robustness of a CFE x and a neural classifier f can be established by checking whether f satisfies local robustness on x for radius δ.*

Proof. If f satisfies local robustness on x with radius δ, all inputs x' obtained from noisy executions that may perturb each component of x up to $\pm\delta$ are guaranteed yield $f(x') = 1$, thus proving that the CFE is δ-robust. Otherwise, there exists an input x' such that $\|x' - x\|_\infty \le \delta$ and $f(x') = 0$, thus proving that the CFE is not robust.

Observation 2. *A complete procedure for deciding the δ-robustness of a CFE can be derived from any complete procedure for verifying local robustness.*

Following Observation 2, we have established that neural networks verification algorithms can be used to check whether a CFE is robust to noisy executions. As we will show in our experiments, this result can be used to generate provable robustness guarantees for a given explanation.

3.2   Robust Semi-factual Explanations

We now turn our attention to robust SFEs and analyse the problem pertaining to the existence of an SFE as per Definition 2.

Proposition 3. *Deciding the existence of an SFE is NP-complete.*

A reduction to verification similar to that presented in Theorem 1 can be devised to decide the existence of a semifactual explanation; the details are therefore omitted. We now formalise robustness to noisy execution for an SFE, following the same rationale used for CFEs.

Definition 5. *Consider an input x_F and a neural classifier f such that $f(x_F) = 0$. Let x be an SFE computed for x_F, i.e., $f(x) = 0$. The SFE x is said to be δ-robust if for all $x' \in \mathcal{X}$ such that $\|x' - x\|_\infty \leq \delta$ we have that $f(x') = 0$.*

Proposition 4. *Deciding whether an SFE is δ-robust is CoNP-complete.*

The proof is similar to that of Proposition 2 and is therefore omitted. Also in this case, a reduction to the verification problem can be devised to determine the robustness of an SFE to noisy execution. Specifically, the problem is reduced to checking whether the neural classifier satisfies local robustness on x for radius δ, following the same steps presented in Theorem 2.

4   Experimental Evaluation

Section 3 laid the foundations for generating formal robustness guarantees for explanations using verification. In this section we demonstrate the practical applicability of our approach and present algorithms, with implementations, to generate CEs with formal robustness guarantees. We illustrate these algorithms in the context of different input data types (tabular and images) and apply them to both fully-connected and convolutional neural classifiers. Our approach can successfully determine whether explanations generated by other methods are robust for user-defined δ's, but in contrast with them, it can generate novel ones that come with formal robustness guarantees. As we show later, the approach scales to neural classifiers with millions of trainable parameters.

Experimental Setup. The approach below is implemented in Python. Our approach is agnostic of the verification engine used and can therefore be instantiated with any complete verifier; the current implementation leverages two complete verification engines, VENUS [5] and VERINET [16]. VENUS solves verification queries by means of a reduction to Mixed-Integer Linear Programming; VERINET instead uses an approach based on interval analysis to compute the output-reachable space of an NN, which is then checked against the local robustness property. Both verifiers are used as black-boxes from their user interface; we refer to the respective papers for more details. We evaluated our approach on two case studies involving neural agents trained to perform credit scoring and traffic sign recognition tasks. Experiments were carried out on an Intel Core i7-6700 (8 cores) with 16GB RAM and running Ubuntu 19.10 (Linux kernel 5.3.0-46).

4.1 Automated Credit Scoring

Our first case study concerns the verification and generation of robust CFEs for a neural agent trained to perform credit scoring tasks. We consider the HELOC dataset [10], which contains anonymised information about home equity line of credit (HELOC) applications made by real homeowners. Each entry contains 23 features that describe the risk profile of an applicant. Entries are labelled as "*bad*" if the corresponding customer resulted to be a late payer, or "*good*" otherwise. The decision task is to predict whether a new customer will repay their HELOC within two years and thus, whether or not to accept the application.

Neural Classifiers. We trained three feed-forward neural networks; each classifier takes a 23-dimensional input x_F and produces an output y which determines whether a customer is assigned a *good* credit score, i.e., they have made their payments without ever being more than 90 days overdue, or *bad* otherwise. All classifiers have 3 hidden layers of size 128 (**nn1**), 256 (**nn2**) and 512 (**nn3**) respectively. All networks were trained using PyTorch 1.4.0 and the Adam optimiser; inputs are normalised within $[-0.5, 0.5]$.

Verifying Robustness of Explanations. We start our analysis with a set of experiments designed to show how verification tools can be used to check the robustness of heuristically-computed explanations. For these experiments we considered Contrastive Explanation Method (CEM) [8], a popular explanation algorithm. CEM uses a gradient-based search to compute SFEs and CFEs for a given input and neural classifier. Our aim is to understand the extent to which explanations provided by CEM are robust. Given a contrastive explanation x, a neural classifier f and a robustness threshold δ, we formulate a verification query to establish whether f satisfies local robustness for x and radius δ. If local robustness is satisfied, then the explanation is guaranteed to be robust. Otherwise, a counterexample to the robustness hypothesis can be returned to show an input for which the explanation is invalidated.

Results. For each of the neural networks considered we used CEM to generate 100 SFEs and 100 CFEs for a total of 200 randomly selected instances

Table 1. Robustness of 100 CFEs (top) and 100 SFEs (bottom) for different robustness thresholds. For each δ, we report the number of explanations that were found to be robust ($\#$), the average time (t, sec) needed to check robustness and the number of timeouts after 1 h (to).

CFEs	$\delta = 0.1$			$\delta = 0.5$			$\delta = 1$			$\delta = 2$			$\delta = 5$		
	$\#$	t	to	$\#$	t	to	$\#$	t	to	$\#$	t	to	$\#$	t	to
nn1	100	0.08	0	56	0.32	0	2	0.52	0	0	1.06	0	0	1.51	0
nn2	100	0.1	0	25	10.69	0	0	17.68	1	0	11.58	0	0	60.59	1
nn3	100	0.19	0	5	156.20	23	0	85.28	4	0	252.23	7	0	381.76	8
SFEs	$\delta = 0.1$			$\delta = 0.5$			$\delta = 1$			$\delta = 2$			$\delta = 5$		
	$\#$	t	to	$\#$	t	to	$\#$	t	to	$\#$	t	to	$\#$	t	to
nn1	100	0.04	0	100	0.04	0	98	0.22	0	1	0.41	0	0	1.18	0
nn2	100	0.1	0	57	0.87	0	2	1.10	0	1	22.28	0	0	14.75	0
nn3	100	0.18	0	48	20.19	0	8	68.66	6	0	41.52	7	0	969.67	37

of the HELOC dataset. For each explanation, we formulated local robustness queries as described above and used VENUS to verify robustness across domains of different sizes. Results are reported in Table 1 for $\delta \in \{0.1, 0.5, 1, 2, 5\}$ (at verification time, each perturbation value is rescaled within the normalisation ranges used for training). Overall, we observe that scalability of our approach does not appear to be an issue for smaller δ's. We notice, however, that checking large domains on bigger networks requires increased computational efforts and results in more timeouts. This is expected given the complexity of the underlying decision problems (cf Sect. 3). We also observe that both SFEs and CFEs obtained via CEM are robust for small δ's. However, their robustness decreases when considering larger domains. This is already evident, e.g., for $\delta = 0.5$, where the number of δ-robust explanations drops considerably, revealing that most of the explanations proposed by the tool are not robust. This is understandable as CEM is not designed to generate robust explanations; however users have no way to determine the extent to which an explanation is robust.

CFEs with Robustness Guarantees. The experiments above showed that present state-of-the-art gradient-based approaches may generate non-robust explanations. We now take a step further and show how our approach can be used to generate explanations endowed with formal robustness guarantees. In the following, we discuss a tighter coupling between explanation generation with verification and argue this simple idea empowers humans users to decide whether to accept an explanation with a low robustness threshold, or ask for a new one with better robustness guarantees.

Remark. The main focus of the proposed algorithm is to quantify the robustness of a CFE. As such, in our experiments we do not enforce additional metrics such as proximity or sparsity. However we stress that these metrics can be easily embedded into our framework; we exemplify this using the actionability metric.

Algorithm 1

Require: input x_F, neural classifier f, parameters ϵ, δ
Ensure: CFE x, certified robustness threshold l
  1: $x \leftarrow$ **none**
  2: $l, u \leftarrow 0, \delta$
  3: /*Determine whether CFE exists*/
  4: **res**, $x \leftarrow$ CHECKLOCALROBUSTNESS(f, x, ϵ)
  5: /*If robustness is violated, a CFE exists; otherwise return*/
  6: **if** res is **false then**
  7:     /*Binary search to determine robustness threshold*/
  8:     **while** $u - l > 0$ **do**
  9:        $m \leftarrow \frac{l+u}{2}$
 10:        **res**, $x' \leftarrow$ CHECKLOCALROBUSTNESS(f, x, m)
 11:        **if** res is **true then**
 12:            $l \leftarrow m$
 13:        **else**
 14:            $u \leftarrow m$
 15: **return** x, l

A procedure to generate robustness guarantees for CFEs is given in Algorithm 1. The algorithm receives an input x_F, a neural classifier f and parameters ϵ, δ. The overall aim of the algorithm is to first decide whether a CFE exists; if one can be found, the algorithm operates further steps to quantify its robustness. After some initialisation steps (l. 1–2), the algorithm performs an initial verification query to establish whether f satisfies robustness on x_F for radius ϵ (l. 4). If the property holds, the algorithm immediately returns as no CFE exists within the analysed distance. Instead, if the property is violated, a CFE x is found and the algorithm moves on to quantify its robustness. The search is initialised with a user-specified robustness threshold δ, defining the target robustness that a user would like to achieve. As δ may not be attainable in general for a given CFE, the algorithm performs a binary search to find the largest radius across which x is robust (l. 8–17). At each step of the search, a verification query checking local robustness of the CFE is performed until either the largest robust radius is found or termination condition is reached.

Results. For each network, we sampled 200 instances from the HELOC dataset evenly split between accepted and rejected applications. We used the VENUS verifier to generate an initial explanation and then computed the largest radius for which the explanation is robust. In practice, the binary search scheme terminates when $u - l \leq 0.0001$.

A summary of the results obtained running Algorithm 1 with $\epsilon \in \{0.1, 0.5, 1, 2\}$ and $\delta = 2$ are shown in Table 2. To begin with, we notice that when ϵ is too small, the algorithm is not able to find CFEs. However, we observe that when ϵ increases, the algorithm is able to identify more CFEs, for which robustness guarantees are successfully computed. Overall, we observe that the explanations generated are characterised by small robustness thresholds on average; this information can be used by regulators and users alike to select only those explanations that have larger thresholds, such as the one we reported in the example above, and filter out others that may be more problematic. Furthermore, [36] showed that SoA explanation methods tend to return explanations that are indistinguishable from adversarial examples. Using the robustness certificates provided by our methodology, users would be able to decide when an explanation can be trusted with confidence (i.e., high robustness threshold) and when instead the explanation may just be an artefact of the model (i.e., low robustness threshold). We conclude with an example to demonstrate our robustness guarantees.

Table 2. Robustness results for CFEs generated for 100 random instances. For each initial ϵ, we report the number of robust explanations ($\#$), their average robustness threshold (l), the average time (t, sec) it took to compute them and the number of timeouts after 1 h (to).

CFEs	$\epsilon = 0.1$				$\epsilon = 0.5$				$\epsilon = 1$				$\epsilon = 2$			
	$\#$	l	t	to	$\#$	l	t	to	$\#$	l	t	to	$\#$	l	t	to
nn1	3	0.02	0.22	0	15	0.04	0.55	0	35	0.02	1.28	0	62	0.03	4.09	0
nn2	6	0.02	0.61	0	16	0.04	1.93	0	30	0.05	66.97	6	53	0.05	120.31	36
nn3	6	0.01	2.79	0	16	0.03	153.18	1	18	0.04	156.77	69	12	0.07	1231.74	88

Example 1. Consider the following rejected application:

$$x_F = [66, 185, 11, 92, 23, 0, 0, 91, 18, 6, 6, 23, 1, 22, 0, 1, 1, 53, 19, 7, 3, 4, 71]$$

Using Algorithm 1, we generated the following CFE:

$$x = [71, 190, 16, 97, 19.6, 4, 4.5, 96, 22.7, 2.1, 3.8, 28, 5.4, 25.2, 5, 0.2, 1.1, 48, 14, 12, 6.7, 3.3, 70.6]$$

for which we were able to prove a robustness threshold of $l = 1.8$. This result can be then used to generate a textual explanation:

"*Modifying x_F to x would result in your application being accepted. Acceptance would still be granted even if each feature in x were to vary up to ± 1.8.*"

The user can then use this information to decide whether to accept this explanation, or ask for a new one with stronger robustness guarantees.

Incorporating Actionability. As already mentioned, Algorithm 1 can be extended to account for additional properties beyond robustness. A particularly desirable property that we consider is *actionability*, where perturbations are permitted only on features that the end-user can reasonably act upon. Generating actionable explanations that are also robust is of crucial importance to guarantee that produced recommendations indeed achieve the goal pursued by the user.

Actionability is typically enforced by allowing changes only input features which are classified as mutable a-priori (e.g., the education level of an applicant may change while his or her ethnicity may not). Such domain knowledge can be seamlessly incorporated into our framework. This simply requires local robustness checks to be performed over domains that are defined by box constraints (as opposed to L_∞), where immutable features are not allowed to change their initial value. Most state-of-the-art verifiers for neural networks support this feature natively; we therefore tested this approach in a setting where only 4 out of 23 features of the HELOC dataset can be modified: number of satisfactory trades, number of total trades, number of trades opened in last twelve months and number of bank trades with high utilisation ratio.

Results. We tested the ability of our approach to generate robust, actionable CFEs for **nn1**. Similarly to the previous set of experiments, we observe CFEs that modify only few features may be impossible to find for small values of ϵ. Indeed, we could prove that no CFE exists for $\epsilon = 0.1$, with their number increasing for larger neighbourhoods: we identified $3, 6, 9$ and 15 CFEs corresponding to ϵ equal to $0.5, 1, 2$ and 5 respectively. Reducing the number of mutable features can, however, be exploited to analyse larger perturbations of input features as the sparsity of perturbations reduces the search space to be explored. As a result, we were able to run experiments using values of ϵ up to 30 and generate 50 robust actionable CFEs taking 9.8s on average.

These experiments confirm that our approach can indeed generate CEs with robustness guarantees that are also actionable. This has important practical implications: our CEs suggest changes that are achievable in practice and are formally guaranteed to yield the expected outcome for any slight perturbation of magnitude less than the robustness threshold identified. We see these results as an important contribution toward complementing existing approaches for XAI.

4.2   Traffic Sign Recognition

We now turn to agents dealing with image classification tasks. In particular, we consider the German Traffic Sign Recognitions Benchmark (GTSRB) dataset [45], which contains images of traffic signs collected under strong variations in visual appearance due to, e.g., illumination and weather conditions. Given such variability, a neural agent may fail to provide robust decisions: a correctly classified image may cease to be so if small photometric changes were applied to it. We then show how SFEs augmented with robustness guarantees can provide formal assurances in the presence of photometric changes.

Neural Classifier. We trained a convolutional neural network to solve the GTSRB classification task. Images in the dataset were rescaled to size 32×32; thus, the network takes a 32×32-dimensional input image x_F and produces a 43-dimensional output y containing the score for each of the 43 classes. The classifier consists of two convolutional layers, each paired with a batch normalisation layer, followed by one fully-connected layer, thus resulting in $\sim$5M tunable parameters;

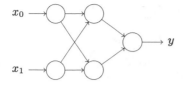

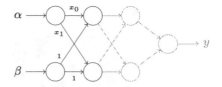

Fig. 1. A neural network.   **Fig. 2.** Augmented neural network.

all layers use ReLU activations. The classifier was trained using Pytorch 1.4.0; no normalisation was applied.

Encoding Photometric Changes. Reasoning about robustness of SFEs for the GTSRB requires a way to encode mathematically the possible effects of photometric changes. It has been observed that such changes can be modelled via standard NN layers [34], as show in the following example.

Example 2. Consider the neural network in Fig. 1. The network receives an input $x = [x_0, x_1]$ and produces an output y. Network weights and biases, as well as activations, are omitted to simplify exposition.

Photometric changes are defined by a linear transformation of the input x defined as $x' = \alpha \cdot x + \beta$, where α controls the contrast and β the brightness of x'. This operation can be encoded by a linear layer where the inputs x_0, x_1 are transformed by α and β before being fed to the original network (Fig. 2). Prepending this additional layer to the original network (shown in grey), we obtain an augmented network that takes as input the parameters encoding the photometric changes, produces a transformed image and then proceeds with the classification. This construction allows the study of the robustness of explanations using standard verifiers, where local robustness is now checked in the space of parameters α, β defining the transformation.

SFEs with Robustness Guarantees. We now generate SFEs with provable robustness guarantees for the neural classifier in question. To assist in this task we use a verification-based procedure similar to Algorithm 1, where users can select domains of interest for parameters α and β. We then check whether classifications are robust across this domain, i.e., the classification of the original input is not affected by the transformations analysed. When this is the case, the user is given the possibility to generate several SFEs by navigating the domain characterised by α and β values which have been proved to be robust. To facilitate this task, we developed the GUI shown in Fig. 3, where the user can use sliders to navigate the space of parameters controlling photometric changes. Notice that each valuation of α and β is formally guaranteed to yield valid SFEs, following our procedure. Otherwise, an explanation is returned to exemplify the circumstances under which the neural classifier fails, as shown in Fig. 4.

Results. We evaluate our approach using 50 randomly selected GTRSB images; for each image, we let the user select three transformation domains of varying

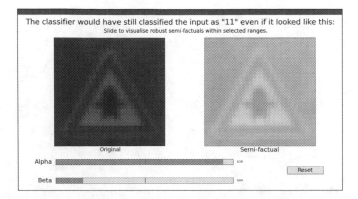

Fig. 3. A GUI to navigate and visualise robust SFEs obtained for different contrast (α) and brightness (β) values.

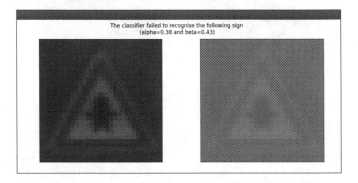

Fig. 4. When the SFE is not robust, a counterexample is visualised.

sizes, thereby resulting in 150 instances. The augmented network, together with the user-proposed bounds are sent to VERINET to solve verification queries. Our approach was able to generate robust SFEs for 11 domains taking an average time of 0.70s per instance; 98 domains were proved not to be robust with an average solving time of 1.42s (41 timeouts in total). These experiments confirm that our approach can be used to generate SFEs with robustness guarantees for convolutional classifiers operating on images. This is an important step toward providing reliable CEs for neural networks used in safety-critical applications such as autonomous driving.

5   Discussion and Conclusions

In this paper we have laid the foundations for a rigorous study of the robustness of CEs with respect to noisy execution. We developed entirely novel approaches to verify the robustness of any candidate CE and indeed to generate CEs with formal robustness guarantees. We have provided an implementation and used it to generate explanations for complex classifiers of millions of tunable parameters.

One consideration with our approach is that robustness guarantees are generated either for norm-bounded (Sect. 4.1) or user-defined (Sect. 4.2) noise models. Such perturbations may fail to account for the shape of decision boundaries in a neural classifier, possibly resulting in conservative estimates of the robustness threshold. As such, we believe our results also motivate interesting discussions on how robustness thresholds could be set in practical applications.

Our results motivate several further research directions. This work showed how formal verification neural networks can play a role towards increasing the reliability of CEs; it would be interesting to investigate synergies between XAI and VNN further. Verification could be integrated more tightly into the explanation generation process to ensure that only CEs with the strongest robustness guarantees are returned. Lastly, it would be interesting to study the implications that robustness (or a lack thereof) may have on human trust within HNMAS.

References

1. Akintunde, M., Botoeva, E., Kouvaros, P., Lomuscio, A.: Formal verification of neural agents in non-deterministic environments. J. Auton. Agents Multi-Agent Syst. **36**(1) (2022)
2. Barrett, S., Rosenfeld, A., Kraus, S., Stone, P.: Making friends on the fly: cooperating with new teammates. Artif. Intell. **242**, 132–171 (2017)
3. Björkegren, D., Blumenstock, J., Knight, S.: Manipulation-proof machine learning. arXiv preprint arXiv:2004.03865 (2020)
4. Black, E., Wang, Z., Fredrikson, M.: Consistent counterfactuals for deep models. In: Proceedings of the International Conference on Learning Representations (ICLR22). OpenReview.net (2022)
5. Botoeva, E., Kouvaros, P., Kronqvist, J., Lomuscio, A., Misener, R.: Efficient verification of neural networks via dependency analysis. In: Proceedings of the 34th AAAI Conference on Artificial Intelligence (AAAI20), pp. 3291–3299. AAAI Press (2020)
6. Brix, C., Müller, M.N., Bak, S., Johnson, T.T., Liu, C.: First three years of the international verification of neural networks competition (VNN-COMP). arXiv preprint arXiv:2301.05815 (2023)
7. Byrne, R.: Counterfactuals in explainable artificial intelligence (XAI): evidence from human reasoning. In: Proceedings of the 28th International Joint Conference on Artificial Intelligence, IJCAI19, pp. 6276–6282 (2019)
8. Dhurandhar, A., et al.: Explanations based on the missing: towards contrastive explanations with pertinent negatives. In: Advances in Neural Information Processing Systems (NeurIPS18), pp. 590–601 (2018)
9. Dutta, S., Long, J., Mishra, S., Tilli, C., Magazzeni, D.: Robust counterfactual explanations for tree-based ensembles. In: Proceedings of the International Conference on Machine Learning (ICML22). Proceedings of Machine Learning Research, vol. 162, pp. 5742–5756. PMLR (2022)
10. FICO Community: Explainable Machine Learning Challenge (2019). https://community.fico.com/s/explainable-machine-learning-challenge

11. Guidotti, D., Leofante, F., Pulina, L., Tacchella, A.: Verification of neural networks: enhancing scalability through pruning. In: Proceedings of the 24th European Conference on Artificial Intelligence (ECAI20), pp. 2505–2512. IOS Press (2020)

12. Guidotti, D., Pulina, L., Tacchella, A.: pyNeVer: a framework for learning and verification of neural networks. In: Hou, Z., Ganesh, V. (eds.) ATVA 2021. LNCS, vol. 12971, pp. 357–363. Springer, Cham (2021). https://doi.org/10.1007/978-3-030-88885-5_23

13. Hancox-Li, L.: Robustness in machine learning explanations: does it matter? In: Proceedings of the 2020 Conference on Fairness, Accountability, and Transparency (FAT*20), pp. 640–647. ACM (2020)

14. Henriksen, P., Hammernik, K., Rueckert, D., Lomuscio, A.: Bias field robustness verification of large neural image classifiers. In: Proceedings of the 32nd British Machine Vision Conference (BMVC21). BMVA Press (2021)

15. Henriksen, P., Lomuscio, A.: Efficient neural network verification via adaptive refinement and adversarial search. In: Proceedings of the 24th European Conference on Artificial Intelligence (ECAI20), pp. 2513–2520. IOS Press (2020)

16. Henriksen, P., Lomuscio, A.: DEEPSPLIT: an efficient splitting method for neural network verification via indirect effect analysis. In: Proceedings of the 30th International Joint Conference on Artificial Intelligence (IJCAI21), pp. 2549–2555. ijcai.org (2021)

17. Jennings, N.R., et al.: Human-agent collectives. Commun. ACM **57**(12), 80–88 (2014)

18. Jiang, J., Leofante, F., Rago, A., Toni, F.: Formalising the robustness of counterfactual explanations for neural networks. In: Proceedings of the 37th AAAI Conference on Artificial Intelligence (AAAI23), pp. 14901–14909. AAAI Press (2023)

19. Johnson, T., et al.: ARCH-COMP20 category report: artificial intelligence and neural network control systems (AINNCS) for continuous and hybrid systems plants. In: Proceedings of the 7th International Workshop on Applied Verification of Continuous and Hybrid Systems (ARCH20), pp. 107–139. EasyChair (2020)

20. Karimi, A., Barthe, G., Balle, B., Valera, I.: Model-agnostic counterfactual explanations for consequential decisions. In: Proceedings of the 23rd International Conference on Artificial Intelligence and Statistics (AISTATS20), pp. 895–905. PMLR (2020)

21. Katz, G., Barrett, C., Dill, D.L., Julian, K., Kochenderfer, M.J.: Reluplex: an efficient SMT solver for verifying deep neural networks. In: Majumdar, R., Kunčak, V. (eds.) CAV 2017. LNCS, vol. 10426, pp. 97–117. Springer, Cham (2017). https://doi.org/10.1007/978-3-319-63387-9_5

22. Kenny, E., Keane, M.: On generating plausible counterfactual and semi-factual explanations for deep learning. In: Proceedings of the 35th AAAI Conference on Artificial Intelligence, AAAI21, pp. 11575–11585. AAAI Press (2021)

23. Kouvaros, P., et al.: Formal analysis of neural network-based systems in the aircraft domain. In: Huisman, M., Păsăreanu, C., Zhan, N. (eds.) FM 2021. LNCS, vol. 13047, pp. 730–740. Springer, Cham (2021). https://doi.org/10.1007/978-3-030-90870-6_41

24. LeCun, Y., Bengio, Y., Hinton, G.: Deep learning. Nature **521**(7553), 436–444 (2015)

25. Leofante, F., Botoeva, E., Rajani, V.: Counterfactual explanations and model multiplicity: a relational verification view. In: Proceedings of the 20th International Conference on Principles of Knowledge Representation and Reasoning (KR23) (2023, to appear)

26. Leofante, F., Lomuscio, A.: Towards robust contrastive explanations for human-neural multi-agent systems. In: Proceedings of the International Conference on Autonomous Agents and Multiagent Systems (AAMAS23), pp. 2343–2345. ACM (2023)
27. Leofante, F., Narodytska, N., Pulina, L., Tacchella, A.: Automated verification of neural networks: advances, challenges and perspectives. CoRR abs/1805.09938 (2018)
28. Liu, C., Arnon, T., Lazarus, C., Strong, C.A., Barrett, C.W., Kochenderfer, M.J.: Algorithms for verifying deep neural networks. Found. Trends Optim. 4(3–4), 244–404 (2021)
29. Lomuscio, A., Maganti, L.: An approach to reachability analysis for feed-forward ReLU neural networks. arXiv preprint arXiv:1706.07351 (2017)
30. Van Looveren, A., Klaise, J.: Interpretable counterfactual explanations guided by prototypes. In: Oliver, N., Pérez-Cruz, F., Kramer, S., Read, J., Lozano, J.A. (eds.) ECML PKDD 2021. LNCS (LNAI), vol. 12976, pp. 650–665. Springer, Cham (2021). https://doi.org/10.1007/978-3-030-86520-7_40
31. McCloy, R., Byrne, R.: Semifactual "even if" thinking. Thinking Reason. 8(1), 41–67 (2002)
32. Miller, T.: Explanation in artificial intelligence: insights from the social sciences. Artif. Intell. 267, 1–38 (2019)
33. Mohammadi, K., Karimi, A., Barthe, G., Valera, I.: Scaling guarantees for nearest counterfactual explanations. In: Proceedings of the AAAI/ACM Conference on AI, Ethics, and Society (AIES21), pp. 177–187. ACM (2021)
34. Mohapatra, J., Weng, T., Chen, P., Liu, S., Daniel, L.: Towards verifying robustness of neural networks against A family of semantic perturbations. In: Proceedings of the IEEE/CVF Conference on Computer Vision and Pattern Recognition (CVPR20), pp. 241–249. IEEE (2020)
35. Mothilal, R.K., Sharma, A., Tan, C.: Explaining machine learning classifiers through diverse counterfactual explanations. In: Proceedings of the International Conference on Fairness, Accountability, and Transparency (FAT*20), pp. 607–617. ACM (2020)
36. Pawelczyk, M., Agarwal, C., Joshi, S., Upadhyay, S., Lakkaraju, H.: Exploring counterfactual explanations through the lens of adversarial examples: a theoretical and empirical analysis. In: Proceedings of the International Conference on Artificial Intelligence and Statistics (AISTATS22). Proceedings of Machine Learning Research, vol. 151, pp. 4574–4594. PMLR (2022)
37. Pawelczyk, M., Broelemann, K., Kasneci, G.: On counterfactual explanations under predictive multiplicity. In: Proceedings of the 36th Conference on Uncertainty in Artificial Intelligence (UAI20). Proceedings of Machine Learning Research, vol. 124, pp. 809–818. AUAI Press (2020)
38. Pawelczyk, M., Datta, T., van den Heuvel, J., Kasneci, G., Lakkaraju, H.: Probabilistically robust recourse: navigating the trade-offs between costs and robustness in algorithmic recourse. In: Proceedings of the 11th International Conference on Learning Representations (ICLR23). OpenReview.net (2023)
39. ProPublica: How We Analyzed the COMPAS Recidivism Algorithm (2016). https://www.propublica.org/article/how-we-analyzed-the-compas-recidivism-algorithm
40. Pulina, L., Tacchella, A.: An abstraction-refinement approach to verification of artificial neural networks. In: Touili, T., Cook, B., Jackson, P. (eds.) CAV 2010. LNCS, vol. 6174, pp. 243–257. Springer, Heidelberg (2010). https://doi.org/10.1007/978-3-642-14295-6_24

41. Rosenfeld, A., Richardson, A.: Explainability in human-agent systems. Auton. Agents Multi Agent Syst. **33**(6), 673–705 (2019)
42. Russell, C.: Efficient search for diverse coherent explanations. In: Proceedings of the International Conference on Fairness, Accountability, and Transparency (FAT*19), pp. 20–28. ACM (2019)
43. Sharma, S., Henderson, J., Ghosh, J.: CERTIFAI: a common framework to provide explanations and analyse the fairness and robustness of black-box models. In: Proceedings of the AAAI/ACM Conference on AI, Ethics, and Society (AIES20), pp. 166–172. ACM (2020)
44. Slack, D., Hilgard, A., Lakkaraju, H., Singh, S.: Counterfactual explanations can be manipulated. In: Advances in Neural Information Processing Systems 34 (NeurIPS21), pp. 62–75 (2021)
45. Stallkamp, J., Schlipsing, M., Salmen, J., Igel, C.: The German traffic sign recognition benchmark: a multi-class classification competition. In: Proceedings of the International Joint Conference on Neural Networks (IJCNN11), pp. 1453–1460. IEEE (2011)
46. Upadhyay, S., Joshi, S., Lakkaraju, H.: Towards robust and reliable algorithmic recourse. In: Advances in Neural Information Processing Systems 34 (NeurIPS21), pp. 16926–16937 (2021)
47. Ustun, B., Spangher, A., Liu, Y.: Actionable recourse in linear classification. In: Proceedings of the Conference on Fairness, Accountability, and Transparency (FAT*19), pp. 10–19. ACM (2019)
48. Wachter, S., Mittelstadt, B., Russell, C.: Counterfactual explanations without opening the black box: automated decisions and the GDPR. Harv. JL Tech. **31**, 841 (2017)
49. Wang, S., Pei, K., Whitehouse, J., Yang, J., Jana, S.: Efficient formal safety analysis of neural networks. In: Advances in Neural Information Processing Systems (NeurIPS18), pp. 6367–6377. Curran Associates, Inc. (2018)

LTL$_f$ Synthesis Under Environment Specifications for Reachability and Safety Properties

Benjamin Aminof[1(✉)], Giuseppe De Giacomo[1,2(✉)], Antonio Di Stasio[2(✉)], Hugo Francon[3(✉)], Sasha Rubin[4(✉)], and Shufang Zhu[2(✉)]

[1] Sapienza University of Rome, Rome, Italy
`benj@forsyte.at`
[2] University of Oxford, Oxford, UK
`{giuseppe.degiacomo,antonio.distasio,shufang.zhu}@cs.ox.ac.uk`
[3] ENS Rennes, Rennes, France
`hugo.francon@ens-rennes.fr`
[4] The University of Sydney, Camperdown, Australia
`sasha.rubin@sydney.edu.au`

Abstract. In this paper, we study LTL$_f$ synthesis under environment specifications for arbitrary reachability and safety properties. We consider both kinds of properties for both agent tasks and environment specifications, providing a complete landscape of synthesis algorithms. For each case, we devise a specific algorithm (optimal wrt complexity of the problem) and prove its correctness. The algorithms combine common building blocks in different ways. While some cases are already studied in literature others are studied here for the first time.

1 Introduction

Synthesis under environment specifications consists of synthesizing an agent strategy (aka plan or program) that realizes a given task against all possible environment responses (i.e., environment strategies). The agent has some indirect knowledge of the possible environment strategies through an environment specification, and it will use such knowledge to its advantage when synthesizing its strategy [2,4,9,24]. This problem is tightly related to planning in adversarial nondeterministic domains [20], as discussed, e.g., in [10,15].

In this paper, we study synthesis under environment specifications, considering both *agent task specifications* and *environment specifications* expressed in Linear Temporal Logic on finite traces (LTL$_f$). These are logics that look at finite traces or finite prefixes of infinite traces. For concreteness, we focus on LTL$_f$ [16,17], but the techniques presented here extend immediately to other temporal logics on finite traces, such as Linear Dynamic Logics on finite traces, which is more expressive than LTL$_f$ [16], and Pure-Past LTL, which has the same expressiveness as LTL but evaluates a trace backward from the current instant [11].

Linear temporal logics on finite traces provide a nice embodiment of the notable triangle among Logics, Automata, and Games [21]. These logics are full-

V. Malvone and A. Murano (Eds.): EUMAS 2023, LNAI 14282, pp. 263–279, 2023.
https://doi.org/10.1007/978-3-031-43264-4_17

fledged logics with high expressiveness over finite traces, and they can be translated into classical regular finite state automata; moreover, they can be further converted into deterministic finite state automata (DFAs). This transformation yields a game represented on a graph. In this game, one can analyze scenarios where the objective is to reach certain final states. Finally, despite the fact that producing a DFA corresponding to an LTL$_f$ formula can require double-exponential time, the algorithms involved—generating alternating automata (linear), getting the nondeterministic one (exponential), determinizing it (exponential), solving reachability games (poly)—are particularly well-behaved from the practical computational point of view [26, 28, 32].

In this paper, however, we consider LTL$_f$ specifications in two contexts which we denote as

$$\exists\varphi \text{ and } \forall\varphi \text{ with } \varphi \text{ an arbitrary LTL}_f \text{ formula.}$$

The first one specifies a *reachability* property: there exists a finite prefix $\pi_{<k}$ of an infinite trace π such that $\pi_{<k} \models \varphi$. This is the classical use of LTL$_f$ to specify synthesis tasks [17]. The second one specifies a *safety* property: every finite prefix $\pi_{<k}$ of an infinite trace π is such that $\pi_{<k} \models \varphi$. This is the classical use of LTL$_f$ to specify environment behaviours [1,13]. The formulas $\forall\varphi$ and $\exists\varphi$ with φ in LTL$_f$ capture exactly two well-known classes of LTL properties in Manna and Pnueli's Temporal Hierarchy [23]. Specifically, $\exists\varphi$ captures the *co-safety properties* and $\forall\varphi$ captures the *safety properties* (in [23], expressed respectively as $\Diamond\psi$ and $\Box\psi$ with ψ an arbitrary Pure-Past LTL formulas, which consider only past operators.)

We let Env and Task denote an environment specification and a task specification, respectively, consisting of a safety ($\forall\varphi$) and/or reachability property ($\exists\varphi$). This gives rise to 12 possible cases: 3 without any environment specifications, 3 with safety environment specifications ($\forall\varphi$), 3 with reachability environment specifications ($\exists\varphi$), and 3 with both safety and reachability environment specifications ($\exists\varphi \wedge \forall\varphi$). For each of these, we provide an algorithm, which is optimal wrt the complexity of the problem, and prove its correctness. When the problem was already solved in literature, we give appropriate references (e.g., Task = $\exists\varphi$ and Env = $true$ is classical LTL$_f$ synthesis, solved in [17]). In fact, we handle all the cases involving reachability in the environment specifications by providing a novel algorithm that solves the most general case of Env = $\exists\varphi_1 \wedge \forall\varphi_2$ and Task = $\exists\varphi_3 \wedge \forall\varphi_4$[1].

These algorithms use the common building blocks (combining them in different ways): the construction of the DFAs of the LTL$_f$ formulas, Cartesian products of such DFAs, considering these DFAs as the game arena and solving games for reachability/safety objectives. Also, all these problems have a 2EXPTIME-complete complexity. The hardness comes from LTL$_f$ synthesis [17], and the membership comes from the LTL$_f$-to-DFA construction, which dominates the complexity since computing the Cartesian products and solving reachability/safety games

---

[1] In fact, this algorithm can solve all cases, but it's much more involved compared to the direct algorithms we provide for each case.

is polynomial[2]. Towards the actual application of our algorithms, we observe that although the DFAs of LTL$_f$ formulas are worst-case double-exponential, there is empirical evidence showing that the determinization of NFA, which causes one of the two exponential blow-ups, is often polynomial in the NFA [27,28,32]. Moreover, in several notable cases, e.g., in all DECLARE patterns [29], the DFAs are polynomial in the LTL$_f$ formulas, and so are our algorithms.

2   Preliminaries

Traces. For a finite set Σ, let Σ^ω (resp. Σ^+, Σ^*) denote the set of infinite strings (resp. non-empty finite strings, finite strings) over Σ. We may write concatenation of sets using $\cdot$, e.g., $\Sigma \cdot \Sigma$ denotes the set of strings over Σ of length 2. The length of a string is denoted $|\pi|$, and may be infinite. Strings are indexed starting at 0. For a string π and $k \in \mathbb{N}$ with $k < |\pi|$, let $\pi_{<k}$ denote the finite prefix of π of length k. For example, if $\pi = \pi_0\pi_1 \ldots \pi_n$, then $|\pi| = n + 1$ and $\pi_{<2} = \pi_0\pi_1$. Typically, Σ will be the set of interpretations (i.e., assignments) over a set *Prop* of atomic propositions, i.e., $\Sigma = 2^{Prop}$. Non-empty strings will also be called *traces*.

Linear-Time Temporal Logic on Finite Traces. LTL$_f$ is a variant of Linear-time temporal logic (LTL) interpreted over *finite*, instead of infinite, traces [16]. Given a set *Prop* of atomic propositions, LTL$_f$ formulas φ are defined by the following grammar: $\varphi ::= p \mid \neg\varphi \mid \varphi \wedge \varphi \mid \bigcirc\varphi \mid \varphi\,\mathcal{U}\,\varphi$ where $p \in$ *Prop* denotes an atomic proposition, $\bigcirc$ is read *next*, and $\mathcal{U}$ is read *until*. We abbreviate other Boolean connectives and operators.

For a finite trace $\pi \in (2^{Prop})^+$, an LTL$_f$ formula φ, and a position i ($0 \le i < |\pi|$), define $\pi, i \models \varphi$ (read "φ *holds* at position i") by induction, as follows:

- $\pi, i \models p$ iff $p \in \pi_i$ (for $p \in$ *Prop*);
- $\pi, i \models \neg\varphi$ iff $\pi, i \not\models \varphi$;
- $\pi, i \models \varphi_1 \wedge \varphi_2$ iff $\pi, i \models \varphi_1$ and $\pi, i \models \varphi_2$;
- $\pi, i \models \bigcirc\varphi$ iff $i < |\pi| - 1$ and $\pi, i + 1 \models \varphi$;
- $\pi, i \models \varphi_1\,\mathcal{U}\,\varphi_2$ iff for some j ($i \le j < |\pi|$), $\pi, j \models \varphi_2$, and for all k ($i \le k < j$), $\pi, k \models \varphi_1$.

We write $\pi \models \varphi$, if $\pi, 0 \models \varphi$ and say that π *satisfies* φ. Write $\mathcal{L}(\varphi)$ for the set of finite traces over $\Sigma = 2^{Prop}$ that satisfy φ. In addition, we define the *weak next* operator $\bullet\varphi \equiv \neg\bigcirc\neg\varphi$. Note that: $\neg\bigcirc\varphi$ is not, in general, logically equivalent to $\bigcirc\neg\varphi$, but we have that $\neg\bigcirc\varphi \equiv \bullet\neg\varphi$.

Domains. A *domain (aka transition system, aka arena)* is a tuple $\mathcal{D} = (\Sigma, Q, \iota, \delta)$, where Σ is a finite alphabet, Q is a finite set of states, $\iota \in Q$ is the initial state, $\delta : Q \times \Sigma \to Q$ is a transition function. For an infinite string

---

[2] For pure-past LTL, obtaining the DFA from a pure-past LTL formula is single exponential [11], and indeed the problems and all our algorithms become EXPTIME-complete.

$w = w_0 w_1 w_2 \ldots \in \Sigma^\omega$ a *run* of $\mathcal{D}$ on w is a sequence $r = q_0 q_1 q_2 \ldots \in Q^\omega$ that $q_0 = \iota$ and $q_{i+1} \in \delta(q_i, w_i)$ for every i with $0 \leq i$. A *run* of $\mathcal{D}$ on a finite string $w = w_0 w_1 \ldots w_n$ over Σ is a sequence $q_0 q_1 \cdots q_{n+1}$ such that $q_0 = \iota$ and $q_{i+1} \in \delta(q_i, w_i)$ for every i with $0 \leq i < n+1$. Note that every string has exactly one run of $\mathcal{D}$.

Deterministic Finite Automaton (DFA). A *DFA* is a tuple $\mathcal{M} = (\mathcal{D}, F)$ where $\mathcal{D}$ is a domain and $F \subseteq Q$ is a set of *final* states. A finite word w over Σ is *accepted* by $\mathcal{M}$ if the run of $\mathcal{M}$ on w ends in a state of F. The set of all such finite strings is denoted $\mathcal{L}(\mathcal{M})$, and is called the *language* of $\mathcal{M}$.

Theorem 1. [17] *Every* LTL$_f$ *formula* φ *over atoms Prop can be translated into a* DFA $\mathcal{M}_\varphi$ *over alphabet* $\Sigma = 2^{Prop}$ *such that for every finite string* π *we have that* $\pi \in \mathcal{L}(\mathcal{M})$ *iff* $\pi \models \varphi$. *This translation takes time double-exponential in the size of* φ.

Properties of Infinite Strings. A *property* is a set P of infinite strings over Σ, i.e., $P \subseteq \Sigma^\omega$. We say that P is a *reachability* property if there exists a set $T \subseteq \Sigma^+$ of finite traces such that if $w \in P$ then some finite prefix of w is in T. We say that P is a *safety* property if there exists a set $T \subseteq \Sigma^+$ of finite traces such that if $w \in P$, then every finite prefix of w is in T. It is worth noting that the complement of a reachability property is a safety property, and vice versa.

An LTL$_f$ formula can be used to denote a reachability (resp., safety) property over $\Sigma = 2^{Prop}$ as follows.

Definition 1. *For an* LTL$_f$ *formula* φ, *let* $\exists\varphi$ *denote set of traces* π *such that some finite prefix of* π *satisfies* φ, *and let* $\forall\varphi$ *denote set of traces* π *such that every finite (non-empty) prefix of* π *satisfies* φ.

Note that $\exists\varphi$ denotes a reachability property, and $\forall\varphi$ denotes a safety property. From now on, "prefix" will mean "finite non-empty prefix". Note also that for an LTL$_f$ formula, $\mathcal{L}(\varphi)$ is a set of finite traces. On the other hand, $\mathcal{L}(\exists\varphi)$ (and similarly $\mathcal{L}(\psi)$ where ψ is a Boolean combination of formulas of the form $\exists\varphi$ for LTL$_f$ formulas φ) is a set of infinite traces. In this paper, we consider $\exists\varphi$, $\forall\varphi$, and $\exists\varphi \wedge \forall\varphi$ to specify both agent tasks and environment behaviours.

Deterministic Automata on Infinite Strings (DA). Following the automata-theoretic approach in formal methods, we will compile formulas to automata. We have already seen that we can compile LTL$_f$ formulas to DFAs. We now introduce automata over infinite words to handle certain properties of infinite words. A *deterministic automaton* (DA, for short) is a tuple $\mathcal{A} = (\mathcal{D}, \alpha)$ where $\mathcal{D}$ is a transition system, say with the state set Q, and $\alpha \subseteq Q^\omega$ is called an *acceptance condition*. An infinite string w is *accepted* by $\mathcal{A}$ if its run is in α. The set of all such infinite strings is denoted $\mathcal{L}(\mathcal{A})$, and is called the *language* of $\mathcal{A}$.

We consider reachability (reach) and safety (safe) acceptance conditions, parameterized by a set of target states $T \subseteq Q$:

- reach(T) = $\{q_0 q_1 q_2 \ldots \in Q^\omega \mid \exists k \geq 0 : q_k \in T\}$. In this case, we call $\mathcal{A}$ a *reachability automaton*.
- safe(T) = $\{q_0 q_1 q_2 \ldots \in Q^\omega \mid \forall k \geq 0 : q_k \in T\}$. In this case, we call $\mathcal{A}$ a *safety automaton*.

Remark 1. Every reachability (resp. safety) property expressible in LTL is the language of a reachability automaton (resp. safety automaton) [16, 22, 25].

3 Problem Description

Reactive Synthesis. Reactive Synthesis (aka Church's Synthesis) is the problem of turning a specification of an agent's task and of its environment into a strategy (aka policy). This strategy can be employed by the agent to achieve its task, regardless of how the environment behaves. In this framework, the agent and the environment are considered players in a turn-based game, in which players move by picking an evaluation of the propositions they control. Thus, we partition the set *Prop* of propositions into two disjoint sets of propositions $\mathcal{X}$ and $\mathcal{Y}$, and with a little abuse of notation, we denote such a partition as *Prop* $= \mathcal{Y} \cup \mathcal{X}$. Intuitively, the propositions in $\mathcal{X}$ are controlled by the environment, and those in $\mathcal{Y}$ are controlled by the agent. In this work (in contrast to the usual setting of reactive synthesis), the agent moves first. The agent moves by selecting an element of $2^{\mathcal{Y}}$, and the environment responds by selecting an element of $2^{\mathcal{X}}$. This is repeated forever, and results in an infinite trace (aka play). From now on, unless specified otherwise, we let $\Sigma = 2^{Prop}$ and *Prop* $= \mathcal{Y} \cup \mathcal{X}$. We remark that the games considered in this paper are games of perfect information with deterministic strategies.

An *agent strategy* is a function $\sigma_{\mathsf{ag}} : (2^{\mathcal{X}})^* \to 2^{\mathcal{Y}}$. An environment strategy is a function $\sigma_{\mathsf{env}} : (2^{\mathcal{Y}})^+ \to 2^{\mathcal{X}}$. A strategy σ is *finite-state* (aka *finite-memory*) if it can be represented as a finite-state input/output automaton that, on reading an element h of the domain of σ, outputs the action $\sigma(h)$. A trace $\pi = (Y_0 \cup X_0)(Y_1 \cup X_1) \cdots \in (2^{\mathcal{Y} \cup \mathcal{X}})^\omega$ *follows an agent strategy* $\sigma_{\mathsf{ag}} : (2^{\mathcal{X}})^* \to 2^{\mathcal{Y}}$ if $Y_0 = \sigma_{\mathsf{ag}}(\epsilon)$ and $Y_{i+1} = \sigma_{\mathsf{ag}}(X_0 X_1 \ldots X_i)$ for every $i \geq 0$, and it *follows an environment strategy* σ_{env} if $X_i = \sigma_{\mathsf{env}}(Y_0 Y_1 \ldots Y_i)$ for all $i \geq 0$. We denote the unique infinite sequence (play) that follows σ_{ag} and σ_{env} as $\mathsf{play}(\sigma_{\mathsf{ag}}, \sigma_{\mathsf{env}})$. Let P be a property over the alphabet $\Sigma = 2^{Prop}$, specified by formula or DA. An agent strategy σ_{ag} (resp., environment strategy σ_{env}) *enforces* P if for every environment strategy σ_{env} (resp., agent strategy σ_{ag}), we have that $\mathsf{play}(\sigma_{\mathsf{ag}}, \sigma_{\mathsf{env}})$ is in P. In this case, we write $\sigma_{\mathsf{ag}} \rhd P$ (resp. $\sigma_{\mathsf{env}} \rhd P$). We say that P is *agent (resp., environment) realizable* if there is an agent (resp. environment) strategy that enforces P.

Synthesis Under Environment Specifications. Typically, an agent has some knowledge of how the environment works, represented as a fully observable model of the environment, which it can exploit to enforce its task [2]. Formally, let Env and Task be properties over alphabet $\Sigma = 2^{Prop}$, denoting the environment specification and the agent task, respectively.

Note that while the agent task Task denotes the set of desirable traces from the agent's perspective, the environment specification Env denotes the set of environment strategies that describe how the environment reacts to the agent's actions (no matter what the agent does) in order to enforce Env. Specifically, Env is treated as a set of traces when we reduce the problem of synthesis under environment specification to standard reactive synthesis.

We require a consistency condition of Env, i.e., there must exist at least one environment strategy $\sigma_{env} \rhd$ Env. An agent strategy σ_{ag} enforces Task *under the environment specification* Env, written $\sigma_{ag} \rhd_{Env}$ Task, if for all $\sigma_{env} \rhd$ Env we have that play$(\sigma_{ag}, \sigma_{env}) \models$ Task. Note that if Env = *true* then this just says that σ_{ag} enforces Task (i.e., the environment specification is missing).

Definition 2 (Synthesis under environment specifications). *Let* Env *and* Task *be properties over alphabet* $\Sigma = 2^{Prop}$, *denoting the environment specification and the agent task, respectively. (i) The* realizability under environment specifications problem *asks, given* Task *and* Env, *to decide if there exists an agent strategy enforcing* Task *under the environment specification* Env. *(ii) The* synthesis under environment specifications problem *asks, given* Task *and* Env, *to return a finite-state agent strategy enforcing* Task *under the environment specification* Env, *or say that none exists.*

In [2] is shown that for any linear-time property[3], synthesis under environment specifications can be reduced to synthesis without environment specifications. Thus, in order to show that Task is realizable under Env it is sufficient to show that Env $\to$ Task is realizable. Moreover, to solve the synthesis problem for Task under Env, it is enough to return a strategy that enforces Env $\to$ Task.

Table 1. Task and Env considered. Note that, from Alg. 7 we get the remaining cases involving reachability environment specifications by suitably setting $\varphi_1, \varphi_2, \varphi_4$ to *true*.

Task	Env	Alg
$\exists \varphi$	*true*	Algorithm 1
$\forall \varphi$	*true*	Algorithm 2
$\exists \varphi_1 \wedge \forall \varphi_2$	*true*	Algorithm 3
$\exists \varphi_1$	$\forall \varphi_2$	Algorithm 4
$\forall \varphi_1$	$\forall \varphi_2$	Algorithm 5
$\exists \varphi_1 \wedge \forall \varphi_2$	$\forall \varphi_3$	Algorithm 6
$\exists \varphi_1 \wedge \forall \varphi_2$	$\exists \varphi_3 \wedge \forall \varphi_4$	Algorithm 7

In the rest of the paper, we provide a landscape of algorithms for LTL$_f$ synthesis considering reachability and safety properties for both agent tasks and

---

[3] Technically, the properties should be Borel, which all our properties are.

environment specifications. However, these synthesis problems are complex and challenging due to the combination of reachability and safety properties. To tackle this issue, one possible approach is to reduce LTL$_f$ synthesis problems to LTL synthesis problems through suitable translations, e.g., [12,14,30,31]. However, there is currently no methodology for performing such translations when considering combinations of reachability and safety properties[4]. Additionally, synthesis algorithms for LTL specifications are generally more challenging than those for LTL$_f$ specifications, both theoretically and practically [13,14,30,31]. In this paper, we show that for certain combinations, we can avoid the detour to LTL synthesis and keep the simplicity of LTL$_f$ synthesis. Specifically, we consider that Task and Env take the following forms: $\exists\varphi_1, \forall\varphi_1, \exists\varphi_1 \wedge \forall\varphi_2$ where the φ_i are LTL$_f$ formulas, and in addition we consider the case of no environment specification (formally, Env = $true$). This results in 12 combinations. Algorithms 1–7, listed in Table 1, optimally solve all the combinations. All these algorithms adopt some common building blocks while linking them in different ways.

Theorem 2. *Let each of* Task *and* Env *be of the forms* $\forall\varphi$, $\exists\varphi$, *or* $\exists\varphi_1 \wedge \forall\varphi_2$. *Solving synthesis for an agent* Task *under environment specification* Env *is 2EXPTIME-complete.*

4   Building Blocks for the Algorithms

In this section, we describe the building blocks we will use to devise the algorithms for the problem described in the previous section.

DAs for $\exists\varphi$ *and* $\forall\varphi$. Here, we show how to build the DA whose language is exactly the infinite traces satisfying $\exists\varphi$ (resp. $\forall\varphi$). The first step is to convert the LTL$_f$ formula φ into a DFA $\mathcal{M}_\varphi = (\Sigma, Q, \iota, \delta, F)$ that accepts exactly the *finite* traces that satisfy φ as in Theorem 1. Then, to obtain a DA $\mathcal{A}_{\exists\varphi}$ for $\exists\varphi$ define $\mathcal{A}_{\exists\varphi} = (2^{\mathcal{X} \cup \mathcal{Y}}, Q, \iota, \delta, \text{reach}(F))$. It is immediate that $\mathcal{L}(\exists\varphi) = \mathcal{L}(\mathcal{A}_{\exists\varphi})$. To obtain a DA $\mathcal{A}_{\forall\varphi}$ for $\forall\varphi$ define $\mathcal{A}_{\forall\varphi} = (2^{\mathcal{X} \cup \mathcal{Y}}, Q, \iota, \delta, \text{safe}(F \cup \{\iota\}))$.

The reason ι is considered a part of the safe set is that the DFA $\mathcal{M}_\varphi$ does not accept the empty string since the semantics of LTL$_f$ precludes this. It is immediate that $\mathcal{L}(\forall\varphi) = \mathcal{L}(\mathcal{A}_{\forall\varphi})$. For $\psi \in \{\exists\varphi, \forall\varphi\}$, we let CONVERTDA($\psi$) denote the resulting DA.

Lemma 1. *Let* φ *be an* LTL$_f$ *formula, and let* $\psi \in \{\exists\varphi, \forall\varphi\}$. *Then the languages* $\mathcal{L}(\psi)$ *and* $\mathcal{L}(\text{CONVERTDA}(\psi))$ *are equal.*

For formulas of the form $\forall\varphi$ we will suppress the initial state in the objective and so CONVERTDA($\forall\varphi$) will be written $(\mathcal{D}_{\forall\varphi}, \text{safe}(T))$, i.e., T contains ι.

Games over DA. The synthesis problems we consider in this paper are solved by reducing them to two-player games. We will represent games by DAs $\mathcal{A} =$

---

[4] In [9] is shown that the case of LTL$_f$ synthesis under safety and reachability properties can be solved by reducing to games on infinite-word automata. This certain case is covered in our paper, nevertheless, we provide a direct approach that only involves games on finite-word automata.

$(\mathcal{D}, \alpha)$ where $\mathcal{D}$ is a transition system, sometimes called an 'arena', and α is an acceptance condition, sometimes called a 'winning condition'. The game is played between an *agent* (controlling $\mathcal{Y}$) and *environment* (controlling $\mathcal{X}$). Intuitively, a position in the game is a state $q \in Q$. The initial position is ι. From each position, first the agent moves by setting $Y \in 2^{\mathcal{Y}}$, then the environment moves by setting $X \in 2^{\mathcal{X}}$, and the next position is updated to the state $\delta(q, Y \cup X)$. This interaction results in an infinite run in $\mathcal{D}$, and the agent is declared the winner if the run is in α (otherwise, the environment is declared the winner).

Definition 3. *An agent strategy σ_{ag} is said to* win the game $(\mathcal{D}, \alpha)$ *if for every trace π that follows σ_{ag}, the run in $\mathcal{D}$ of π is in α.*

In other words, σ_{ag} wins the game if every trace π that follows σ_{ag} is in $L(\mathcal{D}, \alpha)$. For $q \in Q$, let $\mathcal{D}_q$ denote the transition system $\mathcal{D}$ with initial state q, i.e., $\mathcal{D}_q = (\Sigma, Q, q, \delta)$. We say that q is a *winning state* for the agent if there is an agent strategy that wins the game $(\mathcal{D}_q, \alpha)$; in this case, the strategy is said to *win starting from* q.

In the simplest settings, we represent agent strategies as functions of the form $f_{\mathsf{ag}} : Q \to 2^{\mathcal{Y}}$, called positional strategies. An agent positional strategy f_{ag} induces an agent strategy, $\sigma_{\mathsf{ag}} = \mathrm{STRATEGY}(\mathcal{D}_q, f_{\mathsf{ag}})$, as follows: define $\sigma_{\mathsf{ag}}(\epsilon) = f_{\mathsf{ag}}(q)$, and for every finite trace π let ρ be the run of $\mathcal{D}_q$ on π (i.e., starting in state q), and define $\sigma_{\mathsf{ag}}(\pi) = f_{\mathsf{ag}}(q')$ where q' is the last state in ρ (i.e., $q' = \rho_{|\pi|}$). In more complex settings, e.g., in the Algorithm 7, we will construct functions of the form $f_{\mathsf{ag}} : Q \cdot (2^{\mathcal{Y}} \cdot 2^{\mathcal{X}} \cdot Q)^* \to 2^{\mathcal{Y}}$, which similarly induce agent strategies $\mathrm{STRATEGY}(\mathcal{D}_q, f_{\mathsf{ag}})$ where for every finite trace $\pi = Y_0 \cup X_0, \cdots, Y_k \cup X_k$, and run $q_0, \cdots, q_{k+1}$ of π in $\mathcal{D}_q$, define $\sigma_{\mathsf{ag}}(\pi) = f_{\mathsf{ag}}(q_0, Y_0 \cup X_0, q_1, Y_1 \cup X_1, \cdots, q_{k+1})$. Below the agent strategy $\sigma_{\mathsf{ag}} = \mathrm{STRATEGY}(\mathcal{D}_q, f_{\mathsf{ag}})$ returned by the various algorithms will be finite state, in the sense that it is representable as a transducer. For simplicity, with a little abuse of notation, we will return directly σ_{ag}, instead of its finite representation as a transducer.

Dual definitions can be given for the environment, with the only notable difference being that $f_{\mathsf{env}} : Q \times 2^X \to 2^{\mathcal{Y}}$ since the moves of the environment depend also on the last move of the agent (since the agent moves first).

In this paper, besides the terms 'environment' and 'agent', we also consider the terms 'protagonist' and 'antagonist'. If the DA $(\mathcal{D}, \alpha)$ is a specification for the agent, then the agent is called the protagonist and the environment is called the antagonist. On the other hand, if the DA $(\mathcal{D}, \alpha)$ is a specification for the environment, then the environment is called the protagonist, and the agent is called the antagonist. Intuitively, the protagonist is trying to make sure that the generated traces are in $\mathcal{L}(\mathcal{D}, \alpha)$, and the antagonist to make sure that the generated traces are not in $\mathcal{L}(\mathcal{D}, \alpha)$. Define Win_p (resp. Win_a) as the set of states $q \in Q$ such that q is a protagonist (resp. antagonist) winning state. This set is called protagonist's (resp. antagonist) *winning region*. In this paper, all our games (including reachability and safety games) are *determined*. Therefore:

Lemma 2. *For every state $q \in Q$, it holds that $q \in \mathsf{Win}_p$ iff $q \notin \mathsf{Win}_a$.*

The problem of *solving* a game $(\mathcal{D}, \alpha)$ for the protagonist is to compute the winning region Win_p and a function f_p such that $\textsc{Strategy}(\mathcal{D}, f_p)$ wins from every state in $\mathsf{Win}_p{}^5$. To do this, we will also sometimes compute a winning strategy for the antagonist (that wins starting in its winning region).

Solving Reachability Games and Safety Games. We repeatedly make use of solutions to reachability games and safety games given by DAS $\mathcal{A}$. Thus, for a protagonist $p \in \{\mathsf{ag}, \mathsf{env}\}$ let $\textsc{Solve}_p(\mathcal{A})$ denote the procedure for solving the game $\mathcal{A}$, i.e., p is trying to ensure the play is in $\mathcal{L}(\mathcal{A})$; this procedure returns the protagonist's winning region Win_p and a function f_p such that $\textsc{Strategy}(\mathcal{D}, f_p)$ wins starting from every state in Win_p [19].

Product of Transition Systems. Let $\mathcal{D}_i$ $(1 \leq i \leq k)$ be transition systems over alphabet Σ. Their *product*, denoted $\textsc{Product}(\mathcal{D}_1, \cdots, \mathcal{D}_k)$, is the transition system $\mathcal{D} = (\Sigma, Q, \iota, \delta)$ defined as follows: (i) The alphabet is Σ. (ii) The state set is $Q = Q_1 \times \cdots \times Q_k$. (iii) The initial state is $\iota = (\iota_1, \cdots, \iota_k)$. (iv) The transition function δ maps a state $(q_1, \cdots, q_k)$ on input $z \in \Sigma$ to the state $(q_1', \cdots, q_k')$ where $q_i' = \delta_i(q_i, z)$ $(1 \leq i \leq k)$. Also, the *lift* of a set $F_i \subseteq Q_i$ to $\mathcal{D}$ is the set $\{(q_1, \cdots, q_k) : q_i \in F_i\} \subseteq Q$.

Restriction of a Transition System. The restriction of a transition system, defined as the procedure $\textsc{Restriction}(\mathcal{D}, S)$, restricts $\mathcal{D} = (\Sigma, Q, \iota, \delta)$ to $S \subseteq Q$ is the transition system $\mathcal{D}' = (\Sigma, S \cup \{sink\}, \iota, \delta', \alpha')$ where for all $z \in \Sigma$, $\delta'(sink, z) = sink$, $\delta'(q, z) = \delta(q, z)$ if $\delta(q, z) \in S$, and $\delta'(q, z) = sink$ otherwise. Intuitively, $\mathcal{D}'$ redirect all transitions from S that leave S to a fresh *sink* state. We may denote the sink by $\bot{}^6$.

5   Reachability Tasks, No Env Spec

Algorithm 1 solves the realizability and synthesis for the case of reachability tasks and no environment specification. Formally, Task is of the form $\exists\varphi$ where φ is an LTL$_f$ formula, and $\mathsf{Env} = true$. This problem is solved in [17], but here we rephrase the problem in our notation.

Theorem 3. *Algorithm 1 solves the synthesis under environment specifications problem with* $\mathsf{Task} = \exists\varphi, \mathsf{Env} = true$, *where* φ *is an* LTL$_f$ *formula.*

---

[5] Since strategies can depend on the history, and thus on the starting state in particular, there is always a strategy that wins from every state in Win_p.

[6] We remark that (i) when we restrict the transition system of a DA $(\mathcal{D}, \alpha)$ we may need to revise the winning-condition α to express whether reaching $sink$ is good for the protagonist or not (although many times it is not, e.g., when restricting to the winning-region for a safety condition); (ii) in one case, in Algorithm 7, we will add two sink states.

Algorithm 1. Task $= \exists\varphi$, Env $= true$

Input: LTL$_f$ formula φ
Output: agent strategy σ_{ag} that enforces $\exists\varphi$
 1: $\mathcal{A} = \text{CONVERTDA}(\exists\varphi)$, say $\mathcal{A} = (\mathcal{D}_{\exists\varphi}, \text{reach}(T))$
 2: $(W, f_{ag}) = \text{SOLVE}_{ag}(\mathcal{A})$
 3: **if** $\iota \notin W$ **return** "Unrealisable" **endif**
 4: **return** $\sigma_{ag} = \text{STRATEGY}(\mathcal{D}_{\exists\varphi}, f_{ag})$

---

6 Safety Tasks, No Env Spec

Algorithm 2 handles the case Task is of the form $\forall\varphi$ where φ is an LTL$_f$ formula, and Env $= true$. We can use the result in [17] to solve the synthesis for $\forall\varphi$ from the point of view of the environment.

Algorithm 2. Task $= \forall\varphi$, Env $= true$

Input: LTL$_f$ formula φ
Output: agent strategy σ_{ag} that enforces $\forall\varphi$
 1: $\mathcal{A}_1 = \text{CONVERTDA}(\forall\varphi)$, say $\mathcal{A}_1 = (\mathcal{D}_{\forall\varphi}, \text{safe}(T_1))$
 2: $(S_1, f_{ag}) = \text{SOLVE}_{ag}(\mathcal{A}_1)$
 3: **if** $\iota \notin S_1$ **return** "Unrealisable" **endif**
 4: **return** $\sigma_{ag} = \text{STRATEGY}(\mathcal{D}_{\forall\varphi}, f_{ag})$

Theorem 4. *Algorithm 2 solves the synthesis under environment specifications problem with* Task $= \forall\varphi$, Env $= true$, *where φ is an* LTL$_f$ *formula.*

7 Reachability and Safety Tasks, No Env Spec

Algorithm 3 handles the case that Task is of the form $\exists\varphi_1 \wedge \forall\varphi_2$ where φ_1 and φ_2 are LTL$_f$ formulas, and Env $= true$.

Intuitively, the algorithm proceeds as follows. First, it computes the corresponding DA for $\forall\varphi_2$ and solves the safety game over it. The resulting winning area represents the set of states from which the agent has a strategy to realize its safety task. Then, it restricts the game area to the agent's winning area. Finally, it solves the reachability game over the game product of the corresponding DA of $\exists\varphi_1$ and the remaining part of the DA for $\forall\varphi_2$.

In order to obtain the final strategy for the agent we need to refine the strategy f_{ag} to deal with the sink state, call it $\perp_2$, and combine it with g_{ag}. Given f_{ag} computed in Line 3, define $f''_{ag} : Q_1 \times (S_2 \cup \{\perp_2\}) \to 2^{\mathcal{Y}}$ over $\mathcal{D}$ by $f''_{ag}(q, s) = f_{ag}(s)$ if $s \in S_2$, and $f''_{ag}(q, s) = Y$ (for some arbitrary Y) otherwise. In words, f''_{ag} ensures the second component stays in S_2 (and thus in T_2). Recall that g_{ag} over $\mathcal{D}$ ensures that T_1 is reached in the first co-ordinate, while at the same time maintaining the second co-ordinate is in S_2. Finally, let $\text{COMBINE}(\mathcal{D}, R, g_{ag}, f_{ag})$

Algorithm 3. Task $= \exists\varphi_1 \wedge \forall\varphi_2$, Env $= true$

Input: LTL$_f$ formulas φ_1 and φ_2
Output: agent strategy σ_{ag} that realizes $\exists\varphi_1$ and $\forall\varphi_2$
1: $\mathcal{A}_1 = \text{CONVERTDA}(\exists\varphi_1)$, say $\mathcal{A}_1 = (\mathcal{D}_{\exists\varphi_1}, \text{reach}(T_1))$
2: $\mathcal{A}_2 = \text{CONVERTDA}(\forall\varphi_2)$, say $\mathcal{A}_2 = (\mathcal{D}_{\forall\varphi_2}, \text{safe}(T_2))$
3: $(S_2, f_{\mathsf{ag}}) = \text{SOLVE}_{ag}(\mathcal{A}_2)$
4: $\mathcal{D}'_{\forall\varphi_2} = \text{RESTRICT}(\mathcal{D}_{\forall\varphi_2}, S_2)$, say the sink state is $\perp_2$
5: $\mathcal{D} = \text{PRODUCT}(\mathcal{D}_{\exists\varphi_1}, \mathcal{D}'_{\forall\varphi_2})$
6: $(R, g_{\mathsf{ag}}) = \text{SOLVE}_{ag}(\mathcal{D}, \text{reach}(T_1 \times S_2))$
7: **if** $\iota \notin R$ **return** "Unrealisable" **endif**
8: $h_{\mathsf{ag}} = \text{COMBINE}(\mathcal{D}, R, g_{\mathsf{ag}}, f_{\mathsf{ag}})$
9: **return** $\sigma_{\mathsf{ag}} = \text{STRATEGY}(\mathcal{D}, h_{\mathsf{ag}})$

---

denote the final strategy $h_{\mathsf{ag}} : Q_1 \times (S_2 \cup \{\perp_2\}) \rightarrow 2^{\mathcal{Y}}$ defined as follows: $h_{\mathsf{ag}}((q,s)) = g_{\mathsf{ag}}((q,s))$ if $(q,s) \in R$, and $h_{\mathsf{ag}}((q,s)) = f''_{\mathsf{ag}}((q,s))$ otherwise. Intuitively, the agent following h_{ag} will achieve the reachability goal while staying safe, whenever this is possible, and stays safe otherwise.

Theorem 5. *Algorithm 3 solves synthesis under environment specifications problem with* Task $= \exists\varphi_1 \wedge \forall\varphi_2$, Env $= true$, *where the* φ_i *are* LTL$_f$ *formulas.*

8 Reachability Tasks, Safety Env Specs

Algorithm 4 handles the case that Task is of the form $\exists\varphi_1$ and Env $= \forall\varphi_2$, where φ_1, φ_2 are LTL$_f$ formulas. A similar problem of this case was solved in [13], which, more specifically, considers only finite safety of the agent, i.e., the agent is required to stay safe until some point (the bound is related to an additional agent reachability task), and thus can actually be considered as reachability.

Intuitively, the algorithm first computes all the environment strategies that can enforce Env $= \forall\varphi_2$ [7], represented as a restriction of the DA for $\forall\varphi_2$, as in the previous section. Then, based on restricting the game arena on these environment strategies, the algorithm solves the reachability game over the product of the corresponding DA of $\exists\varphi_1$ and the restricted part of the DA for $\forall\varphi_2$.

Theorem 6. *Algorithm 4 solves the synthesis under environment specifications problem with* Task $= \exists\varphi_1$, Env $= \forall\varphi_2$, *where the* φ_i *are* LTL$_f$ *formulas.*

Algorithm 4. Task $= \exists\varphi_1$, Env $= \forall\varphi_2$

Input: LTL$_f$ formulas φ_1, φ_2
Output: agent strategy σ_{ag} that enforces $\exists\varphi_1$ under $\forall\varphi_2$
 1: $\mathcal{A}_1 = \text{CONVERTDA}(\exists\varphi_1)$, say $\mathcal{A}_1 = (\mathcal{D}_{\exists\varphi_1}, \text{reach}(T_1))$
 2: $\mathcal{A}_2 = \text{CONVERTDA}(\forall\varphi_2)$, say $\mathcal{A}_2 = (\mathcal{D}_{\forall\varphi_2}, \text{safe}(T_2))$
 3: $(S_2, f_{\mathsf{env}}) = \text{SOLVE}_{\mathsf{env}}(\mathcal{A}_2)$
 4: $\mathcal{D}'_2 = \text{RESTRICT}(\mathcal{D}_2, S_2)$, say the sink state is $\perp_2$
 5: $\mathcal{D} = \text{PRODUCT}(\mathcal{D}_1, \mathcal{D}'_2)$
 6: $(R, f_{\mathsf{ag}}) = \text{SOLVE}_{\mathsf{ag}}(\mathcal{D}, \text{reach}((T_1 \times S_2) \cup (Q_1 \times \{\perp_2\})))$
 7: **if** $\iota \notin R$ **return** "Unrealisable" **endif**
 8: **return** $\sigma_{\mathsf{ag}} = \text{STRATEGY}(\mathcal{D}, f_{\mathsf{ag}})$

---

9   Safety Tasks, Safety Env Specs

Algorithm 5 handles the case that Task is of the form $\forall\varphi_1$ and Env $= \forall\varphi_2$, where φ_1, φ_2 are LTL$_f$ formulas.

Intuitively, the algorithm proceeds as follows. First, it computes the corresponding DA for $\forall\varphi_2$ and solves the safety game for the environment over it. The resulting winning area represents the set of states, from which the environment has a strategy to enforce the environment specification $\mathcal{L}(\forall\varphi_2)$. It is worth noting that restricting the DA to considering only such winning area, in fact, captures all the environment strategies that enforce $\mathcal{L}(\forall\varphi_2)$ [7]. Based on the restriction, the algorithm solves the safety game over the product of the corresponding DA of $\forall\varphi_1$ and the remaining part of the DA for $\forall\varphi_2$.

Algorithm 5. Task $= \forall\varphi_1$, Env $= \forall\varphi_2$

Input: LTL$_f$ formulas φ_1, φ_2
Output: agent strategy σ_{ag} that enforces $\forall\varphi_1$ under $\forall\varphi_2$
 1: $\mathcal{A}_1 = \text{CONVERTDA}(\forall\varphi_1)$, say $\mathcal{A}_1 = (\mathcal{D}_1, \text{safe}(T_1))$
 2: $\mathcal{A}_2 = \text{CONVERTDA}(\forall\varphi_2)$, say $\mathcal{A}_2 = (\mathcal{D}_2, \text{safe}(T_2))$
 3: $(S_2, f_{\mathsf{env}}) = \text{SOLVE}_{\mathsf{env}}(\mathcal{A}_2)$
 4: $\mathcal{D}'_2 = \text{RESTRICT}(\mathcal{D}_2, S_2)$, call the sink $\perp_2$
 5: $\mathcal{D} = \text{PRODUCT}(\mathcal{D}_1, \mathcal{D}'_2)$
 6: $(S, f_{\mathsf{ag}}) = \text{SOLVE}_{\mathsf{ag}}(\mathcal{D}, \text{safe}((T_1 \times S_2) \cup (Q_1 \times \{\perp_2\})))$
 7: **if** $\iota \notin S$ **return** "Unrealisable" **endif**
 8: **return** $\sigma_{\mathsf{ag}} = \text{STRATEGY}(\mathcal{D}, f_{\mathsf{ag}})$

Theorem 7. *Algorithm 5 solves the synthesis under environment specifications problem with* Task $= \forall\varphi_1$, Env $= \forall\varphi_2$, *where the* φ_i *are* LTL$_f$ *formulas.*

10   Reachability and Safety Tasks, Safety Env Specs

Algorithm 6 handles the case that Task is of the form $\exists\varphi_1 \wedge \forall\varphi_2$ and Env $= \forall\varphi_3$, where $\varphi_1, \varphi_2, \varphi_3$ are LTL$_f$ formulas. As mentioned in the previous section, a similar problem of this case that considers only finite safety of the agent was solved in [13] by reducing Task to reachability properties only. Instead, we provide here an approach to the synthesis problem considering infinite agent safety.

Intuitively, the algorithm proceeds as follows. Following the algorithms presented in the previous sections, it first computes all the environment strategies that can enforce Env $= \varphi_3$, represented as a restriction of the DA for $\forall\varphi_3$. Then, based on restricting the game arena on these environment strategies, the algorithm solves the safety game for the agent over the product of the corresponding DA of $\forall\varphi_2$ and the restricted part of the DA for $\forall\varphi_3$. This step is able to capture all the agent strategies that can realize $\forall\varphi_2$ under environment specification $\forall\varphi_3$. Next, we represent all these agent strategies by restricting the product automaton to considering only the computed agent winning states, thus obtaining $\mathcal{D}'$. Finally, the algorithm solves the reachability game over the product of the corresponding DA of $\exists\varphi_1$ and $\mathcal{D}'$. In order to abstract the final strategy for the agent, it is necessary to combine the two agent strategies: one is from the safety game for enforcing $\forall\varphi_2$ under $\forall\varphi_3$, the other one is from the final reachability game for enforcing $\exists\varphi_1$ while not violating $\forall\varphi_2$ under $\forall\varphi_3$.

Algorithm 6. Task $= \exists\varphi_1 \wedge \forall\varphi_2$, Env $= \forall\varphi_3$

Input: LTL$_f$ formulas $\varphi_1, \varphi_2, \varphi_3$
Output: agent strategy σ_{ag} that enforces $\exists\varphi_1 \wedge \forall\varphi_2$ under $\forall\varphi_3$
1: $\mathcal{A}_1 = \mathrm{CONVERTDA}(\exists\varphi_1)$, say $\mathcal{A}_1 = (\mathcal{D}_1, \mathrm{reach}(T_1))$
2: $\mathcal{A}_2 = \mathrm{CONVERTDA}(\forall\varphi_2)$, say $\mathcal{A}_2 = (\mathcal{D}_2, \mathrm{safe}(T_2))$
3: $\mathcal{A}_3 = \mathrm{CONVERTDA}(\forall\varphi_3)$, say $\mathcal{A}_3 = (\mathcal{D}_3, \mathrm{safe}(T_3))$
4: $(S_3, f_{\mathrm{env}}) = \mathrm{SOLVE}_{\mathrm{env}}(\mathcal{A}_3)$
5: $\mathcal{D}_3' = \mathrm{RESTRICT}(\mathcal{D}_3, S_3)$, call the sink $\perp_3$
6: $\mathcal{D} = \mathrm{PRODUCT}(\mathcal{D}_2, \mathcal{D}_3')$
7: $(S_2, f_{\mathrm{ag}}^s) = \mathrm{SOLVE}_{\mathrm{ag}}(\mathcal{D}, \mathrm{safe}((T_2 \times S_3) \cup (Q_2 \times \{\perp_3\})))$
8: $\mathcal{D}' = \mathrm{RESTRICT}(\mathcal{D}, S_2)$, call the sink $\perp_2$
9: $\mathcal{C} = \mathrm{PRODUCT}(\mathcal{D}_1, \mathcal{D}')$
10: Let $f_{\mathrm{ag}}^{s'} : Q_1 \times (S_2 \cup \{\perp_2\}) \to 2^{\mathcal{Y}}$ map (q_1, q_2) to $f_{\mathrm{ag}}^s(q_2)$ if $q_2 \in S_2$, and is arbitrary otherwise. $\{f_{\mathrm{ag}}^{s'}$ lifts f_{ag}^s to $\mathcal{C}\}$
11: $(R, f_{\mathrm{ag}}^r) = \mathrm{SOLVE}_{\mathrm{ag}}(\mathcal{C}, \mathrm{reach}((T_1 \times S_2 \times S_3) \cup (Q_1 \times (\eta(S_2) \cup \{\perp_2\}) \times \{\perp_3\}))$
     $\{ \eta : Q_2 \times Q_3 \to Q_2$ is the projection onto Q_2, i.e., $(q_2, q_3) \mapsto q_2\}$
12: **if** $\iota \notin R$ **return** "Unrealisable" **endif**
13: Let $f_{\mathrm{ag}} : Q_1 \times (S_2 \cup \{\perp_2\}) \to 2^{\mathcal{Y}}$ on $\mathcal{C}$ map q to $f_{\mathrm{ag}}^r(q)$ if $q \in R$, and to $f_{\mathrm{ag}}^{s'}(q)$ otherwise. $\{f_{\mathrm{ag}}$ does f_{ag}^r on R, and $f_{\mathrm{ag}}^{s'}$ otherwise.$\}$
14: **return** $\sigma_{\mathrm{ag}} = \mathrm{STRATEGY}(\mathcal{C}, f_{\mathrm{ag}})$

Theorem 8. *Algorithm 6 solves synthesis under environment specifications problem with* Task $= \exists\varphi_1 \wedge \forall\varphi_2$, Env $= \forall\varphi_3$, *where the* φ_i *are* LTL$_f$ *formulas.*

11   Reachability and Safety Tasks and Env Specs

Algorithm 7 handles the case that $\mathsf{Env} = \forall \varphi_1 \wedge \exists \varphi_2$ and $\mathsf{Task} = \exists \varphi_3 \wedge \forall \varphi_4$ by solving synthesis for the formula $\mathsf{Env} \rightarrow \mathsf{Task}$ [2], i.e., for $(\exists \neg \varphi_1 \vee \forall \neg \varphi_2) \vee (\exists \varphi_3 \wedge \forall \varphi_4)$. Note that, from the general case, we get all cases involving reachability environment specifications by suitably setting φ_1, φ_2 or φ_4 to $true$. We remark that for the case $\varphi_4 = true$ in which the safety and reachability specifications are presented in the safety-fragment and co-safety fragment of LTL is solved in [10].

We first define two constructions that will be used in the algorithm. Given a transition system $\mathcal{D} = (\Sigma, Q, \iota, \delta)$ and a set of states $T \subseteq Q$, define FLAGGED$(\mathcal{D}, T)$ to be the transition system that, intuitively, records whether a state in T has been seen so far. Formally, FLAGGED$(\mathcal{D}, T)$ returns the transition system $D^f = (\Sigma, Q^f, \iota^f, \delta^f)$ defined as follows: 1. $Q^f = Q \times \{yes, no\}$. 2. $\iota^f = (\iota, b)$, where $b = no$ if $\iota \notin T$, and $b = yes$ if $\iota \in T$. 3. $\delta^f((q, b), z) = (q', b')$ if $\delta(q, z) = q'$ and one of the following conditions holds: (i) $b = b' = yes$, (ii) $b = b' = no, q' \notin T$, (iii) $b = no, b' = yes, q' \in T$. Given a transition system $\mathcal{D} = (\Sigma, Q, \iota, \delta)$ and disjoint subsets V_0, V_1 of Q, define RESTRICTIONWITHSINKS$(\mathcal{D}, V_0, V_1)$ to be the transition system on state set V_0 that, intuitively, behaves like $\mathcal{D}$ on V_0, transitions from V_0 to V_1 are redirected to a new sink state $\bot$, and transitions from V_0 to $Q \setminus (V_0 \cup V_1)$ are redirected to a new sink state $\top$. Formally, RESTRICTIONWITHSINKS$(\mathcal{D}, V_0, V_1)$ is the transition system $(\Sigma, \hat{Q}, \hat{\iota}, \hat{\delta})$ defined as follows: 1. $\hat{Q} = V_0 \cup \{\top, \bot\}$. 2. $\hat{\iota} = \iota$. 3. $\hat{\delta}(q, z) = \delta(q, z)$ if $\delta(q, z) \in V_0$. Otherwise, define $\hat{\delta}(q, z) = \bot$ if $\delta(q, z) \in V_1$, and $\hat{\delta}(q, z) = \top$ if $\delta(q, z) \in Q \setminus (V_0 \cup V_1)$.

Intuitively, at Line 10, S_2 will form part of the agent's winning region since from here safe(T_2) can be ensured. At Line 12, R_3 will also form part of the agent's winning region since from R_3 in $\mathcal{D}'$ reach$(T_3) \cap$ safe(T_4) can be ensured. In the following steps, we identify remaining ways that the agent can win, intuitively by maintaining $T_2 \cap T_4$ either forever (in which case safe(T_2) is ensured), or before the state leaves $T_2 \cap T_4$ either (i) it is in S_2 or R_3 (in which case we proceed as before), or otherwise (ii) it is in S_4 (but not in S_2 nor in R_3) and has already seen T_3 (in which case reach$(T_3) \cap$ safe(T_4) can be ensured).

At the end of the algorithm, we combine the four strategies $f_{\mathsf{ag}}^1, f_{\mathsf{ag}}^2, f_{\mathsf{ag}}^3$ and f_{ag}^4 through procedure COMBINE$(\mathcal{D}^f, f_{\mathsf{ag}}^1, f_{\mathsf{ag}}^2, f_{\mathsf{ag}}^3, f_{\mathsf{ag}}^4, R_1, S_2, R_3, E)$ to obtain the final strategy $f_{\mathsf{ag}} : (Q^f)^+ \rightarrow 2^{\mathcal{Y}}$ as follows. For every history $h \in (Q^f)^+$, if the history ever enters R_1 then follow f_{ag}^1, ensuring reach(T_1), otherwise, writing q for the start state of h: 1. if $q \in S_2$ then use f_{ag}^2, which ensures safe(T_2); 2. if $q \in R_3$ then use f_{ag}^3 until T_3 is reached and thereafter use f_{ag}^4, which ensures safe$(T_4) \cap$ reach(T_3); 3. if $q \in E$ then use f_{ag}^e while the states are in E, ensuring safe(T_2) if play stays in E; if ever, let q' be the first state in the history that is not in E; by construction, this corresponds to $\top$ in $\mathcal{D}^f$ and thus is (i) in S_2 or (ii) in R_3, and so proceed as before, or else (iii) in $(S_4 \setminus T_2) \setminus (R_3 \cup S_2)$ (which can be simplified to $S_4 \setminus (R_3 \cup T_2)$) with flag value yes in which case switch to strategy f_{ag}^4. Intuitively, case (i) ensures safe(T_2), and cases (ii) and (iii) each ensure safe$(T_4) \cap$ reach(T_3); 4. and if none of these, then make an arbitrary move. Note that in spite of being a function of the whole history, f_{ag} can be represented

---

Algorithm 7. Task $= \exists\varphi_3 \wedge \forall\varphi_4$, Env $= \forall\varphi_1 \wedge \exists\varphi_2$

Input: LTL$_f$ formulas $\varphi_1, \varphi_2, \varphi_3, \varphi_4$
Output: agent strategy σ_{ag} that enforces $\exists\varphi_3 \wedge \forall\varphi_4$ under $\forall\varphi_1 \wedge \exists\varphi_2$
1: $\mathcal{A}_1 = \text{CONVERTDA}(\exists\neg\varphi_1)$, say $\mathcal{A}_1 = (\mathcal{D}_1, \text{reach}(B_1))$
2: $\mathcal{A}_2 = \text{CONVERTDA}(\forall\neg\varphi_2)$, say $\mathcal{A}_2 = (\mathcal{D}_2, \text{safe}(B_2))$
3: $\mathcal{A}_3 = \text{CONVERTDA}(\exists\varphi_3)$, say $\mathcal{A}_3 = (\mathcal{D}_3, \text{reach}(B_3))$
4: $\mathcal{A}_4 = \text{CONVERTDA}(\forall\varphi_4)$, say $\mathcal{A}_4 = (\mathcal{D}_4, \text{safe}(B_4))$
5: $\mathcal{D}_p = \text{PRODUCT}(\mathcal{D}_1, \mathcal{D}_2, \mathcal{D}_3, \mathcal{D}_4)$
6: Let Q_p be the state set of $\mathcal{D}_p$, and T_i the lift of B_i to Q_p (for $i \le 4$)
7: $(R_1, f_{\text{ag}}^1) = \text{SOLVE}_{\text{ag}}(\mathcal{D}_p, \text{reach}(T_1))$
8: $\mathcal{D}_p' = \text{RESTRICT}(\mathcal{D}_p, Q \setminus R_1)$
9: $\mathcal{D}^f = \text{FLAGGED}(\mathcal{D}_p', T_3)$
10: $(S_2, f_{\text{ag}}^2) = \text{SOLVE}_{\text{ag}}(\mathcal{D}^f, \text{safe}(T_2))$
11: $(S_4, f_{\text{ag}}^4) = \text{SOLVE}_{\text{ag}}(\mathcal{D}^f, \text{safe}(T_4))$
12: $(R_3, f_{\text{ag}}^3) = \text{SOLVE}_{\text{ag}}(\text{RESTRICT}(\mathcal{D}^f, S_4), \text{reach}(T_3))$
13: $V_0 = (Q^f \setminus (S_2 \cup S_4)) \cup ((S_4 \cap T_2) \setminus (R_3 \cup S_2))$
14: V_1 is all states in $(S_4 \setminus T_2) \setminus (R_3 \cup S_2)$ whose flag is set to *no*
15: $\hat{\mathcal{D}} = \text{RESTRICTIONWITHSINKS}(\mathcal{D}^f, V_0, V_1)$
16: $(E, f_{\text{ag}}^e) = \text{SOLVE}_{\text{ag}}(\hat{\mathcal{D}}, \text{safe}((T_2 \cap T_4) \cup \{\top\}))$
17: $W_{\text{ag}} = S_2 \cup R_3 \cup E$ {Note that $W_{\text{ag}} \subseteq Q^f \cup \{\top\}$}
18: **if** $\iota \notin W_{\text{ag}}$ **return** "Unrealisable" **endif**
19: $f_{\text{ag}} = \text{COMBINE}(\mathcal{D}^f, f_{\text{ag}}^1, f_{\text{ag}}^2, f_{\text{ag}}^3, f_{\text{ag}}^4, R_1, S_2, R_3, E)$ {See the definition below.}
20: **return** $\sigma_{\text{ag}} = \text{STRATEGY}(\mathcal{D}^f, f_{\text{ag}})$

---

by a finite-state transducer. So in the Algorithm 7, as before, with a little abuse of notation we write directly $\sigma_{\text{ag}} = \text{STRATEGY}(\mathcal{D}^f, f_{\text{ag}})$, to mean that we return its representation as a transducer.

Theorem 9. *Algorithm 7 solves the synthesis under environment specifications problem with* Task $= \exists\varphi_3 \wedge \forall\varphi_4$ *and* Env $= \forall\varphi_1 \wedge \exists\varphi_2$, *where* φ_i *are* LTL$_f$ *formulas.*

Comparison to Algorithms 1–6. Note that Algorithm 7 can solve the other six variants by suitably instantiating some of $\varphi_1, \varphi_2, \varphi_3, \varphi_4$ to *true*. Nevertheless, Algorithm 7 is much more sophisticated than Algorithms 1–6. Hence, in this paper, we present the algorithms deductively, starting with simpler variants and moving to the most difficult. Furthermore, instantiating Algorithm 7 does not always give the same algorithms as Algorithms 1–6. For instance, Algorithm 1 for the synthesis problem of Task $= \exists\varphi$ (no environment specification) can be obtained from Algorithm 7 by setting $\varphi_1, \varphi_2, \varphi_4$ to *true*, but we cannot get Algorithm 4 for the synthesis problem of Env $= \forall\varphi$ and Task $= \exists\psi$ in this way. This is because Algorithm 7 solves the synthesis problem by reducing to Env $\rightarrow$ Task [2], but Algorithm 4 directly disregards all environment strategies that cannot enforce Env by first solving a safety game for the environment on Env and removing all the states that do not belong to the environment winning region to get a smaller game arena, hence obtaining optimal complexity. Analogously, in Algorithm 3 for the synthesis problem of Env $=$ *true* and Task $= \exists\varphi_1 \wedge$

$\forall \varphi_2$, we also first disregard all the agent strategies that are not able to enforce $\forall \varphi_2$, obtaining a smaller game arena for subsequent computations, hence getting an optimal complexity in practice compared to constructing the game arena considering the complete state space from the DA of $\forall \varphi_2$.

12   Conclusion

In this paper, we have studied the use of reachability and safety properties based on LTL$_f$ for both agent tasks and environment specifications. As mentioned in the introduction, though we have specifically focused on LTL$_f$, all algorithms presented here can be readily applied to other temporal logics on finite traces, such as Linear Dynamic Logics on finite traces (LDL$_f$), which is more expressive than LTL$_f$ [16], and Pure-Past LTL [11], as long as there exists a technique to associate formulas to equivalent DFAs.

It is worth noting that all the cases studied here are specific Boolean combinations of $\exists \varphi$. It is of interest to indeed devise algorithms to handle arbitrary Boolean combinations. Indeed, considering that LTL$_f$ is expressively equivalent to pure-past LTL, an arbitrary Boolean combination of $\exists \varphi$ would correspond to a precise class of LTL properties in Manna & Pnueli's Temporal Hierarchy [23]: the so-called *obligation* properties. We leave this interesting research direction for future work.

Another direction is to consider best-effort synthesis under assumptions for Boolean combinations of $\exists \varphi$, instead of (ordinary) synthesis under assumptions, in order to handle ignorance the agent has about the environment [3,5,6,8,18].

References

1. Aminof, B., De Giacomo, G., Murano, A., Rubin, S.: Planning and synthesis under assumptions. CoRR (2018)
2. Aminof, B., De Giacomo, G., Murano, A., Rubin, S.: Planning under LTL environment specifications. In: ICAPS, pp. 31–39 (2019)
3. Aminof, B., De Giacomo, G., Lomuscio, A., Murano, A., Rubin, S.: Synthesizing best-effort strategies under multiple environment specifications. In: KR, pp. 42–51 (2021)
4. Aminof, B., De Giacomo, G., Murano, A., Rubin, S.: Synthesis under assumptions. In: KR, pp. 615–616. AAAI Press (2018)
5. Aminof, B., De Giacomo, G., Rubin, S.: Best-effort synthesis: doing your best is not harder than giving up. In: IJCAI, pp. 1766–1772. ijcai.org (2021)
6. Aminof, B., De Giacomo, G., Rubin, S., Zuleger, F.: Stochastic best-effort strategies for Borel goals. In: LICS, pp. 1–13 (2023)
7. Bernet, J., Janin, D., Walukiewicz, I.: Permissive strategies: from parity games to safety games. RAIRO Theor. Inform. Appl. **36**(3), 261–275 (2002)
8. Berwanger, D.: Admissibility in infinite games. In: Thomas, W., Weil, P. (eds.) STACS 2007. LNCS, vol. 4393, pp. 188–199. Springer, Heidelberg (2007). https://doi.org/10.1007/978-3-540-70918-3_17
9. Camacho, A., Bienvenu, M., McIlraith, S.A.: Finite LTL synthesis with environment assumptions and quality measures. In: KR, pp. 454–463 (2018)

10. Camacho, A., Bienvenu, M., McIlraith, S.A.: Towards a unified view of AI planning and reactive synthesis. In: ICAPS, pp. 58–67 (2019)
11. De Giacomo, G., Di Stasio, A., Fuggitti, F., Rubin, S.: Pure-past linear temporal and dynamic logic on finite traces. In: IJCAI, pp. 4959–4965 (2020)
12. De Giacomo, G., Di Stasio, A., Perelli, G., Zhu, S.: Synthesis with mandatory stop actions. In: KR, pp. 237–246 (2021)
13. De Giacomo, G., Di Stasio, A., Tabajara, L.M., Vardi, M.Y., Zhu, S.: Finite-trace and generalized-reactivity specifications in temporal synthesis. In: IJCAI, pp. 1852–1858 (2021)
14. De Giacomo, G., Di Stasio, A., Vardi, M.Y., Zhu, S.: Two-stage technique for LTL$_f$ synthesis under LTL assumptions. In: KR, pp. 304–314 (2020)
15. De Giacomo, G., Rubin, S.: Automata-theoretic foundations of FOND planning for LTL$_f$ and LDL$_f$ goals. In: IJCAI, pp. 4729–4735 (2018)
16. De Giacomo, G., Vardi, M.Y.: Linear temporal logic and linear dynamic logic on finite traces. In: IJCAI, pp. 854–860 (2013)
17. De Giacomo, G., Vardi, M.Y.: Synthesis for LTL and LDL on finite traces. In: IJCAI, pp. 1558–1564 (2015)
18. Faella, M.: Admissible strategies in infinite games over graphs. In: Královič, R., Niwiński, D. (eds.) MFCS 2009. LNCS, vol. 5734, pp. 307–318. Springer, Heidelberg (2009). https://doi.org/10.1007/978-3-642-03816-7_27
19. Fijalkow, N., et al.: Games on graphs (2023)
20. Geffner, H., Bonet, B.: A Coincise Introduction to Models and Methods for Automated Planning. Morgan & Claypool (2013)
21. Grädel, E., Thomas, W., Wilke, T. (eds.): Automata Logics, and Infinite Games: A Guide to Current Research. LNCS, vol. 2500. Springer, Heidelberg (2002). https://doi.org/10.1007/3-540-36387-4
22. Kupferman, O., Vardi, M.Y.: Model checking of safety properties. Formal Methods Syst. Des. **19**(3), 291–314 (2001)
23. Manna, Z., Pnueli, A.: A hierarchy of temporal properties. In: PODC, pp. 377–410 (1990)
24. Pnueli, A., Rosner, R.: On the synthesis of a reactive module. In: POPL, pp. 179–190 (1989)
25. Rabin, M.O., Scott, D.S.: Finite automata and their decision problems. IBM J. Res. Dev. **3**(2), 114–125 (1959)
26. Tabajara, L.M., Vardi, M.Y.: LTLF synthesis under partial observability: from theory to practice. In: GandALF. EPTCS, vol. 326, pp. 1–17 (2020)
27. Tabajara, L.M., Vardi, M.Y.: Partitioning techniques in LTLF synthesis. In: IJCAI, pp. 5599–5606 (2019)
28. Tabakov, D., Vardi, M.Y.: Experimental evaluation of classical automata constructions. In: Sutcliffe, G., Voronkov, A. (eds.) LPAR 2005. LNCS (LNAI), vol. 3835, pp. 396–411. Springer, Heidelberg (2005). https://doi.org/10.1007/11591191_28
29. Westergaard, M.: Better algorithms for analyzing and enacting declarative workflow languages using LTL. In: Rinderle-Ma, S., Toumani, F., Wolf, K. (eds.) BPM 2011. LNCS, vol. 6896, pp. 83–98. Springer, Heidelberg (2011). https://doi.org/10.1007/978-3-642-23059-2_10
30. Zhu, S., De Giacomo, G., Pu, G., Vardi, M.Y.: LTL$_f$ synthesis with fairness and stability assumptions. In: AAAI, pp. 3088–3095 (2020)
31. Zhu, S., Tabajara, L.M., Li, J., Pu, G., Vardi, M.Y.: Symbolic LTL$_f$ synthesis. In: IJCAI, pp. 1362–1369 (2017)
32. Zhu, S., Tabajara, L.M., Pu, G., Vardi, M.Y.: On the power of automata minimization in temporal synthesis. In: GandALF. EPTCS, vol. 346, pp. 117–134 (2021)

Logic-Based Approximations of Preferences

Paolo Baldi[✉]

Department of Human Studies, University of Salento, Lecce, Italy
paolo.baldi@unisalento.it

Abstract. In this exploratory work, we provide a general framework, based on Depth-Bounded Boolean logic, for addressing some of the criticisms towards Savage's approach to the foundations of decision theory. We introduce a sequence of approximating preferences structures and show that, under suitable conditions such preferences give rise to a qualitative probability which is almost representable by a finitely additive probability.

1 Introduction

In his seminal work, first published in 1954, and revisited in 1972 [15], Savage laid down a foundational framework for decision-making under uncertainty. His system is based on acts, which are rendered as functions mapping states into outcomes, and on preferences on such acts, which need to obey certain rationality axioms.

Savage's general setup, as well as his axioms, have been since subjected to wide scrutiny and criticisms. Much controversy has been raised in particular on the so-called *Sure-Thing Principle* (STP), that allows an agent to reach a preference by decomposing it in preferences over two mutually exclusive and jointly exhaustive subcases. In Savage's words, the principle is motivated as follows:

> A businessman contemplates buying a certain piece of property. He considers the outcome of the next presidential election relevant. So, to clarify the matter to himself, he asks whether he would buy if he knew that the Democratic candidate were going to win, and decides that he would. Similarly, he considers whether he would buy if he knew that the Republican candidate were going to win, and again finds that he would. Seeing that he would buy in either event, he decides that he should buy, even though he does not know which event obtains, or will obtain, as we would ordinarily say [15].

The purpose of this work is to provide a logical perspective, both on Savage's well-known framework [15] for the foundation of decision theory, and on its criticisms, arising from the famous scenarios presented by Ellsberg [10] and

Allais [1]. Both of these scenarios provided patterns of preferences deemed plausible, and yet conflicting with Savage's axioms, in particular with the Sure-Thing Principle.

The key observation behind this work is the similarity of STP with what in classical logic is known as the *Principle of Bivalence* (PB). To clarify the meaning of PB, we first present it as a rule in natural-deduction style, as follows [9]:

$$\frac{\overset{[\varphi]}{\vdots} \quad \overset{[\neg\varphi]}{\vdots}}{\psi} \text{(PB)}$$

meaning that, to infer the formula ψ, it suffices to infer it both under the assumption that φ is the case and under the assumption that $\neg\varphi$ is the case. The square brackets around the formulas φ and $\neg\varphi$ signal that those are pieces of information assumed for the sake of deriving ψ, but not actually held true (they are *discharged*, in natural deduction terminology). Following [4], we call this type of information *hypothetical*, in contrast to the *actual* information held by an agent. Let us note that the inference rule (PB) is also called a "logical" sure-thing principle in [2], where analogies and differences with STP are analyzed. In particular, [2] stresses that "STP is a desideratum of rational behavior, but not logically necessary", as is the case instead for PB.

In the light of the development of various non-classical logics, considering PB as logically necessary, without further qualification, is not enough. In particular, choosing suitable pieces of hypothetical information for its application in logical deductions, is a complex matter. This may play an important role in decision-making, as we illustrate in the following.

Example 1. You have an urn with balls that are numbered 1–100, and are colored in unknown proportions. Three balls with numbers x_1, x_2, x_3 are extracted from the urn. You are told that $x_2 = x_1 + 1$ and $x_3 = x_2 + 1$. Ball number x_1 is red and ball number x_3 is blue. You have to choose among the following:

– h: You earn 100 euro, if $x_2 = x_1 + 1$ and $x_3 = x_2 + 1$, 0 otherwise.
– h': You earn 110 euro if it holds that, among the extracted balls
  (δ): "a red ball and a non-red ball have numbers that differ by 1", 0 otherwise.

The information provided is sufficient to assess that h always returns the payoff 100. It might be however less obvious that also h' will always return the highest payoff 110. It suffices to reason by cases: if x_2 is red, then, since $x_3 = x_2 + 1$ and x_3 is not red, δ holds. On the other hand, if x_2 is not red, since $x_2 = x_1 + 1$ and x_1 is red, δ still holds.

We find it plausible that agents might prefer h to h', although the payoff for h' is higher than that for h, and both are certain for the agent. In support of this conjecture, note that in empirical research [18], under similar information, over 80% of subjects claimed that it is impossible to determine whether an assertion of the same logical form as δ is true.

We might say that, in the above example, an agent preferring h to h' is behaving irrationally, or is perhaps attributing a *cost* to the very act of doing inferences, a cost which is not immediately captured neither by classical logic, nor by Savage's standard decision-theoretic framework.

PB is indeed costly for realistic agents, and bounding its use makes logical inference tractable, in the sense of computational complexity [17], in contrast to the intractability (under the usual $P \neq NP$ assumption) of classical propositional logic.

This observation is at the core of a family of logical systems, dubbed Depth-Bounded Boolean logics [8] (DBBLs), which allow only for a limited application of PB, and provide tractable approximations of classical logic.

Building on previous work on uncertainty measures in DBBLs [3,4], we introduce in the following a sequence of preferences approximating Savage's framework, which are based on the limited use of PB and hypothetical information.

This setting allows us to provide a unified account of Savage's axioms, and of the preferences in Allais, in Ellsberg, and in Example 1 above. All such preferences will be considered indeed compatible with (our reformulation of) Savage's axioms, and in particular with the Sure-thing principle, but only at the lowest level of our sequence, where no use of hypothetical information is permitted. Furthermore, following Savage, we show that the sequence of approximating preferences determines a finitely additive measure, in the limit.

The paper is further structured as follows. In Sect. 2 we present our analysis of actual and hypothetical information, based on DBBLs. Section 3 introduces our sequence of approximating preference relations, provides a reformulation of some of Savage's basic axioms in that setting, and analyzes our main examples. Section 4 provides the conditions under which the sequence of approximating preferences determines a finitely additive measure in the limit. Finally, we provide some conclusions and hints at future work.

2   Hypothetical and Actual Information

Before proceeding, we briefly fix some notation. We consider a propositional logical language $\mathcal{L}$, with the usual classical connectives $\wedge, \vee, \rightarrow, \neg$ and set of propositional variables $\{p_1, \ldots, p_n, \ldots\}$. The set of formulas will be denoted by Fm, and lowercase Greek letters will be used to refer to formulas. We denote by $S(\varphi)$ the set of subformulas of φ.

We now recall some crucial ideas of the DBBLs, mentioned in the introduction. These logics permit to distinguish between actual and hypothetical information in logical deduction, and determine a hierarchy, with a parameter k measuring the amount of allowed nested use of hypothetical information.

The 0-depth logic, which will be our main focus here, is a logic that does not allow any application of PB, and is thus concerned only with the manipulation of *actual* information. This logic is proof-theoretically defined in terms of the INTroduction and ELIMination (INTELIM) rules in Table 1. The rules are defined for each connective, both when occurring positively (as the main connective of a formula) and negatively (in the scope of a negation).

Table 1. Introduction and Elimination rules.

$$\frac{\varphi \quad \psi}{\varphi \wedge \psi} \ (\wedge\mathcal{I}) \qquad\qquad \frac{\neg\varphi}{\neg(\varphi \wedge \psi)} \ (\neg\wedge\mathcal{I}1)$$

$$\frac{\neg\psi}{\neg(\varphi \wedge \psi)} \ (\neg\wedge\mathcal{I}2) \qquad \frac{\neg\varphi \quad \neg\psi}{\neg(\varphi \vee \psi)} \ (\neg\vee\mathcal{I})$$

$$\frac{\varphi}{\varphi \vee \psi} \ (\vee\mathcal{I}1) \qquad\qquad \frac{\psi}{\varphi \vee \psi} \ (\vee\mathcal{I}2)$$

$$\frac{\varphi \quad \neg\varphi}{\bot} \ (\bot\mathcal{I}) \qquad\qquad \frac{\varphi}{\neg\neg\varphi} \ (\neg\neg\mathcal{I})$$

$$\frac{\varphi \vee \psi \quad \neg\varphi}{\psi} \ (\vee\mathcal{E}1) \qquad \frac{\varphi \vee \psi \quad \neg\psi}{\varphi} \ (\vee\mathcal{E}2)$$

$$\frac{\neg(\varphi \vee \psi)}{\neg\varphi} \ (\neg\vee\mathcal{E}1) \qquad \frac{\neg(\varphi \vee \psi)}{\neg\psi} \ (\neg\vee\mathcal{E}2)$$

$$\frac{\varphi \wedge \psi}{\varphi} \ (\wedge\mathcal{E}1) \qquad\qquad \frac{\varphi \wedge \psi}{\psi} \ (\wedge\mathcal{E}2)$$

$$\frac{\neg(\varphi \wedge \psi) \quad \varphi}{\neg\psi} \ (\neg\wedge\mathcal{E}1) \qquad \frac{\neg(\varphi \wedge \psi) \quad \psi}{\neg\varphi} \ (\neg\wedge\mathcal{E}2)$$

$$\frac{\neg\neg\varphi}{\varphi} \ (\neg\neg\mathcal{E}) \qquad\qquad \frac{\bot}{\varphi} \ (\bot\mathcal{E})$$

We note in passing that the logic has also a non-deterministic semantics, with evaluations capturing the *information* actually held by an agent rather than *truth*, as a primitive notion [7].

The rules encode the principles for the manipulation of information actually possessed by an agent, for each of the connectives of the language. We refer to [7,8] for further details and motivation. The 0-depth consequence relation is defined as follows.

Definition 1. *Let* $T \cup \{\varphi\} \subseteq Fm$. *$T \vdash_0 \varphi$ if there is a sequence of formulas* $\varphi_1, \ldots, \varphi_m$ *such that* $\varphi_m = \varphi$ *and each* φ_i *is either in T or it is obtained by an application of the rules in Table 1 from formulas φ_j with $j < i$.*

Note that, by direct inspection of the rules in Table 1, we have $\nvdash_0 p \vee \neg p$. In fact, this logic, which is strictly weaker than classical logic, has no tautologies at all. The relation $\vdash_0$ captures inferences that are "trivial" in their reliance solely on actual information. This is also reflected computationally, by the fact that, in contrast to classical propositional logic, $\vdash_0$ can be checked in polynomial time [8].

While 0-depth logic permits only to represent actual information, and lack thereof, classical logical proofs also involve reasoning about hypothetical information. Consider again $\nvdash_0 p \vee \neg p$. It can be easily shown that, on the other hand, $p \vdash_0 p \vee \neg p$ and $\neg p \vdash_0 p \vee \neg p$. Hence, we can show that $p \vee \neg p$ is derivable just by one application of PB, using the hypothetical information p and $\neg p$. In DBBLs this amounts to saying that $\vdash_1 p \vee \neg p$. The consequence $\vdash_k$ for $k > 0$ is formally defined as follows, see also [8].

Definition 2. *Let $k > 0$. Then $T \vdash_k \varphi$ if there is a $\psi \in S(T \cup \{\varphi\})$ such that $T, \psi \vdash_{k-1} \varphi$ and $T, \neg\psi \vdash_{k-1} \varphi$.*

The parameter k is thus a "counter" which keeps track of how many nested instances of reasoning by cases are needed for the agent to decide a sentence of interest.

In this work we use only 0-depth logics, to deal with actual information, alongside with a sequence of (depth-bounded) forests, to represent the further hypothetical information which may be used by an agent.

Let us recall the notion of depth-bounded forests, in a slightly modified form from [4]. We start with a set $Supp \subseteq Fm \cup \{*\}$, which represents the information explicitly provided to the agent. The symbol $*$ is meant to the represent the absence of any information. $Supp$ collects background information, which may be of the form "γ holds", or "the probability of γ_i is p_i" where p_i may be the frequency or objective chance of γ_i. If no such information is available to the agent, we let $Supp = \{*\}$. We further impose that for any $\alpha, \beta \in Supp$, such that $\alpha \neq *, \beta \neq *$ we have[1] $\alpha, \beta \vdash_0 \bot$.

Depth-bounded forests are built, starting from $Supp$ and suitably expanding the nodes with two new children nodes, representing an instance of PB obtained by considering a certain piece of hypothetical information and its negation, respectively.

In the following, for any formula $\gamma \in Fm$, we say that γ *decides* δ if $\gamma \vdash_0 \delta$ or $\gamma \vdash_0 \neg\delta$. By the *depth of a node* in a forest, in the usual graph-theoretic sense, we mean the length of the path from the root of a tree in the forest to the node. We then say that a leaf α is *closed* if α 0-decides each formula $\delta \in S(\alpha)$. A leaf which is not closed is said to be *open*.

Definition 3. *Let $Supp \subseteq Fm \cup \{*\}$. We define recursively, a sequence $(F_k)_{k \in \mathbb{N}}$ of depth-bounded forests based on $Supp$ (DBF, for short), as follows:*

1. *For $k = 0$ we let F_0 be a forest with no edges, and with the set of vertices equal to $Supp$[2].*
2. *The forest F_k, for $k \geq 1$ is obtained expanding at least one leaf α of depth k as follows:*
   - *if α is open, with two nodes $\alpha \wedge \beta$ and $\alpha \wedge \neg\beta$ where β is an undecided subsentence of α.*

---

[1] This assumption is actually dispensable [4], but simplifies the formulation of our main definitions and results.

[2] Clearly, $Supp$ is the set of leaves of F_0.

- *Otherwise, if α is closed, with two nodes $\alpha \wedge \beta$ and $\alpha \wedge \neg\beta$, where $\beta \in Fm$ is a sentence whose variables do not already occur in $Supp \cup \{\alpha\}$, if there are any.*

Let us notice that, when $\mathcal{F}$ is defined over a language Fm with finitely many propositional variables, the DBF may be expanded only up to a certain F_k. In what follows, given a DBF $(F_k)_{k \in \mathbb{N}}$ we will denote by $Supp_k$ the set of leaves of the forest F_k. This represent the information which is available to an agent capable of making k nested use of reasoning by cases. This information will be available to the agent for probabilistic quantification and evaluation in considering which actions to take.

3   Approximating Preferences

Our framework for preference comprises, as Savage's original one, a set of states St, a set of outcomes O, and a set of acts A. The idea is that each act $f \in A$ is a function $f \colon St \to O$.

However, we depart from Savage in various respects, in that we focus on the logical language used to represent states, rather than the more usual set-theoretic presentation.

First, we think of the set of states St as evaluations of the formulas of our logical language, of the form $v \colon Fm \to \{0, 1\}$.

Given any $f \in A$ and $S \subseteq St$ we denote by f_S the restriction of f to S. Note that a function f_S is to be interpreted as the function f when the outcomes outside S are disregarded, but it does not amount to conditioning on S, i.e. to consider the action upon the assumption that S is true, as is done e.g. in [13]. This means that, in determining, say whether f_S is preferred to g_T, both the outcomes and how likely are taken to be S, T matter.

We are now ready to reformulate some of the Savage's axioms in our setting. We focus first on those that deal with preference exclusively, without concern for their role in justifying a probabilistic representation of an agent's belief. Recall that $A \subseteq O^{St}$ and let $\succeq$ by a binary relation over A, standing for a preference between acts. Then, we require, as in Savage P1 [15]:

A1 $\succeq$ is a total *pre-order*, i.e. reflexive and transitive, over A

We then formulate a weak form of the sure-thing principle, which is closer to Savage's informal presentation [15] than to his own axiom P2.

A2 *(Sure-thing)*. The following rules are satisfied:

$$\frac{f_S \succeq g_S \quad f_T \succeq g_T}{f_{S \cup T} \succeq g_{S \cup T}} \qquad \frac{f_S \succ g_S \quad f_T \succeq g_T}{f_{S \cup T} \succ g_{S \cup T}}$$

for any $S, T \subseteq Fm$ with $S \cap T = \emptyset$.

The third axiom is an adaptation of Savage's state independence P3. Before presenting it, let us recall that a set S is said to be *non-null* if there are at least two acts $f_S, f'_S \in A$ with $f_S \succ f'_S$.

A3 *(State independence).* Let $S \subseteq St$ be non-null. Then $\succeq$ satisfies the following
   rule:

$$\frac{f(S) = f'(St) = \{x\} \quad g(S) = g'(St) = \{y\} \quad f' \succeq g'}{fs \succeq gs}$$

Definition 4 (Consistent Preference Structure). *Let $A \subseteq O^{St}$ and $\succeq$ be a binary relation over A. We say that $(A, \succeq)$ is a consistent preference structure iff it satisfies axioms A1-A3 above.*

So far, we have only reformulated Savage's axioms, in a framework which is more congenial to our logical construction. Our key contribution is however, formalizing acts, as seen from the point of view of an agent with bounded inferential resources. Towards this purpose, we assume that the agent does not have direct access to the state space St of A, but only to some information, in a syntactic format, that she has to elaborate upon.

The actual, explicit information, provided to the agent, is here encoded by a set $Supp \subseteq Fm$. On the other hand, the information that she has to (via a reasoning effort) hypothesize about will be rendered by the set of leaves $Supp_k$ of a suitable DBF, say $\mathcal{F} = (F_k)_{k \in \mathbb{N}}$ which is built starting from $Supp$.

Now we can express what it means for an agent to access the acts via some pieces of (actual and/or hypothetical information). First, let us define

$$.b_k(\varphi) = \{\alpha \in Supp_k \mid \alpha \vdash_0 \varphi\}$$

and

$$pl_k(\varphi) = \{\alpha \in Supp_k \mid \alpha \nvdash_0 \neg\varphi\}$$

in analogy with the notion of belief and plausibility function in the theory of Dempster-Shafer belief functions [16]. The set $b_k(\varphi)$ collects all the pieces of information that have been explored by the agent up to depth k, that allow her to immediately (i.e. via $\vdash_0$, without using PB) infer φ. On the other hand, $pl_k(\varphi)$ collects the pieces of information at depth k that do not immediately exclude φ.

For any $f \in A$, $f \colon St \to O$ we will denote by $f^k \colon Supp_k \to \mathcal{P}(O)$ the function associating to each piece of information $\alpha \in Supp_k$ the following subset of O:

$$f^k(\alpha) := f(\{v \in St \mid v(\varphi) = 1, \text{ for each } \varphi \text{ such that } \alpha \in pl_k(\varphi)\} \subseteq O$$

Note that a formula α is here mapped into the *set* of outcomes which are not excluded by α. This is because α, which represent a piece of information the agent *can* actually consider, need not to correspond to a state St (i.e. a logical evaluation assigning a truth value to each formula), and might not provide enough information to determine which particular outcome obtains.

Furthermore, for any $S \subseteq Supp_k$, we denote by f_S^k the restriction of f^k to S. Note that S is here taken to be a subset of *formulas* in $Supp_k$, rather than a subset of the states, i.e. of evaluations.

Definition 5 (Consistent k-Preference Structure). *Let $A \subseteq O^{St}$. We say that $(A_k, \succeq_k)$ is a consistent k-preference structure iff*

- A_k *contains* f_S^k *for each* $S \subseteq Supp_k$, $f \in A$
- $(A_k, \succeq_k)$ *is a consistent preference structure, i.e. it satisfies A1–A3 above.*

We are now ready to define our notion of approximating sequence.

Definition 6. *Let* $\mathcal{F} = (F_k)_{k \in \mathbb{N}}$ *be a DBF sequence, and* $A \subseteq O^{St}$. *We say that* $\mathcal{P} = (A_k, \succeq_k)_{k \in \mathbb{N}}$ *is an* approximating preference sequence *(APS, for short) iff:*

- *For each* $k \in \mathbb{N}$, $(A_k, \succeq_k)$ *is a consistent preference structure.*
- *For every* $k \in \mathbb{N}$, *and every* $\varphi, \psi \in Fm$, $f, g \in Supp$, *we have that* $f^k \succeq_k g^k$ *implies* $f^{k'} \succeq_{k'} g^{k'}$ *for every* $k' \geq k$.

The second condition says that, as k increases, the agent can refine, but cannot revise previously determined preferences. Let us test now our notion of APS with the well-known examples of Ellsberg and Allais. To ease notation, in the following we will often slightly abuse the notation, writing directly $f \succeq_k g$ instead of $f^k \succeq_k g^k$.

Example 2 (Ellsberg). Suppose that an agent is presented an urn filled with balls, and is provided the information that 2/3 of the balls are either yellow or blue $(Y \vee B)$, and the remaining 1/3 are red (R). A ball will be extracted from the urn and an agent is confronted with a choice between acts f, g, h, j. The following table summarizes the setup in the standard Savage framework, where states are represented in the columns, the available acts in the rows, and the cells contain the monetary outcome, say in euros.

Table 2. Ellsberg's one urn scenario.

	R	Y	B
f	100	0	0
g	0	100	0
h	100	0	100
j	0	100	100

Ellsberg [10] points out that the strict preferences $f \succ g$ and $j \succ h$ are plausible: agents will typically prefer, ceteris paribus, a bet whose states they can quantify probabilistically (R and $Y \vee B$ for the acts f and j) over one where this is not the case (Y and B for the acts g and j). In other words, they will display a form of *ambiguity aversion* [12].

On the other hand, these preferences are in violation of Savage STP. Indeed, if we ignore what happens in case a blue ball (B) is picked (i.e. we ignore the third column in Table 2), and we assume that the preference for a payoff of 100 euros is independent of the state in which it occurs, the agent should be indifferent between acts f and h, and g and j. Furthermore, both, f and g, and h and j give the same payoff for B, i.e. 0 and 100, respectively. According to the STP then, a preference for f over h dictates a preference for g over j, in contrast to Ellsberg's preferences.

Let us now formalize the example in our setting. We take a finite language over the variables $\{Y, B, R\}$ which stand for the event that a yellow, blue, red ball is picked, respectively. We denote by γ the sentence expressing the fact that Y, B, R are mutually exclusive and jointly exhaustive. We build a DBF and an APS as follows. We let $Supp = \{(Y \vee B) \wedge \gamma, R \wedge \gamma\}$, since those are the formulas upon which the agent is provided probabilistic information, and $A = \{f, g, h, j\}$. It is easy to show that for any such formula $\alpha \in Supp$ we have $pl_0(\alpha) = \{\alpha\}$. The acts f, g, h, j are again defined as in Table 2. Assume that $f \succ_0 g$ and $j \succ_0 h$. We may consider a decomposition of such preferences only via the formulas in $Supp$. We have (omitting the formula γ, for simplicity): $g_{Y \vee B} \succ_0 f_{Y \vee B}$, $f_R \succ_0 g_R$, $j_{Y \vee B} \succ_0 h_{Y \vee B}$, and $h_R \succ_0 j_R$. These preferences, together with $f \succ_0 g$ and $j \succ_0 h$, do not contradict axiom A2, i.e. our reformulated version of the Sure-thing principle. Note that, since $Y \vee R$ and B are not formulas of $Supp_k$, the functions say $f_{Y \vee R}, h_{Y \vee R}, g_{Y \vee R}, j_{Y \vee R}$ and f_B, h_B, g_B, j_B are not defined.

Now, let us consider the expansion of $Supp$ to a 1-depth forest F_1, and the corresponding 1-depth preference structure over $Supp_1$. Notice that the node $R \wedge \gamma$ in $Supp$ is already closed, and thus need not be expanded. We expand instead the open node $(Y \vee B) \wedge \gamma$ as follows (we omit γ for simplicity):

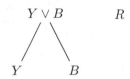

Consider the preference structure $(A_1, \succeq_1)$. With a little abuse of notation, since $((Y \vee B) \wedge \gamma \wedge Y) \vdash_0 Y$, $((Y \vee B) \wedge \gamma \wedge \neg Y) \vdash_0 B$ and $R \wedge \gamma \vdash_0 R$, we just write the formula on the right Y, B, R instead of the corresponding formula on the left, which belongs to $Supp_1$.

Note that, at depth 1, the preferences $f \succ_1 g$ and $j \succ_1 h$ are not allowed by Definition 5. By state independence, we have indeed that $f_{\{Y\}} \approx_1 h_{\{Y\}}$, $f_{\{R\}} \approx_1 h_{\{R\}}$ and $g_{\{Y\}} \approx_1 j_{\{Y\}}$, $g_{\{R\}} \approx_1 j_{\{R\}}$. On the other hand, we have $f_{\{B\}} \approx_1 g_{\{B\}}$, and $h_{\{B\}} \approx_1 j_{\{B\}}$, while $j_{\{B\}} \succ f_{\{B\}}$.

Now, let us further assume that $f_{\{Y\} \cup \{R\}} \succ_1 g_{\{Y\} \cup \{R\}}$. By the previous equivalences, we may use A2 to get $h_{\{Y\} \cup \{R\}} \succ j_{\{Y\} \cup \{R\}}$. By the latter, since we also have $h_{\{B\}} \approx_1 j_{\{B\}}$ we may use A2 to obtain $h \succ_1 j$, which is contrary to the initial assumption $j \succ_1 h$.

Let us now assume $g_{\{Y\} \cup \{R\}} \succeq_1 f_{\{Y\} \cup \{R\}}$. Since $f_B \approx_1 g_B$, by state independence, we obtain by A2, $g = g_{\{Y\} \cup \{R\} \cup \{B\}} \succeq_1 f_{\{Y\} \cup \{R\} \cup \{B\}} = f$, again contradicting the initial assumption that $f \succ_1 g$. In both cases we derived a contradiction with one of the assumptions $f \succ_1 g$ and $j \succ_1 h$.

Example 3 (Allais). Assume you have an urn containing balls numbered from 1 to 100, and a ball will be extracted from the urn. You are offered a choice between the following acts, which are represented in the following table.

Table 3. Allais.

	1	2–10	11–100
f	100	100	100
g	0	500	100
f'	100	100	0
g'	0	500	0

Allais deems the strict preferences $f \succ g$ and $g' \succ f'$ plausible, although they conflict with the sure-thing principle. Indeed, the pairs of acts f and g, and f' and g' have the same outcome, in case balls 11-100 are extracted, namely 100 for the first pair, and 0, for the second. By the sure-thing principle, since the acts f and f', and g and g' have the same outcomes for each extracted ball, f can be preferred to g, if and only f' is preferred to g'.

We formalize this scenario in our setting, building a DBF and an APS. It suffices to consider a finite language over three variables, namely $\{p_1, p_{2-10}, p_{11-100}\}$, standing for the numbers on the extracted ball. We let $Supp = \{\gamma\}$ where γ encodes the fact that $p_1, p_{2-10}, p_{11-100}$ are mutually exclusive and jointly exhaustive. We further let $A = \{f, g, f', g'\}$, where the acts are defined as in Table 3. At depth 0, we may only compare $f_\gamma, g_\gamma, g'_\gamma, f'_\gamma$, since $Supp = \{c\}$. Hence, we may have $f \succeq_0 g$ and $g' \succeq_0 f'$, since no application of A2 can be performed. At depth 1, we replace $Supp$ with $Supp_1 = \{\gamma \wedge \neg p_{11-100}, \gamma \wedge p_{11-100}\}$. We omit γ in the following for simplicity. We have $f_{\neg p_{11-100}} \approx_1 f'_{\neg p_{11-100}}$, $g_{\{\neg p_{11-100}\}} \approx_1 g'_{\{\neg p_{11-100}\}}$, and on the other hand $f_{p_{11-100}} \approx_1 g_{p_{11-100}}$ and $f'_{p_{11-100}} \approx_1 g'_{p_{11-100}}$. By A2 we immediately get that $f_{Supp_1} \succeq_1 g_{Supp_1}$ iff $f'_{Supp_1} \succeq_1 g'_{Supp_1}$, contrary to the Allais' preferences.

Finally, we address Example 1 in our formal setting.

Example 1 (continued). We denote:[3] by p_{in} the assertion "$x_i = n$"; by q_{ij}, the assertion "$x_i = x_j + 1$" and finally by r_i the assertion "the ith extracted ball is red". The initial information provided to the agent is $Supp = \{\gamma\}$, where by γ we denote the formula $r_1 \wedge \neg r_3 \wedge q_{12} \wedge q_{23} \wedge \bigvee_{k=1}^{100} p_{1k}$. The formula δ in Example 1 is encoded instead as:

$$\bigvee_{\substack{i,j \in \{1,2,3\} \\ i \neq j}} r_i \wedge \neg r_j \wedge q_{ij}.$$

We take $A = \{h, h'\}$, where h, h' are defined as in Example 1, with $h(\gamma) = \{100\}$ and $h(\neg \gamma) = \{0\}$, and $h'(\delta) = \{110\}$, $h'(\neg \delta) = \{0\}$. Now, in A_0 we may compare h^0 and h'^0, which both have $Supp = \{\gamma\}$ as their domain. We have then $h^0(\gamma) = \{100\}$ and $h'^0(\gamma) = h'(\{\delta, \neg \delta\}) = \{110, 0\}$ since $\gamma \nvdash_0 \delta$. Hence we may still allow

---

[3] We use a propositional language, to fit the simple general framework put forward in this work, although we might have a more compact representation in a first-order language.

$h \succ_0 h'$. On the other hand, if we consider the 1-depth forest (actually, tree) expanding $Supp = \{\gamma\}$ as follows:

we now have that both $h'^1(\gamma \wedge r_2) = \{110\}$ and $h'^1(\gamma \wedge \neg r_2) = \{110\}$, since $\gamma \wedge r_2 \vdash_0 \delta$ and $\gamma \wedge \neg r_2 \vdash_0 \delta$. Hence h'^1 is constantly equal to 110. On the other hand h^1 is still constantly equal to 100, and assuming that 110 is preferred to 100, we may only have $h' \succeq_1 h$, by state independence.

4   Qualitative Probability and Representation

So far, we have build up the general framework and illustrated how it takes into account various alleged counterexamples, and criticisms of Savage's approach. In particular, our setting shows that a form of idealization is at play in Savage's setting, in essentially disregarding the cost of reasoning by case.

This does not preclude to obtain as a limit, idealized case, Savage's elegant mathematical result, in our framework. Let us recall that one of the main advantages of Savage's framework is its representation theorem for expected utility, which is obtained on the basis of his axioms on preferences among acts. While we are still not able to recover the full representation of expected utility in the limit, in our setting, we will focus here on an important intermediate step towards this result, which has an independent foundational interest.

Let us recall that, on the way to his representation theorem, Savage first manages to obtain a measure of probability, only on the basis of preferences among acts. This is done in two steps: first he derives, from the preference of an agent, an ordering reflecting how likely the agent finds the events of interest, i.e. a *qualitative probability*. Subsequently, he extracts from this relational structure a unique numerical probability representing it.

Let us now recall the notion of qualitative probability over arbitrary boolean algebras, and that of representability, and adapt them to our setting.

Definition 7 (Qualitative probability). *Let $\mathcal{B} = (B, \sqsubseteq, \wedge, \vee, \neg, \bot, \top)$ be a boolean algebra. $(\mathcal{B}, \unrhd)$ is a* qualitative probability *if*

1. *$\unrhd$ is a total preorder over $\mathcal{B}$;*
2. *$\top \rhd \bot$;*
3. *if $\alpha \sqsupseteq \beta$ then $\alpha \unrhd \beta$ and*
4. *if $\alpha \wedge \gamma = \bot$ and $\beta \wedge \gamma = \bot$, then $\alpha \unrhd \beta$ if and only if $\alpha \vee \gamma \unrhd \beta \vee \gamma$.*

Since our sequences are built syntactically, we will use here a different, syntactic definition of qualitative probability.

Definition 8 (synctactic qualitative probability). *Let Fm be the set of formulas over the language $\mathcal{L}$. $(Fm, \unrhd)$ is a (syntactic) qualitative probability if*

1. *$\unrhd$ is a total preorder over Fm;*
2. *$\top \rhd \bot$;*
3. *if $\beta \vdash \alpha$ then $\alpha \unrhd \beta$ and*
4. *if $\alpha \wedge \gamma \vdash \bot$ and $\beta \wedge \gamma \vdash \bot$ then*

$$\alpha \unrhd \beta \text{ if and only if } \alpha \vee \gamma \unrhd \beta \vee \gamma.$$

The two notions are essentially equivalent. Indeed, if we are given a (syntactic) qualitative probability $(Fm, \unrhd)$, we may just define a qualitative probability by quotienting over the logically equivalent formulas, i.e. building the Lindenbaum-Tarski algebra and suitably adapting the $\unrhd$ relation to the equivalence classes. Let us now recall the following, see e.g. [15].

Definition 9 ((Almost) Representability). *A qualitative probability $(\mathcal{B}, \unrhd)$ is said to be*

– representable *if there exists a unique[4] finitely additive probability P such that $\alpha \unrhd \beta$ iff $P(\alpha) \geq P(\beta)$*
– almost representable, *if there exists a unique finitely additive probability P such that $\alpha \unrhd \beta$ implies $P(\alpha) \geq P(\beta)$.*

Savage considers in his system a specific axiom P4 for the purpose of extracting a qualitative probability from preference, and a further axiom P6 for the purpose of representability. In our framework, we obtain qualitative probabilities and representability via a slightly different route, inspired by the reformulation of P4 in [6].

First, we will define a sequence of *comparative beliefs*, determined by an APS.

Definition 10. *Let $\mathcal{F} = (F_k)_{k \in \mathbb{N}}$ be a DBF and $(A_k, \succeq_k)_{k \in \mathbb{N}}$ be an APS. We call comparative plausibility $\unrhd_k$ determined by $\succeq_k$, the relation $\unrhd_k$ defined, for any $\varphi, \psi \in Fm$ by:*

– *$\varphi \unrhd_k \psi$ if $f_\varphi^k \succeq_k g_\psi^k$, for each $f^k, g^k \in Supp_k$ such that $f^k(\varphi) = g^k(\psi) = \{x\}$ for some $x \in O$.*
– *$\varphi \unrhd_k \psi$ if $pl_k(\varphi) \supseteq pl_k(\psi)$.*
– *$\top \rhd_k \bot$*

The idea is that, when we consider acts that have the same outcome, over different pieces of information, the preferences of an agent for one act over the other, only reflects how likely she finds the piece of information to occur. More concretely, if an agent prefers a bet giving her 5 euros if tomorrow it rains, to a bet giving her 5 euros if tomorrow it will be sunny, this can only mean (if she is rational) that she finds rainy weather more likely than sunny weather.

---

[4] Uniqueness is typically nor requested in the definition of representability and almost representability in the literature.

Note that the definition ensures that $\unrhd_k$ is not empty, hence in particular it encodes Savage's axiom (P5).

We now give conditions on an APS, to obtain from the sequences of $\unrhd_k$, a qualitative probability *in the limit*. Before that, we recall, adapting from [4] what we mean by limit.

Definition 11 (Limit structures). *Take a DBF and let $\mathcal{F} = (Supp_k, \unrhd_k)_{k \in \mathbb{N}}$ be a sequence of relational structures, where each $\unrhd_k$ is a binary relation over Fm. We say that the structure $(Fm, \unrhd)$ is the limit of $\mathcal{F}$, where*

$$\varphi \unrhd \psi \text{ iff there is a } k \text{ such that } \varphi \unrhd_n \psi, \text{ for every } n \geq k.$$

Definition 12. *We say that an APS $\mathcal{P} = (A_k, \succeq_k)_{k \in \mathbb{N}}$ over a DBF $\mathcal{F} = \{F_k\}_{k \in \mathbb{N}}$ is:*

- Belief-determining *iff:*
  - *For any $\varphi, \psi \in Fm$ there exists a $k \in \mathbb{N}$ such that either $\varphi \unrhd_k \psi$ or $\psi \unrhd_k \varphi$.*
- Refinable *if whenever $\alpha \unrhd_k \beta$ for some $\alpha, \beta \in Supp_k$ and $k \in \mathbb{N}$, there is a $k' \geq k$ such that*

$$\beta \rhd_{k'} \gamma \text{ for every } \gamma \in Supp_{k'} \text{ that is a descendent of } \alpha.$$

- Coverable *if whenever $\alpha \rhd_k \beta$ for some $\alpha, \beta \in Supp_k$ and $k \in \mathbb{N}$, there is a $k' \geq k$ and $\gamma \in Supp_{k'}$ such that $\gamma \wedge \alpha \vdash \perp$ and*

$$\alpha \vee \gamma \bowtie_{k'} \beta$$

The condition of being belief-determining is our reformulation of axiom P4 in Savage, which is here considered as an axiom of a whole APS, rather than of each Consistent k-Preference Structure, as we did instead for A1–A3. By this condition, indeed, $\unrhd_k$ determines a total order in the limit.

We are now ready to provide our main result.

Theorem 1. *Let $\mathcal{P}$ be an APS over a DBF $\mathcal{F}$ with $Supp = \{*\}$. If $\mathcal{P}$ is belief-determining, then the limit $(Fm, \unrhd)$ of $(F_k, \unrhd_k)_{k \in \mathbb{N}}$ is a qualitative probability.*

Proof. Let us start by showing that, if $\psi \vdash \varphi$, then $\varphi \unrhd \psi$. From $\psi \vdash \varphi$, we get $\neg\varphi \vdash \neg\psi$. We thus have a derivation of $\neg\psi$ from $\neg\varphi$, by using the rules of $\vdash_0$ and applications of PB. Let $k \in \mathbb{N}$ be such that for any $n \geq k$, the set $Supp_n$ collects all the premises of the applications of PB in the proof of $\neg\psi$ from $\neg\varphi$. Hence, for each $\alpha \in Supp_n$, if $\alpha \vdash_0 \neg\varphi$, then $\alpha \vdash_0 \neg\psi$, that is, if $\alpha \nvdash_0 \neg\psi$, then $\alpha \nvdash_0 \neg\varphi$. Hence $pl_n(\varphi) \supseteq_n pl_n(\psi)$, for $n \geq k$. This entails, by Definition 10, $\varphi \unrhd_n \psi$, for each $n \geq k$, hence $\varphi \unrhd \psi$.

We now show that the relation is total. Take $\varphi, \psi \in Fm$. Now, since $\mathcal{P}$ is belief determining, there is a k such that $\varphi \unrhd_k \psi$ or $\psi \unrhd_k \varphi$. Assume the first is the case. Since $\mathcal{P}$ is an APS, we will also have that, for any $n \geq k$, $\varphi \unrhd_n \psi$, hence in particular $\varphi \unrhd \psi$.

Transitivity and reflexivity are immediate, since they follow by A1 for $\succeq_k$, and the fact that $\mathcal{P}$ is an APS.

As for additivity, suppose that $\varphi \wedge \chi \vdash \bot$ and $\psi \wedge \chi \vdash \bot$. We will show that $\varphi \unrhd \psi$ iff $\varphi \vee \gamma \unrhd \psi \vee \gamma$. Let k be such that each $\alpha \in Supp_k$ is closed. We have that $\varphi \vee \chi \succeq_k \psi \vee \chi$ iff $\varphi \unrhd_k \psi$ (adapting the proof of Lemma 11(5) in [4]). By the definition of $\unrhd_k$, this means that for each f, g such that $f^k(\varphi \vee \xi) = g^k(\varphi \vee \psi) = \{x\}$ we have $f_{\varphi \vee \xi} \succeq_k g_{\psi \vee \xi}$. On the other hand, by the reflexivity of $\succeq_k$ (A1), we have $f_\xi \succeq_k f_\xi$ and $g_\xi \succeq_k g_\xi$. Hence, by A2 $f_{\{\varphi\} \cup \{\xi\}} \succeq_k f_{\{\psi\} \cup \{\xi\}}$ iff $f_\varphi \succeq_k g_\psi$. But the latter amounts at saying that $\varphi \unrhd_k \psi$, and the same will hold for any $n \geq k$. Hence we have finally obtained $\varphi \unrhd \psi$ iff $\varphi \vee \xi \unrhd \psi \vee \xi$.

Finally, adapting from [4], we have that, under the refinability and coverability conditions described above, an APS determines a (almost) representable qualitative probability.

Corollary 1. *Let $\mathcal{P}$ be a belief-determining APS.*

- *If $\mathcal{P}$ is refinable, then its limit is almost representable, in the case $\mathcal{A}_\mathcal{L}$ is infinite.*
- *If $\mathcal{P}$ is coverable then its limit is representable, in the case $\mathcal{A}_\mathcal{L}$ is finite.*

Proof. Follows from Theorem 1, and Theorem 20 and 22 in [4].

5   Conclusion

We have introduced a logic-based framework for preference, which approximates Savage's framework, on the basis of the bounded use of hypothetical information. Our approach accommodates in a unified way various traditional challenges to Savage, in particular concerning the Sure-thing principle. Despite their differences, in all the examples considered, we have found indeed a similar pattern: some preferences may be accepted at the bottom level of our sequence, i.e. $\succeq_0$, but they turn out to be inconsistent with Savage-style axioms, when considering $\succeq_k$ for $k > 0$, i.e. when suitable hypothetical information is taken into account. Since DBBLs are computationally tractable, a further natural direction of research for our work is in the computational complexity issues related with the reasoning with the resulting measures of comparative probability. In particular, we aim to compare our setting with other approaches to decision theory, which are logically (in particular, syntactically) and computationally inspired, such as that pursued in [5].

Future work will provide suitable representation theorems for preferences in our framework, in terms of generalized expected utility, both at each level of the approximating sequence, and in the limit. This will be compared with the literature on decision-making under uncertainty, based on weakenings of axioms in the Anscombe-Aumann framework [11]. We further plan to consider logical systems where the preference relation $\succeq_k$ is taken to be part of the language, and investigate their properties, with the aim of obtaining tractable logics of preference.

References

1. Allais, M.: Le comportemement de l'homme rationnel devant le risque: critique des postulats et axiomes de l'ecole americaine. Econometrica **21**(4), 503–546 (1953)
2. Aumann, R.J., Hart, S., Perry, M.: Conditioning and the sure-thing principle, pp. 1–10 (2005)
3. Baldi, P., Hosni, H.: Tractable approximations of probability. J. Logic Comput. **33**, 599–622 (2022)
4. Baldi, P., Hosni, H.: Logical approximations of qualitative probability. In: ISIPTA. Proceedings of Machine Learning Research, vol. 147, pp. 12–21. PMLR (2021)
5. Bjorndahl, A., Halpern, J.Y.: Language-based decisions. Electron. Proc. Theor. Comput. Sci. **335**, 55–67 (2021)
6. Bradley, R.: Decision Theory with a Human Face. Cambridge University Press, Cambridge (2017)
7. D'Agostino, M.: An informational view of classical logic. Theor. Comput. Sci. **606**, 79–97 (2015)
8. D'Agostino, M., Finger, M., Gabbay, D.: Semantics and proof-theory of depth bounded Boolean logics. Theor. Comput. Sci. **480**, 43–68 (2013)
9. D'Agostino, M., Floridi, L.: The enduring scandal of deduction: is propositional logic really uninformative? Synthese **167**, 271–315 (2009)
10. Ellsberg, D.: Risk, ambiguity, and the savage axioms. Quart. J. Econ. **75**(4), 643–669 (1961)
11. Gilboa, I.: Theory of Decision Under Uncertainty. Cambridge University Press, Cambridge (2009)
12. Gilboa, I., Marinacci, M.: Ambiguity and the Bayesian paradigm. In: Arló-Costa, H., Hendricks, V.F., van Benthem, J. (eds.) Readings in Formal Epistemology. SGTP, vol. 1, pp. 385–439. Springer, Cham (2016). https://doi.org/10.1007/978-3-319-20451-2_21
13. Kranz, D., Luce, R.D., Suppes, P., Tversky, A.: Foundations of Measurement, vol. 1. Academic Press, New York (1971)
14. Pearl, J.: The sure-thing principle. J. Causal Inference **4**(1), 81–86 (2016)
15. Savage, L.J.: The Foundations of Statistics, 2nd edn. Dover (1972)
16. Shafer, G.: A Mathematical Theory of Evidence. Princeton University Press, Princeton (1976)
17. Sipser, M.: Introduction to the Theory of Computation. PWS Publishing Company (1997)
18. Stanovich, K.: What Intelligence Tests Miss: The Psychology of Rational Thought. Yale University Press (2009)

A Comparative Analysis of Multi-agent Simulation Platforms for Energy and Mobility Management

Aliyu Tanko Ali[1]([⊠]) [iD], Martin Leucker[1] [iD], Andreas Schuldei[1] [iD],
Leonard Stellbrink[2] [iD], and Martin Sachenbacher[1] [iD]

[1] Institute for Software Engineering and Programming Languages,
University of Lübeck, Ratzeburger Allee 160, Lübeck, Germany
{aliyu.ali,leucker,andreas.schuldei,sachenbacher}@isp.uni-luebeck.de
[2] Institute for Multimedia and Interactive Systems, University of Lübeck,
Ratzeburger Allee 160, Lübeck, Germany
leonard.stellbrink@uni-luebeck.de

Abstract. Effective energy and mobility management benefits from multi-agent simulations (MAS) to model complex interactions among various agent types. Selecting the optimal MAS platform to implement and simulate these interactions is vital for achieving accurate results, scalability to realistic problem sizes, and efficient computational performance. This paper investigates the energy and mobility domain and identifies key parameters such as the number and complexity of agents, parallel computing power, CPU requirements etc., for developing MAS in the context of this domain. It then presents a comprehensive evaluation of various MAS development platforms. Using a multi-level selection and elimination approach, we narrowed down our evaluation to two final candidates. We then implemented key aspects of our model in both platforms to compare them in terms of practical relevance. Our findings reveal that the Agents.jl platform outperforms the Mesa platform in terms of runtime performance, has a smaller memory footprint for large numbers of agents, and offers scalability, making it the most suitable choice for developing MAS for integrated energy and mobility models.

Keywords: Multi-agent simulation · Agent-based models · Mobility transition · Car-sharing

1 Introduction

The shift from internal combustion engine vehicles to battery-powered electric vehicles (EVs) is driving a mobility transition aimed at promoting public transport, car-sharing, and sustainability [13,14]. Car-sharing users play a crucial role in this transition, as they need to adapt their behavior to new circumstances like

This project was funded by the state of Schleswig-Holstein, Germany.

limited range and necessary charging stops, while also the limitations of the electric power grid must be considered. Electric car-sharing providers should learn when to charge cars to maximize renewable energy use and ensure car's availability. This situation creates a need for AI-supported forecasting, peak shaving, and recommendation to dynamically adapt car-sharing behavior [27].

Our ongoing project, "Multi-Agent Simulation of Intelligent Resource Regulation in Integrated Energy and Mobility" (MASIRI)[1], aims to create a multi-agent simulation using intelligent agent modeling based on the psychological behavior of electric car-sharing users. Particularly, we investigate the influence of human experience and behavior on mobility and energy use in vehicle-to-grid (V2G) systems, and how this knowledge can optimize system design.

Multi-agent simulation is a computational technique that simulates the behavior and interactions of multiple agents within an ecosystem [4]. These simulations are built on the principles of agent-based models (ABM) [6], which focuses on representing individual agents and their behaviors to study the emergent properties of a system. The simulation environment provides a platform for agents to interact, communicate, and potentially collaborate or compete with each other. Agents can exchange information, share resources, coordinate their actions, and influence the behavior of other agents.

Various platforms have emerged that aid in the development of MAS in research and industrial contexts [23,25]. However, selecting a MAS development platform suitable for a given scenario is a difficult task, as there is no universally agreed-upon set of criteria for ranking and evaluating these platforms. Researchers rely on using semi-structured techniques, including questionnaires, to compare platforms [3,9,29]. Some studies compare different platforms [10,18,22] and evaluate specific requirements like strengths, performance, and code complexity [7,25]. However, many of these studies are outdated, some platforms are not maintained, and they do not cover our use case area. Several works in the literature, including [8,11,21,31], and [24], have employed agent-based models to explore different scenarios within the realm of electromobility. However, the majority of these studies primarily focus on analyzing EV users and their charging behavior, as well as the role of EVs as a new form of urban mobility. The development of a comprehensive MAS of electromobility in the context of car-sharing and V2G has received comparatively less attention. In this study, we carefully curated a collection of platforms from multiple sources, including diverse projects, comparative studies, and online searches. The primary objective of this extensive curation process was to identify the platform that best aligns with the specific requirements of our project.

The contributions of this paper are as follows: First, it delineates the requirements of MAS for the energy and mobility domain, with a specific focus on a particular use case. Next, it then presents an updated and comprehensive overview of various MAS platforms. Employing a multi-level selection and elimination approach, we narrow down the options from multiple platforms to two final candidates. Subsequently, we implement key aspects of our model in both platforms

---

[1] https://www.imis.uni-luebeck.de/en/forschung/projekte/masiri.

to enable a practical and relevant comparison. Based on the evaluation and comparison, we identify and select the most suitable MAS platform for our specific research purposes.

The remainder of the paper is organized as follows: Sect. 2 introduces MAS for integrated energy and mobility and identifies the resulting requirements for MAS development. Section 3 studies various MAS development platforms, Sect. 4 explains the results from implementing our use case scenario and their evaluation, and finally, Sect. 5 presents the conclusion.

2 MAS for Integrated Energy and Mobility

In our project MASIRI, the model aims to simulate the current and future energy usage and the mobility behavior of the inhabitants of Lübeck, a city in the state of Schleswig-Holstein, Germany, with a population of approximately 220,000 and a car ownership rate of 464 per 1,000 inhabitants. We take into account the growing popularity of private and electric car-sharing, as well as the mobility needs of the residents within their living spaces [12].

Developing MAS in this domain requires various agent types and groups to reflect the different actors involved, including electric cars, their users, and a micro-grid energy system. In our setting, we consider electric cars and charging stations with bi-directional capabilities, meaning that the cars, when not driving, can also serve as energy buffers and feed back energy into the grid (V2G). The car users encompass individuals from diverse age groups, with a variety of car models and sizes to cater to their needs. The micro-grid energy system harnesses renewable energy from different sources, such as wind and solar power, with the latter generated by photovoltaic (PV) panels installed on residential rooftops.

Our model and simulation will be developed by domain experts rather than versatile programmers. As a result, we seek to find a MAS development platform that provides a modeling language based on or similar to popular programming languages like Python or Java. Additionally, we will incorporate historical records of the grid, weather conditions, and car-sharing bookings into the model. This means that the platform should also support the import of data from external sources, such as CSV files. Other requirements regarding MAS development platforms will be identified in Sect. 3.

2.1 Model Description

To scale our model, we utilized the latest available data from the city's statistics department [12]. Based on this data, we identified a total of 150,000 car users, all of whom we assumed to be car-sharing users. In addition, we considered the number of cars in the city, which was recorded as 103,000. For the purpose of our simulation, we assumed that all of these cars were electric, used for car-sharing. Furthermore, we took into account the 50,000 residential buildings in Lübeck and assumed that they are either partially or fully equipped with PV panels, heating systems, and air conditioning units. These buildings, along with the cars and their users, will collectively represent the agents in our simulation. To capture the dynamics and patterns over time, we will simulate a complete year of data records. By incorporating these real-world numbers and characteristics, our simulation aims to accurately represent the scale and size of the agents and their interactions within the modeled system.

Dynamical generation and optimization are necessary for several components of the agents' modules. These include a booking reservation logic (booking algorithm) for users to reserve cars and bi-directional charging of electric car batteries. Optimizing the booking algorithm is crucial to avoid high car unavailability to satisfy users' needs or to serve as an energy buffer. We have already developed a booking reservation algorithm using the Python programming language, and by leveraging linear programming techniques [30], we have successfully optimized both the booking algorithm and the bi-directional charging system. In addition to this, we also plan to use reinforcement learning to train agents on adaptive booking strategies without harming the energy grid.

2.2   Platform Evaluation Scenario

In order to assess the MAS development platforms, we develop a minimum viable product (MVP) that simulates a use case closely resembling our intended final product. For this purpose, we establish the following requirement in the use case:

1. **Users:** Agents who book electric cars for random short-distance trips, following a normal distribution throughout the day.
2. **Cars:** These are electric cars utilized for a car-sharing service, which have a certain driving range depending on their state of charge (SoC). They recharge upon return from a trip and are capable of buffering excess energy when connected to the grid.
3. **Houses:** Residential units with optional features like solar power roofs, heat pumps, air conditioning systems. Private cars contribute to the energy consumption of the houses when they are being recharged.
4. **Random Weather:** The use case involves random sunshine and temperature data at a 5-min resolution, incorporating yearly and daily cycles, seasonal variations, and daytime fluctuations. These patterns include noise to capture realistic yearly and daily variations. By incorporating this data, we have abstracted the energy model (micro-grid) aspect that will be included in the final product. However, it is important to note that in our final product, we intend to conduct a comprehensive study of a micro-grid connection within the given settings.

Figure 1 provides an overview of the simulation use case. The simulation does not consider the positions of houses and users, types of cars, users' age groups, and other details that will be included in our final model. We also do not consider modeling charging stations as we would have in the final model.

Use Case Agent Actions and Interactions: User agents book cars at random times, with more daytime activity and a normal distribution peaking at 14:00

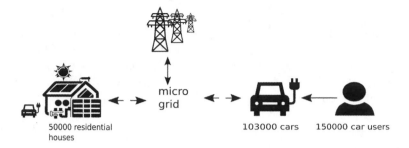

Fig. 1. Use case overview. Arrows indicate temporary or permanent connectivity or availability.

and a 3-h standard deviation. The cars are recharged after each trip, with trip duration determining the required charging. Power consumption and generation data are collected in 5-min intervals, using realistic charging times and battery sizes. Charging times contribute to overall power consumption data.

The house agents generate and consume electricity based on generated weather data. House agents have randomized features, such as air conditioning, solar power, and heat pumps with varying capacities. Larger houses have greater solar power capacity. Power consumption and generation data are collected for each 5-min slot, with car charging times included in the overall data. Electric car batteries buffer excess solar energy, feeding it back to the house when needed, if the car is idle.

In this paper, our primary objective is to evaluate different platforms and identify the most suitable one for our project. Consequently, the simulation use case described herein only considers certain details (of the intended final product) to assess the platforms.

2.3 Expected Features from MAS Platform

As our project is expected to span over multiple years, it is essential for us to have an active and well-maintained platform that can effectively support our evolving needs. The complexity of the project will undoubtedly grow over time, requiring a simulation platform that can keep up with these changes. In this paper and the MASIRI project at large, we identify some general as well as domain-specific features that are crucial. The general features include:

G1 Language familiarity: This is important because of the expertise of the developers. The platform must be one that does not require much time to learn its syntax and ABM implementation.

G2 Scalability: Currently, our plan is to simulate the inhabitants of Lübeck. However, it is possible that the population size may change, leading to a larger population, or that the model might be adapted or modified to analyze another city. Therefore, it is crucial to have a platform that can accommodate scalability when necessary.

G3 Parallelism & distributed computing: Based on our preliminary investigation, we have found that most platforms offer some level of parallel computing features. However, it is important to note that the emphasis on ease of use rather than performance is evident in some platforms [28]. Given that our model comprises various types of agents and is of large size, efficient simulation running time becomes a crucial factor, and therefore, performance is a significant consideration.

G4 Community support: A platform with an active and strong community fosters knowledge sharing and facilitates the exchange of experiences. This community support will be invaluable during the development phase, particularly when it comes to debugging and troubleshooting. The collective expertise and insights of community members can provide valuable guidance and solutions, enabling us to address challenges more efficiently.

G5 Interoperability: The platform should facilitates interface with external libraries, tools, and data sources for domain-specific functionality and streamlined data processing. This feature will enable us to incorporate our already developed booking algorithm, optimization tools, and the historical record.

G6 Visualization & analysis tools: The inclusion of built-in tools dedicated to visualizing and analyzing simulation outputs plays a crucial role in facilitating a deeper understanding of the simulation results and enabling comprehensive performance evaluation. These integrated tools will provide us with intuitive and interactive interfaces to explore, interpret, and visualize complex simulation data in a meaningful way.

G7 Documentation: A wealth of comprehensive resources, including platform documentation, YouTube videos, tutorials, and working examples, will greatly assist us in gaining a thorough understanding of how to effectively utilize the platform. These resources will serve as invaluable tools during the initial stages, providing step-by-step guidance, practical demonstrations, and real-world examples that will aid in our learning process and enable us to make the most of the platform's capabilities.

For our agent-based learning, mobility, and energy use case, the following additional features are crucial:

D1 Learning capabilities: For an ideal platform, it is imperative to encompass support for a diverse range of learning algorithms that enable the training of agents to adapt strategies and optimize energy usage.

D2 OpenStreetMap space: The ability to incorporate geo-spatial data, including the positions of users and cars in relation to each other, house locations, road networks, points of interest, and more, is crucial for accurately simulating real-world mobility and energy systems. It should provide a rich and detailed spatial dataset that enhances the realism and accuracy of our model.

D3 Data integration: The integration of external data plays a pivotal role in the effectiveness and significance of an ABM platform. By seamlessly incorporating real-time or historical data sources, the platform becomes capable of facilitating realistic and dynamic simulations that closely mirror the complexities of real-world situations.

3   Multi-level Selection

To compile a comprehensive list of platforms, we conducted thorough searches across multiple sources, including diverse projects, comparative studies, and online resources. In particular, notable survey articles such as [15] and review articles like [16,23,26], and [1] provided valuable insights and compilations of platforms in the field. Leveraging these sources, we identified platforms based on their specific areas of application, existing projects utilizing the platforms, and studies that conducted comparisons among different platforms. Given the diverse modeling approaches offered by these platforms, we categorized them into the following groups:

– **Language or Environment for MAS (LEM):** Refers to programming languages, frameworks, and software environments that are used to create, simulate, and deploy ABMs.
– **Support Software (SS):** Refers to a software tool, package, or platform that provides specific functionalities and capabilities to facilitate the development, deployment, and management of ABMs.
– **MAS-based Modeling Platform (MMP):** Refers to a software application or platform that specifically focuses on modeling and simulating ABMs. These platforms provide an environment where developers can design and simulate agents, their behaviors, interactions, and the dynamic environment in which they operate.

We then gathered information (summarized in Table 1) on each platform's modeling language, licence, and activity status[2]. The latter was checked through various means, including visiting the platform's website (in search of recent updates, news, and announcements), engaging with the community (such as discussion groups), and examining the GitHub or source code repository.

3.1   First Round of Selection

After careful evaluation, we eliminated platforms for which we could not find essential information, such as licensing details or recent activities. Some platforms, including FAME, SWARM, JACK, Junus, GOAL, Cougaar, and StarLogo (TNG and Nova versions), have not been regularly updated or maintained. This lack of maintenance raises concerns about their reliability, potential bugs, and compatibility with modern operating systems. To mitigate the risk of selecting an inactive platform (or platform that might become inactive) for our project, we decided to also exclude platforms with no activity for more than 2 years. Consequently, FLAME, 2APL, ZEUS, and ActressMAS were also removed from consideration.

---

[2] This information was checked on May 25th, 2023.

Table 1. A table showing different MAS development platforms. The platforms are listed in alphabetical order and not ranked. GPL stands for General Public Licence, AFL for Academic Free License, EPL for Eclipse Public License, and COSL for Cougaar Open Source License.

Name	Modeling language	Licence	Category	Last activity
ActressMAS	C#	Open source	LEM	2021.06.15
Agents.jl	Julia	MIT	MMP	2023.05.19
AgentScript	JavaScript	Various	LEM	2023.01.23
Cougaar	Java	COSL	LEM	2013.10.22
FAME	Jave	Apache v2.0	SS	2021.01.20
FLAME	C/C++	Open source	LEM	2017.05.30
GAMA	GAML	GNU GPL v3	LEM	2021.10.15
GOAL	GOAL	unknown	LEM	2021.11.08
JACK	Java	Commercial license	LEM	2015.07.01
JADE	Java	Open source (Java)	LEM	2022.12.19
Jadex	Java	GNU GPL v2.0	LEM	2022.10.08
Janus	SARL	Apache v2.0	LEM	unknown
Jason	AgentSpeak	GNU GPL v3	LEM	2023.04.02
Mason	Java	AFL	LEM	2022.09.07
MATSim	XML	GNU GPL	MMP	2023.04.01
Mesa	Python 3+	Apache v2.0	MMP	2023.03.08
NetLogo	NetLogo	GNU GPL v2.0	MMP	2023.05.11
Repast4Py	Python	Various	MMP	2023.03.02
SPADE	Python	Open source	SS	2023.12.13
SpaDES	R	GNU GPL v3	SS	2022.02.16
SUMO	Python, Java, C++	EPL v2.0	SS	2023.06.29
StarLogo	Objective C	Various	LEM	2018.11.24
SWARM	Java C	GNU GPL	LEM	2013.08.01
ZEUS	Java	Unknown	LEM	2021.06.20
2APL	2APL	GNU GPL v3.0	LEM	2021.12.01

Platforms such as AgentScript, SPADE, Jason, Jadex, and JADE are actively maintained and continue to receive updates. Unfortunately, we were unable to find information regarding the compatibility of these platforms with the general requirements G4 and G7. SpaDES is based on the R language, while Jason is based on AgentSpeak. Moreover, we found limited documentation and community support forums for these platforms. Consequently, their capacity to fulfill requirements G1, G4, and G7 is further hindered.

We examined different implementations of Repast, specifically focusing on Repast Simphony, a Java-based modeling toolkit, and Repast4Py, a Python-based distributed agent-based modeling toolkit. Since our booking algorithm was already developed in Python, we found the Repast4Py version more appealing. We further evaluated it alongside another Python-based platform, Mesa. Through our analysis, we discovered that Repast offers certain advantages over Mesa in terms of documentation and flexibility in programming languages [5]. However, Mesa provides advantages in terms of simplicity, user-friendliness, and seamless integration with Python libraries and frameworks [20]. The simulation software SUMO [17] was also evaluated as part of our study. It offers a user-friendly graphical user interface (GUI) called "sumo-gui," which simplifies the process of adding road layouts, intersections, vehicles, and users through drag and drop functionality. Additionally, SUMO provides an interface Python library called "TraCI," allowing users to develop Python scripts that can connect to a running SUMO simulation, retrieve information, and control various aspects of the simulation. We encountered challenges when attempting to incorporate the energy model component of our model in a seamless and straightforward manner.

Although some of the remaining platforms are not based on Java or Python, they have extensive documentation and a wealth of working examples available, making them popular within the ABM modeling community. Moving forward, we will provide a brief overview of these platforms.

Mason [19] is a fast, discrete-event, multi-agent simulation library core in Java. It serves as a robust foundation for developing large-scale, custom-purpose simulations in Java, while also catering to the requirements of lightweight simulation applications. It has a comprehensive model library accompanied by an optional suite of visualization tools, catering to both 2D and 3D simulations.

Mesa [20] is a versatile and open-source Python library specifically designed for agent-based modeling (ABM). It offers users a streamlined approach to developing agent-based models by providing built-in core components like spatial grids and agent schedulers. Additionally, Mesa allows for flexible customization through the implementation of personalized components.

NetLogo [28] is an integrated development environment and programming language designed for modeling and simulating complex systems. It features a custom scripting language, NetLogo, and built-in visualization tools. Users can export data to external visualization tools for advanced analysis.

GAMA [2] is an open-source simulation platform and modeling language offering various features for agent creation, communication, and decision-making. GAMA provides visualization and analysis tools and a custom language, GAML, for composing complex models with spatial dimensions. The platform supports running simulations on multiple machines for increased performance.

MATSim [32] is an open-source framework for simulating large-scale transportation systems, modeling individual travelers and vehicles within a network. It is Java-based and features tools for different transport modes, routing algorithms, and activity-based travel demand modeling. MATSim also offers visualization and analysis tools for exploring simulation dynamics and is ideal for predicting policy impacts on transportation systems.

Agents.jl [7] is a Julia library for agent-based modeling within the JuliaDynamics ecosystem. Julia is a high-performance language suitable for computational and numerical science applications. Agents.jl manages and creates spaces, simplifies data collection, and offers visualization options, including OpenStreetMaps and 3D visualizations, through related JuliaDynamics libraries. Julia also enables developers to call methods, functions, or scripts from other languages such as Python or R.

A summary of the pros and cons of the platforms following the initial round of selection is presented in Table 2. This summary highlights the notable advantages and drawbacks of each platform, providing valuable insights to inform the subsequent stages of the selection process.

3.2   Second Round of Selection

In order to evaluate the remaining platforms based on the specified requirements outlined in Subsect. 2.3, and taking into account the pros and cons summarized in Table 2, we employ a rating scale. This rating scale assigns values of $high = 3$, $medium = 2$, and $low = 1$ to each platform, indicating the level of satisfaction for each requirement.

For each platform, we assess its performance against each requirement and assign a corresponding rating. A rating of "*high*" is assigned when a platform fully satisfies a requirement, "*medium*" when it partially satisfies the requirement, and "*low*" when it does not meet the requirement. By applying this rating scale, we calculate a score for each platform, considering the cumulative ratings for all the evaluated requirements as follows:

$$score = 3 \times (highs) + 2 \times (mediums) + 1 \times (lows). \tag{1}$$

The platform with the highest cumulative score signifies that it fulfills the majority of the requirements. The scores for each platform are calculated based on the assigned ratings, and Table 5 showcases the platforms alongside their corresponding scores.

In the end, we observed that Mason (scored 18) and GAMA (scored 18), have relatively smaller user communities compared to other platforms, resulting in limited availability of tutorials and documentation. We encountered challenges in finding comprehensive resources such as kickstart examples, troubleshooting guides, and interactive forums for engaging with developers and users of these platforms. MATSim (scored 19) and NetLogo (scored 18), although they have larger user communities and tutorials, lack community support at a similar level as Mason and GAMA. Additionally, we found limited examples or resources showcasing the implementation of non-transport simulations using MATSim. NetLogo, being a Logo-based language, requires developers to familiarize themselves with its specific syntax. Furthermore, information on integrating external modules or expanding the platform's functionality was scarce during our evaluation process.

Table 2. Pros and Cons.

Platform	Pros	Cons
Mason	Highly customizable and flexible for creating multi-agent simulations. Supports both discrete and continuous modeling	Steep learning curve. Lacks a user-friendly interface. Limited visualization options
Mesa	Easy to use and well-documented. Supports both discrete and continuous modeling. Has a built-in visualization tool	Limited support for advanced features like parallel computing and large-scale simulations
NetLogo	User-friendly and intuitive interface. Supports both discrete and continuous modeling. Has a large library of pre-built models. Good visualization options	Limited support for large-scale simulations. Limited customization options
GAMA	Highly customizable and flexible. Supports both discrete and continuous modeling. Good visualization options	Steep learning curve. Limited community support
MATSim	Strong support for agent-based transportation modeling. Supports large-scale simulations. Good visualization options	Limited support for other types of multi-agent simulations. Steep learning curve
Agents.jl	Highly customizable and flexible. Supports both discrete and continuous modeling. Good support for scientific computing	Recurring issue of packages being redefined constantly. Steep learning curve. Various visualization options

Mesa (scored 23), benefiting from Python's intuitiveness, community support, and familiarity, was more appealing, especially since we already have a module (booking algorithm) that was developed in Python. In addition to this, we found it to be more easy to learn compared to RepastPy. Similarly, Agents.jl (scored 26) is based on Julia, a language that has some similarities in syntax with Python, and the ability to call Python's methods and scripts through packages such as PyCall.jl. Agents.jl is appealing as well due to multiple reasons. Among these reasons is the fact that it benefits from Julia's active user base and the availability of Julia-specific libraries and resources that are interoperable with Python, agents' learning capabilities, speed, scalability [7] etc. Agents.jl and Mesa have the highest and second highest score. As such, we pre-selected Agents.jl and Mesa as the final two platforms for further evaluation.

4 Mesa vs. Agents.jl

We created a minimum viable product (MVP) reflecting our final product to compare the performance and ease of use of Mesa and Agents.jl. This MVP is based on the scenario in Subsect. 2.2. The code is publicly available[3]. During

---

[3] https://github.com/stockh0lm/masiri_mas_framework_benchmark.

development, we sought help from Python and Julia communities for technical details and bug hunting, using chat platforms and web forums. While we found no dedicated Mesa community, there was an Agents.jl discussion channel in the Julia Slack server[4]. Both communities were approachable, helpful, and competent, with fast response times. Although the Julia community was smaller, it did not negatively impact the support received.

It is worth noting that Mesa is single-threaded; therefore, there is no direct way to utilize multi-threaded runs. The only option for achieving concurrent or parallel computing in Mesa is to run multiple computations in parallel and use the intermediate results. This implies that the implementation discussed in this paper utilizes a single thread for Mesa.

4.1   Implementation - Model Speed and Scalability Evaluation

We implemented identical simulations in Mesa and Agents.jl. Mesa, by default, operates in a single-threaded manner. However, in order to enhance its performance and enable parallel agent processing, we incorporated multi-threading functionality in Julia, utilizing varying numbers of concurrent threads. Anticipating more complex final agents, we added a recursive Fibonacci computation for both frameworks to increase computational load. We ran both simulations with agent numbers as powers of two (1, 2, 4, ..., 2048), at which point the Mesa runs took several days, and clear trends were established. We examined Agents.jl's vertical scalability using 1, 2, 4, and 8 threads for different agent numbers. We did not attempt using the Distributed.jl library for Julia, as it would have exceeded our time scope and been challenging to test at the time. The results of this implementation is shown in Tables 3 and 4.

In order to evaluate the RAM consumption and runtime performance (excluding the compile-time of Agents.jl), we incorporated code to measure these metrics and enabled dynamic configuration of the number of agents. The benchmarks were conducted on a Debian GNU-Linux Server with specifications including 12 cores, 32GB RAM, Julia 1.8.5, Agents.jl 5.12, Python 3.11.1, and Mesa 1.2.1. To minimize system-related variability, we recorded the median runtime of four simulation runs, ensuring that the agent numbers varied identically for each run.

Table 3. Comparison of RAM usage in the benchmark for Mesa and Agents.jl. The runs for 10^6 and 10^7 agents were never completed and only started to measure the trend in memory usage.

	Mesa	Agents.jl
1 agent	155.84 MB	555.39 MB
1000000 agents	0.7 GB	0.7 GB
10000000 agents	5.3 GB	3.3 GB

---

[4] https://julialang.slack.com/archives/CBLNLEU74.

Table 4. Single threaded speed comparison of Mesa and Agents.jl.

	Mesa	Agents.jl
1 agent	91 s	0,5 s
32 agents	48 min	2,5 s
2048 agents	52 h	155 s

4.2   Benchmark Results

Mesa required about 160 MB for agent counts up to 2048, while Agents.jl used
between 524 MB and 608 MB in this range, see Fig. 2. Mesa's RAM footprint was
about four times smaller and more consistent than Agents.jl's. In both cases, the
majority of the memory footprint appeared to be caused more by binaries and
libraries than the model and agent data. This manifested only at higher agent
counts of one million, as seen in Table 3. Run time for the models increased with
the number of agents: Mesa ran between 50 s (1 agent) and 52 h (2048 agents).
In Agents.jl the same computations took between 0.2 s and 5 min, as displayed
in Table 4. Mesa is about a thousand times slower than Agents.jl when running
the simulations.

The multi-threading results (also depicted in Fig. 3) showed that run-time
decreased as thread count increased, particularly for higher agent numbers,
where eight threads were roughly twice as fast as one thread. However, the
scalability was not consistently linear, indicating factors such as resource con-
tention, parallelization overhead, or implementation limitations. For low agent
numbers, higher thread counts led to increased run-time, suggesting that the
optimal thread count is dependent on the simulation's complexity and agent
count. Overall, Agents.jl demonstrates promising vertical scalability, but further
optimization is necessary for efficient resource utilization. Based on our evaluation and experience during the simulation of our use case, we have concluded
that Agents.jl is the most suitable platform for implementing our model. One

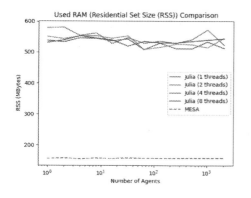

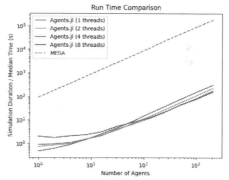

Fig. 2. Used RAM Comparison.   **Fig. 3.** Median Run Time Comparison.

Table 5. Scoring MAS development platforms.

Tools	Language Familiarity	Scalability	Parallelism & distributed computing	Community support	Interoperability	Visualization & analysis tools	Documentation	Learning capabilities	OpenStreet-Map space	Data integration	Score
Mesa	high	medium	low	medium	high	high	high	medium	low	high	23
Agents.jl	low	High	High	High	High	High	High	medium	high	medium	26
Mason	high	high	medium	low	medium	medium	low	low	low	medium	18
MATSim	high	high	medium	low	medium	medium	medium	low	low	medium	19
NetLogo	low	medium	medium	medium	medium	high	medium	medium	low	low	18
GAMA	low	high	medium	low	medium	medium	low	medium	low	high	18

of the key factors that led us to this conclusion is the impressive runtime speed
we observed while using Agents.jl. It has demonstrated superior performance in
handling the computational demands of our simulation, making it the preferred
choice among the evaluated platforms.

5 Conclusion

In this paper, we conducted a study on various MAS development platforms
with the aim of selecting the most suitable candidate for modeling a Multi-
Agent Simulation of Intelligent Resource Regulation in the context of Integrated
Energy and Mobility. We considered both general (G1-G7) and domain-specific
(D1-D3) features during our evaluation process. Through this study, we identified
two final candidates, namely Mesa in Python and Agents.jl in Julia. To assess
their suitability for our project, we developed a MVP in these two platforms
and evaluated their performance, speed, scalability, and memory footprint. Our
evaluation criteria also encompassed determining whether the platforms fulfill
our requirements for both general and domain-specific features.

While Mesa had a smaller memory footprint and a larger community,
Agents.jl offered significantly better runtime performance, which was nearly a
thousand times faster in some cases. Considering these factors, we concluded that
Agents.jl in Julia was the most suitable framework for our project. Its superior
performance, ability to scale with larger models, and integration with Python
code make it a solid choice for implementing our intelligent resource regulation
model.

References

1. Abar, S., Theodoropoulos, G.K., Lemarinier, P., O'Hare, G.M.: Agent based modelling and simulation tools: a review of the state-of-art software. Comput. Sci. Rev.
   24, 13–33 (2017)
2. Amouroux, E., Chu, T.-Q., Boucher, A., Drogoul, A.: GAMA: an environment for
   implementing and running spatially explicit multi-agent simulations. In: Ghose, A.,
   Governatori, G., Sadananda, R. (eds.) PRIMA 2007. LNCS (LNAI), vol. 5044, pp.
   359–371. Springer, Heidelberg (2009). https://doi.org/10.1007/978-3-642-01639-
   4_32
3. Bitting, E., Carter, J., Ghorbani, A.A.: Multiagent systems development kits: an
   evaluation. In: Proceedings of the 1st Annual Conference on Communication Networks & Services Research. Moncton, Canada, pp. 80–92. Citeseer (2003)
4. Bousquet, F., Le Page, C.: Multi-agent simulations and ecosystem management: a
   review. Ecol. Model. **176**(3–4), 313–332 (2004)
5. Collier, N.T., Ozik, J., Tatara, E.R.: Experiences in developing a distributed
   agent-based modeling toolkit with Python. In: 2020 IEEE/ACM 9th Workshop
   on Python for High-Performance and Scientific Computing (PyHPC), pp. 1–12.
   IEEE (2020)
6. Crooks, A.T., Heppenstall, A.J.: Introduction to agent-based modelling. In: Heppenstall, A., Crooks, A., See, L., Batty, M. (eds.) Agent-Based Models of Geograph-
   ical Systems, pp. 85–105. Springer, Dordrecht (2012). https://doi.org/10.1007/978-
   90-481-8927-4_5

7. Datseris, G., Vahdati, A.R., DuBois, T.C.: Agents.jl: a performant and feature-full agent-based modeling software of minimal code complexity. Simulation, p. 00375497211068820 (2022)
8. ElBanhawy, E.Y., Dalton, R., Thompson, E.M., Kottor, R.: Real-time electric mobility simulation in metropolitan areas. A case study: Newcastle-Gateshead, in 1, 533–546 (2012)
9. Garcia, E., Giret, A., Botti, V.: On the evaluation of MAS development tools. In: Bramer, M. (ed.) IFIP AI 2008. ITIFIP, vol. 276, pp. 35–44. Springer, Boston (2008). https://doi.org/10.1007/978-0-387-09695-7_4
10. Garcia, E., Giret, A., Botti, V.: Analysis, comparison and selection of mas software engineering processes and tools. In: Yang, J.-J., Yokoo, M., Ito, T., Jin, Z., Scerri, P. (eds.) PRIMA 2009. LNCS (LNAI), vol. 5925, pp. 361–375. Springer, Heidelberg (2009). https://doi.org/10.1007/978-3-642-11161-7_25
11. Grignard, A., et al.: The impact of new mobility modes on a city: a generic approach using ABM. In: Morales, A.J., Gershenson, C., Braha, D., Minai, A.A., Bar-Yam, Y. (eds.) ICCS 2018. SPC, pp. 272–280. Springer, Cham (2018). https://doi.org/10.1007/978-3-319-96661-8_29
12. Lübeck, H., Bürgermeister, D., et al.: Statistisches Jahrbuch 2019–2022: Lübeck in Zahlen 2019–2022. Hansestadt Lübeck, Fackenburger Allee 29, 23539 Lübeck (2022). https://bekanntmachungen.luebeck.de/dokumente/d/1720/inline
13. Hertzke, P., Müller, N., Schenk, S., Wu, T.: The global electric-vehicle market is amped up and on the rise. McKinsey Center for Future Mobility, pp. 1–8 (2018)
14. Jittrapirom, P., Caiati, V., Feneri, A.M., Ebrahimigharehbaghi, S., Alonso González, M.J., Narayan, J.: Mobility as a service: a critical review of definitions, assessments of schemes, and key challenges (2017)
15. Kravari, K., Bassiliades, N.: A survey of agent platforms. J. Artif. Soc. Soc. Simul. 18(1), 11 (2015)
16. Leon, F., Paprzycki, M., Ganzha, M.: A review of agent platforms. Multi-Paradigm Modelling for Cyber-Physical Systems (MPM4CPS), ICT COST Action IC1404, pp. 1–15 (2015)
17. Lopez, P.A., et al.: Microscopic traffic simulation using sumo. In: 2018 21st International Conference on Intelligent Transportation Systems (ITSC), pp. 2575–2582. IEEE (2018)
18. López, T.S., Brintrup, A., McFarlane, D., Dwyer, D.: Selecting a multi-agent system development tool for industrial applications: a case study of self-serving aircraft assets. In: 4th IEEE International Conference on Digital Ecosystems and Technologies, pp. 400–405. IEEE (2010)
19. Luke, S.: Multiagent simulation and the mason library. George Mason University 1 (2011)
20. Masad, D., Kazil, J.: MESA: an agent-based modeling framework. In: 14th PYTHON in Science Conference, vol. 2015, pp. 53–60. Citeseer (2015)
21. Nijenhuis, B., Doumen, S.C., Hönen, J., Hoogsteen, G.: Using mobility data and agent-based models to generate future e-mobility charging demand patterns (2022)
22. Owen, C., Love, D., Albores, P.: Selection of simulation tools for improving supply chain performance. In: Proceedings of 2008 OR Society Simulation Workshop (2008)
23. Pal, C.V., Leon, F., Paprzycki, M., Ganzha, M.: A review of platforms for the development of agent systems. arXiv preprint arXiv:2007.08961 (2020)
24. Querini, F., Benetto, E.: Agent-based modelling for assessing hybrid and electric cars deployment policies in Luxembourg and Lorraine. Transp. Res. Part A: Policy Pract. 70, 149–161 (2014)

25. Railsback, S.F., Lytinen, S.L., Jackson, S.K.: Agent-based simulation platforms: review and development recommendations. Simulation **82**(9), 609–623 (2006)
26. Rendón Sallard, T., Sànchez-Marrè, M.: A review on multi-agent platforms and environmental decision support systems simulation tools (2006)
27. Thoma, D., Sachenbacher, M., Leucker, M., Ali, A.T.: A digital twin for coupling mobility and energy optimization: the ReNuBiL living lab. In: FM2023 Workshop on Applications of Formal Methods and Digital Twins (2023, to appear)
28. Tisue, S., Wilensky, U.: NetLogo: a simple environment for modeling complexity. In: International Conference on Complex Systems, vol. 21, pp. 16–21. Citeseer (2004)
29. Tran, Q.-N.N., Low, G., Williams, M.-A.: A feature analysis framework for evaluating multi-agent system development methodologies. In: Zhong, N., Raś, Z.W., Tsumoto, S., Suzuki, E. (eds.) ISMIS 2003. LNCS (LNAI), vol. 2871, pp. 613–617. Springer, Heidelberg (2003). https://doi.org/10.1007/978-3-540-39592-8_87
30. Vanderbei, R.J., et al.: Linear Programming. Springer, Cham (2020)
31. Vuthi, P., Peters, I., Sudeikat, J.: Agent-based modeling (ABM) for urban neighborhood energy systems: literature review and proposal for an all integrative ABM approach. Energy Inform. **5**(4), 1–23 (2022)
32. Axhausen, K.W., Horni, A., Nagel, K.: The Multi-agent Transport Simulation MATSim. Ubiquity Press (2016)

Observational Preorders for Alternating Transition Systems

Romain Demangeon[1], Catalin Dima[2(✉)], and Daniele Varacca[2]

[1] LIP6, Sorbonne University Paris, Paris, France
romain.demangeon@sorbonne-universite.fr
[2] LACL, Université Paris-Est Créteil, Créteil, France
{dima,daniele.varacca}@u-pec.fr

Abstract. We define two notions of observational preorders on Alternating transition systems. The first is based on the notion of being able to enforce a property. The second is based on the idea of viewing strategies as a generalised notion of context. We show that alternating simulation as defined by Alur et al. [3] is a sound proof technique for the enforcing preorder and a complete proof technique for the "contextual" preorder. We conclude by comparing alternating simulation with the classic notion of simulation on labelled transition systems.

1 Introduction

Several process calculi have been defined to model concurrent systems, such as the Calculus of Communicating Systems (CCS) [10], or the π-calculus [11]. In these syntactic frameworks, there is a canonical way to define a preorder between terms. It consists in giving an unlabelled "reduction" semantics of the terms, some notions of basic observation, and then define the preorders *contextually*: one term P is less than a term Q if for every context C, if $C[P]$ produces some basic observation, so does $C[Q]$. This definition is often easy to give, and it's also rather convincing. The usual narrative then says that proving that two terms are in the relation is hard, due to the quantification over all contexts. Labelled semantics comes to the rescue by means of theorems that say that labelled similarity is included in (or coincide with) contextual preorder. This is the case for CCS and the π-calculus for instance.

In this paper we address the following question:

> *Can we generalise a notion of contextual preorder*
> *to a setting where there is no syntax around?*

In particular, how can we generalise the notion of context?

We will consider the model of *Alternating Transition Systems* (ATS) proposed by Alur, Henzinger and Kupferman [2]. In this setting, states can be described by boolean properties and a notion of alternation between an *Agent* and an *Opponent* is present. ATSs come with a notion of *strategy*. The Agent and the Opponent follow strategies according to some rules, and the interaction between the strategies produces a run of the system. We then can make several observations on the run, we can for instance observe the sequence of boolean properties encountered during this run.

The first preorder we define is based on the notion of *enforcing a specification* (which slightly generalizes [13,14]). The Agent can enforce a specification if it has a winning strategy for it, that is a strategy such that, whatever the Opponent does, the resulting execution satisfies the specification. After formalising a suitable general notion of specification, we propose to define a preorder as follows: an ATS P is less than an ATS Q if for every specification φ, if Agent can enforce φ on P then she can enforce it on Q.

To define a second preorder, we generalise the definition of contextual preorder to ATS using the intuition that *strategies generalise the notion of context*. With this intuition in mind, we say that an ATS P is less than an ATS Q if for every pair of strategies σ_A, σ_O (of Agent and Opponent), if the run produced by these strategies on P exhibits some properties, so does the run produced by the *same* strategies on Q. One problem with this intuition is that the notion of strategy, as defined by Alur et al., is very much bound to the system. We cannot directly apply a strategy for P to a different system Q. We overcome this difficulty by defining a way of "transfering" a strategy from a system to another.

ATS come also equipped with a notion of *alternating simulation* [3], which is used to define another preorder, called *Alternating Similarity*. The natural question to ask is: *what is the relation between these preorders?* We show that alternating similarity and the generalised contextual preorders coincide, and they are both stronger than the enforcing preorder.

In order to carry out our proofs, we propose a simplified presentation of ATS, using a formalism close to labelled transition systems. In the syntactic models, labels are useful when the system interacts with a context, but they are not necessary to the more powerful notion of strategy. We still like to rephrase the notion of ATS in a labelled setting. In this way we are able to stress the connections between the notion of alternating simulation, and Milner and Park's notion of simulation on LTS. We also argue that the labelled presentation may play some role in future extensions of our work.

Plan. The main contributions of our work are:

1. the introduction of the enforcing preorder on ATS;
2. the introduction of a contextual preorder which compares ATS by matching their strategies; using a *choice correspondence* operation;
3. the translation of the alternating simulation preorder to our labelled presentation of ATS;
4. the proof that two preorders coincide and they are stronger than the third.

Section 2 presents our new definition for Alternating Transition Systems, considering them as agent/opponent games on LTS, and defines the enforcing preorder. Section 3 introduces our version of *alternating simulation*(AS) as a way to compare ATS taking into account just how labels group together outcoming transitions. Section 4 defines a pre-order relation on ATS which compares how strategies for the two ATS can interact. A pair of mapping on states and labels, called choice correspondence, allows one to compare two systems using actions with different labels. We call this the *Morris preorder*. Section 5 shows that the largest alternating simulation and the Morris preorder coincide. We also show that they are both stronger (we conjecture strictly) than the enforcing preorder. We conclude by discussing the symmetric versions of our relations. We also define a name-aware version of the alternating simulation and compare it with Park and Milner's simulation.

2   An Alternating View of Transition Systems

Alternating Transition Systems (ATS) were introduced by Alur, Henzinger and Kupferman [2] to model open systems. In this model, the execution of a system is produced by the action of different agents. They are a very useful model, that has been used extensively in research related with synthesis and verification [1,4,8,15] (to cite only a few). However it lacks the simplicity of the notion of Labelled Transition Systems (LTS) [12] that is at the basis of the semantics of process algebras. In this section we propose to see traditional LTS as a simplified version of ATS.

2.1   Definition

Alur, Henzinger and Kupferman define ATS by having several players that can form *coalitions*. In this paper, to make things simple, we will only consider two players: the *Agent* and the *Opponent*. As in the definition by Alur, Henzinger and Kupferman, these players make choices that produce an eventual execution of the system. However the choices are made on a standard LTS. The intuition is that at each state of the system, the Agent chooses a label l (among all the labels that are allowed in that state), while the Opponent chooses one of the transitions that are labelled by l. A *Labelled Transition System* (LTS) is a tuple $\mathcal{L} = (S, s_0, L, \mathcal{T}, P, \leq, O)$ where

1. S is the set of states and L a the set of labels, with $s_0 \in S$ the initial state.
2. $\mathcal{T} \subseteq S \times L \times S$ is the transition relation.
3. P is the set of atomic observations and $(P, \leq)$ forms a discrete partial order.
4. $O : S \to P$ is the observation function.

We write $s \xrightarrow{l}$ if there exists s' such that $s \xrightarrow{l} s'$.

In Fig. 1, transitions with the same labels are grouped in *bunch* of transitions, making explicit how the game proceed. From state s_0, Agent chooses one bunch of transitions labelled by either l or k; then Opponent chooses a state reachable by a transition taken from the chosen bunch. For instance, if Agent chooses l, Opponent can choose s_2 but not s_4.

A finite or infinite *run* of an LTS is an alternating sequence of states and labels, starting in the inital state, respecting the transition relation. The set of finite runs of an LTS $\mathcal{L}$ is denoted by $runs(\mathcal{L})$. The set of infinite runs of an LTS

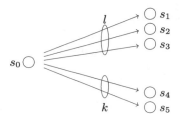

Fig. 1. Bunches of transitions in ATS.

$\mathcal{L}$ is denoted by $runs_\infty(\mathcal{L})$, the set of finite runs ending with a state $runs_\bullet(\mathcal{L})$ and the set of finite runs ending with a label $runs_\rightarrow(\mathcal{L})$. The length of a run ρ is denoted $\ell(\rho)$ (and equals ∞ for infinite runs). Furthermore, for any $k \leq \ell(\rho)$, the $(k+1)$-th item (state or action) in the run ρ is denoted $\rho[k]$, with the first item being denoted $\rho[0]$, while the prefix of length $k+1$ is denoted $\rho[\leq k]$.

The observation function can be extended homomorphycally to a map $O : runs_\infty(\mathcal{L}) \to P^\omega$ which we call the *infinite observation* of the run. Given two infinite observations $Q_1 = (p_0 \ldots p_n \ldots)$, $Q_2 = (r_0 \ldots r_n \ldots)$ where for each $i \geq 0$ we have $p_i, r_i \in P$, we say that $Q_1 \leq Q_2$ if for each $i \geq 0, p_i \leq r_i$. If $(s, l, s') \in \mathcal{T}$ we will write $s \xrightarrow{l} s'$.

As we discuss in details later, the identity of labels is not important. In the presence of the syntax of a process algebras, the identity of a label allows synchronisations of different subsystems. But in the framework we discuss here, labels are just a means of *grouping together* different transitions. We will allow relabelling as long as they produce the same groups (or *bunches*) of transitions.

As the intuition suggests, the successive moves of the Agent and the Opponent produce an infinite execution of the system, as we formalise now.

2.2   Strategies and Observations

Given an LTS $\mathcal{L} = (S, s_0, L, \mathcal{T}, P, \leq, O)$, a *strategy for the Agent* is a function $\sigma_A : runs_\bullet(\mathcal{L}) \to L$ such that if $\sigma_A(s_0 l_0 \ldots s_n) = l_n$ then $s_n \xrightarrow{l_n}$. A *strategy for the Opponent* is a function $\sigma_O : runs_\rightarrow(\mathcal{L}) \to S$ such that if $\sigma_O(s_0 l_0 \ldots s_n l_n) = s'$ then $s_n \xrightarrow{l_n} s'$. For simplicity, we can suppose that each state of an LTS has at least one outgoing transition (towards a sink state if necessary). This allows us to define strategies as total functions.

The combination of two strategies produces an infinite run. Given an LTS $\mathcal{L} = (S, s_0, L, \mathcal{T})$, a strategy for the Agent σ_A, a strategy for the Opponent σ_O, we define an infinite run $r = s_0 l_0 \ldots s_n l_n \ldots \in runs_\infty(\mathcal{L})$, denoted $\rho[\mathcal{L}, \sigma_A, \sigma_O]$, as follows:

- $l_0 = \sigma_A(s_0)$; $l_n = \sigma_A(s_0 \ldots s_n)$;
- $s_{n+1} = \sigma_O(s_0 \ldots s_n l_n)$;

For the purpose of this paper we will define a *specification* to be an *upward closed* set of infinite observations, so that if an infinite observation satisfies a given specification φ, a larger observation satisfies φ also.

Definition 1. *We say that a run r satisfies the specification φ (denoted $r \vDash \varphi$) if $O(r) \in \varphi$.*

2.3   Enforcing Preorder

We want to define a preorder between systems based on the above notion of observation. Given two LTS $\mathcal{L}, \mathcal{L}'$, when can we say that $\mathcal{L}'$ is "better" than $\mathcal{L}$? We propose the following intuition: if Agent can enforce some specification on $\mathcal{L}$, then she must be able to enforce it on $\mathcal{L}'$.

Definition 2. *We say that Agent can enforce a specification φ on $\mathcal{L}$ if*

$$\exists \sigma_A \forall \sigma_O \rho[\mathcal{L}, \sigma_A, \sigma_O] \vDash \varphi.$$

We can now formalise the notion of enforcing preorder:

Definition 3. *Let $\mathcal{L} = (S, s_0, L, \mathcal{T}, P, \leq, O)$ and $\mathcal{L}' = (S', s_0', L', \mathcal{T}', P, \leq, O')$ be two LTSs sharing the same observation order $(P, \leq)$. We say that $\mathcal{L} \leq \mathcal{L}'$ if for any specification φ, if Agent can enforce φ on $\mathcal{L}$ then Agent can enforce φ on $\mathcal{L}'$.*

3   Alternating Simulations

Alur et al. [3] introduce a notion of bisimulation for ATS, called *alternating bisimulation*. This notion has some resemblance to the notion introduced by Park and Milner [10] for LTS, but there are also major differences, not least because the model they apply to are different.

    In this section we propose to define a notion of Alternating (bi)simulation for LTS that follows the intuition explained in the previous section. At first, we will only study the notion of simulation - we will discuss the symmetric relations at the end of the paper.

    The notion of simulation by Park and Milner takes the identity of labels very seriously. There are two main reasons for this. First, we argue that this is due to the fact that LTS usually model syntactic process algebras where labels are important for synchronisation. In our setting, however, labels are only needed to group transitions together. Secondly, in the world of process algebras, labels also play the role of observations. In this paper, we use a more general notion of observation.

    Therefore our definition of simulation will allow "relabelling". This brings us to the following definition.

Definition 4. *Let $\mathcal{L} = (S, s_0, L, \mathcal{T}, P, \leq, O)$ and $\mathcal{L}' = (S', s_0', L', \mathcal{T}', P, \leq, O')$ be two LTSs sharing the same observation order $(P, \leq)$. An Alternating simulation (AS) between them is, is a binary relation $\mathcal{R} \subseteq S \times S'$ such that whenever $s \mathcal{R} s'$, then $O(s) \leq O(s')$ and:*

for all labels l s.t. $s \xrightarrow{l}$, there exists h s.t. $s' \xrightarrow{h}$ and for all t' s.t. $s' \xrightarrow{h} t'$, there exists t s.t. $s \xrightarrow{l} t$ and $t \mathcal{R} t'$.

The largest AS, $\sqsubseteq_{AS}$, is called *alternating similarity*. If there is a AS $\mathcal{R}$ s.t. $s_0 \mathcal{R} s'_0$, we say $\mathcal{L} \sqsubseteq_{AS} \mathcal{L}'$.

Remark 1. Note that, contrary to the notion in [3], we do not require $O(s) = O(s')$ in the first item above. The reason will come up later, when defining the "Morris preorder" in Definition 6.

Example 1.

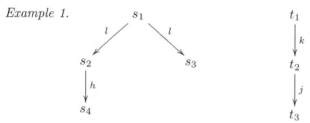

Consider the two LTL depicted above, where all the states have the same observation. (We could also imagine that states with no outgoing transitions have one transition towards a sink state with a special observation). In this case the relation $\{(s_1, t_1), (s_2, t_2), (s_4, t_3)\}$ is an AS. However, there is no AS containing (t_1, s_1). Indeed the only choice to match $t_1 \xrightarrow{k}$ is $s_1 \xrightarrow{l}$. But if now we choose $s_1 \xrightarrow{l} s_3$, we need to have (t_2, s_3), in which case there is no transition in the first system to match the action of the second system.

As one of the main results of this paper, we will show that, alternating simulation is a sound proof technique for the enforcing preorder.

Theorem 1. Let $\mathcal{L} = (S, s_0, L, \mathcal{T}, P, \leq, O)$ and $\mathcal{L}' = (S', s'_0, L', \mathcal{T}', P, \leq, O')$ be two LTSs sharing the same observation order. If $\mathcal{L} \sqsubseteq_{AS} \mathcal{L}'$ then $\mathcal{L} \leq \mathcal{L}'$.

This theorem implies Lemma 1 of [3]. Its proof is based on the simulation game, briefly suggested [3], that we formalize here for our variant of the alternating simulation.

3.1   The Simulation Game

In this section we adapt the classical two-player simulation game between Spoiler and Duplicator to the case of the alternating simulation. We then show that any memoryless winning strategy for Duplicator in this game defines an AS, and vice-versa, any AS gives a memoryless winning strategy for Duplicator.

The simulation game is built from any two LTS $\mathcal{L} = (S, s_0, L, \mathcal{T}, P, \leq, O)$ and $\mathcal{L}' = (S', s'_0, L', \mathcal{T}', P, \leq, O')$. Intuitively, from game positions labelled with pairs of states $(s, s') \in S \times S'$, Spoiler chooses a label $l \in L$ and the game advances to a position labelled (s, s', l) which belongs to Duplicator. Here, Duplicator must reply with a label $l' \in L'$ and then the game proceeds to a position labeled

(s, s', l, l') belonging again to Spoiler. In this new position, Spoiler chooses $t' \in S'$ such that $(s', l', t') \in T'$, the game advancing further to a position (s, s', l, l', t') belonging to Duplicator. Finally, Duplicator must reply in this position with a state $t \in S$ such that $(s, l, t) \in T$, after which the game advances to position (t, t'), and the above sequence of moves can be played again. All positions (s, s') with $O(s) \not\leq O(s')$ are winning for Spoiler, hence Duplicator's objective is to avoid these positions – that is, a safety objective.

Formally, the two-player turn-based simulation game is built as follows: $\mathcal{G} = (\mathcal{Q}_D, \mathcal{Q}_S, q_0, \delta)$ where $\mathcal{Q}_D = S \times S' \times L \cup S \times S' \times L \times L' \times S'$, $\mathcal{Q}_S = S \times S' \cup S \times S' \times L \times L'$, $q_0 = (s_0, s'_0) \in \mathcal{Q}_S$ $Act_D = L' \cup S$, $Act_S = L \cup S'$, and the transition function is:

$$\delta = \{(s, s') \xrightarrow{l} (s, s', l) \mid s \in S, s' \in S', l \in L, s \xrightarrow{l} \}$$

$$\cup \{(s, s', l) \xrightarrow{l'} (s, s', l, l') \mid s \in S, s' \in S', l \in L, l' \in L'\}$$

$$\cup \{(s, s', l, l') \xrightarrow{t'} (s, s', l, l', t') \mid s \in S, s' \in S', l \in L, l' \in L', t' \in S'$$
$$\text{with } (s', l', t') \in T'\}$$

$$\cup \{(s, s', l, l', t') \xrightarrow{t} (t, t') \mid s \in S, s' \in S', l \in L, l' \in L', t \in S, t' \in S'$$
$$\text{with } (s, l, t) \in T \text{ and } (s', l', t') \in T'\}$$

Finally, Duplicator's objective is defined by the set of states $Obj = \{(s, s', \alpha) \in \mathcal{Q}_D \cup \mathcal{Q}_S \mid O(s) \leq O(s')\} \subseteq \mathcal{Q}$.

A strategy for Duplicator is a mapping $\sigma_D : (\mathcal{Q}_S \cdot \mathcal{Q}_D)^* \longrightarrow Act_D$ and a strategy for Spoiler is a mapping $\sigma_S : (\mathcal{Q}_S \cdot \mathcal{Q}_D)^* \times \mathcal{Q}_S \longrightarrow Act_S$. Furthermore, a memoryless strategy for Duplicator is a mapping $\sigma : \mathcal{Q}_D \longrightarrow Act_D$. Due to the particular way in which the states, actions and transitions are constructed, we will identify a memoryless strategy with a pair $(\sigma_{L'}, \sigma_S)$ with $\sigma_{L'} : S \times S' \times L \longrightarrow L'$ and $\sigma_S : S \times S' \times L \times L' \times S' \longrightarrow S$. A run ρ is compatible with a strategy for Duplicator σ if, whenever $\rho[i] \in \mathcal{Q}_D$, then $\rho[i] \xrightarrow{\sigma(\rho[\leq i+1])} \rho[i+2]$.

Note that the AS game $\mathcal{G}$ is a *safety* game, defined by the set of runs $Runs_{Obj} = \{\rho \in runs(\mathcal{G}) \mid \forall i \in \mathbb{N}.\rho[i] \in Obj\}$.

Theorem 2. $\mathcal{L} \subset_{\mathsf{AS}} \mathcal{L}'$ *if and only if Duplicator has a memoryless winning strategy in the simulation game.*

Proof. The proof proceeds by showing that any memoryless winning strategy for Duplicator gives rise to an alternating simulation, and vice-versa. Technically, this requires restating the notion of AS by skolemizing the existential quantifiers in Definition 4. The skolemized version of AS is given by the following proposition:

Proposition 1. *A relation $\mathcal{R}$ is an AS if and only if, for any $s\mathcal{R}s'$, $O(s) \leq O(s')$ and there exist partial functions $\eta : S \times S' \times L \longrightarrow L'$ and $\theta : S \times S' \times L \times S'$ (called an AS pair) such that whenever $s\mathcal{R}s'$:*

1. For each $l \in L$ with $s \xrightarrow{l}$ we have that $\eta(s, s', l)$ is defined and $s' \xrightarrow{\eta(s,s',l)}$.

2. For each $t' \in S'$ with $s' \xrightarrow{\eta(s,s',l)} t'$, we have that $\theta(s, s', l, t')$ is defined.
3. $s \xrightarrow{l} \theta(s, s', l, t') \in T$.
4. $\theta(s, s', l, t') \mathcal{R} t'$.

With this preparation, given $\sigma = (\sigma_{L'}, \sigma_S)$ a memoryless winning strategy for Duplicator, we build the following relation $\mathcal{R} \subseteq S \times S'$:

$s \mathcal{R}_\sigma s'$ iff there exists a run $\rho \in Runs(\mathcal{G})$ which is compatible with $(\sigma_{L'}, \sigma_S)$ such that $(s, s') = \rho[i]$ for some $i \in \mathbb{N}$.

We will show that $\mathcal{R}_\sigma$ is an AS between $\mathcal{L}$ and $\mathcal{L}'$.

Note first that, if $s \mathcal{R}_\sigma s'$ then $O(s) \leq O(s')$ since any run ρ which is compatible with $(\sigma_{L'}, \sigma_S)$ must be winning for Duplicator and therefore visit only positions $(s, s') \in Obj$. We then build, using σ, an AS pair $(\eta_\sigma, \theta_\sigma)$ as required by Proposition 1, as follows: for each $s \in S, s', t' \in S', l \in L$,

$$\eta_\sigma(s, s', l) = \sigma_{L'}(s, s', l) \text{ and } \theta_\sigma(s, s', l, t') = \sigma_S(s, s', l, \sigma_{L'}(s, s', l), t')$$

Then the pair $(\eta_\sigma, \theta_\sigma)$ satisfies the hypotheses of Proposition 1 for $\mathcal{R}_\sigma$:

1. For any (s, s', l), $\eta_\sigma(s, s', l) = \sigma_{L'}(s, s', l)$ is defined and $s' \xrightarrow{\sigma_{L'}(s,s',l)}$.
2. For any (s, s', l, t'), $\theta_\sigma(s, s', l, t') = \sigma_S(s, s', l, \sigma_{L'}(s, s', l), t')$ is defined.
3. $(s, s', l, \sigma_{L'}(s, s', l), t') \xrightarrow{\sigma_S(s,s',l,\sigma(s,s',l),t')} (\sigma_S(s, s', l, \sigma(s, s', l), t'), t') \in \delta$,
   which implies that $s \xrightarrow{l} \sigma_S(s, s', l, \sigma_{L'}(s, s', l), t') \in T$ by definition of $\mathcal{G}$.
4. Any run which reaches (s, s') and is compatible with $(\sigma_{L'}, \sigma_S)$ can be extended to a run which reaches $\sigma_S(s, s', l, \sigma_{L'}(s, s', l), t'), t')$, and therefore $\sigma_S(s, s', l, \sigma_{L'}(s, s', l), t'), t') \mathcal{R}_\sigma t'$.

For the other direction of Theorem 2, the skolemized version of AS will be again of help, by providing us with the Duplicator choices in each state of the simulation game. Namely, given AS $\mathcal{R}$ defined by the AS pair (η, θ) as in Proposition 1, we show that any extension of (η, θ) to a pair of total functions $(\sigma_{L'}, \sigma_S)$ represents a memoryless winning strategy for Duplicator in $\mathcal{G}$. Or, in other words, the tuples where η and θ are undefined cannot be reached by runs which are compatible with these choices.

Formally, take any strategy for Duplicator $(\sigma_{L'}, \sigma_S)$ with $\sigma_{L'} : S \times S' \times L \longrightarrow L'$ and $\sigma_S : S \times S' \times L \times L' \times S' \longrightarrow S$ which is defined as follows:

- For each s, s', l, $\sigma_{L'}(s, s', l) = \eta(s, s', l)$ if $\eta(s, s', l)$ is defined, and is arbitrary otherwise.
- For each s, s', l, l', t', $\sigma_S(s, s', l, \sigma(s, s', l), t') = \theta(s, s', l, t')$ if $\eta(s, s', l)$ and $\theta(s, s', l, t')$ are defined, and is arbitrary otherwise.

Then any finite run ρ which is compatible with $(\sigma_{L'}, \sigma_S)$ visits only states (s, s', α) with $s \mathcal{R} s'$ – and, as a consequence, $(s, s', \alpha) \in Obj$. The proof goes by induction on the length of the run.

The base case is trivial since $s_0 \mathcal{R} s'_0$ and the initial position in $\mathcal{G}$ is compatible with any strategy. So assume ρ is a run of length ≥ 1. If the length of the run is

$4k + 1$, then $\rho = \rho' \cdot (s, s', l)$ for some ρ' with $\ell(\rho') = 4k$ and $\rho'[4k] = (s, s')$, and therefore $s\mathcal{R}s'$ by the induction hypothesis. Furthermore, for $\ell(\rho) = 4k + 2$ we must have $\rho = \rho' \cdot (s, s', l, l')$ and, by the induction hypothesis, $\rho'[4k + 1] = (s, s', l)$ is such that $s\mathcal{R}s'$. But then, by construction of $\sigma_{L'}$, we must have $l' = \sigma_{L'}(s, s', l) = \eta(s, s', l)$. Going one step further, for $\ell(\rho) = 4k + 3$ we must have $\rho = \rho' \cdot (s, s', l, l', t')$ and again $s\mathcal{R}s'$ by the induction hypothesis and $l' = \sigma_{L'}(s, s', l)$. Finally, for $\ell(\rho) = 4k + 4$ and $\rho = \rho' \cdot (t, t')$ compatible with $(\sigma_{L'}, \sigma_S)$, we must have $\rho[4k + 3] = (s, s', l, l', t')$, $s\mathcal{R}s'$, $l' = \sigma_{L'}(s, s', l)$, and $t = \sigma_S(s, s', l, l', t') = \theta(s, s', l, t')$ and hence $t\mathcal{R}t'$.

4   Strategies as Contexts

The previous section does not tell the whole story of alternating simulation, and we explore here the connections with observational preorders from [7].

4.1   Observational Preorders

In a syntactic calculus, there is a standard way to define observational preorder on syntactic terms, which we call here the *Morris-style* definition: $t \leq s$ if for every context C, the observations that can be made on $C[t]$ are (in some sense) included in the observations that can be made on $C[s]$ [7]. In the case of the functional language PCF, for instance, the Morris preorder is defined taking termination as the only observation.

    While the relation is very easy to define, and very convincing, the quantification over all possible contexts makes it hard to directly prove that two terms are in the relation. Some other, easier to handle, notion is then introduced for this purpose. For instance, in the '70 people tried to capture the observation pre-congruence for PCF using domains, and subsequently using game semantics. The holy Grail of this line of research was "full abstraction", a precise characterisation of the Morris preorder.

    In the study of CCS, (bi)-simulation and its large weaponry of up-to techniques, was proven to precise characterise barbed pre-congruence, which can be argued to be a generalisation of the Morris preorder to nondeterministic systems.

    In the exemples mentioned above, contexts can be seen as way of testing a term: you submit a term to different experiments, and observe the results. In the setting studied here, there are no terms, only transition systems. The only way to interact with a transition system is by playing on it. Therefore we argue that the right transposition of contexts, here, are the strategies.

    Let's try to formulate the Morris-style preorder using this intuition. Given two LTS $\mathcal{L}, \mathcal{L}'$ we say that $\mathcal{L} \leq \mathcal{L}'$ if for any strategies σ_A, σ_O the observations of $\rho[\mathcal{L}, \sigma_A, \sigma_O]$ are included in the observations of $\rho[\mathcal{L}', \sigma_A, \sigma_O]$.

    There is a problem with this naive formulation: the definition of strategy does not allow the same strategies to interact with different transition systems. We need to have a way to generalise the notion of "same" strategy. Strategies make choices based on the previous history. We need to put in correspondence different choices, on different histories. We argue then that two strategies are "the same" if they make corresponding choices.

4.2   Choice Correspondence and the Morris Preorder

We have therefore to propose a suitable definition of "choice correspondence" for states and labels:

Definition 5. *Let $\mathcal{L} = (S, s_0, L, \mathcal{T}, P, \leq, O)$ and $\mathcal{L}' = (S', s_0', L', \mathcal{T}', P, \leq, O')$ be two LTSs sharing the same observation order. A choice correspondence is consituted by two mappings:*

$$\begin{cases} f : runs_\bullet(\mathcal{L}) \times runs_\bullet(\mathcal{L}') \to L \to L' \\ g : runs_\to(\mathcal{L}) \times runs_\to(\mathcal{L}') \to S' \to S \end{cases}$$

with the following properties:

- *if $hl \in runs_\to(\mathcal{L})$ and $f(h, h')(l) = l'$ then $h'l' \in runs_\to(\mathcal{L}')$;*
- *if $h's' \in runs_\bullet(\mathcal{L}')$ and $g(h, h')(s') = s$ then $hs \in runs_\bullet(\mathcal{L})$.*

In one direction, the f component builds a correspondence between choices of labels, while in the other direction, the g component builds a correspondence between states. Both mappings take into account the history of the computation.

A choice correspondence allows us to build a run on two LTSs, with just one pair of strategies. Since the corresponding functions act in different directions, we will need one strategy to be defined on each LTS. Then the two other strategies are induced by the correspondence.

Let $\mathcal{L} = (S, s_0, L, \mathcal{T})$ and $\mathcal{L}' = (S', s_0', l', \mathcal{T})$ be two LTSs. Consider (f, g) be a choice correspondence, σ_A a strategy for agent in $\mathcal{L}$ and σ_O' a strategy for opponent in $\mathcal{L}'$.

We define the following:

- a map $\xi' : runs_\to(\mathcal{L}) \to runs_\to(\mathcal{L}')$,
- a strategy σ_O for opponent in $\mathcal{L}$,
- a map $\xi : runs_\bullet(\mathcal{L}') \to runs_\bullet(\mathcal{L})$,
- and a strategy σ_A' for agent in $\mathcal{L}'$.

We do that by induction on the length of the argument. For the base case we put $\xi(s_0') = s_0$ and $\sigma_A'(s_0') = \sigma_A(s_0)$.

For the induction step, let $h'l's' \in runs_\bullet(\mathcal{L}')$, define $h = \xi(h')$, $l = \sigma_A(h)$ and $s = g(hl, h'l')(s')$, then

$$\xi(h'l's') = hls \quad \text{and} \quad \sigma_A'(h'l's') = f(hls, h'l's')(\sigma_A(hls)).$$

The function ξ' and the strategy σ_O are defined analogously.

Note that the definition of σ_A' does not depend on σ_O' and that the definition σ_O does not depend on σ_A. When f, g is clear from the context, we will denote $\sigma_A' = \xi'(\sigma_A)$ and $\sigma_O = \xi(\sigma_O')$. We obtain thus two runs: $\rho[\mathcal{L}, \sigma_A, \xi(\sigma_O')]$ and $\rho[\mathcal{L}', \xi'(\sigma_A), \sigma_O']$.

We can now say that σ_A and $\xi'(\sigma_A)$ are "the same" strategy up to the choice correspondence (f, g) (and similarly for $\xi(\sigma'_O)$ and σ'_O).

The definitions proposed above allow us to give a generalised definition of contextual preorder. Recall that in the in the original definition, $S \leq S'$ if, whatever observations we can make with $C[S]$, it is possible with $C[S']$. Here we don't really care for which term we choose the context as it must be the same for both. The way we defined the choice correspondence forces us to define the strategies on specific systems, and then "transfer it" to the other one. This informal discussion leads us to this formal definition of Morris preorder up to choice correspondence:

Definition 6. *Let $\mathcal{L} = (S, s_0, L, \mathcal{T})$ and $\mathcal{L}' = (S', s'_0, L', \mathcal{T})$ be two LTSs. Consider a choice correspondence (f, g) for $\mathcal{L}$ and $\mathcal{L}'$. We say that $\mathcal{L} \leq_{f,g} \mathcal{L}'$ if for all strategy σ_A for agent in $\mathcal{L}$ and all strategy σ'_O for opponent in $\mathcal{L}'$:*

$$O(\rho[\mathcal{L}, \sigma_A, \xi(\sigma'_O)]) \leq O(\rho[\mathcal{L}', \xi'(\sigma_A), \sigma'_O]).$$

5   The Adequacy Theorems

We can now state the main theorem of the paper.

Theorem 3. . *Let $\mathcal{L} = (S, s_0, L, \mathcal{T})$ and $\mathcal{L}' = (S', s'_0, L', \mathcal{T})$ be two LTSs. The following are equivalent:*

1. *$\mathcal{L} \subset_{\mathsf{AS}} \mathcal{L}'$;*
2. *there exists a choice correspondence (f, g) such that $\mathcal{L} \leq_{f,g} \mathcal{L}'$.*

To prove this theorem we utilize the AS game defined in Subsect. 3.1.

Lemma 1. *Duplicator has a winning strategy in $\mathcal{G}$ if and only if there is a choice correspondence (f, g) for which $\mathcal{L} \leq_{f,g} \mathcal{L}'$.*

For the one direction, we build a choice correspondence (f, g) directly from the definition of a strategy σ_D for Duplicator. We then show that if σ_D is winning, $\mathcal{L} \leq_{f,g} \mathcal{L}'$. For the other direction, from a choice correspondence (f, g) we build a strategy σ_D for Duplicator, which is winning if $\mathcal{L} \leq_{f,g} \mathcal{L}'$. See the appendix for the details.

In general, the strategy we build for Duplicator is aware of all the history, but Theorem 2 requires a memoryless strategy. Therefore, to conclude the Proof of Theorem 3, we need to observe that, $\mathcal{G}$ being a safety game and hence a particular type of parity game, it is memoryless determined [6,9], that is, if Duplicator has a winning strategy, then she has a memoryless winning strategy.

We are finally able to prove Theorem 1. It is a corollary of the following proposition and of Theorem 3.

Proposition 2. *Let $\mathcal{L} = (S, s_0, L, \mathcal{T})$ and $\mathcal{L}' = (S', s'_0, L', \mathcal{T})$. If there exists a choice correspondence (f, g) for which $\mathcal{L} \leq_{f,g} \mathcal{L}'$, then $\mathcal{L} \leq \mathcal{L}'$.*

Proof. Consider a choice correspondence (f, g). Given two strategies σ_A for $\mathcal{L}$ and σ'_O for $\mathcal{L}'$, we are able to build two strategies σ'_A for $\mathcal{L}'$ and σ_O for $\mathcal{L}$. If $\mathcal{L} \leq_{f,g} \mathcal{L}'$ then

$$O(\rho[\mathcal{L}, \sigma_A, \sigma'_O]) \leq O(\rho[\mathcal{L}', \sigma_A, \sigma'_O]).$$

Summarizing, the following formula is true:

$$\forall \sigma_A \forall \sigma'_O \exists \sigma'_A \exists \sigma_O . O(\rho[\mathcal{L}, \sigma_A, \sigma_O]) \leq O(\rho[\mathcal{L}', \sigma'_A, \sigma'_O]).$$

Note, however, that the way we constructed σ'_A depends only on the choice correspondence (f, g) and on the definition of σ_A. We can therefore swap the quantifiers:

$$\forall \sigma_A \exists \sigma'_A \forall \sigma'_O \exists \sigma_O . O(\rho[\mathcal{L}, \sigma_A, \sigma_O]) \leq O(\rho[\mathcal{L}', \sigma'_A, \sigma'_O]).$$

In a sense, the choice correspondence acts as a form of *local skolemization* of the existential quantifiers.

Fix now an upward-closed specification φ and assume that $O(\rho[\mathcal{L}, \sigma_A, \sigma_O]) \leq O(\rho[\mathcal{L}', \sigma'_A, \sigma'_O])$. Then $\rho[\mathcal{L}, \sigma_A, \sigma_O] \vDash \varphi \implies \rho[\mathcal{L}', \sigma'_A, \sigma'_O] \vDash \varphi$.

Therefore if there exists a choice correspondence (f, g) for which $\mathcal{L} \leq_{f,g} \mathcal{L}'$, we can conclude that for all upward-closed specification φ:

$$\forall \sigma_A \exists \sigma'_A \forall \sigma'_O \exists \sigma_O . (\rho[\mathcal{L}, \sigma_A, \sigma_O] \vDash \varphi \implies \rho[\mathcal{L}', \sigma'_A, \sigma'_O] \vDash \varphi).$$

By pushing the quantifiers inward in a suitable way, we obtain that for all upward-closed specification φ:

$$(\exists \sigma_A \forall \sigma_O . \rho[\mathcal{L}, \sigma_A, \sigma_O] \vDash \varphi) \implies (\exists \sigma'_A \forall \sigma'_O . \rho[\mathcal{L}', \sigma'_A, \sigma'_O] \vDash \varphi)$$

which is the definition of enforcing preorder. □

Proposition 3. *The inverse of Theorem 1 does not hold.*

Figure 2, inspired from [13], provides the counterexample for the inverse of Theorem 1. The partial order of observations is $P = \{\bot, p, q, r\}$ where $\leq$ is the identity relation. In both LTS, the Agent has two strategies, one enforcing $\varphi_1 = \{\bot p^\omega, \bot q^\omega\}$ and the other enforcing $\varphi_2 = \{\bot p^\omega, \bot r^\omega\}$. Hence $\mathcal{L}_1 \leq \mathcal{L}_2$ and $\mathcal{L}_2 \leq \mathcal{L}_1$. On the other hand, clearly $\mathcal{L}_1 \not\sqsubseteq_{\mathsf{AS}} \mathcal{L}_2$ and $\mathcal{L}_2 \not\sqsubseteq_{\mathsf{AS}} \mathcal{L}_1$.

6   Complements

6.1   The Quest for Symmetric Relations

We have studied in detail three preorders. What can we say about the symmetric version of them? The symmetric version of the enforcing preorder, that we call *enforcing equivalence*, is easily defined: We say that $\mathcal{L}$ is enforcing equivalent to $\mathcal{L}'$ if for any specification φ, Agent can enforce φ on $\mathcal{L}$ if and only if Agent can enforce φ on $\mathcal{L}'$.

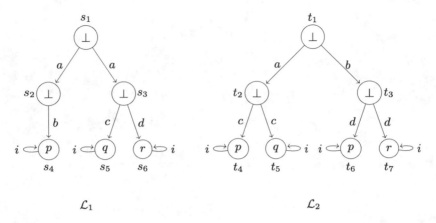

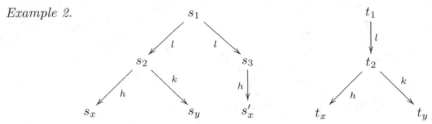

Fig. 2. Two LTS which are enforcing equivalent but for which there exists no alternating simulation in either direction.

The notion of alternating bisimulation is also easily defined as a symmetric alternating simulation. The largest alternating bisimulation is called alternating bisimilarity. As for Park and Milner bisimulation, alternating bisimilarity is stronger than the equivalence generated by alternating similarity, as we show in the following example.

Example 2.

In this model, the observation in states s_x, s'_x, t_x is x, and the observation in s_y, t_y is y. The reader can verify that $\{(s_1, t_1), (s_2, t_2), (s_x, t_x), (s_y, t_y)\}$ and $\{(t_1, s_1), (t_2, s_2), (t_2, s_3), (t_x, s_x), (t_y, s_y), (t_x, s'_x)\}$ are both alternating simulations, but there is no alternating bisimulation containing (s_1, t_1).

It remains open to find a proper definition of Morris equivalence, as we have not yet pinned down the right symmetric generalisation of the notion of choice correspondence. Asking the functions (f, g) to be bijective seems to us too strong a requirement. However just asking the existence of two unrelated choice correspondences would correspond to having two simulations in both direction, and we have just shown that this is weaker than bisimilarity.

This quest for Morris equivalence should also be guided by the bisimulation game, which is the symmetric version of the simulation game in Sect. 3.1, and then stating an appropriate adaptation of Theorem 2 and, consequently, Theorem 3. More specifically, in the bisimulation game, in each position $(s, s') \in S \times S'$, Spoiler first chooses the side where she challenges the simulation (that is, challenges Duplicator with either proving that $s \sqsubset_{AS} s'$ or $s' \sqsubset_{AS} s$), and then proceeds by proposing Duplicator with a label in the chosen transition system. We call this extra intermediary step a *side-challenging step*. The symmetry in the definition of the alternating bisimulation could be solved in the bisimulation game by requiring that Duplicator have *imperfect information*, in the sense that she "forgets" each Spoiler's side-challenging step. But two-player games with imperfect information are not determined in general, hence more study is needed to properly adapt Theorem 2.

6.2 Taking Labels Seriously

To get closer to the world of Park and Milner we propose a definition of simulation that takes into account the identity of the labels.

Definition 7. *A Name-aware alternating simulation (NAAS) on a labelled transition system, is a binary relation $\mathcal{R}$ such that whenever $s \mathcal{R} t$, $O(s) \leq O(t)$ and:*

for all labels l, if $s \xrightarrow{l}$, then $t \xrightarrow{l}$, and for all t' s.t. $t \xrightarrow{l} t'$, there exists s' s.t. $s \xrightarrow{l} s'$ and $s' \mathcal{R} t'$.

The largest NAAS, $\sqsubset_{NA}$, is called name-aware similarity. *If there is a NAAS $s \mathcal{R} t$, we say $s \sqsubset_{NA} t$.*

In the following examples we suppose all the states have the same observation.

Example 3.

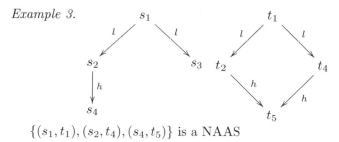

$\{(s_1, t_1), (s_2, t_4), (s_4, t_5)\}$ is a NAAS

Example 4.

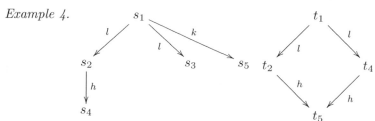

There is no NAAS in either direction.

The example above shows that the NAAS is different from the standard notion of similarity by Park and Milner. Indeed there is a standard simulation between t_1 and s_1: the fact that there is a label more from s_1 is irrelevant.

While the two notions of simulation differ, it can be shown that the symmetric notions coincide.

Definition 8. *A* Name-aware alternating bisimulation *(NAAB) on a labelled transition system, is a binary relation $\mathcal{R}$ such that both $\mathcal{R}$ and $\mathcal{R}^{-1}$ are NAAS. The largest NAAB is called* name-aware bisimilarity.

A Park and Milner simulation *(PMS) on a labelled transition system, is a binary relation $\mathcal{R}$ such that whenever $s \mathcal{R} t$,*

- $O(s) \leq O(t)$
- *for all labels l, and for all states s' if $s \xrightarrow{l} s'$, then there exists t' such that $t \xrightarrow{l} t'.$, there exists s' s.t. $s' \mathcal{R} t'$.*

A Park and Milner bisimulation *(PMB) on a labelled transition system, is a binary relation $\mathcal{R}$ such that both $\mathcal{R}$ and $\mathcal{R}^{-1}$ are PMS.*

Theorem 4. *A binary relation $\mathcal{R} \subseteq S \times T$ is a Name-aware alternating bisimulation if and only if it is a Park and Milner bisimulation.*

Proof. The proof is done in both directions by checking that a NAAB satisfies the conditions for being a PMB, and that a PMB satisfies the conditions for being a NAAB.

7   Conclusions and Future Work

We have generalised the syntactic notion of observational preorder to a setting without syntax, and we also have presented some notions originally defined on alternating transition systems, using standard labelled transition systems. This leads us to a new definition of a coinductive relation, that happens to characterise the Morris preorder.

Alternating bisimulations were used to prove (manually) bisimulation reductions for multi-agent systems [5], which were specified using the ISPL multi-agent modelling language used in the MCMAS tool for model-checking. We plan to provide LTS semantics to such multi-agent modelling languages together with algorithmic tools for deciding or building alternating bisimulation reductions. This will lead us to an extension of this work to the case of alternating transition systems (or concurrent game structures) with imperfect information, which requires a notion of observation-based strategy.

A notion of choice correspondence that takes into account the identity of the labels can be easily defined. We think that the corresponding notion of Morris preorder coincides with name-aware similarity.

Acknowledgments. We thank the anonymous reviewers for their remarks, suggestions and references, among which the papers [13,14] provided us with the inspiration for the counterexample in Proposition 3.

References

1. Alur, R., Henzinger, T.A.: Reactive modules. Formal Methods Syst. Des. **15**(1), 7–48 (1999). https://doi.org/10.1023/A:1008739929481
2. Alur, R., Henzinger, T.A., Kupferman, O.: Alternating-time temporal logic. J. ACM **49**(5), 672–713 (2002)
3. Alur, R., Henzinger, T.A., Kupferman, O., Vardi, M.Y.: Alternating refinement relations. In: Sangiorgi, D., de Simone, R. (eds.) CONCUR 1998. LNCS, vol. 1466, pp. 163–178. Springer, Heidelberg (1998). https://doi.org/10.1007/BFb0055622
4. Atkinson, K., Bench-Capon, T.J.M.: Practical reasoning as presumptive argumentation using action based alternating transition systems. Artif. Intell. **171**(10–15), 855–874 (2007)
5. Belardinelli, F., Condurache, R., Dima, C., Jamroga, W., Jones, A.V.: Bisimulations for verifying strategic abilities with an application to threeballot. In: Larson, K., Winikoff, M., Das, S., Durfee, E.H. (eds.) Proceedings of the 16th Conference on Autonomous Agents and MultiAgent Systems, AAMAS 2017, São Paulo, Brazil, 8–12 May 2017, pp. 1286–1295. ACM (2017)
6. Emerson, E.A., Jutla, C.S.: Tree automata, mu-calculus and determinacy (extended abstract). In: 32nd Annual Symposium on Foundations of Computer Science, San Juan, Puerto Rico, 1–4 October 1991, pp. 368–377. IEEE Computer Society (1991)
7. Morris, J.H.: Lambda-calculus models of programming languages. Ph.D. thesis, M.I.T. (1968)
8. Lomuscio, A., Qu, H., Raimondi, F.: MCMAS: an open-source model checker for the verification of multi-agent systems. Int. J. Softw. Tools Technol. Transf. **19**(1), 9–30 (2017). https://doi.org/10.1007/s10009-015-0378-x
9. Mazala, R.: Infinite games. In: Grädel, E., Thomas, W., Wilke, T. (eds.) Automata Logics, and Infinite Games. LNCS, vol. 2500, pp. 23 38. Springer, Heidelberg (2002). https://doi.org/10.1007/3-540-36387-4_2
10. Milner, R.: A Calculus of Communicating Systems. Lecture Notes in Computer Science, vol. 92. Springer, Heidelberg (1980). https://doi.org/10.1007/3-540-10235-3
11. Milner, R.: Communicating and Mobile Systems - The Pi-Calculus. Cambridge University Press, Cambridge (1999)
12. Nielsen, M., Winskel, G.: Models for Concurrency, pp. 1–148. Oxford University Press (1995). Also published in BRICS Research Series as RS-94-12
13. van Benthem, J.: Extensive games as process models. J. Log. Lang. Inf. **11**(3), 289–313 (2002)
14. van Benthem, J., Bezhanishvili, N., Enqvist, S.: A new game equivalence, its logic and algebra. J. Philos. Log. **48**(4), 649–684 (2019)
15. van der Hoek, W., Roberts, M., Wooldridge, M.J.: Social laws in alternating time: effectiveness, feasibility, and synthesis. Synthese **156**(1), 1–19 (2007)

Synthesising Reward Machines for Cooperative Multi-Agent Reinforcement Learning

Giovanni Varricchione[1(✉)], Natasha Alechina[1], Mehdi Dastani[1],
and Brian Logan[1,2]

[1] Department of Information and Computing Sciences, Utrecht University,
Utrecht, The Netherlands
{g.varricchione,n.a.alechina,m.m.dastani,b.s.logan}@uu.nl
[2] Department of Computing Science, University of Aberdeen, Aberdeen, UK

Abstract. Reward machines have recently been proposed as a means of encoding team tasks in cooperative multi-agent reinforcement learning. The resulting *multi-agent reward machine* is then decomposed into individual reward machines, one for each member of the team, allowing agents to learn in a decentralised manner while still achieving the team task. However, current work assumes the multi-agent reward machine to be given. In this paper, we show how reward machines for team tasks can be synthesised automatically from an Alternating-Time Temporal Logic specification of the desired team behaviour and a high-level abstraction of the agents' environment. We present results suggesting that our automated approach has comparable, if not better, sample efficiency than reward machines generated by hand for multi-agent tasks.

1 Introduction

Reward machines (RMs) [4, 18, 19] have recently been proposed as a way of specifying rewards for reinforcement learning (RL) agents. RMs are Mealy machines used to specify tasks and rewards based on a high-level abstraction of the agent's environment. Providing an explicit encoding of the structure of the task has been shown to increase sample efficiency in reinforcement learning. For example, the RM-based algorithm proposed in [4] has been shown to out-perform state-of-the-art RL algorithms, especially in tasks requiring specific temporally extended behaviours.

Recently, in [12], RMs were proposed as a means of specifying rewards for team tasks in multi-agent reinforcement learning. In cooperative multi-agent reinforcement learning (MARL) [13] the aim is to train a group of agents to perform a team task with the objective of maximising the expected future reward of the team. MARL is more challenging than single-agent RL. As the correctness of the actions of each agent may depend on the actions of other agents in the team, the agents must coordinate their actions [2]. In addition, the agents are learning and updating their policies simultaneously. From the point of view of

V. Malvone and A. Murano (Eds.): EUMAS 2023, LNAI 14282, pp. 328–344, 2023.
https://doi.org/10.1007/978-3-031-43264-4_21

each individual agent, the learning problem is non-stationary; i.e., the optimal policy for each agent is constantly changing [7].

In [12] these problems are addressed by specifying a *multi-agent reward machine* which encodes the abstract structure of the team task. The multi-agent reward machine is then decomposed into individual reward machines, one for each member of the team. The decomposition is carried out by projecting the coalition RM onto the set of observable events of each agent in the team. If the decomposition is done in such a way that the combined behaviour of the individual reward machines is "bisimulation equivalent" to that of the team reward machine, each agent can be trained using its individual reward machine to perform its part of the team task in a decentralised manner while still ensuring that the team task will be achieved by the joint action of the agents. This avoids the problem of non-stationarity, and in [12] an algorithm based on this approach called "Decentralized Q-Learning with Projected Reward Machines" (DQPRM) is shown to be more sample efficient than independent q-learners (IQL) [16] and hierarchical independent learners (h-IL) [17].

However, in [12], the multi-agent reward machine is generated "by hand". Although reward machines are usually specified by hand, some works, such as [5,9], have shown how these can be synthesised *automatically*. Inspired by this line of research, in this paper we show how individual reward machines can be synthesised automatically from a high-level description of the agents' environment and an Alternating-time Temporal Logic (ATL) specification of the desired team behaviour. As in [12], we provide formal guarantees ensuring that the behaviour learned from our automatically synthesised individual RMs is guaranteed to result in coordinated behaviour on the team task. Moreover, as tasks are specified in ATL, we can easily incorporate additional constraints on team goals, e.g., invariant properties, which were not dealt with in [12].

The structure of this paper is as follows. In Sect. 2, we give preliminaries for our work; these include defining reward machines and the syntax and semantics of (imperfect information) ATL. In Sect. 3, we present our approach and show how to synthesise team and individual RMs. Moreover, we provide theoretical results in line to those of [12]. Section 4 provides an empirical evaluation of our work. As the main focus of our approach is to automatize the construction of RMs in multi-agent reinforcement learning, we will show how agents trained with our automatically synthesised RMs have comparable, if not better, performance than those of [12]. Then, in Sect. 5 we present related works, and in Sect. 6 we conclude and indicate possible future directions.

2   Preliminaries

In this section, we briefly introduce reward machines, multi-agent reinforcement learning with reward machines, and Alternating Time Temporal Logic, which form the basis of our approach.

2.1   Multi-agent Environments

We begin by defining a *Multi-Agent Environment* (MAE) that specifies the low-level environment in which the agents act.

Definition 1 (Multi-agent environment). *A multi-agent environment with n agents is a tuple $E = \langle Agt, S_1, \ldots, S_n, A_1, \ldots, A_n, Pr, (Prop_i)_{i \in Agt}, Val \rangle$ where:*

- *Agt is a non-empty finite set of n agents;*
- *S_i is the finite set of states of agent i. We denote the set of joint states, i.e., the cartesian product of all the sets of states, with $S = S_1 \times \cdots \times S_n$;*
- *A_i is the finite set of actions of agent i. We denote the set of joint actions, i.e., the cartesian product of all the sets of actions, with $A = A_1 \times \cdots \times A_n$;*
- *$Pr : S \times A \times S \to \Delta(S)$ is the joint state transition probability distribution and $\Delta(S)$ is the set of all probability distributions over S; $Pr(s'|s, a)$ denotes the probability of transitioning from a joint state $s \in S$ to a joint state $s' \in S$ by performing a joint action $a \in A$;*
- *$(Prop_i)_{i \in Agt}$ is the set of propositional symbols "observable" by agent i, $Prop := \bigcup_{i \in Agt} Prop_i$ is the entire set of observable propositions;*
- *$Val : Prop \to 2^S$ is a valuation function mapping each propositional symbol to the set of joint states in which it is true. For each agent i, we can also obtain its individual valuation function Val_i by taking the restriction of Val onto $Prop_i$ and S_i;*

A joint policy $\pi : S \to \Delta(A)$ maps any state in a MAE E to a probability distribution over the set of joint actions.

When agents are trained individually, we will consider their induced Markov Decision Process (MDP), i.e., $M_i = \langle S_i, A_i, Pr, Prop_i, Val \rangle$.

In the context of a MAE, we might be interested in some specific propositions that can aid us when specifying some task we want the agents to accomplish. In such case, we give a "labelling", used to describe how the evolution of the MAE affects the truth of these propositions. Given a set of propositional symbols $Prop$, we denote with $\overline{Prop}$ the set of literals we derive from it. For a given propositional symbol $p \in Prop$, we denote with, respectively, p^+ and p^- its positive and negative literal.

Definition 2 (Labelling). *Given a MAE $E = \langle Agt, S_1, \ldots, S_n, A_1, \ldots, A_n, Pr, (Prop_i)_{i \in Agt}, Val \rangle$, its labelling is the, naturally induced, function $L : S \times A \times S \to \wp(\overline{Prop})$ mapping transitions in the MAE to the set of associated literals that are brought about by it. To be precise, given joint states $s, s' \in S$ and joint action $a \in A$, we have that $L(s, a, s') := \{p^+ \mid s \notin Val(p) \land s' \in Val(p)\} \cup \{p^- \mid s \in Val(p) \land s' \notin Val(p)\}$. As each agent $i \in Agt$ has its own set of observable propositional symbols $Prop_i$, we can define its individual labelling $L_i : S_i \times A_i \times S_i \to \wp(\overline{Prop_i})$ by analogously taking $L_i(s_i, a_i, s_i) := \{p^+ \mid s_i \notin Val_i(p) \land s_i' \in Val_i(p)\} \cup \{p^- \mid s_i \in Val_i(p) \land s_i' \notin Val_i(p)\}$.*

In this paper we focus on *postcondition labelling*, where $L(s, a, s')$ is the set of literals made true in s' by executing a in s. If, for a given atomic proposition

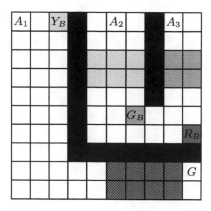

Fig. 1. COOPERATIVEBUTTONS domain from [12].

$p \in Prop$, we have that neither of its literals appear in $L(s, a, s')$, then it means that its truth value has not changed from s to s'.

Example 1. We now give an example of a MAE. The COOPERATIVEBUTTONS environment [12] is a 10×10 gridworld containing walls (some of which can be lowered) and buttons (Fig. 1). There are three agents, i_1, i_2 and i_3. Agents can move **left**, **up**, **right**, **down** or **stay** in the same cell. Movement actions are nondeterministic: if an agent moves in any direction, it may end up in a cell adjacent to the one it was trying to reach with probability 0.2. Walls stop agents from moving to the desired cell, but the coloured ones can be lowered by pressing the corresponding button. The red button requires two agents to press it together in order to lower the red wall. The goal of the agents is to cooperate to allow agent i_1 to reach the *Goal* location. The task can be achieved as follows: first i_1 presses the yellow button, then i_2 the green button, then i_2 and i_3 the red button, and finally i_1 reaches the *Goal* location.

The set of propositional symbols is $Prop = \{Y_B, G_B, A_2^{R_B}, A_3^{R_B}, R_B, Goal\}$. Propositional symbols Y_B, G_B and R_B are true if, respectively, the yellow, green and red button has been pressed, while *Goal* is true if an agent is on the goal location G. If i_2 and i_3 are on the button, then propositional symbols $A_2^{R_B}$ and $A_3^{R_B}$ are respectively true. As soon as both $A_2^{R_B}$ and $A_3^{R_B}$ are true, R_B becomes true as well. Agent i_1's set of propositions is $Prop_{i_1} = \{Y_B, R_B, Goal\}$, agent i_2's is $Prop_{i_2} = \{Y_B, G_B, A_2^{R_B}, R_B\}$, and agent i_3's is $Prop_{i_3} = \{G_B, A_3^{R_B}, R_B\}$. Note that there are no propositions corresponding to exact location of agents in the environment, which would be relevant for the low-level MARL environment.

A joint state corresponds to the pair of coordinates $\langle x_j, y_j \rangle$ of each agent $i_j \in \{i_1, i_2, i_3\}$ and the set of propositions true in it[1]. Individual states for agent i contain only its coordinates and the set of propositions, from $Prop_i$, true in it.

---

[1] For convenience, we will omit the set of propositional symbols true in joint states, and just give them as triples of coordinates. Whenever the set of propositional symbols is needed, we will explicitly state it beforehand.

We now explain how the set of propositional symbols is crucial in order to correctly define the dynamics of MAEs. Suppose that agent i_2 is in cell $\langle 5, 1\rangle$, i.e., in front of the yellow wall. If the agent were to perform (successfully) the down action, then its resulting state would depend on whether Y_B is true or false: in the former case, i_2 reaches cell $\langle 5, 2\rangle$, in the latter it will hit the wall and remain on cell $\langle 5, 1\rangle$.

Finally, as an example of a label for a transition, suppose the initial joint state s is $\langle\langle 1, 0\rangle, \langle 5, 0\rangle, \langle 8, 0\rangle\rangle$ (with no propositional symbol being true) and that the joint action is $\langle$right, stay, stay$\rangle$. In this case, if agent i_1 correctly moves to the right, the next joint state will be $\langle\langle 2, 0\rangle, \langle 5, 0\rangle, \langle 8, 0\rangle\rangle$, meaning that agent i_1 has correctly pressed the yellow button. Therefore, the transition $\langle\langle 1, 0\rangle, \langle 5, 0\rangle, \langle 8, 0\rangle\rangle, \langle$right, stay, stay$\rangle, \langle\langle 2, 0\rangle, \langle 5, 0\rangle, \langle 8, 0\rangle\rangle$ will be labelled with $\{Y_B^+\}$.

2.2   Reward Machines

A *reward machine* (RM) (referred to as a *simple reward machine* in [18]) is a Mealy machine over an alphabet Σ. Intuitively, an RM takes abstract descriptions of an event in the environment as input, and outputs a reward.

Definition 3. *A reward machine is a tuple* $R = \langle U, u^I, \Sigma, t, r\rangle$ *where:*

- *U is a finite non-empty set of states;*
- *u^I is the initial state;*
- *Σ is a finite set of environment events;*
- *$t : U \times \Sigma \to U$ is a transition function that, for every state $u \in U$ and event $e \in \Sigma$, gives the state resulting from observing event e in state u; and*
- *$r : U \times \Sigma \to \mathbb{R}$ is a reward function that for every state $u \in U$ and event $e \in \Sigma$ gives the reward resulting from observing event e in state u.*

In our case, the set of events Σ will correspond to sets of literals over the finite set of propositional symbols *Prop*, as given in the definition of MAEs.

2.3   Multi-Agent RL with RMs

To formally define the *multi-agent reinforcement learning problem with reward machines*, we introduce the notion of a Markov Game with a Reward Machine (MGRM). An MGRM is essentially a product of a multi-agent environment and a reward machine; it is the multi-agent analogous of a Markov Decision Process with Reward Machine (MDPRM), as defined in [18].

Definition 4. *A (cooperative) Markov Game with a Reward Machine is a tuple* $G = \langle Agt, S_1, \ldots, S_n, A_1, \ldots, A_n, Pr, (Prop_i)_{i \in Agt}, Val, L, \gamma, U, u^I, \Sigma, t, r\rangle$ *where:*

- *$Agt, S_j, A_j, Pr, (Prop_i)_{i \in Agt}, Val$ are as in Definition 1;*
- *$L : \mathcal{S} \times \mathcal{A} \times \mathcal{S} \to \wp(\overline{Prop})$ is the labelling function, defined as in Definition 2;*

- – $\gamma \in [0,1]$ is a discount factor;
- – U, u^I, Σ, t, r are as in Definition 3, with $\Sigma = \wp(\overline{Prop})$;
- – If in states $s \in S$, $u \in U$, the agents perform an action $\mathbf{a}$ to move from s to s', then $u' = t(u, L(s, \mathbf{a}, s'))$ and the agents receive a reward $r(u, L(s, \mathbf{a}, s'))$.

The alphabet Σ is a *labelling* L of triples from $S \times A \times S$ by consistent sets of literals over $\overline{Prop}$. In this paper we focus on *postcondition labelling*, where $L(s, \mathbf{a}, s')$ is the set of literals made true in s' by executing $\mathbf{a}$ in s. As each agent $i \in Agt$ has a set of observable variables $Prop_i \subseteq Prop$, we define the set of observable events of agent i as $\Sigma_i := \wp(\overline{Prop_i}) \cap \Sigma$. Notice that Σ_i is defined as the powerset of the literals obtained by considering the propositions observable by i. Similarly, for a coalition $A \subseteq Agt$, we define $\Sigma_A := \bigcup_{i \in Agt} \Sigma_i$. We assume that $\Sigma_{Agt} = \Sigma$, i.e. the grand coalition is able to observe all events. For a given event $e \in \Sigma$ and a subset of events $\Sigma' \subseteq \Sigma$, we denote the restriction of e onto Σ' by $e \restriction \Sigma'$, where $e \restriction \Sigma' \subseteq e$ is the maximal subset[2] (with respect to inclusion) of e that is also in Σ'. This will be used to define the 'part of' the event e that is observable by a given subset of agents.

The (cooperative) multi-agent reinforcement learning problem [3,15] is to learn an optimal group policy $\pi^* : S \to \Delta(A)$ that maximises the expected discounted future reward from any joint state.

2.4 Alternating-Time Temporal Logic

Alternating-time Temporal Logic (ATL) [1] is a standard formalism for specifying the high-level behaviour of agents in multi-agent systems. In this section, we define the syntax and semantics of ATL with imperfect information. We need imperfect information because we cannot assume that the agents can observe all the effects of each other's actions, and it is important for decomposability that each agent bases its choice of actions only on what it can observe.

Let $Agt = \{i_1, \ldots, i_n\}$ be a set of n agents and $Prop$ denote a (finite) set of propositional symbols. Formulas of ATL are defined by the following syntax:

$$\phi, \psi ::= p \mid \neg\phi \mid \phi \vee \psi \mid \langle\!\langle A \rangle\!\rangle \bigcirc \phi \mid \langle\!\langle A \rangle\!\rangle \Box \phi \mid \langle\!\langle A \rangle\!\rangle \phi \,\mathcal{U}\, \psi$$

where $p \in Prop$ is a proposition and $A \subseteq Agt$. Here, $\langle\!\langle A \rangle\!\rangle \bigcirc \phi$ means that coalition A has a strategy to ensure that the next state satisfies ϕ, $\langle\!\langle A \rangle\!\rangle \Box \phi$ that A has a strategy to ensure that ϕ is always true, and $\langle\!\langle A \rangle\!\rangle \phi \,\mathcal{U}\, \psi$ that A has a strategy to ensure that ϕ holds until it eventually enforces ψ.

The models of ATL are concurrent game structures. Imperfect information is modelled by indistinguishability relations between states, one for each agent. The resulting concurrent game structures are called *"epistemic concurrent game structures"*.

---

[2] We assume that Σ' is a subset of events obtained by taking the powerset of a subset of propositional symbols $Prop' \subseteq Prop$. This is to ensure that $e \restriction \Sigma'$ is always well-defined as the unique maximal subevent of e in Σ'.

Definition 5. *An epistemic concurrent game structure (ECGS) is a tuple $M = \langle Agt, Q, Prop, v, (\sim_i | i \in Agt), Act, d, \delta \rangle$ where:*

- *Agt is a non-empty finite set of n agents;*
- *Q is a non-empty finite set of states;*
- *$Prop$ is a finite set of propositional symbols;*
- *$v : Prop \rightarrow \wp(Q)$ is a valuation which associates each proposition in $Prop$ with a subset of states where it is true;*
- *$\sim_i \subseteq Q \times Q$ for each $i \in Agt$ is an equivalence relation. For each state $q \in Q$, we denote with $[q]_i$ the equivalence class of q for $\sim_i$;*
- *Act is a non-empty finite set of actions;*
- *$d : Q \times Agt \rightarrow \wp(Act) \setminus \{\emptyset\}$ is a function which assigns to each $q \in Q$ a non-empty set of actions available to each agent $i \in Agt$, with the constraint that $q_1 \sim_i q_2$ implies that $d(q_1, i) = d(q_2, i)$. We denote joint actions by all agents in Agt available at q by $D(q) = d(q, i_1) \times \ldots \times d(q, i_n)$;*
- *$\delta : (q, \sigma) \mapsto Q$ is a function that gives for every $q \in Q$ and joint action $\sigma \in D(q)$ the state resulting from executing σ in q. We write $q \xrightarrow{\sigma} q'$ to abbreviate $\delta(q, \sigma) = q'$.*

Given an ECGS M, we denote the set of all infinite sequences of states (computations) by Q^ω. For a computation $\lambda = q_0 q_1 \ldots \in Q^\omega$, we use, for any natural $j \in \mathbb{N}$, the notation $\lambda[j]$ to denote the j-th state q_j in the computation λ. Given an ECGS M and a state $q \in Q$, a *joint action by a coalition* $A \subseteq Agt$ is a tuple $\sigma_A = (\sigma_i)_{i \in A}$ such that $\sigma_i \in d(q, i)$ for all $i \in A$. The set of all joint actions for A at state q is denoted by $D_A(q)$. Given a joint action by the grand coalition $\sigma \in D(q)$, σ_A denotes the joint action executed by A: $\sigma_A = (\sigma_i)_{i \in A}$. The set of all possible outcomes of a joint action $\sigma_A \in D_A(q)$ at state q is $out(q, \sigma_A) = \{q' \in Q \mid \exists \sigma' \in D(q) : \sigma_A = \sigma'_A \wedge q' = \delta(q, \sigma')\}$.

In our case, we specifically consider ECGSs in which each action $\mathfrak{a} \in Act$ has a set of (consistent) postconditions $post(\mathfrak{a}) \subseteq \overline{Prop}$ associated to. For any coalition $A \subseteq Agt$, we define $post(\sigma_A) := \bigcup_{i \in A} post(\sigma_i)$. The transition function δ is defined accordingly: $\delta(q, \sigma)$ leads to the state q' in which the propositional symbols of positive and negative literals from $post(\sigma)$ are, respectively, true and false, and $q' \in v(p) \iff q \in v(p)$ for all propositional symbols p without a literal in $post(\sigma)$. For joint actions σ such that $post(\sigma)$ is not consistent, δ is undefined.

Example 2. As an example, we provide an ECGS that abstracts the COOPERATIVEBUTTONS MAE. Obviously, $Agt = \{i_1, i_2, i_3\}$. We take $Q = 2^{Prop}$, where $Prop$ is the original set of propositional symbols from the COOPERATIVEBUTTONS domain, as given in Example 1, which also acts as the set of propositional symbols in the ECGS. v is the naturally induced valuation, i.e., $v(p) = \{q \in Q \mid p \in q\}$. For the equivalence (indistinguishability) relationships $\sim_i$ of agent i, we take the one naturally induced by the set of "observable" propositional symbols $Prop_i$ of agent i as described in Example 1. In other words, for any agent $i \in Agt$, two states q, q' are such that $q \sim_i q'$ if and only if $q \in v(p) \iff q' \in v(p)$ for all $p \in Prop_i$. The set of actions is $Act = \{\texttt{press\_yellow}, \texttt{press\_green}, \texttt{press\_red}, \texttt{to\_goal}, \texttt{nil}\}$, where $\texttt{nil}$ is the "null" action that can be executed by any agent in any state and leads to no consequence. The action $\texttt{press\_yellow}$ can be performed only by agent i_1, whenever Y_B is false. $\texttt{press\_green}$ can be performed only by agent i_2, whenever G_B and Y_B are, respectively, false and true. $\texttt{press\_red}$ can be performed by agents $i2$ and i_3: for the former, whenever Y_B is true, and, for the latter, whenever G_B is true. Finally, $\texttt{to\_goal}$ can be performed only by agent i_1, whenever R_B is true. As for the transition function δ, all valid joint actions have the "intuitive" set of postconditions, e.g., if agent i_1 performs the $\texttt{press\_yellow}$ action and i_2 and i_3 the $\texttt{nil}$ action, then the ECGS moves from state q to state q', where the only difference is that $q \notin v(Y_B)$ and $q' \in v(Y_B)$. The only action that requires "coordination" is $\texttt{press\_red}$, in the sense that δ is defined so that any joint action σ moves the ECGS to a state where R_B is true if and only if $\sigma_{i_2} = \sigma_{i_3} = \texttt{press\_red}$.

We would like to stress how the ECGS differs from the MAE in this example: as one can notice, the ECGS does not contain any information about the precise position of the agents in the environment, unlike the MAE. Moreover, the set of actions are completely different: the MAE's actions describe how the agents "*phisically*" move in the environment, whereas the ECGS's describe how the agents can press buttons or reach the goal. Due to this, having just a "strategy" to achieve the task in the ECGS does not suffice for the agents to be able to also achieve the task in the MAE: they need to learn how to move in the latter environment in order to do so. However, as we will later see, having a "*high-level strategy*" can aid them in learning how to act in the MAE.

Given an ECGS M, a *strategy for a coalition* $A \subseteq Agt$ is a mapping $F_A : Q \to Act^{|A|}$ such that, for every $q \in Q$, $F_A(q) \in D_A(q)$. A computation $\lambda \in Q^\omega$ is consistent with a strategy F_A iff, for all $j \geq 0$, $\lambda[j+1] \in out(\lambda[j], F_A(\lambda[j]))$. We denote by $out(q, F_A)$ the set of all consistent computations λ of F_A that start from q. Some strategies are unrealistic in that they require agents to select different actions in two states that they cannot distinguish. For this reason, the strategies are usually restricted to being uniform:

Definition 6 (Uniform strategy). *A strategy for agent i, F_i, is* uniform *if and only if it specifies the same choices for indistinguishable situations: if $q \sim_i q'$ then $F_i(q) = F_i(q')$. A strategy for a coalition A is* uniform *if and only if it is uniform for each $i \in A$.*

Strong uniformity requires, in addition, that in order for a formula of the form $\langle\!\langle A \rangle\!\rangle \varphi$ to be true in a state q, the same uniform strategy by A should ensure φ from all the states indistinguishable from q by A, i.e., all $q' \in [q]_A$, where $[q]_A$ is the equivalence class of q for $\sim_A := \bigcap_{i \in A} \sim_i$.

Given an ECGS M, a state q of M, the truth of an ATL formula φ with respect to M and q is defined inductively on the structure of φ as follows:

- $M, q \models p$ iff $q \in v(p)$;
- $M, q \models \neg\phi$ iff $M, q \not\models \phi$;

– $M, q \models \phi \vee \psi$ iff $M, q \models \phi$ or $M, q \models \psi$;
– $M, q \models \langle\langle A \rangle\rangle \bigcirc \phi$ iff there exists a uniform strategy F_A such that for all $q' \sim_A q$, for all $\lambda \in out(q', F_A)$: $M, \lambda[1] \models \phi$;
– $M, q \models \langle\langle A \rangle\rangle \square \phi$ iff there exists a uniform strategy F_A such that for all $q' \sim_A q$, for all $\lambda \in out(q', F_A)$ and $j \geq 0$: $M, \lambda[j] \models \phi$;
– $M, q \models \langle\langle A \rangle\rangle \phi \mathcal{U} \psi$ iff there exists a uniform strategy F_A such that for all $q' \sim_A q$, for all $\lambda \in out(q', F_A)$, $\exists j \geq 0$: $M, \lambda[j] \models \psi$ and $M, \lambda[k] \models \phi$ for all $k \in \{0, \ldots, j-1\}$.

Finally, we define a *witness* for a coalitional modality formula (see e.g., [11]). If a formula of the form $\langle\langle A \rangle\rangle \varphi$ is true in a state q, there is a strategy F_A such that all paths generated by this strategy satisfy φ. A *witness* $W(q, F_A)$ for the truth of $\langle\langle A \rangle\rangle \varphi$ in q is a finite tree rooted in q that is generated by executing F_A. For φ of the form $\bigcirc \phi$, the tree is cut off at the first "step", meaning that only states satisfying ϕ and that can be reached from the initial state in one transition are considered. For φ of the form $\phi \mathcal{U} \psi$, the tree is cut off at the states satisfying ψ. For φ of the form $\square \phi$, the tree is cut off at the first repeating state encountered on the branch (intuitively, it represents cyclic paths satisfying ϕ).

We specify tasks for for agent teams using ATL formulas. Hence, in our approach, the ECGS will be the "high-level environment" which abstracts the low-level MAE in which the agents act. For example, the task from the Buttons domain can be specified as $\langle\langle Agt \rangle\rangle \top \mathcal{U}$ *Goal*: this formula is true if the grand coalition *Agt* has a strategy to reach the goal. The ATL formula plays a role similar to that of a planning goal in the synthesis of single-agent reward machines in [9]. However, the use of ATL means we can specify more flexible properties: for example, that *Agt* can bring about ψ while maintaining ϕ, or that *Agt* can maintain some property forever ϕ, etc. We can also talk about abilities of $A \subset Agt$ allowing for, e.g., the presence of opponent coalitions. Nevertheless, in this work we focus on the case in which $A = Agt$, leaving the treatment of a non-fully-cooperative setting to future research. As we always assume that $A = Agt$, we will write just A to refer to the grand coalition.

3   Synthesising MGRMs

In this section, we show how, given an ECGS M, an initial state q of such ECGS, and an ATL formula $\langle\langle A \rangle\rangle \varphi$ specifying a team task, we can synthesise a MGRM from a witness $W(q, F_A)$, where F_A is a strategy for coalition A to enforce φ (if there exists any).

In Fig. 2, we provide a high-level overview of the objects that are used in our approach and how they are related to each other. The MAE and individual agents' environments (represented by Markov Decision Processes), the ECGS and the ATL formula are all given in input, whereas the rest is computed in our approach. We would like to stress the fact that the dynamics of the low-level environments are hidden to the agents, which means that it is not possible for them to compute a policy to perform the task by only having a witness of a high-level strategy for it.

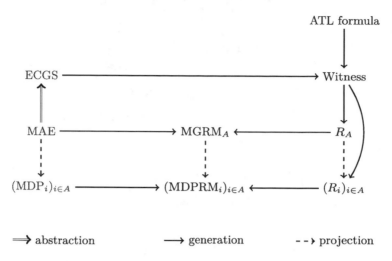

Fig. 2. High-level overview and relationship between the objects used in our approach. Objects in blue can be reused in other tasks.

3.1   Synthesising Reward Machines

Fix an ECGS $M = \langle Agt, Q, Prop, v, (\sim_i | \ i \in Agt), Act, d, \delta \rangle$ with some initial state $q \in Q$ and an ATL formula $\langle\langle A \rangle\rangle\varphi$. We can use an ATL model checker to synthesise a uniform strategy F_A to achieve the task encoded by the ATL formula $\langle\langle A \rangle\rangle\varphi$. For example, Fig. 3 shows a uniform strategy synthesised by the MCMAS model checker [11] for the COOPERATIVEBUTTONS task. From a uniform strategy F_A to achieve $\langle\langle A \rangle\rangle\varphi$ and some initial ECGS state q, we can generate a witness $W(q, F_A)$ for F_A in time polynomial in M and $\langle\langle A \rangle\rangle\varphi$. Then, from the witness, we can synthesise both the coalitional RM R_A and each of the individual RMs R_i, for each agent $i \in A$.

Notice that the witness and the reward machine derived from it are defined in terms of the (high-level) actions of M and are not directly executable in the MAE E or in the individual agents' environments. However, the synthesised RM can be used to guide an agent in learning which low-level actions in E should be performed to accomplish each step in the RM.

Intuitively, for a sub-coalition $B \subseteq A$, states of R_B are equivalence classes of nodes in the witness, plus an extra "error" state. Edge labels (ECGS actions) in the witness are replaced with events corresponding to postconditions of those actions. The reward machines for $\langle\langle A \rangle\rangle\phi \mathcal{U} \psi$ and $\langle\langle A \rangle\rangle\Box\phi$ transit to the error state on events corresponding to a violation of ϕ (we assume that $\neg\phi$ is always observable by A). The error state has a self-loop and no transitions to other states of the reward machine. Finally, the state corresponding to the second last state of the witness for $\langle\langle A \rangle\rangle\phi \mathcal{U} \psi$ transits to the error state only on events that *both* violate ϕ *and* are not postconditions of the last action in the witness (do not achieve ψ).

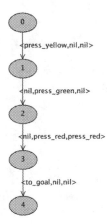

Fig. 3. Strategy for the CooperativeButtons domain. To obtain the corresponding coalition RM, it suffices to modify the action labels with their corresponding postconditions and give 1 as a reward on the transition from state 3 to 4 and 0 on all other transitions.

Reward Machine Synthesis. Given the ECGS $M = \langle Agt, Q, Prop, v, (\sim_i \mid I \in Agt), Act\ d, \delta \rangle$ and a witness $W(q, F_A)$, we construct a reward machine $R_B = \langle U_B, u_B^I, \Sigma_B, t_B, r_B \rangle$ for $B \subseteq A$ as follows:

- $U_B = Q(W(q, F_A))/\sim_B \cup \{u_{err}\}$ is the set of equivalence classes of states in $W(q, F_A)$ with respect to the indistinguishability relation of B, plus u_{err};
- $u_B^I = [q]_B$;
- Σ_B is defined as usual. If $\langle\langle A \rangle\rangle \varphi$ is of the form $\langle\langle A \rangle\rangle \Box \phi$ or $\langle\langle A \rangle\rangle \phi \mathcal{U} \psi$, then we also add the event $\neg \phi$ to Σ_B;
- $t_B(u, e) = u'$ iff there are q_1, q_2 in the set of nodes of $W(q, F_A)$ such that $u = [q_1]_B$ and $u' = [q_2]_B$, with q_1 connected to q_2 through an edge labelled with $F_A(q_1)$, and there is a joint action $\sigma \in D(q_1)$ with $q_1 \xrightarrow{\sigma} q_2$, $\sigma_A = F_A(q_1)$ and such that $e = post(\sigma) \upharpoonright \Sigma_B$. If $\langle\langle A \rangle\rangle \varphi = \Box \phi$ or $\langle\langle A \rangle\rangle \varphi = \langle\langle A \rangle\rangle \phi \mathcal{U} \psi$ and $\neg \phi \in e$, then $u' = u_{err}$ unless $e = post(\sigma) \upharpoonright \Sigma_B$ for an action σ leading to a final state q^f in $W(q, F_A)$. In the latter case the RM transitions to $u' = [q^f]$ in the witness $W(q, F_A)$ (as ϕ needs to hold only strictly before ψ holds);
- For the definition of r_B, there are three different cases:
    1. $r_B(u, e) = 1$ iff $\langle\langle A \rangle\rangle \varphi = \langle\langle A \rangle\rangle \bigcirc \phi$, $u = [q]$, and $e = post(F_A(q)) \upharpoonright \Sigma_B$, or $\langle\langle A \rangle\rangle \varphi = \langle\langle A \rangle\rangle \phi \mathcal{U} \psi$ and $e = post(\sigma) \upharpoonright \Sigma_B$ for an action σ leading to a final state q^f in $W(q, F_A)$.
    2. $r_B(u, e) = -1$ iff $\langle\langle A \rangle\rangle \varphi = \langle\langle A \rangle\rangle \Box \phi$, $u \neq u_{err}$ and $\neg \phi \in e$;
    3. For all other (u, e), $r_B(u, e) = 0$.

3.2   Correctness of the Approach

We now show that the RMs generated by our approach are "correct" decompositions in the sense of [12]. In [12] it is shown that the reward the individual

RMs grant to the agents is always equal to the reward the coalition RM would have granted them. Moreover, it is shown how the probabilities that each agent achieves its subtask bound the probability that the whole coalition achieves the team task. In this Subsection we replicate these results for our approach.

Let A be a coalition of agents, F_A a strategy for the coalition and q the initial state of the ECGS. We define the set of *compatible event sequences* $\Xi_{F_A,s}$ for strategy F_A and initial state q as the set of event sequences that is observed by coalition A while following strategy F_A, i.e. $\Xi_{F_A,q} := \{\xi \mid \exists\lambda \in out(q, F_A) \forall j \in \mathbb{N} \exists\sigma \in D(\lambda[j]) : \sigma_A = F_A(\lambda[j]) \wedge \xi[j] = post(\sigma) \upharpoonright \Sigma_A\}$.

Theorem 1. *Fix a strategy F_A for the coalition of agents $A = \{i_1, \ldots, i_n\}$ and an initial state q. Let $R_A = \langle U_A, u_A^I, \Sigma_A, t_A, r_A\rangle$ be the coalition RM and $R_\otimes = \langle U_\otimes, u_\otimes^I, \Sigma_\otimes, t_\otimes, r_\otimes\rangle$ be the product RM $R_{i_1} \otimes \ldots \otimes R_{i_n}$. Given a compatible event sequence $\xi \in \Xi_{F_A,q}$, then for any step $j \in |\xi|$ we have that $r_A(u_A^j, \xi[j]) = r_\otimes(g(u^j), \xi[j])$, where $u^j = (u_{i_1}^j, \ldots, u_{i_n}^j)$ is the j-th state reached by the product RM following the event sequence ξ, and $g((u_{i_1}, \ldots, u_{i_n})) := \bigcap_{i \in A} u_i$ for any $(u_{i_1}, \ldots, u_{i_n}) \in U_{i_1} \times \cdots \times U_{i_n}$, with U_{i_j} being the set of states of R_{i_j}.*

Proof Sketch. The claim is proven by showing that g is a homomorphism, with respect to the transition and reward functions, from the set of states of the product RM (the parallelization of all the individual RMs) to that of the coalition RM. This can be done via an induction on the length of the input sequence.

To conclude, we state a theorem relating the expected undiscounted future rewards obtained by a coalition to the ones obtained by the agents in such coalition. Consider a coalition $A = \{i_1, \ldots, i_n\}$, a witness $W(q, F_A)$ for some state q of an ECGS and a strategy F_A for some formula $\langle\!\langle A\rangle\!\rangle\varphi$, a joint state s of a MAE and an arbitrary joint policy $\pi = (\pi_1, \ldots, \pi_n)$ for the same MAE. For the coalition RM R_A built from $W(q, F_A)$, we denote by $V_A^\pi(s)$ the sum of expected undiscounted future rewards produced by R_A, given all agents follow their policy as specified by π from the MGRM state s and the initial state u_A^I of R_A. Analogously, for the individual RM R_{i_j} built from the same witness $W(q, F_A)$, we denote by $V_{i_j}^\pi(s)$ the sum of expected undiscounted future rewards produced by R_{i_j} under the same assumptions. Moreover, recall that if $\langle\!\langle A\rangle\!\rangle\varphi$ is of the form $\langle\!\langle A\rangle\!\rangle\bigcirc\phi$ or $\langle\!\langle A\rangle\!\rangle\phi\,\mathcal{U}\,\psi$, then any RM generated from a witness for a strategy for the formula can give a reward of only 0 or 1. Similarly, any RM for a formula of the form $\langle\!\langle A\rangle\!\rangle\Box\phi$ can give a reward of only 0 or -1.

Theorem 2. *If $\langle\!\langle A\rangle\!\rangle\varphi$ is of the form $\langle\!\langle A\rangle\!\rangle\bigcirc\phi$ or $\langle\!\langle A\rangle\!\rangle\phi\,\mathcal{U}\,\psi$, then*

$$\max\{0, V_{i_1}^\pi(s) + \ldots + V_{i_n}^\pi(s) - (n-1)\} \leq V_A^\pi(s) \leq \min\{V_{i_1}^\pi(s), \ldots, V_{i_n}^\pi(s)\}$$

If $\langle\!\langle A\rangle\!\rangle\varphi$ is of the form $\langle\!\langle A\rangle\!\rangle\Box\phi$, then

$$\max\{-V_{i_1}^\pi(s), \ldots, -V_{i_n}^\pi(s)\} \leq -V_A^\pi(s) \leq \min\{1, -V_{i_1}^\pi(s) - \ldots - V_{i_n}^\pi(s)\}.$$

Proof Sketch. Observe that $V_A^\pi(s)$ and $V_{i_j}^\pi(s)$ are, respectively, the probabilities that coalition A and agent i_j complete, if $\langle\langle A \rangle\rangle\varphi$ is of the form $\langle\langle A \rangle\rangle \bigcirc \phi$ or $\langle\langle A \rangle\rangle\phi \mathcal{U}\psi$, or fail, if $\langle\langle A \rangle\rangle\varphi$ is of the form $\langle\langle A \rangle\rangle\Box\phi$, their (sub)task. Since A completes the task if and only if all its agents complete their task, and fails the task if and only if some of its agents fail theirs, the claim follows by applying the Fréchet inequalities for logical conjunctions and disjunctions.

Theorem 2 bounds the probability that a coalition completes or fails (depending on the formula) a task, assuming all agents follow the policy specified by π. For formulas of the form $\langle\langle A \rangle\rangle \bigcirc \phi$ or $\langle\langle A \rangle\rangle\phi \mathcal{U}\psi$, if all agents $i \in A$ are able to (eventually) complete their subtask, then coalition A is able to (eventually) complete the team task: for all agents $V_{i_j}^\pi(s) = 1$, then $\max\{0, V_{i_1}^\pi(s) + \ldots + V_{i_n}^\pi(s) - (n-1)\} = 1$, and so $V_A^\pi(s) = 1$. Similarly, for formulas of the form $\langle\langle A \rangle\rangle\Box\phi$, if agent i_j violates ϕ, then the coalition will violate ϕ: $-V_{i_j}^\pi(s) = 1$, then $\max\{-V_{i_1}^\pi(s), \ldots, -V_{i_n}^\pi(s)\} = 1$, and so $V_A^\pi(s) = -1$. When $\gamma = 1$, optimality of individual policies implies optimality of the joint policy. Note this does not imply the same holds when $\gamma < 1$, thus we leave this case to future research.

4   Evaluation

In this section we present an evaluation of the automatically synthesised reward machines. Specifically, we show how strategies for team goals generated by the model checker MCMAS [11] can be used to produce an RM for each agent in a team of agents, and present results from the two benchmarks from [12], COOPER-ATIVEBUTTONS and 10-Agent RENDEZVOUS[3]. The RENDEZVOUS environment is a 10×10 gridworld in which the agents first have to rendezvous at a common location, and then each agent has to reach its individual goal location.

We compare the performance of DQPRM when using our automatically synthesised RMs and the RMs from [12] in both the COOPERATIVEBUTTONS and RENDEZVOUS environments. We used the same experimental setup as in [12] for these two tasks. In both the COOPERATIVEBUTTONS and RENDEZVOUS environments, if an agent, during its individual training, observes an event that can also be observed by another agent, it is provided with a signal that simulates successful synchronisation with probability 0.3. This is needed to "simulate" the behaviour of other agents during the individual training. For action selection, agents use softmax exploration with a constant temperature of $\tau = 0.2$. The discount factor is $\gamma = 0.9$ and the learning rate $\alpha = 0.8$. For both tasks each experiment consists of 10 episodes: for COOPERATIVEBUTTONS each episode consists of 250000 training steps, while for RENDEZVOUS 150000 training steps. For both tasks a test is run every 1000 training steps to evaluate the agents, with every test running for at most 1000 steps (after which the test is ended and the task is considered failed). Performance is measured as the number of steps necessary to complete the task. For both plots, lines represent median performance, whereas the shaded areas the 25th and 75th percentiles.

---

[3] Code is available at github.com/giovannivarr/SynthesisingRMsMARL.

The results are shown in Fig. 4. As can be seen, agents trained with our automatically generated RMs converge faster than those trained with the hand-crafted ones from [12]. We believe this might be due to the fact that in both tasks the generated RMs have less states than the hand-crafted ones. Though we do not have any formal results about this, we also think this is a side effect of synthesising RMs against defining them by hand, as in the latter case one could include information that might turn out to be superfluous to complete the final task. It might also be the case that one does not include enough information, hence obtaining an RM that is not informative enough to the agent to achieve the task. Regardless, the experimental evaluation suggests that, at least for these scenarios, automated synthesis generates RMs that successfully encode the task.

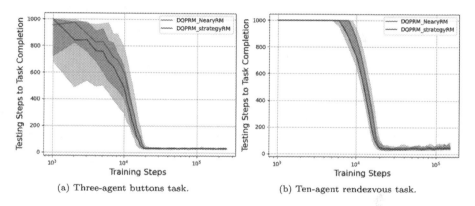

(a) Three-agent buttons task.   (b) Ten-agent rendezvous task.

Fig. 4. COOPERATIVEBUTTONS and RENDEZVOUS [12]. The x-axis shows the number of elapsed training steps (in a logarithmic scale). The y-axis the number of steps required for the learned policies to complete the task – note that the agents have a maximum limit of 1000 steps to complete the task, after which the test is considered "failed".

5   Related Works

There is a large literature on the problem of non-stationarity in MARL [7,8,14, 22]. Some approaches address the problem by training each agent individually. For example, in IQL [16], each agent learns a policy by treating other agents as part of the environment. Others, e.g., [6,21], adopt a hierarchical approach, where a task is decomposed so that agents learn how to cooperate only at the highest level of the hierarchy. This seems to be more efficient than learning how to cooperate in the low-level environment. In a sense, we also employ a hierarchical approach, but in our case there is no need for the agents to *learn* how to cooperate at the high level because the policy learnt using their RM ensures coordination.

An approach employing high-level planning for formally specified single-agent RL tasks was proposed in [10]. First, low-level policies for a set of subtasks are trained, and then high-level planning is used to identify the sequence of subtasks which maximizes the probability of achieving the task, as described by a formal specification, given the current policies. Our work differs from [10] as we consider a multi-agent setting and use a different specification language.

Reward machines were introduced in [18] as a way of improving the sample efficiency of reinforcement learning by providing an RL agent with a high-level abstract description of its task and environment. There have been several proposals for the automated generation of RMs. For example, in [19,20] an RM is learned by an agent through experience in the environment. Closer to our work is [4], where an RM for a single agent is generated using LTL and other logics that are equivalent to regular languages, and [9] where a single-agent RM is generated from a sequential or a partial order plan. However, to the best of our knowledge, our approach is the first to synthesise individual RMs in a multi-agent setting.

6   Conclusions and Future Work

We have given a procedure to synthesise team reward machines for a cooperative MARL task from a given ATL specification. As in [12], the team RM is then decomposed in individual RMs, one per agent in the team, that are used to train such agents individually. We have provided theoretical bounds on the probability of the team completing the task after its agents are trained individually, similarly to what was done in [12]. Empirically, we have shown that the performance we obtain by using our synthesised RMs is broadly similar to that obtained by using hand-crafted ones from [12].

One direction for future work would be to investigate whether the use of multiple or "partially-ordered" strategies improves performance in the multi-agent setting. The RMs we construct are based on witnesses. Essentially, they correspond to sequential plans, each of them representing a single strategy. However, in [9] it was shown that, for single-agent RL, using partial order plans to construct RMs improves performance. In our approach, this would translate to having a witness that, instead of representing a single strategy, shows all possible strategies to achieve the task. In truth, this can already be done in the current version of MCMAS. While this approach can be easily implemented in a single-agent setting, it is not as trivial in a multi-agent one due to various reasons, e.g., it would require the agents to communicate to decide which plan to follow.

Another future direction would be to investigate non-cooperative RL scenarios. In these cases, ATL could be easily employed to produce a strategy for the coalition of agents we are interested in. MCMAS, the model checker we used in this work, is able to generate witnesses for such settings. To the best of our knowledge, this would also be a novelty in the reward machines literature, as RMs have never been employed in a non-cooperative multi-agent setting.

Finally, one could consider to enrich the specification language to ATL*. This would enable even more flexible specification of tasks and generation of strategies for several temporal formulas simultaneously.

References

1. Alur, R., Henzinger, T.A., Kupferman, O.: Alternating-time temporal logic. J. ACM **49**(5), 672–713 (2002)
2. Boutilier, C.: Planning, learning and coordination in multiagent decision processes. In: Proceedings of the 6th Conference on Theoretical Aspects of Rationality and Knowledge, pp. 195–210. Morgan Kaufmann Publishers Inc. (1996)
3. Buşoniu, L., Babuška, R., De Schutter, B.: Multi-agent reinforcement learning: an overview. In: Srinivasan, D., Jain, L.C. (eds.) Innovations in Multi-Agent Systems and Applications - 1. Studies in Computational Intelligence, vol. 310, pp. 183–221. Springer, Heidelberg (2010). https://doi.org/10.1007/978-3-642-14435-6_7
4. Camacho, A., Toro Icarte, R., Klassen, T.Q., Valenzano, R., McIlraith, S.A.: LTL and beyond: formal languages for reward function specification in reinforcement learning. In: Proceedings of the 28th International Joint Conference on Artificial Intelligence, IJCAI-19, pp. 6065–6073. IJAI (2019)
5. Camacho, A., Toro Icarte, R., Klassen, T.Q., Valenzano, R., McIlraith, S.A.: LTL and beyond:formal languages for reward function specification in reinforcement learning. In: Proceedings of the Twenty-Eighth International Joint Conference on Artificial Intelligence, IJCAI-19, pp. 6065–6073. International Joint Conferences on Artificial Intelligence Organization (2019). https://doi.org/10.24963/ijcai.2019/840
6. Ghavamzadeh, M., Mahadevan, S., Makar, R.: Hierarchical multi-agent reinforcement learning. Auton. Agent. Multi-Agent Syst. **13**(2), 197–229 (2006)
7. Hernandez-Leal, P., Kaisers, M., Baarslag, T., de Cote, E.M.: A survey of learning in multiagent environments: dealing with non-stationarity (2019)
8. Hernandez-Leal, P., Kartal, B., Taylor, M.E.: A survey and critique of multiagent deep reinforcement learning. Auton. Agent. Multi-Agent Syst. **33**(6), 750–797 (2019)
9. Illanes, L., Yan, X., Toro Icarte, R., McIlraith, S.A.: Symbolic plans as high-level instructions for reinforcement learning. In: Beck, J.C., Buffet, O., Hoffmann, J., Karpas, E., Sohrabi, S. (eds.) Proceedings of the Thirtieth International Conference on Automated Planning and Scheduling (ICAPS 2020), pp. 540–550. AAAI Press (2020). www.ojs.aaai.org/index.php/ICAPS/article/view/6750
10. Jothimurugan, K., Bansal, S., Bastani, O., Alur, R.: Compositional reinforcement learning from logical specifications. In: Ranzato, M., Beygelzimer, A., Dauphin, Y., Liang, P., Vaughan, J.W. (eds.) Advances in Neural Information Processing Systems, vol. 34, pp. 10026–10039. Curran Associates, Inc. (2021). www.proceedings.neurips.cc/paper_files/paper/2021/file/531db99cb00833bcd414459069dc7387-Paper.pdf
11. Lomuscio, A., Qu, H., Raimondi, F.: MCMAS: an open-source model checker for the verification of multi-agent systems. Int. J. Softw. Tools Technol. Transfer **19**(1), 9–30 (2017)
12. Neary, C., Xu, Z., Wu, B., Topcu, U.: Reward machines for cooperative multiagent reinforcement learning. In: Proceedings of the 20th International Conference on Autonomous Agents and MultiAgent Systems (AAMAS 2021), pp. 934–942. ACM (2021)
13. Panait, L., Luke, S.: Cooperative multi-agent learning: the state of the art. Auton. Agent. Multi-Agent Syst. **11**(3), 387–434 (2005)
14. Silva, F.L.D., Taylor, M.E., Costa, A.H.R.: Autonomously reusing knowledge in multiagent reinforcement learning. In: Proceedings of the 27th International Joint

Conference on Artificial Intelligence, IJCAI-18, pp. 5487–5493. International Joint Conferences on Artificial Intelligence Organization (2018)

15. Sutton, R.S., Barto, A.G.: Reinforcement Learning: An Introduction. MIT press, Cambridge (2018)

16. Tan, M.: Multi-agent reinforcement learning: independent vs. cooperative agents. In: In Proceeedings of the 10th International Conference on Machine Learning, pp. 330–337 (1993)

17. Tang, H., et al.: Hierarchical deep multiagent reinforcement learning with temporal abstraction (2019)

18. Toro Icarte, R., Klassen, T.Q., Valenzano, R., McIlraith, S.A.: Reward machines: exploiting reward function structure in reinforcement learning. J. Artif. Intell. Res. **73**, 173–208 (2022)

19. Toro Icarte, R., Waldie, E., Klassen, T.Q., Valenzano, R.A., Castro, M.P., McIlraith, S.A.: Learning reward machines for partially observable reinforcement learning. In: Advances in Neural Information Processing Systems 32: Annual Conference on Neural Information Processing Systems 2019, pp. 15497–15508 (2019)

20. Xu, Z., et al.: Joint inference of reward machines and policies for reinforcement learning. In: Proceedings of the International Conference on Automated Planning and Scheduling, vol. 30, pp. 590–598 (2020)

21. Yang, J., Borovikov, I., Zha, H.: Hierarchical cooperative multi-agent reinforcement learning with skill discovery. In: Proceedings of the 19th International Conference on Autonomous Agents and MultiAgent Systems, pp. 1566–1574. International Foundation for Autonomous Agents and Multiagent Systems (2020)

22. Zhang, K., Yang, Z., Başar, T.: Multi-agent reinforcement learning: a selective overview of theories and algorithms. In: Vamvoudakis, K.G., Wan, Y., Lewis, F.L., Cansever, D. (eds.) Handbook of Reinforcement Learning and Control. SSDC, vol. 325, pp. 321–384. Springer, Cham (2021). https://doi.org/10.1007/978-3-030-60990-0_12

Adaptive Cognitive Agents: Updating Action Descriptions and Plans

Peter Stringer[1]([⊠]) [iD], Rafael C. Cardoso[2] [iD], Clare Dixon[1] [iD], Michael Fisher[1] [iD], and Louise A. Dennis[1] [iD]

[1] The University of Manchester, Manchester, UK
{peter.stringer,clare.dixon,michael.fisher,
louise.dennis}@manchester.ac.uk
[2] University of Aberdeen, Aberdeen, UK
rafael.cardoso@abdn.ac.uk

Abstract. In this paper we present an extension of Belief-Desire-Intention agents which can adapt their performance in response to changes in their environment. We consider situations in which the agent's actions no longer perform as anticipated. Our agents maintain explicit descriptions of the expected behaviour of their actions, are able to track action performance, learn new action descriptions and patch affected plans at runtime. Our main contributions are the underlying theoretical mechanisms for data collection about action performance, the synthesis of new action descriptions from this data and the integration with plan reconfiguration. The mechanisms are supported by a practical implementation to validate the approach.

Keywords: Beliefs-Desires-Intentions · Action Descriptions · AI Planning

1 Introduction

Long-term autonomy requires autonomous systems to adapt once their capabilities no longer perform as expected. To achieve this, a system must first be capable of detecting such changes and then adapting its internal reasoning processes to accommodate these. For example, deploying an autonomous robot into a dynamic environment can result in actions becoming unreliable over time, as the environment changes, producing unexpected outcomes that were unforeseeable before runtime. The autonomous agent must be capable of observing these changes and adapting accordingly.

Cognitive agents [6,29,35] have explicit reasons for the choices they make. These are often described in terms of the agent's *beliefs* and *goals*, which in turn determine the agent's *intentions*. This view of cognitive agents is encapsulated within the Belief-Desire-Intention (BDI) model [28,29]. Here, *beliefs* represent the agent's (possibly incomplete, possibly incorrect) information about itself, other agents, and its environment, *desires* represent the agent's long-term goals,

© The Author(s), under exclusive license to Springer Nature Switzerland AG 2023
V. Malvone and A. Murano (Eds.): EUMAS 2023, LNAI 14282, pp. 345–362, 2023.
https://doi.org/10.1007/978-3-031-43264-4_22

while *intentions* represent the goals that the agent is actively pursuing (the representation of intentions often includes partially instantiated and/or executed plans and so combines the goal with its intended means).

Our work focuses on cognitive agents programmed in a Belief-Desire-Intention (BDI) [30] programming language providing high-level decision making in an autonomous system, as outlined in [15]. Programs written in these languages use *plans* created in advance by a programmer to select *actions* to execute in the environment. These plans make implicit assumptions about the behaviour of the actions they execute. Therefore, in this context, the challenge becomes to make these assumptions explicit, detect when they no longer hold, and then modify the plans accordingly. Most agent programming languages commonly used for high-level control of autonomous robots, do not support the adaptation of agent programs at runtime to deal with changes in their environment.

Some of these languages use *action descriptions* (sometimes referred to as *capabilities* in the literature), which consist of explicit pre- and post-conditions for all known actions. An action's pre-conditions are the environment conditions which should hold if an action is to execute correctly, whilst post-conditions are the expected changes in the environment made as a direct result of the completed action. We assume the existence of these action descriptions. We also assume that the cognitive agent is able to determine: when an action has finished executing; and whether it has met its post-conditions when it does so. These assumptions allow the system to maintain logs of action performance which can then be mined to detect patterns of failure. Although not all BDI systems can represent action descriptions, some do, and so mechanisms and semantics used for such functionality are discussed in [12,23,33].

Once a failure pattern is detected, we use synthesis methods to update its action description to reflect its actual behaviour. We can then repair or replace actions in any existing plans by using an automated planner to construct patches.

Running Example. Consider an agent navigating around a space to visit some set of waypoints (where, for instance, it needs to perform some kind of inspection tasks). Examples of this kind are common (see [19,27]). We assume the agent has a predetermined route to traverse the waypoints—for instance that the robot should visit waypoint 0, then 1, then 2, then 3 before returning to 0. It also has actions that encode movement between waypoints (e.g., `move(0, 1)` moves the robot from point 0 to point 1). As well as the specific actions needed for the predetermined route, the agent is also aware that it can move between the other waypoints (for instance that it can move from point 0, directly to point 3, `move(0, 3)` and from point 3 to point 1, `move(3, 1)`). If, over time, the route between points 0 and 1 becomes obstructed, we would like the robot to reason that it can replace the instruction to move from 0 to 1 directly, in its plan, with an instruction to move from 0 to 3, and then from 3 to 1.

Our contribution, in this work, is a methodology to detect faulty actions, modify their descriptions and reconfigure BDI plans based on these new descriptions, enabling long term autonomy. Our work applies in general to BDI programming languages which allow action descriptions. We have implemented the methodology in the GWENDOLEN programming language as a prototype to exemplify the approach.

2   Background and Related Work

GWENDOLEN is a BDI programming language that contains a number of features for integrating with autonomous and robotic systems. One of its main distinctive features is that GWENDOLEN agents can be verified using a program model-checker, Agent Java Pathfinder (AJPF) [16]. A full operational semantics for GWENDOLEN is presented in [13]. Its key components are, for each agent, a set of beliefs that are ground first-order formulae and a set of intentions that are stacks of *deeds* associated with some event. Deeds can be the addition or deletion of beliefs, the adoption of new goals, and the execution of primitive actions. A GWENDOLEN agent may have several concurrent intentions and will, by default, execute the first deed on each intention stack in turn. GWENDOLEN is event-driven and events include the acquisition of new beliefs (typically via perception), messages and goals. A programmer supplies plans that describe how an agent should react to events by extending the deed stack of the relevant intention. These plans contain actions for execution.

Plans are of the form `event : guard <- deeds`, where the event is the addition or deletion of a belief or goal, the guard is a term that is evaluated against the agent's belief set and the deeds are transformed into an intention stack if the event occurs and the guard evaluates to true.

If implemented in GWENDOLEN, our example of a robot travelling between waypoints can be represented with the four plans shown in Fig. 1. We use standard BDI syntax in which ! represents a goal and + denotes the addition of this goal. The first of these plans states that if a new goal to be at waypoint 1 has been added (`+!at(1)`) and the agent currently believes it is at waypoint 0 (`B at(0)`) then the agent should move to waypoint 1 (`move(0, 1)`) and adopt the goal to be at waypoint 2 (`+!at(2)`) to continue its patrol route. For example, if the robot starts at waypoint 0 and is sent a goal to reach waypoint 1, then these four plans will keep the robot patrolling around all four waypoints autonomously.

```
+!at(1): {B at(0)} <- move(0, 1), +!at(2);
+!at(2): {B at(1)} <- move(1, 2), +!at(3);
+!at(3): {B at(2)} <- move(2, 3), +!at(0);
+!at(0): {B at(3)} <- move(3, 0), +!at(1);
```

Fig. 1. Four GWENDOLEN plans for a patrolling robot.

While all BDI languages have individual features, they have many similarities. In particular the use of plans (sometimes called *rules*) which have guards controlling when they apply and then execute some sequence of actions, belief updates and goal updates is common to many such languages (e.g., *Jason* [3] and GOAL [23]).

Some BDI languages also employ *action descriptions* (sometimes referred to as *capabilities*) which have their roots in AI planning and STRIPS operators [18].

Definition 1 (Action Description). *We assume a language $\mathcal{L}$ of first-order terms. Action descriptions are a triple $\{Pre\}A\{Post\}$ where A is a term in $\mathcal{L}$ representing an action, $\{Pre\}$ is a set of terms representing the action's pre-conditions and $\{Post\}$ is a set of expressions of the form $+t$ or $-t$ (where t is a term in $\mathcal{L}$). Note: $+t$ means that the term t should be added to the agent's belief base following execution of the action and $-t$ means that the term t should be removed from the agent's belief base.*

Returning to our example, the action description $\{at(0)\}move(0,1)$ $\{-at(0), +at(1)\}$ can be associated with the agent action move(0, 1). This has the pre-condition, $\{at(0)\}$ (the agent is at waypoint 0), and post-conditions $\{-at(0), +at(1)\}$ (the belief that the agent is at waypoint 0 should be removed and the belief that the agent is at waypoint 1 should be added).

In many languages, actions descriptions are used both to control whether an action is executed if it appears in a plan (by checking the action's pre-conditions) and to directly manipulate the agent's belief base using the post-conditions without using perception to check whether the action has completed successfully and established these post-conditions. In some cases it is implicitly assumed that the low-level action execution process checks post-conditions and so a success signal is not sent to the agent unless the post-conditions have been achieved.

Action descriptions/capabilities exist in, among others, the GOAL [24] language and 2APL [11]. A version of GWENDOLEN also exists that contains an implementation of action descriptions [33].

GWENDOLEN does not use its action descriptions to control action execution or to update its belief base. Instead it uses the descriptions to make inferences about action success or failure by comparing the state of the world after an action execution completes with the state of the world described in the post-conditions. This allows the agent to react to action failure as well as, more generally, to plan failure. GWENDOLEN also tracks the performance of actions over time in an *action log*. An example of an action log using the move(0, 1) action is shown in Fig. 2. This shows a log with two entries. Each entry contains the action name, a list of the difference in beliefs before and after the action executed, and finally the outcome for that action once it terminated. The action in Fig. 2 is a move action from waypoint 0 to waypoint 1. In the first entry, the action is believed to have succeeded and the change in beliefs is shown as the addition of the belief $at(1)$ (at waypoint 1) and removal of the belief $at(0)$ which matches the expected post-conditions for that action. In the second entry, the change in beliefs results in the agent believing that it is at waypoint 3, not at waypoint 1 as per the action description, producing a failure as the action outcome.

The action log has a fixed, application specific size, and the oldest entry is removed before adding a new one, once the log reaches its size limit. The presence of this action log opens up the possibility of implementing an *action lifecycle* [34] inspired by the concept of goal life-cycles for BDI languages [22].

Action	Change in Beliefs	Action Outcome
move(0, 1)	+at(1), -at(0)	Success
move(0, 1)	+at(3),-at(0)	Failure

Fig. 2. Example of an action log with the move(0, 1) action for a Gwendolen agent.

An action lifecycle allows actions which fail or are aborted to be moved into a *suspect* state and finally become *deprecated* following repeated failures.

We're not aware of any other BDI language that maintains an action log in this way, but in principle, it should not be difficult to add this functionality to any language that already supports action descriptions.

The automated planning research community has invested considerable effort in the modelling of actions with stochastic outcomes, both theoretically as variants on Markov Decision Procedures [26,36], and practically by capturing such concepts in planners (e.g. [9]) and domain description languages such as in the Planning Domain Definition Language (PDDL) 2.1 [20]. This community deploys action descriptions to flexibly plan on-the-fly for each new goal which avoids the problem faced in BDI languages that an action whose behaviour has changed may result in failing, and therefore useless, plans. The use of a BDI language, with its programmer supplied plans, presumes that bespoke planning for every new goal is undesirable (usually for reasons of efficiency, but also for verifiability). Our approach exploits AI planning techniques to patch the plans that fail as a result of action failure, but seeks to minimize the amount of planning that actually takes place.

Plan failure has been extensively researched in BDI programming languages (e.g., [4,17,31]), however, it has not been linked with action descriptions perhaps because most languages do not use action descriptions as a mechanism to detect action failure. The closest work to our own is in [22] with a proposal for BDI goal life-cycles.

A key component of our approach is synthesising or learning a new action description when an action ceases to perform as expected. We presume this arises because of the dynamic environment in which the agent is operating. Using algorithms to discover the effects of actions has been explored in the AI Planning domain [2]. Most of the resulting techniques operate in environments where it is assumed multiple action descriptions need to be learned at the same time and that the action descriptions themselves have not been changing during the learning period. We have based our approach on ideas from [10] and [21] in which new action descriptions are learned from traces of action behaviour with a weighting mechanism used to guide choice of additions and deletions to the constructed action post-condition.

After learning/synthesizing a new (or updated) action description, it is necessary to refactor the plans from the plan library. The process of updating plans of execution based on a set of conditions (failure or new information) is often referred to as reconfigurability, and it has been frequently applied in the robotics and manufacturing industry [1,5,8,32]. A mechanism for plan library reconfigurability combining BDI agents and automated planning was presented in [7], but it has no account for how failure is detected, and simply ignores the action that caused the failure in subsequent reconfigurations. We leverage this work in ours, if an action is deprecated by the action lifecycle, then any plans involving that action are patched using the mechanism from [7].

To the best of our knowledge, there is no end-to-end framework in cognitive agents for updating action descriptions and patching the associated plans such as is presented here.

3   Framework

Our starting point is the system architecture outlined in [15] in which a cognitive agent performs high-level mission reasoning, such as deciding in which order some set of waypoints are to be visited. In order to do this, it takes input from subsystems for processing sensor data into high-level concepts such as the location of obstacles, and outputs instructions (actions) to control systems such as those for navigation and path planning. This is shown in Fig. 3 together with the action log component that tracks action performance.

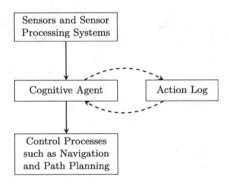

Fig. 3. System architecture overview.

Cognitive agents generally employ a *reasoning cycle* which governs a sense-reason-act process. The action log integrates with the *act* phase and compares the outcomes of executed actions to the post-conditions described in the action's description. If the post-conditions are successful, then a success is logged, and if they are not a failure is logged. In all situations the action log also records the changes in beliefs from the moment when the action was executed, to the moment when it succeeded or failed. These changes are stored as a list of expressions of the form $+t$ or $-t$ where t is a term—that is, in the same format as post-conditions in action descriptions.

Figure 4 shows five entries in an action log. When a new entry is made by an agent following an action execution, the size of the log is checked against the predefined size limit. If the size limit has been reached, then the oldest entry is removed (from the top of the list in this example) before the new entry is added to the bottom. In this case a single action success has been experienced for the move(0, 1) action, followed by four failures. These failures might be caused by, for instance, some obstacle appearing in the path between waypoints 0 and 1. Attempts by the agent to move around the obstacle, using low-level obstacle avoidance techniques have led consistently to the agent finding itself at waypoint 3, each time this action is executed in the route goal.

The agent is able to navigate the rest of the route in this example but finds that the move(0, 1) action leads the agent to believe they have reached waypoint 3, and when executing this action during the next four iterations of the route, the same outcome is recorded.

Our framework extends action descriptions to include a *failure threshold* (Definition 2).

Definition 2 (Action Description (modified)). Action descriptions *are a tuple* $\{Pre\}A\{Post\}[n]$ *where A,* $\{Pre\}$ *and* $\{Post\}$ *are as described in Definition 1 and n is a positive integer representing a failure threshold.*

If the number of failures for the action in the action log exceeds the failure threshold, then the action becomes deprecated. Note that the action log should be of fixed length, so that an action can not become deprecated as the result of a slow build up of occasional failure over time. It only becomes deprecated if its *recent* failures have exceeded the threshold. The definition of recent should be application specific to account for speed with which change/degradation is anticipated in the environment. The threshold should be specific to the action itself, since some actions are naturally more failure prone than others for reasons that may be external to the action itself. Our tolerance of failure therefore varies depending upon the action.

We extend the act phase of the reasoning so that after the execution of an action, the action log is consulted. If the most recent action has not become

Action	Change in Beliefs	Action Outcome
move(0, 1)	+at(1),-at(0)	Success
move(0, 1)	+at(3),-at(0)	Failure
move(0, 1)	+at(3),-at(0)	Failure
move(0, 1)	+at(3),-at(0)	Failure
move(0, 1)	+at(3),-at(0)	Failure

Fig. 4. Example of detecting failures in an action log with size limit equal to 5. The next new entry will be added to the bottom row and the first row would be removed.

deprecated the cycle continues as before. If it has become deprecated, then a new action description is synthesized from the information in the log and relevant plans are patched before the agent continues to the sense phase. This reasoning cycle is shown in Fig. 5.

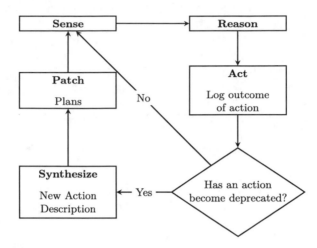

Fig. 5. Extended Sense-Reason-Act cycle to account for action deprecation, synthesis of new action descriptions, and the patching of plans.

We synthesize a new action description by extracting, from the action log, all the failed instances of the deprecated action. We then have a list (probably containing duplicates, as can be observed from Fig. 4) of new candidate post-conditions for the action in the form of the change in beliefs as the action executed. Each item in this list is assigned a weight score based on how recent the item is. The weights for identical items are then summed and that with the highest score selected as the new post-condition for the action. Pseudo-code for this process is shown in Algorithm 1. Line 2 instantiates the initial weight score (n) to 1, and in Line 3 it sets *post_scores* to an empty map. Lines 4–7 will loop through every entry in the action log to find entries that match with the deprecated action (same action) and where the outcome of the entry was reported as a failure. When this happens, the post-conditions of the action are added to the *post_scores* map along with the weight score, which is then incremented by one for the future iterations of the action log. In line 8 we initialise *best* with 0. Lines 9–11 iterate over the keys in the *post_scores* map to select the candidate post-condition with the highest weight score.

If we consider the action log in Fig. 4 and suppose our failure threshold is four, then the agent's 'act' phase should now attempt to synthesize a new action description from the log. It extracts the list of failures which contains four items all of which have identical new post-conditions—namely $\{+at(3), -at(0)\}$. This therefore becomes the new post-condition for the action `move(0, 1)`.

Algorithm 1: Algorithm for synthesizing post-conditions when an action is detected to be deprecated.

---

1 **if** *action is deprecated* **then**
2      $n \leftarrow 1$;
3   *post_scores* $\leftarrow \{\}$ // map of post-conditions to scores
4   **for** *entry* $\in$ *action log* **do**
        // NB. the action log consists of tuples (action, change in beliefs, outcome)
5   **if** *entry*[0] = *action* & *entry*[2] = *Failure* **then**
6   *post_scores*[*entry*[1]] $\leftarrow$ *post_scores*[*entry*[1]] + n;
7              $n \leftarrow n + 1$
8   *best* $\leftarrow 0$;
9   **for** *post* $\in$ *keys*(*post_scores*) **do**
10   **if** *post_scores*[*post*] > *best* **then**
11   *best* $\leftarrow$ *post*

However, suppose the action log is more variable. Initially, attempts to avoid the obstacle between 0 and 1 resulted in the agent arriving at waypoint 3, but suppose the obstacle has become more serious—perhaps sand and debris is piling up as the result of storms—and now the low-level movement behaviour causes an abort that returns the agent to waypoint 0. This results in the action log in Fig. 6.

Action	Change in Beliefs	Action Outcome
move(0, 1)	+at(1),-at(0)	Success
move(0, 1)	+at(3),-at(0)	Failure
move(0, 1)	+at(3),-at(0)	Failure
move(0, 1)		Failure
move(0, 1)		Failure

Fig. 6. Example of an action log with variable post-conditions for the same action (move(0, 1)).

Figure 7 shows this action log extracted into a list of candidate post-conditions, weighted by how recent they are.

Of the two candidate post-conditions $\{+at(3), -at(0)\}$ has a total weight of 3, while $\{\}$ (no change) has a total weight of 7. Therefore the empty post-condition is selected for the new action description.

Once a new action description is stored, we are able to use a plan reconfiguration mechanism to patch any plans containing the action. The work in [7] describes how an AI planning problem can be extracted from a failed action by a process of:

Candidate Post-Condition	Weight
$\{+at(3), -at(0)\}$	1
$\{+at(3), -at(0)\}$	2
$\{\}$	3
$\{\}$	4

Fig. 7. Post-conditions extracted from Fig. 6, added with their respective weights which are calculated based on how recent they are.

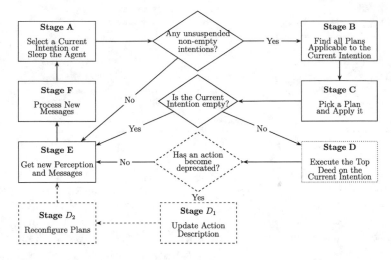

Fig. 8. GWENDOLEN reasoning cycle. Our additions are shown with dashed lines and stages we have modified are shown with dotted lines.

1. using the failed action's pre- and post-conditions as initial and goal states respectively for the planning problem; and
2. using the set of all other action descriptions as an action model for the planner.

This planning problem can then be solved to create a "patch" for any BDI plan containing the failed action. Our framework uses this mechanism with a slight modification. We only seek to replace an action once it has become deprecated (i.e., after some pre-defined number of failures). The set of action descriptions sent to the planner is then created from the agent's current set of action descriptions, including the newly learned description of the deprecated action.

In our example, let us assume that our move(0,1) action has become deprecated. Attempts to move from waypoint 0 to waypoint 1 now result in the agent arriving at waypoint 3 (based on the action log from Fig. 4. A STRIPS-type planner [18] is called with the updated action descriptions and an initial planning state—at(0) (the agent is at waypoint 0)—and goal state—at(1) & ¬ at(0) (the agent should end up at waypoint 1)—created from the pre- and post-conditions of move(0, 1). Among other action descriptions the planner has the new description for move(0,1) available

($\{at(0)\}$move(0, 1)$\{-at(0), +at(3)\}$[4] with [4] representing the failure threshold of the action) as well as an action describing a move from waypoint 3 to
1 ($\{at(3)\}$move(3, 1)$\{-at(3), +at(1)\}$[4]). It is straightforward for the planner to create the plan move(0,1),move(3,1) to solve this problem (note that
move(0,1) now takes us to waypoint 3, not waypoint 1). If we were using plans
similar to the GWENDOLEN plans[1] shown in Fig. 1, this means that the plan
+!at(1):$\{at(0)\}$ <- move(0, 1), +!at(2) contains our deprecated action and
will not succeed in moving the agent to waypoint 1. This patch produced by the
planner, replaces the appearance of move(0, 1) in the original plan producing
the new plan: +!at(1):$\{at(0)\}$ <- move(0, 1), move(3, 1), +!at(2) which
is stored for reuse.

4   Implementation

We implemented our framework in the version of the GWENDOLEN programming
language that creates an action log of action success and failure using action
descriptions [33].[2]

We extended the GWENDOLEN reasoning cycle with a synthesize stage (Stage
D_1) and a reconfigure stage (Stage D_2) which are executed after GWENDOLEN's
equivalent of the act phase which is called Stage D. This reconfigure stage uses
the action log to synthesize new action descriptions and then uses these to patch
the agent's plans. Our extended GWENDOLEN reasoning cycle is shown in Fig. 8
with our additions shown using dashes.

After Stage D (when actions are executed), the last entry of the action log
is checked. If it is an entry for anything other than an action failure nothing
further happens, no action becomes deprecated, and the cycle continues to Stage
E. However, if it is an entry for an action that has failed, the number of entries
containing a failure for this specific action is checked against its failure threshold.
Note that the threshold value of an action is domain specific. If the threshold
has been reached, the reasoning cycle moves to the new Stage D_1 in which a
new action description will be learned and then to Stage D_2 where plans will be
patched.

A fixed length action log may not capture rare, but still consistent, failures, as
the oldest entry is removed when new entries are recorded. A more sophisticated
failure threshold could be developed to measure the significance of each failure
regardless of frequency and act accordingly, although this case was not considered
in the current implementation.

There is also scope for further development to allow greater refinement of failure thresholds, which is not limited to just failure frequency. In the current state,
the punishment for assigning an inappropriate threshold is not considerable, as
agents would quickly reach the threshold again to correct the action description
back to the original description. This is the current state of managing incorrect

---

[1] As noted, many BDI formalisms represent plans in a very similar fashion, so although
we use a GWENDOLEN plan as an example here, the technique is general.
[2] Code available at https://github.com/mcapl/mcapl/tree/reconfig_eumas.

failure detections. However, this method is wholly reliant upon accurate agent perception of the environment and actions could produce further failures if the agent wrongly believes pre-conditions for actions. This system works under the assumption that the agent's perception of the environment remains accurate. Further testing and deployment into a realistic scenario would be required to improve on the current implementation.

Once a new action description is stored we are able to use plan reconfiguration mechanism from [7]. This extracts all the action descriptions from the agent and translates them into STRIPS operators [18]. Let, $\{Pre\}a\{Post\}[n]$ be the old action description for the failed action a. The reconfiguration mechanism computes initial and goal states for a planning problem from $\{Pre\}$ and $\{Post\}$. This planning problem is then given to a STRIPS planner together with the STRIPS operators of the agent's plan descriptions. If the planner computes a new plan this is translated into a sequence of GWENDOLEN actions, a_l, this sequence replaces a everywhere it appears in the agent's plans.

5   Evaluation

We evaluated our approach on a variation of the "waypoint patrol" example we have been using throughout the paper. Our environment consisted of five waypoints and our agent had a plan for a patrol mission to visit each waypoint in turn. The GWENDOLEN plan was:

```
+!at(4):{at(0)} <- move(0, 1),
                   move(1, 2),
                   move(2, 3),
                   move(3, 4);
```

Each move action had a description of the form:

$$\{at(X)\}\text{move(X, Y)}\{-at(X), +at(Y)\}$$

(e.g., $\{at(1)\}$move(1, 2)$\{-at(1), +at(2)\}$. We varied the number of action descriptions for 'move' actions available to the agent. The agent always had descriptions for the four actions in the plan (i.e., move(0, 1), move(1, 2), move(2, 3), move(3, 4)—we refer to these as the *fixed actions*), but also had a random selection of other 'move' actions between the five waypoints—we refer to these as the *variable actions*. Figure 9 illustrates this, with the *fixed* move actions shown by solid lines and the *variable* move actions shown by dashed lines.

We generated random instances of this scenario varying the probability that each of the variable 'move' actions was available. The table presented in Fig. 10 shows how many times (out of ten runs) our framework successfully managed to patch the plan in the event that the move(0, 1) action resulted in the agent finding itself at waypoint 2 rather than waypoint 1.

As is to be expected, we can see that as the number of potential alternative actions increases, so does the chance of successfully patching the failing plan.

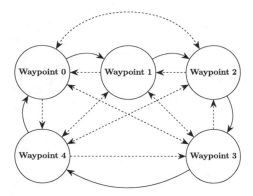

Fig. 9. Waypoint environment. Dashed arrows indicate variable actions only available in *some* instantiations of the problem.

10%	20%	30%	40%	50%	60%	70%	80%	90%	100%
3	7	7	8	9	10	9	10	10	10

Fig. 10. First row represents the probability for each extra move route to be available in the execution. Second row contains the results for how many times our implementation managed to successfully patch a plan when the action move(0, 1) action was deprecated resulting in a move to waypoint 2, rather than waypoint 1

In particular, once more than 50% of the edges in the graph are available as actions, there is a high chance that the agent will be able to synthesize a patch for its plans.

When there was only a 10% probability of each *variable action* being available, the reconfigured plan, when it could be generated, tended to be quite long. For instance, in one instance, the only *variable action* available at runtime was the move(3, 1) action. This resulted in a patch were move(0, 1) was replaced by the sequence move(0, 1), move(2, 3), move(3, 1) (recall that move(0, 1) is now resulting in a move to waypoint 2). This resulted in the patched plan:

```
+!at(4):{at(0)} <- move(0, 1),
                   move(2, 3),
                   move(3, 1),
                   move(1, 2),
                   move(2, 3),
                   move(3, 4);
```

The shortest possible plan patch, can be achieved for when the move(2, 1) action is available to the planner. When possible, the planner always opts for the plan with the lowest "cost" that can achieve the provided goal state. We modelled the plan cost simply as the total number of actions in the plan. In our scenario this provides a good estimation for the lowest cost (in terms of resources consumed by the agent in order to execute the plan) since all of the actions are similar, though this would not necessarily hold true for other action models. This costing approach explains why we tended to generate shorter patches when more actions were available.

6   Discussion and Future Work

One major aspect of future work is to adapt the framework to manage action descriptions containing variables. Many BDI languages use variables and unification in plans, to enable one plan to apply in many situations depending upon the instantiation of its parameters. There are two aspects to this challenge. Firstly when an action is executed in a BDI language, it is almost always the case that its variable parameters are instantiated—so although we might have an action description of the form $\{at(X)\}$move(X, Y)$\{-at(X), +at(Y)\}$ where X and Y are variables, it is only ever called as, say move(0, 1) or move(1, 2). Therefore the process of synthesizing new descriptions from the action log will need to utilize generalisation techniques to abstract from concrete log entries to abstract descriptions. It may also be necessary to split action descriptions by synthesizing new pre-conditions indicating that, in some situations the action still behaves as originally assumed, but in others it does not. Secondly, STRIPS-type planners, while they frequently use action descriptions that contain variable parameters, do not generally plan using initial and goal states that contain variables. This includes the planner embedded in the implementation we used from [7]— therefore this planner would need to be replaced with one capable of handling variables in initial states and goals. The work in [25] contains simple examples that might be adapted for this use.

We would also like to introduce more sophistication into the algorithm for learning new action descriptions. At present all changes in beliefs after an action execution are treated as one group. Consider a situation where two robots are both working in an area. Sometimes, after moving between waypoints the agent also perceives the presence of the second robot. In this case the current action log would sometimes record $\{+at(1), -at(0), +second\_robot\}$ as the belief change and sometimes record $\{+at(1), -at(0)\}$. Algorithm 1 treats these entirely separately and is unable to recognise that $+at(1)$ and $-at(0)$ occur in both. We anticipate that weighting each term appearing in the set of belief changes individually, rather than as a group, would enable the construction of post-conditions that better reflected the actual action behaviour.

At present the planning problem sent to the STRIPS planner is formulated from the description of the failed action alone and does not account for the context in which the action appears. Many BDI plans are expressed in terms of some *guard*, which can be considered a pre-condition for the whole plan, and a *goal* which can be considered a goal state for the plan. We would like to use techniques such as regression planning to infer from the plan's guard and goal, and the pre-conditions and post-conditions of any other actions in the plan, what the actual state of the agent is likely to be at the point the failed action was executed and which of the failed action's post-conditions were actually necessary in order to achieve the goal of the plan. This introduces more flexibility into the patching mechanism, allowing plans to be patched even if an exact replacement for the failing action could not be found. It also reduces the risk that the computed patch might contain additional post-conditions that will break the plan—for instance, suppose our failed action is $\{pr_1\}a_1\{+po_2\}$ and the computed patch is a_2,a_3 where a_3's post-condition is $\{+po_1, +po_3\}$. Now consider a plan e:guard $< -a_1,a_4$ where the description of a_4 is $\{\neg po_3\}a_4\{+po_4\}$. If we replace a_1 in this plan with our patch then a_4 will no longer be applicable and the plan will break. More context-sensitive construction of the planning problem should be able to account for this and avoid creating a patch that will break the plan.

The use of the GWENDOLEN language which is linked to the AJPF model-checking tool and the Model-Checking Agent Programming Languages (MCAPL) framework [14], opens the possibility of verifying the patched plans produced by our framework. While we are interested in exploring this idea, the AJPF model-checker typically performs verification very slowly. If the agent existed in an environment where there were periods of inactivity, then it would be possible for re-verification to take place to ensure that the agent's plans continued to adhere to any specified properties, but in an environment where patching needs to occur quickly then this may not be feasible. If the reconfiguration mechanism was adapted, as suggested above, to be sensitive to the context in which an action was invoked then it should be possible to establish idealised results about the safety of patches, at least in environments where the only things changing the environment are the agent's own actions. It might also be possible to treat actions appearing in plans as sequences of abstract actions of length up to l, with the abstract actions having no specified behaviour during verification. This forces the verification to consider all possible action outcomes, allowing plans to be patched with any sequence of actions of length less than l, but the resulting state space for verification is likely to be unwieldy and include consideration of many action outcomes that are either unlikely or impossible, forcing, in turn, the inclusion of fail-safe plans within the agent to handle behaviour that can never occur resulting in "crufty" code.

The extent to which long-term autonomy can be achieved through the generation of amended action descriptions and the patching of plans is an open question. Scenarios such as we have presented involving navigation around way-points linked in a graph structure are relatively common, and it is reasonable to suppose that over time paths between waypoints might alter. What is unknown is how common it is that changes in the environment or robot capabilities can be compensated for by combinations of (adapted) actions and how common it is that action degradation simply results in a robot that can not usefully perform its mission. It is likely that the proposed framework would need to be combined with mechanisms for weakening mission specifications, for instance, by dropping some goals that were no longer obtainable, while continuing to pursue others.

We have presented here the over-arching template of a framework for adapting BDI agent plans in the face of changed action behaviour. With the additions from the future work described, the framework in this paper should be capable of handling larger scenarios with greater complexity. Also, introducing multiple agents to the scenario undoubtedly increases the complexity of the situation, although this also opens the opportunity for agents to collaborate and share action descriptions.

Acknowledgements. This work has been supported by The University of Manchester's Department of Computer Science and the EPSRC "Robotics and AI for Nuclear" (EP/R026084/1), "Future AI and Robotics for Space" (EP/R026092/1), and Computational Agent Responsibility (EP/W01081X/1) Hubs and the TAS Verifiability Node (EP/V026801). During the course of this work, Michael Fisher was supported by the Royal Academy of Engineering.

References

1. Antzoulatos, N., Castro, E., de Silva, L., Rocha, A.D., Ratchev, S., Barata, J.: A multi-agent framework for capability-based reconfiguration of industrial assembly systems. Int. J. Prod. Res. **55**(10), 2950–2960 (2017)
2. Arora, A., Fiorino, H., Pellier, D., Etivier, M., Pesty, S.: A review of learning planning action models. Knowl. Eng. Rev. **33**, e20 (2018)
3. Bordini, R.H., ubner, J.F.H., Wooldridge, M.: Programming Multi-agent Systems in AgentSpeak Using Jason (2007)
4. Bordini, R.H., Hübner, J.F.: Semantics for the Jason variant of AgentSpeak (plan failure and some internal actions). In: ECAI, pp. 635–640. IOS Press (2010). https://doi.org/10.3233/978-1-60750-606-5-635
5. Borgo, S., Cesta, A., Orlandini, A., Umbrico, A.: A planning-based architecture for a reconfigurable manufacturing system. In: Proceedings of the Twenty-Sixth International Conference on International Conference on Automated Planning and Scheduling, ICAPS 2016, pp. 358–366. AAAI Press, London (2016)
6. Bratman, M.E.: Intentions, Plans, and Practical Reason. Harvard University Press, Cambridge (1987)
7. Cardoso, R.C., Dennis, L.A., Fisher, M.: Plan library reconfigurability in BDI agents. In: Dennis, L.A., Bordini, R.H., Lespérance, Y. (eds.) EMAS 2019. LNCS (LNAI), vol. 12058, pp. 195–212. Springer, Cham (2020). https://doi.org/10.1007/978-3-030-51417-4_10
8. Chen, I.M., Yang, G., Yeo, S.H.: Automatic modeling for modular reconfigurable robotic systems: theory and practice. In: Cubero, S. (ed.) Industrial Robotics, chap. 2. IntechOpen, Rijeka (2006)
9. Cirillo, M., Karlsson, L., Saffiotti, A.: Human-aware task-planning: an application to mobile robots. ACM Trans. Intell. Syst. Technol. **1**(2), 15 (2010)
10. Cohen, P.R., Feigenbaum, E.A.: The Handbook of Artificial Intelligence: Volume 3, vol. 3. Butterworth-Heinemann (2014)
11. Dastani, M.: 2APL: a practical agent programming language. Auton. Agent. Multi-Agent Syst. **16**, 214–248 (2008). https://doi.org/10.1007/s10458-008-9036-y
12. Dastani, M., van Birna Riemsdijk, M., Meyer, J.-J.C.: Programming multi-agent systems in 3APL. In: Bordini, R.H., Dastani, M., Dix, J., El Fallah Seghrouchni, A. (eds.) Multi-Agent Programming. MSASSO, vol. 15, pp. 39–67. Springer, Boston, MA (2005). https://doi.org/10.1007/0-387-26350-0_2
13. Dennis, L.A.: Gwendolen semantics: 2017. Technical report ULCS-17-001, University of Liverpool, Department of Computer Science (2017)

14. Dennis, L.A.: The MCAPL framework including the agent infrastructure layer and agent java pathfinder. J. Open Sour. Softw. **3**(24), 617 (2018)
15. Dennis, L.A., Fisher, M., Lincoln, N.K., Lisitsa, A., Veres, S.M.: Practical verification of decision-making in agent-based autonomous systems. Autom. Softw. Eng. **23**(3), 305–359 (2016)
16. Dennis, L.A., Fisher, M., Webster, M.P., Bordini, R.H.: Model checking agent programming languages. Autom. Softw. Eng. **19**(1), 5–63 (2012). https://doi.org/10.1007/s10515-011-0088-x
17. Ferrando, A., Cardoso, R.C.: Safety shields, an automated failure handling mechanism for BDI agents. In: Proceedings of the 21st International Conference on Autonomous Agents and Multiagent Systems, AAMAS 2022, pp. 1589–1591. International Foundation for Autonomous Agents and Multiagent Systems, Richland (2022). www.ifaamas.org/Proceedings/aamas2022/pdfs/p1589.pdf
18. Fikes, R.E., Nilsson, N.J.: Strips: a new approach to the application of theorem proving to problem solving. Artif. Intell. **2**(3), 189–208 (1971). https://doi.org/10.1016/0004-3702(71)90010-5, www.sciencedirect.com/science/article/pii/0004370271900105
19. Fisher, M., et al.: An overview of verification and validation challenges for inspection robots. Robotics **10**(2) (2021). https://doi.org/10.3390/robotics10020067, www.mdpi.com/2218-6581/10/2/67
20. Fox, M., Long, D.: PDDL2.1: an extension to PDDL for expressing temporal planning domains. JAIR **20**, 61–124 (2003)
21. Guerra-Hernández, A., El Fallah-Seghrouchni, A., Soldano, H.: Learning in BDI multi-agent systems. In: Dix, J., Leite, J. (eds.) CLIMA 2004. LNCS (LNAI), vol. 3259, pp. 218–233. Springer, Heidelberg (2004). https://doi.org/10.1007/978-3-540-30200-1_12
22. Harland, J., Morley, D.N., Thangarajah, J., Yorke-Smith, N.: An operational semantics for the goal life-cycle in BDI agents. Auton. Agent. Multi-Agent Syst. **28**(4), 682–719 (2014). https://doi.org/10.1007/s10458-013-9238-9
23. Hindriks, K.V.: Programming rational agents in GOAL. In: El Fallah Seghrouchni, A., Dix, J., Dastani, M., Bordini, R.H. (eds.) Multi-Agent Programming, pp. 119–157. Springer, Boston (2009). https://doi.org/10.1007/978-0-387-89299-3_4
24. Hindriks, K.V.: Programming cognitive agents in goal (2021)
25. Luger, G.F.: Artificial Intelligence: Structures and Strategies for Complex Problem Solving, 6th edn. Addison-Wesley Publishing Company, USA (2008)
26. Mausam, Weld, D.S.: Planning with durative actions in stochastic domains. JAIR **31**, 33–82 (2008)
27. Menghi, C., Tsigkanos, C., Pelliccione, P., Ghezzi, C., Berger, T.: Specification patterns for robotic missions. IEEE Trans. Softw. Eng. **47**(10), 2208–2224 (2021). https://doi.org/10.1109/TSE.2019.2945329
28. Rao, A.S., Georgeff, M.P.: Modeling agents within a BDI-architecture. In: Proceedings of the 2nd International Conference on Principles of Knowledge Representation and Reasoning (KR&R), pp. 473–484. Morgan Kaufmann (1991)
29. Rao, A.S., Georgeff, M.P.: An abstract architecture for rational agents. In: Proceedings of the 3rd International Conference on Principles of Knowledge Representation and Reasoning (KR&R), pp. 439–449. Morgan Kaufmann (1992)
30. Rao, A.S., Georgeff, M.P.: An abstract architecture for rational agents. KR **92**, 439–449 (1992)
31. Sardina, S., Padgham, L.: A BDI agent programming language with failure handling, declarative goals, and planning. Auton. Agent. Multi-Agent Syst. **23**(1), 18–70 (2011)

32. Støy, K., Brandt, D., Christensen, D.J.: Self-reconfigurable Robots. MIT Press, Cambridge (2010)
33. Stringer, P., Cardoso, R.C., Dixon, C., Dennis, L.A.: Implementing durative actions with failure detection in GWENDOLEN. In: Alechina, N., Baldoni, M., Logan, B. (eds.) EMAS 2021. LNCS, vol. 13190, pp. 332–351. Springer, Cham (2022). https://doi.org/10.1007/978-3-030-97457-2_19
34. Stringer, P., Cardoso, R.C., Huang, X., Dennis, L.A.: Adaptable and verifiable BDI reasoning. In: Cardoso, R.C., Ferrando, A., Briola, D., Menghi, C., Ahlbrecht, T. (eds.) Proceedings of the First Workshop on Agents and Robots for reliable Engineered Autonomy, Virtual event, 4th September 2020. Electronic Proceedings in Theoretical Computer Science, vol. 319, pp. 117–125. Open Publishing Association (2020). https://doi.org/10.4204/EPTCS.319.9
35. Wooldridge, M., Rao, A. (eds.): Foundations of Rational Agency. Applied Logic Series. Kluwer Academic Publishers (1999)
36. Younes, H.L.A., Simmons, R.G.: Solving generalized semi-Markov decision processes using continuous phase-type distributions. In: Proceedings of the AAAI, pp. 742–747. AAAI Press (2004)

Pretty Good Strategies and Where to Find Them

Wojciech Jamroga[1,2] and Damian Kurpiewski[2,3(✉)]

[1] Interdisciplinary Centre for Security, Reliability and Trust, SnT,
University of Luxembourg, Esch-sur-Alzette, Luxembourg
[2] Institute of Computer Science, Polish Academy of Sciences, Warsaw, Poland
d.kurpiewski@ipipan.waw.pl
[3] Faculty of Mathematics and Computer Science, Nicolaus Copernicus University,
Toruń, Poland

Abstract. Synthesis of bulletproof strategies in imperfect information scenarios is a notoriously hard problem. In this paper, we suggest that it is sometimes a viable alternative to aim at "reasonably good" strategies instead. This makes sense not only when an ideal strategy cannot be found due to the complexity of the problem, but also when no winning strategy exists at all. We propose an algorithm for synthesis of such "pretty good" strategies. The idea is to first generate a surely winning strategy with *perfect information*, and then iteratively improve it with respect to two criteria of dominance: one based on the amount of conflicting decisions in the strategy, and the other related to the tightness of its outcome set. We focus on reachability goals and evaluate the algorithm experimentally with very promising results.

Keywords: Strategy synthesis · imperfect information · alternating-time temporal logic · model checking

1 Introduction

As the systems around us become more complex, and at the same time more autonomous, the need for unambiguous specification and automated verification rapidly increases. Many relevant properties of multi-agent systems refer to *strategic abilities* of agents and their groups. For example, functionality requirements can be often understood in terms of the user's ability to complete the selected tasks. Similarly, many security properties boil down to inability of the intruder to obtain his goals. *Logics of strategic reasoning* provide powerful tools to reason about such aspects of MAS [3,7,8,29,40,45]. A typical property that can be expressed says that *the group of agents A has a collective strategy to enforce temporal property φ, no matter what the other agents in the system do*. In other words, A have a "winning strategy" that achieves φ on all its possible execution paths.

Specifications in agent logics can be then used as input to *model checking*, which makes it possible to verify the correct behavior of a multi-agent system by

© The Author(s), under exclusive license to Springer Nature Switzerland AG 2023
V. Malvone and A. Murano (Eds.): EUMAS 2023, LNAI 14282, pp. 363–380, 2023.
https://doi.org/10.1007/978-3-031-43264-4_23

an automatic tool [1, 18, 19, 22, 27, 34, 36, 37]. Moreover, model checking of strategic formulas typically relies on synthesis of a suitable strategy to demonstrate that such a strategy exists.

Verification and reasoning about strategic abilities is difficult for a number of reasons. The prohibitive complexity of model checking and strategy synthesis is a well known factor [7, 8, 10, 26, 39]. This can be overcome to some degree by using efficient symbolic methods and data structures [9, 13, 27, 44]. However, real-life agents typically have limited capabilities of observation, action, and reasoning. That brings additional challenges. First, the theoretical complexity of model checking for imperfect information strategies (sometimes called *uniform strategies*) ranges from **NP**–complete to undecidable [10, 25, 45], depending on the precise setup of the problem. Secondly, practical attempts at verification suffer from state-space and transition-space explosion. Thirdly, there is no simple fixed-point characterisation of typical properties [12, 24]. As a consequence of the latter, most approaches to synthesis and verification boil down, in the worst case, to checking all the possible strategies [16, 17, 35, 38, 43]. Unfortunately, the strategy space is huge – usually larger than the state space by orders of magnitude, which makes brute-force search hopeless.

An interesting attempt at heuristic search through the strategy space has been proposed in [35]. There, a concept of domination between strategies was introduced, based on the "tightness" of the outcome sets induced by the strategies. Formally, strategy s dominates s' if the set of possible executions of s is a strict subset of the executions of s'. The intuition is that those strategies are better which give the agent a better grip on what is going to happen, and better reduce the nondeterminism of the system. Then, the authors of [35] proposed an algorithm for synthesis of uniform strategies, based on depth-first search through the strategy space with simultaneous optimization of dominated partial strategies. The algorithm, dubbed DominoDFS, performed with considerable success on several benchmarks. This might have had two related reasons. First, restricting the set of successor states reduces the possibility of encountering a "bad" successor further on. Perhaps even more importantly, it reduces the space of reachable states, and hence has the potential to considerably speed up the computation.

In this paper, we take the idea of dominance-based optimization, and apply it from a completely different angle. Most importantly, we propose that searching for a "reasonably good" strategy is sometimes a viable alternative to the search for an ideal one (where "ideal" means a surely winning imperfect information strategy). This obviously makes sense when no winning strategy exists, but also when an ideal strategy cannot be found due to the complexity of the problem. Moreover, we propose a procedure for synthesis of such "pretty good" strategies. The algorithm starts with generating a surely winning strategy with *perfect information*. Then, it iteratively improves it with respect to two criteria of dominance: one based on the amount of conflicting decisions in the strategy, and the other related to the tightness of its outcome set. It is worth noting that this is an *anytime* algorithm. Thus, it *always* returns some strategy, provided that a perfect information strategy has been generated in the first phase.

We evaluate the algorithm experimentally on randomly generated concurrent game structures with imperfect information, as well as the scalable Drones benchmark of [35]. The results are compared to the output of DominoDFS and to the fixpoint approximation algorithm of [33], forming a very promising pattern. In particular, for models with relatively small information sets (a.k.a. epistemic indistinguishability classes), our algorithm was able to find *ideal* strategies where the other approaches consistently failed. We note that, according to the theoretical results proposed in [32], approaches relying on search through the space of uniform strategies may be feasible for models with large information sets. At the same time, they are unlikely to succeed for models with small epistemic classes. This makes our new method a potentially good complement to algorithms like DominoDFS.

Outline of the Paper. The structure of the paper is as follows. We begin by introducing the standard semantics of strategic ability in Sect. 2. We also cite the complexity results for model checking and strategy synthesis, and recall the notion of strategic dominance from [35] that will serve as inspiration for our heuristics. In Sect. 3, we propose an abstract template for multicriterial strategic dominance, and instantiate it by two actual dominance relations that will provide the heuristics. Our algorithm for strategy synthesis based on iterated improvement is presented in Sect. 4, and evaluated experimentally in Sect. 5. We also discuss how the algorithm can be extended to synthesis of coalitional strategies in Sect. 6. Finally, we conclude in Sect. 7.

Related Work. A number of frameworks has been aimed at the verification of strategic properties under imperfect information. Regarding the available tools, the state-of-the-art MAS model checker MCMAS [37,38] combines efficient symbolic representation of state-space using Binary Decision Diagrams (BDDs) with exhaustive iteration over uniform strategies. A similar approach based on exhaustive search through strategy space is presented in [17]. A prototype tool SMC [43] employs bounded unfoldings of transition relation with strategy exploration and calls to MCMAS. Strategy search with optimisation of partial strategies has been further used in [14,16,35]. Most relevant to us, the optimisation in [35] was driven by strategic dominance based on the tightness of the outcome set.

Other recent attempts at feasible verification of uniform strategies include [5, 6,31] that propose methods for reduction of models with incomplete information, based respectively on abstraction, bisimulation, and partial-order equivalences. Another method [33] avoids the brute-force strategy search by using fixpoint approximations of the input formulas. A prototype tool STV implementing the DominoDFS algorithm and the fixpoint approximation was reported in [34].

We note that all the above approaches try to directly synthesize an ideal (i.e., uniform surely winning) strategy for the given goal. In contrast, our new algorithm starts with a flawed strategy (namely, surely winning but not uniform), and attempts to do iterative improvement. As we show, this may well end up in producing an ideal solution in cases where the other methods are inconclusive. No less importantly, our algorithm produces reasonably good strategies even when an ideal one cannot be found. The only related work in model checking of multi-agent systems, that we are aware of, is [4, 11] where a theoretical framework was proposed for reasoning about strategies that succeed on "sufficiently many" outcome paths.

2   Preliminaries

In this section we recall the standard formal framework used for reasoning about strategies in MAS. To this end, *alternating-time temporal logic ATL* [2, 3, 45] is often used. We also recall the notion of dominance for partial strategies, that was proposed in [35].

2.1   ATL: What Agents Can Achieve

ATL [2, 3, 45] generalizes the branching-time temporal logic **CTL** [21] by replacing the path quantifiers E, A with *strategic modalities* $\langle\langle A \rangle\rangle$. Formulas of **ATL** allow to express intuitive statements about what agents (or groups of agents) can achieve. For example, $\langle\langle W, E \rangle\rangle F$ win$_{WE}$ says that the players West and Eeast in a game of Bridge can jointly win the game. Formally, the syntax of **ATL** is defined by the following grammar:

$$\phi ::= p \mid \neg\phi \mid \phi \wedge \phi \mid \langle\langle A \rangle\rangle X\phi \mid \langle\langle A \rangle\rangle G\phi \mid \langle\langle A \rangle\rangle \phi \, U \, \phi,$$

where $p \in PV$ is an atomic proposition and $A \subseteq \mathrm{Agt}$ is a group of agents. We read $\langle\langle A \rangle\rangle\gamma$ as "*A can identify and execute a strategy that enforces γ*", X as "*in the next state*", G as "*now and always in the future*", and U as "*until*".

2.2   Models

We interpret **ATL** [3, 45] specifications over a variant of transition systems where transitions are labeled with combinations of actions, one per agent. Moreover, epistemic relations are used to indicate states that look the same to a given agent. Formally, an *imperfect information concurrent game structure*, or simply a *model*, is given by $M = \langle \mathrm{Agt}, St, PV, V, Act, d, o, \{\sim_a \mid a \in \mathrm{Agt}\}\rangle$ which includes a nonempty finite set of agents $\mathrm{Agt} = \{1, \ldots, k\}$, a nonempty set of states St, a set of atomic propositions PV and their valuation $V \colon PV \to 2^{St}$, and a nonempty finite set of (atomic) actions Act. The protocol function $d \colon \mathrm{Agt} \times St \to 2^{Act}$ defines nonempty sets of actions available to agents at each state; we will write $d_a(q)$ instead of $d(a, q)$, and define $d_A(q) = \prod_{a \in A} d_a(q)$ for each $A \subseteq \mathrm{Agt}, q \in St$. Furthermore, o is a (deterministic) transition function that assigns the outcome state $q' = o(q, \alpha_1, \ldots, \alpha_k)$ to each state q and tuple of actions $\langle \alpha_1, \ldots, \alpha_k \rangle$ such that $\alpha_i \in d_i(q)$ for $i = 1, \ldots, k$. Every $\sim_a \subseteq St \times St$ is an epistemic equivalence relation with the intended meaning that, whenever $q \sim_a q'$, the states q and q' are indistinguishable to agent a. By $[q]_a$ we mean the set of states indistinguishable to agent a from the state q. The model is assumed to be *uniform*, in the sense that $q \sim_a q'$ implies $d_a(q) = d_a(q')$. Note that perfect information can be modeled by assuming each $\sim_a$ to be the identity relation.

2.3 Strategies

A strategy of an agent $a \in \mathbb{A}\mathrm{gt}$ is a conditional plan that specifies what a is going to do in every possible situation. The details of the definition depend on the observational capabilities of the agent and its memory. In this paper we consider the case of *imperfect information imperfect recall* strategies (sometimes also called *uniform memoryless strategies*), where an agent can observe only a part of the environment (i.e., perceives some states as indistinguishable) and performs the same action every time a given state is reached.

Formally, a uniform strategy for a is a function $\boldsymbol{\sigma}_a \colon St \to Act$ satisfying $\boldsymbol{\sigma}_a(q) \in d_a(q)$ for each $q \in St$ and $\boldsymbol{\sigma}_a(q) = \boldsymbol{\sigma}_a(q')$ for each $q, q' \in St$ such that $q \sim_a q'$. A *collective uniform strategy* $\boldsymbol{\sigma}_A$ for a coalition $A \subseteq \mathbb{A}\mathrm{gt}$ is a tuple of individual strategies, one per agent from A.

2.4 Outcome Paths

A *path* $\lambda = q_0 q_1 q_2 \dots$ is an infinite sequence of states such that there is a transition between each q_i, q_{i+1}. We use $\lambda[i]$ to denote the ith position on path λ (starting from $i = 0$) and $\lambda[i, j]$ to denote the part of λ between positions i and j. Function $out(q, \boldsymbol{\sigma}_a)$ returns the set of all paths that can result from the execution of a strategy $\boldsymbol{\sigma}_a$, beginning at state q. Formally:

$out(q, \boldsymbol{\sigma}_a) = \{\lambda = q_0, q_1, q_2 \dots \mid q_0 = q$ and for each $i = 0, 1, \dots$ there exists $\langle \alpha^i_{a_1}, \dots, \alpha^i_{a_k} \rangle$ such that $\alpha^i_a \in d_a(q_i)$ for every $a \in \mathbb{A}\mathrm{gt}$, and $\alpha^i_a = \boldsymbol{\sigma}_A|_a(q_i)$ for every $a \in A$, and $q_{i+1} = o(q_i, \alpha^i_{a_1}, \dots, \alpha^i_{a_k})\}$.

Moreover, the function $out^{\mathrm{ir}}(q, \boldsymbol{\sigma}_a) = \bigcup_{a \in A} \bigcup_{q \sim_a q'} out(q', \boldsymbol{\sigma}_a)$ collects all the outcome paths that start from states that are indistinguishable from q to at least one agent in A.

2.5 Semantics of ATL

Given a model M and a state q, the semantics of **ATL** formulas is defined as follows:

- $M, q \models p$ iff $q \in V(p)$,
- $M, q \models \neg \phi$ iff $M, q \not\models \phi$,
- $M, q \models \phi \wedge \psi$ iff $M, q \models \phi$ and $M, q \models \psi$,
- $M, q \models \langle\!\langle A \rangle\!\rangle X \phi$ iff there exists a uniform strategy $\boldsymbol{\sigma}_A$ such that for all $\lambda \in out^{\mathrm{ir}}(q, \boldsymbol{\sigma}_A)$ we have $M, \lambda[1] \models \phi$,
- $M, q \models \langle\!\langle A \rangle\!\rangle G \phi$ iff there exists a uniform $\boldsymbol{\sigma}_A$ such that for all $\lambda \in out^{\mathrm{ir}}(q, \boldsymbol{\sigma}_A)$ and $i \in \mathbb{N}$ we have $M, \lambda[i] \models \phi$,

- $M, q \models \langle\!\langle A \rangle\!\rangle \psi \, U \, \phi$ iff there exists a uniform σ_A such that for all $\lambda \in out^{ir}(q, \sigma_A)$ there is $i \in \mathbb{N}$ for which $M, \lambda[i] \models \phi$ and $M, \lambda[j] \models \psi$ for all $0 \leq j < i$.

The standard boolean operators (logical constants $\top$ and $\bot$, disjunction $\vee$, and implication $\rightarrow$) are defined as usual. Additionally, we define *"now or sometime in the future"* as $F\varphi \equiv \top \, U \, \varphi$. It is easy to see that $M, q \models \langle\!\langle A \rangle\!\rangle F\phi$ iff there exists a collective uniform strategy σ_A such that, on each path $\lambda \in out^{ir}(q, \sigma_A)$, there is a state that satisfies ϕ.

2.6   Model Checking and Strategy Synthesis

It is well known that model checking of **ATL** based on uniform memory-less strategies is $\mathbf{\Delta_2^P}$-complete with respect to the size of the explicit (global) model [10,30,45], i.e., on top of the usual state-space and transition-space explosion which arises from the composition of the agents' local models. This concurs with the results for solving imperfect information games and synthesis of winning strategies, which are also known to be hard [20,26,41]. Note that model checking **ATL** corresponds very closely to strategy synthesis for reachability/safety games. In fact, most model checking algorithms for **ATL** try to build a winning strategy when checking if such a strategy exists.

It is also known that both strategy synthesis and **ATL** model checking for imperfect information are not only theoretically hard, they are also difficult in practice. In particular, imperfect information strategies do not admit straightforward fixpoint algorithms based on standard short-term ability operators [12,23]. That makes incremental synthesis of strategies impossible, or at least difficult to achieve. Some practical attempts to overcome the barrier have been reported in [14–16,28,33,35,42]. Up until now, experimental results confirm that the initial intuition was right: model checking of strategic modalities for imperfect information is hard, and dealing with it requires innovative algorithms and verification techniques.

We emphasize that, at the same time, model checking for perfect information strategies (i.e., ones that can specify different choices at indistinguishable states) is much cheaper computationally, namely **P**-complete in the size of the model [3].

2.7   Partial Strategies and Strategy Dominance

A *partial strategy* for a is a partial function $\sigma_a \colon St \rightharpoonup Act$ that can be extended to a strategy. The domain of a partial strategy is denoted by $dom(\sigma_a)$. The set of all partial strategies for $A \subseteq \mathbb{A}gt$ is denoted by Σ_A.

Let $q \in dom(\sigma_A)$ for some $\sigma_A \in \Sigma_A$. The *outcome* of σ_A from q consists of all the maximal paths $\lambda \in dom(\sigma_A)^* \cup dom(\sigma_A)^\omega$ that follow the partial strategy. Formally we have:

$$\lambda \in out(q, \sigma_A) \text{ iff } \lambda_1 = q \wedge \forall_{i \leq |\lambda|} \lambda_i \in dom(\sigma_A)$$
$$\wedge \, \forall_{i < |\lambda|} \exists_{\beta \in d_{\mathbb{A}gt \setminus A}(\lambda_i)} o(\lambda_i, (\sigma_A(\lambda_i), \beta)) = \lambda_{i+1}$$

where $|\lambda|$ denotes the length (i.e., the number of states) of λ and λ is either infinite or cannot be extended. For each $i \in \mathbb{N}$ let λ_i denote the i–th element. Let $Q \subseteq dom(\sigma_A)$. A partial strategy σ_A is Q-loopless, if the set $\bigcup_{q \in Q} out(q, \sigma_A)$ contains only finite paths. For each $p \in PV$ we say that σ_A is p-free if $V(p) \cap dom(\sigma_A) = \emptyset$.

In what follows, we often refer to partial strategies simply as strategies and assume a fixed CEGM and $A \subseteq \mathbb{A}\mathrm{gt}$.

The paper [35] proposed a notion of strategic dominance defined with respect to a given context. Assume that we want to compare two partial strategies σ_A and σ'_A. First, we fix a context strategy σ^C_A, such that after executing it the control can be given to strategy σ_A or σ'_A. Then, we say that σ_A dominates σ'_A, iff the sets of input states[1] of both strategies are equal, and the set of output states of strategy σ_A is a subset of the set of output states of strategy σ'_A.

3   Two Notions of Dominance for Iterated Strategy Improvement

In [35], partial strategies are optimized according to only one criterion, namely the tightness of their outcome sets. In contrast, we propose to use two dimensions for optimization: tightness of the outcome *and* uniformity of the actions selected within the strategy. This is because, unlike [35], we start the synthesis with a perfect information strategy. Thus, our algorithm optimizes strategies that can include any number of conflicts, in the sense that it might prescribe different actions within the same information set $[q]_a$.

3.1   Multi-criterial Domination: Abstract Template

Consider a set of partial strategies Σ of agent a, based on the same epistemic class of a. That is, there exists $q \in St$ such that $dom(\sigma) \subseteq [q]_a$ for every $\sigma \in \Sigma$. Let $\sigma_1, \sigma_2 \in \Sigma$. We begin with an abstract definition of domination that looks at two criteria $\mathcal{C}_1, \mathcal{C}_2$. The idea is that σ_2 dominates σ_1 if it improves on $\mathcal{C}_1$ without deteriorating with respect to $\mathcal{C}_2$.

Definition 1 $((\mathcal{C}_1, \mathcal{C}_2)$-domination). *Let each $\mathcal{C}_i$ be a criterion associated with a total order $\preceq_{\mathcal{C}_i}$ on the partial strategies in Σ. The strict variant $\prec_{\mathcal{C}_i}$ of the ordering is defined in the obvious way, by $\preceq_{\mathcal{C}_i} \setminus (\preceq_{\mathcal{C}_i})^{-1}$. We say that σ_1 is $(\mathcal{C}_1, \mathcal{C}_2)$-dominated by σ_2 iff it holds that $\sigma_1 \prec_{\mathcal{C}_1} \sigma_2$ and at the same time $\sigma_1 \preceq_{\mathcal{C}_2} \sigma_2$.* ☐

Definition 2 (Better and best domination). *Consider partial strategies σ_2, σ'_2 that both $(\mathcal{C}_1, \mathcal{C}_2)$-dominate σ_1. We say that σ_2 better $(\mathcal{C}_1, \mathcal{C}_2)$-dominates σ_1 iff $\sigma'_2 \prec_{\mathcal{C}_1} \sigma_2$, i.e., σ_2 performs better than σ'_2 with respect to the primary criterion $\mathcal{C}_1$. Note: the fact that σ_2 better dominates σ_1 than σ'_2 does not imply that σ_2 dominates σ'_2, because σ_2 may perform poorer than σ'_2 on the secondary criterion $\mathcal{C}_2$.*

---

[1] i.e., initial states of the strategy.

Moreover, σ_2 best dominates σ_1 with respect to $(\mathcal{C}_1, \mathcal{C}_2)$ iff it dominates σ_1 and no other strategy in Σ better dominates σ_1. The set of strategies that best dominate σ_1 with respect to $(\mathcal{C}_1, \mathcal{C}_2)$ will be denoted by $Best_{\mathcal{C}_1, \mathcal{C}_2}(\sigma_1)$. □

3.2 Outcome- and Uniformity-Dominance

In the following, we assume a shared set of input nodes $In \subseteq dom(\sigma_1), dom(\sigma_2)$. The set of states reachable from In by partial strategy σ_i is denoted by $Reach(In, \sigma_i)$. Furthermore, we define the *domain of relevance* of σ_i as $RDom(In, \sigma_i) = dom(\sigma_i) \cap Reach(In, \sigma_i)$. That is, $RDom(In, \sigma_i)$ excludes from the domain of σ_i the states that cannot be reached, and hence are irrelevant when reasoning about potential conflicts between choices.

The *outcome criterion* is given by relation $\preceq_{\mathcal{O}(In)}$ such that $\sigma_1 \preceq_{\mathcal{O}(In)} \sigma_2$ iff $Reach(In, \sigma_2) \subseteq Reach(In, \sigma_1)$, i.e., σ_2 has at least as tight set of reachable outcome states as σ_1.

We will now proceed to the other criterion, related to uniformity of strategies. First, we define the *conflict set* of σ_i on states $Q \subseteq St$ as $Conflicts(Q, \sigma_i) = \{(q, q') \in Q \times Q \mid \sigma_i(q) \neq \sigma_i(q')\}$, i.e., the set of all pairs of states from Q where σ_i specifies conflicting choices.

Now, the *uniformity criterion* is given by relation $\preceq_{\mathcal{U}(In)}$ such that $\sigma_1 \preceq_{\mathcal{U}(In)} \sigma_2$ iff $Conflicts(RDom(In, \sigma_2), \sigma_2) \subseteq Conflicts(RDom(In, \sigma_1), \sigma_1)$. In other words, all the conflicts that σ_2 encounters in its domain of relevance must also appear in σ_1 (but not necessarily vice versa).

Definition 3 (Outcome- and uniformity-domination). *We say that σ_1 is outcome-dominated by σ_2 on input In iff it is $(\mathcal{O}(In), \mathcal{U}(In))$-dominated by σ_2. Likewise, σ_1 is uniform-dominated by σ_2 on input In iff it is $(\mathcal{U}(In), \mathcal{O}(In))$-dominated by σ_2. The concepts of better and best domination apply in a natural way.* □

4   Iterated Strategy Synthesis

In this section, we propose an algorithm for strategy synthesis, based on the following idea: first generate a surely winning perfect information strategy (if it exists), and then iteratively improve it with respect to the dominance relations proposed in Sect. 3. Of the two relations, uniformity-dominance has higher priority. The iterative improvement terminates when the procedure reaches a fixpoint (i.e., no more improvement is possible anymore) or when the time limit is exceeded. After that, the optimized strategy is returned and checked for uniformity.

We will now define our procedure in more detail.

Definition 4 (Input). *The input of the algorithm consists of: model M, state q in M, and formula $\langle\langle a \rangle\rangle F\varphi$. We define the set of initial states as $Q_0 = [q]_{\sim_a}$, i.e., the states that agent a considers possible when the system is in q.*

Algorithm 1. Synthesis algorithm $strat\_synth(M)$

Generate a winning perfect information strategy σ
if σ doesn't exist **then**
    return **false**
end if
Create an empty list $PStr$
Create a list IS of information sets in $M \dagger \sigma$
for $i = 1$ to $|IS|$ **do**
    Take the info set (i, Q_i) and generate the corresponding partial strategy σ_i as a
    restriction of σ to Q_i and add it to $PStr$
    $In_i := Q_i \cap Reach\big(Reach(Q_0, \sigma) \setminus Q_i, (\sigma \setminus \sigma_i) \big)$
    $RDom_i := Q_i \cap Reach(In_i, \sigma_i)$
    $Out_i := Reach(In_i, \sigma_i) \setminus Q_i$
    $Conflicts_i := Conflicts(RDom_i, \sigma_i)$
end for
Optimize the resulting list of partial strategies $PStr$
return $PStr$

Definition 5 (Data structures). *The algorithm uses the following data structures:*

- *The model;*
- *A list of* information sets *for agent a, represented by pairs (id, Q_{id}) where $id \in \mathbb{N}$ is the identifier of the info set, and $Q_{id} \subseteq St$ is an abstraction class of the $\sim_a$ relation;*
- *A list of* partial strategies $PStr$ *represented by the following tuples:*

$$(id, \sigma_{id}, In_{id}, RDom_{id}, Conflicts_{id}, Out_{id})$$

where id is the identifier of the information set on which the strategy operates, σ_{id} is the current set of choices, In_{id} the set of input states, $RDom_{id}$ is the domain of relevance of σ_{id} from In_{id}, $Conflicts_{id}$ is the current set of conflicts, and Out_{id} is the set of output states, i.e., the states by which σ_{id} can pass the control to another partial strategy.

The main part of the procedure is defined by Algorithms 1, 2 and 3. Algorithm 1 tries to generate a perfect information strategy by employing a standard algorithm, e.g., the well-known fixpoint algorithm of [3]. If successful, it produces:

- An ordered list of epistemic indistinguishability classes, also known as *information sets*, for agent a. The list is generated by means of depth-first search through the transition network, starting from the initial state. Note that the information sets are restricted to the pruning of model M by strategy σ, denoted $M \dagger \sigma$ in the pseudocode. That is, only states reachable by σ from the initial state will be taken into account when looking at potential conflicts between a's choices;
- The ordered list of partial strategies extracted from σ, following the same ordering that was established for the information sets.

Algorithm 2. Single sweep optimization algorithm $optimize\_once(PStr)$

$OldPStr := PStr$
for $i = 1$ **to** $|\mathcal{IS}|$ **do**
    repeat
        $OldPStr_i := PStr(i)$
        if exists σ that uniform-best dominates $PStr(i)$ in In_i **then**
            update $PStr(i)$ by taking $\sigma_i := \sigma$ and recomputing the sets $RDom_i$, Out_i,
            and $Conflicts_i$
        end if
        if exists σ that outcome-best dominates $PStr(i)$ in In_i **then**
            update $PStr(i)$ by taking $\sigma_i := \sigma$ and recomputing the sets $RDom_i$, Out_i,
            and $Conflicts_i$
        end if
    until $PStr(i) = OldPStr_i$
    update σ with the current contents of $PStr$
    for every $j \neq i$ **do**
        update the input states of $PStr(j)$ by $In_j := Q_j \cap Reach\big(Reach(Q_0, \sigma) \setminus$
        $Q_j, (\sigma \setminus \sigma_j) \big)$
    end for
end for
return $PStr$

Algorithm 3. Optimization algorithm $optimize(PStr)$

---

repeat
    $OldPStr := PStr$
    $Pstr := optimize\_once(PStr)$
until timeout or (PStr = OldPStr)
return $PStr$

After that, Algorithm 1 calls Algorithm 3.

Algorithm 3 proceeds in cycles. In each cycle it calls Algorithm 2, which optimizes the partial strategies one by one, following the ordering established by Algorithm 1. Moreover, each partial strategy is optimized first with respect to the uniformity-dominance, and then according to the outcome-dominance; this proceeds in a loop until a fixpoint is found. Algorithm 3 terminates when no improvement has been seen in the latest iteration, or the timeout is reached.

It is worth emphasizing that, except for the first phase (generation of a perfect information strategy), this is an anytime algorithm. It means that the procedure will return *some* strategy even for models whose size is beyond grasp for optimal model checking algorithms. This is a clear advantage over the existing approaches [14, 16, 33, 35, 37, 38, 43] where the algorithms typically provide no output even for relatively small models.

5   Experimental Evaluation

We evaluate the algorithm of Sect. 4 through experiments with two classes of models: randomly generated models and the Drones benchmark of [35].

5.1   First Benchmark: Random Models

As the first benchmark for our experiments, we use randomly generated models of a given size. The models represent a single agent playing against a nondeterministic environment. The models are generated according to the following procedure. First, we begin by generating a directed graph with several, randomly chosen, connections. The size of the graph is given by the parameter. Subsequently, we introduce additional connections between randomly selected nodes from distinct paths, in order to increase the complexity of the resulting model. Winning states are selected from the set containing the final states from each of the paths.

Once the graph is generated, it is used to construct the model. Each node represents a unique state, and a connection between two nodes indicates the presence of at least one transition between them. The transitions are generated using the following approach: for each node, a subset of outgoing connections is randomly chosen. From this subset, a set of transitions is created with actions selected randomly. As a result, some transitions will be influenced not only by the agent but also by the nondeterministic environment. This process is repeated multiple times. In the final step of the model generation algorithm, atomic propositions are randomly assigned to states, and epistemic classes are generated at random.

The number of connections, actions, winning states and epistemic classes is given as the function of the number of states in the model.

5.2   Second Benchmark: Drone Model

As the second benchmark we use the Drone Model from [35] with some minor modifications. In this scenario drones are used to measure the air quality in the specified area. The motivation is clear, as nowadays many cities face a problem of air pollution.

A model is described using three variables:

- Number of drones;
- Initial energy for each drone;
- Map size, i.e., the number of places in the area.

Every drone is equipped with a limited battery, initially charged to some energy level. Each action that the drone performs uses one energy unit. When the battery is depleted, the drone lands on the ground and must be picked up.

In our scenario, in contrast to the original one, the map is randomly generated as a directed graph. This introduces randomization into the model generation

		Strategy Perfect Info			Simplified Strategy				Approximation		Domino DFS	
#st	G. time	G. time	#str	#ep	G. time	#str	#ep	%ir	Time	Conclusive	Time	True
10	0.014	0.031	10	5	42.033	7	0	100%	0.018	50%	0.57	100%
100	0.176	0.546	92	61	60.210	83	0	100%	0.519	20%	90	TIMEOUT
1000	9.401	22.001	882	629	61.865	780	0	100%	3.136	0%	90	TIMEOUT

Fig. 1. Random Model results with logarithmic epistemic classes

		Strategy Perfect Info			Simplified Strategy				Approximation		Domino DFS	
#st	G. time	G. time	#str	#ep	G. time	#str	#ep	%ir	Time	Conclusive	Time	True
10	0.009	0.023	10	5	24.048	6	3	20%	0.017	80%	1.14	100%
100	0.202	0.489	94	58	54.253	66	36	10%	0.197	0%	90	TIMEOUT
1000	10.817	25.239	917	584	61.496	614	347	10%	2.647	0%	90	TIMEOUT

Fig. 2. Random Model results with linear epistemic classes

process, enabling us to thoroughly test our algorithms. It is guaranteed that the graph is connected, and each node can be reached from the initial one. Furthermore, each node has no more than four neighbors: one for each direction of the world. Along with the map, pollution readings are also randomly generated and assigned to each place. Readings can have one of the two values: pollution or no pollution.

Each drone holds information about its current energy level, the set of already visited places and its current position on the map. When in a coalition, the drones share their data between themselves, as it is often done in real-life applications. The indistinguishability relations are given by a faulty GPS mechanism: some of the places on the map are indistinguishable for the drone. In that way, epistemic classes are defined.

At each step, the drone can perform one of the listed actions:

- Fly in one of four directions: North, West, South or East;
- Wait, i.e., stay in the current place.

As mentioned before, each action costs the drone one unit of its energy level. Due to the unpredictable nature of the wind, when performing the *fly* action the drone can be carried away to a different place from the one it intended.

5.3   Running the Experiments

In the experiments, we have tested 10 cases for each benchmark and each configuration, and collected the average results. Due to the randomized nature of the models, it was possible that the model generation produces a structure where no winning perfect information strategy existed. Such models were disregarded in the output of the experiments. We note in passing that, for the Randomized Model benchmark, winning perfect information strategies existed in approximately 70% of cases.

			Strategy Perfect Info			Simplified Strategy				Approximation		Domino DFS	
Map	#st	G. time	G. time	#str	#ep	G. time	#str	#ep	%ir	Time	Conclusive	Time	True
5	330	0.078	0.043	38	13	36.003	13	1	60%	0.036	0%	9.012	90%
10	10648	3.420	1.284	74	33	42.478	30	5	60%	1.895	0%	90	TIMEOUT

Fig. 3. Drone Model results

For each test case, first the perfect information strategy was randomly chosen, and then its optimized version was generated according to Algorithm 3. We compared our results with two other methods: fixpoint approximation from [33] and DominoDFS from [35]. Both algorithms were implemented in Python as well as the strategy optimization algorithm. The code is available online at https://github.com/blackbat13/stv.

Random Model was tested in two different configurations that differ only by the function that binds the size of epistemic classes. In the first configuration, the maximum size of the epistemic classes was given by $\log_2 n$, where n is the number of states in the model. In the second configuration, the size of the epistemic classes was at most 10% n, i.e., linear wrt to the size of the state space.

For both benchmarks, only singleton coalitions were considered. In particular, for Drone Model, we only generated models with a single drone acting against the environment.[2] The initial energy of the drone was defined as the number of places in the map times two, in order to increase the likelihood of generating a model in which the drone can visit all the places on the randomly generated map.

The experiments were conducted on an Intel Core i7-6700 CPU with dynamic clock speed of 2.60–3.50 GHz, 32 GB RAM, running under 64bit Linux Debian.

5.4   Results

The output of the experiments is presented in Figs. 1, 2 and 3. Figures 1 and 2 present the results for the Random Model benchmark; Fig. 3 presents the results for the Drone Model benchmark. All running times are given in seconds. The timeout was set to 90 s. In case of strategy optimization, this was split into two parts: 30 s for the strategy generation, and 60 s for its optimization.

The first columns present information about the model configuration, its size and generation time. The next seven columns describe the output of our algorithms, i.e., the randomly generated strategy with perfect information and its optimized version. The last part of the tables contains the reference results from the algorithms used for comparison: lower and upper fixpoint approximation and DominoDFS method.

The table headers should be interpreted as follows:

– *Map*: number of places on the map (for Drone Model);
– *#st*: number of states in the model;

---

[2] Preliminary experiments for coalitions of drones are presented in Sect. 6.

Algorithm 4. Optimization algorithm for coalition $optimize\_coal(PStr, A)$

---
repeat
   $OldPStr := PStr$
   for $agent$ in A **do**
     $Pstr := optimize\_once(PStr)$
   end for
until timeout or (PStr = OldPStr)
return $PStr$

- $G.time$: generation time for the model/strategy;
- $\#str$: number of states reachable in the strategy;
- $\#ep$: number of states in which the strategy uniformity was broken;
- $\%ir$: percentage of cases in which optimized strategy was a uniform strategy;
- $Time$: time used by the Approximation/Domino DFS algorithm;
- $Conclusive$: percentage of cases in which the result of fixpoint approximation was conclusive, i.e. when both the upper bound and the lower bound computations yield the same outcome;
- $True$: percentage of cases in which Domino DFS returned a winning strategy (timeout was reached in all the other cases).

As the results show, our method performed very well in comparison to the reference algorithms. The DominoDFS method ended mostly with timeout for larger models, and the fixpoint approximations gave mostly inconclusive results. In contrast, our optimized strategies obtained pretty good elimination of conflicts, and in many cases produced ideal, i.e., fully uniform strategies.

The results also show clearly that our optimization algorithm works best in situations when the size of the epistemic classes is relatively small. For the logarithmic size of the epistemic classes, the optimized strategy was always a uniform strategy (!). As for the setting with the linear size, the optimization-based algorithm was not as good, but still gave a reduction of conflicts of about 40%. Even in that case, it produced ideal strategies in 10–20% of instances. It is also worth pointing out that, for the Drone benchmark, our optimization returned a uniform strategy in about 60% cases.

We note, again, that our algorithm is an anytime algorithm, which means that it always returns *some* strategy, regardless of the given timeout.

6 Coalitional Strategies

So far, we have focused on the synthesis of individual strategies. In fact, our synthesis algorithm in Sect. 4 works only for singleton coalitions. This is because it relies on the fact that the domains of partial strategies are closed with respect to indistinguishability relations of the involved agents. While such a closure is guaranteed for information sets of single agent, the union of information sets of several agents typically does not satisfy the property.

Map	#st	G. time	Strategy Perfect Info			Simplified Strategy			
			G. time	#st	#ep	G. time	#st	#ep	%ir
3	667	0.85	0.397	35	11	12.031	9	1	60%
5	31122	69.265	107.428	587	728	60.8	87	58	40%

Fig. 4. Drone model results for coalitions

One way out is to *define* the domains of partial strategies by the closure. The domains would in that case correspond to common knowledge neighborhoods for the coalition. Unfortunately, this will not work well in practice: for most models, the common knowledge closure will produce the whole state space, and thus make the computation infeasible.

Another simple idea is to optimize coalitional strategies agent-wise, alternating between the agents. In that case, we optimize the individual strategies being parts of σ_A one by one, using the optimization template from Sect. 4. The resulting procedure is presented as Algorithm 4.

The output of our experimental evaluation for synthesis of coalitional strategies is presented in Fig. 4. For the experiments, the Drone benchmark was selected with coalition of two drone agents. As the results show, our algorithm obtained a high level of optimization of the initial, perfect information, strategy. Most importantly, the procedure produced ideal strategies in 60% and 40% of the instances, respectively, thus providing a conclusive answer to the model checking question in about half of the cases.

7   Conclusions

In this paper, we propose an anytime algorithm to synthesize "reasonably good" strategies for reachability goals under imperfect information. The idea is to first generate a surely winning strategy with *perfect information*, and then iteratively improve it with respect to its uniformity level and the tightness of its outcome set. We evaluate the algorithm experimentally on two classes of models: randomly generated ones and ones modeling a group of drones patrolling for air pollution. The results show high optimization rates, especially for models with relatively small indistinguishability classes. For such models, the procedure produced ideal strategies in a large fraction of the instances, thus providing a conclusive answer to the model checking question.

The fact that our method works well for models with small epistemic classes suggests that it should complement, rather than compete, with methods based on search through the space of uniform strategies (which usually work better for models with *large* information sets). Depending on the kind of the model, a suitable algorithm should be used.

Acknowledgements. The work was supported by NCBR Poland and FNR Luxembourg under the PolLux/FNR-CORE projects STV (POLLUX-VII/1/2019 and C18/IS/12685695/IS/STV/Ryan), SpaceVote (POLLUX-XI/14/SpaceVote/2023 and

C22/IS/17232062/SpaceVote) and PABLO (C21/IS/16326754/PABLO). The work of Damian Kurpiewski was also supported by the CNRS IEA project MoSART.

References

1. Alur, R., et al.: MOCHA: modularity in model checking. Technical report, University of Berkeley (2000)
2. Alur, R., Henzinger, T.A., Kupferman, O.: Alternating-time temporal logic. In: Proceedings of the 38th Annual Symposium on Foundations of Computer Science (FOCS), pp. 100–109. IEEE Computer Society Press (1997)
3. Alur, R., Henzinger, T.A., Kupferman, O.: Alternating-time temporal logic. J. ACM **49**, 672–713 (2002). https://doi.org/10.1145/585265.585270
4. Aminof, B., Malvone, V., Murano, A., Rubin, S.: Graded modalities in strategy logic. Inf. Comput. **261**, 634–649 (2018). https://doi.org/10.1016/j.ic.2018.02.022
5. Belardinelli, F., Condurache, R., Dima, C., Jamroga, W., Jones, A.: Bisimulations for verification of strategic abilities with application to ThreeBallot voting protocol. In: Proceedings of the 16th International Conference on Autonomous Agents and Multiagent Systems (AAMAS), pp. 1286–1295. IFAAMAS (2017)
6. Belardinelli, F., Lomuscio, A.: Agent-based abstractions for verifying alternating-time temporal logic with imperfect information. In: Proceedings of AAMAS, pp. 1259–1267. ACM (2017)
7. Berthon, R., Maubert, B., Murano, A., Rubin, S., Vardi, M.Y.: Strategy logic with imperfect information. In: Proceedings of LICS, pp. 1–12 (2017). https://doi.org/10.1109/LICS.2017.8005136
8. Berthon, R., Maubert, B., Murano, A., Rubin, S., Vardi, M.Y.: Strategy logic with imperfect information. ACM Trans. Comput. Log. **22**(1), 5:1–5:51 (2021). https://doi.org/10.1145/3427955
9. Bryant, R.E.: Graph-based algorithms for Boolean function manipulation. IEEE Trans. Comput. **35**(8), 677–691 (1986)
10. Bulling, N., Dix, J., Jamroga, W.: Model checking logics of strategic ability: complexity. In: Dastani, M., Hindriks, K., Meyer, J.J. (eds.) Specification and Verification of Multi-agent Systems, pp. 125–159. Springer, Boston (2010). https://doi.org/10.1007/978-1-4419-6984-2_5
11. Bulling, N., Jamroga, W.: What agents can probably enforce. Fund. Inform. **93**(1–3), 81–96 (2009)
12. Bulling, N., Jamroga, W.: Alternating epistemic mu-calculus. In: Proceedings of IJCAI-11, pp. 109–114 (2011)
13. Burch, J.R., Clarke, E.M., McMillan, K.L., Dill, D.L., Hwang, L.J.: Symbolic model checking: 10-20 states and beyond. In: Proceedings of 4th Annual IEEE Symposium on Logic in Computer Science (LICS), pp. 428–439. IEEE Computer Society (1990)
14. Busard, S.: Symbolic model checking of multi-modal logics: uniform strategies and rich explanations. Ph.D. thesis, Universite Catholique de Louvain (2017)
15. Busard, S., Pecheur, C., Qu, H., Raimondi, F.: Improving the model checking of strategies under partial observability and fairness constraints. In: Merz, S., Pang, J. (eds.) ICFEM 2014. LNCS, vol. 8829, pp. 27–42. Springer, Cham (2014). https://doi.org/10.1007/978-3-319-11737-9_3
16. Busard, S., Pecheur, C., Qu, H., Raimondi, F.: Reasoning about memoryless strategies under partial observability and unconditional fairness constraints. Inf. Comput. **242**, 128–156 (2015). https://doi.org/10.1016/j.ic.2015.03.014

17. Calta, J., Shkatov, D., Schlingloff, H.: Finding uniform strategies for multi-agent systems. In: Dix, J., Leite, J., Governatori, G., Jamroga, W. (eds.) CLIMA 2010. LNCS (LNAI), vol. 6245, pp. 135–152. Springer, Heidelberg (2010). https://doi.org/10.1007/978-3-642-14977-1_12

18. Čermák, P., Lomuscio, A., Mogavero, F., Murano, A.: MCMAS-SLK: a model checker for the verification of strategy logic specifications. In: Biere, A., Bloem, R. (eds.) CAV 2014. LNCS, vol. 8559, pp. 525–532. Springer, Cham (2014). https://doi.org/10.1007/978-3-319-08867-9_34

19. Cermák, P., Lomuscio, A., Murano, A.: Verifying and synthesising multi-agent systems against one-goal strategy logic specifications. In: Proceedings of AAAI, pp. 2038–2044 (2015)

20. Chatterjee, K., Doyen, L., Henzinger, T., Raskin, J.F.: Algorithms for omega-regular games of incomplete information. Log. Methods Comput. Sci. **3**(3), 4 (2007)

21. Clarke, E., Emerson, E.: Design and synthesis of synchronization skeletons using branching time temporal logic. In: Kozen, D. (ed.) Logic of Programs 1981. Lecture Notes in Computer Science, vol. 131, pp. 52–71. Springer, Cham (1981). https://doi.org/10.1007/bfb0025774

22. Dembiński, P., et al.: √erics: a tool for verifying timed automata and estelle specifications. In: Garavel, H., Hatcliff, J. (eds.) TACAS 2003. LNCS, vol. 2619, pp. 278–283. Springer, Heidelberg (2003). https://doi.org/10.1007/3-540-36577-X_20

23. Dima, C., Maubert, B., Pinchinat, S.: The expressive power of epistemic μ-calculus. CoRR abs/1407.5166 (2014)

24. Dima, C., Maubert, B., Pinchinat, S.: Relating paths in transition systems: the fall of the modal mu-calculus. In: Italiano, G.F., Pighizzini, G., Sannella, D.T. (eds.) MFCS 2015. LNCS, vol. 9234, pp. 179–191. Springer, Heidelberg (2015). https://doi.org/10.1007/978-3-662-48057-1_14

25. Dima, C., Tiplea, F.: Model-checking ATL under imperfect information and perfect recall semantics is undecidable. CoRR abs/1102.4225 (2011)

26. Doyen, L., Raskin, J.F.: Games with imperfect information: theory and algorithms. In: Lecture Notes in Game Theory for Computer Scientists, pp. 185–212. Cambridge University Press (2011)

27. Gammie, P., van der Meyden, R.: MCK: model checking the logic of knowledge. In: Alur, R., Peled, D.A. (eds.) CAV 2004. LNCS, vol. 3114, pp. 479–483. Springer, Heidelberg (2004). https://doi.org/10.1007/978-3-540-27813-9_41

28. Huang, X., van der Meyden, R.: Symbolic model checking epistemic strategy logic. In: Proceedings of AAAI Conference on Artificial Intelligence, pp. 1426–1432 (2014)

29. Jamroga, W.: Logical Methods for Specification and Verification of Multi-agent Systems. ICS PAS Publishing House (2015)

30. Jamroga, W., Dix, J.: Model checking ATL_{ir} is indeed Δ_2^P-complete. In: Proceedings of EUMAS. CEUR Workshop Proceedings, vol. 223 (2006)

31. Jamroga, W., Penczek, W., Dembiński, P., Mazurkiewicz, A.: Towards partial order reductions for strategic ability. In: Proceedings of the 17th International Conference on Autonomous Agents and Multiagent Systems (AAMAS), pp. 156–165. IFAAMAS (2018)

32. Jamroga, W., Knapik, M.: Some things are easier for the dumb and the bright ones (beware the average!). In: Proceedings of the Twenty-Eighth International Joint Conference on Artificial Intelligence IJCAI, pp. 1734–1740 (2019). https://doi.org/10.24963/ijcai.2019/240

33. Jamroga, W., Knapik, M., Kurpiewski, D., Mikulski, Ł.: Approximate verification of strategic abilities under imperfect information. Artif. Intell. **277** (2019). https://doi.org/10.1016/j.artint.2019.103172

34. Kurpiewski, D., Jamroga, W., Knapik, M.: STV: Model checking for strategies under imperfect information. In: Proceedings of the 18th International Conference on Autonomous Agents and Multiagent Systems AAMAS 2019, pp. 2372–2374. IFAAMAS (2019)

35. Kurpiewski, D., Knapik, M., Jamroga, W.: On domination and control in strategic ability. In: Proceedings of the 18th International Conference on Autonomous Agents and Multiagent Systems AAMAS 2019, pp. 197–205. IFAAMAS (2019)

36. Kurpiewski, D., Pazderski, W., Jamroga, W., Kim, Y.: STV+reductions: towards practical verification of strategic ability using model reductions. In: Proceedings of AAMAS, pp. 1770–1772. ACM (2021)

37. Lomuscio, A., Qu, H., Raimondi, F.: MCMAS: an open-source model checker for the verification of multi-agent systems. Int. J. Softw. Tools Technol. Transf. **19**(1), 9–30 (2017). https://doi.org/10.1007/s10009-015-0378-x

38. Lomuscio, A., Raimondi, F.: Model checking knowledge, strategies, and games in multi-agent systems. In: Proceedings of International Joint Conference on Autonomous Agents and Multiagent Systems (AAMAS), pp. 161–168 (2006). https://doi.org/10.1145/1160633.1160660

39. Mogavero, F., Murano, A., Perelli, G., Vardi, M.: Reasoning about strategies: on the model-checking problem. ACM Trans. Comput. Log. **15**(4), 1–42 (2014)

40. Mogavero, F., Murano, A., Vardi, M.: Reasoning about strategies. In: Proceedings of FSTTCS, pp. 133–144 (2010)

41. Peterson, G., Reif, J.: Multiple-person alternation. In: Proceedings of the 20th Annual Symposium on Foundations of Computer Science (FOCS), pp. 348–363. IEEE Computer Society Press (1979)

42. Pilecki, J., Bednarczyk, M.A., Jamroga, W.: Synthesis and verification of uniform strategies for multi-agent systems. In: Bulling, N., van der Torre, L., Villata, S., Jamroga, W., Vasconcelos, W. (eds.) CLIMA 2014. LNCS (LNAI), vol. 8624, pp. 166–182. Springer, Cham (2014). https://doi.org/10.1007/978-3-319-09764-0_11

43. Pilecki, J., Bednarczyk, M., Jamroga, W.: SMC: synthesis of uniform strategies and verification of strategic ability for multi-agent systems. J. Log. Comput. **27**(7), 1871–1895 (2017). https://doi.org/10.1093/logcom/exw032

44. Raimondi, F., Lomuscio, A.: Automatic verification of multi-agent systems by model checking via ordered binary decision diagrams. J. Appl. Log. **5**(2), 235–251 (2007)

45. Schobbens, P.Y.: Alternating-time logic with imperfect recall. Electron. Notes Theor. Comput. Sci. **85**(2), 82–93 (2004)

A Multi-agent Sudoku Through the Wave Function Collapse

Carlos Marín-Lora[(✉)] and Miguel Chover

GAMERS - Video Games Research Group, Institute of New Imaging Technologies,
Universitat Jaume I, Castellón de la Plana, Spain
{cmarin,chover}@uji.es

Abstract. Sudoku is a logic puzzle that involves filling a 9×9 grid with digits from 1 to 9 without repeating any number in the same row, column, or subgrid. Translating this traditional newspaper puzzle into a video game raises technical challenges as generating a complete and valid grid, creating puzzles with solutions based on the difficulty level, and implementing user interaction mechanisms. This research paper presents the specification and implementation of Sudoku as a video game using the entropies from the wave function collapse technique and a multi-agent game development methodology. The main focus of the development is to consider each of the 81 cells as autonomous agents, computing the possibilities space for each agent and establishing the information transfer mechanisms based on the game's constraints.

Keywords: Multi-agent systems · Entropy · Wave function collapse · Game development · Game logic

1 Introduction

Sudoku is a logic game based on the challenge of completing a 9×9 grid with numbers from 1 to 9, ensuring that each row, column, and sub-grid contains all numbers without repeating. The full implementation of Sudoku as a video game is a challenge that varies in difficulty depending on the approach chosen, the programming language used, and the level of experience of the programmer.

The first step in its implementation goes through the generation of the puzzle. There are methods such as elimination and filling, backtracking, symmetry-based generation, and backtracking algorithms [8,19]. These methods allow the creation of Sudoku grids with different difficulty levels and aesthetic styles, ensuring that they comply with the game rules and guaranteeing a unique solution. The choice of method will depend on the specific requirements and purposes of the video game and the selection of programming language and data structures suitable for the grid generation and manipulation process. Although not strictly necessary, data structures such as lists, vectors, or arrays can help to efficiently organize the grid data and simplify the operations required to validate

V. Malvone and A. Murano (Eds.): EUMAS 2023, LNAI 14282, pp. 381–395, 2023.
https://doi.org/10.1007/978-3-031-43264-4_24

the solution and apply the generation methods. However, for an experienced programmer familiar with Sudoku concepts, the implementation can be moderate to easy, while for a novice programmer, it can be more challenging. Implementing a game with a matrix nature as this without loops and complex data structures presents an exciting intellectual and technical challenge. Although the efficiency of the computer application is likely to be poorer than using them, learning techniques to solve it can provide new and interesting approaches.

In recent years, the development of applications with the multi-agent systems (MAS) methodology has brought innovative approaches in various areas of computer science, and videogames are one of the fields that have experienced a greater impact, where they have been applied to improve content generation and the resolution of complex problems [14,21]. In this sense, and using a methodology for the creation of video games such as MAS [1,10], this work presents an alternative approach for the procedural implementation of the game through the procedural generation method of the *Wave Function Collapse* (WFC) [5].

The goal is to explore how interaction and cooperation between multiple agents within a shared environment can be applied in the Sudoku generation and provide challenging and varied solutions for players. Furthermore, we will examine how this implementation affects different levels of complexity. To accomplish this, we will discuss the key concepts of the methodology and their application to the game. We will also describe the proposed architecture for our implementation and discuss the challenges and benefits of this approach. Through testing, we will evaluate the performance and effectiveness of our MAS.

With all this in mind, the paper is organized as follows. Section 2 presents the work context and the technical foundations of this development. Subsequently, Sect. 3 describes and specifies the system architecture. Section 4 outlines the most relevant mechanics of this implementation, and a description of the application performance is presented in Sect. 5. Finally, Sect. 6 presents the general conclusions of the work and the lines of future work.

2   Background

2.1   Game's Overview

Sudoku is a logic game played on a grid of 9×9 squares divided into nine blocks of 3×3 squares each. The game's goal is to fill the grid with the numbers from 1 to 9 so that each row, column, and 3×3 subgrid contains all the numbers from 1 to 9 without repeating. It is considered a game of logic and problem-solving that has become popular worldwide due to its simplicity and ability to provide mental challenges at different difficulty levels. Sudoku puzzles can be found in newspapers, magazines, websites, and mobile apps.

A conventional Sudoku game starts with some squares already solved, which limits the possible combinations and makes the game's difficulty level flexible. From these initial values, the player must deduce which number should go in each empty square using the game's constraints. There are variants of Sudoku that present different challenges and strategies. For instance, *Sudoku X* works on a 9×9 grid with two additional diagonals that must contain the numbers 1 to 9 without repeating [15], while *Samurai Sudoku* consists of five overlapping 9×9 grids, each with its own rules [2].

2.2   Math Involvement

In mathematical terms, Sudoku is a combination and permutation problem. A 9×9 Sudoku grid has 81 squares, each of which can contain one of nine possible numbers. Therefore, the number of possible Sudoku grids is 9^{81}, which is an incredibly large number: about 6.67×10^{77}. However, not all grids are valid per se, as they must also comply with the rules and constraints of the game. That is, each row, column and 3×3 subgrid must contain all numbers from 1 to 9 without repeating. Although the exact number of valid Sudoku grids is unknown with certainty, it is estimated that there are about 65.47×10^9 valid grids.

To solve more complicated Sudoku grids, mathematical techniques such as graph theory and mathematical logic can be applied. For instance, graph theory can be used to represent the Sudoku grid as a bipartite graph, where nodes represent the squares and edges connect squares that are in the same row, column, or subgrid. They can also be applied to search for feasible solutions. Mathematical logic techniques can also be applied to deduce which are the possible solutions for each box, using techniques such as mutual exclusion and constraint inference. These techniques rely on logical deduction to reduce the number of possible solutions for each cell, which can speed up the resolution [3,17].

Finally, in terms of creating Sudoku grids, mathematical techniques can be applied to design grids that have special properties, such as a minimum number of initial numbers or a particular difficulty. For instance, combinatorial design techniques can be used to create symmetrical or asymmetrical Sudoku grids, which can add an element of aesthetics to the game [19].

2.3   Wave Function Collapse

WFC is a concept in quantum physics that refers to the collapse of the wave function of a particle into a measured state. In very general terms, the idea is that the unobserved state of a particle can be in any potential state. As soon as the particle is observed, the possibilities vanish and the wave function collapses. For computer graphics and video games, it has interestingly been applied as a method of procedural content creation. The aim is to generate content automatically and randomly, such as landscapes, game levels, or architectural structures, using algorithms, constraints, and predefined rules that return coherent and structurally defined results [6,20].

The original algorithm was developed by Maxim Gumin as a texture synthesis method based on single-setup or sample-sample images [4]. Although its application in different contexts relies on the potential states that the algorithm scatters, be they textures, 3D models, or numerical values. The basic idea is that starting from a discrete space such as a mesh or grid and a finite set of possible values, the algorithm initializes each grid cell with potentially all possible values.

That is, with maximum entropy [7,18]. This means that if a cell collapses to a value, the neighboring cells will also see their entropy reduced according to the pre-established restrictions. As the algorithm is executed, the probability wave is collapsed to a particular state, eliminating the least probable options and retaining the most probable ones. This process is repeated until a final configuration is reached, which can be used as a result regardless of the context.

2.4   Video Game Development as MAS

The relationship between MAS and video games is not new. In the literature, one can find multiple references to games that use this methodology to solve specific mechanics [12,14]. However, this paper relies on game engine able to produce games that meet the requirements of a MAS following its formal definition to make a description of the game and its essential elements [9,10]. That is, it uses the methodology to generate complete games as MAS.

In this model, the objects or actors of the game are like autonomous agents Ag that interact with each other within a shared environment Env to describe complex systems. Following this analogy and based on the formal definition of MAS, the game represents the environment and the actors are the agents of the multi-agent games. From the environment state, the actors can perceive information and react to specific states based on their predefined tasks.

The behavior associated with the tasks is determined by sets of behavioral rules and predefined logical semantics. The construction of the games is based on a single type of actor and no hierarchical relationships between them. Each of them has the same structure of properties and behavioral rules with which they can interact with the game environment. All this without a scene graph, which simplifies the internal architecture of the engine [1,16]. The definition of the behavior is established through formal semantics based on predicate logic with a level of abstraction for the definition of the actor's behavior that makes complex data structures such as vectors or matrices unnecessary. This semantics consists of only five conditions and four actions to define the games using predicate formulas and without requiring logical operators, matrices, or loops, since the game loop performs cyclic evaluations of the behavior rules, simply using the IF-THEN-ELSE structure [11,13].

3   Description and Specification

From an expert programmer's point of view, it seems strange not to consider developing a game like Sudoku without using data structures such as lists, vectors, or matrices to represent the grid. However, it is not strictly necessary. Following the methodology of video game development such as MAS [10], a spatial placement of 81 agents interacting with their neighbors within their shared environment can be envisioned.

Practically all current game engines have an interactive graphical interface to prepare the spatial arrangement of the elements that compose a level. In the case of Sudoku, the initial layout consists of generating the 9×9 grid of agents Ag and initializing them within the game environment Env .

Following the video game development methodology discussed above, the logic evaluation of the agents Ag is performed by evaluating their behavioral rules at each iteration of the game loop. That is, the game engine will evaluate the rules of all the agents once per iteration and perform the necessary actions. For this reason, for this implementation, it is necessary to use states that delimit the actions to be performed depending on the phase in which the game is, whether it is the grid generation, the level generation, or the user interaction. Next, the game's features and the elements that compose it are described and specified.

```
Env {                                            Ag {
    State (string) = "WFC_ENTROPY"                   State (string) = "WFC_ENTROPY"
    Level (int) = 41                                 Row (int)= -1
    Auction (int) = 1                                Column (int) = -1
    Entropy (int) = 9                                Block (int) = -1
    AgRow (int) = -1                                 Auction (int) = 1
    AgColumn (int) = -1                              Entropy (int) = 9
    AgBlock (int) = -1                               EntropyX (bool) = true
    AgValue (int) = -1                               Value (int) = 0
    Propagated (int) = 0                         }
    Collapsed (int) = 81
}
```

3.1 Environment Description

The environment Env is the shared space in which the game takes place. It is composed by a set of variables that are accessible to every agent Ag that exists in it. In the environment designed for this game, there are variables that control aspects such as the phase in which it is located, the difficulty level, information about the selected agent Ag, or other control variables. The $State$ variable is key since it delimits the evaluation of the agent's behavior rules to the phase in which the game is located. For example, the first phase is the grid generation with the WFC method, so those states begin with the prefix WFC. Similarly, the ones related to level generation start with LEVEL. The contents of the environment Env are presented above.

3.2 Agent Description

At a simplistic level, in this game, each agent Ag is the representation of a particular value and its space of possibilities within this environment. In terms of variables and characteristics, the agent has variables that determine its position on the grid, a state controller to drive the evaluation of the logic at each phase, and variables to control the entropy of the agent before it collapses to a particular value. Initially, the agents have maximum entropy (9) and no collapse, meaning zero value (0). The structure of an agent Ag is described at the section's beginning. It should be noted that for simplicity and ease of reading, the boolean entropy control variables have been grouped from one value to a single variable ($EntropyX$).

4   Game Implementation and Mechanics

For this particular version of Sudoku, four phases have been visualized that could be said to be organized sequentially. In the first phase, a spatial layout of the game's matrix structure is established and the agents' information is initialized. In the second phase, a pseudo-random grid is constructed to meet the game constraints based on the collapse of the agents in the environment. In the third phase, and from the grid obtained, the agents are randomly collapsed or expanded until the selected difficulty level is completed. After each expansion, it is verified that the puzzle has at least one solution path. At this point, the player has a valid level with which to start playing in the last phase. That phase is the game itself, where the user's interactions with the game are controlled.

4.1   Spatial Layout of the Grid

The Sudoku implementation using the multi-agent game engine approach, based on agents instead of conventional data structures, offers a distinct, flexible, and adaptable alternative [10]. This approach stands out for its ability to adapt to distributed environments, its efficiency, and scalability. It provides an innovative way of approaching the generation of complex games such as Sudoku, taking full advantage of the capabilities of MAS and even promoting parallel performance [21]. In this sense, the structure is generated by assembling and spatially arranging the 81 grid agents and initializing their information. Which consists of their positioning relative to their neighbors. In other words, their row, column, and subgrid. Figure 1 shows on the left the initial arrangement of the 81 agents with their information highlighted, and on the right a representation of an agent's neighborhood relationships (331). Any potential change in the agent state will affect only its row (green), column (yellow), and subgrid (blue) neighbors.

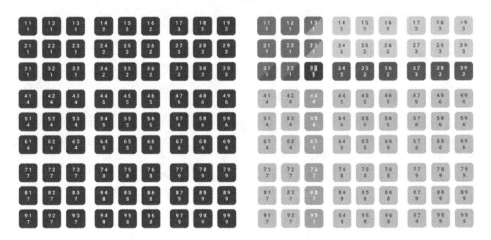

Fig. 1. Grid structure with the agents' codes (left) and the 331 agent neighborhood relationship as an example (right).

4.2   Grid Generation

With the structure established in the previous phase, it is time to generate a valid puzzle that meets the constraints of the game. Remember, each agent can take an integer value between 1 and 9, but that value cannot reappear in its neighborhood (row, column, subgrid). For this task, let's use the WFC procedural generation techniques. This technique starts from a finite set of possible values or assets, either digits, textures, or 3D models. These assets have associated with them pre-established neighborhood constraints that try to ensure continuity when generating procedural patterns. In the present case, a set of values represented by the digits 1 to 9 and by the neighborhood constraints.

Starting from the uncollapsed agents with the lowest entropy, and auction process selects and collapses one to a random value among its entropy. The information about the collapsed value is propagated through its neighborhood, reducing the entropy values of its neighboring agents, that is, the agents sharing row, column and subgrid. Following the previous example, Fig. 2 shows the grid of agents with maximum entropy on the left, and on the right the collapse of agent 331 to value 9. As can be seen, the neighbors have had their entropy reduced to 8 potential values. As long as the grid is not completed, the next steps consist of repeating the same process. Since there are not lists or other similar data structures, the method to select the next agent is to make an auction. To do this, first the agents with the lowest entropy are identified and second, these agents generate a random number. The selected agent will be the one that meets the lowest entropy condition and the lowest auction value. The winner will collapse to one of its potential values within its entropy and propagate this change in its neighborhood.

This method relies primarily on the game engine's game loop. Each action is performed depending on the state of the environment and the agents. This

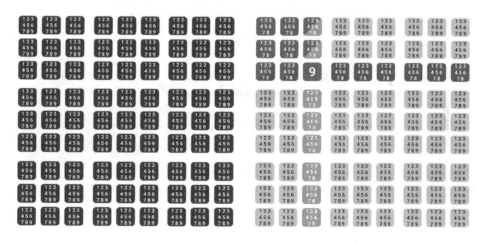

Fig. 2. Example of the grid with maximum entropy (left) and collapse of the first agent and propagation of information in its neighborhood (right).

process is repeated until there are no more uncollapsed agents or until there is no valid solution. That is, when there is an agent with 0 entropy. In that case, the puzzle is reset and it starts again. Other methods could be used to search for solution paths, but as will be seen later, restarting this phase is a fast and robust solution. The agent's behavior rules that control this process are presented next:

WFC ENTROPY: These are the agent's actions while the environment has the *"WFC ENTROPY"* state. The agent also has three sub-states for this rule: *"WFC ENTROPY"*, *"WFC AUCTION"* and *"WFC COLLAPSE"*. These sub-states are sequential and executed in consecutive iterations of the game loop. Their tasks are, respectively, to determine which are the agents with the lowest entropy, to perform a random auction to select an agent among those with the lowest entropy, and finally to collapse the selected agent. At the end of the process or if it does not meet the entropy or auction cutoff criteria, the agent goes to a waiting state or *"IDLE"*. If the search for the lowest entropy founds an agent with entropy 0, it goes to the *"WFC RESET"* state to undo the grid and start over.

```
1 if(Env.State == "WFC_ENTROPY")          18        Env.Auction = Ag.Auction;
2   if(Ag.State == "WFC_ENTROPY")         19        Ag.State = "WFC_COLLAPSE";
3     if(Env.Entropy > Ag.Entropy)        20      else
4       Env.Entropy = Ag.Entropy;         21        Ag.State = "IDLE";
5       Ag.State = "WFC_AUCTION";         22      end
6     else                                23    end
7       Ag.State = "IDLE";                24    if(Ag.State == "WFC_COLLAPSE")
8     end                                 25      if(Env.Auction == Ag.Auction)
9     if(Env.Entropy == 0)                26        Env.AgRow = Ag.Row;
10      Env.collapsed = 81;               27        Env.AgColumn = Ag.Column;
11      Ag.State = "IDLE";                28        Env.AgBlock = Ag.Block;
12      Env.State = "WFC_RESET";          29        Env.State = "WFC_COLLAPSE";
13    end                                 30      end
14  end                                   31      Ag.State = "IDLE";
15  if(Ag.State == "WFC_AUCTION")         32    end
16    Ag.Auction = Rand(0,100000);        33 end
17    if(Env.Auction > Ag.Auction)
```

Behavior Rule 1.1 – Agent's "WFC ENTROPY" rule.

WFC RESET: If in *"WFC ENTROPY"* any agent with entropy 0 is found, the process must be restarted. This behavior rule is in charge of restarting the agent and resetting the environment state when all are ready.

```
1 if(Env.State == "WFC_RESET")     5   if(Env.Collapsed == 0)
2   Ag.Entropy = 9;                6     Env.State = "WFC_ENTROPY";
3   Ag.EntropyX = true;            7   end
4   Env.Collapsed -= 1;            8 end
```

Behavior Rule 1.2 – Agent's "WFC RESET" rule.

WFC COLLAPSE: The agent selected in *"WFC ENTROPY"* is collapsed to a random value within its probability space and the environment information is updated. The next step is to propagate the information to its neighbors.

```
1 if(Env.State == "WFC_COLLAPSE")        8        Env.Propagate -= 1;
2   if(Env.Row == Ag.Row)                9        Env.State = "WFC_PROPAGATE";
3     if(Env.Column == Ag.Column)       10      end
4       if(Env.Block == Ag.Block)       11    end
5         Ag.Value = Rand(Ag.EntropyX); 12  end
6         Env.AgValue = Ag.Value;       13 end
7         Env.Collapsed += 1;
```

Behavior Rule 1.3 – Agent's "WFC COLLAPSE" rule.

WFC PROPAGATE: Finally, *"WFC PROPAGATE"* is responsible for propagating the agent's collapse information among its neighbors. That is, it eliminates the collapsed value of the entropy of the non-collapsed agents that share row, column, or subgrid. Finally, a check is made to see if the grid is complete or if there are missing agents to be collapsed. In the first case, it is passed to the *"LEVEL RANDOM"* level generation state, and in the second case it is returned to *"WFC ENTROPY"* to repeat the process with the remaining agents.

```
 1 if(Env.State == "WFC_PROPAGATE")     14      end
 2   if(Ag.value != 0)                  15    end
 3     if(Ag.Row == Env.AgRow)          16    Env.Propagate -= 1;
 4       Ag.EntropyX = false;           17    if(Env.Propagate == 0)
 5       Ag.Entropy -= 1;               18      if(Env.Collapsed < 81)
 6     end                              19        Env.State = "WFC_ENTROPY";
 7     if(Ag.Column == Env.AgColumn)    20      else
 8       Ag.EntropyX = false;           21        Env.State = "LEVEL_RANDOM";
 9       Ag.Entropy -= 1;               22        Ag.State = "LEVEL_AUCTION";
10     end                              23      end
11     if(Ag.Block == Env.AgBlock)      24    end
12       Ag.EntropyX = false;           25 end
13       Ag.Entropy -= 1;
```

Behavior Rule 1.4 – Agent's "WFC PROPAGATE" rule.

4.3   Level Generation

With a complete and valid grid according to the game constraints, the puzzle begins to be generated according to a preset difficulty level.

In this sense, starting from a specific number of agents set by a value to denote the difficulty level, the opposite process of the previous phase is started. That is, one of the collapsed agents is randomly selected, uncollapsed and its information is expanded in its neighborhood. If after this step there is no agent with entropy 1, the expansion is undone and a collapsed agent is randomly selected again.

This process is looped until the number of collapsed agents equals the selected difficulty level. An example of a grid generated in the first phase can be seen in Fig. 3 on the left, which is converted into a puzzle ready to be played with a difficulty level of 40 collapsed agents and 41 to be discovered.

Similarly, as in the previous phase, this process is directly dependent on the game loop of the engine since the rules evaluation is performed autonomously by each agent at each iteration of the loop. Next, the behavioral rules of the agents controlling this process are presented.

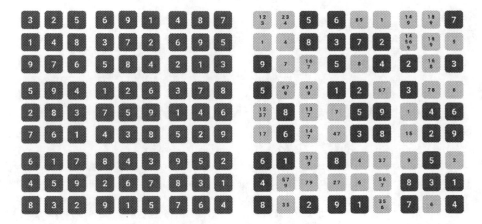

Fig. 3. Example of a complete and valid grid generated (left) and a puzzle ready to play with level 41 (right).

LEVEL RANDOM: This rule is used to select an agent for decollapse. The selection method is the random auction, as in the previous phase. In the first iteration, the auction is made and, if it is the winner, in the second iteration it is established as the agent to be decollapsed.

```
 1 if(Env.State == "LEVEL_RANDOM")        11   if(Ag.State == "LEVEL_COLLAPSE")
 2   if(Ag.State == "LEVEL_AUCTION")      12     if(Env.Auction == Ag.Auction)
 3     if(Ag.Value != 0)                  13       Env.AgRow = Ag.Row;
 4       Ag.Auction = Rand(0,100000);     14       Env.AgColumn = Ag.Column;
 5       if(Env.Auction > Ag.Auction)     15       Env.AgBlock = Ag.Block;
 6         Env.Auction = Ag.Auction;      16       Env.State = "LEVEL_COLLAPSE";
 7         Ag.State = "LEVEL_COLLAPSE";   17     end
 8       end                              18     Ag.State = "IDLE";
 9     end                                19   end
10   end                                  20 end
```

Behavior Rule 1.5 – Agent's "LEVEL RANDOM" rule.

LEVEL COLLAPSE: If the agent is the selected one, this rule decollapses it and moves the state to the propagation sub-phase *"LEVEL PROPAGATE"*.

```
 1 if(Env.State = "LEVEL_COLLAPSE")        8       Env.Collapsed -= 1;
 2   if(Env.Row == Ag.Row)                 9       Env.State = "LEVEL_PROPAGATE";
 3     if(Env.Column == Ag.Column)        10     end
 4       if(Env.Block == Ag.Block)        11   end
 5         Env.AgValue = Ag.Value;        12   end
 6         Ag.EntropyX = true;            13 end
 7         Ag.Entropy += 1;
```

Behavior Rule 1.6 – Agent's "LEVEL COLLAPSE" rule.

LEVEL PROPAGATE: This rule applies to the collapsed agent's neighbors, whose entropy is increased by the collapsed value. After this, a check is made to see if there are more collapsed agents than the game's difficulty level. If so, the process is repeated and if not, the next and last *"PLAY"* phase is switched. In addition, if any agent with 0 entropy is found, the last collapse is undone and the process is repeated selecting another agent.

```
1 if(Env.State = "LEVEL_PROPAGATE")    14      end
2   if(Ag.Value != 0)                  15    end
3     if(Ag.Row == Env.AgRow)          16    if(Env.Collapsed > Env.Level)
4       Ag.EntropyX = true;            17      Env.State = "LEVEL_RANDOM";
5       Ag.Entropy += 1;               18      Ag.State = "LEVEL_AUCTION";
6     end                              19    else
7     if(Ag.Column == Env.AgColumn)    20      Env.State = "PLAY";
8       Ag.EntropyX = true;            21    end
9       Ag.Entropy += 1;              22    if(Ag.Entropy == 0)
10    end                              23      Env.State = "LEVEL_UNCOLLAPSE";
11    if(Ag.Block == Env.AgBlock)      24    end
12      Ag.EntropyX = true;            25 end
13      Ag.Entropy += 1;
```

Behavior Rule 1.7 – Agent's "LEVEL PROPAGATE" rule.

LEVEL UNCOLLAPSE: If the last collapse had to be undone, the entropy of the selected agent is increased and it is switched to the sub-state that controls the expansion of information in its neighbors *"LEVEL EXPAND"*.

```
1 if(Env.State = "LEVEL_UNCOLLAPSE")    8          Env.Collapsed += 1;
2   if(Env.Row == Ag.Row)              9          Env.State = "LEVEL_EXPAND"
3     if(Env.Column == Ag.Column)      10        end
4       if(Env.Block == Ag.Block)      11      end
5         Ag.Value = Env.AgValue;      12    end
6         Ag.EntropyX = false;         13 end
7         Ag.Entropy -= 1;
```

Behavior Rule 1.8 – Agent's "LEVEL UNCOLLAPSE" rule.

LEVEL EXPAND: In the same way as in the *"LEVEL PROPAGATE"*, the information is transferred by its neighbors but in this case, removing the value of the decollapsed agent from its entropy.

```
1 if(Env.State = "LEVEL_EXPAND")     10      end
2   if(Ag.Value != 0)                11      if(Ag.Block == Env.AgBlock)
3     if(Ag.Row == Env.AgRow)        12        Ag.EntropyX = false;
4       Ag.EntropyX = false;         13        Ag.Entropy -= 1;
5       Ag.Entropy -= 1;             14      end
6     end                            15    end
7     if(Ag.Column == Env.AgColumn)  16    Env.State = "LEVEL_RANDOM";
8       Ag.EntropyX = false;         17 end
9       Ag.Entropy -= 1;
```

Behavior Rule 1.9 – Agent's "LEVEL EXPAND" rule.

4.4   User Interaction

With the puzzle ready to play, it only remains to specify the logic of the user's interaction with the game. And for this, and the simplicity of this text, it is assumed that the agent selection is done by pointer and the value selection is done by numeric keypad with values from 0 to 9. Where 0 corresponds to the action of resetting the value of the agent. In this sense, the following is the behavior rules that model this logic in the specification system:

PLAY: This rule controls the user's interaction in two ways: the agent's selection by pointer and the value choice to be placed in the agent by a keyboard.

```
 1 if(Env.State == "PLAY")          12    end
 2   if(pointer(Ag))                13    if(keyboard(x))
 3     if(Env.Row != 0)             14      if(Env.AgRow != 0)
 4       Env.AgRow = 0;             15        Ag.Value = x;
 5       Env.AgColumn = 0;          16        Env.Collapsed += 1;
 6       Env.AgBlock = 0;           17        Env.AgRow = 0;
 7     else                         18        Env.AgColumn = 0;
 8       Env.AgRow = Ag.Row;        19        Env.AgBlock = 0;
 9       Env.AgColumn = Ag.Column;  20      end
10       Env.AgBlock = Ag.Block;    21    end
11     end                         22 end
```

Behavior Rule 1.10 – Agent's "PLAY" rule.

5   Results

From the presented description and specification, the game has been implemented in the Unity game engine, specifically in its version 2022.2.1.f1. The result is a fully functional game deployed for the Android mobile platform. In Fig. 4 you can see on the left a game capture with the puzzle ready to be played, and on the right, the same puzzle but already solved. In the screenshot on the left, the entropy values of each of the agents can also be observed for debugging and validation purposes.

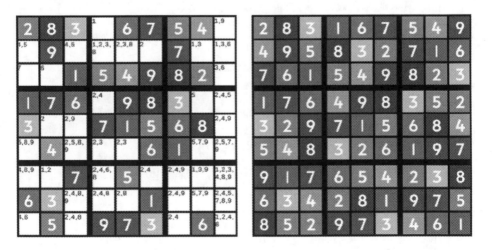

Fig. 4. Screenshot of the game implementation in Unity with the puzzle ready to play with level 41 (left) and the same puzzle solved (right).

Table 1. Seconds taken to grid build (WFC) and level creation (LEVEL) phases.

AGENTS	WFC										AVG
41	2.82	1.64	2.04	1.64	1.64	1.64	4.46	3.76	1.64	1.64	**2.29**
51	1.64	1.64	6.44	1.64	2.80	3.48	1.64	2.40	1.64	1.64	**2.50**
61	1.64	1.64	4.62	2.04	1.64	1.64	3.16	1.64	1.64	1.64	**2.13**
71	1.64	3.16	1.64	3.96	2.04	1.64	2.78	1.64	1.64	2.04	**2.22**
LEVEL											
41	0.84	0.84	0.84	0.84	0.84	0.84	0.84	0.84	0.84	0.84	**0.84**
51	1.04	1.04	1.04	1.04	1.06	1.06	1.06	1.04	1.04	1.04	**1.05**
61	1.30	1.24	1.32	1.32	1.28	1.28	1.26	1.28	1.28	1.28	**1.28**
71	1.66	1.94	1.78	1.64	1.80	1.78	2.02	1.72	1.68	1.74	**1.78**
TOTAL											
41	3.66	2.48	2.88	2.48	2.48	2.48	5.30	4.60	2.48	2.48	**3.13**
51	2.68	2.68	7.48	2.68	3.86	4.54	2.70	3.44	2.68	2.68	**3.54**
61	2.94	2.88	5.94	3.36	2.92	2.92	4.42	2.92	2.92	2.92	**3.41**
71	3.30	5.10	3.42	5.60	3.84	3.42	4.80	3.36	3.32	3.78	**3.99**

The efficiency of the implementation is one of the unknowns of the process. A benchmark with 10 executions of the game over 4 levels of difficulty has been performed to estimate the effect of the methodology. Where each level involves more agents without collapsing initially. The results of these measurements can be seen in Table 1.

From Table 1, arises that the generation process with the WFC method has no relation with the selected level. Since the dimensions of the problem are constant and the variability in the average times is due to the restart that was decided to implement when, given the pseudo-random component of the phase, it is not possible to continue with the generation, and the process is restarted. The situation changes in the case of the level, where an increase in times is observed as the number of agents without collapse increases. It has been observed that in the first level, no backtracking events are observed, but from level 51 onwards entropy recalculations begin to be observed. At the last level, a range of 10–20 backtracking and recalculation events have been observed.

Overall, the average level generation times until the player can start interacting range from 3 to 4 s. These are not prohibitive times, but to smooth that transition an airport shuffle or panel effect has been arranged to provide feedback to the player about what is happening while the puzzle is being generated.

6   Conclusions and Future Work

This paper has presented a procedural implementation of the Sudoku game using a methodology to generate games such as MAS. The main goal was to propose a solution for a game with a matrix nature using MAS. The results obtained show that this approach generates a fully functional video game, offering valid and varied Sudokus to the players.

This approach has represented a challenge since it has made it possible to approach a complex matrix game such as Sudoku innovatively. Furthermore, the successful implementation of Sudoku as a MAS supports the feasibility and effectiveness of this approach. The generation of games using MAS opens up new possibilities, as it can allow expanding the range of methodologies for game construction as this approach offers a distinct, flexible, and adaptable alternative to distributed and scalable environments. In addition to helping developers to acquire computational thinking skills different from the traditional ones.

In this sense, one of the next research lines lies on the definition of a formal scripting language that encapsulates the methodology for generating games as MAS, its integration within a game engine created specifically on it, and on a commercial engine such as Unity.

Acknowledgements. This work has been developed with the support of valgrAI - Graduate School and Research Network of Artificial Intelligence and the Generalitat Valenciana, and co-funded by the European Union. Furthermore, with Grant PDC2021-120997-C31 funded by MCIN/AEI/10.13039/501100011033 by the "European Union NextgenerationEU/PRTR". Grant to Consolidated Research Groups (CIAICO/2021/037) of the Department of Innovation, Universities, Science and Digital Society (Generalitat Valenciana).

References

1. Chover, M., Marín-Lora, C., Rebollo, C., Remolar, I.: A game engine designed to simplify 2D video game development. Multimed. Tools Appl. **79**, 12307–12328 (2020)
2. Danbaba, A.: Construction and analysis of samurai sudoku. Int. J. Math. Comput. Sci. **10**(4), 165–170 (2016)
3. Felgenhauer, B., Jarvis, F.: Mathematics of sudoku I. Math. Spectr. **39**(1), 15–22 (2006)
4. Gumin, M.: Wave Function Collapse: Bitmap & tilemap generation from a single example with the help of ideas from Quantum Mechanics. GitHub (2016). www.github.com/mxgmn/WaveFunctionCollapse
5. Karth, I., Smith, A.M.: WaveFunctionCollapse is constraint solving in the wild. In: Proceedings of the 12th International Conference on the Foundations of Digital Games, pp. 1–10, August 2017
6. Kleineberg, M.: An infinite, procedurally generated city, assembled out of blocks using the Wave Function Collapse algorithm with backtracking. GitHub (2018). www.github.com/marian42/wavefunctioncollapse
7. Machta, J.: Entropy, information, and computation. Am. J. Phys. **67**(12), 1074–1077 (1999)
8. Maji, A.K., Jana, S., Roy, S., Pal, R.K.: An exhaustive study on different sudoku solving techniques. Int. J. Comput. Sci. Issues (IJCSI) **11**(2), 247 (2014)
9. Marín-Lora, C., Chover, M., Sotoca, J.M.: Prototyping a game engine architecture as a multi-agent system. In: 27th International Conference in Central Europe on Computer Graphics, Visualization and Computer Vision (WSCG 2019) (2019)

10. Marín-Lora, C., Chover, M., Sotoca, J.M., García, L.A.: A game engine to make games as multi-agent systems. Adv. Eng. Softw. **140**, 102732 (2020)

11. Marín-Lora, C., Chover, M., Sotoca, J.M.: A game logic specification proposal for 2D video games. In: Rocha, Á., Adeli, H., Reis, L.P., Costanzo, S., Orovic, I., Moreira, F. (eds.) WorldCIST 2020. AISC, vol. 1159, pp. 494–504. Springer, Cham (2020). https://doi.org/10.1007/978-3-030-45688-7_50

12. Marín-Lora, C., Chover, M., Sotoca, J.M.: A multi-agent specification for the Tetris game. In: Matsui, K., Omatu, S., Yigitcanlar, T., González, S.R. (eds.) DCAI 2021. LNNS, vol. 327, pp. 169–178. Springer, Cham (2022). https://doi.org/10.1007/978-3-030-86261-9_17

13. Marín-Lora, C.: Game Development Based on Multi-agent Systems (Doctoral dissertation, Universitat Jaume I) (2022)

14. Nystrom, R.: Game programming patterns. Genever Benning (2014)

15. Provan, J.S.: Sudoku: strategy versus structure. Am. Math. Mon. **116**(8), 702–707 (2009)

16. Rebollo, C., Marín-Lora, C., Remolar, I., Chover, M.: Gamesonomy vs Scratch: two different ways to introduce programming. In: 15th International Conference On Cognition And Exploratory Learning In The Digital Age (CELDA 2018). Ed. IADIS Press (2018)

17. Russell, E., Jarvis, F.: Mathematics of sudoku II. Math. Spectr. **39**(2), 54–58 (2006)

18. Sbert, M., Feixas, M., Rigau, J., Viola, I., Chover, M.: Applications of information theory to computer graphics. In: Eurographics (Tutorials), pp. 625–704, August 2007

19. Simonis, H.: Sudoku as a constraint problem. In: CP Workshop on Modeling and Reformulating Constraint Satisfaction Problems, vol. 12, pp. 13–27. Citeseer, October 2005

20. Stalberg, O.: Townscaper. Steam (2021). www.store.steampowered.com/app/1291340/Townscaper/

21. Wooldridge, M.: An Introduction to Multiagent Systems. John wiley & sons, Hoboken (2009)

AGAMAS: A New Agent-Oriented Traffic Simulation Framework for SUMO

Mahyar Sadeghi Garjan, Tommy Chaanine, Cecilia Pasquale[ID],
Vito Paolo Pastore[ID], and Angelo Ferrando[✉][ID]

Department of Informatics, Bioengineering, Robotics and Systems Engineering,
University of Genoa, Genoa, Italy
{mahyar.sadeghigarjan,tommy.chaanine,cecilia.pasquale,
vito.paolo.pastore,angelo.ferrando}@unige.it

Abstract. Simulating everyday traffic scenarios is not an easy task. Many aspects have to be taken into consideration and properly modelled, from static components, like traffic lights, to dynamic components, like vehicles. Due to their intrinsic autonomy and distribution, such components have already been designed as software agents, and integrated into existing traffic simulators, such as SUMO. The needing for agent-based modelling is even more evident when autonomous vehicles are present in the simulation. In this paper, we present an Agent-Based Traffic Simulation framework, where the simulation components can be defined as JADE agents. We present the engineering of our framework, and we show how it represents a new alternative for creating Agent-Based simulations in the largely used SUMO traffic simulator. We also demonstrate its applicability by employing the framework in one case study involving autonomous vehicles.

Keywords: Agent-Based Traffic Simulation · JADE · SUMO

1 Introduction

The transportation of goods and passengers plays a crucial role in our society. As a consequence, the demand for traffic mobility has grown significantly in recent decades, bringing benefits to human development but causing, as a side effect, an increase in road congestion. Indeed, traffic jams are becoming more frequent every day [10, 25, 27]. The reasons may vary, but at the heart of the matter, we always find a human component. This is true both in urban scenarios, as well as in highway ones. The traffic problem can be tackled from different perspectives; many efforts have been made by researchers to develop traffic control strategies for both urban and highway networks [9, 15, 21]. Nowadays, the most advanced traffic control strategies involve the use of intelligent devices as actuators of different control actions, ranging from smart traffic lights [13, 14, 23] to Connected and Autonomous Vehicles (CAVs) [5, 6, 16]. The former depends on static objects (the traffic lights) and can be mainly deployed in urban scenarios, while the latter can be also deployed in highway scenarios, and depends on dynamic objects

(CAVs) that act as safety cars to enforce a certain speed on vehicular traffic to prevent congestion in different scenarios. In both cases, new and intelligent components are added to the traffic flow, with the objective of preventing/solving traffic jams. Such components need to be autonomous, reactive, proactive, and in some cases, even rational. Namely, such components need to be *agents*.

Some work recognising static and dynamic intelligent components in traffic scenarios as agents have been recently released [8,12,19]. Nonetheless, we are still far away from a large use of such intelligent systems in everyday life, and the possibility of deploying them as agents may be an important stepping stone to achieving such a goal. Because of that, it is problematic to foresee the possible implications of their use. To overcome this issue, traffic simulations have been exploited [3]; where both autonomous and non-autonomous components can be deployed and experimented with together.

In such scenarios, the logic is usually hard-coded inside the simulation; mainly because the existing tools do not support an easy-to-use integration with agent technologies. For this reason, even though from an engineering perspective it would be advantageous to exploit software agents to handle the autonomous components in the simulation, it is usually hardly the case.

Various tools exist to simulate traffic scenarios, amongst them we may find SUMO [11], Aimsun [1], Matsim [18], and PTV Vissim [17] (to cite the most widely used ones). Unfortunately, no existing and maintained framework bridges the gap between such traffic simulators and the agent world.

This paper tries to fill this gap, by introducing a general-purpose AGent-oriented trAffic siMulAtor in Sumo (AGAMAS). We opted for SUMO as a traffic simulator, as it is open source and largely adopted by the traffic simulation community. AGAMAStransparently integrates JADE [2] software agents in SUMO. Amongst the available agent-based frameworks, we opted for JADE because based on Java, highly customisable, and natively decentralised.

2   Background

Tackling daily life traffic issues can be costly. Traffic congestion is an example that can be solved by enlarging the size of the highways. However, this approach is expensive in terms of time and resources. Traffic control, on the other hand, offers cheaper and short-term solutions in which it is possible to enhance the traffic flow. Modelling the traffic results in traffic flow prediction, incident detection and eventually better control of the traffic. However, gauging the effectiveness of these models requires traffic simulation software tools. Traffic model simulations allow for fast, safe, reproducible, and cost-effective experiments.

Simulation of Urban MObility, or SUMO [11], is a multi-modal traffic simulator, designed to handle large networks. It is microscopic, continuous, and portable, and it was developed by the German Aerospace Centre for modelling inter-modal traffic systems like vehicles, public transport and pedestrians. Since 2001, it has been available as an open-source project. In 2017 it became an Eclipse Foundation project.

SUMO can simulate and analyse road traffic and traffic management systems, in addition to route finding, visualisation, importing networks and calculating emissions. It allows the generation (virtually) of detectors' observations and to model the flow of traffic at intersections. SUMO is used in research concerning traffic prediction, traffic lights and vehicular communication systems, and to analyse new traffic strategies before they are implemented in the real world. Moreover, SUMO can be enhanced with custom models, providing many APIs for online control of the simulation. Since traffic scenarios are highly dynamic, having online (and continuous) access to the environment is a paramount feature. These online communications are necessary to build flexible and reactive agent-based solutions. For this reason, in AGAMAS, we opted for SUMO as a simulated traffic environment where to introduce our software agents.

3   Related Work

A similar framework to AGAMASwas introduced back in 2010 [24], and it's named TRasMapi. Traffic simulation software has seen huge improvements since then. However, TRasMapi is not updated and cannot provide access to the features that have been introduced into SUMO during the last decade. Moreover, TRasMapi was used to build more abstract frameworks. In [22], for instance, TRasMapi was used to implement artificial transportation systems in which it was used to allow synchronisation between an agent-based population and SUMO that could instantiate an Artificial Society (AS) of heterogeneous drivers and intelligent traffic light management solutions. Since [22] is based on TRasMapi, it is no longer compatible with recent versions of SUMO.

Another tool that allows implementing agents in SUMO is ITSUMO [20], in which agents are implemented as cellular automata. ATSim [4] is another related framework, providing the possibility to create an agent-based traffic simulation system to support global system throughput on a macro-level view. However, unlike AGAMAS, ATSIM combines JADE with commercial traffic simulation suite AimSun [1]; while AGAMASand SUMO are open source.

AGAMAShas a proper definition of agents in the traffic simulation in terms of connectivity and autonomy. Agents in JADE perform actions based on their behaviours, while the resulting computations can be decentralised (thanks to JADE containers). Most of the recent publications have disregarded this fact due to the lack of a proper library to implement autonomous objects as agents. For example, in [7], the cooperation among autonomous vehicles is performed in a centralised way. Hence, one action is chosen for all the vehicles in the network.

4   Agent-Based Traffic Simulation in AGAMAS

The urge to have an Agent-Based simulation with new capabilities in terms of interacting with the SUMO environment and also having access to its recent (more sophisticated) APIs was the motivation for this work. Two of the main properties of an agent are sensing the environment and performing actions to change the latter itself. Hence, both requirements should be taken into consideration in the development of a new Agent-Based traffic simulation framework. As previously mentioned, JADE and SUMO are the two main components of AGAMAS. The former, for what concerns the software agents' development, while the latter, for what concerns the traffic simulation. Figure 1 demonstrates the architecture of the above-mentioned framework. Real-time interaction with the environment is provided by Traci APIs (based on TCP connections). Traci is a short form of "Traffic Control Interface". It provides the bridge to a running simulation in SUMO, allowing to retrieve values of simulated objects and change their behaviour online. Since this connection is continuous, it offers real-time interaction with the environment. AGAMAS' agents have continuous access to the environment and its simulated objects.

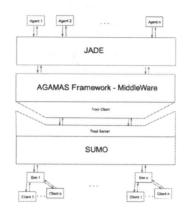

Fig. 1. The Architecture of AGAMAS.

Note that, even though technological, this aspect is quite relevant. Indeed, in order to handle such a continuous connection, AGAMAS' agents need to run in parallel with SUMO. This requires AGAMASto be thread-safe, especially in what concerns the interactions between the JADE agents and SUMO. Specifically, it is necessary for the Traci instantiation to be thread-safe.

In the case of Java, the available Traci library is called libtraci[1] and is fully supported and maintained by the SUMO development team. Libtraci has recently been extended to support concurrent interactions[2] with SUMO. Because of that, AGAMAShas been safely built on top of it.

---

[1] https://sumo.dlr.de/docs/Libtraci.html.

[2] This feature has been recently added to libtraci thanks to the effort of the SUMO team and the authors of this work.

4.1   Perceptions and Actions of Agents

Agents, of any type, should have the capability to sense the environment and perform actions upon the latter. Here, we discuss in detail, how agents interact with the simulated environment.

Perceptions and Actions in AGAMASare propagated through Traci. As reported in Fig. 1, Traci is the bridge to connect JADE agents with SUMO, and it is divided into two main parts: (i) Traci server, and (ii) Traci client. Based on the AGAMAS' architecture, Traci server is on the simulation side (*i.e.*, SUMO), and starts listening to the queries (sent by the agents) as soon as the simulations start. Traci client is a part of the middleware and performs the role of the communication module.

APIs in Traci client are accessible using the SUMO Command Module. Although, in AGAMAS, the developer does not need to deal directly with either the TCP connections or the Command Modules. Overall, the APIs offered by Traci which are built upon Command Modules can be divided into two parts: GET: They retrieve values from the simulation. Agents in the framework perceive the simulated environment through these APIs. SET: They change values of variables, or the behaviour, of a simulated object. Using these APIs, agents are able to perform their actions in the environment.

In the older version of Traci, it was required to manually deal with the connections and the commands, hence, making it difficult to submit queries. However, in AGAMAS, instead of building the communication module from scratch, libtraci is exploited. As previously mentioned, libtraci is the implementation of Traci in Java and it simplifies utilising the APIs.

Perceptions of any agent can be gathered through this package by calling the desired GET queries. To perform an action, SET APIs of an object in the simulation can be called.

4.2   AGAMAS' Architecture

In this section, we dive more into the details of the middleware, demonstrating how an agent can be created. AGAMASis an Agent-Oriented Traffic Simulation framework. The aim of this framework is to introduce autonomous objects into the simulation, with message-exchanging capabilities that simplify the implementation of an agent-oriented traffic simulation by abstracting away the basic and necessary functionalities of SUMO and JADE integration. Using the framework, it is possible to focus more on the agent aspect of the simulation, rather than its actual implementation.

Although every simulated object can be represented as an agent, AGAMAS-concentrates especially on autonomous vehicles due to their importance. Moreover, autonomous vehicles are the most challenging objects in traffic simulations, and the most natural ones to be specified as agents.

One of the main features of AGAMASis to provide the possibility to have a cluster of vehicles. In this paper, an autonomous vehicle cluster is defined as a cluster of vehicles, controlled by an agent in JADE. Based on this concept, it is possible to have autonomous vehicles with a specific range of decentralised computations. Such a simplification in AGAMASis useful when describing complex behaviours that affect a swarm of identical vehicles. This becomes relevant when multiple objects in the simulation are not rational (at the object level), but their cluster is (at the collective level).

After an initial configuration phase, the simulation is ready to be populated by objects (as agents). For instance, it is possible to create multiple agents, where each agent handles one (or many) vehicle(s) in the SUMO simulation. Naturally, such a number of vehicles is arbitrary and it is determined by the application's requirements. By creating a cluster with one vehicle, in fact, we are inserting a fully autonomous vehicle in the simulation. It is also possible to handle multiple SUMO vehicles with a single JADE agent. Representing multiple vehicles as a single agent will lead to highly sophisticated cooperation due to agent-based communications among the clusters and single autonomous vehicles and the simplicity of submitting queries for all the vehicles in a cluster.

As an example, in Listing 1.1, it is shown how to create a cluster of vehicles as an agent, and how to monitor their speed using a JADE cyclic behaviour:

Listing 1.1. An example of creating an agent with a cluster of two vehilces.

```
1   public static void main(String[] args) {
2       String[] command = new String[]{"sumo-gui", "--delay", "10.0",
3       "-c", "path_to_sumocfg_file"};
4       SUMOMAS sm = new SUMOMAS(false, command, 5000);
5       List<String> ids = new ArrayList<String>();
6       ids.add("1"); ids.add("2");
7       //vehicle type parameters should be passed to the cluster
8       AV_Cluster avc = sm.createCluster(ids, vehicles_type,
9       route_id, departure_time, departure_lane, departure_position,
10      departure_speed, arrival_lane, arrival_pos, arrival_speed,
11      from_TAZ, to_TAZ, line, person_capacity, person_number);
12      ArrayList<SumoVehicle> vehicles=avc.getSumoVehicles();
13      SumoVehicle vehicle_1=vehicles.get(1);
14      avc.addBehaviour(new CyclicBehaviour() {
15          @Override
16          public void action() { System.out.println(avc.getSpeed()); }
17      });
18      avc.addBehaviour(new OneShotBehaviour() {
19          @Override
20          public void action() { vehicle_1.changeLane(1, 9); }
21      });
22      sm.runSim();
23  }
```

Above, a cluster with two vehicles is created by passing the list of specified IDs (line 6), and other vehicle-type parameters that can be found in the SUMO documentation. SUMOMAS, after setting up the agent, and adding its corresponding vehicles to the simulation, returns the agent in charge of the resulting cluster (line 8). Users do not need to deal with adding the vehicles to the simulation and starting up the agents themselves. Furthermore, AGAMAShandles the agent's life cycle in the simulation. That is, it kills the agent when all of its vehicles exit the simulation (*i.e.*, when the simulated objects stop existing in the SUMO simulated environment).

Each cluster agent in AGAMAShas access to the SUMO Vehicle class (part of libtraci); the latter provides additional functionalities for each vehicle of the cluster. However, in order to simplify the APIs, AGAMASabstracts this aspect away from the user. In fact, all the operations performed on the cluster are automatically propagated (and if needed replicated) to the under-the-hood set of SUMO vehicles. Thanks to this, the user can focus on programming the agent as a cluster, without the need of programming the single low-level vehicles' behaviour.

Once the agent has been created (exploiting the SUMOMAS class), it is exactly a JADE agent. Because of that, we can program it as it is customary for JADE agents. For instance, in Listing 1.1, line 14, we add a cyclic behaviour to the agent. With it, we can log the speed of the agent; that is, the speed of the vehicles belonging to its cluster. This simple code logs the speed of all the vehicles in the cluster. This is obtained by calling the getSpeed() method on the cluster agent (line 16), which returns a list with a size equals to the number of vehicles inside the cluster. The order of the so returned speeds in the list is the same as the ID list passed upon agent creation.

5   Experiments

The case study on which we experimented AGAMASconsists of a deadlock handling scenario, as shown in Fig. 2. This case study has been inspired by [26].

In this case study, we explore the use of AGAMASto develop CAVs capable of solving a simple deadlock scenario. In more detail, the case study consists in a traffic simulation where all vehicles are CAVs, but two kinds exist: the normal ones (the green) and the emergency ones (the red). The problem we tackle with AGAMASis to develop these CAVs as JADE agents, where the objective is for the emergency vehicles to not get delayed by normal ones on their road.

Let us assume we have one single emergency vehicle (CAV_EM), and various normal vehicles. Amongst the latter, we have one vehicle that is currently an obstacle for the emergency one (CAV_Slow_0). In order to avoid making the emergency vehicle to stop, CAV_Slow_0 needs to free the lane. To do so, since we are in a scenario where all the vehicles are CAVs, it can communicate with its closest CAV on its right (CAV_Slow_1 in this case), as depicted in Fig. 2. Such communication is devolved to create a gap for letting CAV_Slow_0 change lane (and so freeing the lane for the emergency vehicle). In more detail, by using AGAMAS' APIs (partially provided by libtraci), and by message exchange amongst the JADE agents, the emergency vehicle sends a message to the CAV blocking its lane (CAV_Slow_0 in this instance). Upon receiving such a message, CAV_Slow_0, in turn, asks CAV_Slow_1 to decrease its own speed (to create a gap to be filled by CAV_Slow_0). Figure 2 demonstrates such message passing.

Now that, even though the process of freeing the lane for the emergency vehicle is clear, we need to focus on when the communication amongst the CAVs should indeed start. Specifically, we need to determine the ideal distance for the emergency vehicle to ask the obstacle to change lanes. That is if the emergency vehicle sends a message when closer to the obstacle than the ideal distance, then the obstacle may not have the time to free the lane. This is related to the concept of ideal travel time; that is the time the emergency vehicle can travel

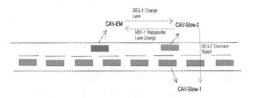

Fig. 2. Simple Deadlock. Emergency Vehicle cannot travel faster

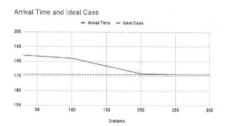

Fig. 3. Distance to send the message to the obstacle vehicle vs. Travel time

the route, all the way, constantly, with its maximum speed (so without any obstacle forcing it to decrease its speed or, in the worst case, stop). This travel time is measurable in a free lane with an emergency vehicle, travelling with the maximum desired speed. Figure 3 reports the experimental results we obtained; where, if the emergency vehicle sends a message before getting closer than 200 m[3] to the obstacle vehicle, then it can travel without being slowed down.

6   Conclusions and Future Work

In this work, we proposed AGAMAS, an Agent-Oriented Traffic Simulation framework that combines the JADE agent development system, with the SUMO traffic simulator. We presented AGAMAS, its engineering, and its main components. Specifically, we showed how AGAMASexploits the Traci API to obtain a highly-usable and extendable implementation. AGAMASrepresents a stable solution that allows exploiting the newest features of SUMO.

Future directions will include further extensions of AGAMAS. We presented the core of AGAMAS, but we are interested in further enriching its own library to simplify the creation of autonomous objects in traffic simulation (as we did for the cluster creation case study). The experiments we carried out showed the effectiveness of AGAMAS, but we plan to simulate more challenging scenarios (*i.e.*, scenarios that involve more autonomous behaviours), where its full potential can be exploited.

---

[3] Naturally, this value depends on the simulation parameters (e.g., vehicles' speed).

References

1. Barceló, J., Casas, J.: Dynamic network simulation with AIMSUN. In: Kitamura, R., Kuwahara, M. (eds.) Simulation Approaches in Transportation Analysis. Operations Research/Computer Science Interfaces Series, vol. 31, pp. 57–98. Springer, Boston, MA (2005). https://doi.org/10.1007/0-387-24109-4_3
2. Bellifemine, F.L., Caire, G., Greenwood, D.: Developing Multi-Agent Systems with JADE. John Wiley & Sons, Hoboken (2007)
3. Chao, Q., et al.: A survey on visual traffic simulation: models, evaluations, and applications in autonomous driving. Comput. Graph. Forum **39**(1), 287–308 (2020). https://doi.org/10.1111/cgf.13803
4. Chu, V.H., Görmer, J., Müller, J.P.: ATSim: combining AIMSUM and jade for agent-based traffic simulation. In: Proceedings of the 14th Conference of the Spanish Association for Artificial Intelligence (CAEPIA) (2011)
5. Čičić, M., Pasquale, C., Siri, S., Sacone, S., Johansson, K.H.: Platoon-actuated variable area mainstream traffic control for bottleneck decongestion. Eur. J. Control **68**, 100687 (2022)
6. Čičić, M., Xiong, X., Jin, L., Johansson, K.H.: Coordinating vehicle platoons for highway bottleneck decongestion and throughput improvement. IEEE Trans. Intell. Transp. Syst. **23**(7), 8959–8971 (2021)
7. Dong, J., Chen, S., Ha, P.Y.J., Li, Y., Labi, S.: A DRL-based multiagent cooperative control framework for CAV networks: a graphic convolution Q network. arXiv: Artificial Intelligence (2020)
8. Gerostathopoulos, I., Pournaras, E.: Trapped in traffic?: A self-adaptive framework for decentralized traffic optimization. In: Litoiu, M., Clarke, S., Tei, K. (eds.) Proceedings of the 14th International Symposium on Software Engineering for Adaptive and Self-Managing Systems, SEAMS@ICSE 2019, Montreal, QC, Canada, 25–31 May 2019, pp. 32–38. ACM (2019). https://doi.org/10.1109/SEAMS.2019.00014
9. Hamilton, A., Waterson, B., Cherrett, T., Robinson, A., Snell, I.: The evolution of urban traffic control: changing policy and technology. Transp. Plan. Technol. **36**(1), 24–43 (2013)
10. Johansson, O., Pearce, D., Maddison, D.: Blueprint 5: True Costs of Road Transport. Routledge, Abingdon (2014)
11. Lopez, P.A., et al.: Microscopic traffic simulation using sumo. In: The 21st IEEE International Conference on Intelligent Transportation Systems. IEEE (2018). www.elib.dlr.de/124092/
12. Nguyen, J., Powers, S.T., Urquhart, N., Farrenkopf, T., Guckert, M.: An overview of agent-based traffic simulators. CoRR abs/2102.07505 (2021). www.arxiv.org/abs/2102.07505
13. de Oliveira, L.F.P., Manera, L.T., Luz, P.D.G.D.: Smart traffic light controller system. In: Alsmirat, M.A., Jararweh, Y. (eds.) Sixth International Conference on Internet of Things: Systems, Management and Security, IOTSMS 2019, Granada, Spain, 22–25 October 2019, pp. 155–160. IEEE (2019). https://doi.org/10.1109/IOTSMS48152.2019.8939239
14. de Oliveira, L.F.P., Manera, L.T., Luz, P.D.G.D.: Development of a smart traffic light control system with real-time monitoring. IEEE Internet Things J. **8**(5), 3384–3393 (2021). https://doi.org/10.1109/JIOT.2020.3022392
15. Pasquale, C., Sacone, S., Siri, S., Ferrara, A.: Traffic control for freeway networks with sustainability-related objectives: review and future challenges. Annu. Rev. Control **48**, 312–324 (2019)

16. Piacentini, G., Goatin, P., Ferrara, A.: Traffic control via platoons of intelligent vehicles for saving fuel consumption in freeway systems. IEEE Control Syst. Lett. **5**(2), 593–598 (2020)

17. PTV, A.: VISSIM 5.30-05 user manual. Germany. Karlsruhe: PTV AG (2011)

18. Rieser, M., Dobler, C., Dubernet, T., Grether, D., Horni, A., Lammel, G., Waraich, R., Zilske, M., Axhausen, K.W., Nagel, K.: Matsim user guide. MATSim, Zurich (2014)

19. Sarné, G.M.L., Postorino, M.N.: Agents meet traffic simulation, control and management: a review of selected recent contributions. In: Santoro, C., Messina, F., Benedetti, M.D. (eds.) Proceedings of the 17th Workshop From Objects to Agents co-located with 18th European Agent Systems Summer School (EASSS 2016), Catania, Italy, 29–30 July 2016. CEUR Workshop Proceedings, vol. 1664, pp. 112–117. CEUR-WS.org (2016). www.ceur-ws.org/Vol-1664/w19.pdf

20. da Silva, B.C., Junges, R., de Oliveira, D., Bazzan, A.L.C.: ITSUMO: an intelligent transportation system for urban mobility. Adaptive Agents and Multi-Agent Systems (2004)

21. Siri, S., Pasquale, C., Sacone, S., Ferrara, A.: Freeway traffic control: a survey. Automatica **130**, 109655 (2021)

22. Soares, G., Kokkinogenis, Z., Macedo, J.L., Rossetti, R.J.F.: Agent-based traffic simulation using sumo and jade: an integrated platform for artificial transportation systems. In: International Conference on Simulation of Urban Mobility (2013)

23. Tan, D., Younis, M.F., Lalouani, W., Lee, S.: PALM: platoons based adaptive traffic light control system for mixed vehicular traffic. In: 2021 IEEE Smart-World, Ubiquitous Intelligence & Computing, Advanced & Trusted Computing, Scalable Computing & Communications, Internet of People and Smart City Innovation (SmartWorld/SCALCOM/UIC/ATC/IOP/SCI), Atlanta, GA, USA, 18–21 October 2021, pp. 178–185. IEEE (2021). https://doi.org/10.1109/SWC50871.2021.00033

24. Timóteo, I.J.P.M., Araujo, M.R., Rossetti, R.J.F., Oliveira, E.C.: TraSMAPI: an API oriented towards multi-agent systems real-time interaction with multiple traffic simulators. In: 13th International IEEE Conference on Intelligent Transportation Systems, Funchal, Madeira, Portugal, 19–22 September 2010, pp. 1183–1188. IEEE (2010). https://doi.org/10.1109/ITSC.2010.5625238

25. Treiber, M., Kesting, A.: Traffic Flow Dynamics: Data, Models and Simulation, pp. 983–1000. Springer-Verlag, Berlin, Heidelberg (2013). https://doi.org/10.1007/978-3-642-32460-4

26. Wang, N., Wang, X., Palacharla, P., Ikeuchi, T.: Cooperative autonomous driving for traffic congestion avoidance through vehicle-to-vehicle communications. In: IEEE Vehicular Networking Conference (VNC) (2017)

27. Zhang, K., Batterman, S.: Air pollution and health risks due to vehicle traffic. Sci. Total Environ. **450**, 307–316 (2013)

Coordinating Systems of Digital Twins with Digital Practices

Luca Sabatucci[1][(✉)], Agnese Augello[1], Giuseppe Caggianese[2], and Luigi Gallo[2]

[1] Institute for High Performance Computing and Networking, National Research Council of Italy, Palermo, Italy
{luca.sabatucci,agnese.augello}@icar.cnr.it
[2] Institute for High Performance Computing and Networking, National Research Council of Italy, Naples, Italy
{giuseppe.caggianese,luigi.gallo}@icar.cnr.it

Abstract. Digital Twin is a promising paradigm to support the development of socio-technical systems for the digital transformation of society. For example, smart cities and healthcare applications gain advantages from this new paradigm. Currently, researchers are investigating methodologies that exploit Digital Twins as general-purpose abstractions for complex modelling and simulation. Taking inspiration from the *Social Practice theory*, this paper explores the idea of explicitly representing the physical and social context in socio-technical systems. To this aim, we introduce the concept of digital practice as an additional brick of a methodology for modelling and implementing socio-technical systems via digital twins and agents. We illustrate this preliminary idea by exploiting an assistance scenario for the elderly.

Keywords: Digital Twins · Digital Practices · Social Practices · Socio-Technical Systems · Ambient Assisted Living

1 Introduction

A Digital Twin (DT) is a digital model of a physical entity (an object, a space, or a complex aggregation) updated through the bidirectional exchange of information between the physical and virtual systems [25].

Digital twins have evolved from advanced manufacturing and Industry 4.0 [6] to become popular instruments to be employed in a range of socio-technical applications, from smart cities [11,23] to health applications [1,14].

They originated as integrated software architectures to monitor and control heterogeneous devices, machines, plants, and factories where individual products are connected through a network [6]. Now, digital twins encountered advanced artificial intelligence techniques to add the possibility to predict and optimize complex behaviour by taking advantage of seamless integration between IoT and data analytics, allowing for rapid analysis and real-time decisions made through accurate analytics [12].

V. Malvone and A. Murano (Eds.): EUMAS 2023, LNAI 14282, pp. 406–414, 2023.
https://doi.org/10.1007/978-3-031-43264-4_26

Recently, also healthcare systems are incorporating the concept of digital twins, posing the ambitious definition of mirroring persons' health, including physical, mental, and social aspects, on top of the clinical data [1]. Human Digital Twins represent a copy (or counterpart in cyberspace) of a real person [24]. Futuristic scenarios see every newborn will be genome sequenced and her model continuously updated with data captured by ambient, body-worn, and embedded sensors. More concretely, a human digital twin in healthcare and assistive scenarios allows us to put humans into the loop. For example, in surgery, having an updated model of the patient's body could be of capital importance for the surgeon before and during an operation.

Also, Software Engineering highlighted the role of digital twins in the digital transformation of our society [22]. Conceiving complex software systems utilizing digital twins will lead humans to be more and more intertwined with technologies and, on the other hand, to augment their capabilities. Moreover, the academy and industry agree to introduce an integration view on digital twins [15], in which a system can be conceived as the composition/collaboration of several discrete digital twins [19]. Also, it is possible to imagine a composite digital twin as a combination of discrete digital twins by unifying multiple individual components (or parts) [15].

This paper stems from the need to define a social perspective for digital twins. We believe that state-of-the-art still misses capturing the *context*, i.e. the physical and social setting. This work looks at the concept of Social Practice (SP) [21], a theory that studies contextual behavioural patterns, determining actions to do, and incorporating means to be addressed. Recently, this theory was used to simplify the deliberation processes of virtual agents [3,4,8,13].

We introduce the concept of Digital Practice (DP) as "a digital twin of a social practice". It is a digital entity that makes the dynamic relationships between physical entities in a social environment explicit, taking the context into account. We intend to push Digital Practices as the third component of a methodology for designing socio-technical systems via digital twins and agents. The responsibility of Digital Practices is to monitor the dynamic physical setting and to coordinate agents and digital twins for addressing social goals. We use an assistive scenario for the elderly to illustrate the main idea.

The paper is organized as follows: Sect. 2 introduces the baselines for our work. Section 3 presents the design paradigm where agents and digital twins are first-class citizens and digital practices provide the social perspective. Some conclusions are sketched in Sect. 4.

2 Preliminary Concepts

The idea we push on in this paper is that a socio-technical system may be conceived as a system of agents and digital twins. To create a unifying methodology, we take inspiration from sociological and cultural theories, particularly *Social Practice theory* [13,21].

2.1   Digital Twins and Agents

There are at least two main motivations for a synergy between digital twins and agents.

First, the novel term Cognitive Digital Twin is always more frequent in literature, recalling DTs that autonomously perform intelligent tasks. The interest to incorporate cognition and optimization capabilities into a digital twin has been caught by the agent community who provided integrated solutions to resolve unknown situations via prediction and reasoning [10].

Second, the academy and industry agree to support the idea of a social perspective of digital twins. The Industrial Internet Consortium [15] defined a discrete digital twin as a single entity. In contrast, a composite digital twin combines many discrete digital twins representing an entity comprising multiple components or parts. Indeed, several digital twin systems are conceived with increasingly complex and collaborative interdependencies [19], and multi-agent systems could be an extremely useful tool when representing relationships among several digital twins.

The literature proposes an increasing number of papers that exploit agents for implementing digital twins showing how the digital twin paradigm is moving towards a process of 'agentification' for different reasons: 1) extending digital twin with high-level reasoning capabilities for implementing prediction and adaptation [10], 2) agents allow implementing societies of digital twins [19], and 3) DTs provide a powerful engineering abstraction to design agents' interactions with the physical environment [20].

We adopt the point of view suggested in Mariani et al. [16] of a system made of agents and digital twins but with a clear separation of concerns and responsibilities: agents are responsible for autonomous actions and decision-making, whereas DTs provide a general abstraction for accessing to the physical world.

2.2   Social Practice Theory

According to this theory, social order is embedded within shared structures of knowledge, shaped by cultural values, which enables a symbolic organization of reality according to the specific situation.

These structures, consisting of several interconnected elements, allow people to give meaning to the world and act in a certain way. In particular, social practices are routinised behaviours involving individuals acting in a context that considers bodily and mental activities, material artefacts, knowledge, emotions, skills, etc. They refer to everyday activities and how humans typically and habitually perform them within a society (such as going to work, cooking, ...).

Social Practice (SP) aims to integrate the individual perspective with the social perspective, considering (and explaining) how context relates to individuals' experiences, culture and capabilities. A practice forms a *pattern* whose existence depends on the existence and specific interconnections of many individuals, which cannot be reduced to any of these. We refer to social practices because they are similar for groups of individuals at different points in time and space.

Interestingly, a Practice is seen as a concrete (even if intangible) entity in which individuals play a role in enacting it. As observed by [9], social practices could represent a starting point for systems needing context. Social Practice theory has inspired the creation of a model for cognitive agents [8], which outlines the main elements of a practice, including 1) a *Context* that describes the physical elements in the environment, such as the *Resources* that are used in the Practice, the involved *Actors*, *Affordances* which enable social actions, the *Time* under which the practice takes place, and *Places* where objects and actors are usually located. 2) a *Meaning*, which describes the *Purpose* of the actions, *Promotes*, i.e. values that are supported by the practice, *Counts-as* rules, i.e. the interpretation of facts in the context 3) *Expectations* in the practice, such as possible *Plan Patterns*, *Norms*, *Strategies*), *Start* and *End* conditions for the practice; 4) *Activities*, including *Competences* that the agent needs to possess to perform *Possible Actions* within the Practice.

3   Digital Practices: Towards a Design Methodology for Agents and Digital Twins

The level of granularity for modelling the DTs is one of the first decisions to be made when using them to define a socio-technical system. One possibility is to conceive the whole system (for instance, the whole caregiving centre) as a small number of big DTs. Each of them will represent an extensive portion of the field of interest (including in the same model many aspects, such as physical spaces, resources and people). In this case, the designer is going to select a coarse-grained approach. It is worth underlying that scalability could be an issue: designing huge complex models requires considering all the relationships among the embedded entities. In our scenario, representing the whole caregiving centre through a unique digital twin needs considering different locations, guests' positions and behaviours, and potential interactions among all its occupants (carers, nurses, elderly people and visitors).

Conversely, a fine-grained level of granularity is more natural from a design point of view, because it allows reasoning in a bottom-up style similar to when designing with object-oriented languages. Actually, this approach could be imagined as an extension of the object-oriented paradigm, where objects have a physical dimension. Past experiences [17] show a fine-grained approach was successful in designing manufacturing systems and smart cities. In our scenario, the patient, the caregiver, the wearable device and the physical space could be modelled as different DTs.

The fine-grained approach addresses scalability and reusability, but it poses other problems to solve: simpler objects yield DTs with simpler internal models, but, in a dynamic context, designers must take into account the possible interactions among them. Consequently, models grow in complexity to introduce interaction rules. Moreover, defining a strict coupling degrades the level of reusability in similar contexts.

We propose a design methodology that is based on the finer level of granularity and tries to solve some of the potential issues by shifting out the interaction logic from digital twin models, thus increasing flexibility and reusability. We set the following desiderata for modelling dynamic digital twin systems: 1) interaction as a first-class citizen of the methodology and 2) modelling interactions considering the context in which they can occur.

3.1   Digital Practice

We introduce the concept of Digital Practice (DP) for developing a dynamic social perspective for digital twins. A digital practice adds a digital perspective to the original concept of social practice.

A Digital Practice is defined as the digital twin of a Social Practice. It is structured as:

- a set of **Roles** for human and software agents. In particular, humans are stakeholders whereas agents are responsible for enacting autonomous and proactive behaviours within the practice.
- **Context**: digital twins are central for representing entities of the physical setting (humans, resources and spaces), used to define the activation rule of the practice, i.e. the specific situation in which the practice activates.
- **Time and Space**: essential to delineate the practice's activation rule.
- **Domain Knowledge**: allows disambiguating the meaning in the practice; it is typically represented as a set of beliefs and rules concerning a domain of interest, allowing the software system to perform automatic reasoning and pattern matching.
- a **Goal Model**: it represents the final purpose of the practice, merging meaning and social expectation (the feeling that something will or should happen in a context); it includes goals, and soft goals linked together by relationships. Goals represent states of the world to be addressed, whereas soft goals represent qualities and values the practice promotes.
- a set of **Capabilities**: what the digital entities can do (are expected to) do in the digital practice.
- **Digital Affordances**: expressing ways of conveying to end-users what actions are possible in the context and how to interact with the system.
- an **Orchestration Plan**: it describes a usual flow of actions to address the final purpose. This is not necessarily a static plan.
- **Norms/Conditions**: they hold in the social setting and describe what is considered acceptable and not.

3.2   Designing an Ambient Assisted Living for the Elderly

We use a caregiving centre scenario to describe the work's motivation and objective. We suppose to develop an Ambient Assisted Living (AAL) for caregiving centres where trained caregivers help older adults with daily activities, socialization, and rehabilitation [2,5,7].

IoT devices allow monitoring of physical locations and people activities in a care facility. Environmental sensors can collect audio and video data about events happening in the rooms, while wearable technology can offer real-time biological data and localization.

In this scenario, DTs may represent patients, mirroring the person's health condition, psychological state and stress levels. They also can be used for tracing guests' movements and behaviour within the building.

Also, some physical spaces (e.g. the living room) are modelled as DTs because monitoring/controlling environmental conditions and activities in these places could be important to ensure a good level of assistance.

To obtain more precise data (for some patients), the system should use wearable devices. Following the fine-grained approach, we model wearable devices as DTs because they have a relevant model to be periodically updated. This choice allows the patient's DT and the device's DT to exist and evolve independently. However, a wearable DT makes sense only if a couple [patient - device] will be dynamically formed, i.e. when a patient is effectively wearing it.

Here, we report a scenario of fall management. We identified a digital practice (see Fig. 1) that includes a patient (Elderly Individual DT), his smartwatch (Wearable DT), physical spaces (Living DT), and caregivers (Digital Caregiver DT). The practice activates when the patient suffering the Alzheimer's disease leaves the living room, and no caregivers are following him. The purpose is to monitor his movements and prevent risks. The plan is to alert caregivers when the patient leaves the room and "send" the nearest caregivers if something dangerous is going to happen.

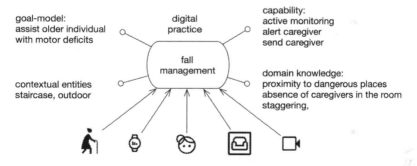

Fig. 1. The Fall Management digital practice aims at assisting an older individual when no caregivers are present.

3.3   Some Considerations

Despite the concept of digital practice is still at a preliminary phase, in this short paper we want to highlight there is a clear value in explicitly modelling at the digital level those aspects that concern the social practice at the physical level. From a methodological point of view, digital practice is a first-class design abstraction, different from agents and digital twins. Whereas digital twins run at a physical layer, agents act at a business layer, digital practices exist at a higher social layer and their components (roles, goal models, norms, activation rules) affect underlying elements.

Encapsulating Physical and Social Setting. This work conveys the idea that agents 'live' in a physical/social context. Whereas the physical layer can be represented by digital twins, it is up to digital practices to define the social setting in which interactions happen, and the way they occur, according to stakeholders' meanings and expectations.

Some examples of DPs for the assistive scenario are the following: an elderly patient with degraded motor skills can be near a stair: this situation triggers the activation of an emergency protocol, providing an affordance to secure the elderly. Otherwise, some devices in a specific situation can provide an *affordance* for the older person to remember to take medication. Finally, a ramp for disabled residents starts operating when a wheelchair gets on it.

Therefore, a specific behaviour should activate when external conditions hold. These may depend on the state of physical things in the scene or other factors (i.e. social expectations). For example, in the staircase scenario, the interaction happens in the *proximity* of two digital twins.

Generating Dynamic Aggregates. The final goal of a digital practice is to trigger agents' dynamic behaviour due to what is happening in the physical world. In the digital practice definition, there are roles and digital twins. As for agent's groups [18], roles can be dynamically assigned to agents. Similarly, the digital practice does not prescribe which instances of digital twins to consider (supposing a dynamic environment). Indeed, the context evolves in unforeseeable ways. In the caregiving centre application, designers could not always anticipate all the combinations of [patient-wearable] that may appear and how they behave and interact. Digital practices aim to abstractly encapsulate these behavioural patterns, thus activating and deactivating them dynamically on the occurrence.

4   Conclusions

This paper focused on digital twins as a software engineering paradigm for dealing with systems with an essential physical component, mainly where humans are in the loop. The objective is to conceive a design paradigm where agents and digital twins are first-class abstractions.

We introduce a fine-grained perspective in which the system is seen as interacting autonomous entities, some with a physical counterpart and others consisting only of virtual essence. To model interactions and synergies among different entities, we took inspiration from sociological and cultural theories, explicitly relying on *Social Practice theory*. This allows us to model the concept of Digital Practice aiming to integrate the individual perspective with the social perspective, considering (and explaining) how the context influences individual behaviours.

From a methodological point of view, digital practice is a first-class design abstraction. It is quite different from both agents and digital twins. This is because digital practices exist at a higher layer and affect underlying elements (agents and digital twins that run a business and physical layers).

References

1. Ahmadi-Assalemi, G., et al.: Digital twins for precision healthcare. Cyber Def. Age AI Smart Soc. Augment. Humanit. 133–158 (2020)
2. Andrich, R., et al.: ACube: user-centred and goal-oriented techniques. Fondazione Bruno Kessler-IRST, Technical report, p. 66 (2010)
3. Augello, A.: Unveiling the reasoning processes of robots through introspective dialogues in a storytelling system: a study on the elicited empathy. Cogn. Syst. Res. **73**, 12–20 (2022)
4. Augello, A., Gentile, M., Dignum, F.: Social practices for social driven conversations in serious games. In: De Gloria, A., Veltkamp, R. (eds.) GALA 2015. LNCS, vol. 9599, pp. 100–110. Springer, Cham (2016). https://doi.org/10.1007/978-3-319-40216-1_11
5. Bellagente, P., et al.: Easy implementation of sensing systems for smart living. In: 2017 IEEE International Systems Engineering Symposium (ISSE), pp. 1–6. IEEE (2017)
6. Brettel, M., Friederichsen, N., Keller, M., Rosenberg, M.: How virtualization, decentralization and network building change the manufacturing landscape: an industry 4.0 perspective. Int. J. Inf. Commun. Eng. **8**(1), 37–44 (2014)
7. Camarinha-Matos, L.M., Ferrada, F., Oliveira, A.I., Rosas, J., Monteiro, J.: Care services provision in ambient assisted living. IRBM **35**(6), 286–298 (2014)
8. Dignum, F.: Social practices: a complete formalization. arXiv preprint arXiv:2206.06088 (2022)
9. Dignum, V., Dignum, F.: Contextualized planning using social practices. In: Ghose, A., Oren, N., Telang, P., Thangarajah, J. (eds.) COIN 2014. LNCS (LNAI), vol. 9372, pp. 36–52. Springer, Cham (2015). https://doi.org/10.1007/978-3-319-25420-3_3
10. Eirinakis, P., et al.: Enhancing cognition for digital twins. In: 2020 IEEE International Conference on Engineering, Technology and Innovation (ICE/ITMC), pp. 1–7. IEEE (2020)
11. Ford, D.N., Wolf, C.M.: Smart cities with digital twin systems for disaster management. J. Manag. Eng. **36**(4), 04020027 (2020)
12. Fuller, A., Fan, Z., Day, C., Barlow, C.: Digital twin: enabling technologies, challenges and open research. IEEE Access **8**, 108952–108971 (2020)
13. Holtz, G.: Generating social practices. J. Artif. Soc. Soc. Simul. **17**(1), 17 (2014)
14. Liu, Y., et al.: A novel cloud-based framework for the elderly healthcare services using digital twin. IEEE Access **7**, 49088–49101 (2019)
15. Malakuti, S., et al.: Digital twins for industrial applications: definition. Business Values, Design Aspects, Standards and Use Cases: An Industrial Internet Consortium Whitepaper (2020)
16. Mariani, S., Picone, M., Ricci, A.: About digital twins, agents, and multiagent systems: a cross-fertilisation journey. In: Melo, F.S., Fang, F. (eds.) Autonomous Agents and Multiagent Systems. Best and Visionary Papers. AAMAS 2022. LNCS, vol. 13441, pp. 114–129. Springer, Cham (2022). https://doi.org/10.1007/978-3-031-20179-0_8

17. Michael, J., Pfeiffer, J., Rumpe, B., Wortmann, A.: Integration challenges for digital twin systems-of-systems. In: Proceedings of the 10th IEEE/ACM International Workshop on Software Engineering for Systems-of-Systems and Software Ecosystems, pp. 9–12 (2022)

18. Odell, J.J., Van Dyke Parunak, H., Fleischer, M.: Modeling agent organizations using roles. Softw. Syst. Model. **2**, 76–81 (2003)

19. Orozco-Romero, A., Arias-Portela, C.Y., Saucedo, J.E.A.M.: The use of agent-based models boosted by digital twins in the supply chain: a literature review. In: Vasant, P., Zelinka, I., Weber, G.-W. (eds.) ICO 2019. AISC, vol. 1072, pp. 642–652. Springer, Cham (2020). https://doi.org/10.1007/978-3-030-33585-4_62

20. Picone, M., Mamei, M., Zambonelli, F.: WLDT: a general purpose library to build IoT digital twins. SoftwareX **13**, 100661 (2021)

21. Reckwitz, A.: Toward a theory of social practices: a development in culturalist theorizing. Eur. J. Soc. Theory **5**(2), 243–263 (2002)

22. Saracco, R.: Digital twins: bridging physical space and cyberspace. Computer **52**(12), 58–64 (2019)

23. Seuwou, P., Banissi, E., Ubakanma, G.: The future of mobility with connected and autonomous vehicles in smart cities. Digit. Twin Technol. Smart Cities 37–52 (2020)

24. Shengli, W.: Is human digital twin possible? Comput. Methods Programs Biomed. Update **1**, 100014 (2021)

25. VanDerHorn, E., Mahadevan, S.: Digital twin: generalization, characterization and implementation. Decis. Support Syst. **145**, 113524 (2021)

On Admissible Behaviours
for Goal-Oriented Decision-Making
of Value-Aware Agents

Andrés Holgado-Sánchez[✉][ID], Joaquín Arias[ID], Mar Moreno-Rebato[ID],
and Sascha Ossowski[ID]

CETINIA, Universidad Rey Juan Carlos de Madrid, 28933 Móstoles, Spain
{andres.holgado,joaquin.arias,mar.rebato,sascha.ossowski}@urjc.es

Abstract. The emerging field of *value awareness engineering* claims
that software agents and systems should be value-aware, i.e. they should
be able to explicitly reason about the value-alignment of their actions.
Values are often modelled as preferences over states or actions which are
then extended to plans. In this paper, we examine the effect of different
groundings of values depending on context and claim that they can be
used to prune the space of courses of actions that are aligned with them.
We put forward several notions of such value-admissible behaviours and
illustrate them in the domain of water distribution.

Keywords: Value alignment · Value-admissible behaviours · Value
awareness engineering · Water distribution

1 Introduction

A key requirement for trustworthy AI is to consider ethical aspects in the design
and implementation of AI systems. In particular, it is considered of utmost
importance that autonomous AI agents and systems include a systematic way of
aligning their decisions with human values. While value-based decision-making is
a widely discussed problem in sociology, only recently it has found its way into
computer science [17]. The emerging field of *value awareness engineering* [8]
claims that software agents and systems should be value-aware, i.e. they should
be able to explicitly reason about the value-alignment of their actions.

Proposals for modelling value-based decision processes of autonomous agents
are often based on preferences over states or actions [7,9], which are then
extended to sequential decisions. Other approaches [2,3] set out from observed
sequences of actions (plans) and then learn preferences over states or actions
through (inverse) reinforcement learning [10].

In this paper, we are concerned with the role of values in plan selection of
autonomous value-aware agents. In particular, we argue that values not only
induce preferences over plans, but may also be used to discard certain courses of
actions right away depending on a particular value grounding. For this purpose,

V. Malvone and A. Murano (Eds.): EUMAS 2023, LNAI 14282, pp. 415–424, 2023.
https://doi.org/10.1007/978-3-031-43264-4_27

we put forward several notions of value-admissible behaviours, and illustrate them with regard to different groundings of the value of equity in water distribution, taking into account real-world (legal) restrictions.

This paper is structured as follows. Section 2 presents a discussion of related work. Section 3 introduces the value-related world model for this paper, and puts forwards our notion of value-admissible plans. In Sect. 4 we present a use case regarding equitable domestic water distribution in a drought scenario, providing legal considerations around the value of equity. We also describe and analyze the results of applying the proposed value-alignment framework to the example. Finally, Sect. 5 presents our conclusions and points to future lines of work.

2   Related Work

The practical reasoning community was among the first to formally represent values for computation. Weide et al. [17] introduced *value preferences* represented as *agent perspectives* that consist of preorder relationships between states to represent the agent's ideas on how states promote or demote certain values. However, they use that preference to perform actions in reasoning schemes and do not analyze sequences of decisions.

An approach more concerned about abstraction and generality of value representation is introduced by Montes and Sierra [9]. It conceives states as representative of values through a function evaluation, and relies on a taxing example in order to illustrate a more general framework for optimizing value-alignment of normative systems. Still, their analysis does not consider the effects of choosing different value semantics functions or other criteria that would characterize value-admissible plans. Similarly, Lera-Leri et al. [7] proposed an extended formalization of a value system where the focus is put on numerically assessing the value of both *taking* or *not taking* actions (instead of states). This framework, though indeed useful for the value system aggregation problem is, again, not focusing on analyzing sequences of decisions/actions.

Techniques on reinforcement learning (RL) [16] are considered state of the art in most decision-making scenarios, though human values have been introduced scarcely into those systems. There are examples of policies learning values such as fairness jointly with efficiency in multi-agent systems [6]. The approach defines a suitable special reward function based on the Coefficient of Variation (CV) that, for each agent, intends to maximize its default bounded reward subject to that reward being similar to the other's, in a resource allocation problem. A similar approach was developed in [5] to consider equality in social dilemmas. Finally, [14] brings forward a powerful model for both multi-value-aware and multi-norm-compliant MDPs, but it relies heavily on the algorithmic value concept in RL to define the criteria of best value-promoting plans.

As specifying rewards manually requires domain expertise and is a process prone to optimization, IRL (Inverse Reinforcement Learning) [10] has been used which learns the reward from value-aligned trajectories. However,

Arnold et al. [1] show that IRL by itself may not be adequate for agents to learn values, suggesting the use of an external process to actually infer the norms or guidelines shaping the value-aligned decisions.

3   Value Aligning Sequences of Decisions

We define goal-oriented decision-making as a model based on a Multi-Agent System (MAS) [9], where the world is modelled as a labelled transition system, called **decision world** $(\mathcal{S}, \mathcal{A}, \mathcal{T})$ with the following elements.

- **States** $\mathcal{S}$, representing the MAS completely in each situation.
- **Actions** $\mathcal{A}$, representing the MAS joint actions or decisions.
- **Transitions** $\mathcal{T} \subset \mathcal{S} \times \mathcal{A} \times \mathcal{S}$, representing available actions connecting each pair of states. We will denote them with $s \xrightarrow{a} t$, where $s, t \in \mathcal{S}$ and $a \in \mathcal{A}$.
- **Paths** $\mathcal{P}$, representing joint transitions (sequences of decisions), e.g. a path of length n from s_0 to s_n would be represented as: $P = s_0 \xrightarrow{a_1} s_1 \xrightarrow{a_2} \ldots \xrightarrow{a_n} s_n$.
- **Goal States** $\mathcal{G} \subset \mathcal{S}$, representing states where agents satisfy their needs or aims in the problem.
- **Plans**, representing paths that we consider solutions to our problems, i.e. those going from a given initial state s_0, to a goal state $s_g \in \mathcal{G}$.

We are interested in identifying which plans adhere the better with a value v under consideration. We assume v is firstly grounded in states for then, constructing path-level criteria.

3.1   State-Level Alignment: Value Preferences

Following Weide et al. [17] or Sierra et al. [15], we assume a value preference among states based on a preorder relation $\sqsubseteq_v$, which we call **perspective** or **value preorder**, i.e. given s and s', two states, $s \sqsubseteq_v s'$ means that s' is at least as preferred as s w.r.t. the value v.

Another approach is using a numeric value to quantify the above relation. Citing [9], the semantics of a value v in state s is an *unbounded* **semantics function** $f_v : \mathcal{S} \longrightarrow \mathbb{R}$, where f_v is directly proportional to the promotion of v.[1] The relationship between those approaches is fairly straight-forward: $s' \sqsubseteq_v s'' \iff f_v(s') \leq f_v(s'')$. Examples of statistical functions that can be used to define semantics functions for the value of equity are the following:

1. Maximum-Minimum difference (**Mn**): Difference between maximum and minimum values of the state. Inversely proportional to equality.
2. Sample Standard Deviation (**SSD**): Standard deviation as dispersion metric is inversely proportional to equality.

---

[1] Original definition from Montes and Sierra [9] assumes that the range of all value semantics functions is bounded in $[-1, 1]$, so $f_v(s) \approx -1, 0, +1$ indicates that state s strongly opposes, is neutral or strongly promotes the value v, respectively. This would represent an (unnecessary strict) *absolute* value promotion metric.

3. Median Absolute Deviation (**MAD**). It is a robust version of the SSD, unaffected by outsiders.
4. Coefficient of Variation (**CV**) [6]. Defined as the sample standard deviation over the mean (in absolute value). Values closer to 0 mean greater equality.
5. Gini Index (**GI**) [5,9][2]. Inequality in an economic system is usually represented with this function as it has unique important properties [12].

3.2   Plan-Level Alignment and Admissibility

In literature, the value-alignment of a path (and a of plan, by extension) is given by a human [2] or calculated by aggregating values of states [9] or actions [7]. However, it is important to notice that, from the point of view of the decision-making of a value-aware agent, not all courses of action need to be considered. For instance, in a water distribution scenario, all assignments that, at some point in time, leave stakeholders without a minimum amount of water necessary for basic needs, should not be considered even if they lead to a final state in which water distribution is equitable. These "lower bounds" on the value alignment determine the paths that are *admissible* under a certain value. They can either be determined in absolute or in relative terms, and based on preference preorders or semantics functions, as we will argue in the sequel.

Given an aggregation function agg, and a semantics function f_v, we define the semantics of a value for a path $P = s_0 \xrightarrow{a_1} \ldots \xrightarrow{a_n} s_n$ as: $agg_v(P) = agg(\{f_v(s_0), \ldots, f_v(s_n)\})$. This is called its **aggregated alignment**. Examples of aggregation functions (agg) are the mean, the (discounted) sum, the maximum, etc. This aggregation concept was already mentioned as a modelling aspect in [9].

Value-admissible behaviours for a value v are given by a constraint criterion on the set of all plans $\mathcal{P}$. It characterizes the subset of plans $B(\mathcal{P}, \sqsubseteq_v)$ that are admissibly aligned with the value, based on state/action-level alignment $\sqsubseteq_v$. In this paper we are concerned with three very general classes of such behaviours:

a) **Local behaviour.** Admits plans which are constructed by only visiting the next states that are the most preferable:

$$B_{local}(\mathcal{P}, \sqsubseteq_v) = \{P \in \mathcal{P} \mid \forall s \xrightarrow{a} t \in P, \nexists s \xrightarrow{a'} t' \in Q \in \mathcal{P} \cdot t \neq t' \wedge t \sqsubseteq_v t'\}$$

b) **Goal behaviour.** Admits plans leading to the goal states that are the most preferable. Here, $out(P)$ denotes the final and goal state of P.

$$B_{goal}(\mathcal{P}, \sqsubseteq_v) = \{P \in \mathcal{P} \mid \nexists Q \in \mathcal{P} \cdot out(Q) \neq out(P) \wedge out(P) \sqsubseteq_v out(Q)\}$$

---

[2] Note that the $[-1, 1]$-bounded semantics function used in [9] is defined in terms of the Gini index, i.e., $f_{eq} = 1 - 2 \cdot GI(s)$. Similarly, the rest of the semantics functions we have enumerated can be bounded to that interval if needed. For this theory, we just consider these functions as *quantifiers* of value preorders.

c) **Aggregated behaviour**. This strategy admits plans with the highest overall alignment according to an *agg* aggregation function.

$$B_{agg_v}(\mathcal{P}, \sqsubseteq_v) = \{P \in \mathcal{P} \mid \not\exists Q \in \mathcal{P}\backslash\{P\} \cdot agg_v(P) \le agg_v(Q)\}$$

Requiring value-admissibility of such behaviours obviously reduces the space of plans that a value-aware agent can choose from. In some situations (e.g. in Sect. 4.2 while using certain semantics functions) this may even lead to a unique admissible plan. Therefore, we can introduce some relaxation over the above criteria, by admitting some more states of plans that are admissibly close to abiding to them. This relaxation can be more easily stated by quantifying the preorder, i.e. using (not necessarily bounded) semantics functions. As an example, we detail the *epsilon-local* behaviour:

ϵ-**Local Behaviour**. Given a set of plans $\mathcal{P}$, $\epsilon \in \mathbb{N}$, and the semantics function for a value v, f_v, the ϵ-**local behaviour**, B_ϵ is defined as:

$$B_\epsilon(\mathcal{P}, f_v) = \{P \in \mathcal{P} \mid \forall s \xrightarrow{a} t \in P, \ f_v(t) \ge \max\{f_v(t') \mid \exists t \xrightarrow{a'} t' \in Q \in \mathcal{P}\} - \epsilon\}\}$$

This behaviour extends the local one by admitting not only the next most preferable state(s) but the ϵ-most preferred at each step; i.e., among the next possible states, we would admit traversing those with up to an ϵ decrement in semantics value w.r.t the most valued one(s).

4 Example: Equity in Water Distribution

To illustrate our approach to value alignment, we draw upon a use case in the domain of water distribution. This domain has being explored deeply, i.e. with socio-cognitive agents [11], though with no value-awareness in mind yet. In the following we first summarise legal aspects and values related to water use, and then present a simple example considering a situation of water distribution in a drought scenario, where the value of equity is to be maintained.

4.1 Legal and Values Considerations for Water Distribution

Preserving values in the context of water distribution is indeed of the maximum importance and representative of general situations. At the European level, the Parliamentary Assembly of the Council of Europe declared that access to water must be recognized as a fundamental human right because it is essential for life on the planet and it is a resource that must be shared by humanity[3]. Providing such access is, in turn, a commitment under the UN Sustainable Development Goal No. 6 of the 2030 Agenda "Ensure availability and sustainable management of water and sanitation for all".[4]

---

[3] Council of Europe Parliamentary Assembly Resolution No. 1693 (2009).

[4] SDG 6 of the United Nations 2030 Agenda for Sustainable Development https://www.un.org/sustainabledevelopment.

As we have seen above, water is an essential good for human life, so universal access to it must be guaranteed; but water is also a scarce resource with economic value, which contributes simultaneously to social, environmental, and economic objectives.[5] Currently, the water volume allocation for agriculture is 70%. In water stress scenarios, it will undoubtedly be necessary to reallocate this percentage to other uses[6] and, consequently, to improve water management, including digitization in this sector. This will require a better allocation of water in situations of scarcity and theorizing about different models.

In Spain, the average household water consumption was 133 litres per inhabitant per day.[7] The main use of water is irrigation and agricultural use, which accounts for approximately 80.5% of this demand, followed by urban supply, which represents 15.5%. The remainder is for industrial use [4]. Of all the water uses, the priority is urban water supply.[8] The regulations have established that the net or average consumption endowment, as a minimum objective, must be at least 100 litres per inhabitant per day.[9]

From the legal point of view, water (surface and groundwater) is a public good (i.e., it is not subject to private ownership). Urban water supply is configured as a public service, extensively regulated (including its price through the corresponding tariff) and, as such, it has the characteristics inherent to such services: equal access, provision, and quality, the existence of basic common conditions, universality and continuity, solidarity, transparency and control with user participation [13]. In turn, the legislation establishes general principles applicable to water management, from which stand out management unit, integral treatment, deconcentration, decentralization, coordination, efficiency and user participation.[10]

4.2 Use Case

In our use case, in a situation of drought, water needs to be distributed from a reservoir to 4 equally populated and distant villages using a tanker vehicle with $11kl$ of capacity. We consider a goal of distributing a total of $44kl$ from the reservoir to the villages. For each trip, we must decide which village is visited and supplied with water. For simplicity, the vehicle always discharges the entire capacity of its tank when arriving to a village.

The problem can be modelled with the basic elements of the decision world introduced in Sect. 3 as follows:

---

[5] https://www.oecd.org/water/Recomendacion-del-Consejo-sobre-el-agua.pdf.

[6] In agriculture (https://www.bancomundial.org/es/topic/water-in-agriculture).

[7] Statistics on Water Supply and Sanitation Year 2020, see https://www.ine.es/prensa/essa_2020.pdf.

[8] Royal Decree 1/2001, of July 20, approving the Revised Text of the Water Law, Article 60.

[9] Royal Decree 3/2023, of January 10, establishing the technical-sanitary criteria for the quality of drinking water, its control, and supply, Article 9.

[10] Royal Decree 1/2001, of July 20, approving the Revised Text of the Water Law, Article 14.

- **States**: a state is a list of four values where each value represents the amount of water delivered to each village, i.e. $[11, 11, 0, 0]$.
- **Actions**: an action indicates the village visited by the vehicle, identified by a number from 1 to 4 (one for each village).
- **Transitions**: Depending on goals, we will have different transitions, though they all model that the truck delivers its $11kl$ to the village indicated by the action. An example of a transition would be $[0, 0, 11, 11] \xrightarrow{4} [0, 0, 11, 22]$.

Depending on the particular context, the value of equity in this scenario can be grounded in different semantics functions. We intend to examine the impact of choosing a specific semantics function in relation to different notions of value-admissible behaviour. For this purpose, we consider three different semantics functions inspired by statistical ones from Sect. 3: $f_1 = -$ Mm, $f_2 = -$ SSD and $f_3 = -$ MAD, and the three main behaviours proposed in Sect. 3.2, i.e., Local, Goal, and Aggregated (considering the **sum** as the aggregation function, no "*epsilon*" versions considered yet).

Figure 1 shows the state-transition diagram for our use case. For simplicity, we collapsed states ordering the variables from highest to lowest, so each path represents much more distributions, but all equivalent in the end. In the figure, plans pertaining to local behaviours are represented by red edges, the ones from the aggregated behaviours by blue edges, and goal states are indicated by green nodes.

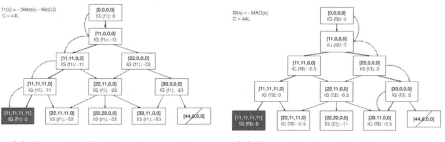

(a) Semantics function $f_1 = -Mn$.   (b) Semantics function $f_3 = -MAD$.

Fig. 1. Plans admissible to deliver $44kl$ under local, goal, and aggregated behaviours. The *local plans* are represented by red edges; the aggregated plans, by blue edges; and the goal plans are those going from the initial state to the green nodes, which mark the most value-aligned goal states. (Color figure online)

In line with the discussion put forward in Sect. 4.1, we can assume that the *local behaviour* is strongly aligned with the value of equity, as an agent adhering to that type of behaviour can justify its actions by claiming that it is always promoting equity to the best it can at each moment. Figure 1a shows that, for f_1, there is one single plan admissible under all the behaviours. Indeed, the goal-admitted plan (reaching the green state) coincides with the plans admitted by the local and aggregated behaviours.

By contrast, Fig. 1b indicates that considering the semantics function f_3 there is only one goal-admissible plan, which does not coincide with the local-admissible plan. Both plans are aggregate-admissible.

It is worth noting that with Schur-Concave semantics functions, such as $f_2 = -$ SSD or the modified Gini Index from [9], the three behaviours admit the same single plan (Fig. 1a). This plan certifies a local behaviour which is aligned with the value while keeping the highest overall final alignment score according to the semantics of the value. This situation, however, is not the norm, as under f_3, the local plan reaches the state $[33, 11, 0, 0]$ instead of $[11, 11, 11, 11]$. This means that we cannot generally assume that just adhering to equitable principles will lead us into the most equitable goal. Still, the local plan is also admissible as aggregated behaviour, so it does preserve equity in that sense.

In general, the left blue plan can probably be conceived as most aligned with the value of equity (it is a goal plan, therefore reaches an equitable goal, and it is also part of the aggregated behaviours, so achieves overall equity). But notice that, to follow that plan, the second decision would need to be less equity-aligned than the other option, implying that it might not fully comply with legal requirements.

These problems may be addressed using the ϵ-local behaviour introduced in Sect. 3.2. With this behaviour, under certain circumstances, a small enough $\epsilon > 0$ may be tolerated (e.g. when all the villages get the Spanish minimum legal amount of water per inhabitant: $133l/inhab.$) in the hope for finding better future alignment.

5   Conclusions and Future Work

In this paper, we analyze water allocation and human rights legislation to analyze value-aligned decision-making in a water scarcity scenario where preserving the value of equity is a legal requirement. Based on recent work, we formalize the value alignment problem with state-level preferences and semantics functions, characterizing not only the aggregated alignment of general paths but also plan value-admissibility criteria with the concept of behaviours. With a small water distribution in a drought situation example, we observe that a behaviour that conforms to the legislation (trying to preserve equity in each action) may lead to less equal states in the long term. As such, we ended up proposing a relaxed behaviour that could contemplate better future equity-aligned decisions without losing the law's intentions regarding the value.

In future work, we propose using reinforcement learning considering value-admissibility behaviours. Different tasks can be investigated, such as learning an approximately optimal policy adhering to different behaviours simultaneously or one that adheres to the ϵ-local behaviour while maximizing others (e.g. aggregated/goal behaviour). Lastly, we highlight the problem of defining suitable value-aligned aggregation functions for generic (goal-oriented) decision-making problems.

Acknowledgements.. This work has been supported by grant VAE: TED2021-131295B-C33 funded by MCIN/AEI/ 10.13039/501100011033 and by the "European Union NextGenerationEU/PRTR", by grant COSASS: PID2021-123673OB-C32 funded by MCIN/AEI/ 10.13039/501100011033 and by "ERDF A way of making Europe", and by the AGROBOTS Project of Universidad Rey Juan Carlos funded by the Community of Madrid, Spain.

References

1. Arnold, T., Kasenberg, D., Scheutz, M.: Value alignment or misalignment - what will keep systems accountable? In: AAAI Workshop on AI, Ethics, and Society (2017)
2. Christiano, P., Leike, J., Brown, T.B., Martic, M., Legg, S., Amodei, D.: Deep reinforcement learning from human preferences (2023)
3. Fürnkranz, J., Hüllermeier, E., Cheng, W., Park, S.H.: Preference-based reinforcement learning: a formal framework and a policy iteration algorithm. Mach. Learn. **89**, 123–156 (2012). https://doi.org/10.1007/s10994-012-5313-8
4. Government, S.: Strategic project for economic recovery and transformation of digitalization of the water cycle. Report 2022. Technical report, Ministry for the Ecological Transition and Demographic Challenge (2022)
5. Guo, T., Yuan, Y., Zhao, P.: Admission-based reinforcement-learning algorithm in sequential social dilemmas. Appl. Sci. **13**(3) (2023). https://doi.org/10.3390/app13031807. www.mdpi.com/2076-3417/13/3/1807
6. Jiang, J., Lu, Z.: Learning fairness in multi-agent systems. In: Advances in Neural Information Processing Systems, vol. 32 (2019)
7. Lera-Leri, R., Bistaffa, F., Serramia, M., Lopez-Sanchez, M., Rodriguez-Aguilar, J.: Towards pluralistic value alignment: aggregating value systems through l_p-regression. In: Proceedings of the 21st International Conference on Autonomous Agents and Multiagent Systems, AAMAS 2022, Richland, SC, pp. 780–788. International Foundation for Autonomous Agents and Multiagent Systems (2022)
8. Montes, N., Osman, N., Sierra, C., Slavkovik, M.: Value engineering for autonomous agents. CoRR abs/2302.08759 (2023). https://doi.org/10.48550/arXiv.2302.08759
9. Montes, N., Sierra, C.: Synthesis and properties of optimally value-aligned normative systems. J. Artif. Intell. Res. **74**, 1739–1774 (2022). https://doi.org/10.1613/jair.1.13487
10. Ng, A.Y., Russell, S.J.: Algorithms for inverse reinforcement learning. In: Proceedings of the Seventeenth International Conference on Machine Learning, pp. 663–670 (2000)
11. Perello-Moragues, A., Poch, M., Sauri, D., Popartan, L.A., Noriega, P.: Modelling domestic water use in metropolitan areas using socio-cognitive agents. Water **13**(8) (2021). https://doi.org/10.3390/w13081024. www.mdpi.com/2073-4441/13/8/1024
12. Plata-Pérez, L., Sánchez-Pérez, J., Sánchez-Sánchez, F.: An elementary characterization of the Gini index. Math. Soc. Sci. **74**, 79–83 (2015)
13. PricewaterhouseCoopers: La gestión del agua en españa. análisis y retos del ciclo urbano del agua (2018). www.pwc.es/es/publicaciones/energia/assets/gestion-agua-2018-espana.pdf

14. Rodriguez-Soto, M., Serramia, M., Lopez-Sanchez, M., Rodriguez-Aguilar, J.A.: Instilling moral value alignment by means of multi-objective reinforcement learning. Ethics Inf. Technol. **24**, 9 (2022). https://doi.org/10.1007/s10676-022-09635-0
15. Sierra, C., Osman, N., Noriega, P., Sabater-Mir, J., Perelló, A.: Value alignment: a formal approach. CoRR abs/2110.09240 (2021). arxiv.org/abs/2110.09240
16. Sutton, R.S., Barto, A.G.: Reinforcement Learning: An Introduction. MIT Press, Cambridge (2018)
17. van der Weide, T.L., Dignum, F., Meyer, J.-J.C., Prakken, H., Vreeswijk, G.A.W.: Practical reasoning using values. In: McBurney, P., Rahwan, I., Parsons, S., Maudet, N. (eds.) ArgMAS 2009. LNCS (LNAI), vol. 6057, pp. 79–93. Springer, Heidelberg (2010). https://doi.org/10.1007/978-3-642-12805-9_5

Multi-tasking Resource-Constrained Agents Reach Higher Accuracy When Tasks Overlap

Andreas Kalaitzakis[(✉)] and Jérôme Euzenat

Univ. Grenoble Alpes, Inria, CNRS, Grenoble INP, LIG, 38000 Grenoble, France
{Andreas.Kalaitzakis,Jerome.Euzenat}@inria.fr

Abstract. Agents have been previously shown to evolve their ontologies while interacting over a single task. However, little is known about how interacting over several tasks affects the accuracy of agent ontologies. Is knowledge learned by tackling one task beneficial for another task? We hypothesize that multi-tasking agents tackling tasks that rely on the same properties, are more accurate than multi-tasking agents tackling tasks that rely on different properties. We test this hypothesis by varying two parameters. The first parameter is the number of tasks assigned to the agents. The second parameter is the number of common properties among these tasks. Results show that when deciding for different tasks relies on the same properties, multi-tasking agents reach higher accuracy. This suggests that when agents tackle several tasks, it is possible to transfer knowledge from one task to another.

Keywords: Cultural knowledge evolution · Knowledge transfer · Multi-tasking

1 Introduction

Agents have been previously shown to improve their accuracy as a result of cultural knowledge evolution. The latter studies agents that evolve their knowledge representations, based on their perception and the feedback they receive from other agents. Recent work on cultural knowledge evolution focuses on agents tackling a single task: taking an abstract decision within an abstract domain. In [3], agents are forced to take identical decisions regarding a set of environment objects. Eventually, agents learn to agree over a single decision task, yet not necessarily on the same basis. For example, two agents may both decide to visit *Barcelona*. Agent α may base its decision on the *temperature* property, while agent β may base its decision on the *ticket_price* property.

However, several tasks may exist. We build on previous works by introducing agents capable of taking abstract decisions within several domains. To do so,

This work has been partially supported by MIAI @ Grenoble Alpes (ANR-19-P3IA-0003).

agents classify objects into ontology classes and associate these classes with different decisions for different tasks. We consider that realistic agents should not be able to develop ontologies containing all class descriptions. Thus, we limit the number of classes to be maintained within an agent's ontology. When this limit is reached, agents will try to forget knowledge that is not relevant to the tasks they favor. Deciding for different tasks may rely on a set of common properties. For example, the property *temperature* may be used in order to choose a destination (task 1). The same property may also be used to decide whether to wear a T-shirt (task 2). However, the property *temperature* may be completely irrelevant to choosing a movie (task 3). We assume that when this set is not empty, agents carrying several tasks may develop multi-purpose knowledge, i.e., knowledge that can be transferred among different tasks. Based on this, we formulate the following hypothesis: multi-tasking agents tackling tasks that rely on the same properties, are more accurate than multi-tasking agents tackling tasks that rely on different properties. We test this hypothesis by varying two parameters. The first parameter is the number of tasks assigned to each agent. The second parameter the number of common properties shared among the different tasks. Two variations of the second parameter are examined. Tasks either rely on the same properties, or rely on different ones. We then evaluate agent ontologies based on their contribution to promote successful interactions and provide accurate decisions. Based on this evaluation, the following is shown: when agents tackle tasks based on common properties, knowledge built by an agent while tackling one task, improves its accuracy on another task. We thus conclude that it is possible to transfer knowledge from one task to another.

After discussing related work in Sect. 2, preliminaries regarding the entities that constitute the environment as well as the notation that describes it, are introduced in Sect. 3. In Sect. 4, an outline of the experiment is provided, including how agents learn their initial ontologies, interact with each other and adapt when they disagree. Section 5 presents our hypothesis and the protocol used to test it. Results are presented in Sect. 6 and conclusions are provided in Sect. 7.

2   Related Work

It has been shown that referential games [9] facilitate the establishment of communication protocols between communicating agents. [11] argues that a communication protocol emerges when agents attempt to minimize the computational complexity of semantic interpretation. [7] studies a framework where two agents develop a language in order to succeed in a referential game. [6] shows that implicit cultural transmission leads to greater language compositionality. While our work relies on successfully communicating agents, our focus is on how this successful communication allows for better task completion.

Different examples of multi-tasking agents exist in literature. Indicatively, multi-task learning has been shown to significantly improve classification in a variety of areas, e.g., adversary robustness [10], visual interconceptual similarity [4] and phenotype learning [5]. Agents have also been used to study the impact of multi-task learning on emerging communication protocols. In [12], cooperative multi-agent reinforcement learning is considered. Our work is related to these works, since they consider agents that perform several tasks. However our focus is not on agents that improve their accuracy individually. Here we study agents that improve their accuracy through social transmission.

Social transmission among agents has been studied in [3] and [13]. In [13], the authors examine how concepts are organized and how their collective behavior can be established autonomously. In [3], a two-stage experiment is used, where agents first learn a classifier and then interact in pairs. Through an adaptation mechanism, it is shown that the agents achieve better knowledge, without adopting identical ontologies. We differentiate from these, by introducing memory-limited agents that tackle several tasks.

3   Experimental Framework

3.1   Environment

Agents evolve in an environment populated by objects described by a set $\mathcal{P}$ of boolean properties. Objects are therefore described by the presence or absence of a property $p \in \mathcal{P}$, denoted by p and $\neg p$ respectively. Hence, there are $2^{|\mathcal{P}|}$ object types, that are gathered in a set $\mathcal{I}$.

3.2   Tasks

The term task refers to a piece of work, carried out by an agent. Here, we will concentrate on a set of decision tasks: making a decision about an object. There may be different tasks $t \in \mathcal{T}$ associated to a different set of possible decisions $\mathcal{D}_t$. Each object o can be considered with respect to any task $t \in \mathcal{T}$. A function $h^*(o, t) \rightarrow \mathcal{D}_t$ provides the correct, unknown to agents, decision for an object o with respect to a task t. For example, $h^*(tomato, coloring)$ will provide the decision red.

3.3   Agents

Agents are autonomous, co-existing entities, able to perceive and distinguish objects based on their properties. In this context, a population of multi-tasking agents $\mathcal{A}$ is assigned different subsets of $\mathcal{T}$. To tackle these tasks, agents build and evolve private ontologies, expressed in $\mathcal{ALC}$ [2]. Each agent α uses its ontology to compute a function $h^\alpha(o, t) \rightarrow \mathcal{D}_t$ which, given an object o and a task t, provides a decision $h^\alpha(o, t)$. The right part of Fig. 1 shows an example of a multi-task ontology constructed by an agent α. The bottom part represents the private ontology $\mathcal{O}^\alpha$ of agent α, allowing it to classify objects of the environment. The top part shows a set of decision ontologies, each one containing the valid decisions for a respective task t. An agent α learns at most one decision for an object o and a task t. Thus, each leaf of $\mathcal{O}^\alpha$ cannot be aligned more than once with the same decision ontology.

4   Experiment Outline

In this paper, we examine if knowledge can be transferred from one task to another. To this end, a two-stage experiment is used. In the first stage, agents induce private ontologies based on randomly selected labeled examples. In the second stage, agents go through a fixed number of interactions. For each interaction, two randomly selected agents will have to decide with respect to an object o and a task t. When agents disagree, one of the two agents adapts its ontology.

More details about how agents learn, are assigned tasks, interact, release resources and adapt their ontologies are presented in Subsects. 4.1, 4.2, 4.3, 4.4 and 4.5 respectively.

4.1   Initial Ontology Induction

We approach multi-task learning as a problem of inducing an ontology capable of providing a decision for any task $t \in \mathcal{T}$. Different algorithms may be used, affecting the final accuracy of agents. This paper does not examine how different learning algorithms impact the achieved accuracy. This paper examines how cultural evolution improves the accuracy of multi-tasking agents. Thus, details about the learning algorithm are omitted. A learning example can be seen in Fig. 1. By the end of its initial ontology induction phase, the agent α is able to classify an object described by $p_1 \sqcap p_2$ but unable to decide about the task t_1.

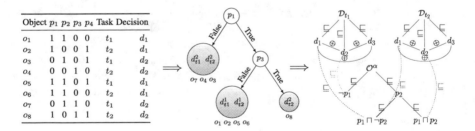

Fig. 1. Given a set of labeled examples, agents will induce a decision tree. The latter is subsequently transformed into an ontology. Each color represents a different decision. (Color figure online)

4.2   Task Assignment

Agents are assigned with different subsets of $\mathcal{T}$ of the same size. The latter varies from 1 to $|\mathcal{T}|$ and remains constant for the duration of an experiment. Based on it, all possible task permutations of the same size are initially produced. Each permutation corresponding to a different subset of $\mathcal{T}$, is then assigned to an even number of agents. Thus, the number of agents is always a multiple of the number of the different subsets of $\mathcal{T}$.

4.3   Interaction

For each interaction, two randomly selected agents α and β are asked to provide a decision for an object o with respect to a task t. The agents provide their decisions based on the respective functions $h^\alpha(o,t)$ and $h^\beta(o,t)$. If an agent is unable to provide a decision, then one decision is randomly selected. The agents will then disclose their decisions to each other. If $h^\alpha(o,t) = h^\beta(o,t)$, the agents agree and their interaction is considered as successful. On the contrary, their interaction ends as a failure. In this case, one of the two agents may adapt its ontology. In order to decide which agent will adapt, an evaluation set is randomly selected. It contains samples labeled with respect to the task t. The agents are evaluated against this set and a score is assigned to each one of them. The agent with the lowest score may adapt its ontology.

4.4   Resources Release

When an agent's resources are exhausted, it tries to forget knowledge as follows (Fig. 2). Leaf nodes that satisfy the following criteria are removed: (a) they have the same immediate parent node (b) they are associated with the same decision regarding all tasks assigned to the agent. The process is repeated recursively, as long as leaf nodes satisfying (a) and (b) exist.

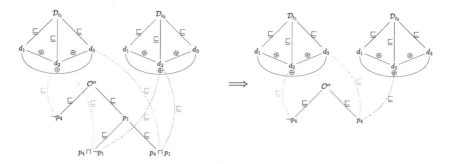

Fig. 2. Let an agent α assigned the task t_2, with t_2 relying on the property set $\mathcal{P}_{t_2}$. The property $p_1 \notin \mathcal{P}_{t_2}$, thus p_1 does not allow for distinguishing different decisions for the task t_2. In this example, the agent has associated the same decision (in red), to both $p_4 \sqcap \neg p_1$ and $p_4 \sqcap p_1$. These two classes can be removed without any loss of accuracy with respect to t_2. For the task t_2, the parent node will now be associated with the decision d_2 (red). For the task t_1, the parent node will now be associated with one of two decisions previously associated with its former descendent nodes. Here, the decision d_3 (gray) was randomly selected. (Color figure online)

4.5   Adaptation

Our adaptation mechanism extends the one presented in [3]. Based on it, an agent can either replace an existing decision or split a class into two sub-classes

(Fig. 3). The agent does this on the basis of a property that distinguishes the current object from the objects classified by the class to be split. Only the decisions concerning the current task are affected.

5   Experimental Setting

5.1   Hypothesis

– Multi-tasking agents tackling tasks that rely on the same properties, are more accurate than multi-tasking agents tackling tasks that rely on different properties.

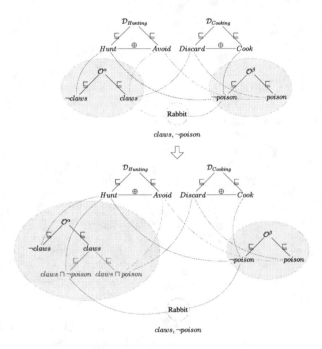

Fig. 3. The agent α will split the class *claws* into two sub-classes using the property *poison*. The first $(claws \sqcap \neg poison)$ will be associated with the decision of the agent β. The second $(claws \sqcap poison)$ will be associated with all decisions previously associated with the class *claws*.

5.2   Parameters

The experiment is executed under 6 setups. Each setup is run 20 times and its results are averaged. One run consists of 80000 interactions with each interaction taking place among two randomly selected agents. The total population of agents is 18. Their environment contains 64 different object types, each one perceivable through 6 different binary properties. The agents are initially trained with respect to 3 tasks. Taking 1 out of 4 decisions with respect to each task relies on 2 properties. These properties are either the same for all tasks, or different for each task. Agents induce an initial ontology based on a random 10 % of all existing labeled examples. The agents are assigned 1 to 3 tasks. Agent evaluation is based on 60% of all samples.

5.3   Measures

Success rate, as introduced in [3] is defined as the proportion of successful interactions, over all performed interactions until the nth interaction. Task accuracy adapts the accuracy measure introduced in [3] to different tasks. It is defined as the proportion of object types for which a correct decision would be taken with respect to a task t, by an agent α on the nth iteration of the experiment.

$$tacc(\alpha, n, t) = \frac{|\{o \in \mathcal{I} : h_n^\alpha(o,t) = h^*(o,t)\}|}{|\mathcal{I}|}$$

6   Results and Discussion

We hypothesize that when tasks rely on common properties, it is possible for agents to build multi-purpose knowledge. To test this hypothesis, the accuracy of the following two populations was compared. The first consists of agents assigned up to 3 tasks for which all properties are shared. The second consists of agents assigned up to 3 tasks for which no properties are shared. Figure 4 depicts the

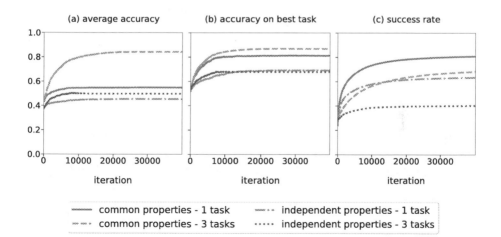

Fig. 4. (a) average accuracy, (b) accuracy on best task and (c) success rate for different number of assigned tasks and common properties.

evolution of the agents (a) average accuracy, (b) accuracy on their best task and (c) success rate, for different number of tasks and common properties. Figure 4a shows that assigning more tasks to agents, significantly improves their average accuracy. This improvement is higher when agents tackle tasks that rely on the same properties. On the one hand, when tasks rely on different properties, agents tackling 3 tasks are 9% more accurate than agents tackling 1 task. On the other hand, when tasks rely on common properties, agents tackling 3 tasks are 55% more accurate than agents tackling 1 task. This shows that agents tackling tasks relying on a common set of properties, may improve their accuracy on one task by carrying out another task. Results thus support our hypothesis.

Figure 4b shows two things. First, agents tackling tasks that rely on the same properties achieve a higher accuracy on their best task, compared to agents tackling tasks that rely on different properties. This indicates that while the agents may abstain from some tasks, their ontologies contain multi-purpose knowledge, acquired during the initial ontology induction phase. This further supports our hypothesis. Second, when tasks rely on different properties, the effect of the number of tasks assigned to each agent on the accuracy for its best task, is statistically insignificant ($p > 0.05$). This indicates that when tasks rely on different properties, learning to decide with respect to one task is not related to learning to decide with respect to a different task.

Figure 4c shows that tackling less tasks or having tasks that rely on common properties improves the success rate. This is due to two reasons. The first is that the fewer the assigned tasks, the fewer are the decisions over which agents need to agree. The second is that the more tasks rely on common properties, the less non relevant knowledge may be present to an agent's initially induced ontology. Furthermore, while success rate improves over the course of the experiment, it does not converge to 1. This indicates that the final ontologies do not allow agents to reach consensus. This can be explained by the limitation of resources: agents may lack the resources required to learn to decide accurately for all assigned tasks and objects. As a result, they are able to decide accurately for different subsets of the existing object types at a given time. Thus, unless the different subsets coincide for all agents, consensus cannot be achieved. The latter is true even when agents interact over the same single task.

6.1 Statistical Analysis

Analysis of variance shows that the number of common properties among different tasks, has a statistically significant impact ($p < 0.05$) on all measures. The number of assigned tasks has a statistically significant impact on (1) the success rate and (2) the average accuracy. When tasks rely on common properties, the latter has a statistically significant impact on the agents accuracy on their best task.

7   Conclusion

We hypothesize that agents tackling tasks that rely on common properties, benefit from the formation of multi-purpose knowledge. We test this hypothesis by introducing agents that learn and evolve ontologies with respect to several tasks. The experimental results support this hypothesis. On the one hand, it is shown that when agents tackle tasks that rely on common properties, knowledge is transferred from one task to another. On the other hand, when these tasks rely on different properties, tackling additional tasks does not affect the agents accuracy on their best task. Thus, deciding between tackling one or several tasks depends on the agents objective and the environment setup. The agent objective corresponds to whether they seek to optimize their accuracy on average or on their best task. The environment setup corresponds to whether the tasks depend on common properties or not. The experiments rely on minimal hypotheses about the environment, hence the results apply to a wide range of environment. These may serve as an insight on how agents evolve their knowledge within more complex environments. For example, one may consider environments where some tasks share properties, while other tasks are completely independent.

Data Availability. The cultural evolution simulator used for our experiments can be found in [1]. Settings, results and the data analysis notebook are available in [8].

References

1. Lazy lavender (2023). https://gitlab.inria.fr/moex/lazylav
2. Baader, F., Calvanese, D., McGuinness, D., Nardi, D., Patel-Schneider, P.F. (eds.): The Description Logic Handbook: Theory, Implementation, and Applications. Cambridge University Press, Cambridge (2003)
3. Bourahla, Y., Atencia, M., Euzenat, J.: Knowledge improvement and diversity under interaction-driven adaptation of learned ontologies. In: Proceedings of the 20th ACM International Conference on Autonomous Agents and Multi-Agent Systems (AAMAS), London, United Kingdom, pp. 242–250 (2021)
4. Fan, J., Gao, Y., Luo, H.: Integrating concept ontology and multitask learning to achieve more effective classifier training for multilevel image annotation. IEEE Trans. Image Process. **17**(3), 407–426 (2008)
5. Ghalwash, M., Yao, Z., Chakraporty, P., Codella, J., Sow, D.: Phenotypical ontology driven framework for multi-task learning. In: Proceedings of the Conference on Health, Inference, and Learning, CHIL 2021, New York, USA, pp. 183–192 (2021)
6. Harding Graesser, L., Cho, K., Kiela, D.: Emergent linguistic phenomena in multi-agent communication games. In: Proceedings of the 2019 Conference on Empirical Methods in Natural Language Processing and the 9th International Joint Conference on Natural Language Processing (EMNLP-IJCNLP), Hong Kong, China, pp. 3700–3710 (2019)
7. Havrylov, S., Titov, I.: Emergence of language with multi-agent games: learning to communicate with sequence of symbols. In: 5th International Conference on Learning Representations (ICLR 2017, Workshop Track), Toulon, France (2017)
8. Kalaitzakis, A.: 20230505-MTOA experiment description (2023). https://sake.re/20230505-MTOA

9. Lewis, D.K.: Convention: A Philosophical Study. Wiley-Blackwell, Cambridge (1969)
10. Mao, C., et al.: Multitask learning strengthens adversarial robustness. In: Vedaldi, A., Bischof, H., Brox, T., Frahm, J.-M. (eds.) ECCV 2020. LNCS, vol. 12347, pp. 158–174. Springer, Cham (2020). https://doi.org/10.1007/978-3-030-58536-5_10
11. Steels, L.: What triggers the emergence of grammar? In: AISB 2005: Proceedings of the Second International Symposium on the Emergence and Evolution of Linguistic Communication (EELC 2005), Hatfield, United Kingdom, pp. 143–150 (2005)
12. Thomas, J., Santos-Rodriguez, R., Anca, M., Piechocki, R.: Multi-lingual Agents Through Multi-headed Neural Networks, vol. 4, Tromsø, Norway (2023)
13. Wang, J., Gasser, L.: Mutual online ontology alignment. In: Proceedings of the 1st ACM International Conference on Autonomous Agents and Multi-Agent Systems (AAMAS), Bologna, Italy (2002)

Election Manipulation on Social Networks with Abstention

Vincenzo Auletta$^{(\boxtimes)}$![ORCID], Diodato Ferraioli$^{(\boxtimes)}$![ORCID], and Carmine Viscito

Università degli Studi di Salerno, 84084 Fisciano, SA, Italy
{auletta,dferraioli}@unisa.it, c.viscito@studenti.unisa.it

Abstract. The Election Manipulation through the diffusion of (fake) news on social networks has been a subject that recently attracted the interest of many works in both in the communities of AI and social choice theory. However, all these works assume that each voter has to express her vote, not considering the possibility that she could abstain. One of the reasons of this omission is the lack of a satisfying modeling of how people choose to abstain. In this work, we try to fill this gap by presenting an innovative model for abstention that will match most of the real-world observations about the topic. Next, we will provide experimental evidence that abstention opportunity will help the manipulator to control the elections, by comparing how well-known algorithms and heuristics behave in the setting with and without abstention.

Keywords: Information Diffusion · Voting · Graph Algorithms

1 Introduction

"We have three major voter suppression operations under way". These words were spelled out by a senior official of the Trump campaign for the 2016 presidential election [24]. The three campaigns were aimed to convince groups of people (idealistic white liberals, young women, and African Americans) among which the competitor, Hillary Clinton, would win with a large margin, to do not vote[1].

This is just an example of how social networks are nowadays largely used for manipulating the outcome of an election. Similar examples can be found in literature with respect to more or less all the electoral events occurred in the last years [12,22,23]. Since the literature in AI and in social choice theory focuses on how elections can be bribed, and how much specific electoral rules are robust against these manipulations [8–10,18], it appears natural to analyse

---

*Supported by the Italian MIUR PRIN 2017 Project ALGADIMAR "Algorithms, Games, and Digital Markets" and by "GNCS-INdAM".

[1] E.g., a cartoon with a text "Hillary Thinks African Americans are Super Predators" was planned to be delivered to certain African American voters through Facebook "dark posts" – non-public posts whose viewership is controlled by the campaign [24].

V. Malvone and A. Murano (Eds.): EUMAS 2023, LNAI 14282, pp. 435–444, 2023.
https://doi.org/10.1007/978-3-031-43264-4_29

within this computational viewpoint how manipulation arising from the spread of (mis)information on social networks can impact on the election outcome.

This line of research has been started by Wilder and Vorobeychik [38] that consider that voters in a two-candidate election are arranged in a social network, and they will support the sponsored candidate as soon as they receive information spread by a subset of carefully chosen senders, a.k.a., *seeds*. They showed that, even if selecting the best set of seeds can be a computationally hard problem, however a set of seeds guaranteeing an efficient approximation of the optimal choice can be efficiently computed. These results have been extended to more complex settings, focusing, e.g., on different models of information diffusion, different voting rules, and more complex sets of messages to spread [1,13,14].

Unfortunately, none of these works is able to capture the specific manipulation tentative described above. Indeed, all these works assume that each voter has to express a vote and she cannot abstain, and they do not consider the advantage for the sponsored candidate that this choice could guarantee.

Our Contribution. One of the main reasons about this gap is due to the lack of a satisfying model about the reasons behind abstention. Indeed, voting appears to be irrational, since the cost of voting usually outweighs the chance of being influential in the electoral result, and thus the benefit that from one's own vote can arise [16]. While a large amount of literature (see Related Works) tried to provide some justification for this irrational behavior, most of these proposals fail to match aspects that are actually observed on real-world elections.

Our first contribution in this work is then to design a model for abstention that provides a closer fit to real-world scenarios. Specifically, our model improves over previous ones: it matches real-world observations whenever previous models do, but, our model predicts also an higher turnout of about 60% that essentially matches the one observed in most of the recent elections [15].

Next we considered the problem of election manipulation in a setting where agents may decide to abstain. Clearly, the hardness results proved for the simpler setting without abstention extend to our setting. However, we will run several simulations showing that, in practice, manipulating an election when abstention is allowed is easier than when agents are forced to vote.

Related Works. Several models have been proposed in order to justify why people votes despite of the large unbalance between the cost of voting and the benefit that our single vote can lead to. For example, Riker and Ordeshook [34] propose to include in the model a variable representing the sense of civic duty: this does not explain why electors' behaviour change from an election to another and from one type of election to another. Alternative approaches were proposed that model voters as regret minimizers [21], i.e., voters are assumed to choose a strategy that minimize the chance of having a large regret, or as players in an opportune game-theoretic framework [29,33]. Unfortunately, these approaches appear not to match with data coming from observations of real-world elections. Abstention has been moreover assumed to be related with asymmetric information available to voters [20,32]. However, no agreement has been found on how to model this aspect, and different proposed models lead to very different predictions. An orthogonal approach assume that the differences in turnout can be motivated by the disagreement within the electorate, and the partial knowledge about this disagreement available to voters [19]. However, these models turn out to be often unpractical, since they do not allow for easy predictions. Finally, other works focus on the evolutionary aspects related to vote participation [35]: these models still fail to explain the difference of behavior among elections.

Recently, Guage and Fu [25] proposed a model that merges most of the above ideas: they consider both information asymmetry and disagreement within the electorate, and they evaluate this model within an evolutionary framework. Moreover, they postulate the existence of an underdog effect, in which voters are happier when they are able to lead to the victory the less favourite candidate. This model has been observed to better match the behaviors of voters in real-world elections. Still, it fails to match the turnout size observed in real-world.

As discussed above, none of these models has been considered in the recent line of work about election manipulation in social networks via the choice of information seeds [1,13,14,38]. Note anyway that this is not the only election manipulation approach on social network that has been considered in literature. For instance, Sina et al. [36] consider a manipulator willing to modify the relationship among voters to make the desired candidate win an election. Auletta et al. [2–4] focus on a manipulator controlling the order in which information is disclosed to voters, and they prove that the manipulator can lead the minority to become a majority in different settings, and a bare majority to become a consensus [6] (the last result holds only when there are only two candidates [5,7]). Bredereck and Elkind [11] finally provide results for each of the above discussed manipulation approaches, seeding, changing network relationship, and controlling when information is disclosed.

2 Definitions

We consider an election scenario with n voters an m candidates. In this work we will follow [38] and [25], and we will consider only the case of $m = 2$ candidates, that we will denote as A and B. We assume that the n voters are arranged on the vertices of a *social graph* $G = (V, E)$, that models the social relationships among voters. To each edge $e = (u, v) \in E$ is associated a weight $p(e) \in [0, 1]$ measuring the strength of the relationship among u and v. Each voter u moreover has a *preferred candidate* $c_u \in \{A, B\}$.

A manipulator is provided with a budget b and she can choose a subset A_0 of at most b voters from which to spread information. As in [1,13,38], the information is assumed to spread according to the *Independent Cascade Model* [27]: at each time step $t \geq 0$, for each node $u \in A_t$ and each neighbour v of u not in $\bigcup_{i=0}^{t} A_i$, v is inserted in A_{t+1} with probability $p(u, v)$. Note that the procedure terminates after T steps where T is the first time step t such that A_{t+1} is empty. Nodes in $\bigcup_{i=0}^{t} A_i$ are called *active* nodes, and they represent the one that received the information spread by the manipulator.

For each voter $u \in V$, we let $a_u \in \{0, 1\}$ to denote the decision of u about whether to vote ($a_u = 1$) or to abstain ($a_u = 0$). In the former case, the voter is assumed to vote for the preferred candidate c_u. More details about how the decision is taken are given below. However, we stress that this also depends on the message received from the manipulator. To distinguish the decision taken by a voter u when she does not receive this message from the decision that she takes upon the reception of this message, we will denote the latter as $\bar{a}_u$.

For a candidate c, the votes that this candidate would achieve without manipulation is $V_c = \sum_{u:\, c_u = c} a_u$. Similarly, the votes that c would achieve when the manipulation is active is $\overline{V}_c = \sum_{u:\, c_u = c} \bar{a}_u$. The *margin of victory* of candidate c without manipulation is $M_c = V_c - V_{\bar{c}}$, where $\bar{c} = \{A, B\} \setminus \{c\}$. Similarly, the margin of victory of candidate c due to the manipulation is $\overline{M}_c = \overline{V}_c - \overline{V}_{\bar{c}}$. The increment in the margin of victory of c due to the manipulation is then $\Delta_c = \overline{M}_c - M_c$. The goal of the manipulator is then to select the set A_0^* of seeds of size at most b that maximizes the expected increment in the margin of victory Δ_c for the desired candidate c, where expectation is taken over the random coin tosses of the diffusion model. Roughly speaking, the manipulator would like to decrease the distance with the winner or increase the distance with the competitor as much as possible.

3   Modeling Abstention

Our model is inspired by the model proposed by Guage and Fu [25]. It describes the behavior of a voter as a trade-off between benefits and costs. If the preferred candidate loses, it would be better not to vote, since there are no benefits. However, if the preferred candidate wins, one feels like as her own vote was helpful to the cause, and she enjoys the benefits associated with winning. A peculiar feature of the model moreover is that the benefits deriving from voting for a candidate who wins are influenced by how much one expects the candidate to actually win the election. Specifically, the feeling of being useful to the victory is larger, and thus the happiness of the voter, when her preferred candidate was not the favourite one, but it happens to win. This *underdog effect* leads the model to assume that the benefit arising from the victory of the preferred candidate decreases with the size of the majority if this candidate is favourite and increases otherwise. Note also that the payoff for voting when the election ends in a tie is always positive and it may even exceed the payoff for voting when the preferred candidate wins: indeed, when candidates are tied, it is appropriate to think that one's vote prevented the candidate from losing and each single vote was crucial.

Specifically, the model of Guage and Fu [25] assumes that a voter u whose preferred candidate is c receives the following payoff from voting: -1 if c loses; $\frac{1}{2}$ if c ties; $1 - w(P_u - 0.5)$ if c wins, where P_u is the likelihood that u assigns to the victory of her preferred candidate and w is a scaling factor weighting the strength of the underdog effect. The benefit from non-voting is instead assumed to be simply 0. Hence, the expected benefit received on voting will be $U_u = (1 - w(P_u - 0.5))P(V_c > V_{\bar{c}}) + \frac{1}{2}P(V_c = V_{\bar{c}})(1 - w(P_u - 0.5)) - P(V_c < V_{\bar{c}})$, where all the probabilities depend on the voter u's information. Hence, u will vote when U_u is at least 0, and she will abstain otherwise.

The authors analyse this model in a very simple setting: they indeed assume that the information is symmetric among supporters of the same candidate and asymmetric among supporters of different candidates, and they look for the perception that these voters should take. According to an evolutionary viewpoint, this choice should be one of the *self-fulfilling* perceptions, namely those perceptions that happens to become true. By analysing the model according to these intuitions, the authors are able to prove several properties that turn out to match the ones observed in real-world elections (see [25] for details): e.g., since the probability of a tie decreases as the number of agents increases, this leads to a decrease in the turnout for large elections; the turnout decreases when there is one candidate that is supposed to have a very large margin of victory.

Our Model. The main difference between our model and [25], consists in adding a cost whenever we abstain, motivated by the *happiness* in having the preferred candidate to win (without any effort from the voter) or the *regret* that one voter may develop on discovering that her own vote may have been useful to make her preferred candidate to win. Specifically, we assume that the benefit that the voter achieves from voting are exactly the same as in [25]. However, when the voter i abstains, she receives a benefit of U/N if the desired candidate wins, and a benefit of $-1 + D/N$ otherwise, where D is the difference between the number of votes for the preferred candidate c and the ones for $\bar{c}$, and N is the number of voters. Roughly speaking, if the desired candidate c will win, the voter is happy, and her happiness increases with the margin of victory; if c will lose, she regrets for not voting, and the regret increases as candidates are closer to each other.

We can define the expected benefit U_u achieved from voting exactly as above. Similarly, we can define the expected benefit from abstention as $\overline{U}_u = \frac{D}{N}P(V_c > V_{\bar{x}}) - \left(1 - \frac{D}{N}\right)P(V_c \leq V_{\bar{x}})$. People will vote only if $U_u \geq \overline{U}_u$. In order to analyse our model we adopt the same simplifying assumption of [25] and we consider asymmetry among supporters of different candidates, but symmetry within the set of supporters of the same candidate: we suppose that each voter believes that q_c is the probability that a supporter of c will submit a vote, and $q_{\bar{c}}$ to be the same quantity with respect to $\bar{c}$. With this belief one can evaluate whether to vote or not by simply computing the probability that one candidate defeats the other: e.g., $P(V_c > V_{\bar{x}}) = \sum_{k=0}^{N_{\bar{c}}} \binom{N_{\bar{c}}}{k} q_{\bar{c}}^k (1 - q_{\bar{c}})^{N_{\bar{c}}-k} \sum_{j=k+1}^{N_c} \binom{N_c}{j} q_c^j (1 - q_c)^{N_c-j}$, where N_c is the total number of supporters of candidate c, i.e. $N_c = |\{u : x_u = c\}|$.

In order to validate our model we follow the same approach as in [25]. Specifically, for fixed values of N (we next show only the case for $N = 1000$) and w (next we follow [25] and focus on the case $w = 0$), we plot for every choice of q_A and q_B the threshold that separates abstention from voting for the supporters of each of the two candidates. In those regions where the expected payoff for voting is positive, groups would like to increase the frequency with which they vote, while in the negative regions, they would like to increase the frequency with which they abstain. Hence, self-fulfilling equilibria must be searched exactly in the region in which both groups have positive utility. Figure 1 then shows that this predicts a turnout of about 65%, that matches the one observed in most of the real-world elections. Interestingly, while our model is the first to correctly

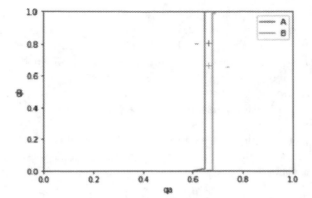

Fig. 1. The figure depicts for each voter the threshold among the case in which voting is beneficial or not. Note that for supporters of A is convenient to vote when q_A is on the right of the threshold, while for supporters of B is convenient to vote when q_B is on the left of the threshold. The figure refers to the case $p_A = 0.6$.

predicts this turnout, it maintains all the other properties as in [25]. For example, by redrawing Fig. 1 for different values of $p_A \in [0.5, 1]$, or for different values of N, one may observe that turnout decreases with the increase of the population size or of the perceived distance among the two candidates.

The role played by the voter perception p_c turns out to be relevant for the voting decision, and consequently for the outcome of the election. For example, a candidate supported by a large majority may want to hide or weaken this information, otherwise many of their own supporters may be induced to abstain (since their vote appears to be useless), by decreasing in this way her margin of victory. On the other side, revealing this information would have a beneficial effect on supporters of the competitors since it may discourage them to vote. In this work we focus on this kind of manipulation. Namely, we assume that the manipulator will spread a message $\tilde{p}_c$ advertising a false poll describing a margin of victory of one candidate towards the other one that is different from the real one. Each voter u receiving the message will then takes her voting decision (i.e., it will set a_u) based on the model above with respect to the voter perception $\tilde{p}_c$, instead that according to the publicly known poll p_c. All voters that do not receive the fake poll, still take their decision according to p_c.

4   Election Manipulation

Wilder and Vorobeychik [38] showed that a simple hill-climbing greedy algorithm is able to return a set of seeds that guarantees a margin of victory for the desired candidate that is at least $\frac{1}{2}\left(1 - \frac{1}{e}\right)(1 - \varepsilon)$. Essentially, the algorithm works by iteratively selecting the seed that produces the largest increment in the expected number of influenced nodes, until b seeds have been chosen. Note that this increment can be approximated up to a $1 - \varepsilon$ multiplicative factor in polynomial-time through a Monte-Carlo algorithm. Moreover, this greedy approach is known to provide the desired approximation guarantee whenever the objective function, in this case the margin of victory, is a monotone and submodular function in the number of seeds. Unfortunately, this approach cannot give the same approximation guarantee when applied to the case with abstention. Indeed, the margin of victory can fail to be monotone: if our message turns out to advertise a smaller gap among candidates than the actual one, and with a newly added seed this message happens to be sent mostly to supporters of the competitor, this will reduce the margin of victory of the desired candidate.

This greedy approach is also quite unpractical since the amount of Monte-Carlo simulations necessary to guarantee a good approximation is usually very large. For this reason, many heuristics have been proposed to reduce the computational cost of the seed selection algorithm. Many of them are simply based on choosing as seeds the most central nodes in the networks. Several centrality measures have been proposed to this aim, such as *degree, betweenness*, or *PageRank* centrality. We next focus mostly on the simplest of these measure, i.e., degree centrality, that assigns to each node a measure that is proportional to the number of neighbors of that node.

We tested the performances of the above algorithms on a bunch of different networks, both synthetic and real. First of all we considered Preferential Attachment networks over 1000 nodes. In these networks nodes are assumed to join the network sequentially, and each node will chose a neighbor among the nodes already in the network. In particular, with probability p this node is chosen with a probability that is proportional to the degree of these nodes, so that a rich-get-richer effect occurs, and with probability $1 - p$ this node is chosen uniformly at random. It is known that networks generated in this way have a power law degree distribution, that is known to be a typical feature of real social networks [17]. Here we set the value of the parameter p equal to 0.75.

We also consider in our tests some networks that are publicly available on KONECT [28] and SNAP [31]. Specifically we will consider: `Eurorads` [37]: a sparse undirected network with 1174 nodes and 1417 edges; `Arenas-Email` [26]: a slightly denser undirected network with 1133 nodes and 5451 edges; `Email-EU-Core` [30,39]: a much denser and directed network consisting of 1005 nodes and 25571 edges. For each of these four networks, each node has been randomly assigned to be a supporter of one of the two candidates and edge probabilities have been randomly drawn from [0, 1]. W.l.o.g. we assume that the candidate supported by the manipulator is A and the seed set has been selected as the set of 10 nodes with the highest degree. From each of these seeds, the manipulator has been supposed to advertise a fake poll stating $\tilde{p}_A \in \{0.6, 0.7, 0.8\}$. We assume that each node that does not receive this message has a perception that is equivalent to the fraction of voters supporting A. For each of this settings we repeated our simulation 50 times. Over these simulations, we will collect the number of times in which candidate A actually wins and the average margin of victory. We compared the outcome of our manipulation, with the one in which the manipulator cannot lead the voters to abstain, but only to change their preferred candidate: essentially each node that receives the message, and that in our model would decide to do not vote, is supposed instead to vote for the less preferred candidate. As for the remaining voters (that would abstain even without the reception of the fake news), we assume that they will still abstain.

The number of times that candidate A wins and the average margin of victory increase, e.g. in Eurorads the first goes from 0 to 12 over 50 simulations, and the second goes from -7 to -4 when $\tilde{p}_A = 0.6$. Similar results for $\tilde{p}_A = 0.7$: e.g. in Eurorads we have an increase from 38 to 47 in the number of victories, and from 3 to 4 in the average margin of victory. It is interesting to note that when $\tilde{p}_A = 0.8$, we instead can have that the effect of abstention can be negative: e.g., in Eurorads the number of victories decreases from 50 to 48 and the margin of victory decreases from 12 to 9: these bad performances are easily explained with the fact that with such a large value of the advertised poll almost all nodes receiving it are induced to abstain. Hence, in the setting in which this abstention is allowed, the election is run over the few remaining candidates only. In this way the margin of victory cannot be large, or at least it cannot be as large as when the election is run among all candidates. Moreover, in some cases this margin of victory can be smaller than 0 when evaluated on the few voters that are not influenced by the message, but this is not the case when all the people deciding to do not vote are instead force to vote for their less preferred candidate. These improvement of the manipulation power when abstention is allowed occurs even if the seeds are simply selected according to their degree. Better performances are achieved with smarter algorithms. E.g. when $\overline{p}_A = 0.7$ on Eurorads, we achieve an higher percentage of victories with the greedy namely 49 over 50 simulations, and the expected margin of victory improves from 4 to 6.

5   Conclusion

In this work we took a preliminary analysis of the problem of election manipulation in social networks when the goal of the manipulator is instead to convince the supporters of the competitor to do not vote. To this aim, we first provided a formal model of how voters decide to abstain that extends and improves the model in [25]. The model is defined for elections with only two candidates and assume that all the supporters of a candidate have the same belief with respect to the outcome of the election. It would be interesting to extend the model to elections with more than two candidates or with a larger asymmetry among different social groups even if they support the same candidate.

Next, we started the analysis of the manipulation problem in our model. Our goal here has been to show that abstention can help the manipulator to achieve better results. We had some preliminary hints in this directions, through our simulations run on several networks and different settings. Clearly, more experiments would be necessary to verify the extent at which this claim holds. Moreover, it would also be interesting to analyse more in details the theoretical aspects of the problem: e.g., to design efficient approximation algorithms or to formally prove inapproximability results.

References

1. Abouei Mehrizi, M., Corò, F., Cruciani, E., D'Angelo, G.: Election control through social influence with voters' uncertainty. J. Comb. Optim. **44**(1), 635–669 (2022)
2. Auletta, V., Caragiannis, I., Ferraioli, D., Galdi, C., Persiano, G.: Minority becomes majority in social networks. In: Markakis, E., Schäfer, G. (eds.) WINE 2015. LNCS, vol. 9470, pp. 74–88. Springer, Heidelberg (2015). https://doi.org/10.1007/978-3-662-48995-6_6
3. Auletta, V., Caragiannis, I., Ferraioli, D., Galdi, C., Persiano, G.: Information retention in heterogeneous majority dynamics. In: Devanur, N.R., Lu, P. (eds.) WINE 2017. LNCS, vol. 10660, pp. 30–43. Springer, Cham (2017). https://doi.org/10.1007/978-3-319-71924-5_3
4. Auletta, V., Caragiannis, I., Ferraioli, D., Galdi, C., Persiano, G.: Robustness in discrete preference games. In: AAMAS, pp. 1314–1322 (2017)
5. Auletta, V., Ferraioli, D., Fionda, V., Greco, G.: Maximizing the spread of an opinion when Tertium Datur Est. In: AAMAS, pp. 1207–1215 (2019)
6. Auletta, V., Ferraioli, D., Greco, G.: Reasoning about consensus when opinions diffuse through majority dynamics. In: IJCAI, pp. 49–55 (2018)
7. Auletta, V., Ferraioli, D., Greco, G.: On the effectiveness of social proof recommendations in markets with multiple products. In: ECAI, pp. 19–26 (2020)
8. Bartholdi, J.J., Tovey, C.A., Trick, M.A.: The computational difficulty of manipulating an election. Soc. Choice Welfare **6**, 227–241 (1989)
9. Bartholdi III, J.J., Orlin, J.B.: Single transferable vote resists strategic voting. Soc. Choice Welfare **8**(4), 341–354 (1991)
10. Bartholdi III, J.J., Tovey, C.A., Trick, M.A.: How hard is it to control an election? Math. Comput. Model. **16**(8–9), 27–40 (1992)
11. Bredereck, R., Elkind, E.: Manipulating opinion diffusion in social networks. In: Proceedings of the International Joint Conference on Artificial Intelligence (IJCAI), pp. 894–900 (2017)
12. Bruno, M., Lambiotte, R., Saracco, F.: Brexit and bots: characterizing the behaviour of automated accounts on twitter during the UK election. EPJ Data Sci. **11**(1), 17 (2022)
13. Castiglioni, M., Ferraioli, D., Gatti, N., Landriani, G.: Election manipulation on social networks: seeding, edge removal, edge addition. J. Artif. Intell. Res. **71**, 1049–1090 (2021)
14. Corò, F., Cruciani, E., D'Angelo, G., Ponziani, S.: Exploiting social influence to control elections based on positional scoring rules. Inf. Comput. **289**, 104940 (2022)
15. Desilver, D.: US trails most developed countries in voter turnout. Pew Res. Cent. **21** (2018)
16. Downs, A.: An economic theory of political action in a democracy. J. Polit. Econ. **65**(2), 135–150 (1957)
17. Easley, D., Kleinberg, J.: Networks, Crowds, and Markets: Reasoning About a Highly Connected World. Cambridge University Press, Cambridge (2010)
18. Faliszewski, P., Hemaspaandra, E., Hemaspaandra, L.A.: How hard is bribery in elections? J. Artif. Intell. Res. **35**, 485–532 (2009)
19. Feddersen, T., Sandroni, A.: A theory of participation in elections. Am. Econ. Rev. **96**(4), 1271–1282 (2006)
20. Feddersen, T.J., Pesendorfer, W.: Abstention in elections with asymmetric information and diverse preferences. Am. Polit. Sci. Rev. **93**(2), 381–398 (1999)

21. Ferejohn, J.A., Fiorina, M.P.: The paradox of not voting: a decision theoretic analysis. Am. Polit. Sci. Rev. **68**(2), 525–536 (1974)
22. Ferrara, E.: Disinformation and social bot operations in the run up to the 2017 French presidential election. First Monday **22**(8) (2017)
23. Giglietto, F., et al.: Mapping Italian news media political coverage in the lead-up to 2018 general election. Available at SSRN 31799300 (2018)
24. Green, J., Issenberg, S.: Inside the trump bunker, with days to go. BusinessWeek (2016)
25. Guage, C., Fu, F.: Asymmetric partisan voter turnout games. Dyn. Games Appl. **11**(4), 738–758 (2021)
26. Guimera, R., Danon, L., Diaz-Guilera, A., Giralt, F., Arenas, A.: Self-similar community structure in a network of human interactions. Phys. Rev. E **68**(6), 065103 (2003)
27. Kempe, D., Kleinberg, J., Tardos, É.: Maximizing the spread of influence through a social network. In: KDD, pp. 137–146 (2003)
28. Kunegis, J.: KONECT: the Koblenz network collection. In: Proceedings of the 22nd International Conference on World Wide Web, pp. 1343–1350 (2013)
29. Ledyard, J.O.: The pure theory of large two-candidate elections. Public Choice **44**(1), 7–41 (1984)
30. Leskovec, J., Kleinberg, J., Faloutsos, C.: Graph evolution: densification and shrinking diameters. ACM Trans. Knowl. Discov. Data (TKDD) **1**(1), 2-es (2007)
31. Leskovec, J., Krevl, A.: SNAP datasets: Stanford large network dataset collection (2014). www.snap.stanford.edu/data
32. Matsusaka, J.G.: Explaining voter turnout patterns: an information theory. Public Choice **84**(1–2), 91–117 (1995)
33. Palfrey, T.R., Rosenthal, H.: A strategic calculus of voting. Public Choice **41**(1), 7–53 (1983)
34. Riker, W.H., Ordeshook, P.C.: A theory of the calculus of voting. Am. Polit. Sci. Rev. **62**(1), 25–42 (1968)
35. Sieg, G., Schulz, C.: Evolutionary dynamics in the voting game. Public Choice **85**(1–2), 157–172 (1995)
36. Sina, S., Hazon, N., Hassidim, A., Kraus, S.: Adapting the social network to affect elections. In: AAMAS, pp. 705–713 (2015)
37. Šubelj, L., Bajec, M.: Robust network community detection using balanced propagation. Eur. Phys. J. B **81**, 353–362 (2011)
38. Wilder, B., Vorobeychik, Y.: Controlling elections through social influence. In: AAMAS, pp. 265–273 (2018)
39. Yin, H., Benson, A.R., Leskovec, J., Gleich, D.F.: Local higher-order graph clustering. In: Proceedings of the 23rd ACM SIGKDD International Conference on Knowledge Discovery and Data Mining, pp. 555–564 (2017)

Supporting Adaptive Multi-Agent Systems with Digital Twins Environments

Samuele Burattini[(✉)] [ID]

Alma Mater Studiorum - University of Bologna, Via dell'Università 50,
47522 Cesena, FC, Italy
samuele.burattini@unibo.it

Abstract. Adaptability is an essential feature of autonomous agents, especially when considering the interaction with the real world which is, by definition, dynamic and unpredictable. To support adaptation in real-world scenarios self-describing Digital Twins with simulation and prediction abilities could be exploited to build the environment of a multi-agent system. A roadmap is presented, reflecting on the role of the environment in the development of multi-agent systems, its potential integration with Digital Twins and suggesting the need for a generalised model for adaptive agents that could leverage the features offered by such Digital Twins environment.

Keywords: Adaptability · Digital Twins · Multi-Agent Systems

1 Introduction

Agents are defined as software entities situated in an environment that they can perceive and autonomously act upon to achieve their design objectives [26]. Autonomy is often further linked to the ability of an agent to *adapt* either to changes in the environment or to improve its behaviour over time [13].

Adaptability is then a fundamental and defining feature of agents although often hard to obtain (and measure) practically. Fully adaptable agents may even end up displaying undesired behaviour, especially when considering the emergent behaviour of a Multi-Agent System (MAS) [7] and the combination of adapting and predefined constrained behaviour is still an open issue.

Adaptive agents are especially relevant when employed in scenarios where the dynamics of the environments are not stable. This is the case of cyber-physical systems, where software agents need to interact with the real world which intrinsically exhibits a high degree of unpredictability. The use of agents in industry has always been of interest to support automation scenarios [11] but is yet to deliver the full potential due to the strict requirements of such settings [3,12] and the complexity of the interaction of agents and the real world.

In the past few years, Digital Twins (DTs) emerged from the manufacturing domain as modelling tools to represent physical assets with the highest possible

V. Malvone and A. Murano (Eds.): EUMAS 2023, LNAI 14282, pp. 445–451, 2023.
https://doi.org/10.1007/978-3-031-43264-4_30

fidelity [6], enabling bidirectional communication between the real and digital worlds. The concept is rapidly spreading over different domains and applications and has been further extended to give the DT the ability to augment the capabilities of an asset for example by making predictions about its behaviour.

In this context, following the principle that the environment can be used as a first-class abstraction to program Multi-Agent Systems (MAS) [25], Digital Twins could be used to model such environment, providing a bridge for MAS to operate in the real world. From a MAS perspective, DTs could encapsulate the technical details that concern communication with sensors and actuators, provide a detailed and up-to-date description of the state and capabilities of an asset, and explicitly support exploration and reasoning through simulated or predictive outcomes of agent-twin interactions. The development of DTs environments for multi-agent systems calls for conceptual and technological integration but also for a new way to intend adaptability not only as an internal ability of the agents but as driven by the features offered by the environment.

This contribution aims to provide an overview of the background this research is based on, highlight the first steps that are being developed towards the integration of MAS and DTs and lay out the open research issues that will be explored in future works.

2   Background

This work has its roots in the literature about the role of the environment in MAS and the development of Digital Twins as a modelling tool for physical assets that enable bidirectional communication between software applications and the real world.

2.1   The Role of the Environment in Multi-Agent Systems

Every agent definition mentions an *environment* in which the agent is placed. The role of such an environment is then of fundamental interest in MAS research. Specifically, the environment can offer three different levels of support to the development of multi-agent systems: (i) at a basic level it can be seen as the deployment context, (ii) at an abstraction level it can be used to shield agents from technical details, (iii) at an interaction-mediation level it can be used to regulate access to shared resources and mediate interaction among agents [25].

The Agents & Artifacts (A&A) meta-model [22] introduces the notion of software artifact as the basic building block to shape the environment and represent resources and tools that agent can modify, share and interact with.

Artifacts have a unique identity, a type, and are described by a set of *observable properties* that agents can perceive, *operations* that agents can exploit to perform actions and *events* that can signal changes. Artifacts are also logically grouped in *workspaces* that define the topology of the environment.

From an engineering point of view artifacts model function-oriented components that can be exploited by goal-oriented ones. From a designing point of view, being inspired by theories of human behaviour (such as Activity Theory [21,24] and Distributed Cognition [9]) artifacts have the additional role of supporting information discovery and exchange to support agent activities [18]. The environment design is then crucial to allow agents to effectively explore it, adapt to its current state and find means to reach their goals and is now considered a cardinal dimension of Multi-Agent Oriented Programming [1].

2.2 Digital Twins

The idea of Digital Twins has been introduced around twenty years ago in the field of manufacturing [6] and expanded to several domains with the introduction of Internet of Things (IoT) technologies, and the movement of Industry 4.0 [16]. In its more recent interpretation, the valuable abstraction of a DT can be applied to several assets, not only machines or products monitored by sensors, but also people or processes that are relevant to a specific domain [10].

At its core, the idea is to create a virtual representation of any physical asset and keep it synchronised with its real counterpart. The Digital Twin should allow to interact with the physical asset as if it was the asset itself as well as augment it with additional features and functionalities. Although there is not a unified architecture for Digital Twins, a generally accepted view is a five-dimensional model [23] that includes:

1. a *physical layer* that is related to a unique asset in the real world possibly observed by sensors and equipped with actuators,
2. a *connection layer* supporting the data exchange through networking,
3. a *data layer* for processing and storage of the DT data,
4. a *model layer* that represents the behaviour of the asset,
5. a *service layer* that exposes the information collected from the DT to external applications as well offering additional services such as prediction and simulation services.

Implementing this layered architecture requires deep knowledge of several supporting technologies, from the IoT and network stack related to the physical side of the twin to the machine learning or modelling techniques required to create the model layer of the DT and the data processing techniques that make it possible to keep it up to date and store historical information.

From an agent perspective, the *service layer* though is the most interesting because it shields the agent from the technical details and allows it to interact with the DT, discover its current state as its potential future ones.

3   Building Digital Twins Environments

Several works analyse the relationship between Multi-Agent Systems and Digital Twins [14,16,20]. Different approaches view agents either as part of the Digital Twin itself, to model its behaviour, or as an external application layer.

This work follows the latter perspective, to isolate responsibilities between MAS and the DTs. Specifically, the DTs can be considered general-purpose representations of physical entities that can be used in several applications. The

MAS will implement instead the business logic to manage the DTs and achieve application goals in the considered domain.

This separation of concerns is especially relevant when considering modelling a complex application domain using several Digital Twins as suggested by the idea of a *Web of Digital Twins* (WoDT) [20]. The proposal is to build an ecosystem of Digital Twins capable of describing themselves in terms of their current properties, available actions and events as well as relationships with other DTs. These linked self-describing DTs can populate a (distributed) Knowledge Graph [8] with near-real-time data about the corresponding physical assets.

From an agent perspective, the Knowledge Graph that is generated by the WoDT can be seen as a hypermedia environment [4] where agents can interact using standard Web technologies, furthermore, exploiting a semantic representation of the environment could also benefit the level of abstraction used when programming the MAS behaviour [2].

Building Digital Twins environments for MAS along this vision requires effort in three parallel directions

- *WoDT Infrastructure Support*: an infrastructure is required to actively start developing networks of linked Digital Twins capable of providing a semantic description of their features. This is being worked on in the form of a software library to create Digital Twins that follow the five dimensional model and expose a semantic description of their features [19] as well as a platform to deploy them and enable discovery from external applications.
- *DTs in MAS environment*: investigating bridges between MAS and DTs through the environment dimension is necessary both on a conceptual and technical level. There are different possibilities to achieve this [14] and some are starting to be developed in the MAS community [15] although this still needs to sediment towards a universally accepted approach.
- *MAS and the Web*: when considering the complexity of the Web of Digital Twins, the integration of DTs in MAS environments needs to take in account the distributed nature of the environment and the use of standard web technologies. Studying how agents interact with the Web is an active development line [5] that can yield interesting results for the research on DTs as well.

4   Future Works

Once the conceptual and technical integration between MAS and the Web of Digital Twins has been achieved, many open challenges still remain to effectively leverage DTs environments. Given the context of cyber-physical systems where both DTs and MAS can be applied, adaptability to changes in the environment is a key feature to be investigated and build more robust industrial MAS. To understand how DTs environments could support this process in this section the two challenges that are more relevant to develop adaptive multi-agent systems in DTs environment are highlighted: the first one, more on the agent side, is to understand what does it mean to build an adaptive MAS and what are the requirements to support adaptability in general, the second one, on the DTs side, is to understand how to offer support for those requirements.

4.1   Towards a Generalised Model for Adaptive MAS

Although adaptability is considered amongst the defining features of a software agent, there are several different models of agents and several techniques have been applied to solve the problem of adapting agent behaviour to either unpredictable changes or to learn entirely new behaviours.

To investigate how the environment design can play a role in supporting adaptation, a generalised model of adaptive MAS could be defined. This can be crucial in understanding what are the key elements that needs to be available for the agent to be more robust to changes and identify requirements for the design of the environment in order to support adaptation.

In particular, the focus will be on generalising those kinds of MAS where the behaviour is (at least partially) defined, but requires to either cope with changes or discover *better* means to achieve goals. This effectively excludes agent systems that are only based on learning that tackle the problem of adaptation with a very different perspective and do not include the design of the environment as first-class abstraction. Such systems are indeed useful for several domains where it's infeasible to define a policy beforehand. Instead, in the context of Multi-Agent Oriented Programming it is more often the case in which a predefined policy is imposed by the business logic of the application but the system is still desired to be robust and resilient towards changes over time.

4.2   Exploiting Digital Twins Capabilities for Adaptation

While exploring the general relationship between adaptation and the environment, Digital Twins models and technologies can be refined in order to exhibit those capabilities that are considered essential to support adaptation.

Among the ones that are already part of the original concept of a Digital Twin, it will be relevant to understand how to create self-describing DTs that expose a *knowledge-level* [17] representation of their state and capabilities so that agents can reason upon them. This DT description may need to be aligned with semantic vocabularies that the agents can understand as well as possibly be delivered to different agents with different capabilities or goals using different representation formats. Furthermore, the data required by agents to perform their reasoning may include features of the Digital Twin itself, such as the *fidelity* of an information that is reported from the physical asset.

Finally modelling the simulation and prediction capabilities of a DT to expose them as a service for agents to safely explore the environment and its dynamics is an interesting challenge, especially when involving multiple DTs connected in a complex and open ecosystem such as the Web of Digital Twins. For example an agents may need to understand whether acting on a DT will result in its goal achievement without having undesired side effects on other linked DTs. This would require to assemble some form of simulation scenario or virtual environment the agent could safely explore before acting on the "real" DTs.

References

1. Boissier, O., Bordini, R., Hubner, J., Ricci, A.: Multi-Agent Oriented Programming: Programming Multi-Agent Systems Using JaCaMo. Intelligent Robotics and Autonomous Agents series, MIT Press (2020). www.books.google.it/books?id=GM_tDwAAQBAJ
2. Burattini, S., Ciortea, A., Meshua, G., Ricci, A.: Agents & artifacts at the knowledge level. In: Engineering Multi-Agent Systems, 11th International Workshop (2023). www.emas.in.tu-clausthal.de/2023/papers/EMAS_2023_paper_3263.pdf
3. Calvaresi, D., Marinoni, M., Sturm, A., Schumacher, M., Buttazzo, G.: The challenge of real-time multi-agent systems for enabling IoT and CPS. In: Proceedings of the International Conference on Web Intelligence, pp. 356–364 (2017)
4. Ciortea, A., Boissier, O., Ricci, A.: Engineering world-wide multi-agent systems with hypermedia. In: Weyns, D., Mascardi, V., Ricci, A. (eds.) EMAS 2018. LNCS (LNAI), vol. 11375, pp. 285–301. Springer, Cham (2019). https://doi.org/10.1007/978-3-030-25693-7_15
5. Ciortea, A., Mayer, S., Gandon, F., Boissier, O., Ricci, A., Zimmermann, A.: A decade in hindsight: the missing bridge between multi-agent systems and the world wide web. In: Proceedings of the International Conference on Autonomous Agents and Multiagent Systems (2019)
6. Grieves, M., Vickers, J.: Digital twin: mitigating unpredictable, undesirable emergent behavior in complex systems. In: Kahlen, F.-J., Flumerfelt, S., Alves, A. (eds.) Transdisciplinary Perspectives on Complex Systems, pp. 85–113. Springer, Cham (2017). https://doi.org/10.1007/978-3-319-38756-7_4
7. Guessoum, Z.: Adaptive agents and multiagent systems. IEEE Distrib. Syst. Online 5(7) (2004). https://doi.org/10.1109/MDSO.2004.10
8. Hogan, A., et al.: Knowledge graphs. ACM Comput. Surv. (CSUR) 54(4), 1–37 (2021)
9. Hutchins, E.: Distributed cognition. Int. Encycl. Soc. Behav. Sci. Elsevier Sci. 138, 1–10 (2000)
10. Jones, D., Snider, C., Nassehi, A., Yon, J., Hicks, B.: Characterising the digital twin: a systematic literature review. CIRP J. Manuf. Sci. Technol. 29, 36–52 (2020)
11. Karnouskos, S., Leitao, P.: Key contributing factors to the acceptance of agents in industrial environments. IEEE Trans. Ind. Inf. 13(2), 696–703 (2016)
12. Leitão, P., Mařík, V., Vrba, P.: Past, present, and future of industrial agent applications. IEEE Trans. Ind. Inf. 9(4), 2360–2372 (2012)
13. Maes, P.: Modeling adaptive autonomous agents. Artif. Life 1(1_2), 135–162 (1993)
14. Mariani, S., Picone, M., Ricci, A.: Agents and digital twins for the engineering of cyber-physical systems: opportunities, and challenges. In: Engineering Multi-Agent Systems, 10th International Workshop (2022). www.emas.in.tu-clausthal.de/2022/papers/paper7.pdf
15. Mariani, S., Picone, M., Ricci, A.: Towards developing digital twin enabled multi-agent systems. In: Engineering Multi-Agent Systems, 11th International Workshop (2023). www.emas.in.tu-clausthal.de/2023/papers/EMAS_2023_paper_9236.pdf
16. Minerva, R., Lee, G.M., Crespi, N.: Digital twin in the IoT context: a survey on technical features, scenarios, and architectural models. Proc. IEEE 108(10), 1785–1824 (2020)
17. Newell, A.: The knowledge level. Artif. Intell. 18(1), 87–127 (1982)
18. Omicini, A., Ricci, A., Viroli, M.: Artifacts in the A&A meta-model for multi-agent systems. Auton. Agents Multi-Agent Syst. 17(3), 432–456 (2008). https://doi.org/10.1007/s10458-008-9053-x

19. Picone, M., Mamei, M., Zambonelli, F.: Wldt: a general purpose library to build IoT digital twins. SoftwareX **13**, 100661 (2021)
20. Ricci, A., Croatti, A., Mariani, S., Montagna, S., Picone, M.: Web of digital twins. ACM Trans. Internet Technol. **22**(4) (2022). https://doi.org/10.1145/3507909
21. Ricci, A., Omicini, A., Denti, E.: Activity theory as a framework for MAS coordination. In: Petta, P., Tolksdorf, R., Zambonelli, F. (eds.) ESAW 2002. LNCS (LNAI), vol. 2577, pp. 96–110. Springer, Heidelberg (2003). https://doi.org/10.1007/3-540-39173-8_8
22. Ricci, A., Piunti, M., Viroli, M.: Environment programming in multi-agent systems: an artifact-based perspective. Auton. Agents Multi-Agent Syst. **23**(2), 158–192 (2011). https://doi.org/10.1007/s10458-010-9140-7
23. Tao, F., et al.: Five-dimension digital twin model and its ten applications. Comput. Integr. Manuf. Syst. **25**(1), 1–18 (2019)
24. Vygotsky, L.S., Cole, M.: Mind in society: Development of higher psychological processes. Harvard University Press (1978)
25. Weyns, D., Omicini, A., Odell, J.: Environment as a first class abstraction in multiagent systems. Auton. Agents Multi-Agent Syst. **14**(1), 5–30 (2007). https://doi.org/10.1007/s10458-006-0012-0
26. Wooldridge, M., Jennings, N.R.: Intelligent agents: theory and practice. knowl. Eng. Rev. **10**(2), 115–152 (1995)

A Step Forward to Widespread BDI AOP: JaKtA

Martina Baiardi[(✉)] [ORCID]

Department of Computer Science and Engineering (DISI), Alma Mater
Studiorum—Univerisità di Bologna, Via dell'Università 50, 47522 Cesena, FC, Italy
m.baiardi@unibo.it
https://www.unibo.it/sitoweb/m.baiardi/en

Keywords: BDI · AgentSpeak(L) · DSL · Kotlin · JaKtA

1 AOP and the Mainstream

The Agent-Oriented Programming (AOP) is a paradigm introduced thirty years
ago [6] to model autonomous entities with a *mental state*: agents. Agents are a
form of abstraction used to model complex systems: they are designed to perform
tasks and interact with each other. Each agent has an explicit representation of
the world that depends on the environment in which are situated and they delib-
erate about the best course of action to take to achieve their goals. The typical
approach to model the agents' mental state, and consequently their behaviour,
is through symbolic techniques; one notable example is the BDI model [5], which
exploits logics to describe agents with three elements: *Beliefs*, *Desires*, and *Intentions*. Beliefs describe the agent's internal state and keep track of changes that
occur in the environment in which they act. Desires represent the motivational
state of the system, in other words, they are the primary goal that the system
wants to achieve. Each agent is designed with a set of plans, each one composed
of a set of actions, chosen to concur to the achievement of their goals. An agent
chooses a plan depending on the belief set they hold on their mental state. Agents
can execute more than one plan at a time: Intentions represent the plans chosen
by an agent, and they also keep track of their progress.

Today, several languages that support AOP can be found [2] and, specifically
for BDI, common choices are Jason [1], Jadex [4] and GOAL [3]. However, despite
having been available for several years, no BDI/AOP programming language
shows up in commonly used programming languages' popularity indexes such
TIOBE[1], PYPL[2] (PopularitY of Programming Language) and Stackoverflow
Developer Survey[3].

In this short paper, we try to identify some potential factors hindering the
diffusion of the BDI/AOP paradigm and propose a potential improvement path.

---

[1] https://archive.is/C316B.
[2] https://archive.ph/4VakY.
[3] https://archive.is/LTfhl.

© The Author(s), under exclusive license to Springer Nature Switzerland AG 2023
V. Malvone and A. Murano (Eds.): EUMAS 2023, LNAI 14282, pp. 452–457, 2023.
https://doi.org/10.1007/978-3-031-43264-4_31

2   The Missing Pieces

In this section, We highlight some of the reasons that we believe are preventing the spreading of the BDI/AOP paradigm.

2.1   Learning Curve vs. Ergonomics

Currently, there are many AOP technologies, typically found in the form of stand-alone languages or libraries. Custom languages (Fig. 1) have great ergonomics, because they are conceived to model the BDI paradigm's entities, but, compared to libraries, they generally have a steeper learning curve, as users need to learn and adapt to a new custom syntax and software ecosystem. The result is a barrier that prevents developers to understand how to model agents, even if the problem they need to solve is suitable to be resolved by exploiting AOP. On the other hand, the adoption of a library leads to a gentler learning curve as it inherits the syntax and ecosystem of a mainstream language, but at the price of a much worse ergonomy: a general-purpose language syntax does not usually capture BDI/AOP abstractions as first-level entities, and, in turn, this leads to lower clarity, code cleanliness, and maintainability.

We believe that there is a need for BDI/AOP technologies that strike a balance between ergonomics and ease of adoption, one example is the definition of internal Domain-Specific Languages (DSLs). Such technologies would offer a custom syntax while leveraging the existing ecosystem and syntax familiarity of a mainstream language.

2.2   Tooling

Tooling is a major factor in a programming language's success. Developers are more likely to adopt a technology that allows them to leverage well-known development tools (IDEs, code suggestions, syntax highlighters, linters...) and rich ecosystems of libraries. Tools are so important to practitioners that some believe the tooling built around a programming language to be even more important than the language itself[4]. However, these features are tough to find in AOP custom languages: each one needs the custom implementation of tools that support developers and, moreover, someone has to maintain them, which is a time-valuable task for researchers.

We believe that having access to robust tooling is crucial for developers working with AOP. By leveraging mainstream programming languages, BDI/AOP libraries inherit the vast array of existing development tools and ecosystems. This approach not only eliminates the need for custom tooling development but also ensures ongoing support and maintenance from a wider community. As a result, developers can leverage efficient and effective tools while enjoying the benefits of the BDI/AOP paradigm, fostering wider adoption and empowering to harness the full potential of these programming approaches (Fig. 1).

---

[4] https://archive.is/kXi9M.

2.3   Middleware/Runtime Requirements

The majority of BDI/AOP languages rely on specific runtimes, such as the Java Virtual Machine (JVM) or the Python interpreter. This solution, however, is not always applicable, because BDI/AOP systems may be designed to execute on heterogeneous architectures and with specific constraints impeding the use of the required runtime. For instance, a web application would require agents to be executed within a browser, while a wearable-oriented application may require agents to run with constrained resources (making, e.g., unfeasible the use of a JVM).

BDI/AOP technologies should provide seamless compatibility across diverse platforms and architectures, ensuring that systems can be implemented and executed effortlessly, regardless of the specific runtime or constraints of the target device. Achieving this goal would empower developers to embrace the BDI/AOP paradigm without being limited by the availability of specific runtimes, thereby promoting the adoption and widespread use of this paradigm across various domains and architectures.

2.4   Concurrency Model

Often, current BDI/AOP languages offer limited configuration options regarding concurrency. Ideally, developers should be able to write their BDI/AOP code regardless of the underlying concurrency model, which should be pluggable. In most cases, instead, agent description languages are strictly coupled with their execution model, and the developer must adapt to it. Concurrency types should support at least sequential execution, parallel execution, or simulated time:

- Sequential execution is valuable for scenarios that prioritize better debugging capabilities or devices with limited resources: being able to execute agents sequentially allows for easier traceability and debugging of the agent's behaviour, simplifying the identification and resolution of potential issues. Additionally, resource-constrained devices can benefit from sequential execution to optimize resource utilization and improve overall performance.
- Parallel execution, on the other hand, is essential for scenarios where high performance and parallelism are crucial. By enabling the system to execute concurrently, agents can leverage the available hardware resources and improve overall system efficiency.
- Simulated time execution is particularly useful for testing and simulation purposes. It allows developers to control and manipulate time, facilitating the simulation of complex scenarios and enabling the testing of agent behaviours under various conditions. Simulated time execution provides a controlled environment for experimentation, ensuring that agents perform as expected in different time-dependent situations.

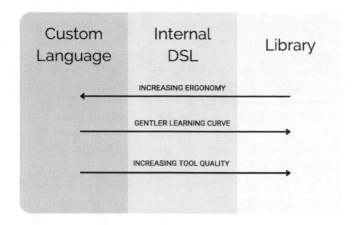

Fig. 1. Comparisons between different BDI/AOP technologies types.

3 The JaKtA Approach

To address these missing pieces, we propose JaKtA, a BDI framework for Multi-Agent Systems (MASs) hosted in Kotlin language, and already available as an experimental tool with a permissive open source license[5]. The main purpose of the framework is to reduce developers' barriers to learning the BDI/AOP paradigm by:

1. Providing access to BDI/AOP abstractions to a large (and expanding) community of developers already acquainted with a mainstream language syntax, for whom the learning curve will be gentle;
2. Offering an ergonomy akin to the one of a dedicated programming language by leveraging advanced Kotlin features. Kotlin, in fact, directly supports the creation of internal DSLs. DSLs are specifically designed to assist developers during the creation of complex domain entities;
3. Inheriting the whole existing, rich, and actively maintained tooling of Kotlin;
4. Running on multiple runtimes via multiplatform compilation using a single and shared code base;
5. Decoupling BDI entities' definition from their execution. In this way, the same system description could be transparently executed single-threaded, multi-threaded, with simulated time, or even with a custom combination of them.

Currently, JaKtA provides evidence that the first three points can indeed be achieved: gentler learning curve, ergonomics, and tooling. Kotlin has been chosen as the host language because of its expanding community, as results from languages popularity indexes, and being Kotlin the reference language for the Android mobile platform since 2019[6]. We believe that providing rich BDI/AOP

---

[5] https://github.com/jakta-bdi/jakta.
[6] https://archive.is/1IplY.

support for a language whose popularity will likely continue to grow in the foreseeable future is a good opportunity to allow more developers access to the paradigm. Moreover, the direct support to DSLs offered by Kotlin allows us to provide a syntax that is very close to the one of a custom language, while still being a mainstream language, and consequently, exploit all the language features, including syntax, libraries and tooling.

The JaKtA architecture is specifically designed to be modular, this means that the DSL definition is completely decoupled from the entities model: developers can easily customize and extend the DSL definition, without compromising domain entities' behaviour.

4   The Future Directions

As future research directions, we will focus on two main features to include in JaKtA: *(i)* the Kotlin Multiplatform support, and *(ii)* the implementation of the library's concurrency management.

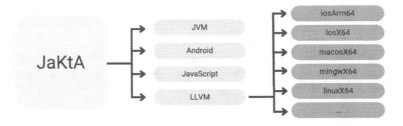

Fig. 2. JaKtA's future multi-target approach leveraging Kotlin multiplatform.

The multiplatform adoption will enable the framework to compile for several platforms, including native, JVM, and web applications (Fig. 2) and, consequently, to be executed on heterogeneous architectures. The concurrency model management, instead, will enable users to define a MASs without considering the underlying concurrency model, and then choosing separately how to execute the system.

References

1. Bordini, R.H., Hübner, J.F.: BDI agent programming in agentspeak using *Jason*. In: Toni, F., Torroni, P. (eds.) CLIMA 2005. LNCS (LNAI), vol. 3900, pp. 143–164. Springer, Heidelberg (2006). https://doi.org/10.1007/11750734_9
2. Calegari, R., Ciatto, G., Mascardi, V., Omicini, A.: Logic-based technologies for multi-agent systems: summary of a systematic literature review. In: Dignum, F., Lomuscio, A., Endriss, U., Nowé, A. (eds.) 20th International Conference on Autonomous Agents and Multiagent Systems, Virtual Event, AAMAS 2021,United Kingdom, 3–7 May 2021, pp. 1721–1723. ACM (2021). https://doi.org/10.5555/3463952.3464214

3. Hindriks, K.V.: Programming rational agents in GOAL. In: El Fallah Seghrouchni, A., Dix, J., Dastani, M., Bordini, R.H. (eds.) Multi-Agent Programming, pp. 119–157. Springer, Boston, MA (2009). https://doi.org/10.1007/978-0-387-89299-3_4
4. Pokahr, A., Braubach, L., Lamersdorf, W.: Jadex: a BDI reasoning engine. In: Bordini, R.H., Dastani, M., Dix, J., El Fallah Seghrouchni, A. (eds.) Multi-Agent Programming. MSASSO, vol. 15, pp. 149–174. Springer, Boston, MA (2005). https://doi.org/10.1007/0-387-26350-0_6
5. Rao, A.S., Georgeff, M.P.: Modeling rational agents within a BDI-architecture. In: Allen, J.F., Fikes, R., Sandewall, E. (eds.) Proceedings of the 2nd International Conference on Principles of Knowledge Representation and Reasoning (KR 1991), Cambridge, MA, USA, 22–25 April 1991, pp. 473–484. Morgan Kaufmann (1991)
6. Shoham, Y.: Agent-oriented programming. Artif. Intell. **60**(1), 51–92 (1993). https://doi.org/10.1016/0004-3702(93)90034-9

A Brief Overview of an Approach Towards Ethical Decision-Making

Mashal Afzal Memon[(✉)] [iD]

Università degli Studi dell'Aquila, L'Aquila, Italy
mashalafzal.memon@graduate.univaq.it

Abstract. Ethics in decision-making reflects traits such as transparency, equity, and trust. However, when considering ethics in the decision-making process of autonomous agents, the significant challenge is how autonomous agents should interact to reach an agreement, knowing that their ethical preferences may differ. On that account, this study explores two fields to propose an approach to ethical decision-making: *automated negotiation*, the field concerning interaction among multiple agents to reach an agreement, and *machine ethics*, the field concerned with adding or ensuring moral behaviors from agents. Although agents can negotiate and decide on a solution automatically, whether they can propose an ethically correct decision is still a subject matter. To this end, this study proposes the concept of introducing ethics in the decision-making process of intelligent agents for ethical decision-making. In particular, we propose a research framework that addresses how user ethical preferences can be converted into quantifiable measures and further used by autonomous agents during negotiation for ethical decision-making.

Keywords: Adaptation and Learning · Automated negotiation · Ethical behavior of multi-agent systems

1 Introduction

Artificial intelligence has played an essential role in the development of future generation of intelligent agents capable of autonomous decision making [11,30]. Although the next generation of intelligent agents promises many advantages, their increased degree of freedom raises concerns about their moral behavior during decision-making [4]. Since the early 2000s, Picard emphasized the need for embedding morality into autonomous machines: *"the greater the freedom of a machine, the more it will need moral standards"* [28]. Consequently, the development of autonomous systems that can ensure the morality of their behavior has attracted the interest of the research community, leading to the birth of the field of *"Machine ethics"* [16]. When considering ethics in the decision-making process, a significant challenge is how autonomous agents should interact in order to reach a situational agreement, knowing that their ethical preferences may differ in general.

V. Malvone and A. Murano (Eds.): EUMAS 2023, LNAI 14282, pp. 458–464, 2023.
https://doi.org/10.1007/978-3-031-43264-4_32

Negotiation is a process between multiple agents in which a decision is made jointly by communication, i.e., through exchange of dialogues, bids, and offers to reach an agreement that is accepted by all agents [8,32]. In the context of *"Automated negotiation"*, designing agents capable of effectively acquiring and integrating user ethical preferences into the decision-making process is a key challenge [6,13,21]. To this end, we focus on combining ethics with automated negotiation to propose an approach where autonomous agents negotiate with each other based on user ethical preferences for ethical decision-making. In particular, in this study, we propose a research framework that focuses on describing how user ethical preferences can be converted into quantifiable measures to be then used by autonomous agents during negotiation for ethical decision-making.

The remainder of the paper is structured as follows. In Sect. 2, we detail the related work to our study. Section 3 describes our research framework. Section 4 provides a discussion with an overview of the future research direction and Sect. 5 concludes the proposed study.

2   Related Work

In this section, we discuss related work that covers both the theoretical fundamentals and the current state-of-the-art for automated negotiation and ethical decision-making.

Challenges of introducing ethics in automated decision-making – In the following, we discuss more theoretical works that highlight the difficulties of introducing ethics into autonomous systems. In [26], Moor defines four different levels of ethical agents. At the lower levels, agents do not have any ethics explicitly added to their software, but may have an ethical impact on other agents, humans, and the environment due to their actions or design (e.g., autopilots can impact the safety of passengers). At higher levels, Moor identifies *explicit ethical agents*, who use available ethical knowledge in their decision process. At the higher level, Moor also introduces the concept of *fully ethical agents*, which are capable of making explicit judgments and justifying them, i.e., human-like ethical reasoning. In addition to the technical challenges related to the development of these agents [10,15,29], the uncertainty of different moral principles makes it difficult to identify a single ethical theory that can be followed to develop such intelligent systems [4,9,27]. In [14], Floridi describes digital ethics as two separate components. The first, *hard ethics*, represents the ethical rules described by the higher authorities, which are (in principle, should be) commonly accepted. The second, *soft ethics*, encompasses user morals, which can reflect on user personal preferences during decision-making. This vision poses the challenge of how to embed user ethical preferences into decision-making, not only in those situations in which humans interact with autonomous agents but also when the latter interact between themselves on behalf of humans.

Automated negotiation – In the following, we discuss studies that consider negotiation between autonomous agents for automated decision-making. In multi-agent systems, rules have been an effective technique for modeling negotiation. In [23], the seller and buyer agents negotiate the price using fuzzy rules to find the best bidding strategy. Agents learn during negotiation by interacting with opponents to modify and create new rules. A similar idea has been discussed in [18], where agents use associative rules during negotiation to adjust parameters such as time, value intervals to offer, and negotiation issues to reduce the number of interactions by generating associative rules. Although these studies present negotiation based on rules, negotiation based on user ethical preferences is still unexplored. Furthermore, the study in [20] defines various stages of the life cycle of the negotiating agent, and the studies in [7,25,31], propose multiple approaches to automate the negotiation process based on different stages of the life cycle of the negotiating agents. However, none of these studies considers user ethical preferences in negotiation, which is the main focus of our approach.

Ethical decision-making – We discuss below the studies that consider ethics during the decision-making process. The architecture of an artificial moral agent is proposed in [22], which combines the moral values of different stakeholders to make an ethical decision. The agent makes a decision by forming a single ethical theory from different moral values. It is assumed that moral values are classified and that agents utilize them to take a collaborative decision that leads to an agreement. However, in our study, where agents' moral values differ from each other and are unknown to opponents, rather than forming a single conclusion to agree, agents self-adapt their behavior and negotiate to reach an agreement until it satisfies their moral values. In [12], the study proposes an ethical reasoner to conduct decision-making. In this work, the ethical reasoner follows a predetermined ethical theory, and the possible actions that the system can undertake are ranked according to their adherence to the ethical theory. However, the proposed study does not consider the morality of users as part of decision-making, as the ethical principles followed by the system are decided by the system designers. Therefore, in our study, we focus on user morals for ethical decision-making instead of explicit ethical theories and rules.

3   Research Framework

This section describes the focus areas and research questions that result from the state-of-the-art. Figure 1 shows a visual representation of our framework.

Automated negotiation is a compelling research field that groups three familiar research fields into one, namely, game theory, economics, and artificial intelligence [5]. The significance of automated negotiation is receiving great attention in the current age, as intelligent agents that negotiate with each other and represent human users are likely to be more efficient [13,21]. On the other hand, machine ethics is a field that combines computational logic with moral philosophy [4]. A well-known obstacle in this field is the lack of general agreement on which specific ethical values should be followed by autonomous decision-making agents [10,15], as individuals differ in their moral judgements [4,27].

Traditionally, in a multi-agent environment, agents can be cooperative and communicate with each other to perform a shared task [13,21], or they can be selfish and compete with others to maximize their own utility [5,17]. In the

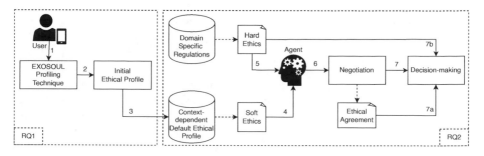

Fig. 1. A visual representation of the research framework. The dotted boxes highlight the elements dedicated to each research question. The solid box represents the component, the knowledge base represents the rules and ethical profile, the file icon represents the instance, the solid arrow represents the data flow, and the dotted arrow represents the connection between the instance and the parent element.

former case, the system can only follow the ethical principles decided by the system designers (thus disregarding plurality of opinions); whereas, in the latter case, the selfish behavior of agents will purposely lead them to ignore the ethical principles of others, as to maximize their own benefits according to their own ethical beliefs. For that, we employ the concept of ethics as proposed by Floridi [14], according to which soft ethics encompasses user ethical preferences and hard ethics represents explicit ethical rules. In our work, mimicking human behavior, we consider autonomous systems as independent and competing over shared resources but willing to negotiate to reach an agreement as long as it does not violate their own ethical boundaries. Note that it does not make much sense to hope that the agreement is reached once and for all; rather, it is situational in that it relates to or depends on specific circumstances, state of affairs, or environments. To this end, the research questions that model this study are:

RQ1: How does human ethical preferences can be represented as quantifiable measures?

This research question focuses on profiling human according to their ethical preferences (i.e., soft ethics as mentioned above). To reflect human ethical preferences in the decision-making process of autonomous agents, it is important to represent them as quantifiable measures. For that reason, within the EXOSOUL project[1] [1–3,19], we exploit a personalized ethical profiling technique to collect individual's preferences through a survey (1) that aims to gather data on the moral preferences of users in the digital world. The resultant profile of this survey (2) is then used to develop a context-dependent ethical profile (3) that the autonomous agent uses for negotiation purposes, as shown in Fig. 1.

RQ2: How can we design autonomous agents that take human ethical preferences into account when negotiating for decision making?

---

[1] https://exosoul.disim.univaq.it/.

This research question focuses on detailing the process of combining human ethical preferences with automated negotiation. For that reason, in [24], we propose an approach in which an autonomous system adapts its behavior and adjusts its autonomy according to the input it receives from the user as an ethical profile (4). We assume to create a context-dependent profile from the general profile obtained through [1,2]. It is worth mentioning that even agents negotiate on the basis of soft ethics; we consider that each agent involved in the process is in compliance with domain specific rules (i.e. hard ethics as mentioned above) to avoid illegal actions (5). According to user ethical preferences, when the user shows priority towards herself, the agent self-adapts and becomes self-interested, and hence negotiates (6) to reach an agreement until it satisfies its ethical beliefs; however, if self-prioritization according to user ethical preferences is not important, the agent becomes cooperative and coordinates to reach an agreement if the opponent offers satisfy its ethical preferences. During negotiation, each received offer is then evaluated according to the ethical principles of the user profile. The negotiation ends when an ethical agreement is reached or no offer satisfies the ethical beliefs of the involved parties. When no agreement is reached, we consider the agents to follow domain-specific rules to apply a fall-back strategy for decision-making (7).

4   Discussion

This section provides a discussion and an overview of future steps. Our work highlights the need to consider ethics in the decision-making process of autonomous systems. This will help to ensure that autonomous systems behave ethically while enabling effective decision-making. To this end, as a first step, we propose to ingrain the ethical beliefs of the user into the system through an ethical profile [1–3,19]. Context-dependent ethical profiling is one of the future research directions of this work. For ethics-based negotiation, in [24], we then propose an approach to utilize the context-dependent ethical profile during negotiation. To this end, we consider the adoption of reinforcement learning as an appropriate technique. By employing reinforcement learning in negotiation, the agent will engage in a continuous loop to learn through user ethical preferences and adapt its negotiation strategy.

5   Conclusion

This study introduces an ethical perspective in the decision-making process of autonomous agents for ethical decision-making and details how an autonomous agent can represent user ethical preferences during negotiation. Negotiation resolves possible conflicts and results in ethical decisions that satisfy the user's ethical beliefs. In the future, we plan to implement this study and validate its effectiveness in real-world scenarios.

Acknowledgements. The authors would like to thank the entire multidisciplinary team of the EXOSOUL@univaq project for enlightening debates and joint work on digital ethics for autonomous systems.

References

1. Alfieri, C., Donati, D., Gozzano, S., Greco, L., Segala, M.: Ethical preferences in the digital world: the EXOSOUL questionnaire. In: HHAI 2023: Augmenting Human Intellect, pp. 290–299. IOS Press (2023)

2. Alfieri, C., Inverardi, P., Migliarini, P., Palmiero, M.: Exosoul: ethical profiling in the digital world. In: HHAI2022: Augmenting Human Intellect, pp. 128–142. IOS Press (2022)

3. Autili, M., Ruscio, D.D., Inverardi, P., Pelliccione, P., Tivoli, M.: A software exoskeleton to protect and support citizen's ethics and privacy in the digital world. IEEE Access **7**, 62011–62021 (2019). https://doi.org/10.1109/ACCESS. 2019.2916203

4. Awad, E., et al.: The moral machine experiment. Nature **563**(7729), 59–64 (2018)

5. Baarslag, T., Hendrikx, M.J., Hindriks, K.V., Jonker, C.M.: Learning about the opponent in automated bilateral negotiation: a comprehensive survey of opponent modeling techniques. Auton. Agents Multi-Agent Syst. **30**(5), 849–898 (2016)

6. Baarslag, T., Kaisers, M.: The value of information in automated negotiation: a decision model for eliciting user preferences. In: Proceedings of the 16th Conference on Autonomous Agents and Multiagent Systems, pp. 391–400 (2017)

7. Bachrach, Y., et al.: Negotiating team formation using deep reinforcement learning. Artif. Intell. **288**, 103356 (2020)

8. Bagga, P., Paoletti, N., Stathis, K.: Deep learnable strategy templates for multi-issue bilateral negotiation. In: Proceedings of the 21st International Conference on Autonomous Agents and Multiagent Systems, pp. 1533–1535 (2022)

9. Bogosian, K.: Implementation of moral uncertainty in intelligent machines. Minds Mach. **27**(4), 591–608 (2017)

10. Bostrom, N., Yudkowsky, E.: The ethics of artificial intelligence. In: Artificial Intelligence Safety and Security, pp. 57–69. Chapman and Hall/CRC (2018)

11. Buiten, M.C.: Towards intelligent regulation of artificial intelligence. Eur. J. Risk Regul. **10**(1), 41–59 (2019)

12. Cardoso, R.C., Ferrando, A., Dennis, L.A., Fisher, M.: Implementing ethical governors in BDI. In: Alechina, N., Baldoni, M., Logan, B. (eds.) EMAS 2021. Lecture Notes in Computer Science, vol. 13190, pp. 22–41. Springer, Cham (2021). https://doi.org/10.1007/978-3-030-97457-2_2

13. Chen, S., Weiss, G.: Automated negotiation: an efficient approach to interaction among agents. In: Interactions in Multiagent Systems, pp. 149–177. World Scientific (2019)

14. Floridi, L.: Soft ethics and the governance of the digital. Philos. Technol. **31**(1), 1–8 (2018)

15. Floridi, L.: Establishing the rules for building trustworthy AI. Nat. Mach. Intell. **1**(6), 261–262 (2019)

16. Guarini, M.: Introduction: machine ethics and the ethics of building intelligent machines. Topoi **32**(2), 213–215 (2013)

17. Hoen, P.J., Tuyls, K., Panait, L., Luke, S., La Poutré, J.A.: An overview of cooperative and competitive multiagent learning. In: Tuyls, K., Hoen, P.J., Verbeeck, K., Sen, S. (eds.) LAMAS 2005. LNCS (LNAI), vol. 3898, pp. 1–46. Springer, Heidelberg (2006). https://doi.org/10.1007/11691839_1

18. Hu, J., Deng, L.: An association rule-based bilateral multi-issue negotiation model. In: 2011 Fourth International Symposium on Computational Intelligence and Design, vol. 2, pp. 234–237. IEEE (2011)

19. Inverardi, P., Palmiero, M., Pelliccione, P., Tivoli, M.: Ethical-aware autonomous systems from a social psychological lens. In: Proceedings of the 6th International Workshop on Cultures of Participation in the Digital Age: AI for Humans or Humans for AI? CEUR Workshop Proceedings, vol. 3136, pp. 43–48 (2022)

20. Kiruthika, U., Somasundaram, T.S., Raja, S.: Lifecycle model of a negotiation agent: a survey of automated negotiation techniques. Group Decis. Negot. **29**(6), 1239–1262 (2020)

21. Kraus, S.: Agents that negotiate proficiently with people. In: Salerno, J., Yang, S.J., Nau, D., Chai, S.-K. (eds.) SBP 2011. LNCS, vol. 6589, pp. 137–137. Springer, Heidelberg (2011). https://doi.org/10.1007/978-3-642-19656-0_21

22. Liao, B., Slavkovik, M., van der Torre, L.: Building jiminy cricket: an architecture for moral agreements among stakeholders. In: AAAI Conference on AI, Ethics, and Society, pp. 147–153 (2019)

23. Mahan, F., Isazadeh, A., Khanli, L.M.: Using an active fuzzy ECA rule-based negotiation agent in e-commerce. Int. J. Electr. Commer. Stud. **2**(2), 127–148 (2011)

24. Memon, M.A., Scoccia, G.L., Inverardi, P., Autili, M.: Don't you agree with my ethics? let's negotiate! In: Augmenting Human Intellect - Proceedings of the Second International Conference on Hybrid Human-Artificial Intelligence (HHAI). Frontiers in Artificial Intelligence and Applications, vol. 368, pp. 385–388. IOS Press (2023)

25. Mohammadi Ashnani, F., Movahedi, Z., Fouladi, K.: Modeling opponent strategy in multi-issue bilateral automated negotiation using machine learning. Int. J. Web Res. **3**(2), 16–25 (2020)

26. Moor, J.H.: The nature, importance, and difficulty of machine ethics. IEEE Intell. Syst. **21**(4), 18–21 (2006)

27. Nallur, V., Collier, R.: Ethics by agreement in multi-agent software systems. In: 14th International Conference on Software Technologies, Prague, Czech Republic, 26–28 July 2019, pp. 529–535. SCITEPRESS (2019)

28. Picard, R.W.: Affective Computing. MIT press, Cambridge (2000)

29. Ryan, M., Stahl, B.C.: Artificial intelligence ethics guidelines for developers and users: clarifying their content and normative implications. J. Inf. Commun. Ethics Soc. **19**(1), 61–86 (2020)

30. Totschnig, W.: Fully autonomous AI. Sci. Eng. Ethics **26**(5), 2473–2485 (2020)

31. Wu, L., Chen, S., Gao, X., Zheng, Y., Hao, J.: Detecting and learning against unknown opponents for automated negotiations. In: Pham, D.N., Theeramunkong, T., Governatori, G., Liu, F. (eds.) PRICAI 2021. LNCS (LNAI), vol. 13033, pp. 17–31. Springer, Cham (2021). https://doi.org/10.1007/978-3-030-89370-5_2

32. Zuckerman, I., Rosenfeld, A., Kraus, S., Segal-Halevi, E.: Towards automated negotiation agents that use chat interfaces. In: The Sixth International Workshop on Agent-Based Complex Automated Negotiations (ACAN) (2013)

On Verifying Unbounded Client-Server Systems

Tephilla Prince[✉]

Indian Institute of Technology Dharwad, Dharwad, India
tephilla.prince.18@iitdh.ac.in

Keywords: Petri Nets · Temporal Logic · Bounded Model Checking

1   Introduction

Formal verification of Petri nets is well studied and there are existing state-of-the-art verification tools such as KREACH [5], Petrinizer [6], QCOVER [2] and ICOVER [7]. Several communication protocols, services and applications are unbounded client-server systems. Existing tools are not specifically suited for verifying unbounded client-server systems as they do not allow the user to explicitly specify client and server properties as well as their unboundedness. Moreover, the tools specify properties in logics such as LTL or CTL, which are not unsuitable. It is necessary to find suitable logics to express properties of unbounded client-server systems where the number of clients is not known a priori. In this work, we make the following key contributions:

- We describe a running example of unbounded client-server systems and narrow down a suitable formal model for it.
- We introduce a monodic logic $\mathcal{L}^1_{UCS}$ for easily expressing properties of unbounded client-server systems explained with a running example.[1]

1.1   Modeling Unbounded Client-Server Systems

We consider as a running example, the Autonomous Parking System (APS) that manages parking lots through communication between the system (server) and the vehicle (client). This system has been successfully implemented by the industry [3,13]. This is a type of single server multiple client system, where the clients are distinguishable and unbounded. The service being offered is the finite set of parking lots available for occupancy by the clients. In this section, the objective is to identify a formal model for the combined interactions between the server and unboundedly many clients in the running example. The formal model should not be specific to the APS case study however, it needs to be generic enough to apply to other unbounded client-server systems as well.

---

[1] A preliminary version of this work is accepted only for presentation, not publication at the Indian Conference on Logic and its Applications (ICLA) 2023.

V. Malvone and A. Murano (Eds.): EUMAS 2023, LNAI 14282, pp. 465–471, 2023.
https://doi.org/10.1007/978-3-031-43264-4_33

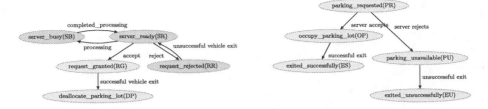

Fig. 1. State diagram of server   **Fig. 2.** State diagram of client

We begin by describing the state diagrams for the server and client given in Fig. 1 and Fig. 2 respectively. Initially, the system is in the state *server_ready (SR)*, when it is ready to service the client. We assume a steady inflow of parking requests. When a client inquires about parking space, the client is in the *parking_requested (PR)* state. The server non-deterministically chooses to either grant or reject the parking request based on local information such as space availability, the priority of incoming requests, etc. We assume two disjoint workflows for each scenario. First, if the server accepts the request, the server is in *request_granted (RG)* state and simultaneously, the client goes to *occupy_parking_lot (OP)* state. Eventually, the client gives up its allocated parking space, is in *exit_successfully (ES)* and simultaneously the server is in *deallocate_parking_lot (DP)* state. This marks the successful exit of the client from the system. Second, if the server rejects the request, the client is in *parking_unavailable (PU)* state and the server is in *request_rejected (RR)* state. The only option is for the client to exit. After granting the request, the server can go to *server_busy (SB)* state. Theoretically, this description allows for an unbounded number of client requests to be processed by the server. It is not difficult to observe that the combined interactions between the server and clients described above can be interleaved and formally modeled as a single net.

The **requirements** for the formal model are as follows. The **distinguishable clients** in the running example necessitate **distinguishable tokens** for **client identifiers**. Since there are unbounded clients, a fresh client identifier is issued when a new client enters the system. When clients exit, the identifiers need to be purged. The server process is always present. The server (client) processes are in the server (client) places. There is only communication between the server and clients. In case of synchronizing places in the net, the union of client identifiers is necessitated with restriction on the arcs based on the type of process.

Petri nets are suitable to model *concurrent* behaviour of the clients. The places correspond to the local states of the client and server, which are a disjoint set of server places and client places. The transitions correspond to their combined interactions. The tokens correspond to the client's requests. A candidate model is the colored Petri net [9] which satisfies the above requirements. However, we do not prefer the colored Petri net, for two reasons. First, they allow arbitrary expressions over user-defined syntax labelling the arcs, which is overkill for our requirement. This is because the underlying modeling language (such as CPN Modeling Language in CPN Tools [10]) is highly expressive. Second, the lack of tools to automatically *unfold* the formal model of the system for verification. Recall that our long-term goal is the automatic verification of unbounded client-server systems. Suppose we represented the formal model as a colored Petri net such as using CPN Tools, there are no existing tools that can automatically *unfold* an *unbounded* colored Petri net created using CPN Tools. Existing tools can only unfold *bounded* colored Petri nets [1,4].

2   Restricted ν-Nets

We consider a model that satisfies all the requirements listed in Sect. 1.1. The second candidate model is a type of ν-net [12], which is a coloured Petri net defined over a system of component nets, which use a labelling function λ, to handle synchronization between multiple component nets. We restrict the ν-nets to a single component, providing a simplified definition while doing away with the labelling function used in ν-nets. We begin with some definitions that are necessary for describing the restricted ν-net. Given an arbitrary set A, we denote by $\mathcal{MS}(A)$, the set of finite multisets of A, given by the set of mappings $m : A \to \mathbb{N}$. We denote by $S(m)$ the support of m, defined as follows: $S(m) = \{a \in A | m(a) > 0\}$.

A restricted ν-net is a coloured Petri Net $N = (P, T, F)$, where

- P and T are finite disjoint sets of places and transitions, respectively,
- $F \colon (P \times T) \cup (T \times P) \to \mathcal{MS}(\text{Var})$ defines the set of arcs of the net, satisfying $\nu \notin pre(t)$ for every $t \in T$, where $pre(t) = \bigcup_{p \in P} S(F(p,t))$ (Fig. 3).

For a transition t of the net, we define, $post(t) = \bigcup_{p \in P} S(F(t,p))$ and $Var(t) = pre(t) \bigcup post(t)$, where, Var is a finite set of variables used for labelling arcs. Distinguishable tokens (identifiers) are taken from an arbitrary infinite set Id. Fresh names (identifiers) are created in the net using a special variable $\nu \in Var$ that appears only in post-condition arcs. A marking of a restricted ν-net $N = (P, T, F)$ is a function $M : P \to (\mathcal{MS}(Id))$. We denote by $S(M)$ the set of names in M. i.e., $S(M) = \bigcup_{p \in P} S(M(p))$. A mode of a transition t is a mapping $\sigma : Var(t) \to Id$, instantiating every variable in the adjacent arcs of t to some identifier. A transition is **identifier-preserving** if $post(t) \backslash \{\nu\} \subseteq pre(t)$. Let N be a restricted ν-net and M a marking of N. We say that M **enables** the transition t with mode σ whenever:

- If $\nu \in Var(t)$ then $\sigma(\nu) \notin S(M)$
- $\sigma(F(p,t)) \subseteq M(p)$ for all $p \in P$.

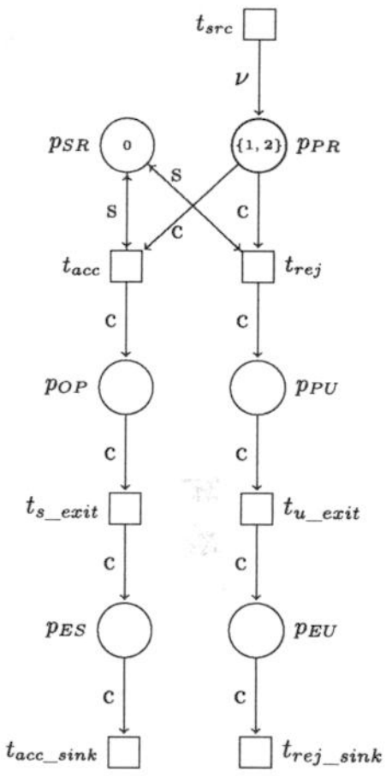

Fig. 3. A restricted ν-net modeling APS

Notice that $\sigma(\nu) \notin S(M)$ for the enabling of transition, that causes the creation of fresh (equal) identifiers in all the places reached by arcs labelled by the special variable ν.

The reached marking of net N after firing of t with mode σ is denoted by $M \xrightarrow{t(\sigma)} M'$ $M'(p) = M(p) - \sigma(F(p,t)) + \sigma(F(t,p))$ for every $p \in P$. The transitions t_{acc}, t_{rej}, t_{s_exit}, t_{u_exit}, t_{acc_sink}, t_{rej_sink}, represent the accept, reject, exit successfully, exit unsuccessfully and the two sink transitions respectively. All of them are *identifier-preserving* transitions. The firing of transition t_{src} acts as the source. The arc labelled ν ensures that a new client identifier is generated in place p_{PR}. The place p_{PR} contains a set of clients requesting for parking. In the unsuccessful scenario, the transition t_{rej} is fired when the server rejects the request, which brings the vehicle to *parking_ unavailable* state represented by place p_{PU}. On firing of transition t_{u_exit}, the vehicle goes to *exited_ unsuccessfully* state represented by place p_{EU}. The firing of transition t_{rej_sink} is the sink transition for the rejected parking requests. This ensures that the rejected vehicle identifier exits the system and is never reused. If the client arrives after it has exited, it is always issued a fresh identifier. Notice that there are arcs labelled s to indicate the server which has identifier 0, which is necessary for the acceptance or rejection of a parking request. The token with identifier 0 is permanently present in each marking exactly at server place p_{SR}. The ν arc ensures that new identifiers are generated, essentially giving an unbounded number of agents in the ν-net. The arcs labelled c carry the client identifiers from one client place to another. The net behaves as a standard ν-net component with autonomous transitions as described in [11].

3   The Monodic Logic $\mathcal{L}^1_{UCS}$

The monodic logic $\mathcal{L}^1_{UCS}$ is an extension of Linear Temporal Logic (LTL), and both a syntactic and semantic subclass of MFOTL [8]. A *monodic* formula is a well-formed formula with at most one free variable in the scope of a temporal modality. Let P_s be the set of atomic propositions of the server and P_c be the set of client predicates. The set of *client formulae*, Δ, is the *boolean and temporal modal closure* of atomic client formulae P_c:

$$\alpha, \beta \in \Delta ::= p(x), p \in P_c \mid \neg\alpha \mid \alpha \vee \beta \mid \alpha \wedge \beta \mid \mathbf{X}_c\alpha \mid \mathbf{F}_c\alpha \mid \mathbf{G}_c\alpha \mid \alpha \ \mathbf{U}_c \ \beta$$

The set of *server formulae*, Ψ, is the *boolean and temporal modal closure* of $\Phi = \{(\exists x)\alpha, (\forall x)\alpha \mid \alpha \in \Delta\}$ and atomic server formulae P_s:

$$\Psi ::= q \in P_s \mid \neg\psi \mid \phi \in \Phi \mid \psi_1 \vee \psi_2 \mid \psi_1 \wedge \psi_2 \mid \mathbf{X_s}\psi \mid \mathbf{F_s}\psi \mid \mathbf{G_s}\psi \mid \psi_1 \ \mathbf{U_s} \ \psi_2$$

where $\psi, \psi_1, \psi_2 \in \Psi$. To give a flavour of $\mathcal{L}^1_{UCS}$ and its expressibility, we enumerate some properties of APS that are not easily expressible in Linear Temporal Logic (LTL). Let P_s be the set of atomic propositions of the server and P_c be the set of client predicates. In the APS running example, they are defined as follows: $P_c = \{PR, OP, PU, ES, EU\}$. $P_s = \{SR\}$.

1. When a vehicle requests a parking space, it is always the case that for every vehicle, it eventually exits the system, either successfully after being granted a parking space, or unsuccessfully, when its request is denied.

$$\psi_1 = \mathbf{G}_s(\forall x)\Big(PR(x) \Rightarrow \mathbf{F}_c \ (ES(x) \ \lor \ EU(x))\Big)$$

2. It is always the case that if the client occupies a parking lot, it will eventually exit the parking lot.

$$\psi_2 = \mathbf{G}_s(\forall x)\Big(OP(x) \Rightarrow \mathbf{F}_c(ES(x))\Big)$$

3. There may be clients who have requested parking and who wait in the parking unavailable state until they can exit the system.

$$\psi_3 = \mathbf{G}_s(\exists x)\Big(PR(x) \ \land \mathbf{F}_c\big(PU(x) \ \mathbf{U}_c \ EU(x)\big)\Big)$$

It can be observed that there are no free variables in the scope of $\mathbf{G_s}$ and exactly one free variable in the scope of the client modalities. It is also possible to construct $\mathcal{L}^1_{UCS}$ specifications with propositions from P_s and server transitions. The ease of expressibility of the client and server behaviour is the key motivation behind the logic $\mathcal{L}^1_{UCS}$.

We consider the *unbounded client-server systems* where all clients are of the same type. At any instant, the number of clients is *bounded*, but their cardinality is *unknown* and *dynamic*. We refer to the clients that are present in the system at any point in time as *live agents* (clients). The *live window* of a particular client begins when it enters the system and ends when the client exits the system. Hence, if there are several *live agents*, their *live windows* would overlap each other. This is inter-

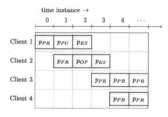

Fig. 4. Snapshot of the running example *(APS)*

esting as it allows us to reason about the *live clients* which satisfy particular properties simultaneously.

Example 1. *Figure 4 depicts the snapshot of the system with 4 distinguishable clients, with overlapping* live *windows. While the system is* unbounded, *there are a finite number of clients at an instant. Each row shows the local state of that client. For each instance, the local state of the client is in the cell i.e., client 1 is at state p_{PR} at instance 0. For client 1, the* left *boundary, when it enters the system is at instance 0 and its* right *boundary is at instance 2, when it exits the system. This corresponds to the client requesting parking and getting rejected. There may be multiple clients in the same local state (client 3 and client 4 are in state p_{PR} at instance 4). There may be clients who are live at the bound 5 and have not exited the system, such as clients 3 and 4. This is an interesting case, where the bound equals the current right boundary for the client.*

4 Conclusion

We have formally modeled unbounded client-server systems and described a monodic logic for specifying their properties. Future work includes implementing an algorithm to formally verify these systems and compute its complexity.

Acknowledgements. I would like to thank my supervisors Ramchandra Phawade and S. Sheerazuddin for their valuable inputs on this work.

References

1. Bilgram, A., Jensen, P.G., Pedersen, T., Srba, J., Taankvist, P.H.: Improvements in unfolding of colored petri nets. In: Bell, P.C., Totzke, P., Potapov, I. (eds.) RP 2021. LNCS, vol. 13035, pp. 69–84. Springer, Cham (2021). https://doi.org/10.1007/978-3-030-89716-1_5

2. Blondin, M., Finkel, A., Haase, C., Haddad, S.: Approaching the coverability problem continuously. In: Chechik, M., Raskin, J.-F. (eds.) TACAS 2016. LNCS, vol. 9636, pp. 480–496. Springer, Heidelberg (2016). https://doi.org/10.1007/978-3-662-49674-9_28

3. Cai, Z., Zhou, Y., Qi, Y., Zhuang, W., Deng, L.: A millimeter wave dual-lens antenna for IoT-based smart parking radar system. IEEE Internet Things J. **8**, 418–427 (2021). https://doi.org/10.1109/JIOT.2020.3004403

4. Dal Zilio, S.: MCC: a tool for unfolding colored petri nets in PNML format. In: Janicki, R., Sidorova, N., Chatain, T. (eds.) PETRI NETS 2020. LNCS, vol. 12152, pp. 426–435. Springer, Cham (2020). https://doi.org/10.1007/978-3-030-51831-8_23

5. Dixon, A., Lazić, R.: KReach: a tool for reachability in petri nets. In: Biere, A., Parker, D. (eds.) TACAS 2020. LNCS, vol. 12078, pp. 405–412. Springer, Cham (2020). https://doi.org/10.1007/978-3-030-45190-5_22

6. Esparza, J., Ledesma-Garza, R., Majumdar, R., Meyer, P., Niksic, F.: An SMT-based approach to coverability analysis. In: Biere, A., Bloem, R. (eds.) CAV 2014. LNCS, vol. 8559, pp. 603–619. Springer, Cham (2014). https://doi.org/10.1007/978-3-319-08867-9_40

7. Geffroy, T., Leroux, J., Sutre, G.: Occam's razor applied to the petri net coverability problem. Theor. Comput. Sci. (2018). https://doi.org/10.1016/j.tcs.2018.04.014

8. Hodkinson, I.M., Wolter, F., Zakharyaschev, M.: Decidable fragment of first-order temporal logics. Ann. Pure Appl. Logic **106**(1–3), 85–134 (2000)

9. Kurt Jensen and Lars Michael Kristensen: Coloured petri nets - modelling and validation of concurrent systems. Springer (2009). https://doi.org/10.1007/b95112

10. Jensen, K., Kristensen, L.M., Wells, L.: Coloured petri nets and CPN tools for modelling and validation of concurrent systems. Int. J. Softw. Tools Technol. Transf. **9**(3–4):213–254 (2007). https://doi.org/10.1007/s10009-007-0038-x

11. Rosa-Velardo, F., de Frutos-Escrig, D.: Name creation vs. replication in petri net systems. In: Kleijn, J., Yakovlev, A. (eds.) ICATPN 2007. LNCS, vol. 4546, pp. 402–422. Springer, Heidelberg (2007). https://doi.org/10.1007/978-3-540-73094-1_24

12. Rosa-Velardo, F., de Frutos-Escrig, D.: Name creation vs. replication in petri net systems. Fundam. Informaticae, **88**(3), 329–356 (2008). http://content.iospress.com/articles/fundamenta-informaticae/fi88-3-06
13. Yan, G., Yang, W., Rawat, D.B., Olariu, S.: Smartparking: a secure and intelligent parking system. IEEE Intell. Transp. Syst. Mag. **3**, 18–30 (2011). https://doi.org/10.1109/MITS.2011.940473

Capacity ATL: Reasoning About Agent Profiles and Applications to Cybersecurity

Gabriel Ballot[✉]

Télécom Paris - EDF R&D, Palaiseau, France
`gabriel.ballot@telecom-paris.fr`

Abstract. Cybersecurity is a context in which at least two agents, namely a defender and an attacker, interact to achieve conflicting objectives. As such, its analysis with game theory is natural. Most game theoretic approaches for cybersecurity rely on analytical games described by a reward function depending on agent actions, and the goal is often to find equilibriums (e.g, Nash equilibrium). However, these techniques imply a new analysis for each particular system or network. Contrarily, defining *Multi-Agent System (MAS)* formalisms adapted to describe multi-step attacks can help generically design defense systems. Moreover, model checking defender strategic abilities in the *MAS* offers guarantees on active cyber defenses leveraged by the security team, including honeypots (i.e, deception mechanisms) and *Moving Target Defenses* (i.e, system reconfiguration). The existing formalisms do not capture all the aspects of active defenses, so we developed *Capacity Alternating-time Temporal Logic* to reason about strategic abilities under imperfect information of the agents' capacities. During my thesis, we plan to explore further the use of *MAS* verification for active cybersecurity.

1 Introduction

Model checking is a formal verification technique for ensuring system correctness by checking a property (i.e, a desired quality of the system) for all possible system computations. It has been successfully applied to computer systems to guarantee properties without relying on an expert's knowledge or intuition. Model checking is based on three components: a formal system model describing its states and behavior, a formal specification of the system's correctness, and a model-checking algorithm to verify if the specification holds on the system's model. Since the early 2000s and the supremacy of systems interconnection, not only closed systems are analyzed with verification techniques, but also open systems where multiple agents interact. The modeling and specification formalisms have evolved to be sometimes more expressive or more specific, for instance, from *Computation Tree Logic (CTL)* [11] expressing properties on infinite computation trees to *Alternating-time Temporal Logic (ATL)* [1] and *Strategy Logic (SL)* [19] that express agents strategic abilities on *Concurrent Game Structure (CGS)*. A *CGS* is a Kripke structure where transitions are labeled with a tuple of actions (one for each agent), and, in each state, each agent decides its next action, thus triggering a particular transition. *ATL* properties ask whether agent coalitions have a strategy (what action to do in each state) to enforce properties in a specific temporal horizon. For example, *ATL* property $readCmd \rightarrow \langle controler \rangle (\neg write) \, \mathcal{U} \, read$ would express that "when `read` command arrives, the memory controller can prevent any write in the register until the read happens". This thesis explores how strategic system verification can be a powerful tool for finding optimal defense strategies in cybersecurity.

System security has been analyzed through analytical game theory to derive optimal defender actions in a specific system [10]. However, strategic verification of *Multi-Agent Systems (MASs)* provides a framework to analyze generic systems. *MAS* verification and attack modeling give all the elements to reason on systems under complex multi-step attacks. The cybersecurity community investigates the use of *active defenses* to create more reactive and proactive defense systems. An active defense system implies the defender has actions to counter the attacker. Consequently, the defender must decide what action to use and when: it means having a *strategy*. However, the defender must identify and reason about the current attackers to find meaningful strategies. We focus on two active defense types: *honeypots* and *Moving Target Defenses (MTDs)*. Honeypots mimic attractive computer resources to lure attackers, make them waste time, and study their capacities. *MTD* is a defense paradigm aiming to periodically change the system configuration to shift the attack surface [20]. *MTDs* tend to break the longstanding asymmetry between the attacker and the defender, that is, the attacker can spend an unlimited time planning an attack while the defender sets its defenses once. *MTDs* are characterized by three elements *(i)* the moving parameter (i.e, a configuration parameter that will change), it can be the data format, an application binary, the instruction set, the CPU architecture, the protocol, or the network topology, *(ii)* the set of valid values for the moving parameter, for instance, the set of valid addresses for an IP address shuffling *MTD*, and the way to choose the next configuration, and *(iii)* the reconfiguration period or the triggering condition. In a preliminary work [3], we characterized the *MTD* time and cost impact on the attacker using *Markov Decision Processes*. *MTDs* are mostly designed to change configurations periodically. However, we believe *MTDs* need a rational activation condition, not just based on time, because the cost might be high for the regular user, especially when no malicious activity is detected. In particular, *MTDs* must rely on precise detection mechanisms to gather meaningful information about the attacker's profile. Enhanced adaptive honeypots can provide this intelligence.

2   Capacity Alternating-Time Temporal Logic

ATL does not deal with different agent profiles, while it is essential for precise active defenses like adaptive honeypots and *MTDs*. Consequently, we introduce *Capacity Alternating-time Temporal Logic (CapATL)*, a logic extending *ATL*, to reason about the strategic abilities of agents in a new game structure that captures the information about agent profiles. We call it *Capacity Concurrent Game Structure (CapCGS)*.

A *CapCGS* is a *CGS* where agents are given a set of capacities that specify the actions that the agent can do. For instance, an agent can have a set of two possible capacities, *beginner* or *advanced*, and the *beginner* capacity might only be able to perform simple actions $\{\alpha_1, \alpha_2\}$ while the *advanced* capacity lets the agent do $\{\alpha_2, \alpha_3\}$. At the beginning of the play, each agent is secretly given one of its possible capacities and keeps it during the whole game. Agents cannot observe others' capacity assignments or actions during the play. However, they can observe the history (i.e, the list of game states during the play) and infer knowledge about other agents' capacities. Indeed, if the history is $q_1 q_2$ and the only transition between q_1 and q_2 uses the action α_3 for the opponent, then he must have the capacity *advanced*. This game structure reflects some natural aspects of *MAS*: agents can have different profiles that restrict their actions. This can happen in various situations, such as different client versions in protocol analysis, different robots in heterogeneous fleets, different personality traits in social structure modeling, or different attacker profiles in a cybersecurity setting.

CapATL extends *ATL* with a *knowledge* operator $\mathcal{K}_{\mathsf{cap}}^a$ to ask whether an agent a has some knowledge about the capacity of agents in the game. As in *ATL* [1], a temporal formula specifies in what temporal horizon a subformula should hold. For example, $\mathcal{N} \ell$ is true if the atomic proposition ℓ holds in the *next* state, and $\ell_1 \, \mathcal{U} \, \ell_2$ is true if ℓ_1 holds *until* ℓ_2 holds. Moreover, $\langle \cdot \rangle$ is the strategic operator. It expresses the existence of a strategy to enforce a temporal formula whatever the opponents' actions. For instance, $\langle Y \rangle \mathcal{N} \phi$ asks whether the agents in Y can enforce ϕ in the next state, and $\langle Y \rangle \phi_1 \, \mathcal{U} \, \phi_2$ is true if Y has a strategy to enforce ϕ_1 until ϕ_2 holds.

Semantically, depending on agents' actions, a *CapCGS* will give outcomes ρ of the form $\rho = q_1 \xrightarrow{\boldsymbol{\alpha}_1} q_2 \xrightarrow{\boldsymbol{\alpha}_2} \ldots$, where $\{q_1, q_2, \ldots\}$ are states and $\{\boldsymbol{\alpha}_1, \boldsymbol{\alpha}_2, \ldots\}$ are tuples of actions, i.e, $\boldsymbol{\alpha}_i = (\alpha_{i,1}, \ldots, \alpha_{i,k})$ where k is the number of agents in the *CapCGS*. Thus, an outcome ρ is an infinite path, i.e, a list of states and transitions of the *CapCGS* taken during the play. Since agents cannot change their capacities during the play, each agent a must have at least one capacity c_a such that, for all $i > 0$, $\alpha_{i,a}$ is a possible action for the capacity c_a. We call complete capacity assignment a function λ that assigns a capacity $\lambda(a)$ to each agent a. Thus, given an outcome ρ, we can compute the set of complete capacity assignments $F(\rho)$ that are compatible with ρ. However, agents do not observe the path ρ, but only the states of the path and their own actions. For each agent a, we can define an indistinguishability relation $\sim_a$ such that $\rho \sim_a \rho'$ iff, for all $i > 0$, $q_i = q_i'$ and $\alpha_{i,a} = \alpha_{i,a}'$ where $\rho' = q_1' \xrightarrow{\boldsymbol{\alpha}_1'} q_2' \xrightarrow{\boldsymbol{\alpha}_2'} \ldots$ and $\boldsymbol{\alpha}_i' = (\alpha_{i,1}', \ldots, \alpha_{i,k}')$. Thus, given a path ρ, the knowledge of an agent a, i.e, the set of possible capacity assignment from a's point of view, is $F(\rho, a) := \bigcup_{\rho' \sim_a \rho} F(\rho')$. A formula $\mathcal{K}_{\mathsf{cap}}^a(a' \mapsto c)$ is true given a path ρ if, according to a, every possible complete capacity assignment $\lambda \in F(\rho, a)$ verifies $\lambda(a') = c$.

CapATL model-checking problem is, given a formula ϕ and a *CapCGS*, to find the set of state q such that $q \models \phi$. This problem is decidable and the

precise complexity class is yet to be studied. However, *CapATL* model checking is not polynomial, so it is significantly more complex than *ATL*. Indeed,
even for reachability objectives, the problem of having a compatible complete
capacity assignment arises. Moreover, the knowledge operator in *CapATL* differs
from the one in *Alternating-time Temporal Epistemic Logic (ATEL)* [15,16] since
CapATL deals with imperfect knowledge of agents' capacities and actions, while
ATEL tackles incomplete information about states. This significant difference
impacts the model-checking problem complexity: imperfect information about
states leads to undecidability when agents have perfect recall [9], whereas model
checking is decidable when imperfect information concerns capacities, even with
perfect recall.

3   Case Study

In cybersecurity, identifying the attacker as soon as possible is extremely valuable. Cyber honeypots are decoy systems that aim to lure the attacker from
real resources and collect intelligence about the attacker's behavior and capacities. Honeypots are generally characterized by five attributes [14]: the level of
interaction with the attacker, the *adaptability* during a session of interaction,
the *deployment environment* (on the internet or a private network), the *resource*
type, the *services* implemented, and the virtual or real *implementation*. Adaptive
and interactive honeypots emulate real services and evolve during the interaction
with the attacker. For example, RASSH uses reinforcement learning to keep the
attacker of a fake SSH server active as long as possible [21].

We aim to design a honeypot using a *CapCGS* model and verify its design
using a *CapATL* objective. This objective can include safety (avoiding bad states)
and liveness (eventually reaching good states) properties, but also knowledge
properties like identifying the attacker profile and not being identified as a honeypot. The honeypot is a virtual network with several actions, such as modifying
the topology, the services on different machines, introducing vulnerabilities, etc.
Engineers can imagine a honeypot as a set of challenges and make it more realistic
by incorporating them into a larger system with several attack paths. They can
provide, directly or through a transformation, a *CapCGS* model of the honeypot.
This model relates the honeypot states and the transitions linked to the actions
of the attacker and the defender. We can annotate the states where the attacker
gets a fake reward (e.g, a fake password file) with an atomic proposition *win* and
the states where the attacker compromises the honeypot for real (e.g, he manages to escape from the virtual environment) with an atomic proposition *hacked*.
These atomic propositions will be used to formalize the safety and liveness objectives. Relying on public databases like [18], we extract attacker profiles, denoted
c_1 to c_n, and link them to their respective actions. For instance, c_1 is 'external
employee' and c_2 is 'internal employee', which implies c_2 has the action 'plug USB
device' while c_1 does not. The defender can also have two capacities, *honeypot*
and *real*, where *honeypot* allows some actions that are not possible in a real system, like modifying the output of the `top` Linux command. The last step is to formalize a *CapATL* security objective. For instance, we want the defender to have

a strategy such that the honeypot is never hacked, the attacker cannot identify the system as a honeypot, and when the reward is given to the attacker, we can identify its capacity (i.e, the attacker profile). This property is expressed in *Cap-ATL* as follows: $\langle D \rangle (\neg hacked)\, \mathcal{U}\, (\neg hacked \wedge \neg \mathcal{K}^A_{\mathsf{cap}}(D \mapsto honeypot) \wedge (win \implies (\mathcal{K}^D_{\mathsf{cap}}(A \mapsto c_1) \vee \cdots \vee \mathcal{K}^D_{\mathsf{cap}}(A \mapsto c_n))))$ where the defender is D and the attacker A. Thus, *CapATL* tackles, among others, the attack attribution problem—i.e, finding the attacker capacity—which is one of the primary purposes of honeypots. Using *CapATL* has three main advantages: *(i)* we have strong guarantees on the adequation of the honeypot to the specifications, *(ii)* we automatically access the honeypot adaptation strategy through model checking, and *(iii)* the method is generic and can apply to any adaptive honeypot.

4 Future Works

There are several directions to continue working on *CapATL*. First, we need to identify the precise complexity class of the model-checking problem and provide an efficient algorithm. However, no efficient algorithm can polynomial, which is not satisfactory for real-world applications. We would like to investigate logical fragments and restrictions on the strategies class to find a PTIME problem. In particular, inspired by [17], we can investigate bounded memory agents with dynamic recall. More practically, we want to implement a honeypot verified with *CapATL*, this would validate the applicability of *CapATL*, and it could rely on an optimized algorithm. In the future, we plan to look at quantitative aspects such as in [2] but for capacity aspects. Indeed, the attacker capacity might be quantified through different scores such as network, system, social engineering, *etc.* Moreover, we will get back to *MTD* and exploit the possible symbiosis between adaptive honeypots and *MTD* using strategic verification of *MAS*. Moreover, we can extend our idea to Strategy Logic (SL) [12]. In this way, we can gain expressive power and provide more powerful solution concepts. Since SL is in general non-elementary we can also study some fragments of the logic such as SL[SG] [8]. Furthermore, we can also explore the more realistic setting for games with imperfect information, but unfortunately, as mentioned earlier, the model checking problem with imperfect information for strategic logics is undecidable in general. Given the relevance of this setting, even partial solutions to the problem can be useful, such as abstractions either on the information [4–6] or on the strategies [7] or on the formulas [13]. In conclusion, we can embed the mentioned techniques to provide a more powerful and useful framework.

Acknowledgement. This work was carried out within SEIDO Lab, a joint research laboratory covering research topics in the field of smart grids, e.g, distributed intelligence, service collaboration, cybersecurity, and privacy. It involves researchers from academia (Télécom Paris, Télécom SudParis, CNRS LAAS) and industry (EDF R&D).

The author thank Vadim Malvone, Jean Leneutre, and Youssef Laarouchi for their contribution to the work.

References

1. Alur, R., Henzinger, T.A., Kupferman, O.: Alternating- time temporal logic. English. J. ACM **49**(5), 672–713 (2002). ISSN: 0004–5411. https://doi.org/10.1145/585265.585270

2. Aminof, B., et al.: Graded modalities in strategy logic. Inf. Comput. **261**, 634–649 (2018). https://doi.org/10.1016/j.ic.2018.02.022

3. Ballot, G., et al.: Reasoning about moving target defense in attack modeling formalisms. In: Proceedings of the 9th ACM Workshop on Moving Target Defense. MTD 2022. Los Angeles, CA, USA: Association for Computing Machinery, pp. 55–65 (2022). ISBN: 9781450398787, https://doi.org/10.1145/3560828.3564009

4. Belardinelli, F., Ferrando, A., Malvone, V.: An abstraction-refinement framework for verifying strategic properties in multi-agent systems with imperfect information. Artif. Intell. **316**, 103847 (2023). https://doi.org/10.1016/j.artint.2022.103847

5. Belardinelli, F., Lomuscio, A., Malvone, V.: An abstraction- based method for verifying strategic properties in multi-agent systems with imperfect information. In: The Thirty-Third AAAI Conference on Artificial Intelligence, AAAI 2019, Honolulu, Hawaii, USA, 2019. AAAI Press, pp. 6030–6037 (2019). https://doi.org/10.1609/aaai.v33i01.33016030

6. Belardinelli, F., Malvone, V.: A three-valued approach to strategic abilities under imperfect information. In: Calvanese, D., Erdem, E., Thielscher, M., (eds.) Proceedings of the 17th International Conference on Principles of Knowledge Representation and Reasoning, KR 2020, Rhodes, Greece, 2020, pp. 89–98 (2020). https://doi.org/10.24963/kr.2020/10

7. Belardinelli, F., et al.: Approximating perfect recall when model checking strategic abilities: theory and applications. J. Artif. Intell. Res. **73**, 897–932 (2022). https://doi.org/10.1613/jair.1.12539

8. Belardinelli, F., et al.: Strategy logic with simple goals: tractable reasoning about strategies. In: Kraus, S., (ed.) Proceedings of the Twenty-Eighth International Joint Conference on Artificial Intelligence, IJCAI 2019, Macao, China, August 10–16, pp. 88–94 (2019). https://www.ijcai.org/, https://doi.org/10.24963/ijcai.2019/13

9. Dima, C., Tiplea, F.L.: Model-checking ATL under imperfect information and perfect recall semantics is undecidable. CoRR abs/1102.4225 (2011). https://hal.science/hal-01699948

10. Do, C.T et al.: Game theory for cyber security and privacy. ACM Comput. Surv. 50(2) (2017). ISSN: 0360–0300, https://doi.org/10.1145/3057268

11. Emerson, E.A., Clarke, E.M.: Using branching time temporal logic to synthesize synchronization skeletons. Sci. Comput. Program. **2**(3), 241–266 (1982). ISSN: 0167–6423. https://doi.org/10.1016/0167-6423(83)90017-5, https://www.sciencedirect.com/science/article/pii/0167642383900175

12. Mogavero, F.., et al.: Reasoning about strategies: on the model-checking problem. ACM Trans. Comput. Logic **15**(4), 34:1–34:47 (2014). https://doi.org/10.1145/2631917

13. Ferrando, A., Malvone, V.: Towards the verification of strategic properties in multi-agent systems with imperfect information. In: Agmon, N. (ed.) Proceedings of the 2023 International Conference on Autonomous Agents and Multiagent Systems, AAMAS 2023, London, United Kingdom, 29 May 2023–2, June 2023 ACM, 2023, pp. 793–801. https://doi.org/10.5555/3545946.3598713. URL: https://dl.acm.org/doi/10.5555/3545946.3598713

14. Fraunholz, D., Zimmermann, M., Schotten, H.D.: An adaptive honeypot configuration, deployment and maintenance strategy. In: 2017 19th International Conference on Advanced Communication Technology (ICACT), pp. 53–57 (2017). https://doi.org/10.23919/ICACT.2017.7890056

15. Van Der Hoek, W., Wooldridge, M.: Tractable multiagent planning for epistemic goals. In: The First International Joint Conference on Autonomous Agents & Multiagent Systems, AAMAS 2002, July 15–19, 2002, Bologna, Italy, Proceedings. ACM, pp. 1167–1174 (2002). https://doi.org/10.1145/545056.545095

16. Jamroga, W., van der Hoek, W.: Agents that know how to play. Fundamenta Informaticae **63**(2–3), 185–219 (2004)

17. Jamroga, W., Malvone, V., Murano, A.: Natural strategic ability under imperfect information. In: Elkind, E., et al., (eds.) Proceedings of the 18th International Conference on Autonomous Agents and MultiAgent Systems, AAMAS 2019, Montreal, QC, Canada, May 13–17, 2019. International Foundation for Autonomous Agents and Multiagent Systems, pp. 962–970 (2019). http://dl.acm.org/citation.cfm?id=3331791

18. Mitre Att&ck. https://attack.mitre.org/. Accessed 30 Jan 01 2023

19. Mogavero, F., et al.: Reasoning about strategies: on the model-checking problem. English. ACM Trans. Comput. Logic **15**(4), 1–47 (2014). ISSN: 1529–3785. https://doi.org/10.1145/2631917

20. Okhravi, H., et al.: Finding focus in the blur of moving-target techniques. IEEE Secur. Priv. **12**(2), 16–26 (2014). https://doi.org/10.1109/MSP.2013.137

21. Pauna, A., Bica, I.: RASSH - reinforced adaptive SSH honeypot. In: 2014 10th International Conference on Communications (COMM). IEEE, pp. 1–6 (2014). https://doi.org/10.1109/ICComm.2014.6866707

Value-Awareness Engineering: Towards Learning Context-Based Value Taxonomies

Andrés Holgado-Sánchez[✉][iD]

CETINIA, Universidad Rey Juan Carlos de Madrid, 28933 Móstoles, Spain
andres.holgado@urjc.es

Abstract. The emerging field of *value awareness engineering* claims that software agents and systems should be value-aware, i.e. they should be able to explicitly reason about the value-alignment of their actions. Existing approaches characterize values in various ways, from which we defend the recently introduced context-based value taxonomies, which allow a very rich context-dependent value representation while providing alignment explainability. We propose further work in the area, that would strive mainly on the feasibility for a system to learn value taxonomies from streams of value-aware preferences (using CEP rule learning), so the result is human-readable and representative of a complex value system.

Keywords: Value awareness engineering · Value Learning · Context-based value taxonomies · Complex Event Processing

1 Introduction and Related Work

Value awareness in autonomous systems is an issue that is becoming increasingly important due to the proliferation of AI-based systems that impact people. The emerging field of *value awareness engineering* [10] claims that software agents and systems should be value-aware, i.e. they should be able to explicitly reason about the value-alignment of their actions. Value-alignment problems have being approached in various ways, mostly depending on the application domain considered. In this future research we will focus in state transition systems either for decision-making or value learning in a multi- or single-agent scope. In these and other scenarios, authors came up with different value representations: Weide *et al.* [16] or Sierra and Osman [15] represent values as preordered preference relations; Montes and Sierra [11] used semantics functions, or numerical state alignment metrics; Lera-Leri *et al.* [9] approached the value system aggregation problem through action-based value promotion representation; [1] delved into argumentation techniques that explicitly reference values; [13] constructed a reinforcement learning method to align to norms and values, given by environment rewards; Furnkranz *et al.* [6] and Chirstiano *et al.* [3] represented human preferences with the same technique but parting from trajectories or plans. In the

V. Malvone and A. Murano (Eds.): EUMAS 2023, LNAI 14282, pp. 479–485, 2023.
https://doi.org/10.1007/978-3-031-43264-4_35

three months prior to submitting this report, authors have studied the problem in unpublished work [7,8] around the value-alignment and admissibility concept that we summarize here.

From all the approaches visited, we find the context-based value taxonomy concept by Nardine Osman and Mark d'Inverno [12] inspiring for future research in the area of value learning. This mathematical representation characterizes values by a directed acyclic graph with nodes representing intermediate value concepts derived from automatically satisfied properties from the world states, with relative importance from some condomain dependent on a context.

We argue that this representation has advantages over other approaches, as provides both explainability and computational advantages over all other visited scenarios. Authors also state that this taxonomy can cover most of all the other representations discussed. The point is that, with value taxonomies, a machine can hold specific and clear reasoning with values, apart from optimizing some abstract utility metric or relying on arbitrary human advice of what states or actions or even transitions are aligned or not. The challenge strives then, in how would we be able to learn such useful and meaningful taxonomies in an efficient way, for a single value or groups of them (*value systems*).

We end up proposing to adapt a work on Automatic CEP (Complex Event Processing) rule learning, with temporal and spatial relations, by Ralf Bruns *et al.* [2], in order to learn these context-based value taxonomies, by reading streams of agent actions/state information in order to learn not only semantics functions ([11]) or value aggregation ([9]), but hopefully to elicit aligned agent behaviours in Multi-Agent Systems.

2   Value Awareness as Value-Alignment and Admissibility

On the way towards the value learning objective we have studied other simpler approaches and problems, identifying some issues with existing representations. In [7] we first studied a water allocation problem and the value of equity. Similarly as in [11], we first modelled a MAS (Multi-Agent System) as a goal-oriented decision-making *world* composed of states $\mathcal{S}$ (representing the states of all agents in the MAS), actions $\mathcal{A}$ (representing all possible joint actions) and transitions $\mathcal{T} \subset \mathcal{S} \times \mathcal{A} \times \mathcal{S}$ (eliciting available connections from each state to others via the considered set of actions). We also considered goal states $\mathcal{G} \subset \mathcal{S}$ and plans, which are paths leading to goal states.

We then defined a **state-level preference-based value-alignment** criterion using a mathematical *preorder*, similarly as in [15,16]. It assumed each state has meaning towards value-alignment, grounded via a generic preference relation that compares pairs of states. For instance, $s_1 \sqsubseteq_v s_2$ would represent that state s_2 is more preferable than s_1.

We also considered to quantify those relations in the scenarios where defining state value *semantics functions* [11] is feasible. Specifically, a function $f_v : \mathcal{S} \to \mathbb{R}$ is a semantics function if it is directly proportional to the preservation or alignment of value v in every state. $f_v(s)$ would be the (value) *semantics* of s or the semantics of v in state s. We then defined the concept of **semantics value of a path** as an aggregation function evaluation over the semantics of the path's traversed states (e.g. examples of aggregation are the sum, the mean, etc.).

However, analyzing the legal background of the particular value of equity in water distribution, we realized that certain aggregations might not be acceptable from a legal point of view. In particular, legal requirements may often request to do the appropriate actions in each moment and only looking for the immediate outcome, instead of focusing on an rather long term optimization. Due to this fact, we defined then another concept, which is **value-admissible behaviours**:

Definition 1 (Value-Admissible Behaviour). *A value-admissible behaviour for a value v is a constraint criteria for plans $\mathcal{P}$ that characterizes the subset $B(\mathcal{P}, \sqsubseteq_v)$ that are admissibly aligned with the value, based on state/action-level alignment via a preorder $\sqsubseteq_v$.*

In [8] we trained some policies with reinforcement learning that were able to adhere to specific behaviours regarding equity while having the objective to maximize the expected average path alignment (i.e. semantics of paths). We showed the relevance and the computational feasibility of considering value-admissibility towards value aligning sequences of decisions.

However, limitations exist for reinforcement learning techniques when trying to cope with value-admissible behaviours. Most surveyed RL algorithms ([3,4,6,8,13], for different reasons) will have problems to correctly represent behaviours when the Markov assumption for the policy holds no more (i.e. when the behaviour admissibility depends explicitly on past states/actions).

3   Learning Value-Awareness with Value Taxonomies

So far we discussed some ways to achieve value-aligned decision making within newly introduced value-admissible behaviours. But we took for granted that values are encoded as state preferences inside agents, and we as a society might not know how to model certain complex values with such detail. We want to analyze what aspects the agents consider when taking decisions, regarding their *value system* [14]. We claim that these state preferences, and admissible behaviours should be learned by analyzing (human) agent actions and plans.

A new fine-grained representation needs to be used in order to gather properties of states into value alignment criteria. We found **context-based value taxonomies** [12] a nice candidate towards that end. Instances of value taxonomies (Definition 2) will be able not only to define state-level value preference representation or path value-admissibility, but also to provide mechanisms of explainability with regard to value-alignment based on relevant state or path properties. Moreover, different taxonomies may be used to context-aware *aggregate values* [9] together (i.e. solidarity and equity could both be abstract value concepts for another taxonomy for the value of *reciprocity*). An example of a context-based taxonomy from [12] is seen in Fig. 1a.

Definition 2 ((Context-based) Value Taxonomy). *A (context-based) value taxonomy* $V(c) = (N, E, I_c)$*, based on a context c is defined as a directed acyclic graph, where:*

1. *The set of nodes* $N = N_l \cup N_\varphi$ *represents value concepts, and it is composed of two types of nodes:*
   i) *those that are specified through labels, representing abstract value concepts like 'fairness' or 'reciprocity';*
   ii) *those that are specified through concrete properties of states, such as the Gini Index [7, 11] in allocation problems.*
2. *The set of edges* E : $N \times N$ *is a set of directed edges* $(n_p, n_c) \in E$ *that represent the relation between value concepts* n_p *and* n_c *(parent and child nodes, respectively) illustrating that the value concept* n_p *is a more general concept than* n_c*.*
3. *The importance function* $I_c : N \to COD$ *assigns an importance value from the codomain* COD *to value concepts in* N*, depending on the context c.. The condomain could be an interval* $[-1, 1]$*, for instance.*

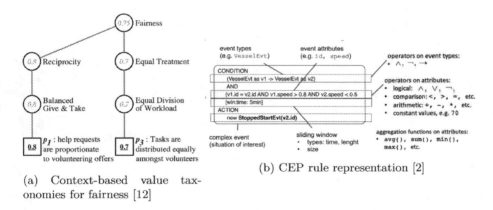

(a) Context-based value taxonomies for fairness [12]

(b) CEP rule representation [2]

Fig. 1. A context-based value taxonomy for fairness [12] (left) and the suggested CEP rule learnable elements [2] (right)

The alignment of an entity e's actions (or states, or behaviours) with a context-based value taxonomy $V(c)$ is then specified in Eq. (1):

$$\mathcal{A}(e, V(c)) = \bigoplus_{p \in N_{\Phi,c}} f(sd(p, e), I_c(p)), \tag{1}$$

where $N_{\Phi,c}$ represents the property nodes of the taxonomy $V(c)$ and $sd(p, e)$ represents the degree of satisfaction of property p with respect to the e's actions. The function f is used to take into account the importance of property nodes when considering their degree of satisfaction, whereas $\oplus$ is used to aggregate those values for all property nodes in $V(c)$.

The work in [12] does not specify a concrete "aggregation language" to define the aggregation function $\oplus$ and the function f. This "aggregation language" may not have a clear accepted definition and we consider that learning it is the way to go to have a proper relevant taxonomic definition of our values. To do so, we propose using work by Bruns *et al.* [2], in the context of CEP rule learning. Specifically, we propose to learn instantiations of aggregation languages where (in Fig. 1b) *CONDITIONS* would characterize taxonomy contexts and *ACTIONS* would consist of calculating a suitable $\mathcal{A}(e, V(c))$ as in (1).

The learning of such instantiations could be accomplished by observing the state transitions that take place in a given system or environment and comparing those transitions with possible alternative ones that an agent (or group of agents) would have chosen. The idea here is that state transitions are partially due to the values an agent has, since they are the results of the actions an agent has chosen based on its values. Other possible actions would lead to other possible state transitions but are not preferred by the agent with respect to her value system. The resulting framework is shown in Fig. 2.

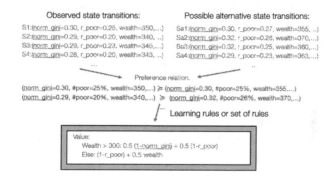

Fig. 2. Schema of the proposed taxonomy-based value learning from events.

Readings of such streams of preferences would lead us to learn no only taxonomies for state preferences, but also identifying admissible behaviours regarding different agent perspectives. Although a bias might arise considering that values are not the only force striving action, this could be sorted out with recent work assessing how much norms and values really influence behaviour [5,11].

4   Conclusions

This extended abstract aims at reviewing work around decision-making with awareness of values, identifying a future line of work for a thesis around the topic of value learning. We defend that an useful value representation providing both explainability and computational resourcefulness are the context-sensitive value taxonomies; and that an useful value taxonomy learning method could be borrowed from Automatic CEP (Complex Event Processing) rule learning.

We claim that this technique would be able to process streams of value-aware agent preferences and actions to characterize complete value systems and value-admissible behaviours in any general decision-making context.

Acknowledgements. This work has been supported by grant VAE: TED2021-131295B-C33 funded by MCIN/AEI/ 10.13039/501100011033 and by the "European Union NextGenerationEU/PRTR".

References

1. Bench-Capon, T., Atkinson, K., McBurney, P.: Using argumentation to model agent decision making in economic experiments. Auton. Agents Multi-Agent Syst. **25**, 183–208 (2012)
2. Bruns, R., Dunkel, J., Seremet, S.: Learning ship activity patterns in maritime data streams: enhancing cep rule learning by temporal and spatial relations and domain-specific functions. IEEE Trans. Intell. Transp. Syst. (2023). https://doi.org/10.1109/TITS.2023.3282246
3. Christiano, P., Leike, J., Brown, T.B., Martic, M., Legg, S., Amodei, D.: Deep reinforcement learning from human preferences (2023)
4. Dalal, G., Dvijotham, K., Vecerik, M., Hester, T., Paduraru, C., Tassa, Y.: Safe exploration in continuous action spaces (2018)
5. Fagundes, M.S., Ossowski, S., Cerquides, J., Noriega, P.: Design and evaluation of norm-aware agents based on normative markov decision processes. Int. J. Approximate Reasoning **78**, 33–61 (2016). https://doi.org/10.1016/j.ijar.2016.06.005, https://www.sciencedirect.com/science/article/pii/S0888613X16300871
6. Fürnkranz, J., Hüllermeier, E., Cheng, W., Park, S.H.: Preference-based reinforcement learning: a formal framework and a policy iteration algorithm. Mach. Learn. **89**, 123–156 (2012)
7. Holgado-Sánchez, A., Arias, J., Moreno-Rebato, M., Ossowski, S.: Value-admissible behaviours in goal-oriented value-aware decision-making. In: Submitted to the 20th European Conference on Multi-Agent Systems (EUMAS 2023) (2023)
8. Holgado-Sánchez, A., Billhardt, H., Ossowski, S.: Learning value-aligned actions in goal-oriented decision-making. In: Submitted to Value Engineering in AI (VALE 2023) Workshop, Affiliated with the 26th European Conference on Artificial Intelligence (ECAI 2023)
9. Lera-Leri, R., Bistaffa, F., Serramia, M., Lopez-Sanchez, M., Rodriguez-Aguilar, J.: Towards pluralistic value alignment: aggregating value systems through Lp-regression. In: Proceedings of the 21st International Conference on Autonomous Agents and Multiagent Systems, pp. 780–788. AAMAS 2022, International Foundation for Autonomous Agents and Multiagent Systems, Richland, SC (2022)
10. Montes, N., Osman, N., Sierra, C., Slavkovik, M.: Value engineering for autonomous agents. CoRR abs/2302.08759 (2023). https://doi.org/10.48550/arXiv.2302.08759, https://doi.org/10.48550/arXiv.2302.08759
11. Montes, N., Sierra, C.: Synthesis and properties of optimally value-aligned normative systems. J. Artif. Intell. Res. **74**, 1739–1774 (2022). https://doi.org/10.1613/jair.1.13487
12. Osman, N., d'Inverno, M.: A computational framework of human values for ethical AI (2023)

13. Rodriguez-Soto, M., Serramia, M., Lopez-Sanchez, M., Rodriguez-Aguilar, J.A.: Instilling moral value alignment by means of multi-objective reinforcement learning. Ethics Inf. Technol. **24**(1), 1–17 (2022). https://doi.org/10.1007/s10676-022-09635-0
14. Schwartz, S.H.: Universals in the content and structure of values: theoretical advances and empirical tests in 20 countries. In: Advances in Experimental Social Psychology, vol. 25, pp. 1–65. Elsevier (1992)
15. Sierra, C., Osman, N., Noriega, P., Sabater-Mir, J., Perelló, A.: Value alignment: a formal approach. CoRR abs/2110.09240 (2021), https://arxiv.org/abs/2110.09240
16. van der Weide, T.L., Dignum, F., Meyer, J.-J.C., Prakken, H., Vreeswijk, G.A.W.: Practical reasoning using values. In: McBurney, P., Rahwan, I., Parsons, S., Maudet, N. (eds.) ArgMAS 2009. LNCS (LNAI), vol. 6057, pp. 79–93. Springer, Heidelberg (2010). https://doi.org/10.1007/978-3-642-12805-9_5

Virtual Environments via Natural Language Agents

Andrea Gatti[✉][iD]

DIBRIS - University of Genoa, Genoa, Italy
andrea.gatti@edu.unige.it

Abstract. VEsNA is a framework for managing Virtual Environments via Natural Language Agents. It allows users to interact with agents using natural language and makes it easy to understand the action of agents through a modern virtual interface.

Keywords: Multi-agent Systems · Natural Language Processing · Virtual Reality

1 Introduction and Motivation

The recent advent of ChatGPT has led to much discussion in the world of scientific research. In addition to generating answers that are indeed plausible, much of the credit for these discussions goes to the rapid spread of the tool. If we check Google Trends[1] for Google searches containing "ChatGPT" by comparing them with two very close research fields, "Chatbot" and "Generative Artificial Intelligence", we obtain the graph visible in Fig. 1.

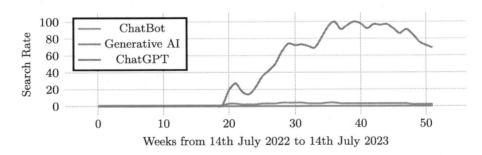

Fig. 1. Google Trend Analysis between "ChatGPT", "ChatBot" and "Generative AI"

---

[1] https://trends.google.com/trends/explore?date=2021-01-01%202023-07-13&q=ChatGPT,%2Fm%2F01305y,%2Fg%2F11khkg2rwf&hl=it. visited on 2023, July 14th.

V. Malvone and A. Murano (Eds.): EUMAS 2023, LNAI 14282, pp. 486–492, 2023.
https://doi.org/10.1007/978-3-031-43264-4_36

This gap between the popularity of the tool and the corresponding areas of research suggests that general interest increases when research finds interfaces that make the technology accessible in a natural way to non-expert users. Chat-GPT presents itself with an interface to which users have long been accustomed.

For this very purpose, VEsNA[2] is introduced, a framework for Virtual Environments via Natural Language Agents. VEsNA allows users to interact with a virtual environment by writing messages in natural language. Within the virtual environment live static objects that can be added or removed, and intelligent virtual agents with a physical body. We presented a first version of the framework in [12] at the AREA (Second Workshop on Agents and Robots for reliable Engineered Autonomy) workshop[3]in the context of IJCAI (International Joint Conferences on Artificial Intelligence Organization) on July 24Th, 2022 and we extended this work in [11].

2   Background

VEsNA exploits three opensource technologies: Rasa for the Natural Language Processing part, JaCaMo for the Multiagent Systems part and Godot for the Virtual Environment part.

Rasa. Rasa [18] is an open-source generative conversational AI platform that allows users to implement their own chatbot. Users define a set of *intents* with which a message can be sent and a set of *actions* that the chatbot can perform. The simplest actions only involve a message on the chat, but more complex actions can be written in Python as complete classes. *Intents* and *actions* are ordered within user-defined *stories* that describe the possible course of a conversation.

Godot. Godot *is a free, all-in-one, cross-platform game engine that makes it easy to create 2D and 3D games.* [13] Godot makes it possible to manage a virtual environment by handling objects as nodes in a tree. Nodes have different types with different characteristics that implement different physical qualities. It is also open to virtual reality and allows scripts to be attached to nodes. Scripts can be written either in GDScript, Godot's native language, or in C# via a plugin that compiles the written code.

JaCaMo. JaCaMo [4,5] *"is a framework for Multi-Agent Programming that combines three separate technologies, each of them being well-known on its own and developed for a number of years so they are fairly robust and fully-fledged"* [6]. JaCaMo uses Jason for programming autonomous agents, Cartago for programming environmental artifacts and Moise for programming multi-agent organisations. It allows the programming of multi-agent systems following the BDI paradigm. Jason extends the AgentSpeak(L) language and allows agents to be programmed in a logic programming language. Agents can be extended using artefacts written in Java.

---

[2] https://github.com/driacats/VEsNA.
[3] https://areaworkshop.github.io/AREA2022/.

3   Related Work

Our work aims to study the intersection of software agents, Virtual Reality and Natural Language Processing. The section is subdivided into three parts: (1) Software Agents and Virtual Reality, (2) Software Agents and Natural Language Processing and (3) Software Agents, Virtual Reality and Natural Language Processing.

Software Agents and Virtual Reality. One of the first appearance of logic programming and Virtual Reality together is in 1999 with LogiMOO [19]. LogiMOO exploits Prolog for distributing group-work over the internet in user-crafted virtual places, where virtual objects and agents live.

In the Master Thesis by N. Poli dating back 2018 [17], simple Belief-Desire-Intention agents were implemented using a lightweight Prolog engine, tuProlog [9], that overcame some limitations of UnityProlog[4], an existing Prolog interpreter compatible with Unity3D. A roadmap to exploit game engines to model MAS that also discusses the results achieved in [17] has been published by S. Mariani and A. Omicini in 2016 [16].

The ThinkEngine [1] is a plugin for Unity that allows developers to program "Brains" using Answer Set Programming, ASP [14,15].

A. Brännström and J. C. Nieves in [7] introduce UnityIIS, a lightweight framework for implementing intelligent interactive systems that integrate symbolic knowledge bases for reasoning, planning, and rational decision-making in interactions with humans. This is done by integrating Web Ontology Language (OWL)-based reasoning [3] and ASP-based planning software into Unity.

Software Agents and Natural Language Processing. One of the first works combining Software Agents and Natural Language Processing dates back almost thirty years ago: E. Csuhaj-Varjú described a multi-agent framework for generating natural languages, motivated by grammar systems from formal language theory [8].

Ten years later, a project about understanding a natural language input using multiagent system techniques was presented by M. M. Aref [2]. In 2004, V. Y. Yoon et al. proposed in [21] a natural language interface for a multi-agent system.

More recently, and more consistently with our work, S. Trott et al. described an implemented system that supports deep semantic natural language understanding for controlling systems with multiple simulated robot agents [20].

Software Agents, Virtual Reality and Natural Language Processing. The proposed work represents a natural evolution of the seminal work described in [11] and [12] that, to the best of my knowledge, is the first to integrate Software Agents, Virtual Reality and Natural Language Processing together. There, together with professor V. Mascardi, I introduce a prototype of VEsNA, a framework for managing Virtual Environments via Natural Language Agents. VEsNA is a general-purpose, domain-free and flexible framework that allows users to

---

[4] https://github.com/ianhorswill/UnityProlog.

interact with a virtual environment by adding and removing objects using natural language.

In [10], together with professor V. Mascardi and Angelo Ferrando, I presented a policy for Rasa [18] that works as online runtime verification monitor.

4   Design and Implementation

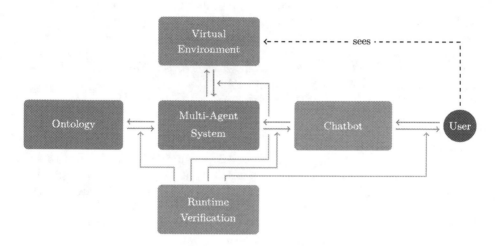

Fig. 2. Architecture of VEsNA

VEsNA is a general-purpose, domain-free, scalable and flexible framework that allows users to interact with a virtual environment using natural language. A schema of the architecture is visible in Fig. 2. Users see a chat and a virtual scene viewed from the outside as the interface. First, the framework enables natural language communication between users and the multi-agent system (MAS). Within the MAS, one agent, called *prompter*, is solely responsible for adding and removing objects from the scene. Second, the framework enables communication between the MAS and virtual reality. The *prompter* and Godot communicate with structured messages in JSON format using a Websocket connection. The *prompter*, in particular, is able to add objects with a global reference to the entire scene (e.g., *"Add a table in front on the right"*) or by referring to one of the objects already in the scene (e.g., *"Add a chair to the left of the table"*). Objects added by the *prompter* are static and cannot be moved.

The framework also allows intelligent agents to be added to the scene. MAS implements the brain of the agents while Godot implements the physical body. The brain and its body also communicate with JSON messages exchanged using the Websocket protocol. We call the brain and body pair *embodied agent*. Each *embodied agent* has its own private port for internal communications. Thus, the brain has access only to that information to which the physical body has access and not to all the information in the scene. When users add an *embodied agent* to the scene the prompter creates a new agent in the MAS and a new body in the scene and tells both a port on which to communicate. From the time the agent is created forward all instructions that come from the user to the agent are routed directly to the agent.

The agent is able to move and see objects, although vision is very rudimentary for the time being. The agent part of the *embodied agent* does not take advantage of all the capabilities of JaCaMo and in particular only performs the actions it knows without yet being able to put them together to find a nontrivial solution.

The framework implements connections between components with well-defined JSON messages that allow for the eventual replacement of one of the components with an equivalent API-compliant one. The framework also implements a runtime verification monitor to ensure the correctness of communications between user and chatbot, presented in [10].

5   Conclusions and Future Work

The framework is in an early stage of development that makes it possible to understand its potential even though it is still in a very primordial stage. The case study that will be considered for implementation is the theater. In this context the *embodied agents* will be the actors and the static objects will be the props instead, and the framework will act as an assistant director helping a hypothetical playwright virtually visualize the plot he or she is writing. The theatrical context will also allow us to study different types of goals, from the least to the most abstract. If in scripts each actor has a sequence of lines and directions that he or she interprets with limited freedom, in canovacci, on the other hand, he or she has more freedom, knowing only the final goal of his or her character and some indications about character and relationships with the other actors. The framework should therefore provide a sufficiently nourished set of actions that can be performed by the actors, actions that can be both physical and communicative with the other actors. It will also need to be able to take in input and handle complex, abstract goals and check during execution whether changes have occurred that necessitate a change of plan. Actors will be influenced in their actions by their own emotions and the relationships they have with other agents and will communicate with each other using natural language, which is also understandable to users.

The framework will also implement an ontology for describing agent knowledge and a runtime verification system that checks the correctness of messages exchanged between components.

When this part of the implementation achieves stability and usability, then new challenges will be faced, particularly immersing users in virtual reality by making them part of the scene and allowing them to communicate directly with *embodied agents* without having a chat as an intermediary. A project in this area of research has potential spin-offs in entertainment (for the creation and enjoyment of content with opportunities for interaction), training (if immersed in virtual reality, users can be exposed to realistic situations that allow them to learn how to handle or execute certain instructions), and rehabilitation (if immersed in virtual reality, users can perform rehabilitation exercises together with a nonhuman instructor).

References

1. Angilica, D., Ianni, G., Pacenza, F.: Declarative AI design in unity using answer set programming. In: IEEE Conference on Games, CoG 2022, Beijing, China, August 21–24, 2022, pp. 417–424. IEEE (2022). https://doi.org/10.1109/CoG51982.2022.9893603
2. Aref, M.M.: A multi-agent system for natural language understanding. In: IEMC 2003. Managing Technologically Driven Organizations: The Human Side of Innovation and Change (IEEE Cat. No.03CH37502), pp. 36–40 (2003). https://doi.org/10.1109/KIMAS.2003.1245018
3. Bechhofer, S., et al.: OWL web ontology language reference. recommendation. In: World Wide Web Consortium (W3C) (2004). http://www.w3.org/TR/owl-ref/
4. Boissier, O., Bordini, R.H., Hubner, J., Ricci, A.: Multi-agent Oriented Programming: Programming Multi-agent Systems Using JaCaMo. MIT Press, Cambridge (2020)
5. Boissier, O., Bordini, R.H., Hübner, J.F., Ricci, A., Santi, A.: Multi-agent oriented programming with JaCaMo. Sci. Comput. Program. **78**(6), 747–761 (2013). https://doi.org/10.1016/j.scico.2011.10.004
6. Boissier, O., Bordini, R.H., Hübner, J.H., Ricci, A., Santi, A.: Jacamo project. http://jacamo.sourceforge.net/
7. Brännström, A., Nieves, J.C.: A Framework for developing interactive intelligent systems in unity. In: Amit Chopra, J.D., Zalila-Wenkstern, R. (eds.) Engineering Multi-Agent Systems (EMAS 2022) (2022). https://emas.in.tu-clausthal.de/2022/papers/paper12.pdf
8. Csuhaj-Varjú, E.: Grammar systems: a multi-agent framework for natural language generation. In: Paun, G. (ed.) Mathematical Aspects of Natural and Formal Languages, World Scientific Series In Computer Science, vol. 43, pp. 63–78. World Scientific (1994). https://doi.org/10.1142/9789814447133_0004
9. Denti, E., Omicini, A., Ricci, A.: Multi-paradigm java-prolog integration in tuProlog. Sci. Comput. Program. **57**(2), 217–250 (2005). https://doi.org/10.1016/j.scico.2005.02.001
10. Ferrando, A., Gatti, A., Mascardi, V.: RV4Rasa: a formalism-agnostic runtime verification framework for verifying chat-bots in rasa. In: Proceedings of the 6th International Workshop on Verification and Monitoring at Runtime Execution (VORTEX 2023), July 18, 2023, Seattle, WA, USA. ACM, New York, NY, USA (2023)
11. Gatti, A., Mascardi, V.: Towards VEsNA, a framework for managing virtual environments via natural language agents. In: Cardoso, R.C., Ferrando, A., Papacchini, F., Askarpour, M., Dennis, L.A. (eds.) Proceedings of the Second Workshop on Agents and Robots for reliable Engineered Autonomy, AREA@IJCAI-ECAI 2022, Vienna, Austria, 24th July 2022. EPTCS, vol. 362, pp. 65–80 (2022). https://doi.org/10.4204/EPTCS.362.8
12. Gatti, A., Mascardi, V.: VEsNA, a framework for virtual environments via natural language agents and its application to factory automation. Robotics **12**(2), 46 (2023). https://doi.org/10.3390/robotics12020046

13. Godot: Godot: Online Resource. https://godotengine.org
14. Lifschitz, V.: Action languages, answer sets, and planning. In: Apt, K.R., Marek, V.W., Truszczynski, M., Warren, D.S. (eds.) The Logic Programming Paradigm. Artificial Intelligence, pp. 357–373. Springer, Heidelberg (1999). https://doi.org/10.1007/978-3-642-60085-2_16
15. Lifschitz, V.: Answer Set Programming. Springer, Cham (2019). https://doi.org/10.1007/978-3-030-24658-7
16. Mariani, S., Omicini, A.: Game engines to model MAS: a research roadmap. In: Santoro, C., Messina, F., Benedetti, M.D. (eds.) 17th Workshop "From Objects to Agents" co-located with 18th European Agent Systems Summer School (EASSS 2016), Catania, Italy, July 29–30, 2016. CEUR Workshop Proceedings, vol. 1664, pp. 106–111. CEUR-WS.org (2016). http://ceur-ws.org/Vol-1664/w18.pdf
17. Poli, N.: Game Engines and MAS: BDI & artifacts in Unity, Master's thesis, Alma Mater Studiorum Universita di Bologna (2018)
18. Rasa: Rasa. https://rasa.com
19. Tarau, P., Bosschere, K.D., Dahl, V., Rochefort, S.: LogiMOO: an extensible multi-user virtual world with natural language control. J. Log. Program. **38**(3), 331–353 (1999). https://doi.org/10.1016/S0743-1066(98)10028-6
20. Trott, S., Appriou, A., Feldman, J., Janin, A.: Natural language understanding and communication for multi-agent systems. In: 2015 AAAI Fall Symposia, Arlington, Virginia, USA, November 12–14, 2015, pp. 137–141. AAAI Press (2015). http://www.aaai.org/ocs/index.php/FSS/FSS15/paper/view/11675
21. Yoon, V.Y., Rubenstein-Montano, B., Wilson, T., Lowry, S.: Natural language interface for a multi agent system. In: 10th Americas Conference on Information Systems, AMCIS 2004, New York, NY, USA, August 6–8, 2004, p. 215. Association for Information Systems (2004). http://aisel.aisnet.org/amcis2004/215

Reasoning About Smart Parking

Silvia Stranieri[✉] [iD]

University of Naples Federico II, Naples, Italy
silvia.stranieri@unina.it

Abstract. Efficient parking management can lead to reduced traffic congestion, lower fuel consumption, decreased air pollution, improved overall urban mobility, and it constitutes a challenge in the automotive field. This work faces the problem by following both algorithmic and formal approaches, relying on practical implementation and rigorous analysis and verification.

1 Introduction

In today's era, the Internet of Things (IoT) is increasingly becoming an essential part of our daily lives [19]. The integration of IoT can be observed in various aspects, including autonomous vehicles [34], smart cities [18], and autonomous vehicular networks [2]). This trend is expected to continue, as evidenced by a study [31] predicting that by 2050, nearly 65% of the population will reside in urban areas. This projected increase in urban population would inevitably lead to a rise in the number of vehicles on city roads, consequently exacerbating several related issues such as traffic congestion, as indicated by a study [30] ranking Rome as one of the European cities with the longest traffic jam delays. Furthermore, this surge in vehicles also contributes to increased gas emissions [29] and a greater demand for parking spaces.

The parking problem refers to the challenges and issues associated with efficiently managing parking spaces in urban areas. IoT offers promising solutions to address the parking problem by leveraging interconnected devices, sensors, and data analysis. Smart parking systems equipped with IoT technology can collect real-time data about parking space availability, occupancy, and duration. Furthermore, parking behavior analysis and prediction based on collected data can help optimize parking space allocation, traffic flow management, and pricing strategies. The detection of available parking slots poses a significant challenge in vehicular ad hoc networks, impacting various aspects. Firstly, the search for an unoccupied parking slot by drivers is a major cause of traffic congestion, as they repeatedly navigate the same roads until they find an available spot. Additionally, the psychological stress experienced by drivers must be considered. Lastly, the issue of environmental pollution is crucial. As highlighted in a study by [20], assessing vehicle energy consumption and urban air quality is essential.

In addressing complex problems, such as those encountered in various domains including technology, science, and society, employing different approaches becomes essential for gaining comprehensive insights and achieving

V. Malvone and A. Murano (Eds.): EUMAS 2023, LNAI 14282, pp. 493–499, 2023.
https://doi.org/10.1007/978-3-031-43264-4_37

optimal solutions. This notion holds true when tackling challenges using both algorithmic and formal methods. By approaching the same problem from multiple perspectives, we can leverage the unique strengths of each approach and gain a deeper understanding of the problem's intricacies.

In literature, the parking problem is mainly treated with algorithmic methods, which offer a practical and efficient approach to problem-solving [1,5–8,11,12,14–16,32], but also with formal methods, that provide a rigorous and systematic approach to problem-solving, drawing upon mathematical models, logical specifications, and formal strategic reasoning [3,17,21,22,26,28].

The thesis [33] advances the state of the art by employing techniques from both approaches. Indeed, when applied to the same problem, algorithmic and formal methods allows us to benefit from the strengths of each approach. Algorithmic methods provide practical implementations, while formal methods offer rigorous analysis and verification. This complementary nature enables us to thoroughly explore problem spaces, refine solutions, and make informed decisions.

2   An Algorithmic Solution

Extensive research has been conducted on solving a well-known optimization problem by drawing inspiration from the behavior of real ants in nature. This optimization problem is commonly referred to as the ant colony optimization problem (ACO). The aim is to utilize this solution approach in a decentralized manner to tackle the parking problem. However, the approach deviates from traditional ACO principles. In typical ACO scenarios, ants are attracted to paths with a higher concentration of pheromone, a chemical substance released by ants that have previously traversed the same path. In contrast, in the proposed scenario, the pheromone acts as a deterrent for drivers to avoid overcrowded situations. Specifically, when a driver follows a particular path, the associated pheromone is updated to inform other drivers that the path may be congested. This mechanism ensures that when a driver needs to choose a path, they will opt for the one with less congestion by following the pheromone trail. As a result, a context-aware and self-organizing network is established, promoting an even distribution of vehicles among available parking slots. This approach also contributes to lower gas emissions as drivers can avoid multiple rounds of searching for a parking space.

More precisely, the model configuration can be seen in Fig. 1, where each driver, that has to park his car, has a starting region that is known, and a destination region towards which he wants to get as close as possible. Hence, the graph configuration depends on a fixed destination region for any driver taking part of the parking process.

For each parking region of the model, and each edge connecting nodes, w is the distance to walk to reach the destination region, and a is the number of available parking spots in the region, while d is the distance to travel by road to reach the destination node of the arc from the source one, and p is the probability with which each vehicle will visit the destination node of the arc from

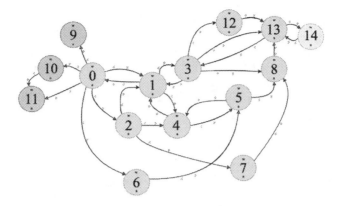

Fig. 1. Parking regions graph.

the source one. Since it is a probability, it is a value between zero and one. As in the standard ACO, this parameter works as the pheromone but, differently form ACO, it has a repulsive power, rather than an attractive one.

In order to avoid drivers choosing the wrong edges, a coloring mechanism is provided. "Wrong edges" means edges that push the driver irreversibly away from the destination, rather than getting him closer to it. Since, at the very beginning of the execution, there is no pheromone yet to inform drivers of which edges should be picked and which should not, a graph coloring is needed to prevent wrong choices that would lead to a bad exploration of the graph. Precisely, a parameter θ is defined, which indicates the maximum distance that is reasonable to walk from the parking slot to the destination: (i) the red nodes are those that do not lead to the destination node, and hence they should be avoided; (ii) the green nodes are the ones that bring to the destination or to a parking region within the distance θ; (iii) the yellow is associated to those nodes v having only one outgoing arc, which is directed only to a node having v among its adjacent nodes. Such a configuration might be source of annoying loops, and for this reason it is imposed that yellow nodes should be visited only once by each vehicle, unless a parking slot is made available in the region: in this last case, a further visit is allowed to complete possibly the parking process. Clearly, as in the standard version of ACO, at the beginning, the graph does not provide a meaningful pheromone information, indeed it has value 1 on every edge. In this phase, the edge chosen by the driver, among the available ones with the same amount of pheromone, is the one that maximizes the ratio $\frac{a}{d*w}$.

Moreover, in order to make simulate the repulsion mechanism, the pheromone on an edge is decreased when a vehicle moves to the pointed node and it is increased when a vehicle leaves the source node. When each vehicle has performed a movement, a total evaporation occurs, meaning that the pheromone is updated so to make attractive again the edges already visited.

Finally, every time a vehicle visits a node already seen, a constraint relaxation is applied, that increases the parameter θ.

3   A Formal Solution

With a formal approach, cars are treated as individual entities in a multi-player game, engaging in competition for parking spots at entry gates. The proposed algorithm is based on priorities for the allocation of parking spaces and it ensures a Nash equilibrium solution. The model definition is explained as follows.

Definition 1. *The Parking Game Structure (PGS) is a tuple $\mathcal{G} = (G, Agt, S, F, T, R)$, where:*

- *$G = \{g_1, g_2, ..., g_n\}$ is set of gates;*
- *$Agt = \{Agt_k\}_{k \in G}$, where $Agt_k = \{a_1, a_2, ..., a_{l_k}\}$ be the set of agents at the gate $k \in G$ (i.e., the* cars *waiting for parking at k), with $\bigcap_{i=1}^n A_i = \emptyset$. We let $l_k = |Agt_k|$ be the number of cars at the gate k; $l_k = |Agt_k|$ be the number of cars at the gate k;*
- *$S = \{s_1, s_2, ..., s_m\}$ is the set of parking slots;*
- *$F = \{F_k\}_{k \in G}$, where $F_k = (f_1, f_2, ..., f_{l_k})$ is the list of* resilience *values for the agents in Agt_k, with $f_i \in [0,1]$ for each $i \in Agt_k$;*
- *$T = \{T_k\}_{k \in G}$, where $T_k = (t_1, t_2, ..., t_{l_k})$ is the list of* time limits *for the agents in Agt_k, where $t_i \in \mathbb{N}$ represents the time the agent i has available for parking starting from gate g_k;*
- *$R = \{R_k\}_{k \in G}$, where $R_k = (r_1, r_2, ..., r_m)$ is the list of* reaching-times *for the gate k, where $r_i \in \mathbb{N}$ represents the time needed to reach the parking slot i from gate g_k, for each $i \in S$.*

The resilience values for the agents have a twofold usage: first, they create an ordering system among the agents, which is essential in determining their prioritization; second, these indexes significantly impact the final preemption order, which can have a significant effect on the overall outcome. The intuition is that the higher the resilience the less the priority for the agent. Such resilience indexes are supposed to be unique, meaning $f_i \neq f_j, \forall 1 \leq i < j \leq n$. The indexes in the set F can either be manually set or automatically determined. In the case of agents, the resilience index represents their capability. Therefore, a lower index value indicates a higher priority.

A *strategy* for an agent involves choosing an appropriate slot. A *strategy profile* is a set of n strategies, one for each player, represented as an n-tuple $\bar{s} = (\bar{s}_1, ..., \bar{s}_n)$. It is important to note that it is possible for multiple players to choose the same strategy. Next, the *costs associated* with the strategy profile $\bar{s}$ is defined as a tuple of costs, denoted as $\bar{c} = (\bar{c}_1, ..., \bar{c}_n)$. Let $B > 0$ be a constant value denoting the highest cost any agent may have for parking.

Definition 2. *Let $a_i \in Agt$ be an agent and $\bar{s} = (\bar{s}_1, ..., \bar{s}_n)$ be a strategy profile. The cost $\bar{c} = (\bar{c}_1, ..., \bar{c}_n)$ is such that:*

$$\bar{c}_i(\bar{s}) = \begin{cases} f_i(t_i - r_i); & \text{if } (i)(t_i - r_i) \geq 0 \ \& \\ \quad (ii)(\nexists k \neq i : f_k < f_i \wedge s_k = s_i \wedge (t_k - r_k) \geq 0) \\ B, \text{ otherwise} \end{cases}$$

The cost value c_i is considered finite if agent a_i has sufficient time to reach the parking slot s_i and the slot has not been occupied by another agent a_k with lower resilience ($f_k < f_i$). In this case, the finite value of c_i reflects the amount of time remaining for the agent after reaching the assigned slot, relative to the total amount of time available to him. On the other hand, if the cost value is assigned as highest, B, it represents the worst outcome for agent a_i, meaning that they were unable to park at slot s_i. The utility of agent i for the strategy profile $\bar{s}$ is $u_i(\bar{s}) = B - \bar{c}_i(\bar{s})$.

That is, $u_i(\bar{s})$ is the difference between the highest cost B and her actual cost c_i given the strategies $\bar{s}$. Finally, the *social welfare* is the sum of utilities of among all agents in the system.

A strategy profile s is a Nash Equilibrium [27] if for all players i and each alternate strategy s_i', we have that $u_i(s_i, s_{-i}) \geq u_i(s_i', s_{-i})$.

In other words, no player i can change his chosen strategy from s_i to s_i' and thereby improve his utility, assuming that all other players stick the strategies they have chosen in s. Observe that such a solution is self-enforcing in the sense that once the players are playing such a solution, it is in every player's best interest to stick to his or her strategy. Then, the total cost, denoted as π, of a strategy $\bar{s}$ is defined as the sum of all the cost values in the tuple $\bar{s}$, that is $\pi(\bar{s}) = \sum_{i \in Ag} c_i$.

Experimental results prove that the algorithm presented in this study efficiently determines a Nash equilibrium for allocating parking slots within a quadratic time frame. It surpasses the performance of a greedy solution by successfully satisfying a greater number of parking requests and achieving higher social welfare. Notably, the Nash algorithm exhibits exceptional effectiveness when the number of cars matches the number of slots, making it the preferred choice for meeting agent demands with significantly superior performance.

4   Conclusions

This work explores the parking problem from both an algorithmic and a formal point of view. Algorithms excel at optimizing processes, allocating resources, and making informed decisions based on available data. They involve designing and implementing step-by-step procedures or algorithms to accomplish specific tasks. Formal methods offer a high level of precision, allowing for the verification, validation, and formal specification of systems and processes. They enable the construction of mathematical models that accurately represent the problem and its constraints, enabling rigorous analysis and verification of system properties. By applying formal methods, we can detect and prevent potential issues, guarantee correctness, ensure safety, and evaluate the performance of systems.

Acknowledgement. This papers is based on the Phd Thesis [33] and the works [1, 4,9,10,13,23–25]. This work is partially supported by the PRIN project RIPER (No. 20203FFYLK).

References

1. Agizza, M., Balzano, W., Stranieri, S.: An improved ant colony optimization based parking algorithm with graph coloring. In: Barolli, L., Hussain, F., Enokido, T. (eds.) AINA 2022. LNNS, vol. 451, pp. 82–94. Springer, Cham (2022). https://doi.org/10.1007/978-3-030-99619-2_8
2. Alsarhan, A., Al-Ghuwairi, A.R., Almalkawi, I.T., Alauthman, M., Al-Dubai, A.: Machine learning-driven optimization for intrusion detection in smart vehicular networks. Wirel. Pers. Commun. **117**(4), 3129–3152 (2021)
3. Aminof, B., Murano, A., Rubin, S., Zuleger, F.: Verification of agent navigation in partially-known environments. Artif. Intell. **308**, 103724 (2022)
4. Arif, M., Balzano, W., Fontanella, A., Stranieri, S., Wang, G., Xing, X.: Integration of 5G, VANETs and blockchain technology. In: TrustCom, pp. 2007–2013 (2020)
5. Balzano, M., Balzano, W., Sorrentino, L., Stranieri, S.: Smart destination-based parking for the optimization of waiting time. In: Barolli, L., Amato, F., Moscato, F., Enokido, T., Takizawa, M. (eds.) WAINA 2020. AISC, vol. 1150, pp. 1019–1027. Springer, Cham (2020). https://doi.org/10.1007/978-3-030-44038-1_94
6. Balzano, W., Barbieri, V., Riccardi, G.: Smart priority park framework based on DDGP3. In: AINA, pp. 674–680. IEEE Computer Society (2018)
7. Balzano, W., Galiano, W., Stranieri, S.: PaSy - management of a smart-parking system based on priority queues. In: Barolli, L., Woungang, I., Enokido, T. (eds.) AINA 2021. LNNS, vol. 227, pp. 81–90. Springer, Cham (2021). https://doi.org/10.1007/978-3-030-75078-7_9
8. Balzano, W., Lapegna, M., Stranieri, S., Vitale, F.: Competitive-blockchain-based parking system with fairness constraints. Soft. Comput. **26**(9), 4151–4162 (2022)
9. Balzano, W., Murano, A., Sorrentino, L., Stranieri, S.: Network signal comparison through waves parameters: a local-alignment-based approach. In: M&N, pp. 1–6. IEEE (2019)
10. Balzano, W., Murano, A., Sorrentino, L., Stranieri, S.: A smart compact traffic network vision based on wave representation. In: Barolli, L., Takizawa, M., Xhafa, F., Enokido, T. (eds.) WAINA 2019. AISC, vol. 927, pp. 870–879. Springer, Cham (2019). https://doi.org/10.1007/978-3-030-15035-8_85
11. Balzano, W., Murano, A., Vitale, F.: V2V-EN - vehicle-2-vehicle elastic network. Procedia Comput. Sci. **98**, 497–502 (2016)
12. Balzano, W., Prosciutto, E., di Covella, B.S., Stranieri, S.: A resource allocation technique for VANETs inspired to the Banker's algorithm. In: Barolli, L. (ed.) 3PGCIC 2022. LNCS, vol. 571, pp. 222–231. Springer, Cham (2022). https://doi.org/10.1007/978-3-031-19945-5_22
13. Balzano, W., Stranieri, S.: ACOp: an algorithm based on ant colony optimization for parking slot detection. In: Barolli, L., Takizawa, M., Xhafa, F., Enokido, T. (eds.) WAINA 2019. AISC, vol. 927, pp. 833–840. Springer, Cham (2019). https://doi.org/10.1007/978-3-030-15035-8_81
14. Balzano, W., Stranieri, S.: COVID-prevention-based parking with risk factor computation. In: Barolli, L., Yim, K., Enokido, T. (eds.) CISIS 2021. LNNS, vol. 278, pp. 121–130. Springer, Cham (2021). https://doi.org/10.1007/978-3-030-79725-6_12
15. Balzano, W., Vitale, F.: DiG-park: a smart parking availability searching method using V2V/V2I and DGP-class problem. In: AINA, pp. 698–703. IEEE Computer Society (2017)

16. Balzano, W., Vitale, F.: PAM-SAD: ubiquitous car parking availability model based on V2V and smartphone activity detection. In: De Pietro, G., Gallo, L., Howlett, R.J., Jain, L.C. (eds.) KES-IIMSS 2017. SIST, vol. 76, pp. 232–240. Springer, Cham (2018). https://doi.org/10.1007/978-3-319-59480-4_24

17. Berthon, R., Maubert, B., Murano, A., Rubin, S., Vardi, M.Y.: Strategy logic with imperfect information. ACM Trans. Comput. Log. **22**(1), 5:1–5:51 (2021)

18. Ghazal, T.M., et al.: IoT for smart cities: machine learning approaches in smart healthcare-a review. Future Internet **13**(8), 218 (2021)

19. Greengard, S.: The Internet of Things. MIT Press, Cambridge (2021)

20. Höglund, P.G.: Parking, energy consumption and air pollution. Scie. Total Environ. **334**, 39–45 (2004)

21. Jameel, F., Zafar, N.A.: Formal modeling and automation of e-payment smart parking system. In: ICoDT2, pp. 1–6. IEEE (2021)

22. Latif, S., Rehman, A., Zafar, N.A.: NFA based formal modeling of smart parking system using TLA+. In: ICISCT, pp. 1–6. IEEE (2019)

23. Malvone, V., Stranieri, S.: Towards a model checking tool for strategy logic with simple goals. In: Proceedings of the 22nd Italian Conference on Theoretical Computer Science, Bologna, Italy, 13–15 September 2021, vol. 3072 of CEUR Workshop Proceedings, pp. 311–316. CEUR-WS.org (2021)

24. Maubert, B., Murano, A., Pinchinat, S., Schwarzentruber, F., Stranieri, S.: Dynamic epistemic logic games with epistemic temporal goals. In: ECAI, vol. 325 of Frontiers in Artificial Intelligence and Applications, pp. 155–162. IOS Press (2020)

25. Maubert, B., Pinchinat, S., Schwarzentruber, F., Stranieri, S.: Concurrent games in dynamic epistemic logic. In: IJCAI, pp. 1877–1883. ijcai.org (2020)

26. Murano, A., Stranieri, S., Mittelmann, M.: Multi-agent parking problem with sequential allocation. In: ICAART, pp. 484–492. SCITEPRESS (2023)

27. Nisan, N., Roughgarden, T., Tardos, E., Vazirani, V.V.: Algorithmic Game Theory. Cambridge University Press, Cambridge (2007)

28. Noviello, F., Mittelmann, M., Murano, A., Stranieri, S.: Parking problem with multiple gates. In: Mathieu, P., Dignum, F., Novais, P., De la Prieta, F. (eds.) PAAMS 2023. Lecture Notes in Computer Science, vol. 13955, pp. 213–224. Springer, Cham (2023). https://doi.org/10.1007/978-3-031-37616-0_18

29. Pope Iii, C.A., et al.: Lung cancer, cardiopulmonary mortality, and long-term exposure to fine particulate air pollution. Jama **287**(9), 1132–1141 (2002)

30. Statista. Cities with the longest traffic jam delays in Europe in 2019, based on average number of hours lost per year (2019)

31. Statista. Proportion of population in cities worldwide from 1985 to 2050 (2021)

32. Stranieri, S.: An indoor smart parking algorithm based on fingerprinting. Future Internet **14**(6), 185 (2022)

33. Stranieri, S.: Vehicular ad Hoc Networks: an algorithmic and a game-theoretic approach. Ph.D. thesis, Universitá di Napoli, Federico II (2022)

34. Wiseman, Y.: Autonomous vehicles. In: Research Anthology on Cross-Disciplinary Designs and Applications of Automation, pp. 878–889. IGI Global (2022)

Towards the Optimization of Speculative PDES Platforms in Shared-Memory Multi-core Machines

Federica Montesano[✉][iD]

University of Rome Tor Vergata, Rome, Italy
federica.montesano@alumni.uniroma2.eu

Abstract. Speculative parallel discrete event simulation on shared-memory machines has become a hot field to study due to its exploitation of massively parallel computing systems. This paper reviews various aspects taken into account during the first two year of the PhD, believing in their relevance also in the context of agent-based simulation. In particular, it first focuses on memory-awareness to improve performance of speculative PDES platforms, it then introduces a new incremental state saving mechanism leveraging operating system's services and finally it describes a way of collecting a global committed state during run-time execution with minimum delay.

Keywords: parallel discrete event simulation · shared-memory machines · load-sharing · parallel computing · agent-based simulation · communication · cooperation · coordination

1 Introduction

Parallel discrete event simulation (PDES) [1,5,15] provides the support for simulating large and complex discrete-event systems and along its life researchers have been designing solutions to exploit computing resources in order to improve overall performance and scalability.

In PDES, a model is typically partitioned into *Logical Processes* (LPs), which are executed across multiple processing units and which process *events*. In traditional PDES, threads manage a subset of LPs for a medium-long amount of time before finding a new binding. To the contrary, a share-everything approach [8,9,11] allows any thread to manage any LP at any time, allowing the simulation to progress more rapidly due to a short-term binding between threads and LPs. The latter is the approach we refer to throughout the paper.

LPs need to be synchronized in order to guarantee correctness. Each LP has a virtual clock to advance its simulation time, to order events to be processed and to send events to other LPs through message passing interface (MPI). Synchronization among LPs is violated if a LP receives out-of-order events, meaning events in the past (the timestamp of the event received is lower than the current LP's clock). We refer to this as a *causality violation*. Consequently, to ensure

© The Author(s), under exclusive license to Springer Nature Switzerland AG 2023
V. Malvone and A. Murano (Eds.): EUMAS 2023, LNAI 14282, pp. 500–506, 2023.
https://doi.org/10.1007/978-3-031-43264-4_38

correct synchronization, a PDES system must satisfy a necessary and sufficient condition widely known as Local Causality Constraint (LCC) [10]. To satisfy LCC a synchronization technique must be adopted.

Synchronization techniques fall into two categories: *conservative* and *optimistic*. The former strictly avoids causality violations to happen, the latter tolerates some causality violations and support state saving and state restoring mechanism to cope with the violations. Optimistic synchronization is the mechanism we refer to throughout the paper, based on the Time Warp algorithm [6].

As a first aspect taken into consideration there is spatial/temporal locality. As stated at the beginning, our paradigm is share-everything, meaning that there is no pre-determined partitioning of LPs among threads and that every thread picks an available LP and processes events destined to it. But nothing comes without a cost, and some limitations of this approach lie in the need of concurrently scanning a global pool of events instead of a per-thread queue, and also in the lack of memory-awareness in both the just mentioned pool and the actual access to the LPs' state. Even though the non-blocking nature of our global pool reduces some problems related to concurrent access to the pool [11,12], the above limitations practically hinder scalability, so we developed a mechanism to fully exploit caching hierarchy also in a NUMA-aware way without increasing the probability of causality violations, as explained in Sect. 2.

As mentioned, optimistic synchronization implies that some mechanism to restore the correct state of the simulation is implemented. Checkpointing techniques for PDES have been extensively studied in the literature. There are two main strategies: periodic state saving [17–19] and incremental state saving [2,20]. The former copies the entire LP's state periodically, the latter copies portions of LP's state based on what has been actually accessed (see Fig. 1). We explored a new incremental state saving mechanism exploiting the operating systems' memory protection facility, in order to minimize the intrusiveness given by instrumentation techniques.

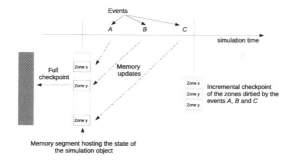

Fig. 1. Incremental state saving in speculative PDES platforms

As a last aspect considered in this paper, we describe the problem of inspecting a portion of the simulation state during run-time execution. The problem to tackle in a speculative environment is ensuring that the state being accessed is a committed one, in order to avoid accessing to a potentially incorrect state due to causality violations. We define a state as committed if the virtual time of every LP is lower than or equal to the last computed *global virtual time* (GVT) [7,16]. The global virtual time is either the smallest local vitual time or the smallest timestamp of all messages in transit.

Output collection and simulation state inspection (also referred to as state swapping) have not been comprehensively studied in the literature [3]. Our contribution has been to develop a mechanism to allow an effective access to the committed global state without hampering simulation execution and in a prompt manner.

The objective of this paper is to present some results achieved during the first two years of PhD regarding the optimization of several aspects of speculative PDES in shared-memory platforms to suggest possible application of some techniques to enhance agent-based simulation performance.

In particular, we present solutions for:

1. exploiting in a better way cache and memory hierarchy without hampering progress of the simulation or causing over-speculation [14] to improve overall performance, in Sect. 2
2. improving state saving/restoring in an optimistic environment in order to reduce memory usage through incremental state saving leveraging memory protection services[1], in Sect. 3
3. collecting the committed global state through state swapping, balancing the workload of the worker threads, in a prompt manner and without hampering actual simulation execution [13], in Sect. 4.

2   Locality Based Load-Sharing and NUMA Awareness

In order to fully exploit the benefits of speculative PDES we have leveraged the concepts of spatial and temporal locality in the following manner: on one hand we favor batch processing of events destined to LPs which are more likely to be in closest cache components respect to a worker thread, on the other hand we develop a window-based mechanism to control the extent of local picking of events to avoid over-speculation by tuning the window's width through conditions regarding both the commit rate of the simulation and the event execution's granularity. This is depicted in Fig. 2.

Furthermore, we consider an additional aspect regarding memory locality, that is NUMA awareness: our locality improvement has been extended to take into consideration also NUMA placement of LPs when trying to pick an event. Locality based load-sharing is relevant for agent-based simulation to reduce the communication overhead between agents. We compared our solution with our baseline speculative simulation platform USE [8], reaching overall better performance in terms of throughput (up to 30% speedup) with negligible overhead.

---

[1] The paper Marotta, Montesano, Pellegrini and Quaglia: *Incremental Checkpointing of Large State Simulation Models with Write-Intensive Events via Memory Update Correlation on Buddy Pages* is currently under review.

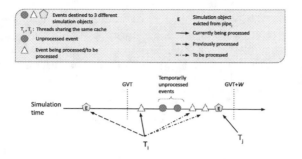

Fig. 2. Spatial/Temporal locality approach

3 Incremental State Saving Exploiting Memory Protection

Incremental state saving has been studied using profiling and/or instrumentation techniques [4] in order to detect actually written memory locations and manage the state saving in a more fine-grained way [23]. Our contribution is based on the exploitation of operating systems' write-protection service and on the concept of buddy pages. In fact, we consider two pages A, B as buddies if they are contiguous and aligned in the segment layout. If these pages are both write-accessed, we group these two pages into a larger page C, actually managed by the checkpointing operation even if just one of the single pages has been write-accessed. During the simulation execution, the write-protection service is switched on/off when saving/restoring the state in order to support the incremental state saving.

The idea of coalescing pages has been adopted to reduce the costs of the write-protection, since its execution brings the operating systems to flush internal memory structures, risking to cause too much overhead. We compared our solution to an instrumentation-based one, observing a higher throughput respect to the instrumentation-based technique (22% speedup), and a large memory reduction respect to the full checkpointing mechanism (about a third of the full checkpoint). Despite the low level solution, it is likely that its application in agent-based simulation would still have benefits in terms of overall efficiency of the state saving procedure.

4 Effective Access to the Committed Global State

In the scenario of fully-shared speculative PDES, when considering the state swapping problem we have to be sure that the portion of state we are considering is committed. An additional problem is caused by the promptness of the approach chosen to make the threads switch from the simulation context to the state swapping context. The latter aspect is very important both for real-time applications and agent-based simulation, to guarantee prompt decisions based on the simulation output. In fact, since agent-based simulation is used to model social/emergency situations or biological dynamics, one might want to promptly have access to the simulation output in order to make some decisions. Since this aspect has not been fully dealt with, we have developed a mechanism to support the access to a committed global state exploiting Linux kernel's facilities, in particular:

1. we developed a two-contexts based mechanism to promptly alert all threads and make them switch from the simulation context to a new context, designated to the collection of the committed state of all LPs, namely state swap activities;
2. the above mentioned mechanism to alert the threads is based on the operating system's service called Inter Processor Interrupt [21,22], which allows to send an interrupt to one or more threads with minimum delay, all managed in several kernel level modules;
3. we developed a mechanism to balance the workload [24] among the threads dedicated to the committed state collection, in order to avoid that a thread which is faster than others in swapping its states returns too early to simulation context, leading to over-optimism in its execution.

We compared our solution with a synchronous signaling mechanism to make threads switch to the state swapping context, showing the effectiveness of our solution in terms of promptness and intrusiveness. In fact, our mechanism takes around 10/30 µs against 300 ms of the synchronous approach to switch from simulation context to state swapping context, and 1 ms against 10 ms to switch back.

5   Conclusions

An overview of the results achieved during the first two years of PhD has been proposed. In particular, a special attention to memory locality has been paid in order to fully exploit the capabilities of speculative PDES. Continuing, a new perspective on the implementation of incremental state saving has been introduced, exploiting memory protection services, along with a memory segment management scheme based on buddies to reduce the costs associated with the mentioned service. Finally, we developed a mechanism to promptly alert threads while executing the simulation to make them switch into another context and start state swapping operation in order to produce a committed global state of the simulation, without impeding the actual progress of the simulation.

Future research directions include integrating low level memory pages management mechanisms to further improve the state swapping operation, and also dynamically adjust resource usage, mainly LPs' state, in order to reduce the memory used by the simulation.

References

1. Andelfinger, P., Köster, T., Uhrmacher, A.: Zero lookahead? Zero problem. The window racer algorithm. In: Proceedings of the 2023 ACM SIGSIM Conference

on Principles of Advanced Discrete Simulation, SIGSIM-PADS 2023, pp. 1–11. Association for Computing Machinery, New York (2023). https://doi.org/10.1145/3573900.3591115

2. Carnà, S., Ferracci, S., Santis, E.D., Pellegrini, A., Quaglia, F.: Hardware-assisted incremental checkpointing in speculative parallel discrete event simulation. In: 2019 Winter Simulation Conference, WSC 2019, National Harbor, MD, USA, 8–11 December 2019, pp. 2759–2770. IEEE (2019). https://doi.org/10.1109/WSC40007.2019.9004901

3. Cucuzzo, D., D'Alessio, S., Quaglia, F., Romano, P.: A lightweight heuristic-based mechanism for collecting committed consistent global states in optimistic simulation. In: 11th IEEE International Symposium on Distributed Simulation and Real-Time Applications, DS-RT 2007, pp. 227–234. IEEE Computer Society (2007). https://doi.org/10.1109/DS-RT.2007.18

4. Economo, S., Cingolani, D., Pellegrini, A., Quaglia, F.: Configurable and efficient memory access tracing via selective expression-based x86 binary instrumentation. In: 24th IEEE International Symposium on Modeling, Analysis and Simulation of Computer and Telecommunication Systems, MASCOTS 2016, London, United Kingdom, 19–21 September 2016, pp. 261–270. IEEE Computer Society (2016). https://doi.org/10.1109/MASCOTS.2016.69

5. Fujimoto, R.M.: Parallel discrete event simulation. Commun. ACM **33**(10), 30–53 (1990). https://doi.org/10.1145/84537.84545

6. Fujimoto, R.M.: Performance of time warp under synthetic workloads. In: Proceedings of the Multiconference on Distributed Simulation, pp. 23–28. Society for Computer Simulation (1990)

7. Fujimoto, R.M., Hybinette, M.: Computing global virtual time in shared-memory multiprocessors. ACM Trans. Model. Comput. Simul. **4**, 425–446 (1997). https://doi.org/10.1145/268403.268404

8. Ianni, M., Marotta, R., Cingolani, D., Pellegrini, A., Quaglia, F.: The ultimate share-everything PDES system. In: Proceedings of the 2018 ACM SIGSIM Conference on Principles of Advanced Discrete Simulation, SIGSIM-PADS 2018, pp. 73–84. Association for Computing Machinery, New York (2018). https://doi.org/10.1145/3200921.3200931

9. Ianni, M., Marotta, R., Pellegrini, A., Quaglia, F.: Towards a fully non-blocking share-everything PDES platform. In: 21st IEEE/ACM International Symposium on Distributed Simulation and Real Time Applications, DS-RT 2017, Rome, Italy, 18–20 October 2017, pp. 25–32. IEEE Computer Society (2017). https://doi.org/10.1109/DISTRA.2017.8167663

10. Jefferson, D.R.: Virtual time. ACM Trans. Program. Lang. Syst. **7**(3), 404–425 (1985). https://doi.org/10.1145/3916.3988

11. Marotta, R., Ianni, M., Pellegrini, A., Quaglia, F.: A lock-free o(1) event pool and its application to share-everything PDES platforms. In: Proceedings of the 20th International Symposium on Distributed Simulation and Real-Time Applications, DS-RT 2016, pp. 53–60. IEEE Press (2016). https://doi.org/10.1109/DS-RT.2016.33

12. Marotta, R., Ianni, M., Pellegrini, A., Quaglia, F.: A conflict-resilient lock-free calendar queue for scalable share-everything PDES platforms. In: Proceedings of the 2017 ACM SIGSIM Conference on Principles of Advanced Discrete Simulation, SIGSIM-PADS 2017, pp. 15–26. Association for Computing Machinery, New York (2017). https://doi.org/10.1145/3064911.3064926

13. Marotta, R., Montesano, F., Quaglia, F.: Effective access to the committed global state in speculative parallel discrete event simulation on multi-core machines. In: Proceedings of the 2023 ACM SIGSIM Conference on Principles of Advanced Discrete Simulation, SIGSIM-PADS 2023, Orlando, FL, USA, 21–23 June 2023, pp. 107–117. ACM (2023). https://doi.org/10.1145/3573900.3591117

14. Montesano, F., Marotta, R., Quaglia, F.: Spatial/temporal locality-based load-sharing in speculative discrete event simulation on multi-core machines. In: SIGSIM-PADS 2022: SIGSIM Conference on Principles of Advanced Discrete Simulation, Atlanta, GA, USA, 8–10 June 2022, pp. 81–92. ACM (2022). https://doi.org/10.1145/3518997.3531026

15. Pellegrini, A., Quaglia, F.: The ROme OpTimistic simulator: a tutorial. In: an Mey, D., et al. (eds.) Euro-Par 2013. LNCS, vol. 8374, pp. 501–512. Springer, Heidelberg (2014). https://doi.org/10.1007/978-3-642-54420-0_49

16. Pellegrini, A., Quaglia, F.: Wait-free global virtual time computation in shared memory timewarp systems. In: 26th IEEE International Symposium on Computer Architecture and High Performance Computing, SBAC-PAD 2014, Paris, France, 22–24 October 2014, pp. 9–16. IEEE Computer Society (2014). https://doi.org/10.1109/SBAC-PAD.2014.38

17. Quaglia, F.: Event history based sparse state saving in time warp. In: Unger, B.W., Ferscha, A. (eds.) Proceedings of the 12th Workshop on Parallel and Distributed Simulation, PADS 1998, Banff, Alberta, Canada, 26–29 May 1998, pp. 72–79. IEEE Computer Society (1998). https://doi.org/10.1109/PADS.1998.685272

18. Quaglia, F.: Combining periodic and probabilistic checkpointing in optimistic simulation. In: Fujimoto, R.M., Turner, S.J. (eds.) Proceedings of the Thirteenth Workshop on Parallel and Distributed Simulation, PADS 1999, Atlanta, GA, USA, 1–4 May 1999, pp. 109–116. IEEE Computer Society (1999). https://doi.org/10.1109/PADS.1999.766167

19. Quaglia, F.: A cost model for selecting checkpoint positions in time warp parallel simulation. IEEE Trans. Parallel Distrib. Syst. **12**(4), 346–362 (2001). https://doi.org/10.1109/71.920586

20. Rönngren, R., Liljenstam, M., Ayani, R., Montagnat, J.: Transparent incremental state saving in time warp parallel discrete event simulation. In: Proceedings of the Tenth Workshop on Parallel and Distributed Simulation, PADS 1996, pp. 70–77. IEEE Computer Society, USA (1996). https://doi.org/10.1145/238788.238818

21. Silvestri, E., Milia, C., Marotta, R., Pellegrini, A., Quaglia, F.: Exploiting interprocessor-interrupts for virtual-time coordination in speculative parallel discrete event simulation. In: Proceedings of the 2020 ACM SIGSIM Conference on Principles of Advanced Discrete Simulation, SIGSIM-PADS 2020, pp. 49–59. Association for Computing Machinery, New York (2020). https://doi.org/10.1145/3384441.3395985

22. Stallings, W.: Operating Systems: Internals and Design Principles, 7th edn. Prentice Hall Press, USA (2011)

23. Toccaceli, R., Quaglia, F.: DyMeLoR: dynamic memory logger and restorer library for optimistic simulation objects with generic memory layout. In: 2012 ACM/IEEE/SCS 26th Workshop on Principles of Advanced and Distributed Simulation, pp. 163–172. IEEE Computer Society, Los Alamitos (2008). https://doi.org/10.1109/PADS.2008.23

24. Vitali, R., Pellegrini, A., Quaglia, F.: Load sharing for optimistic parallel simulations on multi core machines. ACM SIGMETRICS Perform. Eval. Rev. **3**, 2–11 (2012). https://doi.org/10.1145/2425248.2425250

Decidability Borders of Verification of Communicating Datalog Agents

Francesco Di Cosmo[✉][ID]

Free University of Bozen-Bolzano, Bolzano, Italy
fdicosmo@unibz.it

Abstract. We present our recent results in charting the decidability boundary of formal verification of Communicating Datalog Agents, a multi-agent system grounded in logic programming.

Keywords: Logic Programming · Data-Centricity · Petri-Nets

1 Introduction

In Declarative Networking [5], multi-agent systems (MASs) grounded in logic programming have been put forward to simplify the modeling, implementation, and analysis of network services, protocols, and distributed systems [4,24,29]. These agents are data-centric, i.e., their steps are limited to evaluations of queries on databases (DBs), and several languages to specify them are available [1,4,25,26]. An example are Communicating Datalog Agents (CDAs) [10]: a set of data-centric agents, programmed in a specialization of the Datalog query language, affected by the environment via the reception of input DBs, exchanging relational messages on a network of point-to-point channels and are. While the logic perspective facilitates the development of analysis techniques, in spite of previous works [12,13,15,30], a comprehensive study of the decidability and complexity of verification of models like CDAs is lacking. In this paper, we present our results towards closing this gap and, taking into account the characteristic of CDAs, we provide an articulated decidability border of formal verification.

2 CDA Model

While we introduce CDAs assuming familiarity with Datalog with negation, the reader can find preliminaries in footnotes or referring to [2]. A *CDA* is a set V of agents interacting in a *CDA network* $Net = (V, E, N)$ (Fig. 1a), where (V, E) is a directed graph, whose edges $(v, u) \in E$ represent communication channels from v to u, and N is a function assigning to each agent v a relational representation of the local network, in the form of a *network DB* $N(v)$ over the *network signature* $\mathcal{N} = \{\text{name}/1, \text{neigh}/1\}$.[1] The DB $N(v)$ contains the name of

---

[1] A *signature* $\mathcal{A}$ is a finite set $\{A_1/a_1, \ldots, A_n/a_n\}$ where, for $i \in \{1, \ldots, n\}$, A_i is a *symbol* and $a_i \in \mathbb{N}$ is its *arity*. Given a countably infinite set Δ, called *domain*, of constants, a *fact* over $\mathcal{A}$ is a formula $A_i(c_1, \ldots, c_{a_i})$, where $c_J \in \Delta$ for each $J \in \{1, \ldots, a_i\}$. A *DB* over $\mathcal{A}$ is a finite set of facts over $\mathcal{A}$.

V. Malvone and A. Murano (Eds.): EUMAS 2023, LNAI 14282, pp. 507–513, 2023.
https://doi.org/10.1007/978-3-031-43264-4_39

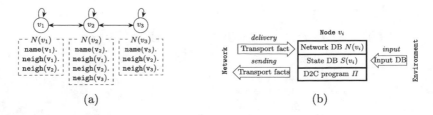

Fig. 1. A CDA network (a), and an arbitrary data-centric CDA node v_i (b).

v and of it neighbors. We focus on connected networks whose edge set is closed under reflexivity and symmetry. This class contains, e.g., complete networks.

Channels are used to send and deliver messages, i.e., facts over a dedicated *message signature* $\mathcal{Q}$. For example, if $\mathcal{Q} = \{Q_0/0, Q_1/1, Q_2/2\}$, a channel (v, u) may contain one message T_0, two copies of the message $Q_1(a)$, for some $a \in \Delta$, and one message $Q_2(v, u)$, sent by v and still to be delivered to u.[2] CDA communication is *asynchronous*, i.e., at each step, only one channel delivers only one message. However, the message to be delivered can be chosen according to several *channel types*: a *perfect* channel delivers all of the sent messages in the same order they were sent; a *lossy* channel may lose some message (which is never delivered), but preserve order; an *unordered* channel delivers all sent messages, but in an arbitrary order. Networks have only one channel type.

The environment provides input DBs to agents according to a *policy* among *interactive* (the input DB is updated non-deterministically at each computation step), *autonomous* (the input DB is non-deterministically chosen and fixed at the first computation step) *closed* (the input DB is always empty).

Each agent (Fig. 1b) is equipped with a relational memory in the form of a *state DB* over a dedicated *state signature* $\mathcal{S}$ and may receive additional information from the environment in the form of an *input DB* over a dedicated *input signature*. Agents *react* to the reception of a message by computing a Datalog-like program Π over the incoming message, the state DB (called *previous*), and the input DB.[3], returning a new state DB, that substitutes the previous one, and a set of outgoing messages that are cast on the channels.[4]

The Datalog-like language used to program agents is D2C, which, in its simplest form, extends Datalog with stratified negation and inequalities by adding labeled literals, i.e., formulas $L@t$, where L is a literal[5] and t is a term, and the construct **prev**. A *D2C program* Π is a finite set of rules

---

[2] Notice that agent names are considered constants in Δ and can appear in facts.

[3] Notice that reactions to changes in the information provided by the environment can still be modeled by sending on the self-loop channel a dedicated message.

[4] In case of ordered channels, the outgoing messages are sent in non-deterministic order. This way, only the order among the messages sent at different steps is relevant. While more sophisticated *casting policies* may be enforced, their relevance is limited, since ordered channels cause almost immediately undecidable verification [8].

[5] Fixed a countably infinite set $\mathcal{V}$ of variables, such that $\Delta \cap \mathcal{V} = \emptyset$, a *term* is a constant or a variable. An *atom* over $\mathcal{A}$ is a formula $A(t_1, \ldots, t_a)$ such that $A/a \in \mathcal{A}$

```
H if B₁,...,Bₙ prev P₁,..., Pₘ, C₁,..., Cₕ.
```

where: 1) the B_is are literals over the state signature (used to query the state DB being computed), input signature (used to query the input DB), or labeled message literals (used to query the incoming message, where the labels represent the name of the sender); 2) the P_is are literals over the state signature (used to query the previous state DB); 3) the C_is are inequality constraints of the form $t_1 \neq t_2$, where t_1 and t_2 are terms; 4) H is a state atom (used to add state facts to the state DB being computed) or labeled message facts (used to produce messages, where the labels represent the name of the recipient). Common Datalog-like assumptions on *safeness* and *stratification* apply (see [10]). For example, the following program incorporates the content of the input predicate I and of the incoming message msg in the state predicate S and, if an incorporated tuple was available also in the previous state DB, then it is sent to all neighbors.

```
S(X) if I(X). S(X) if Msg(X)@Y. Msg(Y)@X if neigh(X),S(Y) prev S(Y).
```

Summarising, a computation of a CDA iterates the following cycle until all channels are empty: 1) asynchronously and according to the channel type, a message m from a node u is delivered to a node v; 2) an input DB I is retrieved according to the policy; 3) a copy S of the state DB of v is provisionally stored as *previous state DB*; 4) v computes the program Π over m, I, and S, producing a new state DB S^+ and a set O of outgoing messages; 5) S^+ substitutes the state DB of v and the messages in O are cast on the channels. To enable startup, initially, all self-loops channels contain the message start.

3   CDA Verification

We chart the decidability boundary of formal verification of CDAs against properties like termination and sometimes (always) convergence: *termination* asks whether the CDA can reach a configuration where all channels are empty; *sometimes (always) convergence* asks whether, for at least one run (for all runs), the CDA reaches a configuration where the agents do not change their state DB anymore. Some relevant related properties are *divergence* (whether agents do not converge), *control-state reachability* (whether the agents reach a target configuration) and *reachability* (whether also channels reach a target configuration).

All of them can be expressed in the CTL_{CDA} language [10], which specializes CTL temporal operators (to analyze the temporal behavior of the system) and FO (to query the local state of agents) to the MAS setting. By focusing on verification of CTL_{CDA}, we can naturally consider sophisticated fragments based on the usage of temporal operators and the signatures of FO queries.

In general, verification of CDA against any of the aforementioned property is undecidable, This is because, thanks to the iterations of the computation cycle, CDA agents can simulate two counter machines (2CMs) [27], whose termination

---

and, for each $i \in \{1, \ldots, a\}$, t_i is a term. A *positive literal* over $\mathcal{A}$ is an atom φ over $\mathcal{A}$. A *negative literal* over $\mathcal{A}$ is a formula **not** φ, where φ is an atom over $\mathcal{A}$.

Table 1. Decidability of termination of prev-aware CDA. B indicates a bounded data-source; PF indicates that the signature cannot occur in the scope of **prev**; ⊤ indicates no constraint.

Input	PF	BPF	BPF	PF	⊤	B	BPF	BPF	PF	B	B
State	B	⊤	B	PF	BPF	B	PF	BPF	BPF	BPF	PF
Channel	B	BPF	PF	BPF	BPF	B	PF	⊤	PF	PF	B
Status	D	U	U	U	U	D	D	U	D	U	D

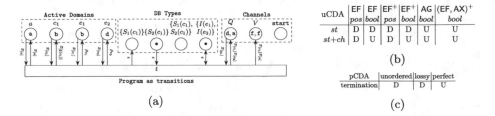

(a)

uCDA	EF pos	EF bool	EF+ pos	EF+ bool	AG bool	(EF, AX)+ bool
st	D	D	D	D	U	U
st+ch	D	U	D	U	U	U

(b)

pCDA	unordered	lossy	perfect
termination	D	D	U

(c)

Fig. 2. A transition in the encoding of a uCDA as a DPN (a), decidability of CTL_{CDA} fragments against unordered uCDA (b), and of termination against pCDA (c). A + indicates nesting of the temporal operators; *pos* and *bool* indicate positive and boolean combinations of temporal operators; *st* and *st + ch* indicate whether FO queries range over the state or also over the message signature.

problem is undecidable. This holds true for any channel type. Thus, we search relevant CDA fragments enjoying decidable verification. These are obtained by constraining the characteristic features of CDAs, e.g., the data-sources sizes, the structure of the program, and the expressiveness of messages.

4   Quest for Decidability

The first constraint we consider is *data-boundedness* [6]. A CDA C is *c-channel bounded* if, for all channels, all reachable configurations contain at most c messages. C is *s-state bounded* if, for all the agents, all reachable state DBs contain at most s different constants. A similar *b-input bounded* constraint can be enforced on the environment, so that it provides only input DBs with at most b constants. By taking advantage of CDA uniformity, we showed that verification of CTL_{CDA} properties of totally (i.e., channel, state, and input) bounded CDAs is PSPACE-complete in the size of the initial configuration and in the number of agents [9,10]. However, even with unordered channels, lifting any of the boundedness conditions results in undecidability (already of termination). The only exception is the lifting of input boundedness over interactive environments: in this case, the agents cannot take advantage of the unbounded input.

Envisaging this peculiarity, we formalized interactive *prev-aware* CDAs [16,19], a generalization of CDAs with unordered channels in which also input and message literals can occur in the scope of **prev**. These are defined by combinations of data-boundedness constraints and type of literals allowed in the scope of **prev**. Table 1 summarizes the decidability border of termination of prev-aware CDAs. In fact, each prev-aware case is a sub-case of a decidable fragment or a generalization of an undecidable one. Decidability is proved by taking advantage of previous results on bounded CDAs and by noticing that constraints on **prev** allow us to forget with impunity the data-values in the various data-sources. This allows to tune abstractions and encodings in suitable computation models with good verification properties, e.g., Petri Nets (PN) [28]. Undecidability is proved via reductions from undecidable problems like satisfiability of stratified Datalog with inequalities [2] or termination of 2CMs. We do so even in very weak fragments, e.g., where all sources of information, except the channels, are bounded and only message symbols can occur in the scope of **prev**. In fact, by exploiting rules like the following, the agent either receives messages in a desirable order, encoding 2CM computations in the channels, or signals an `error` flag.

`error not msg2@X prev msg1@X.`

Inspired by monadic Datalog [7,14] we studied the impact of lifting channel boundedness while weakening the message expressiveness. This is done by bounding the arity messages. Three cases are relevant, i.e., propositional, unary, and binary CDAs (pCDAs, uCDAs, bCDAs), in which the messages have arity 0, at most 1, and at most 2, respectively. Via previous results, verification of bCDAs is undecidable. Instead, reachability-like properties of pCDAs and uCDAs turn out decidable. In fact, we showed [17,18] that pCDAs enjoy of a close correspondence to Communicating Finite State Machines [11], on which reachability is decidable as soon as the channels are not perfect [3]. For uCDAs, we recently tuned an encoding (Fig. 2a) into data PNs (DPN) [22,23,31]. By reducing to data aware PN coverability, we are able to show the decidability border of the extensions of coverability problems in Fig. 2b. This indicates that also pCDA can be encoded in PNs and studied taking advantage of the vast related literature.

5   Conclusions

By exploiting various techniques, we have charted a detailed decidability boundary of verification of CDAs, constraining the characteristic features of the CDA model itself. As a matter of facts, as soon a CDA fragment is capable, even in the most exotic way, to maintain an arbitrary (unbounded) order among tuples, verification of CTL_{CDA} properties becomes undecidable. Nevertheless, we detected relevant decidable fragments. This is the case of uCDAs, which can be seen as a declarative formulation of Petri Nets with data and, thus, can be used to analyse important data-aware concurrent computation models. Hence, we aim implementing a verification tool for this fragment. Currently, we are working towards charting the impact of additional CDA features, most notably the network size and topology. We also plan to extend the programming language towards full Answer Set Programming languages, like *Clingo* [20]; this would enable the integration of CDA verification in frameworks for the analysis of agents learned, e.g., via inductive logic programming tools, like ILASP [21]. Moreover, we plan to implement a tool for the verification of decidable properties of uCDAs.

References

1. Abiteboul, S., Bienvenu, M., Galland, A., Antoine, É.: A rule-based language for web data management. In: Lenzerini, M., Schwentick, T. (eds.) Proceedings of the 30th ACM SIGMOD-SIGACT-SIGART Symposium on Principles of Database Systems, PODS 2011, June 12–16, 2011, Athens, Greece, pp. 293–304. ACM (2011)
2. Abiteboul, S., Hull, R., Vianu, V.: Foundations of Databases. Addison-Wesley, Boston (1995). http://webdam.inria.fr/Alice/
3. Aiswarya, C.: On network topologies and the decidability of reachability problem. In: Georgiou, C., Majumdar, R. (eds.) NETYS 2020. LNCS, vol. 12129, pp. 3–10. Springer, Cham (2021). https://doi.org/10.1007/978-3-030-67087-0_1
4. Alvaro, P., Ameloot, T.J., Hellerstein, J.M., Marczak, W., Van den Bussche, J.: A declarative semantics for Dedalus. Technical report UCB/EECS-2011-120, EECS Department, University of California, Berkeley (2011). http://www.eecs.berkeley.edu/Pubs/TechRpts/2011/EECS-2011-120.html
5. Ameloot, T.J.: Declarative networking: recent theoretical work on coordination, correctness, and declarative semantics. SIGMOD Rec. **43**(2), 5–16 (2014)
6. Belardinelli, F., Lomuscio, A., Patrizi, F.: Verification of agent-based artifact systems. J. Artif. Intell. Res. **51**, 333–376 (2014)
7. Benedikt, M., Bourhis, P., Gottlob, G., Senellart, P.: Monadic datalog, tree validity, and limited access containment. ACM Trans. Comput. Log. **21**(1), 6:1–6:45 (2020)
8. Brand, D., Zafiropulo, P.: On communicating finite-state machines. J. ACM **30**(2), 323–342 (1983)
9. Calvanese, D., Di Cosmo, F., Lobo, J., Montali, M.: Convergence verification of declarative distributed systems (extended version). Submitted to an international journal
10. Calvanese, D., Di Cosmo, F., Lobo, J., Montali, M.: Convergence verification of declarative distributed systems. In: Monica, S., Bergenti, F. (eds.) Proceedings of the 36th Italian Conference on Computational Logic, Parma, Italy, 7–9 September 2021. CEUR Workshop Proceedings, vol. 3002, pp. 62–76. CEUR-WS.org (2021)
11. Chambart, P., Schnoebelen, P.: Mixing lossy and perfect Fifo channels. In: van Breugel, F., Chechik, M. (eds.) CONCUR 2008. LNCS, vol. 5201, pp. 340–355. Springer, Heidelberg (2008). https://doi.org/10.1007/978-3-540-85361-9_28
12. Chen, C., Jia, L., Xu, H., Luo, C., Zhou, W., Loo, B.T.: A program logic for verifying secure routing protocols. In: Ábrahám, E., Palamidessi, C. (eds.) FORTE 2014. LNCS, vol. 8461, pp. 117–132. Springer, Heidelberg (2014). https://doi.org/10.1007/978-3-662-43613-4_8
13. Chen, C., Loh, L.K., Jia, L., Zhou, W., Loo, B.T.: Automated verification of safety properties of declarative networking programs. In: Proceedings of the 17th International Symposium on Principles and Practice of Declarative Programming (PPDP), pp. 79–90 (2015)
14. Cosmadakis, S.S., Gaifman, H., Kanellakis, P.C., Vardi, M.Y.: Decidable optimization problems for database logic programs (preliminary report). In: Simon, J. (ed.) Proceedings of the 20th Annual ACM Symposium on Theory of Computing, 2–4 May 1988, Chicago, Illinois, USA, pp. 477–490. ACM (1988)

15. Deutsch, A., Sui, L., Vianu, V., Zhou, D.: Verification of communicating data-driven web services. In: Vansummeren, S. (ed.) Proceedings of the Twenty-Fifth ACM SIGACT-SIGMOD-SIGART Symposium on Principles of Database Systems, 26–28 June 2006, Chicago, Illinois, USA, pp. 90–99. ACM (2006)

16. Di Cosmo, F.: Verification of Prev-Free communicating Datalog programs (extended version). Submitted to an international conference

17. Di Cosmo, F.: Verification of sometimes termination of lazy-bounded declarative distributed systems (extended version), submitted to ESSLLI 2021 Student Session Best Paper Proceedings

18. Di Cosmo, F.: Verification of sometimes termination of lazy-bounded declarative distributed systems. In: Pedersen, M.Y., Pavlova, A. (eds.) Proceedings of the ESSLLI Student Session 2021, 32nd European Summer School in Logic, Language and Information July 26 - August 13, pp. 13–23 (2021). https://tinyurl.com/2s3v2am2

19. Di Cosmo, F.: Verification of Prev-Free communicating Datalog programs. In: Dovier, A., Formisano, A. (eds.) Proceedings of the 38th Italian Conference on Computational Logic, Udine, Italy, 21–23 June 2023. CEUR Workshop Proceedings, vol. 3428. CEUR-WS.org (2023)

20. Gebser, M., Kaminski, R., Kaufmann, B., Schaub, T.: Multi-shot ASP solving with clingo. Theory Pract. Log. Program. **19**(1), 27–82 (2019)

21. Law, M., Russo, A., Broda, K.: The ILASP system for learning answer set programs. https://www.ilasp.com/ (2015)

22. Lazic, R., Newcomb, T.C., Ouaknine, J., Roscoe, A.W., Worrell, J.: Nets with tokens which carry data. Fundam. Informaticae **88**(3), 251–274 (2008)

23. Lazic, R., Schmitz, S.: The complexity of coverability in ν-petri nets. In: Grohe, M., Koskinen, E., Shankar, N. (eds.) Proceedings of the 31st Annual ACM/IEEE Symposium on Logic in Computer Science, LICS 2016, New York, NY, USA, 5–8 July 2016, pp. 467–476. ACM (2016)

24. Loo, B.T., et al.: Declarative networking. Commun. ACM **52**(11), 87–95 (2009)

25. Loo, B.T., Condie, T., Hellerstein, J.M., Maniatis, P., Roscoe, T., Stoica, I.: Implementing declarative overlays. Oper. Syst. Rev. **39**(5), 75–90 (2005)

26. Ma, J., Le, F., Wood, D., Russo, A., Lobo, J.: A declarative approach to distributed computing: specification, execution and analysis. Theory Pract. Logic Program. **13**, 815–830 (2013)

27. Minsky, M.L.: Computation: Finite and Infinite Machines. Prentice-Hall, Hoboken (1967)

28. Murata, T.: Petri nets: properties, analysis and applications. Proc. IEEE **77**(4), 541–580 (1989)

29. Nigam, V., Jia, L., Loo, B.T., Scedrov, A.: Maintaining distributed logic programs incrementally. Comput. Lang. Syst. Struct. **38**(2), 158–180 (2012)

30. Ren, Y., et al.: FSR: formal analysis and implementation toolkit for safe interdomain routing. Comput. Commun. Rev. **41**(4), 440–441 (2011)

31. Rosa-Velardo, F., de Frutos-Escrig, D.: Decidability and complexity of Petri nets with unordered data. Theor. Comput. Sci. **412**(34), 4439–4451 (2011)

LTL$_f$ Best-Effort Synthesis for Single and Multiple Goal and Planning Domain Specifications

Gianmarco Parretti$^{(\boxtimes)}$

Sapienza Università di Roma, Rome, Italy
parretti@diag.uniroma1.it

Abstract. We study best-effort strategies (aka plans) in fully observable nondeterministic domains (FOND) for goals expressed in Linear Temporal Logic on Finite Traces (LTL$_f$). The notion of best-effort strategy has been introduced to also deal with the scenario when no agent strategy exists that fulfills the goal against every possible nondeterministic environment reaction. Such strategies fulfill the goal if possible, and do their best to do so otherwise. We present a technique for synthesizing best-effort strategies and propose some possible extensions of best-effort synthesis for multiple goal and planning domain specifications.

Keywords: Linear Temporal Logic on Finite Traces (LTL$_f$) · Planning in Nondetermninistic Domains · Best-Effort Strategies · Multiple Goals · Multiple Planning Domains

1 Introduction

Recently there has been quite some interest in synthesis [17,21] for realizing goals (or tasks) φ against environment specifications $\mathcal{E}$ [3,4], especially when both φ and $\mathcal{E}$ are expressed in Linear Temporal Logic on finite traces (LTL$_f$) [15,16], the finite trace variant of LTL [22], a logic specification language that is commonly adopted in Formal Methods [6]. In this setting, synthesis amounts to finding an agent strategy that wins, i.e., generates a trace satisfying φ, whatever is the (counter-)strategy chosen by the environment, which in turn has to satisfy its specification $\mathcal{E}$. This form of synthesis can be seen as an extension of FOND planning [18,19], as shown in, e.g., [9,14].

Obviously, a winning strategy for the agent may not exist. To handle this possibility, the notion of best-effort strategy has been introduced [1]. Best-effort strategies formally capture the idea that the agent could do its best by adopting a strategy that wins against a maximal set (though not all) of possible environment strategies. Best-effort strategies for LTL$_f$ goals and assumptions have some notable properties: (*i*) they always exist, (*ii*) if a winning strategy exists, then best-effort strategies are winning strategies, (*iii*) best-effort strategies can

V. Malvone and A. Murano (Eds.): EUMAS 2023, LNAI 14282, pp. 514–520, 2023.
https://doi.org/10.1007/978-3-031-43264-4_40

be computed in 2EXPTIME, as computing winning strategies (best-effort synthesis is indeed 2EXPTIME-complete). In [5] an algorithm for LTL$_f$ best-effort synthesis has been presented. This algorithm is based on creating, solving, and combining the solutions of three distinct games (with three different objectives) played over a game arena obtained from the deterministic finite-state automata (DFAs) of the LTL$_f$ specifications of the agent goal φ and environment $\mathcal{E}$.

This work studies LTL$_f$ best-effort synthesis in nondeterministic planning domains with full observability (FOND). We begin by motivating why using best-effort strategies in nondeterministic planning domains. Next, we present a technique, based on those in [5,14], for synthesizing best-effort strategies in nondeterministic planning domains. Finally, we propose some further extensions to best-effort synthesis by leveraging existing works on synthesis for LTL$_f$ goals and assumptions.

2   Preliminaries

LTL$_f$ and Automata. *Linear Temporal Logic on Finite Traces* (LTL$_f$) is a formalism for expressing temporal specifications over finite traces. For instance, the LTL$_f$ formula $\Diamond(G)$, where G is a Boolean formula, expresses that G eventually holds. We refer to [15] for more details.

Best-Effort Synthesis for LTL$_f$ Goals and Assumptions [5]. Best-effort synthesis concerns computing a strategy ensuring that the agent does its best to achieve a goal. Formally, best-effort strategies are maximal in the *dominance* order. Specifically, let φ and $\mathcal{E}$ be LTL$_f$ formulas denoting an agent goal and an environment assumption, respectively, and σ_1 and σ_2 be agent strategies. σ_1 *dominates* σ_2, written $\sigma_1 \geq_{\varphi|\mathcal{E}} \sigma_2$, if for every $\sigma_{env} \rhd \mathcal{E}$, $\pi(\sigma_2, \sigma_{env}) \models \varphi$ implies $\pi(\sigma_1, \sigma_{env}) \models \varphi$. Furthermore, σ_1 *strictly dominates* σ_2, written $\sigma_1 >_{\varphi|\mathcal{E}} \sigma_2$, if $\sigma_1 \geq_{\varphi|\mathcal{E}} \sigma_2$ and $\sigma_2 \not\geq_{\varphi|\mathcal{E}} \sigma_1$.

Intuitively, $\sigma_1 >_{\varphi|\mathcal{E}} \sigma_2$ means that σ_1 does at least as well as σ_2 against every environment strategy enforcing $\mathcal{E}$ and strictly better against one such strategy. Then, an agent using a strategy σ_2 strictly dominated by another strategy, say σ_1, is not doing its best to achieve the goal. In fact, the agent could achieve the goal against a strictly larger set of environment strategies if it used σ_2 instead. Within this framework, a best-effort strategy is one which is not strictly dominated by any other strategy. Then, best-effort synthesis for LTL$_f$ goals and assumptions concerns computing an agent strategy σ for which there is no other strategy σ' such that $\sigma' >_{\varphi|\mathcal{E}} \sigma$.

Notably, best-effort strategies always exist and are winning strategies when the problem admits one [5]. Furthermore, Best-effort synthesis is 2EXPTIME-complete and best-effort strategies can be computed in 2EXPTIME, as winning strategies [16]. For further details, we refer to [5].

FOND Planning for LTL$_f$ Goals. Planning in *Fully Observable Nondeterministic* (FOND) domains for LTL$_f$ goals concerns computing a strategy to fulfill a temporally extended goal expressed as an LTL$_f$ formula in a planning domain where the agent has full observability, regardless of how the environment non-deterministically reacts to agent actions. This paper aims at extending existing approaches to planning in FOND domains [8,9,14] with best-effort strategies.

3   Best-Effort Synthesis in Nondeterministic Domains

It is often argued in the literature on planning in nondetermnistic domains that an agent should act even when a winning strategy does not exist, see, e.g., [10,11]. Best-effort strategies provide an interesting approach to this issue, as they always exist and guarantee task completion if the task is realizable. To motivate utilizing best-effort strategies in nondeterministic domains, consider the following example.

Example 1 (adapted from [20]). Consider a robotic autonomous agent and a human operator working on a cooperative assembly task in a shared workspace. In the shared workspace, the robot can move blocks among locations. After every robot action, the human can react by also moving blocks among locations to interfere with the robot, hence introducing nondeterminism to robot actions.

Consider a robot assigned the *task* of assembling an arch of blocks. It is easy to see that the agent has *no winning strategy* to assemble the arch since the human can always disassemble it. Therefore, standard synthesis [14,16] would conclude the task as *unrealizable*, hence "giving up". However, the robot still has the chance to fulfill the goal, should the human cooperate or even perform flawed reactions due to, e.g., lack of adequate training. Therefore, instead of simply giving up, the agent should try its best to pursue the goal by exploiting human reactions. *Best-effort strategies* precisely capture this intuition.

In principle, the framework in [5] can also capture best-effort synthesis in nondeterministic planning domains. In particular, one can re-express FOND domains in LTL$_f$ [3,15,20] and then use directly the LTL$_f$ best-effort synthesis approach. However, doing so does not allow to take full advantage of the specificity of planning domains as environment assumptions, as LTL$_f$ formulas $\mathcal{E}$ representing planning domains are typically large.

Instead, one could directly transform the domain specification into a DFA and solve suitable DFA games for constructing a best-effort strategy. Based on this intuition, we devised a synthesis technique for computing best-effort plans based on solving and combining the solutions of two variants of reachability DFA games, namely adversarial and cooperative, played over the same arena. Intuitively, the adversarial variant requires the agent to reach the goal regardless of environment reactions. In contrast, the cooperative variant only requires the agent to reach the goal should the environment cooperate. The game arena is obtained through *synchronous product* of the DFAs of the planning domain and agent goal. We implemented our synthesis technique by utilizing the symbolic LTL$_f$ framework in [13,25] and the symbolic encoding of planning domains in [20]. An empirical evaluation on a scalable variant of the pick-and-place domains described in Example 1 shows that our technique exhibits orders of magnitude greater scalability than standard best-effort synthesis for LTL$_f$ goals and assumptions. We also observed that LTL$_f$ best-effort synthesis in nondeterministic domains maintains the same complexity as LTL$_f$ FOND planning, i.e., 2EXPTIME-complete and EXPTIME-complete in the size of the goal and domain, respectively [14].

4   Extensions

4.1   Best-Effort Synthesis in Multiple Planning Domains

Many works in the planning and synthesis literature argued that it is not realistic in complex AI scenarios to have a single environment specification, e.g., see [1,2,12]. The scenario in which the agent is provided with two refining models of the environment, namely *expected* and *exceptional*, is already of interest [1]. In such a scenario, the agent should enforce goal completion against all expected environment behaviors, while still providing a satisfactory response to exceptional environment behaviors. That is, the agent should adopt a strategy that is best-effort under both the expected and exceptional environment. In its most general form, this problem is called *best-effort synthesis under multiple environment assumptions* [2].

A natural variation of this problem is *best-effort synthesis under multiple planning domain specifications*. An agent using a strategy that is best-effort under each planning domain specification implements *adaptive behaviors* to changes in its environment. To see this, consider the following variant of Example 1 in Sect. 3.

Example 2. Assume having a robotic autonomous agent assigned to an assembly task in a shared workspace and consider the following two scenarios:

– **Scenario 1.** The agent works on its own on the assembly task, and the effect of all its actions have deterministic effects. Here, we assume that the agent has a winning strategy to assemble the arch.
– **Scenario 2.** As Scenario 1, except that the agent shares its workspace with the human operator, who can also move objects among locations.

In this example, an agent using a best-effort strategy for both Scenarios 1 and 2 is both able to assemble autonomously the arch when the human does not interfere and to deal with the nondeterminism arising from the presence of a human operator. Observe that any strategy synthesized in any of the scenarios above without considering the other does not implement this behavior. To see this, observe that if the agent has only a strategy for Scenario 1, then it will not be able to deal with the nondeterminism coming from the human operator; similarly, if the agent has only a strategy for Scenario 2, it might rely too much on the human operator, without being able to complete the task on its own.

4.2   Best-Effort Synthesis for Multiple Goal Specifications

On the other hand, existing works in the literature argued that providing an agent with multiple goal specifications is reasonable, e.g., [7,24]. Best-effort synthesis provides an interesting approach to this problem as well, as it allows to instruct an agent to use a strategy that does *simultaneously* its best to achieve each goal. An agent using such a strategy can *adapt* its course of actions to environment reactions, depending on which goals are realizable and which are not. To see this, consider the following example.

Example 3. Consider an autonomous agent assigned the task of delivering packages between rooms in a building. In this domain, the robot can move between two rooms only if the door that connects them is open. Assume that in the building, there is a kid who has keys to close some doors, possibly preventing the agent from moving between rooms. At each time step, the kid can also move between rooms and close doors for which he has a key. Consider that the agent has the following tasks:

- **Goal 1.** Reach room R_1 and deliver package P_1;
- **Goal 2.** Reach room R_2 and deliver package P_2.

Assume that the kid has keys to close all doors leading to room R_2 and cannot prevent the agent from reaching room R_1. Then, the agent has a winning strategy for enforcing Goal 1, while it has only a best-effort strategy for Goal 2. In this domain, a best-effort strategy for the agent is first to move to R_1 and, after satisfying Goal 1, try its best to reach R_2.

Again, a best-effort strategy for any of the two goals above without considering the other is not guaranteed to implement this behavior. Indeed, an agent using a best-effort strategy for Goal 1 only, may never reach R_2; instead, an agent using a best-effort strategy for Goal 2 only, may irreparably prevent the realizability of Goal 1 as, e.g., the kid might lock the agent in room R_2.

5   Conclusions and Future Work

This work studied LTL_f best-effort synthesis in nondeterministic domains and proposed some possible extensions. Being best-effort synthesis a new research subject, many other extensions can be developed, and the list presented here is not exhaustive. In fact, a natural extension is to combine the two approaches described in Sects. 4.1 and 4.2. That is, an agent might be provided with multiple goal and domain specifications, and it must synthesize a strategy that is best-effort for each given *goal-domain* pair. Another promising extension is considering maximally permissive strategies [23], which allow the agent to choose a best-effort strategy during execution instead of committing to a single solution beforehand, such that the agent can better adapt to environment reactions. We leave for future work the development of adequate synthesis techniques to solve the problems mentioned above.

Acknowledgements. We thank the contributions of all the co-authors (in alphabetical order): Benjamin Aminof, Giuseppe De Giacomo, Sasha Rubin, and Shufang Zhu. This work has been carried out while Gianmarco Parretti was enrolled in the Italian National Doctorate on Artificial Intelligence run by Sapienza University of Rome. This work has been partially supported by the ERC-ADG White- Mech (No. 834228), the EU ICT-48 2020 project TAILOR (No. 952215), the PRIN project RIPER (No. 20203FFYLK), and the PNRR MUR project FAIR (No. PE0000013).

References

1. Aminof, B., De Giacomo, G., Lomuscio, A., Murano, A., Rubin, S.: Synthesizing strategies under expected and exceptional environment behaviors. In: IJCAI, pp. 1674–1680 (2020)
2. Aminof, B., De Giacomo, G., Lomuscio, A., Murano, A., Rubin, S.: Synthesizing best-effort strategies under multiple environment specifications. In: Proceedings of the International Conference on Principles of Knowledge Representation and Reasoning, pp. 42–51 (2021)
3. Aminof, B., De Giacomo, G., Murano, A., Rubin, S.: Planning and synthesis under assumptions. arXiv (2018)
4. Aminof, B., De Giacomo, G., Murano, A., Rubin, S.: Planning under LTL environment specifications. In: ICAPS, pp. 31–39 (2019)
5. Aminof, B., De Giacomo, G., Rubin, S.: Best-effort synthesis: doing your best is not harder than giving up. In: IJCAI, pp. 1766–1772 (2021)
6. Baier, C., Katoen, J.P., Guldstrand Larsen, K.: Principles of Model Checking. MIT Press, Cambridge (2008)
7. Camacho, A., Bienvenu, M., McIlraith, S.A.: Finite LTL synthesis with environment assumptions and quality measures. In: KR (2018)
8. Camacho, A., Bienvenu, M., McIlraith, S.A.: Towards a unified view of AI planning and reactive synthesis. In: ICAPS, pp. 58–67 (2019)
9. Camacho, A., McIlraith, S.A.: Strong fully observable non-deterministic planning with LTL and LTL$_f$ goals. In: IJCAI, pp. 5523–5531 (2019)
10. Cimatti, A., Pistore, M., Roveri, M., Traverso, P.: Weak, strong, and strong cyclic planning via symbolic model checking. AIJ $1–2$(147), 35–84 (2003)
11. Cimatti, A., Roveri, M., Traverso, P.: Strong planning in non-deterministic domains via model checking. In: AIPS, pp. 36–43 (1998)
12. Ciolek, D.A., D'Ippolito, N., Pozanco, A., Sardiña, S.: Multi-tier automated planning for adaptive behavior. In: ICAPS, pp. 66–74 (2020)
13. De Giacomo, G., Parretti, G., Zhu, S.: Symbolic LTLf best-effort synthesis. In: EUMAS (2023)
14. De Giacomo, G., Rubin, S.: Automata-theoretic foundations of FOND planning for LTLf and LDLf goals. In: IJCAI, pp. 4729–4735 (2018)
15. De Giacomo, G., Vardi, M.Y.: Linear temporal logic and linear dynamic logic on finite traces. In: IJCAI, pp. 854–860 (2013)
16. De Giacomo, G., Vardi, M.Y.: Synthesis for LTL and LDL on finite traces. In: IJCAI, pp. 1558–1564 (2015)
17. Finkbeiner, B.: Synthesis of reactive systems. Dependable Softw. Syst. Eng. **45**, 72–98 (2016)
18. Geffner, H., Bonet, B.: A Concise Introduction to Models and Methods for Automated Planning (2013)
19. Ghallab, M., Nau, D.S., Traverso, P.: Automated Planning - Theory and Practice (2004)
20. He, K., Wells, A.M., Kavraki, L.E., Vardi, M.Y.: Efficient symbolic reactive synthesis for finite-horizon tasks. In: ICRA, pp. 8993–8999 (2019)
21. Pnueli, A., Rosner, R.: On the synthesis of a reactive module. In: POPL, pp. 179–190 (1989)

22. Pnueli, A.: The temporal logic of programs. In: FOCS, pp. 46–57 (1977)
23. Zhu, S., De Giacomo, G.: Act for your duties but maintain your rights. In: Proceedings of the International Conference on Principles of Knowledge Representation and Reasoning, pp. 384–393 (2022)
24. Zhu, S., De Giacomo, G.: Synthesis of Maximally permissive strategies for LTLf specifications. In: IJCAI, pp. 2783–2789. ijcai.org (2022)
25. Zhu, S., Tabajara, L.M., Li, J., Pu, G., Vardi, M.Y.: Symbolic LTL_f synthesis. In: IJCAI, pp. 1362–1369 (2017)

Neurosymbolic Integration of Linear Temporal Logic in Non Symbolic Domains

Elena Umili[(✉)]

Sapienza University of Rome, Rome, Italy
umili@diag.uniroma1.it

Abstract. Linear Temporal Logic (LTL) is widely used to specify temporal relationships and dynamic constraints for autonomous agents. However, in order to be used in practice in real-world domains, this high-level knowledge must be *grounded* in the task domain and integrated with perception and learning modules that are intrinsically continuous and subsymbolic. In this short paper, I describe many ways to integrate formal symbolic knowledge in LTL in non-symbolic domains using deep-learning modules and neuro-symbolic techniques, and I discuss the results obtained in different kinds of applications, ranging from classification of complex data to DFA induction to non-Markovian Reinforcement Learning.

Keywords: Neurosymbolic AI · Linear Temporal Logic · Deep Learning

1 Introduction

Linear Temporal Logic (LTL) [10] is a modal logic widely used in different domains, such as Robotics [7] and Business Process Management [5], for specifying temporal relationships, dynamic constraints, and performing automated reasoning. However, exploiting LTL knowledge in real-world applications can be difficult due to the knowledge's symbolic "crispy" nature. This short paper explores different techniques to relax the knowledge to make it applicable in continuous domains where symbols are grounded through Deep Learning modules and the symbol grounding function and/or the symbolic temporal specification can be unknown or partially known. In particular, we propose two different techniques: (i) one based on Logic Tensor Networks [2,13] and (ii) one based on Probabilistic Finite Automaton [12]. We apply the first approach to classifying sequences of images, and we show that our approach requires less data and is

This work is partially supported by the ERC Advanced Grant WhiteMech (No. 834228), by the EU ICT-48 2020 project TAILOR (No. 952215), by the PRIN project RIPER (No. 20203FFYLK) and by the PNRR MUR project PE0000013-FAIR.

V. Malvone and A. Murano (Eds.): EUMAS 2023, LNAI 14282, pp. 521–527, 2023.
https://doi.org/10.1007/978-3-031-43264-4_41

less prone to overfitting than purely deep-learning-based methods. We use the second approach to learn DFA specifications from traces with gradient-based optimization, showing that it can learn larger automata and is more resilient to noise in the dataset than prior work. Finally, we propose an extension of our second approach [11] that we apply to non-Markovian Deep Reinforcement Learning problems [1]. This third contribution has shown to be more sample efficient of methods based on Recurrent Neural Networks (RNN), and, at the same time, it requires less prior knowledge than methods based on LTL, such as Reward Machines [3] and Restraining Bolts [4].

2   Problem Formulation

We consider the problem of integrating some symbolic background knowledge expressed as an LTLf formula ϕ in a non-symbolic environment producing at each run a sequence of images $I = i_0, i_1, ..i_{l-1}$ and some high-level label over the sequence. Each image in the sequence is the 'rendering' of a symbolic interpretation over the formula alphabet P. This means that there exists a function $sg : \mathcal{I} \rightarrow 2^P$, where $\mathcal{I}$ is the space of images, that maps each image into the truth values of symbols in P, we call this function *symbol grounding function*. We aim to exploit deep learning perception and symbolic reasoning in our system to leverage both subsymbolic data and symbolic knowledge.

3   Models

3.1   Recurrent Logic Tensor Networks

Logic Tensor Networks (LTN) [2] are a neuro-symbolic framework that can reason and learn by exploiting both structured symbolic knowledge and raw data. It implements Real Logic, which is fuzzy relaxation of First Order Logic (FOL). Thanks to continuous logic, neural networks can co-exist in the logic framework and actually implement logic elements, grounding every atom in a real tensor.

LTN can be used for querying, reasoning, and learning: here we focus on learning. LTN can learn from both data and symbolic knowledge by imposing the knowledge available, and searching for the groundings that maximize the satisfiability of that knowledge. This is done by defining a loss objective inverse to the given formula's satisfaction level and optimizing the system's trainable weights by back-propagation.

In our prior work [13], we use the same concept of *learning by best satisfiability*, but we apply it to the DFA generated by the LTLf formula. The neural computational graph implementing the automaton has therefore a *recurrent* structure, like a Long short-term memory (LSTM) neural network, and can be applied to sequences of any length. This feature is missing in the current implementation of LTN, and it is very convenient for imposing logic specifications that are extended in the time dimension.

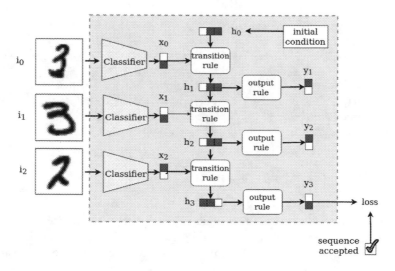

Fig. 1. Design of the Recurrent Logic Tensor Network used in [13].

Our framework is based on three fuzzy predicates: *Symbol*, *State*, and *Output*. The predicate $Symbol(p, t)$ denotes whether the t-th image in the sequence belongs to class p. We ground this predicate with a convolutional neural network, as shown in Fig. 1. At any time t we are in a state q_k of the automaton, we encode this information with another fuzzy predicate *State*, where $State(q_k, t)$ is true if we are in state q_k at time t. Finally, the fuzzy predicate *Output* represents the machine's output in a given time, denoting with $Output(o_i, t)$ whether the machine gives output o_i at time t. In particular, the output can be a symbol in the binary alphabet $\{Acc, Rej\}$ if our temporal specification is a DFA, or a symbol in the alphabet $\{o_0, o_1, ..., o_{N_O - 1}\}$ in case the temporal specification is a Moore Machine.

We use these predicates to define a knowledge base (KB) composed of three axioms: (i) the initial condition, (ii) the transition rule, and (iii) the output rule. In particular, the initial condition only specifies the initial state and does not depend on the classifier predictions. The transition rule calculates the next state given the current automaton state and the symbol prediction over the current image. The output rule calculates the current output given the current state. These two rules are applied recursively as many times as many images compose the sequence.

By applying the rules in the KB, we can monitor the satisfaction of the formula ϕ during time, and, if we know some labels specifying which image sequences are accepted by the formula and which are not, we can impose this information defining a loss on the fuzzy automaton output.

3.2   Probabilistic Relaxation of DFA: DeepDFA

In another prior work [12], we propose a different neural architecture based on Probabilistic Finite Automata (PFA). PFAs are easier to integrate with neural networks since we can calculate the probability that a sequence is accepted by applying matrix multiplications. In particular, we represent a PFA in matrix form as a *transition matrix* M_t, an *input vector* v_i and an *output vector* v_o. Given a string $x = x[0]x[1]...x[l-1]$, the probability that the string is accepted is calculated as follows.

$$v_i \times M_t[x[0]] \times M_t[x[1]] \times ... \times M_t[x[l-1]] \times v_o \qquad (1)$$

In our work, we have designed a recurrent neural network with parameters including a transition matrix and an output vector, resembling the working of a PFA, that we call DeepDFA [12]. Since DFAs can also be represented in the same matrix form, the architecture can impose as background knowledge both DFA and PFA specifications. Differently from the framework presented in Sect. 3.1, this model can only be applied to tasks where the symbols are assumed to be *mutually exclusive*, i.e., at each time step one and only one symbol is true, and the others are false. Another important difference between Recurrent LTN and DeepDFA is that the latter can also be employed to *learn* the DFA specification from traces, and not only to impose it as outside background knowledge. In particular, to learn a DFA from traces with DeepDFA, we have used a specific activation function that smoothly approximates one-hot vectors to drive the PFA to be a DFA during training while maintaining the differentiability of the model.

3.3   DeepDFA with Probabilistic Grounded Symbols

Finally, we propose a slightly different model in [11] that extends DeepDFA to probabilistic grounded symbols. The latter adds to DeepDFA the calculation of the expectation value over the next DFA state using the symbol's probabilities at each time step. It is a more general framework applicable in non-symbolic environments, that we have texted in the context of non-Markovian Reinforcement Learning domains.

4   Applications

4.1   Exploiting LTL Knowledge in Image Sequence Classification

In prior work [13], we used the recurrent LTN architecture explained in Sect. 3.1 to increase the performance of a sequence classifier in visual tasks. In particular, we considered the task of classifying a sequence of images as compliant or not with a given formula, by exploiting the formula knowledge and a set of sequence-level labels expressing if the sequence of images is compliant or not with the formula. Note that we do not assume *any* knowledge of the symbol grounding function. Symbols are grounded in the images implicitly by our framework while it tends to maximize the conformance of the predicted DFA outputs with the sequence labels we have in the dataset. Compared with a purely deep-learning-based approach that cannot exploit the formula knowledge, our approach reaches higher accuracy, even if we decrease the number of samples in the dataset, showing that our way of embedding logical knowledge in the network is very effective.

4.2   Neural DFA Induction from Traces

In another work [12], we tested DeepDFA in learning DFA specifications from labeled sequences of images. Our approach has shown to be very effective in learning compact DFA from data by minimizing the binary cross-entropy loss between the model predictions and the labels. In particular, we compared DeepDFA with a classical combinatorial algorithm for DFA induction based on SAT [15], and we found that our framework can maintain high performances even with large target DFA and with a small percentage of errors in the training data, while the SAT-based approach performs very poorly in these cases. We also compared DeepDFA with another kind of *hybrid* method between RNNs and DFAs: L* extraction [14]. The latter consists of training an RNN on the same task and extracting an equivalent DFA from the RNN. We found that applying this method to some complex languages can be tricky, since it can require training many different RNN architectures before finding the best one for the specific language. Instead, our method has only one hyperparameter, resulting in similar performances and a very much lighter fine-tuning.

4.3   Application to Reinforcement Learning: Visual Reward Machines

Non-Markovian Reinforcement Learning (RL) tasks are arduous, because intelligent agents must consider the entire history of state-action pairs to act rationally in the environment. A common approach to this kind of task uses RNNs to pre-process experience data sequences and automatically extract a state representation for the RL algorithm [6,8,9]. However, there are no theoretical guarantees the resulting state representation will be Markovian. Another kind of approach, such as Reward Machines (RM) [3], uses LTL to specify the temporally-extended tasks and compose a Markovian state representation [4]. However, this approach requires prior knowledge of both the symbol grounding function mapping the environment observations in the specification's symbols and the temporal property. This limits the applicability of this approach in real-world domains. In a previous work [11], we defined Visual Reward Machines (VRM) as a neurosymbolic framework based on the model described in Sect. 3.3. VRMs compose the state representation as RMs, so as to have the same theoretical guarantees in the limit, and they are equivalent to RMs in case of complete knowledge of the task. However, VRMs are still applicable in the case of *missing knowledge* because they can integrate the available prior knowledge with the data they observe in the environment to learn the missing modules (the symbol grounding function and/or the DFA). Compared with methods based on RNNs, our approach reaches higher values of cumulative discounted rewards in visual non-symbolic tasks where RMs cannot be applied.

5   Conclusions

In conclusion, I described many prior works on integrating Linear Temporal Logic in non-symbolic (visual) domains, showing the advantage of relying on both prior structured knowledge and unstructured data acquired in the environment. We remark that future artificial systems should be able to acquire and integrate both these two sources of knowledge from human users and/or the environment, since this is a fundamental milestone of AI systems to achieve complex tasks, and this is the main objective behind our current and future research. In particular, many improvements on the described systems are still possible, such as, for example, integrating richer temporal formalisms such as Alternating-Time Temporal Logic and Signal Temporal Logic, which we let as future research.

References

1. Bacchus, F., Boutilier, C., Grove, A.: Rewarding behaviors, pp. 1160–1167. Portland, OR (1996). https://behaviors.pdf
2. Badreddine, S., d'Avila Garcez, A., Serafini, L., Spranger, M.: Logic tensor networks. Artif. Intell. **303**, 103649 (2022). https://doi.org/10.1016/j.artint.2021.103649
3. Camacho, A., Toro Icarte, R., Klassen, T.Q., Valenzano, R., McIlraith, S.A.: LTL and beyond: formal languages for reward function specification in reinforcement learning. In: Proceedings of the Twenty-Eighth International Joint Conference on Artificial Intelligence, IJCAI 2019, pp. 6065–6073. International Joint Conferences on Artificial Intelligence Organization (2019). https://doi.org/10.24963/ijcai.2019/840
4. Giacomo, G.D., Iocchi, L., Favorito, M., Patrizi, F.: Foundations for restraining bolts: reinforcement learning with LTLF/LDLF restraining specifications (2019)
5. Giacomo, G.D., Masellis, R.D., Grasso, M., Maggi, F.M., Montali, M.: Monitoring business metaconstraints based on LTL and LDL for finite traces. In: BPM (2014)
6. Ha, D., Schmidhuber, J.: Recurrent world models facilitate policy evolution. In: Bengio, S., Wallach, H., Larochelle, H., Grauman, K., Cesa-Bianchi, N., Garnett, R. (eds.) Advances in Neural Information Processing Systems, vol. 31. Curran Associates, Inc. (2018). https://proceedings.neurips.cc/paper/2018/file/2de5d16682c3c35007e4e92982f1a2ba-Paper.pdf
7. He, K., Wells, A.M., Kavraki, L.E., Vardi, M.Y.: Efficient symbolic reactive synthesis for finite-horizon tasks. In: 2019 International Conference on Robotics and Automation (ICRA), pp. 8993–8999 (2019). https://doi.org/10.1109/ICRA.2019.8794170
8. Heess, N., Hunt, J.J., Lillicrap, T.P., Silver, D.: Memory-based control with recurrent neural networks. CoRR abs/1512.04455 (2015). https://arxiv.org/abs/1512.04455

9. Kapturowski, S., Ostrovski, G., Dabney, W., Quan, J., Munos, R.: Recurrent experience replay in distributed reinforcement learning. In: International Conference on Learning Representations (2019). https://openreview.net/forum?id=r1lyTjAqYX
10. Pnueli, A.: The temporal logic of programs. In: 18th Annual Symposium on Foundations of Computer Science, Providence, Rhode Island, USA, 31 October - 1 November 1977, pp. 46–57. IEEE Computer Society (1977). https://doi.org/10.1109/SFCS.1977.32
11. Umili, E., Argenziano, F., Barbin, A., Capobianco, R.: Visual reward machines. In: Proceedings of the 17th International Workshop on Neural-Symbolic Learning and Reasoning, La Certosa di Pontignano, Siena, Italy, 3–5 July 2023, pp. 255–267 (2023). https://ceur-ws.org/Vol-3432/paper23.pdf
12. Umili, E., Capobianco, R.: DeepDFA: a transparent neural network design for DFA induction (2023). https://doi.org/10.13140/RG.2.2.25449.98401
13. Umili, E., Capobianco, R., Giacomo, G.D.: Grounding LTLF specifications in images. In: Proceedings of the 16th International Workshop on Neural-Symbolic Learning and Reasoning as part of the 2nd International Joint Conference on Learning & Reasoning (IJCLR 2022), Cumberland Lodge, Windsor Great Park, UK, 28–30 September 2022, pp. 45–63 (2022). https://ceur-ws.org/Vol-3212/paper4.pdf
14. Weiss, G., Goldberg, Y., Yahav, E.: Extracting automata from recurrent neural networks using queries and counterexamples. In: Dy, J., Krause, A. (eds.) Proceedings of the 35th International Conference on Machine Learning. Proceedings of Machine Learning Research, vol. 80, pp. 5247–5256. PMLR (2018). https://proceedings.mlr.press/v80/weiss18a.html
15. Zakirzyanov, I., Morgado, A., Ignatiev, A., Ulyantsev, V.I., Marques-Silva, J.: Efficient symmetry breaking for sat-based minimum DFA inference. In: LATA (2019)

On Theoretical Questions of Machine Learning, Multi-Agent Systems, and Quantum Computing with Their Reciprocal Applications

Mahyar Sadeghi Garjan[(✉)]

Department of Informatics, Bioengineering, Robotics and Systems Engineering,
University of Genoa, Genoa, Italy
S5283082@studenti.unige.it

Abstract. Recent advances in Multi-Agent Systems (MAS) have shown the importance of this field in computer science. Applications can vary in many different research areas in which the problems can be tackled with distributional AI, like economics, sociology, and psychology. However, there are still challenges and open questions to be answered. Cooperation among agents, implies the existence of a complex connection. Connections can be analysed using GNNs. On the other hand, an agent, per se, should be flexible and adapted to the environment which can be done using RL. In this proposal we are mentioning some challenges and open questions that can be raised by combining these methods in MAS. Additionally, quantum computing is introduced that can fasten the computational effort of ML and MAS programs.

Keywords: Multi-Agent Systems · Machine Learning · Reinforcement Learning · Quantum Computing

1 Introduction

Recent advances in Multi-Agent Systems (MAS) have shown the importance of this field in computer science. Applications can vary in many different research areas in which the problems can be tackled with distributional AI, like economics, sociology, and psychology. However, there are still challenges and open questions to be answered. Particularly in MAS, due to the recent commercial activities of the companies, most of the frameworks and tools are not free. Hence, it slows down, especially, the implementation phase of a MAS research. An instance is traffic control in which with introducing Connected Autonomous Vehicles(CAVs) we are able to enhance the traffic flow on highways and increase safety. Having said this, in a recent research [5], we came up with a free tool, AGAMAS, which is specialised in introducing Autonomous Vehicles (AVs) as agents in Jade that can interact with a simulated environment, called SUMO. AGAMAS provides the basis to implement safety CAVs to influence the traffic flow and speed. Figure 1 represents the architecture of this framework and 2 demonstrates one application of it in which a cluster of vehicles in SUMO that are controlled by a single agent in Jade, have created a block to prevent normal vehicles from their normal flow.

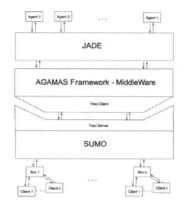

Fig. 1. The Architecture of AGAMAS.

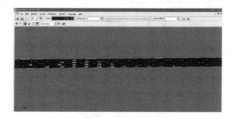

Fig. 2. An application of the AGAMAS in SUMO- Red vehicles are controlled by one agent in Jade that are blocking the normal green vehicles from their normal flow by forcing them to decrease their speed

We used the same framework to devise a control-oriented multi-lane highway model [1] using clusters of CAVs, in which by introducing cluster of CAVs we were able to avoid congestion by forcing other normal vehicles to change their lanes. Considering the experience from our recent researches, more interesting and general questions arose:

1. What would happen if agents were more cooperative and more intelligent?
2. Is it reasonable if we applied ML algorithms to make predictions of accidents in different sections of a highway, so the CAVs could manage the traffic flow to avoid jams in the highway more efficiently?

3. What would be the benefits of applying Reinforcement Learning (RL) instead of explicitly telling agents what actions they should perform?
4. How can we facilitate the cooperation of CAVs, or in general agents in any other domains?

These questions can be generalised to any other domains that agents are playing a crucial role in. However, since agents provide a different approach for programming, it can be exploited in other problems in which the elements of the phenomenon sense the environment and perform actions autonomously. Furthermore, the so-called agents may not be powerful, solely, when it comes to learning behaviours to perform best possible actions and adapting to the environment. As a result, equipping agents with RL can improve them considerably with the intention of making them more intelligent.

In the following sections these concepts will be described in detail to demonstrate why these tools can be useful and how they can be improved, hence, proving a motivation for this proposal.

2   Agents and Learning

Agents are cooperative. In fact, cooperative nature of agents makes MAS to tackle certain problems. However, cooperation among them, implies the existence of a complex connection. Connections can be analysed using GNNs. On the other hand, an agent, per se, should be flexible and adapted to the environment which can be done using RL. As a result, this section will be divided into two main parts of RL and GNNs, in particular.

2.1   Reinforcement Learning

RL is one of the most important branches of AI. Due to its capacity for self-adaption and decision-making in dynamic environments, reinforcement learning has been widely applied in multiple areas, such as healthcare, data markets, autonomous driving, and robotics [4]. Agents' behaviours can be improved by the means of RL. RL is widely applied on the game domain in which the player tries to achieve the highest reward by choosing the actions that highly likely can lead to this aim. As a result, combining RL with MAS can lead to much more efficient results.

Designing some agent-based programs, especially in larger scales in terms of number of the agents to be used and amount of cooperation they acquire, can be a complex task. Studying RL algorithms and exploiting it, particularly in MAS, can tackle this issue by making agents learn and adapt to the environment more efficiently. However, there are open questions that require significant amount of research work, like:

1. How to determine whether an agent is doing good, intelligent exploration?
2. What metrics should be used to evaluate the agents' behaviours, while exploiting the environment randomly as initial steps?

3. How well do exploration methods generalize across environments?
4. How can this generalization be measured?
5. Can ensembles of policies and/or value functions enable faster or safer exploration?

In any case, equipping agents with RL raises its own questions, especially when it comes to safety issues which are dependent on the amount of autonomy agents can have to choose their actions.

MAS and RL can benefit from each other and their improvements will affect the other significantly. An open question in RL is designing algorithms that make a trade-off between exploration and exploitation. Exploration, simply, means that agents should try actions or states that they haven't seen yet. On the other hand, exploitation is choosing actions that lead to highest reward [3]. Hence, exploitation prevents the agent from trying different states that may result in even higher rewards.

2.2   Graph Neural Networks- GNNs

One of the main features of the agents is their cooperation. Cooperation entails the existence of a highly complex and meaningful connection. GNNs, as a powerful tool, can be exploited to enhance, analyse, and understand the cooperation among agents. Taking this into consideration, we can improve agent-agent communication and collaboration. A study case has demonstrate the effectiveness of this approach in which the final aim is to find the most efficient interaction of agents that can lead to optimal cooperation by the means of RL and GNNs to improve the cooperation of CAVs, by considering CAVs as nodes of the graph and connection among them as edges [2]. Although GNNs are powerful methods in analysing any phenomenon that can be described as graphs, but, still, there are some questions that should be addressed to achieve further advances in this field. Heterogeneity, scalability, and interpretability of the GNNs are some of the problems that are needed to be tackled with further research.

3   Quantum Computing (QC) Impact on MAS and ML

Quantum computing utilizes a qubit as the basic unit of computation. The qubit represents a quantum superposition state between two basis states, which denoted as $|0\langle$ and $|1\rangle$ [7]. Considering this, by increasing the qubits, number of the possible states will increase exponentially which provides the capability to compute very complex computational problems, like cryptography [6].

Needless to say, taking the recent advances in QC into account, migration from conventional digital computers to quantum computers is inevitable. One of the the most revolutionary fields that will shape our future is application of QC in ML and MAS. A remarkable example is the variational quantum circuit (VQC) architecture, also known as a quantum neural network (QNN), which integrates a quantum circuit into a classical deep neural network [7].

Quantum computing will allow us to accelerate the training and inference speed while saving computing resources [7]. Hence, we could build up much more complex agents with remarkable capability of learning and adapting to the environment.

As it is demonstrated in paper [7], Quantum Multi-Agent Reinforcement Learning (QMARL) framework enhances 57.7% of total reward than classical frameworks. When it comes to RL, the final goal is to increase the reward as much as possible. Training RL algorithms in an organization of agents, in a highly complex environment with considerable number of parameters, is out of classical computers' capability. Hence, new methods, like QMARL, should be utilized and designed.

Indeed, QC hardwares are not yet available for the public, but, still, computer scientist, specialised in ML and MAS, should prepare themselves for the near future with their contribution to answering to some fundamental questions, raised by science community. Some of these questions are listed below:

1. What is the classical analogue of my quantum machine learning algorithm?
2. How well my QML algorithm performs compared to their corresponding classical algorithms?

First question demands theoretical research work to see if new quantum-based methods correspond to conventional algorithms. Second question, on the other hand, requires experiments for comparison of QC methods and classical approaches. However, most theoretical questions raise when we want to come up with quantum-friendly versions of conventional algorithms. Hence, a lot of researches should be done in this area.

4   Conclusion

Throughout this proposal, some general topics have been mentioned that have great potentials to improve and combine with other tools. All the challenges that we have encountered in the ongoing SEED project, in university of Genova, that mainly has focused on the application of MAS, ML, and, in particular, RL, in traffic control, including lack of sufficient tools for implementing CAVs, have lead us to design and contribute more in the above-mentioned topics, especially in creating AGAMAS. Cooperation and intelligence of the agents can be improved significantly with exploiting other methods, like RL and GNNs. However, these specific areas contain their own special challenges, like the trade-off between exploration and exploitation in RL methods. QC, on the other hand, in few years, will have significant impact on computer science. Exploiting quantum computers and adjusting the conventional methods with this newly emerged computational tool requires inevitable research effort that may shape our future.

Although in this proposal we have mentioned challenges in traffic, but there are a lot of interesting areas that MAS and ML can be applied. Besides the applications, it would be very interesting if we could tackle theoretical questions and form mathematical models for what have been mentioned in this proposal.

References

1. Chaanine, T., Ferrando, A., Caterina Pasquale, C., Paolo Pastore, V., Sadeghi Garjan, M., Siri, S.: A control-oriented highway traffic model with multiple clusters of CAVs. In: IEEE Intelligent Transportation Systems Society Conference Management System (2023)
2. Chen, S., Dong, J., Ha, P., Li, Y., Labi, S.: Graph neural network and reinforcement learning for multi-agent cooperative control of connected autonomous vehicles. Comput.-Aided Civil Infrastruct. Eng. **36**(7), 838–857 (2021)
3. Colas, C., Sigaud, O., Oudeyer, P.Y.: Decoupling exploration and exploitation in deep reinforcement learning algorithms. In: International Conference on Machine Learning, pp. 1039–1048 (2018)
4. Lei, Y., Ye, D., Shen, S., Sui, Y., Zhu, T., Zhou, W.: New challenges in reinforcement learning: a survey of security and privacy. Artif. Intell. Rev. **56**, 7195–7236 (2022)
5. Sadeghi Garjan, M., Chaanine, T., Caterina Pasquale, C., Paolo Pastore, V., Ferrando, A.: Agamas: a new agent-oriented traffic simulation framework for sumo. In: 20th European Conference on Multi-Agent Systems (2023)
6. Yang, Z., Zolanvari, M., Jain, R.: A survey of important issues in quantum computing and communications. IEEE Commun. Surv. Tutor. (2023)
7. Yun, W.J., et al.: Quantum multi-agent reinforcement learning via variational quantum circuit design. In: 2022 IEEE 42nd International Conference on Distributed Computing Systems (ICDCS), pp. 1332–1335. IEEE (2022)

Optimal Rescue Sequences in Disastrous Incidents

Rabeaeh Kiaghadi[✉]

Carl von Ossietzky Universität Oldenburg, 26129 Oldenburg, Germany
Rabeaeh.kiaghadi@uni-oldenburg.de

Abstract. With embedded technology becoming able to pursue autonomous decision-making in complex environments, reliable multi-agent robotic systems drawing optimal decisions in autonomous search and rescue (SAR) missions, without human involvement, become feasible. The objective of this study is to design a control algorithm and provide simulation for an autonomous robotic system in the event of a hazardous incident where the environment is highly stochastic and supply injured people/patients with help. Therefore, time management plays the key role in the number of patients saved as their health condition follows a probabilistic degrading figure. We have modeled robot and patients utilizing an interactive continuous Markov chain, followed by a Genetic-based algorithm for the robot to plan a path with the close to the theoretically possible maximum expected number of the patient rescued.

Keywords: Search and rescue missions · Stochastic model-based optimization · Time-critical decision making · Multi-agent Operation

1 Introduction

Every day, our world faces perilous incidents. In the majority of instances, rescue operations encounter challenges stemming from decision making under massive uncertainty, where the uncertainties pertain to the health states of the casualties and to the environment. Significant financial and life losses may be induced by suboptimal search and rescue sequences such that decision making plays a key role. Moreover, time emerges as one of the most vital factors and time management the top priority in any decision-making process for such incidents where lives are at stake [13,15,16]. Otherwise, the consequences will be irrecoverable. However, there are scenarios where human efficiency reaches its limits. Thus, The necessity for a secure alternative solution in such circumstances has become of crucial importance. This is where robots set foot in.

2 Related Works

The robotic world is a diverse domain and every task requires a specific robotic system. Among those, Robustness, scalability and flexibility, as well as distributed sensing, make swarm robotic systems well suited for rescue missions in

V. Malvone and A. Murano (Eds.): EUMAS 2023, LNAI 14282, pp. 534–539, 2023.
https://doi.org/10.1007/978-3-031-43264-4_43

real-world applications [2,6,9]. However, performance of a multi agent robotic system in a disastrous incidents relies on having a proper vision for modeling the system in advance considering most, if not all, of possible constraints and states the system would find itself in. On the other hand, dealing with probability and uncertainty is inevitable in real systems [1,5,20]. Thus, predicting the future behavior of such stochastic systems makes it possible to provide an optimal strategy in order to reduce the cost of the project [12]. The closer the model is to the real system, the more optimal these strategies can become. Brilliant studies has addressed tools and modeling systems for this matter to be done. [4,8]. Review of recent scholarly conducted studies in domains of Swarm Intelligence and Multi agents [3,7,14], Time-Critical Approaches [19], Exploration-Exploitation Trade-off under uncertainties [18] as well as Probabilistic model checking [10,11] has led us to aim for providing an integrated optimization method for swarm robotics performing search and rescue (SAR) missions in dynamic probabilistic environment.

3   Problem Statement and Contribution

The above analysis reveals that strategic decisions in SAR are characterized by the massive uncertainties inherent to the problem domain. A central such uncertainty is the survival probability of patients sustaining different injuries when they have to wait for rescue. We are addressing this issue by providing optimal route planning for rescue robots when differentiated time-dependent survival probabilities are known for the different casualities, thus solving a complex stochastic optimization problem. A time-variant survival function is allocated to each patient which predicts the diminishing likelihood of their survival as time passes. The desired task for our agent is to maximize the expected number of rescued patients considering time as its primary budget resource.

Due to the high complexity level of this Search and rescue operation, we made several assumptions for this step of modeling one agent and a number of patients to be rescued:

- Robot is informed of approximately how many persons to look for.
- Severity of injured people is categorized into several levels.
- Robot is also informed of the injury classes.
- A supervisor (i.e. drone equipped with GPS) informs the robot about the location of patients!

To provide a mathematical model of our problem, we utilized interactive continuous Markov chain modeling in order to formalize the problem through states/locations and transitions of robots and patients:

In patient's model Fig. 1, patient can be in the state of 'Alive/Waiting to be rescued', 'Dead' or 'Rescued'. In the first state, patient's health condition is degrading based on a survival probability function $SP_{P_i}(t)$ assigned to each patient, potentially leading to sudden death with a rate of $-\dot{SP}_{P_i}(t)$ at time t; once the patient has died, it however remains dead. On the other hand, the

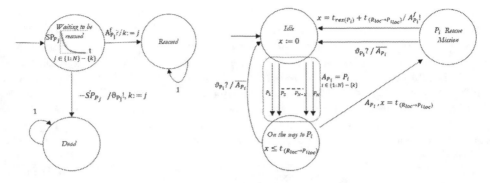

Fig. 1. Patient model   **Fig. 2.** Robot model

transition between states 'waiting to be rescued' and 'Rescued' requires a signal received from robot indicating that this particular patient is saved. Similar to 'Dead' state, rescued patient stays in the state 'Rescued'.

In parallel, the robot has three main location to be in (Fig. 2). Before making any decision, it will be in the state 'Idle' where the clock is reset. When the robot makes one of the possible decisions to rescue a patient (action A_{P_i}), it starts to move toward that particular patient with the required time to reach him/her being counted. Once it reaches the patient, there is still more time needed for the rescue mission to be finished. If the patient dies before the rescue mission is done, robot receives a signal from supervisor, cancels the decision (action $\bar{A}_{P_i}$), updates its location and becomes 'Idle' again in order to asses the current situation and make another decision. The same can happen when robot is on its way to the patient. In case of rescue mission being successful, patient will be added to $finalsequenceList$, sends the signal of $A_{P_i}^f$ and goes back to 'idle' for another decision making process.

4   Methodology

We have formulated our problem as a path planning approach where we are not looking for the minimum length path but for maximum number of patients rescued path. Our algorithm consists of a modified genetic algorithm with heuristic cost function updating the current plan based on changes in accumulated likelihood of other patients staying alive. Since the state of patients' health condition varies over time, it is the robot who should decide which path enables it to rescue as many patients as possible at the end of its time budget. For this to be done, our algorithm considers all changes at each step of robot's path and robot re-plans when it is necessary. Similar to actual search and rescue missions, the severity of patients' condition is classified into distinct categories, including high, medium, low, and lost. As a result, our problem has been broken down into four interconnected problems based on these priority levels. Moreover, the cost in path planning varies from simple Euclidean distance to some cumulative metric resulted from a robot moving [17]. Here, we aim to maximize the cumulative predicted survival probability, where we have utilized genetic algorithm as part of our approach, to prioritize our rescue sequence in order to approximate the maximum of cumulative survival probability.

Algorithm 1: Rescue Mission Algorithm

Data: Coordination of Robot and patients, Patients Health grade
Inputs : $R, P_i, (x,y)_i, f_{Survival_{P_i}}, T$

```
/*Initialization
```
$Finalsequence \leftarrow 0$;
for $i = 1 : P_i$ **do**

> ```
> /*Generate Severity Matrix
> ```
> $Severity_{(mat(4 \times P))} = Severity(f_{Survival_{P_i}}(T + T_s))$;
> $RedList \leftarrow P_{Lost} \leftarrow Severity_{mat}.row(4)$;
> ```
> /*Update Lost list
> ```
> **for** $Severity_{mat}.row(j) = 1 : 3$ **do**
>
> > **if** $Severity_{mat}.row(j)! = empty$ **then**
> >
> > > $PriorityList = P_{Seq}\left\{ argmax \sum_{i=1}^{P_{SL}} f_{Survival_{P_i}}\left(T_{Current} + T_{R_{loc} \rightarrow P_{i_{loc}}}\right) \right\}$
> > > ```
> > > /*Approximation of argmax by modified genetic algorithm
> > > ```
> > > **break**
> >
> > **end**
>
> **end**
>
> $Finalsequence \leftarrow PriorityList(P_{Seq}(end))$ /*Update final list
> $T \leftarrow T + T_{Rescue} + \frac{|R_{loc} - P_{Seq}(end)|}{v_R}$ /*Update time
> $P_i \leftarrow P_i - P_{Seq}(end) - P_{Lost}$ /*Update Patients list
> $P_i \leftarrow P_i + P_{New}$ /*Update Patient list in case of new ones
> $(x,y)_R \leftarrow (x,y)_{P_{Seq}(end)}$ /*Update Robot coordination

end

---

5   Simulation and Early Results

Simulation of the proposed approach has been conducted by a simulator as well as an implementation of Algorithm 1 written in MATLAB. Its output is an animated trajectory of the robot going from one patient to another. Here, we present examples of the final rescue sequence and dependency of the robot's strategy on its own speed, distance and rescue time required for patients (Figs. 3, 4 and 5).

As it is visible in figures, the environment is highly stochastic that the strategy has to be changed at any point of time. Also, since it is not predictable that when each patient would die, it plays the most significant rule in the results compared to the other parameters such as robot's speed and required rescue time. Although it is expected that increment in robot's speed or a decrease in the rescue time would result in greater number of patients rescued, the outcome is still highly dependent on the stochastic nature of the environment including the sudden death of patients. Therefore, the result are the approximated optimal path through step by step assessment and planning as the timeline of sudden death reveals.

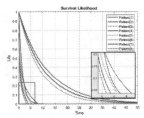

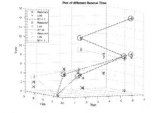

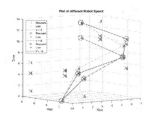

Fig. 3. Patients' Survival Functions

Fig. 4. Different Rescue Time

Fig. 5. Different Robot Speed

6   Conclusion and Future Work

According to our current understanding and based on our problem-solving journey, as we are dealing with a complex planning problem in stochastic domain where robot has to change its locally aimed decision and destination at any step in order to reach its global goal of rescuing as many patients as possible, Genetic algorithm has been adapted here as an starting point option to tackle such problems. Our prioritized and modified Genetic algorithm results is an optimized path leading to an approximation of the theoretically possible maximum number of saved patients. In the near future, we step forward to tackle the multi agent decision making problem in similar environment where the consensus of robots becomes part of the equation.

However, in an actual incident, where robots are not the only agents performing search and rescue operations, ethical aspects and personal attitudes comes into play. Currently, our strategy embedded into the decision-making is totally utilitarian based on a defined scheme of assigning equal values to the lives of patients, without any differentiation based on, e.g., an altruistic personal will to sacrifice for others or societally agreed preference based on, e.g., age or gender. Consequently, this system aims to be fully autonomous with restricted interaction between patients and robotic agents. It might become a matter of concern whether the optimal sequence of rescue mission provided by robots' calculation would be reliable/acceptable by human agents to follow regarding their moral beliefs. If ethical aspects and personal attitudes should be taken into consideration, the design of Human-Machine interfaces permitting to express and respect these will be an interesting future topic to study.

References

1. Al-Hussaini, S., Gregory, J.M., Gupta, S.K.: Generating task reallocation suggestions to handle contingencies in human-supervised multi-robot missions. IEEE Trans. Autom. Sci. Eng. (2023). https://doi.org/10.1109/TASE.2022.3227415
2. Balta, H., et al.: Integrated data management for a fleet of search-and-rescue robots. J. Field Robot. **34**(3), 539–582 (2017)
3. Delmerico, J., et al.: The current state and future outlook of rescue robotics. J. Field Robot. **36**(7), 1171–1191 (2019)

4. Galstyan, A., Lerman, K.: Analysis of a stochastic model of adaptive task allocation in robots. In: Brueckner, S.A., Di Marzo Serugendo, G., Karageorgos, A., Nagpal, R. (eds.) ESOA 2004. LNCS (LNAI), vol. 3464, pp. 167–179. Springer, Heidelberg (2005). https://doi.org/10.1007/11494676_11

5. Grenyer, A., Schwabe, O., Erkoyuncu, J.A., Zhao, Y.: Multistep prediction of dynamic uncertainty under limited data. CIRP J. Manuf. Sci. Technol. **37**, 37–54 (2022). https://doi.org/10.1016/j.cirpj.2022.01.002

6. Gómez, N., Peña, N., Rincón, S., Amaya, S., Calderon, J.: Leader-follower behavior in multi-agent systems for search and rescue based on PSO approach. In: SoutheastCon 2022, pp. 413–420 (2022). https://doi.org/10.1109/SoutheastCon48659.2022.9764133

7. Hao, B., Zhao, J., Du, H., Wang, Q., Yuan, Q., Zhao, S.: A search and rescue robot search method based on flower pollination algorithm and q-learning fusion algorithm. PLoS ONE **18**(3), e0283751 (2023)

8. Ibe, O.: Markov processes for stochastic modeling. Newnes (2013)

9. Jácome, M.Y., Alvear Villaroel, F., Figueroa Olmedo, J.: Ground robot for search and rescue management. In: Botto-Tobar, M., Zambrano Vizuete, M., Montes León, S., Torres-Carrión, P., Durakovic, B. (eds.) Applied Technologies, pp. 399–411. Springer, Cham (2023). https://doi.org/10.1007/978-3-031-24985-3_29

10. Konur, S., Dixon, C., Fisher, M.: Analysing robot swarm behaviour via probabilistic model checking. Robot. Auton. Syst. **60**(2), 199–213 (2012)

11. Kwiatkowska, M., Norman, G., Parker, D.: Probabilistic model checking and autonomy. CoRR abs/2111.10630 (2021)

12. Lerman, K., Martinoli, A., Galstyan, A.: A review of probabilistic macroscopic models for swarm robotic systems. In: Şahin, E., Spears, W.M. (eds.) SR 2004. LNCS, vol. 3342, pp. 143–152. Springer, Heidelberg (2005). https://doi.org/10.1007/978-3-540-30552-1_12

13. Maheswaran, R.T., Rogers, C.M., Sanchez, R., Szekely, P.: Decision-support for real-time multi-agent coordination. In: Proceedings of the 9th International Conference on Autonomous Agents and Multiagent Systems, vol. 1, pp. 1771–1772 (2010)

14. Notomista, G., et al.: A resilient and energy-aware task allocation framework for heterogeneous multirobot systems. IEEE Trans. Rob. **38**(1), 159–179 (2021)

15. Nourbakhsh, I., Sycara, K., Koes, M., Yong, M., Lewis, M., Burion, S.: Human-robot teaming for search and rescue. IEEE Pervasive Comput. **4**(1), 72–79 (2005). https://doi.org/10.1109/MPRV.2005.13

16. Nourjou, R., Smith, S.F., Hatayama, M., Okada, N., Szekely, P.: Dynamic assignment of geospatial-temporal macro tasks to agents under human strategic decisions for centralized scheduling in multi-agent systems. Int. J. Mach. Learn. Comput. **4**(1), 39 (2014)

17. Sanchez-Ibanez, J.R., Perez-del Pulgar, C.J., García-Cerezo, A.: Path planning for autonomous mobile robots: a review. Sensors **21**(23), 7898 (2021)

18. Subbarayalu, V., Vensuslaus, M.A.: An intrusion detection system for drone swarming utilizing timed probabilistic automata. Drones **7**(4), 248 (2023)

19. Unhelkar, V., Shah, J.: Contact: deciding to communicate during time-critical collaborative tasks in unknown, deterministic domains. In: Proceedings of the AAAI Conference on Artificial Intelligence, vol. 30 (2016)

20. Wehbe, R., Williams, R.K.: Probabilistically resilient multi-robot informative path planning (2022)

Efficient Algorithms for LTL$_f$ Synthesis

Marco Favorito$^{(\boxtimes)}$ (iD)

Banca d'Italia, Rome, Italy
marco.favorito@bancaditalia.it, marco.favorito@gmail.com

Abstract. The use of temporal logic on finite traces, like Linear Temporal Logic (LTL) has shown to be very powerful for AI. The focus on finite traces was also motivated by the difficulties of finding good algorithms for automata determinization in the infinite trace setting as LTL, a crucial step in the LTL synthesis problem, while such difficulties in the finite setting disappear. For this reason, synthesis of LTL on finite traces (LTL$_f$) has gained a lot of traction in the research community due to its generality and relevance to other fields. This work aims to study efficient algorithms for solving LTL$_f$ synthesis. We first focus on a compositional approach for computing the deterministic finite automaton (DFA), which will be used together with efficient backward fixpoint computation to solve the DFA game. Then, we consider a family of forward LTL$_f$ synthesis techniques that build the DFA on-the-fly, while searching for a solution, thus possibly avoiding the full DFA construction. Our contributions brought to the realization of efficient tools that achieved the best scores in the 2023 edition of SYNTCOMP.

Keywords: Linear Temporal Logic on Finite Traces · LTL$_f$ Synthesis · Two-Player Games · AND-OR Graph Search

1 Intorduction

One of the grand challenges of Artificial Intelligence (AI) is to equip intelligent agents with autonomous capability of deliberating the execution of complex courses of action to accomplish desired tasks [24,37]. This problem is related to reactive synthesis in Formal Methods: we have an agent acting in an adversarial environment such that the agent controls certain variables (the agent actions) and the environment controls the others (the environment reactions); given a specification of the task, the agent has to find a strategy (plan/policy/controller/program) to choose its actions to fulfil the task in spite of all possible environment reactions [34]. The agent and the environment interact in a *two-player game*, a notion also used in model checking in Verification [1,8], which in turn are at the base of ATL interpretation structures [3], often used in modelling multi-agent systems [39].

In Formal Methods, the most common formalism for specifying tasks is Linear Temporal Logic (LTL) [33] typically used also in model checking [5]. A finite

© The Author(s), under exclusive license to Springer Nature Switzerland AG 2023
V. Malvone and A. Murano (Eds.): EUMAS 2023, LNAI 14282, pp. 540–546, 2023.
https://doi.org/10.1007/978-3-031-43264-4_44

trace variant of LTL, LTL$_f$ [16], became popular in AI. The interest in finite traces is due to the observation that typically, intelligent agents are not dedicated to a single task all their life but are supposed to accomplish one task after another. In particular the synthesis problem for LTL$_f$ has been studied in [17], where it has been shown that the complexity characterization of the problem in the case of LTL$_f$ on finite traces is the same as the one for infinite trace, namely, 2EXPTIME-complete. Also the procedure for computing it is analogus [32]. Starting from the logical specification, we get a nondeterministic automaton (NFA in the finite case, Büchi in the infinite case), we determinize it (in the infinite case, we change the automaton, e.g., to a parity one, since Büchi automata are not closed under determinization, indeed deterministic Büchi automata are strictly less expressive than nondeterministic ones), and then we solve the corresponding game (DFA games for finite traces, parity games for the infinite ones) considering which propositions are controllable and which are not. However, in the case of infinite traces, the determinization remains a very difficult step, and there are no good algorithms yet to perform it [22]. In fact, the problem is highly intractable: from a 9-state NBW, its DRW counterpart has 1,059,057-state DRW [2], and there are no symbolic algorithms for it. Moreover, solving parity games requires computing nested fixpoints (possibly exponentially many). In the finite case, determinization is much easier: it requires the usual subset constructions and good algorithms are available. Indeed, in most cases, the resulting DFA is actually manageable, a phenomenon often observed when determinization is applied to automata finite words [38]. So effective tools can indeed be developed.

Our work aims to concretize the envisioned potential of LTL$_f$ synthesis by providing efficient algorithms for solving the problem. First, we focus on an efficient approach for the transformation of LTL$_f$ formulas into deterministic finite automata (DFA), which is at the core of the automata-theoretic technique for LTL$_f$ synthesis [17]. Our approach is *compositional*, i.e. we inductively transform each LTL$_f$ subformula into a DFA and combine them through automata operators. By relying on efficient semi-symbolic automata representations, we empirically show the effectiveness of our approach and the competitiveness with similar tools [14]. Secondly, we devise a forward-based approach to LTL$_f$ synthesis. The idea is to build the DFA on-the-fly, exploiting the notion of *formula progression* [4,18], while computing a winning strategy for the agent. Our approach can be more efficient than the classical approach based on backward fixpoint computation, which requires the construction of the full DFA upfront (in the worst case, doubly exponentially larger than the size of the formula). Empirical evaluation shows the tool often performs better than the state-of-the-art tools [15].

The topic of LTL$_f$ synthesis has amassed so much interest that the 2023 Reactive Synthesis Competition (SYNTCOMP) has offered an LTL$_f$ track. The symbolic LTL$_f$ synthesis tool Syft [41], when backed by our tool Lydia, yielding LydiaSyft [21], achieved second place in the 2023 edition of SYNTCOMP, whereas our forward-search approach to LTL$_f$ synthesis [20] ranked first[1]. These

---

[1] http://www.syntcomp.org/syntcomp-2023-results/.

impressive results witness the impact of our research. These research works have been part of the author's PhD thesis [19].

2   Compositional LTL$_f$-to-DFA

There are different ways to compute the equivalent DFA from an LTL$_f$ formula φ. The classical approach [16] works as follows: first, compute an equivalent Alternating Finite Automaton (AFA) [12], then compute its equivalent Nondeterministic Finite Automaton (NFA), [35], and then determinize the result to compute the DFA. One of the best practical implementations of the translation from LTL$_f$ to DFA, proposed by [41]. Their tool Syft encodes LTL$_f$ formulas into First-Order Logic formulas, represented as Mona programs [27–29], and uses the Mona tool to perform the actual translation. Another work [6] proposed a hybrid approach to the problem of DFA construction from LTL$_f$ formulas: first, they decompose the outermost conjunction in the input formula φ, where φ is assumed to be in the form $\varphi = \bigwedge_{i=1}^{n} \varphi_i$, in n-subformulae $\varphi_1 \ldots \varphi_n$. Then, they transform each φ_1 into DFA $\mathcal{A}_{\varphi_i}$ in explicit-state representation using Mona. Finally, they start doing the product between all the automata $\mathcal{A}_\varphi$.

In our work [14], we took a step further from the compositional approach proposed in [6]. In particular, our contribution is a fully compositional approach to handle both LTL$_f$ formulae and LDL$_f$ formulas. That is, we don't make any assumption on the structure of the formula, as done by Bansal et al., which stops the decomposition step at the outermost conjunction. We process all the subformulas recursively up to the leaves of the syntax tree, and then we compose the partial DFA of the subformulas using common operations over automata (e.g. union, intersection, concatenation) according to the LTL$_f$/LDL$_f$ operator being processed. The main advantage of doing so is that the partial results can be aggressively minimized at every step, hence keeping the automata as small as possible and therefore reducing the computational load of the overall procedure.

Since the transformation rules are defined over Linear Dynamic Logic on finite traces (LDL$_f$) [16], the input LTL$_f$ formula φ is first translated into an equivalent (linear-size) LDL$_f$ formula. The elementary formula tt (resp. ff) is translated into a DFA with only one accepting (resp. rejecting) state with a self-loop. Boolean operators are processed with the analogous automata-theoretic operations: e.g. conjunction is implemented as automata intersection, disjunction as union, and negation as complementation. The temporal operator $\langle \rho \rangle \psi$ is handled according to the regular expression ρ. Due to lack of space, we cannot describe it in full detail, and the interested reader should refer to [14]. On the implementation side, Lydia uses the semi-symbolic DFA representation provided by Mona. In Mona, the transitions of a DFA are symbolically represented as a shared multi-terminal binary decision diagram (shMBDD) [9], where the transition relation of a DFA is encoded as a binary decision diagram (BDD) with multiple terminal nodes. The alphabets of these DFA are the sets of bit vectors of length k, i.e. $\mathbb{B}^k$, for some k. In our case, each bit is associated to an atomic proposition appearing in the LDL$_f$ formula. In addition to a compact representation of transitions of DFA, the Mona DFA library provides efficient implementations of standard automata operations. These operations include product, (existential) projection, determinization, and minimization. We extended the library to include the Kleene closure, the concatenation, and the universal projection. Intuitively, these operations are needed in the modelling of nondeterminism of the $\mathcal{U}$-operator semantics. Finally, the built DFA, which is *minimal* and *explicit* in the state space, is transformed into a symbolic automaton to make it processable by Syft for efficient symbolic computation for solving the DFA game.

3   Forward LTL$_f$ Synthesis

The main drawback of approaches based on backward fixpoint computation for adversarial reachability of the DFA accepting state is that it requires computing the entire DFA of the LTL$_f$ specification, which in the worst case can be doubly exponential in the size of the formula. Thus, the DFA construction step becomes the main bottleneck. A natural idea is to consider a forward search approach that expands the arena on-the-fly while searching for a solution, possibly avoiding the construction of the entire arena. Forward-based approaches are at the core of the best solution methods designed for other AI problems: Planning with fully observable non-deterministic domains (FOND) [23,24], where the agent has to reach the goal, despite that the environment may choose adversarially the effects of the agent actions, and Planning in partially observable nondeterministic domains (POND), also known as *contingent planning*, where the search procedure must be performed over the *belief-states* [7,25,36]. However, techniques developed for such problems cannot be applied to ours; an attempt has been made by encoding the problem into PDDL [26], as [10,11], but unfortunately this might result in a PDDL specification with exponential size.

For these reasons, researchers have been looking into forward search techniques specifically conceived for solving LTL$_f$ synthesis. The first most notable attempt in this direction is [40]. In that work, the authors present an on-the-fly synthesis approach via conducting a so-called Transition-based Deterministic Finite Automata (TDFA) game, where the acceptance condition is defined on transitions instead of states. The main issue of that approach is the full enumeration of agent-environment moves, which are exponentially many in the number of variables. Moreover, due to the fact that the acceptance condition is defined on transitions, every generated transition has to be checked for acceptance.

In our works [15] and [20], we investigated LTL$_f$ forward synthesis adopting an AND-OR graph search as in FOND Planning [30,31], but over a doubly exponential search space, as for contingent planning [7]. We develop specific techniques to create the search space on-the-fly while exploring it, such that we can possibly decide realizability before reaching the double-exponential blowup.

In detail, in our first work in this direction, [15], we proposed a technique to create on-the-fly the DFA corresponding to the LTL$_f$ specification. This technique avoids a detour to automata theory and instead builds directly deterministic transitions from a current state. In particular, this technique exploits

LTL formula progression to separate what happens now (label) and what should happen next accordingly (successor state). Crucially, we exploited the structure that formula progression provides to branch on propositional formulas (representing several evaluations) instead of individual evaluations. This drastically reduces the branching factor of the AND-OR graph to be searched (recall that in LTL$_f$ synthesis, both the agent choices and the environment choices can be exponentially many). More specifically, we label transitions/edges with propositional formulas on propositions controlled by the agent (for OR-nodes) and by the environment (for AND-nodes). Every such propositional formula captures a set of evaluations leading to the same successor node. We leverage Knowledge Compilation (KC) techniques, and in particular Sentential Decision Diagrams (SDDs) [13], to effectively generate such propositional formulas for OR-nodes and AND-nodes, and thus reduce the branching factor of the search space. The implemented tool, Cynthia, showed to perform better than other tools such as Ltlfsyn [40], and the state-of-the-art approaches Lisa and Lydia.

Nevertheless, for certain types of problem instances, Cynthia's approach can get stuck with demanding compilations of the state formulas needed both for state equivalence checking and for search node expansion. Moreover, the requirement of having an irreducible representation of agent-environment moves can be of little usefulness if the branching factor of the search problem is already high, resulting in an even greater compilation overhead.

For this reason, in our following work on the same line of research [20], we considered different realizations of the previous AND-OR graph search framework, in which we consider two primitive operations: *state-equivalence checking* and *search node expansion*. We formalized and discussed two well-known instances of equivalence checks; one based on Binary Decision Diagrams [9], and the other on a computationally-cheap syntactical equivalence between state formulas. Furthermore, we propose a novel search graph expansion technique based on a procedure inspired by the famous Davis-Putnam-Logemann-Loveland (DPLL) algorithm. This overcomes the limitation of previous works [40] and [14]. The main benefits of this approach is to focus the computational power for actually exploring the search space, rather than wasting time either slavishly enumerating the exponentially many variable assignments [40] or by finding the minimal representation of the available search moves [15]. The new tool, called Nike showed its surprising effectiveness. Indeed, as stated earlier, Nike won the LTL$_f$ Realizability Track in the 2023 edition of SYNTCOMP.

4   Conclusion

Our work, both theoretical and practical, laid the foundations for efficient LTL$_f$ synthesis algorithms. We contributed with novel approaches, both for the effective construction of the DFA that can be used for the classical backward fixpoint computation and also for a forward approach that possibly avoids the exploration of the entire DFA game. The impressive results at the 2023 edition of SYNT-COMP show the impact of our work.

References

1. de Alfaro, L., Henzinger, T.A., Majumdar, R.: From verification to control: dynamic programs for omega-regular objectives. In: LICS, pp. 279–290. IEEE Computer Society (2001)
2. Althoff, C.S., Thomas, W., Wallmeier, N.: Observations on determinization of büchi automata. Theor. Comput. Sci. **363**(2), 224–233 (2006)
3. Alur, R., Henzinger, T.A., Kupferman, O.: Alternating-time temporal logic. J. ACM **49**(5), 672–713 (2002)
4. Bacchus, F., Kabanza, F.: Planning for temporally extended goals. Ann. Math. Artif. Intell. **22**(1–2), 5–27 (1998)
5. Baier, C., Katoen, J.: Principles of Model Checking. MIT Press, Cambridge (2008)
6. Bansal, S., Li, Y., Tabajara, L.M., Vardi, M.Y.: Hybrid compositional reasoning for reactive synthesis from finite-horizon specifications. In: AAAI, pp. 9766–9774. AAAI Press (2020)
7. Bertoli, P., Cimatti, A., Roveri, M., Traverso, P.: Strong planning under partial observability. Artif. Intell. **170**(4–5), 337–384 (2006)
8. Bloem, R., Jobstmann, B., Piterman, N., Pnueli, A., Sa'ar, Y.: Synthesis of reactive(1) designs. J. Comput. Syst. Sci. **78**(3), 911–938 (2012)
9. Bryant, R.E.: Symbolic Boolean manipulation with ordered binary-decision diagrams. ACM Comput. Surv. **24**(3), 293–318 (1992)
10. Camacho, A., Baier, J.A., Muise, C.J., McIlraith, S.A.: Finite LTL synthesis as planning. In: ICAPS, pp. 29–38. AAAI Press (2018)
11. Camacho, A., McIlraith, S.A.: Strong fully observable non-deterministic planning with LTL and LTLf goals. In: IJCAI, pp. 5523–5531 (2019). https://www.ijcai. org/
12. Chandra, A.K., Kozen, D., Stockmeyer, L.J.: Alternation. J. ACM **28**(1), 114–133 (1981)
13. Darwiche, A.: SDD: a new canonical representation of propositional knowledge bases. In: IJCAI, pp. 819–826. IJCAI/AAAI (2011)
14. De Giacomo, G., Favorito, M.: Compositional approach to translate LTLf/LDLf into deterministic finite automata. In: ICAPS, pp. 122–130. AAAI Press (2021)
15. De Giacomo, G., Favorito, M., Li, J., Vardi, M.Y., Xiao, S., Zhu, S.: Ltlf synthesis as AND-OR graph search: Knowledge compilation at work. In: IJCAI, pp. 2591–2598 (2022). https://www.ijcai.org/
16. De Giacomo, G., Vardi, M.Y.: Linear temporal logic and linear dynamic logic on finite traces. In: IJCAI, pp. 854–860. IJCAI/AAAI (2013)
17. De Giacomo, G., Vardi, M.Y.: Synthesis for LTL and LDL on finite traces. In: IJCAI, pp. 1558–1564. AAAI Press (2015)
18. Emerson, E.A.: Temporal and modal logic. In: Handbook of Theoretical Computer Science, Volume B: Formal Models and Sematics (B), pp. 995–1072. Elsevier and MIT Press (1990)
19. Favorito, M.: Automata-theoretic techniques for reasoning and learning in linear-time temporal logics on finite traces (2022)
20. Favorito, M.: Forward LTLf synthesis: DPLL at work (2023). https://doi.org/10. 48550/arXiv.2302.13825
21. Favorito, M., Zhu, S.: Lydiasyft: a compositional symbolic synthesizer for LTLf specifications (2023)
22. Fogarty, S., Kupferman, O., Vardi, M.Y., Wilke, T.: Profile trees for büchi word automata, with application to determinization. Inf. Comput. **245**, 136–151 (2015)

23. Geffner, H., Bonet, B.: A Concise Introduction to Models and Methods for Automated Planning, Synthesis Lectures on Artificial Intelligence and Machine Learning. Morgan & Claypool Publishers (2013)
24. Ghallab, M., Nau, D., Traverso, P.: Automated Planning and Acting. Cambridge University Press, Cambridge (2016)
25. Goldman, R.P., Boddy, M.S.: Expressive planning and explicit knowledge. In: AIPS, pp. 110–117. AAAI (1996)
26. Haslum, P., Lipovetzky, N., Magazzeni, D., Muise, C.: An Introduction to the Planning Domain Definition Language. ynthesis Lectures on Artificial Intelligence and Machine Learning. Morgan & Claypool Publishers, S (2019)
27. Henriksen, J.G., et al.: Mona: monadic second-order logic in practice. In: Brinksma, E., Cleaveland, W.R., Larsen, K.G., Margaria, T., Steffen, B. (eds.) TACAS 1995. LNCS, vol. 1019, pp. 89–110. Springer, Heidelberg (1995). https://doi.org/10.1007/3-540-60630-0_5
28. Klarlund, N.: Mona & fido: the logic-automaton connection in practice. In: Nielsen, M., Thomas, W. (eds.) CSL 1997. LNCS, vol. 1414, pp. 311–326. Springer, Heidelberg (1998). https://doi.org/10.1007/BFb0028022
29. Klarlund, N., Møller, A., Schwartzbach, M.I.: MONA implementation secrets. Int. J. Found. Comput. Sci. **13**(4), 571–586 (2002)
30. Mattmüller, R.: Informed progression search for fully observable nondeterministic planning = Informierte Vorwärtssuche für nichtdeterministisches Planen unter vollständiger Beobachtbarkeit. Ph.D. thesis, University of Freiburg, Germany (2013)
31. Mattmüller, R., Ortlieb, M., Helmert, M., Bercher, P.: Pattern database heuristics for fully observable nondeterministic planning. In: ICAPS, pp. 105–112. AAAI (2010)
32. Mazala, R.: Infinite games. In: Grädel, E., Thomas, W., Wilke, T. (eds.) Automata Logics, and Infinite Games. LNCS, vol. 2500, pp. 23–38. Springer, Heidelberg (2002). https://doi.org/10.1007/3-540-36387-4_2
33. Pnueli, A.: The temporal logic of programs. In: FOCS, pp. 46–57. IEEE Computer Society (1977)
34. Pnueli, A., Rosner, R.: On the synthesis of a reactive module. In: POPL, pp. 179–190. ACM Press (1989)
35. Rabin, M.O., Scott, D.S.: Finite automata and their decision problems. IBM J. Res. Dev. **3**(2), 114–125 (1959)
36. Reif, J.H.: The complexity of two-player games of incomplete information. J. Comput. Syst. Sci. **29**(2), 274–301 (1984)
37. Reiter, R.: Knowledge in Action: Logical Foundations for Specifying and Implementing Dynamical Systems. MIT press, Cambridge (2001)
38. Tabakov, D., Vardi, M.Y.: Experimental evaluation of classical automata constructions. In: Sutcliffe, G., Voronkov, A. (eds.) LPAR 2005. LNCS (LNAI), vol. 3835, pp. 396–411. Springer, Heidelberg (2005). https://doi.org/10.1007/11591191_28
39. Wooldridge, M.J.: An Introduction to MultiAgent Systems, 2nd edn. Wiley, Hoboken (2009)
40. Xiao, S., Li, J., Zhu, S., Shi, Y., Pu, G., Vardi, M.Y.: On-the-fly synthesis for LTL over finite traces. In: AAAI, pp. 6530–6537. AAAI Press (2021)
41. Zhu, S., Tabajara, L.M., Li, J., Pu, G., Vardi, M.Y.: Symbolic LTLf synthesis. In: IJCAI, pp. 1362–1369 (2017). https://www.ijcai.org/

Agent Behavior Composition
in Stochastic Settings

Luciana Silo[1,2(✉)]

[1] Sapienza Università di Roma, Rome, Italy
silo@diag.uniroma1.it
[2] Camera dei Deputati, Rome, Italy

Abstract. Behavior composition problem is particularly relevant for multi-agent systems and aims at building a complex target behavior using several agent behaviors. In this work, we develop a framework that models the agent behaviors in stochastic settings both when the target is represented as a Finite State Machine and when it is represented as an LTL$_f$ formula.

Keywords: Behavior Composition · Markov Decision Processes · Decision Theory

1 Introduction

The behavior composition problem is well-known and extensively investigated in agents and multi-agent settings. It consists of realizing a desired target behavior using a set of agent's behavior, i.e., services. Behaviors are an abstraction of sequences of actions made by agents. The composition and the reuse of components has been largely studied in Service Oriented Computing, under the name of "service composition". Service composition aims at composing complex services by orchestrating (i.e., controlling and coordinating) services that are already at disposal. When service composition takes into account the behavior of the component service it becomes related to what we call here "behavior composition" [6]. This framework takes inspiration from several works where the agent's behaviors are described by finite transition systems [1–3,6]. The approach used in these works is known in the literature as the "Roman model" where each available service is modeled as a finite-state machine (FSM), in which at each state, the service offers a certain set of actions, and each action changes the state of the service in some way. The designer is interested in generating a new service (referred to as a target) from the set of existing services. The target service (the requirement) is specified using an FSM, too. The composition is synthesized by building a *controller* or an *orchestrator* that uses existing services to satisfy the requirements of the target service.

Nevertheless, there is an inherent limitation of the approach based on the classical Roman model, the assumption that the services that can be used to realize the target service, behave *deterministically*. This assumption is often unrealistic because in practice the set of services might show non-deterministic behavior due, for example, to the complexity of the domain, or due to an inherent uncertainty on the dynamics of such a system. Hence, the deterministic service model is not expressive enough to capture crucial facets of the system being modeled. Moreover, the above-mentioned techniques work only when the target is fully realizable, i.e. the specification can either be satisfied or not, with no middle ground.

In this work, we study composition in stochastic settings, in which not only the target but also the services are allowed to behave stochastically. Additionally, we also represent the target service using the flexible formalism named DECLARE [8], directly based on Linear Temporal Logic on finite traces (LTL$_f$) [7].

In both cases, an optimal solution for the composition can be found, by solving an appropriate probabilistic planning problem (a Markov decision process - MDP) derived from the services and requirement specifications, taking into the account the probability associated with each action, and rewards. By solving this problem we have a solution that coincides with the exact solution if a composition exists; otherwise it provides an approximate solution that maximizes the expected sum of values of the target service's request.

2   Formalization of the Problem

In this section, we formalize the problem when the target service is fully defined (FSM) and when it is defined by specifying constraints between the task (LTL$_f$ formula).

2.1   Stochastic Policy

Before stating the problem, we formally define a *stochastic service* as a tuple $\tilde{S} = \langle \Sigma_s, \sigma_{s0}, F_s, A, P_s, R_s \rangle$, formed by:

- Σ_s is the finite set of service states;
- $\sigma_{s0} \in \Sigma$ is the initial state;
- $F_s \subseteq \Sigma_s$ is the set of the service's final state;
- A is the finite set of services' actions;
- $P_s : \Sigma_s \times A \rightarrow Prob(\Sigma_s)$ is the transition function;
- $R_s : \Sigma_s \times A \rightarrow \mathbb{R}$ is the reward function.

In short words, the stochastic service is the stochastic variant of the service defined in the classical Roman model, and it can be seen as a Markov Decision Process[1]. The *target service* (also seen as a Markov Decision Process) is defined as $\mathcal{T} = \langle \Sigma_t, \sigma_{t0}, F_t, A, \delta_t, P_t, R_t \rangle$ [3], where:

- Σ_t is the finite set of service states;

---

[1] An MDP is a tuple $\mathcal{M} = \langle S, A, T, R \rangle$ formed by: a set S of states, a set A of actions, a transition function $T : S \times A \rightarrow Prob(S)$, and a reward function $R : S \times A \rightarrow \mathbb{R}$.

- $\sigma_{t0} \in \Sigma$ is the initial state;
- $F_t \subseteq \Sigma$ is the set of the service's final state;
- A is the finite set of services' actions;
- $\delta_t : \Sigma \times A \to \Sigma$ is the service's deterministic and partial transition function;
- $P_t : \Sigma_t \to \pi(A) \cup \emptyset$ is the action distribution function;
- $R_t : \Sigma_t \times A \to \mathbb{R}$ is the reward function.

A *stochastic system service* $\tilde{\mathcal{Z}}$ is a stochastic service where $\tilde{\mathcal{Z}} = \langle \Sigma_z, \sigma_{z0}, F_z, A, P_z, R_z \rangle$ is defined as follows:

- $\Sigma_z = \Sigma_1 \times \cdots \times \Sigma_n$;
- $\sigma_{z0} = (\sigma_{10}, \ldots, \sigma_{n0})$;
- $F_z = \{(\sigma_1, \ldots, \sigma_n) \mid \sigma_i \in F_i, 1 \le i \le n\}$;
- $A_z = A \times \{1, \ldots n\}$ is the set of pairs (a, i) formed by a shared action a and the index i of the service that executes it;
- $P_z(\boldsymbol{\sigma'} \mid \boldsymbol{\sigma}, (a, i)) = P(\sigma_i' \mid \sigma_i, a)$, for $\boldsymbol{\sigma} = (\sigma_1 \ldots \sigma_n)$, $\boldsymbol{\sigma'} = (\sigma_1' \ldots \sigma_n')$ and $a \in A_i(\sigma_i)$, with $\sigma_i \in \Sigma_i$ and $\sigma_j = \sigma_j'$ for $j \ne i$;
- $R_z(\boldsymbol{\sigma}, (a, i)) = R_i(\sigma_i, a)$ for $\boldsymbol{\sigma} \in \Sigma_z$, $a \in A_i(\sigma_i)$.

We define the set of joint histories of the target and the system service as $H_{t,z} = \Sigma_t \times \Sigma_z \times (A \times \Sigma_t \times \Sigma_z)^*$. A joint history $h_{t,z} = \sigma_{t,0}\sigma_{z,0}a_1\sigma_{t,1}\sigma_{z,1}a_2 \ldots$ is an element of $H_{t,z}$. The projection of $h_{t,z}$ over the target (system) actions is $\pi_t(h_{t,z}) = h_t$ ($\pi_z(h_{t,z}) = h_z$).

An orchestrator $\gamma : \Sigma_t \times \Sigma_z \times A \to \{1, \ldots, n\}$, is a mapping from a state of the target-system service and user action $(\sigma_t, \sigma_z, a) \in \Sigma_t \times \Sigma_z \times A$ to the index $j \in \{1, \ldots, n\}$ of the service that must handle it. Crucially, since stochasticity comes also from the services, the orchestrator *does* affect the probability of an history $h_{t,z}$. Moreover, in general, there are *several* system histories associated with a given target history. We say that a target history h_t is realizable by an orchestrator γ if for all joint histories $h_{t,z}$ such that $h_t = \pi_t(h_{t,x})$, the orchestrator is well-defined, i.e., it can perform all the actions requested by the target for every possible evolution of the stochastic system service.

The solution technique of the given problem is based on finding an optimal policy for the *composition MDP*. The composition MDP is a function, which consists of the cartesian product between the system service and the target service defined as follows: $\mathcal{M}(\tilde{\mathcal{Z}}, \tilde{T}) = \langle S_{\tilde{\mathcal{M}}}, A_{\tilde{\mathcal{M}}}, T_{\tilde{\mathcal{M}}}, R_{\tilde{\mathcal{M}}} \rangle$ [5], where:

- $S_{\tilde{\mathcal{M}}} = \Sigma_{\tilde{\mathcal{Z}}} \times \Sigma_{\tilde{T}} \times A \cup \{s_{\mathcal{M}0}\}$;
- $A_{\tilde{\mathcal{M}}} = \{a_{\mathcal{M}0}, 1, \ldots, n\}$;
- $T_{\tilde{\mathcal{M}}}(s_{\mathcal{M}0}, a_{\mathcal{M}0}, (\sigma_{z0}, \sigma_{t0}, a)) = P_t(\sigma_{t0}, a)$;
- $T_{\tilde{\mathcal{M}}}((\sigma_z, \sigma_t, a), i, (\sigma_z', \sigma_t', a')) = P_t(\sigma_t', a') \cdot P_z(\sigma_z' \mid \sigma_z, \langle a, i \rangle)$, if $P_z(\sigma_z' \mid \sigma_z, \langle a, i \rangle) > 0$ and $\sigma_t \xrightarrow{a} \sigma_t'$ and 0 otherwise;
- $R_{\tilde{\mathcal{M}}}((\sigma_z, \sigma_t, a), i) = R_t(\sigma_t, a) + R_z(\sigma_z, \langle a, i \rangle)$, if $(a, i) \in A(\sigma_z)$ and 0 otherwise.

This definition take into account also the probability of transitioning to the system successor state σ_z' from σ_z doing the system action $\langle a, i \rangle$, i.e. $P_z(\sigma_z' \mid \sigma_z, \langle a, i \rangle)$, and in the reward function, take into account also, the reward observed from doing system action $\langle a, i \rangle$ in σ_z, and sum it to the reward signal coming from the target. By construction, if ρ is an optimal policy, then the orchestrator γ such that $\gamma(\sigma_z, \sigma_t, a) = \rho(\langle \sigma_z, \sigma_t, a \rangle$ is an optimal orchestrator.

To summarize, given the specifications of the set of stochastic services and the target service, first compute the composition MDP, then find an optimal policy for it, and then deploy the policy in an orchestration setting and dispatch the request to the chosen service according to the computed policy.

2.2   Stochastic Constraint-Based Policy

In the following, we formally define the target process specification as an LTL$_f$[2] formula φ over the set of propositions $\mathcal{P}$, which specifies the allowed traces of the process. We can define this specification via DECLARE, a language and framework for the declarative constraint-based modeling of processes [8]. DECLARE provides a set $\mathcal{P}$ of propositions representing the atomic tasks which are units of work in the process. This permits to model the process as a set of logical conditions, so as to more easily specify those processes in which human experience plays a key role or in which the rules of precedence between operations cannot simply be modeled as a sequence. Observe that the set of finite traces that satisfies the specification φ together with the DECLARE assumption $\xi_{\mathcal{P}}$ can be captured by a single deterministic process DFA $\mathcal{A}_\varphi$, obtained by *(i)* generating the corresponding NFA (exponential step), *(ii)* transforming it into a DFA (exponential step) [9], and *(iii)* trimming the resulting DFA by removing every state from which no final state is reachable (polynomial step).

The obtained DFA is indeed a process in the sense that at every step, depending only on the history (i.e., the current state), it exposes the set of actions that are legally executable and eventually lead to a final state (assuming fairness of the execution, which disallows remaining forever in a loop). The LTL$_f$ formula transformed into a deterministic finite automaton (DFA) is defined as $\mathcal{A}_\varphi = \langle \mathcal{P}, Q, q_0, F, \delta \rangle$ where:

- $\mathcal{P}$ is the alphabet;
- Q is a finite set of states;
- q_0 is the initial state;
- $F \subseteq Q$ is the set of accepting states;
- $\delta : Q \times \mathcal{P} \to Q$ is the transition function.

Note that the DFA alphabet is the same as the set of traces that satisfies the formula φ.

The stochastic services are defined as before, and they can perform the process actions in $\mathcal{P}$. To make our model richer, we allow services to execute a broader set of actions, i.e. $\mathcal{P}'$ s.t. $\mathcal{P} \subseteq \mathcal{P}'$, that are specific to the model of the factory that aims to realize the manufacturing process. The composition MDP is a function that consists of the cartesian product between

---

[2] LTL$_f$ is a variant of Linear Temporal Logic (LTL) interpreted over finite traces, instead of infinite ones [7].

the stochastic system service $\tilde{Z}$ and the DFA $\mathcal{A}_\varphi$ of the LTL$_f$ formula φ, i.e., $\mathcal{M}(\tilde{Z}, \mathcal{A}_\varphi) = \langle S_\mathcal{M}, A_\mathcal{M}, T_\mathcal{M}, R_\mathcal{M}, \lambda \rangle$ [4], where:

- $S_\mathcal{M} = \Sigma_z \times Q$ is the product of the states of the system service and the DFA states;
- $A_\mathcal{M}$ is the set of the MDP actions consisting on the product between the DFA action and the service that performs the action;
- $T_\mathcal{M}((\boldsymbol{\sigma}, q), \langle a, i \rangle, (\boldsymbol{\sigma'}, q')) = P_z(\boldsymbol{\sigma'} \mid \boldsymbol{\sigma}, \langle a, i \rangle)$ if $\langle a, i \rangle \in \hat{A}_z(\boldsymbol{\sigma}) \wedge \left((a \in \mathcal{P} \wedge q \xrightarrow{a} q') \vee q' = q \right)$, 0 otherwise, this means that the transition function $T_\mathcal{M}$ takes into account also the probability of transitioning to the system successor state $\boldsymbol{\sigma'}$ from $\boldsymbol{\sigma}$ doing the system action $\langle a, i \rangle$, i.e. $P_z(\boldsymbol{\sigma'} \mid \boldsymbol{\sigma}, \langle a, i \rangle)$, and q' is the successor state of q in $\mathcal{A}_\varphi$ after reading a if it is a process action ($a \in \mathcal{P}$), otherwise it is a service custom action and the automaton remains in the same state ($q' = q$);
- $R_\mathcal{M}((\boldsymbol{\sigma}, q), \langle a, i \rangle, (\boldsymbol{\sigma'}, q'))$ is the reward function that models the process specification φ, it is equal to 1 if $q' \in F$, or $R_z(\sigma_i, a, \sigma_i')$, if $\langle a, i \rangle \in \hat{A}_z(\boldsymbol{\sigma})$, else 0; particularly the reward function returns 1 if the automaton component of the state is an accepting state $q' \in F$, where F is the set of accepting states;
- λ is the discount factor that determines how important future rewards are to the current state.

An optimal policy for the composition MDP can be computed as before, i.e., such that the overall expected sum of rewards is minimized. A solution to this composition MDP induces an orchestrator that coincides with the exact solution if a composition exists. Otherwise, it provides an approximate solution that maximizes the expected discounted sum of values of user requests that can be serviced. Leveraging on the solution policy, the *controller* dispatches the requests to the specific service.

3   Conclusion and Future Works

This project extends the works that use the "Roman model", considering stochastic settings for agent behaviors. This permits to outline a composition that is more "realistic", thanks to the fact that is able to capture the uncertainty of real systems. Moreover, we define the composition when the target behavior is fully defined as an FSM, and when it is represented using model constraints, i.e., DECLARE language. Besides the development of this work, we considered several future research directions, aiming to enrich the theoretical framework with interesting features such as exception handling, modularity of the target specification, possibility to specify safety constraints. Moreover, we are currently developing other interesting extensions. First of all, we are integrating our framework with learning techniques in order to achieve greater scalability and investigation on how to reach the resilience of the system. This can greatly benefit the performance of the framework since, instead of computing the cartesian product (that is high time and memory-consuming), we can directly learn the orchestrator policy on the induced (but unknown) MDP. Then, we are studying the problem combing techniques from LTL$_f$ synthesis, service composition *à la* Roman Model, and stochastic shortest paths on transitions with different costs.

References

1. Berardi, D., Calvanese, D., De Giacomo, G., Hull, R., Mecella, M.: Automatic composition of transition-based semantic web services with messaging. In: VLDB, vol. 5, pp. 613–624 (2005)
2. Berardi, D., Calvanese, D., De Giacomo, G., Lenzerini, M., Mecella, M.: Automatic composition of *E*-services that export their behavior. In: Orlowska, M.E., Weerawarana, S., Papazoglou, M.P., Yang, J. (eds.) ICSOC 2003. LNCS, vol. 2910, pp. 43–58. Springer, Heidelberg (2003). https://doi.org/10.1007/978-3-540-24593-3_4
3. Brafman, R.I., De Giacomo, G., Mecella, M., Sardina, S.: Service composition in stochastic settings. In: Esposito, F., Basili, R., Ferilli, S., Lisi, F. (eds.) AI*IA 2017. LNCS, vol. 10640, pp. 159–171. Springer, Cham (2017). https://doi.org/10.1007/978-3-319-70169-1_12
4. De Giacomo, G., Favorito, M., Leotta, F., Mecella, M., Monti, F., Silo, L.: AIDA: a tool for resiliency in smart manufacturing. In: Cabanillas, C., Pérez, F. (eds.) CAiSE 2023. LNBIP, vol. 477, pp. 112–120. Springer, Cham (2023). https://doi.org/10.1007/978-3-031-34674-3_14
5. De Giacomo, G., Favorito, M., Leotta, F., Mecella, M., Silo, L.: Digital twins composition in smart manufacturing via Markov decision processes. Comput. Ind. **149**, 103916 (2023)
6. De Giacomo, G., Patrizi, F., Sardina, S.: Automatic behavior composition synthesis. Artif. Intell. **196**, 106–142 (2013)
7. De Giacomo, G., Vardi, M.Y.: Linear temporal logic and linear dynamic logic on finite traces. In: IJCAI 2013 Proceedings of the Twenty-Third international joint conference on Artificial Intelligence, pp. 854–860. ACM (2013)
8. Pesic, M., Schonenberg, H., Van der Aalst, W.M.: DECLARE: full support for loosely-structured processes. In: 11th IEEE International Enterprise Distributed Object Computing Conference (EDOC 2007), pp. 287–287. IEEE (2007)
9. Rabin, M.O., Scott, D.: Finite automata and their decision problems. IBM J. Res. Dev. **3**(2), 114–125 (1959)

Author Index

V. Malvone and A. Murano (Eds.): EUMAS 2023, LNAI 14282, pp. 553–554, 2023.
https://doi.org/10.1007/978-3-031-43264-4

Printed in the United States
by Baker & Taylor Publisher Services